The Making of an Industrial Society

Whickham
1560–1765

DAVID LEVINE
AND
KEITH WRIGHTSON

D0209706

CLARENDON PRESS · OXFORD
1991

Oxford University Press, Walton Street, Oxford OX2 6DP
Oxford New York Toronto
Delhi Bombay Calcutta Madras Karachi
Petaling Jaya Singapore Hong Kong Tokyo
Nairobi Dar es Salaam Cape Town
Melbourne Auckland
and associated companies in
Berlin Ibadan

Oxford is a trade mark of Oxford University Press

Published in the United States
by Oxford University Press, New York

© David Levine and Keith Wrightson 1991

All rights reserved. No part of this publication may be reproduced,
stored in a retrieval system, or transmitted, in any form or by any means,
electronic, mechanical, photocopying, recording, or otherwise, without
the prior permission of Oxford University Press

British Library Cataloguing in Publication Data
Levine, David 1946–
The making of an industrial society: Whickham 1560–1765.
– (Oxford studies in social history).
1. (Metropolitan County) Tyne and Wear. Whickham, history
I. Title II. Wrightson, Keith 1948–
942.873
ISBN 0–19–820066–8

Library of Congress Cataloging in Publication Data
Levine, David, 1946–
The making of an industrial society: Whickham, 1560–1765/David
Levine and Keith Wrightson.
p. cm.—(Oxford studies in social history)
Includes bibliographical references and index.
1. Whickham (England)—Economic conditions. 2. Whickham
(England)—Social conditions. 3. Whickham (England)—Industries—
History. I. Wrightson, Keith. II. Title. III. Series.
HC258.W47L48 1991
330.9428'73—dc20 90–39320
ISBN 0–19–820066–8

Typeset by Cambrian Typesetters, Frimley, Surrey
Printed and bound in Great Britain by
Bookcraft Ltd, Midsomer Norton, Bath

To the people of the Durham
coalfield, past and present

PREFACE

The recent historiography of early modern England has been distinguished by an interpretative emphasis upon continuity. This book, in contrast, is concerned primarily with change. It seeks to delineate and to interpret processes of economic and social change by focusing on a single parish in the Durham coalfield, the parish of Whickham, over a period of two centuries. Its central concern, however, is somewhat broader than this geographical focus might seem to imply. Put simply, it is an attempt to reconstruct the making of Britain's first industrialized society.

Such a statement clearly demands justification. In making it, we should say immediately that we are not choosing wilfully to ignore the fact that throughout the period of study (and increasingly in the later seventeenth and early eighteenth centuries) the economies and societies of many English regions were deeply penetrated by industrial activity. We would be blinkered indeed to ignore such realities, for the whole thrust of the recent historiography of industrialization in England has been to emphasize this fact. The concept of the Industrial Revolution as a swift and fundamental transformation of the English economy has now been displaced by an emphasis on slow, uneven incremental change and on continuity with earlier developments. What was formerly seen as *the* great historical watershed of modern times, conventionally located in the two generations after c.1780, has been reduced to 'at most, a modest acceleration in a long period of economic growth that began in the seventeenth century and became impressive only after 1815'.[1]

That the emergence of Britain's industrial economy was a long, protracted process with deep roots is not a contention that we would wish to challenge. Our point is that, in our enhanced awareness of the slow spread of manufacturing industry in the

[1] F. W. Botham and E. H. Hunt, 'Wages in Britain during the Industrial Revolution', *Economic History Review*, 2nd ser., 40 (1987), 380. For trends in the historiography of the Industrial Revolution, see D. Cannadine, 'The Past and the Present in the English Industrial Revolution 1880–1980', *Past and Present*, 103 (1984).

English countryside between the sixteenth and the eighteenth centuries, we should not lose sight of the peculiar precocity of certain sectors of the industrial economy, and in particular of the coal industry of north-east England with which we are principally concerned.

Most of the industries of early modern England were characterized by small-scale, decentralized production. They utilized the labour of by-employed cottagers and smallholders in the 'putting-out system'. They employed largely traditional techniques, required little investment in fixed capital, and were technologically sluggish. In contrast, the coal industry of the north-east was characterized from an early date by highly centralized, large-scale productive units. It employed a large, geographically concentrated force of full-time wage-labourers. It involved massive capital investment by the standards of the day and witnessed the deployment of considerable technological ingenuity, notably in the techniques of drainage and transportation. Moreover, it spawned a variety of related industrial enterprises in the Tyneside region which made use of the fuel it provided and shared some of its structural characteristics.

In the context of a survey of English industrial activity in 1600, or even in 1750, the coal industry of the north-east might well appear anomalous, even as compared with the extractive industries of other regions. But it was a singularly important anomaly: important in the short term for the fuel it supplied to the households and workshops of the towns of southern and eastern England, above all the growing metropolis of London; vitally important in the long term for the role it was eventually to play in the ushering-in of a new industrial age. For if there were immense immediate benefits to be gained from the exploitation of the vast stocks of accumulated energy that England's coal deposits represented, the coal industry of early modern England was also a portent of economic transformation. Handicraft-industrialization did not revolutionize production in England; the use of coal did. Britain became the first industrial economy because it was the first fully to exploit inanimate energy resources for the powering of machinery. This was the essence of what E. A. Wrigley has recently called the transition from an 'advanced organic economy' to a 'mineral-based energy economy'. Without coal, such a transition was unthinkable. Without an appreciation of the absolute centrality of the coal industry, and particularly that of north-east England, in that transition, the emergence of modern industrial society in Britain simply cannot be understood.[2]

If the industrialization of north-east England was to prove a vital anomaly, it was also a remarkably early anomaly. J. U. Nef's tentative suggestion that the late sixteenth and early seventeenth centuries experienced an 'early industrial revolution' based upon coal is clearly hyperbolic when viewed in the national context.[3] But it appears a good deal less extravagant in the specific Tyneside locality. For Tyneside might lay claim to the distinction of having been the first thoroughly industrialized local economy in Britain, one based as much on capital investment as on the use of wage-labour, and in which the agrarian economy, far from existing in symbiosis with industry, had been thoroughly subordinated to its demands. If this might seem to overstate the significance of the coal-centred industrialization of the society of the northern coalfield, such an emphasis is both understandable and justified. The prior existence of an already mature coal industry was crucial to the development of the economic forces which ultimately distinguished British economic history from that of other countries. Similarly, the extraordinarily early experience of industrialization in the northern coalfield was a vital chapter in the development of industrial society in Britain.

It was a general awareness of the peculiar historical experience of Tyneside and the northern coalfield, derived initially from our reading of Nef and the other classical histories of the coal industry, that attracted us, in 1978, to the research that has culminated in this book. It seemed to us that, while the economic and technological histories of the area had been effectively delineated, there was room still for a closer, more detailed, elucidation of the process of economic change. More important, however, was the fact that the opportunity that the region afforded to attempt a *social* history of industrialization had not been taken up for any period before the late eighteenth century.

In the absence of such research, we felt that our understanding of the nature of English society in the early modern period was impaired in two ways. First, our received conceptions of England's

[2] Flinn, *Coal Industry*. 451 ff., cf. E. A. Wrigley, *Continuity, Chance and Change: The Character of the Industrial Revolution in England* (Cambridge, 1988).
[3] Nef, i. 165 ff.

social structure, and of the conventional typology of local societies that composed it, appeared to have no place for the distinctive local society that had apparently sprung up on the northern coalfield in the first half of the seventeenth century. Yet it was there. Secondly, we felt that a closer examination of the structures and dynamics of that society—above all in the relatively neglected late seventeenth and early eighteenth centuries—might help us to appreciate more fully the course of socioeconomic change in the early modern period.

To this extent, we wanted to fill a blank space on the historical map. But we also perceived an opportunity not only to explore the currently fashionable themes of the social history of early modern England in a new context, but also to examine some of the classical questions of historical sociology—questions intimately connected with the attempt to understand the nature of industrial society. In what ways did the early experience of industrialization in the northeast mould the contours of local society? What developments took place in its occupational structure, in the division of labour, in the nature and degree of social stratification, in modes of social integration, in social identities and patterns of social relations? The historiography of early modern England had yielded no social history of industrial development, or none that was empirically based rather than conjectural. The theory of industrial society current in kindred disciplines lacked historical depth. Given this situation, the early industrialization of Tyneside presented 'a standing challenge to the social historian', and one that we found attractive.[4]

These were our general intentions. Our method was to select an area of the northern coalfield for intensive analysis over a period of two centuries, starting on the eve of the Elizabethan expansion of the coal industry and culminating on the eve of the Industrial Revolution proper. Such an approach needs no excuse. Closeness of focus has its limitations; but in our experience it is simply the most fruitful way of pursuing social history, permitting as it does the intensive analysis of particular sources, their interlinkage to provide answers to questions that would otherwise remain inaccessible, the establishment of causal connections and relationships between developments of different types, and above all the opportunity to

[4] Quoting E. Hughes, *North Country Life in the Eighteenth Century: The North-East, 1700–1750* (Oxford, 1952), p. xiv.

place alongside the activities of history's major players the experiences and contributions of its 'immense supporting cast'.[5] It is, however, a long and arduous road to historical understanding; for, given the richness of England's archival resources, the accumulation of detailed information for even a single parish can prove enormously time-consuming.

Our original intention was to study not one parish, but a whole area of the coalfield. The choice of Whickham and its immediate neighbours presented no difficulty, for their names leapt out at us from Nef's pages as the parishes most deeply involved in the early development of the coalfield. We rapidly discovered, however, that such a thoroughgoing area study was simply too great a task even for collaborative researchers. Accordingly, we reluctantly confined ourselves to the parish of Whickham itself, while endeavouring to remain alive to those developments in its immediate environs and in the broader coalfield without which some aspects of its history would have been inexplicable.

Even so, the research for this book occupied some seven years. In the first two years David Levine worked virtually alone, visiting record offices, locating sources, and evaluating their potential. He was primarily responsible for the identification and preliminary exploration of most of the major sources on which our book is based. Thereafter, the research was divided between us, partly on the grounds of geographical convenience and partly on those of subject matter and experience. David Levine worked the sources located in the central record offices in London and concentrated on Whickham's economic development. He also undertook the reconstitution of the parish registers of Whickham, which was completed in Toronto and analysed in Cambridge. Keith Wrightson's fief included the repositories of the north-east and the social dimensions of Whickham's history.

None of this would have been possible without generous financial help from the Social Science and Humanities Research Council of Canada (SSHRC) and the University of St Andrews research fund. It would have been far more difficult than it was but for the courteous assistance of the staffs of the various record offices and libraries listed in our bibliography, the permission granted by the rector of Whickham to use the records of parochial registration

---

[5] Quoting E. P. Thompson, 'Folklore, Anthropology and Social History', *Indian Historical Review*, 3 (1978), 251.

and administration, the advice and encouragement of Joyce Ellis, the late Michael Flinn, H. T. Dickinson, Robert Malcolmson, David Saunders, John Smith, David Stoker, and Lorna Weatherill, and the kindness of Rita and Alec Cassie.

Progress up to 1983 was steady but slow, given our separate commitments and our inability to spend more than part of the year on this project. After almost five years we were still uncertain as to whether the material that we were uncovering was adequate for our objectives. At that critical stage of our work we benefited enormously from grants from the Wolfson Foundation and the SSHRC, which enabled us to employ Christine Issa as a research assistant for several months in the summer of 1983. Her vital contribution was the exploration of the massive and largely uncalendared Strathmore Papers, housed in the Durham County Record Office, and her discoveries there provided the final confirmation that it would be possible to carry the analysis of Whickham's industrial history firmly into the eighteenth century.

Up to this point we had been able to communicate with one another only by means of frequent letters and occasional meetings. In 1983–4 we were at last enabled to work together in Toronto as a result of the award to Keith Wrightson of a Canadian Commonwealth Research Fellowship, tenable at the Ontario Institute for Studies in Education (OISE). In September 1983 we were finally able to pool the results of our work, and to commence piecing together the material.

As we did so, however, any hope that we might have entertained of simply sitting down to write our book in the form of a series of virtually self-contained thematic chapters rapidly evaporated. It was apparent to us that such an approach would inevitably fragment the understanding that we were gradually gaining of the dynamics of Whickham's development. We had expected to be dealing, for the most part, with the analysis of an early industrial society in being. We found that, across the whole period of our study, we were dealing with an industrial society in the making, and that its story was far more complex than we had anticipated. This realization came home most forcibly in the autumn of 1983, when we tacked an 1856 six-inch Ordnance Survey map of Whickham and its environs on to the wall of our work room in OISE and began slowly to assemble in chronological order, and to identify on the map, the landholdings, pits, and other locations that occurred repeatedly in our documents. This exercise gave us a vivid sense of the restlessness of economic and social change in Whickham and of its spatial dimensions. It also made it abundantly clear that any form of static or 'synchronic' approach to Whickham's experience would be totally artificial in its outcome. If we were to recapture something of the processes at work in Whickham, then we must adopt a suitably dynamic form of exposition.

The remainder of the year was spent working towards that end. In October 1983 David Levine presented the initial analysis of Whickham's demographic development in a paper to the conference of the Social Science–History Association. Later, in the intervals between his teaching duties, he wrote a working paper on the history of the coal industry in Whickham, and began the analysis of the paybills and listings discovered among the Strathmore Papers. (A first version of his work on the 1752 colliery paybills was presented at the SSHA meeting later in 1984.) Meanwhile, Keith Wrightson spent most of the year working on the pre-1700 material and wrote the first version of what became our second chapter as a paper delivered at the University of Michigan. In the spring of 1984 we also wrote together an article on 'Death in Whickham', which we have published separately.[6] And as all this proceeded, we devoted many hours to the discussion of the emerging structure and central arguments of our proposed book.

Since 1984 we have been separated by the Atlantic Ocean once more, but the discussions that took place in 1983–4 have been kept airborne quite literally by letter. Further research necessary to consolidate particular themes or to tie up loose ends, and the remainder of the preparatory analysis of the records, was completed by Keith Wrightson, with the frequent and much appreciated assistance of Eva Wrightson. And lastly, since it was logistically impossible for us literally to write together, Keith Wrightson undertook in 1986–8 the final assembly of our material and the writing of the text of our book, incorporating David Levine's working papers as he did so. Each draft chapter was closely and vigorously discussed as it emerged, such discussion contributing to the shaping of the next, and our manuscript was finalized in this manner. In these final stages we benefited from the generosity of

[6] K. Wrightson and D. Levine, 'Death in Whickham', in J. Walter and R. Schofield (eds.), *Famine, Disease, and the Social Order in Early Modern Society* (Cambridge, 1989).

Tom Arkell, Joyce Ellis, P. E. H. Hair, John Hatcher, Christine Issa, Marcus Knight, Sara Mendelson, Brian Outhwaite, and Richard Tuck, all of whom supplied us with material from their own researches; the professional skills of Liz Wright and Ruth Easthope, who typed the manuscript; and the advice of Jeremy Boulton, Adam Fox, Rab Houston, Sheilagh Ogilvie, Nicholas Rogers, and Sir Keith Thomas, general editor of this series, all of whom read and commented upon the entire text.

The resulting book, with its four long chapters, subdivided into sections, may seem eccentric in form, and a word of justification is perhaps needed. As we have already explained, our principal problem in attempting to apprehend and to communicate the social experience of industrialization in Whickham was that of the sheer dynamism of the situation revealed in the records. In our dialogue with the sources and with each other, and in our attempts to conceptualize and to write Whickham's history, we came to realize that the task could best be accomplished by means of a set of overlapping analytical narratives, each of which would approach the development of the parish from a different perspective. A narrative approach seemed to us the only way to explain how Whickham's economy and society were structured and restructured over time and space, and the manner in which the contingencies of particular events and situations contributed to that process. But at the same time, that narrative must of necessity be an analytical narrative; for a purely narrative approach, if such a thing is ever possible, would be inadequate to our explanatory purposes. Narrative is 'embedded in and presupposes, knowledge of general principles, relationships and processes', and we wanted to make such matters explicit.[7] The form eventually devised could be justified on theoretical grounds as an effort to grasp and to express 'the time–space relations inherent in the constitution of all social interaction', or as a means of handling the 'problematic of structuring': the set of problems arising from the way in which 'social action and social structure create and contain one another' in a continuous process of construction and reconstruction of the social world.[8] But it was not adopted in

---

[7] Quoting from a review by Mary Fulbrook in *Social History*, 10 (1985), 137.

[8] Quoting A. Giddens, *Central Problems in Social Theory: Action, Structure and Contradiction in Social Analysis* (London, 1979), 3; and P. Abrams, *Historical Sociology* (Shepton Mallet, 1982), pp. xv–xvii, 108.

conscious response to such theoretical premisses. We found it necessary simply to render Whickham's recorded history intelligible.

This, then, was our procedure in the execution of a truly collaborative project. Like all collaborations, it was not without its practical difficulties and its moments of intellectual conflict. On the whole, however, we are surprised at how little we have been at variance over the interpretation of Whickham's history, and how much our separate findings and insights have stimulated us to develop a common understanding of its dynamics.

It is unlikely that either of us would have begun this project alone. We would certainly not have seen it through to completion individually, or without the assistance of others. The full measure of what we have gained by working together cannot easily be expressed, but we believe that this book at least represents the way in which collaborative research and intellectual partnership, difficult as they may be, can produce results beyond our separate grasps.

D.L. and K.W.

Cambridge and Toronto
September 1989

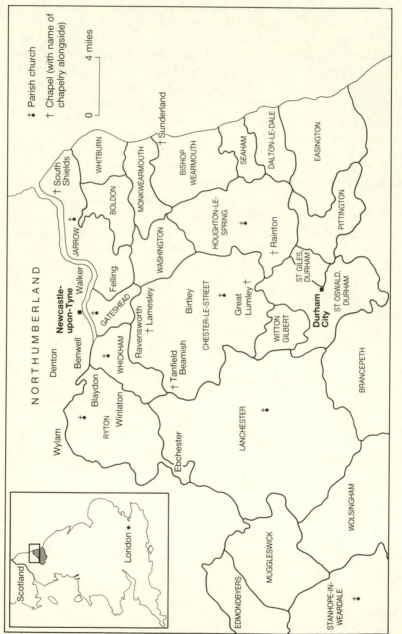

MAP 1. Parishes of northern County Durham

CONTENTS

LIST OF FIGURES

LIST OF MAPS

LIST OF TABLES

ABBREVIATIONS

BL	British Library
CSPD	Calendar of State Papers Domestic
DPD	Durham University Department of Paleography and Diplomatic
DRO	Durham County Record Office
Flinn, *Coal Industry*	M. W. Flinn, with the assistance of David Stoker, *The History of the British Coal Industry*, ii, *1700–1830: The Industrial Revolution* (Oxford, 1984).
GPL	Gateshead Public Library
HMC	*Historical Manuscripts Commission Reports*, Salisbury
Nef	J. U. Nef, *The Rise of the British Coal Industry*, 2 vols. (London, 1932).
NEIMME	North of England Institute of Mining and Mechanical Engineers
Ncle. UL	University of Newcastle-upon-Tyne Library
NRO	Northumberland County Record Office
PRO	Public Record Office
TWA	Tyne and Wear Archives

1

England's Peru: The Industrial Development of Whickham

England's a perfect World! has Indies too!
Correct your Maps: Newcastle is Peru.

William Ellis, *News from Newcastle* (1651)

In 1836 the lessees of the manor of Whickham, County Durham, sank a pit in the western part of their territories in the hope of finding a new seam of coal. Having no record of former workings, they were greatly surprised to discover an underground complex of 'bords and pillars' from a forgotten colliery undertaking—the 'bords' or work-rooms hewn through the thick seam by the pitmen of an earlier generation, the massive pillars of unwrought coal left standing to support the roof.[1] Those great pillars had in all likelihood performed their essential function for two centuries or more. In their accidental discovery, the mining engineers of the Industrial Revolution era had come face to face with the handiwork of some of those predecessors who had laid the foundations of the modern coal industry of Tyneside. It was mineral wealth hewn with pick and wedge from just such workings as these, dragged on sleds to the 'eye' of the pit and 'wound' to the surface for delivery to the coal barons of Newcastle, that had first won for Tyneside its reputation as 'the black Indies': England's Peru.

1. COALS FROM NEWCASTLE

'The history of medieval Durham', it has been said, 'is the history of the Bishopric; the history of modern Durham is the history of its coal industry.'[2] That modern history can be dated from the final

---

[1] NEIMME, Buddle Papers, vol. 20, 93–4.
[2] H. R. Trevor-Roper, 'The Bishopric of Durham and the Capitalist Reformation', *Durham University Journal*, 38, NS 8 (1945–6), 46.

third of the sixteenth century, a period that initiated 'the rapid development of the north-eastern coal industry . . . on the foundation of a flourishing, though comparatively small, medieval industry'.[3]

Coal had been mined in Durham and Northumberland since at least the thirteenth century, and by the fourteenth century the output of Tyneside collieries already constituted an important element in the trade of the city of Newcastle. The coastal trade from the Tyne to the ports of eastern and southern England, above all to the city of London, was firmly established, and in addition an embryonic export trade existed with the Netherlands, France, and the Baltic.[4]

Important as it is to appreciate the antecedents of sixteenth-century developments, however, it is vital that we recognize the full significance of the sharp discontinuity presented by the developments of the late sixteenth and early seventeenth centuries. The quantities of coal shipped from the Tyne in the fourteenth and fifteenth centuries were small in comparison with what was to come.[5] Moreover, shipments from Newcastle in 1513 were no greater than those recorded in 1377.[6] Between 1509 and 1533 it would appear that there was a definite stirring of demand for Tyneside coal, which meant that levels of production at the latter date were somewhat higher than before, and such an anticipatory quickening is well worthy of note.[7] It is to the late sixteenth century, however, that we must look for the dramatic irruption of the Tyneside industry into English economic history.

The history of the coal industry in Britain as a whole between 1560 and 1700 was described by J. U. Nef as a story of 'revolutionary growth'. According to Nef's estimates, national output of coal in the period 1560–1690 may have increased fourteen-fold.[8] In the opinion of D. C. Coleman, this national estimate, given the difficulties of the surviving evidence of coal production, must be described as 'a guess: no more, no less'.

---

[3] J. B. Blake, 'The Medieval Coal Trade of North East England: Some Fourteenth-Century Evidence', *Northern History*, 2 (1967), 2.

[4] A. E. Smailes, *North England* (London and Edinburgh, 1960), 129–30; Nef. i. 6; Blake, 'Medieval Coal Trade', 1–2, 9 ff., 12 ff.

[5] Ibid. 21; Nef, i. 9.   [6] Smailes, *North England*, 129.

[7] I. S. W. Blanchard, 'Commercial Crisis and Change: Trade and the Industrial Economy of the North-East, 1509–1532', *Northern History*, 8 (1973), 73, 83.

[8] Nef, i. 19–20, 76.

Indeed, Nef himself was anxious, more anxious than his critics have allowed, to stress the 'considerable hesitation' with which he put forward his figures and the 'wide margins of error' to which he recognized them to be subject.[9] What is not in doubt is the very considerable growth of the British coal industry and the leading role of the north-eastern industry in that process. As Nef's severest critic acknowledges, by the later seventeenth century contemporary foreign observers regarded the precocity of the coal industry as the most striking of English economic phenomena, and by 1700 almost half of England's coal can be said with confidence to have been produced in Durham and Northumberland.[10]

In the case of the Tyneside industry's expansion, we stand on somewhat firmer statistical ground. Precise calculation of the levels of output in the north-eastern counties is rendered impossible by the fact that the principal statistical series surviving to the historian is provided by the records of coastal shipments contained in the Newcastle port books. Even allowing for the problems of inadequate information on foreign exports, 'land sales' to local consumers, evasion of duties, and the lack of standardization of contemporary weights and measures, however, the 'sea-scale', export orientation of the Tyneside industry makes it permissible to use the port books of Newcastle as a rough and ready proxy for trends in Tyneside production. They provide the following annual tonnages:[11]

Michaelmas 1563–Michaelmas 1564	32,951
Michaelmas 1574–Michaelmas 1575	56,487
Michaelmas 1591–Michaelmas 1592	112,124
Michaelmas 1597–Michaelmas 1598	162,552

[9] D. C. Coleman, *Industry in Tudor and Stuart England* (London, 1975), 46; Nef, i. 19.

[10] Coleman, *Industry*, 45–6; cf. Flinn, *Coal Industry*, 26, 28. Flinn adds that in 1700 the production of the north-eastern coalfield 'exceeded that of the next three largest regions put together'. For further comment on the disagreement between Nef and Coleman, see E. Kerridge, 'The Coal Industry in Tudor and Stuart England: A Comment', *Economic History Review*, 2nd ser., 30 (1977), 340–2; and N. K. Buxton, *The Economic Development of the British Coal Industry* (London, 1978), 11–12. It is to be hoped that Dr John Hatcher's forthcoming volume in the *History of the British Coal Industry* will cast new light on both the expansion of national output c.1500–1700 and the specific contribution of the north-eastern coalfield.

[11] Nef, i. 21. For the difficulties involved in such calculations, see Nef, i. 36 and ii. app. D. Cf. Flinn, *Coal Industry*, 29–33. For a recent recalculation of the size of the north-eastern coal trade, see B. Dietz, 'The North-East Coal Trade, 1550–1750: Measures, Markets and the Metropolis', *Northern History*, 22 (1986).

Michaelmas 1608–Michaelmas 1609   239,271
Christmas 1633–Christmas   1634   452,625
    June 1658–June   1659   529,032
Christmas 1684–Christmas   1685   616,016

These Newcastle statistics indicate what is by any standard a quite extraordinary discontinuity, and one that was most marked in the reigns of Elizabeth and James I. Nef pointed out that 'between 1565 and 1625 the annual shipments doubled every fifteen years', and hazarded the opinion that in these years 'the shipments of coal from Newcastle probably increased at a more rapid rate than at any other period in their history'.[12] Inevitably, perhaps, such conclusions have been challenged. D. C. Coleman, critical of Nef's statement that between 1563–4 and 1684–5 Newcastle shipments 'multiplied nearly nineteenfold', has pointed out that Nef compared the figures for single years only. Using four- or five-year averages for groups of years in the 1590s and 1690s, Coleman calculates 'an increase in Newcastle's coastal exports of coal *not* of nineteen-fold but of rather over three-fold'.[13] Clearly there is some force in Coleman's point. Yet in assessing the growth of Tyneside output we must also note that Coleman excludes from consideration the first thirty years of growth, which were critical in Nef's assessment of its scale.[14] Moreover, the most recent re-examination of the Newcastle figures, while suggesting that Nef underestimated the level of mid-sixteenth-century shipments, none the less suggests a tenfold increase between that date and the early 1680s.[15] Uncertain as we may be about the precise rates of growth of the Tyneside industry, the fact remains that its growth was prodigious. As Nef wrote, in his own attempt to place these developments in perspective,

To a modern mind, accustomed to thinking of production in terms of millions, an output of 25,000 tons will seem insignificant. But the historical student must divest himself of present-day habits of thought. He must measure early developments, not by the standards current in his age, but by those current in the age he strives to recreate.[16]

This is perhaps a sufficient answer to those who might undervalue the changes of the Elizabethan and early Stuart period. Moreover,

[12] Nef, i. 25.
[13] Nef, i. 19; Coleman, *Industry*, 46–7.
[14] Kerridge, 'Coal Industry', 341.
[15] Dietz, 'North-East Coal Trade', 286, 293.
[16] Nef, i. 362.

contemporaries themselves had no doubt of the significance of what was happening around them. As early as 1575, a contemporary reported that 'the commodity of Newcastle and such like coals is of late years known to be of more value than in times past'.[17] In 1649 William Gray of Newcastle, reflecting on the economic development of his city, remarked that its great trade in coal 'began not past fourscore years since'.[18] These two were aware enough that the 1570s marked a turning point, one that historians are better placed to descry as the decisive moment in the transition from the medieval to the early modern stage in the development of Tyneside's industrial economy.

In order to achieve this transformation, several interconnected processes must have been set in train. First, demand for coal must have risen. Second, new collieries and more pits must have been worked. Third, certain pre-existing restrictions on the extraction of coal had to be overcome. Let us look more closely at these developments.

In the later Middle Ages there is little evidence that demand for coal was high or that it was severely checked by limitations on supply. The coal shipped from Newcastle in the fourteenth century appears to have been used to supply heat for limeburning and for ironworking in smithies, as fuel in England's royal castles, and to a limited extent as domestic fuel in the towns of the south and east.[19] It was produced in relatively small-scale collieries in the immediate vicinity of Newcastle, many of which lay on the lands of the Bishopric of Durham and were held by the coalmasters on restrictive terms. Coal mining leases were short, rents were high, and permitted output was generally limited. The bishops husbanded their mineral resources carefully. They were prepared neither to invest heavily in coal production themselves nor to grant leases that might encourage such investment on the part of others.[20] Nevertheless, restrictive as the environment of enterprise was, there is little reason to believe that coal production was insufficient to meet the limited needs of the day.

In the course of the sixteenth century this situation began to

---

[17] F. W. Dendy (ed.), *Extracts from the Records of the Company of Hostmen of Newcastle-upon-Tyne*, Surtees Soc. no. 105 (Newcastle, 1901), p. xxix.

[18] W. Gray, *Chorographia: or, a Survey of Newcastle-upon-Tyne in 1649* (Newcastle, 1813), 33.

[19] Blake, 'Medieval Coal Trade', 2 ff.

[20] Nef, i. 135 ff., 320; Blake, 'Medieval Coal Trade', 22–3.

change, and the initial impulse for change appears to have been increased demand. It was not so much that entirely new uses for coal were discovered, though there were some, as that demand increased prodigiously in certain of the traditional markets for coal—above all in domestic heating. As has been said of the development of the coal industry in a later century, 'without new sources of demand, the growth of the market for coal would necessarily be limited to the rate of growth of the population living in areas with easy access to coal supplies'.[21] This indeed appears to have been the key to the developments of the sixteenth and earlier seventeenth centuries.

In 1575 a report on Newcastle's coal trade indicated some of the forces at work as perceived by contemporaries:

the commodity of Newcastle and such like coals is of late years known to be of more value than in times past, for wood being grown to dearth and the severity of it felt more every day, causes many of the said coals to be used for fuel in London and in other places in this realm by those who in time past used nothing but wood for fuel.[22]

This Elizabethan assessment was echoed and elaborated by a mid-seventeenth-century Newcastle commentator, who argued:

Coales in former times was onely used by smiths and for burning of lime; woods in the south parts of England decaying, and the city of London, and other cities and townes growing populous, made the trade for coale increase yearely and many great ships of burthen built, so that there was more coales vented in one yeare then was in seven yeares, forty yeares by-past; this great trade hath made this port to flourish in all trades.[23]

Contemporaries, then, identified the growing needs of England's urban population in general and that of London in particular, exacerbated by a 'timber crisis', as the crucial factors spurring demand for Tyneside coal in the later sixteenth century. There is good reason to believe that they were close to the truth. Recent research has made it abundantly clear that English population growth rates in these years were very high. Indeed, the population was growing so rapidly at the end of the sixteenth century that 'it was not until after 1786 that Elizabethan rates of growth were exceeded'.[24] Moreover, while the population of England as a whole

---

[21] Flinn, *Coal Industry*, 212.

[22] Dendy, *Hostmen*, p. xxix.   [23] Gray, *Chorographia*, 33.

[24] E. A. Wrigley and R. S. Schofield, *The Population History of England, 1541–1871: A Reconstruction* (London, 1981), 213.

increased, the proportion of the population living in towns grew considerably faster, the greater part of this urban increase being accounted for by the extraordinary growth of London. Throughout the period 1550–1750 London grew faster than the general population—from an estimated 85,000 inhabitants in 1550 to 200,000 in 1600, 475,000 in 1670, 575,000 in 1700, and 675,000 in 1750. The swelling population of the metropolis and of the lesser towns and cities of south-eastern England needed fuel, and there can be no doubt that their requirements created the surging demand for Tyneside coal.[25]

As we have seen, contemporaries believed that urban demand for household fuel could not be supplied by depleted timber resources. Although coal burning was regarded as disagreeable because of its 'noysome smells', Londoners of modest means had little choice but to use it since firewood prices rose more rapidly than the average cost of other commodities. Figures provided by Nef indicate that, using the 1550s as a base, general commodities had risen in price by 50 per cent by the period 1583–92, while firewood went up by 70 per cent. Thereafter the discrepancy became much greater, so that a 2.2-fold increase in general commodity prices by 1633–42 should be set beside a 4.8-fold increase for firewood.[26]

In the light of recent research it would appear that, while England's woodlands undoubtedly contracted in the sixteenth and seventeenth centuries, the actual extent of a *national* 'timber crisis' should not be exaggerated. Such a crisis was never more than local.[27] Nevertheless, London and the other towns of the south-east were precisely the localities where wood shortage was most stringent in

[25] P. Clark and P. Slack, *English Towns in Transition, 1500–1700* (Oxford, 1976), 83; Wrigley and Schofield, *Population History*, 166. Estimates of London's population vary and we are grateful for the advice of Dr Jeremy Boulton of the Cambridge Group for the History of Population and Social Structure on this difficult issue. Those quoted include Boulton's own estimate for 1550 and figures from R. Finlay and B. Shearer, 'Population Growth and Suburban Expansion', in A. L. Beier and R. Finlay (eds.), *London 1500–1700: The Making of the Metropolis* (London, 1986), 39, 49; and E. A. Wrigley, 'Urban Growth and Agricultural Change: England and the Continent in the Early Modern Period', *Journal of Interdisciplinary History*, 5 (1985), 686. For further evidence of the London–Newcastle link, see Dietz, 'The North–East Coal Trade', 287–9.

[26] Nef, i. 157. Calculation based on figures given in Nef, i. 158.

[27] K. Thomas, *Man and the Natural World: Changing Attitudes in England 1500–1800* (London, 1983), 193. For a recent reappraisal of the fuel shortage problem and full bibliographical references, see B. Thomas, 'Was There an Energy Crisis in Great Britain in the 17th Century?' *Explorations in Economic History*, 23 (1986), 124–52.

its effects, and there can be no doubt that the inhabitants of the metropolis turned increasingly to coal. By the 1590s coal had become a crucial commodity for London, a complaint being made to the Privy Council in 1595 on behalf of 'the poor who do use the same for their chiefest fuel'. By the 1620s the supplying of Tyneside coal for London's hearths could be described as 'a matter of great necessitie and much concernings the generall good of the king-dome'.[28]

Domestic heating, however, was not the only source of increased demand, for industrial demand for coal also rose. While it now seems that Nef described the industrial uses of coal in Tudor and Stuart England in somewhat hyperbolic terms, there remains much to commend in his thesis of a coal-driven industrial expansion. Historians are increasingly aware of the proliferation of industrial activities in Elizabethan and early Stuart England, and in particular of the so-called 'consumer industries' founded by enterprising 'projectors' aiming at the domestic production of formerly imported goods.[29] In these numerous, albeit individually quite small-scale, activities, coal had a role to play. Coal had long been used to fuel a number of industrial processes, and this role certainly expanded in the course of the later sixteenth and seventeenth centuries. It was used extensively in lime-burning, smithying, and metalworking, in salt- and soap-boiling, starch- and candle-making, malting and brewing, food processing and sugar-refining, textile finishing, smelting, brick- and tile-making, and in glassworks, as well as in the manufacture of alum, copperas, saltpetre, and gunpowder. It remains plausible, therefore, that by the end of the seventeenth century as much as a third of Britain's coal output may have been employed in industrial processes of one sort or another.[30] That many such industries were urban, and in particular metropolitan, in location only serves to reinforce our understanding of the growing demand for Tyneside coal.

The fact that these rising needs were met by the Tyneside

---

[28] Nef, i. 197; PRO DURH 5/7/101.

[29] Nef wrote, albeit 'very tentatively', of an 'early industrial revolution': Nef, i. 165 ff. For the proliferation of 'consumer' industries, see J. Thirsk, *Economic Policy and Projects: The Development of a Consumer Society in Early Modern England* (Oxford, 1978). To write of a 'consumer society' in this period, though currently fashionable, is at least as hyperbolic as Nef's 'early industrial revolution'. However, the facts of increased industrial activity remain, and demand recognition.

[30] Nef, i. 220.

industry derived initially from the economics of transportation. England was rich in coal deposits, and in many parts of the country these had long been worked to supply local needs. Coal, however, is an exceptionally bulky commodity in relation to its value, and this placed very severe limitations on the geographical areas within which it could be marketed at an attractive price. Given the nature of contemporary road transportation, it was reckoned that the price of coal doubled with every two miles that it was carried overland from the pit head.[31] The possibility of water carriage, however, could transform the situation. Newcastle owed its early pre-eminence in the coal trade to the fact that coal was mined close to the banks of the river Tyne, for the most part in the riverside parishes of County Durham. This simple reality made possible the supply of distant consumers at a price sufficiently low to render coal attractive as an alternative fuel. In 1675, for example, it was claimed that the cost of carrying coal some three hundred miles by water from the Tyne to London was no greater than that of carrying it three or four miles overland.[32]

By that date, the growing coal trade had brought into being a highly articulated transportation infrastructure. On Tyneside itself coal was brought to the riverside 'staithes' by wain or waggon and loaded into the keelboats which carried it seven or eight miles downriver for transfer to the colliers lying in the mouth of the Tyne at Shields. The colliers then undertook the two-week voyage to London, where the coal was discharged on to lighters and taken to the dockside warehouses of the merchants who controlled the London end of the trade.[33] In 1615 there were already some four hundred colliers plying the east coast in a seasonal trade which saw few sailings during the treacherous months of mid-winter.[34] As the trade expanded, the vessels that served it grew both in size and in number; a statement of 1703 claimed that some six hundred ships were working from Newcastle alone.[35]

---

[31] Ibid. 103. Cf. J. Langton, *Geographical Change and Industrial Revolution: Coalmining in South West Lancashire, 1590–1799* (Cambridge, 1979), 45. Langton estimates that in the Lancashire case a two-mile overland journey quadrupled the pit-head price, which was lower than in the north-east.

[32] Nef, i. 103.   [33] Ibid. 386 ff. Cf. Flinn, *Coal Industry*, 163 ff.

[34] R. Galloway, *Annals of Coal Mining and the Coal Trade* (London, 1898; reprinted Newton Abbot, Devon, 1971), 138.

[35] Flinn, *Coal Industry*, 177; Nef, i. 390. The seasonal nature of the trade declined only in the eighteenth century: see Flinn, *Coal Industry*, 174–5.

The growth of the Tyneside coal industry, then, was firmly based on the growing needs of London and on the geographical circumstances that enabled the north-eastern coalfield to meet those needs. First, however, pits needed to be sunk, coal had to be won, and earlier constraints upon the expansion of output had to be broken through. In considering these vital aspects of the growth of the Tyneside coal industry, there is much to be gained by adopting a narrower and a sharper focus. Let us therefore turn our attention from the growth of the Newcastle coal trade to the role played in supplying that trade by a single, and a singularly important, Durham parish: the parish of Whickham.

2. WHICKHAM AND THE GRAND LEASE

Whickham lies on the south bank of the river Tyne, some four miles to the west of the city of Newcastle.[36] The historic parish was large in extent, encompassing almost six thousand acres, and irregular in shape, stretching some four miles east to west at its widest point and some four miles north to south at its deepest. It was bounded to the north by the river Tyne, to the east by the Team, which separated it from the parish of Gateshead, and to the west by the Derwent, which marked the boundary of Ryton parish. To the south-east the Blackburn flowed between Whickham and the chapelry of Lamesley, while to the south-west, beyond Marley Hill, Whickham adjoined the chapelry of Tanfield.

As might be expected in a northern parish of this size, settlement in Whickham was scattered. The principal township of Whickham was located on a steep hill which rises abruptly from the meadowland bordering the Tyne. It was described in 1787 in the following terms:

The town of Whickham hangs on the brow of a hill, with an open eastern aspect . . . The prospect is remarkably beautiful, comprehending part of Gateshead, with the Church, the tower of St Nicholas in Newcastle, the castle and much of the town on the margin of the river . . . while through

---

[36] The following topographical account of Whickham is based, unless otherwise stated, on W. Bourn, *Whickham Parish: Its History, Antiquities and Industry* (Carlisle, 1893); R. Surtees, *The History and Antiquities of the County Palatine of Durham*, 4 vols. (London, 1816–40), ii. 237–56; W. Fordyce, *The History and Antiquities of the County Palatine of Durham*, 2 vols. (Newcastle, 1857), ii. 687–95.

the deep vale the river Tyne forms a fine canal of seven or eight miles in extent, and flows with solemn majesty as if conscious of the wealth which loads its bosom.[37]

Two miles to the north-east of Whickham town, at the confluence of the Team and the Tyne, lay the hamlet of Dunston, while to the north-west Swalwell lay close to the mouth of the Derwent. These were the three principal concentrations of population, but they were supplemented by many other scattered dwellings and by the outlying seats of a number of gentry families.[38] For administrative purposes, the parish was divided into four 'quarters': Whickham, Swalwell, Fellside, and Lowhand. Manorially it was yet more complex. The principal manor of Whickham, a possession of the bishop of Durham, included more than one-third of the acreage of the parish. Farnacres manor occupied the area between Lobley Hill and the Team in the eastern, Lowhand, quarter. The small manors of Axwell-cum-Swalwell and Hollinside lay close to the Derwent, to the north-west and west of Whickham manor respectively, while on the high ground of Fellside quarter in the south-west lay the Gibside estate, formerly the manor of Marley Hill.

This brief outline of the topography of Whickham serves to introduce the parish. To appreciate its importance in the history of the coal industry, however, we must understand something of its geology. In 1715 a test bore revealed that within some three hundred feet beneath the town street of Whickham lay no fewer than six seams of coal. The greatest of these, the famous High Main seam, lay little more than 10 fathoms (60 feet) down, and was described as being approximately 4 yards thick.[39] To the east, on Farnacres manor in the Team valley, the High Main lay only 7 fathoms (42 feet) beneath the surface, while on the 700 foot plateau in the southernmost quarter of Whickham it could be reached some 36 fathoms (216 feet) beneath the Gibside estate.[40]

[37] W. Hutchinson, *The History of Antiquities of the County Palatine of Durham*, 3 vols. (Newcastle, 1785–94), ii. 447–8.

[38] In the 17th c. these included those of the Liddells of Farnacres, the Claverings of Axwell, the Hardings of Hollinside, and the Blakistons of Gibside.

[39] NEIMME, T. E. Forster Collection, Shelf 49, vol. 4, 'Amos Barnes' View Book', 198.

[40] Ibid. 208; NEIMME, Watson Collection, Shelf 8, no. 8, 'View Book', 10; J. Gibson, *Plan of the Collieries on the Rivers Tyne and Wear* (London, 1787), gives the mean depth of working at Marley Hill as 36 fathoms. The account of a 'view' of the Gibside–Northbanks colliery in 1717 states that the main coal lay approximately 250 feet below the surface: DRO D/ST V. 36.

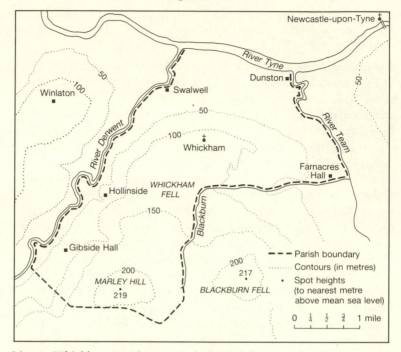

MAP 2. Whickham Parish: principal physical features

It was the High Main seam that provided the greater part of the coal mined on Tyneside prior to the eighteenth century, and it was accessible to the industry of the early modern period in a restricted area only. To the east of Gateshead the coal measures lay buried beneath a considerable thickness of barren strata at depths inaccessible to the mining technology of the age. To the west, beyond the neighbouring parish of Ryton, they lay beneath the Permian rocks of the Pennine spurs at depths of up to 900 feet. Beyond the Tyne, in a line from just north of Newcastle to Lemington, the Ninety Fathom Dyke, a great fault in the coalfield, set the northern limit of the workable area. The accessible seams of early modern Tyneside can thus be envisaged as forming 'a shallow basin round the rim of which they outcropped south of the source of the River Team on the high ground in the Pontop and Tanfield area'.[41] Whickham lay close to the centre of that basin. Moreover,

---

[41] Smailes, *North England*, 19–20; Flinn, *Coal Industry*, 19.

its geographical configuration was such that mining operations in much of the parish could be afforded free drainage north to the Tyne, west to the Derwent, and eastwards to the Team, a fact of vital importance in the age before steam-powered drainage.

Given these facts, and the immediate proximity of navigable water, it is scarcely surprising to learn that Whickham was involved in coal-mining from a very early date. Indeed, it can be said to have been at the very heart of the nascent Tyneside industry. The earliest known lease of mines in Whickham manor was granted by Bishop Hatfield in 1356, and it seems likely that coal had been worked at an even earlier date.[42] In 1492 Whickham provides the first reference to attempts to work coal in the north-eastern coalfield below the zone of free drainage; an entry in the roll of the stock-keeper of the bishop of Durham recording a payment for 'two great chains' to be employed in drawing coals and water from a mine in the manor.[43] Prior to the sixteenth century, in fact, it seems probable that the greater part of the coal shipped from Newcastle was worked in Whickham and Gateshead, and it has been argued that as the industry quickened in the 1520s output became further concentrated in the well drained and productive Whickham mines.[44]

A letter to Cardinal Wolsey during his tenure of the bishopric (1523–9) helps to provide an assessment of the scale of Whickham's participation at this stage. Wolsey was informed 'that ther be thre cole pytts at a township of yours callid Whikam . . . where be alreddy gotyn a gret substance of colis to the nombre of 25 score kele, every kele contayning 20 chald . . .'.[45] If this reference is to the output of a single annual mining season, and if each chaldron can be taken to have been of approximately thirty-four hundredweight, then the mines of Whickham can be said to have been shipping something like 17,000 tons of coal down river in at least one year in the later 1520s.[46] Nef calculated that some forty years later, in 1563–4, the coastal shipments from Newcastle amounted to 32,951 tons. If the Henrician level of production at Whickham was simply maintained, then it seems possible that Whickham manor might

[42] DPD Ch. Comm. MS 244329, 'Memorandum on Leases of Whickham Coal Mines', 1.

[43] Bourn, *Whickham*, 25.

[44] Smailes, *North England*, 133; Blanchard, 'Commercial Crisis', 80–1.

[45] Galloway, *Annals*, 84.

[46] Nef, ii. 369, suggests that the mid-16th-c. chaldron contained approx. 34 cwt.

have supplied more than half of the Tyneside vend on the eve of the Elizabethan expansion of the coal trade.[47]

Whatever the precise output of Whickham's pits, it is clear that the parish was well placed to play a prominent role in the Elizabethan and Jacobean growth of the Tyneside coal industry. This it did, and its experience is illustrative of both the problems that had to be solved if output was to be increased and the manner in which they were faced and overcome.

Among the several constraints upon coal production in the late sixteenth and early seventeenth centuries, the most immediately important were the interconnected problems of capital requirements, profitability, access to potential collieries, and technology. In the first place, coal-mining was an exceptionally expensive and risky activity. In the early days of the industry seams located very close to the surface could be worked by sinking a shallow 'bell-pit', perhaps some twenty feet in depth, and working round it for a radius of some sixteen to twenty feet at the base until the danger of collapse necessitated the abandonment of the pit and the sinking of another.[48] Such simple pits could be worked inexpensively. A small colliery utilizing such methods near Durham in the 1530s, for example, employed only five men, at an aggregate cost of 21*d*. a day, to work pits that rarely lasted a year and could be sunk for a cost of less than 5*s*.[49]

By the turn of the sixteenth and seventeenth centuries, however, the days of easy, cheap extraction were already over in the sea-sale collieries of Tyneside. Deeper shafts needed to be sunk, from which 'levels' could be driven to give access to the coal-faces where the coal was worked by the 'bord and pillar' method. Drainage 'adits' needed to be driven through to nearby hillsides to remove water, while beneath the levels where free drainage was possible chain-

---

[47] Nef, i. 21. Dietz, in 'The North-East Coal Trade', employs a different estimate of the chaldron and suggests that *c.*1550 Newcastle's shipments may have been around 51,000 tons. If we recalculate the Whickham output using Dietz's chaldron, it rises to *c.*21,000 tons—still a very substantial proportion of the Tyneside vend. A further alternative has been suggested to us by Dr John Hatcher. In his view, the chaldron referred to in the Wolsey letter may have been not the Newcastle sea-scale chaldron but a smaller measure. This might indicate a lower output of *c.*12,500 tons. He further suggests that Whickham's output was stable between this date and the early 1560s, at which time it constituted (on Hatcher's estimates) about one-third of *total* Tyneside production.

[48] Flinn, *Coal Industry*, 73, 79; Nef, i. 8.

[49] Galloway, *Annals*, 102.

pumps might be required. When workings had reached distances too far from the initial shaft to permit easy haulage of coal to the eye of the pit, a new shaft needed to be sunk, often connected to existing workings.[50] All this had implications for the amount of capital needed for successful mining, in terms of both the initial outlay in prospecting and sinking, and the constant flow of running investment necessary to keep a colliery in operation.

Contemporaries were well aware of these realities and were equally aware of the risk that the expenditure they undertook might not be recovered. 'This is the uncertainty of mines,' opined William Gray of Newcastle, 'a great charge, the profit uncertain.' He cited the case of Huntingdon Beaumont, who had come from the south in the early years of the seventeenth century with £30,000 to invest in his mine, but lost all and returned home on a 'light horse'.[51] But there were plenty of other examples to point the moral. From Whickham alone we have several. Thomas Liddell of Farnacres leased part of the glebe from the rector in 1597 and 'bestowed exceedinge great chargs in tryinge and seekinge for coals and in wyninge the myne and so att last to his great costs gott coles ther'. He claimed that he had still not recovered his investment by 1611.[52] In 1610 Ralph Cole, a Gateshead coalmaster, leased Axwell Houses colliery for a £200 fine and an annual rent of £75 for the first two pits sunk, promising to pay a further £37.10s. per annum for any additional pit brought into production. He was too confident. Five years later, he had failed to cover his charges and expressed his willingness to surrender the lease.[53]

Coal-mining was an expensive and risky undertaking in the conditions of the day: 'a great charge, the profit uncertain'. It could, none the less, be massively profitable, and there were those on Tyneside who were prepared to take the risks involved. Above all, the merchant 'hostmen' of Newcastle were ideally placed to appreciate the potential harvest to be reaped. The hostmen were those members of Newcastle's company of Merchant Venturers who engaged in the shipping of coal.[54] Already the profits of the

---

[50] N. R. Elliott, 'A Geographical Analysis of the Tyne Coal Trade', *Tijdschrift voor Economische en Sociale Geografie*, 59 (1968), 72; Nef, i. 351 ff.

[51] Gray, *Chorographia*, 31.   [52] PRO DURH 2/10/54.

[53] PRO DURH 2/11/76, 2/16/15.

[54] Prior to 1600 the hostmen had no separate legal identity. By Newcastle's Great Charter of 1600 they were formally incorporated as a trading company and the right to trade in coal was restricted to members. In 1604 a decree of the Council of the

coal trade were theirs, for by an Act of Parliament of 1529 exclusive rights to trade in coal from the Tyne had been granted to the citizens of Newcastle.[55] Already they had extensive experience in the formation of partnerships to work the collieries that supplied the trade. Their appreciation of the potentialities of the developing southern markets for coal can easily be imagined. Certainly they had the capital to invest, in partnerships if not individually, and they had the incentive to deploy it. What they needed above all was access to coal-bearing land in the vicinity of the river which could be worked profitably within the limitations of contemporary technology. Since, under English law, deposits of coal belonged to the owner of the soil, this meant either the acquisition of such land or the negotiation of favourable mining leases from local landlords.

In their efforts to expand output to meet the needs of their trade in the late sixteenth century, partnerships of hostmen proceeded to obtain such leases and to finance the establishment of new collieries, notably on the south bank of the Tyne to the west of the Derwent confluence in the parish of Ryton. In the early seventeenth century further new pits were sunk on the north bank of the river—in Newburn, Denton, Elswick, and Benwell for example.[56] From the outset, however, they were more than aware that their requirements could best be met by an expansion of operations in the manors of Whickham and Gateshead. Here could be found proven collieries of unparalleled richness and ideal location. Before their potential could be realized, however, the hostmen needed to obtain access to those collieries on terms that would permit their unrestricted exploitation and guarantee as nearly as possible their profitability.

Such ambitions were frustrated by the long-established policies of the bishops of Durham. Both Whickham and Gateshead were episcopal manors. In the County Palatine of Durham the bishop held title to all minerals save those in the lands of freeholders, and, as has already been noted, it was episcopal policy to grant mining leases only on highly restrictive terms. In the earliest known lease of

North, ratified by a new charter, established the right of any burgess who could pay the entrance fee to join the hostmen's company. Thereafter the company 'ceased to be the private preserve of the great coal merchants, and became merely the regulatory body for the trading by any competent burgess of the town in the coal market': R. Tuck, 'Civil Conflict in School and Town 1500–1700', in B. Mains and A. Tuck (eds.), *Royal Grammar School, Newcastle-upon-Tyne: A History of the School in its Community* (Stocksfield, 1986), 13–14, 17.

[55] Nef, i. 21.   [56] Ibid. 26; ii. 18, 44 ff.; Smailes, *North England*, 133.

Whickham mines, for example, Bishop Hatfield's lease of 1356, the lessees' output from the five mines granted to them was not to exceed one keel of coal per day. They were to employ no more than five 'barrowmen' and were obligated to compensate the manorial tenants for any damage done to their lands either by mining or by the carriage of coal. The Bishop, for his part, agreed that his forester would provide such timber as was needed for the pits and the construction of riverside staithes, and undertook to grant no further leases to competitors during the twelve-year period of the agreement. In return, he received the very substantial entry fine of five hundred marks.[57]

Two centuries later little had changed. In a lease of 12 July 1550, Bishop Tunstall granted 'all the coole mynes att Whickham' to a partnership of seven gentlemen from Whickham and Gateshead for twenty-one years. The lessees agreed to work 'according to [the] usage and custome' of the bishopric, and were allowed to draw sixteen score corves from each pit per work day 'and not above', though they were permitted to exceed this daily quota if bad weather prevented work at other times. The rent was set at £20 'for every pytt' and subletting was prohibited. The Bishop agreed to provide timber from his woods 'for upholdinge of the shafts', but it was to be cut at the lessees' expense. They were also granted 'sufficient way leave' to carry their coals to the staithes.[58]

Between the time of Bishop Hatfield in the middle of the fourteenth century and that of his mid-Tudor successor, there was no significant change in episcopal practice. We see here no recipe for expansion, and indeed little room for significant growth. As two recent historians have commented, such episcopal leases 'left no room for individual initiative in organizing production', and 'seriously curtailed the production and supply of coal in north-eastern England'.[59] Only with the expiry of the Tunstall lease were there some signs of change. In 1570 Bishop Pilkington granted another twenty-one-year lease at an annual rent of £30. This lease stipulated that 'not passing thre pitts' were to be worked at any one time. Pilkington's lease differs from that of his predecessor,

---

[57] W. Page (ed.), *The Victoria County History of the County of Durham* (London, 1907), ii. 322. The capacity of a 'keel' at this date is unknown. It says much for the potential value of Whickham's mines that the lessees (Sir Thomas Grey and John Pulhore, rector of Whickham) were prepared to pay such a sum for the 12-year lease.

[58] DRO D/ST 4/2.

[59] Blanchard, 'Commercial Crisis', 82; Blake, 'Medieval Coal Trade', 22.

however, in that it demises mines in a specific location—Cross Moor, or part thereof—and not, as was the earlier case, 'all the coole mynes att Whickham'.[60] A further lease survives from 1575 in which Pilkington demised another mine at the annual rent of £18 for a term of twenty-one years. Again, this lease is of interest in that it specifies that the coal was to be worked in a particular area of the manor—Southfield.[61]

This practice might have made it possible for the bishop to permit an increase in the supply of Whickham coal simply by granting a large number of such leases. Stinting of production could be maintained, but more of the manor might have been opened up to exploitation at any one time. The bishop's control over mineral rights did not therefore preclude expansion, though it did place significant obstacles in its way. Indeed, it is conceivable that the bishop and his stewards might have learned to adapt their cautious administrative policies to the heady realities of the Elizabethan boom in the coal trade. There is little sign, however, that they had done so by the mid-1570s. To judge by a subsequent report, it seems likely that only four pits were working in Whickham manor at the close of Bishop Pilkington's reign in 1576.[62] His successor, Bishop Barnes, was allowed no opportunity to learn.

The crucial breakthrough in the exploitation of the mineral wealth of Whickham came with the granting of what soon became known as the Grand Lease.[63] On 1 February 1578 Elizabeth I, in pursuance of her accustomed policy of milking ecclesiastical revenues in order to meet the Crown's pressing financial needs, obtained from the newly elevated Bishop Thomas Barnes a lease of 'all mines as well opened as not opened' in the manors of Whickham and Gateshead. The lease was for the unprecedented period of seventy-nine years, it laid down no restraints on mining, and the annual rent was a mere £117.15s. 8d.[64] It seems likely that this lease

[60] G. P. L. Cotesworth MSS CN/1/312. Cf. Fordyce, *Durham*, ii. 689; Bourn, *Whickham*, 24.

[61] G. P. L. Cotesworth MSS CN/1/312. Cf. Galloway, *Annals*, 92.

[62] B. L. Lansdowne MS 66, no. 84, f. 219. Cf. Lansdowne MS 66, no. 87.

[63] The following account of the Grand Lease is based on DPD Ch. Comm. MS 244329; Nef, i. 150 ff.; Trevor-Roper, 'Bishopric of Durham'; Tuck, 'Civil Conflict'.

[64] DPD Ch. Comm. MS 244329, 2. The lease involved the taking over of the existing mining leases mentioned in n. 62 above. Their rents were apparently paid in addition to the rent of the Grand Lease until Bishop Barnes's death in 1587, but not thereafter: Nef, i. 154. It was later alleged that the holders of the Grand Lease forced out the earlier lessees by harassing their operations until they surrendered their leases: Dendy, *Hostmen*, 8.

was obtained by the Queen at the behest of Thomas Sutton, Master of the Ordnance in the North, for the ink was scarcely dry upon the document before on 19 April 1578 the Queen assigned her rights to Sutton in return for a substantial payment. By virtue of his office, Sutton was in an excellent position to appreciate the potential value of such a lease. Moreover, he was a speculative financier of genius, already on his way to becoming the richest commoner in England. As a client of the Queen's favourite, Robert Dudley, Earl of Leicester, and the latter's brother the Earl of Warwick, he was also admirably placed to bring influence to bear at court in the achievement of this great coup.[65]

In the next few years Sutton firmed up his position. On 20 June 1581 the lease was renewed, again for seventy-nine years and to the Queen in the first instance, but now with full rights of lordship over the manor of Whickham in addition to the mining rights. Less than a year later, on 26 April 1582, it was renewed yet again, on the same terms as in 1581 but this time for a period of no less than ninety-nine years.[66] Whether Sutton's original intention was to work the mines himself is not clear. Initially he appears to have sublet the rights that he had obtained in Whickham to Newcastle merchants who operated the pits as a single colliery.[67] The Newcastle hostmen, however, were deeply chagrined by the success of this well connected interloper. They hampered his opportunity to take full advantage of his new position by simply refusing to make him a freeman of Newcastle, thereby excluding him from direct participation in the coal trade, and they remained obdurate on this point in the face of Sutton's attempts to bring the influence of his powerful patrons to bear in pressing his case. If this was a deliberate tactic, intended to squeeze him out by forestalling the possibility of his becoming the overwhelmingly dominant figure in both the production and shipment of coal, it worked. By the end of 1582, Sutton was offering to sell his rights to the mayor and burgesses of Newcastle.[68]

At this point a delicate legal problem arose. The mayor and burgesses found that the city was in fact legally incapable of purchasing the lease, for it had never been formally incorporated.

[65] DPD Ch. Comm. MS 244329, 2. For Sutton, see Nef, i. 151; Trevor-Roper, 'Bishopric of Durham', 53–5; Tuck, 'Civil Conflict', 12.

[66] DPD Ch. Comm. MS 244329, 3.

[67] Nef, i. 151.

[68] Trevor-Roper, 'Bishopric of Durham', 55; Tuck, 'Civil Conflict', 12.

Dismayed, they swiftly put in train steps to acquire incorporation, spending 'great sums in procuring a new charter to make the town capable' as the mayor later testified. Meanwhile, lest this golden opportunity be lost, the mayor, Henry Anderson, and one of the aldermen, William Selby, were provided with funds to buy the lease in their own names on the understanding that they would transfer their rights to the mayor and burgesses when the new charter had been obtained. Part of the huge purchase price of £12,000 was obtained from the common treasury of the city, which put up £5,500, while the rest was provided by loans from private individuals among those burgesses with a personal interest in the coal trade.[69] Accordingly, on 12 November 1583, on the petition of Thomas Sutton, the Queen granted all her interest in the lease to Anderson and Selby.[70] As a result of this expedient, full rights of lordship in the manor of Whickham became the property of Anderson and Selby in partnership with those of the hostmen who contributed personally to the purchase (for already by 1585 the loans advanced were being regarded in Newcastle as secured by shares in the lease and were indeed being traded in the city[71]). An inner ring of Newcastle burgesses had thus succeeded in arrogating to themselves the spoils of the Grand Lease, an achievement that 'may be said to have constituted an epoch in the history of the Tyne coal trade'.[72]

The story, however, was not quite over. In 1589 Newcastle received its charter of incorporation. Anderson and Selby, however, declined to transfer their lease, arguing that all the merchants involved in the coal trade were shareholding participants in the benefits. Such claims cut no ice with the aggrieved citizens who had contributed indirectly to the purchase through the common treasury of the city but had received nothing in return.[73] In 1591 an indignant complaint alleged that the Grand Lease was already worth £1,500–£1,600 above the annual rent, but that this wealth, which should benefit the city as a whole, served 'but to enrich 8 or 10 private men'. The Grand Lessees, having obtained what amounted

---

[69] Tuck, 'Civil Conflict', 12–13. Cf. Nef, i. 151–2.

[70] DPD Ch. Comm. MS 244329, 3.

[71] Tuck, 'Civil Conflict', 13. Within a few years shares in the Grand Lease were also being bequeathed by will. See e.g. J. C. Hodgson (ed.), *Wills and Inventories from the Registry at Durham*, pt. III, Surtees Soc. no. 112 (Newcastle, 1906), 172, 177.

[72] Quoting Galloway, *Annals*, 93.   [73] Tuck, 'Civil Conflict', 13.

to 'the Monopolie of Coals', were further accused of using their position to force up prices. They 'geve themselves almost wholly to Collyerie and deale litle with other merchandies', it was claimed, for now they were 'the Lords of Coal'.[74]

Matters came to a head in 1592, when a guild meeting open to all the freemen of Newcastle demanded that the lease be transferred to the city. The Mayor (Henry Anderson himself) played for time by referring the matter to the Council of the North in York.[75] For several years the dispute festered in the city. But meanwhile the aggrieved citizens acquired an exceptionally powerful ally. Because the price of coal had risen in the aftermath of the Grand Lease, the authorities of the City of London were deeply unhappy. As early as 1590 the lord mayor of London had brought the matter to the attention of Lord Burghley and put the blame upon the monopolistic practices of the Newcastle hostmen. As the battle raged in Newcastle in the 1590s, London re-entered the fray. In a document of 1595, the London authorities complained that, while Sutton's tenure of the Grand Lease had raised coal prices from 4s. to 6s. per chalder, the subsequent engrossment of the whole commodity of coal by the Newcastle hostmen had seen prices pushed up to 7s., 8s., and now 9s. per chalder. The inner ring of hostmen were alleged to have shut down some collieries in order to 'diet' the trade, and to have abused their commanding position in the coal trade to subject other coal-owners and shipmasters to their control, all of this in the pursuit of huge and excessive profits gouged from the purses of London consumers.[76]

The 'Lords of Coal' were not slow to defend themselves against these charges. They pleaded that prices had not risen so sharply as was alleged, and blamed such increases as had taken place on rising costs of production and transportation. They denied that they had closed pits to force up prices. On the contrary, they claimed that 'ther ar nowe for thes last three or fower yeares more colles wrought then could be gotten carried to the water by reason of the unseasonableness of the yeares'.[77] The discontent of London, however, could not be ignored. In 1598 the Privy Council acted at

---

[74] BL Lansdowne MS 66, no. 86. [75] Tuck, 'Civil Conflict', 13.

[76] Ibid. 13–14; Dendy, *Hostmen*, 2–4.

[77] BL Harleian MS 6850, no. 39. This document has been erroneously dated to 1591. It is clearly a reply to the 1595 complaint printed by Dendy and quoted above. Other internal evidence also suggests a date in the mid-1590s.

last, by establishing a committee of enquiry. A year later, a deal was struck with the hostmen. The Privy Council undertook to arrange for the hostmen, who were at present merely members of the Newcastle company of Merchant Venturers, to be formally incorporated as a separate trading company—a position that would give them exclusive rights to trade in coal from Newcastle. In return, the hostmen, who no longer needed to fear competition, agreed to assign the Grand Lease to the mayor and burgesses of Newcastle. They further undertook not to enhance the price of first-class coals at London beyond 10s. per chalder; and finally, they submitted to the imposition of a levy upon the coal trade, whereby the Crown would receive 1s. per chalder on all coals shipped to English ports and 5s. per chalder on coals shipped overseas.[78]

Acquiescence in a levy that provided a welcome supplement to the coffers of the Crown at a time of pressing financial need was perhaps the key concession. It enabled the hostmen to preserve their gains in all essentials while apparently acceding to the demands of their fellow citizens and their London customers. As recently as 1591 they had protested vociferously against a proposal to levy only 8d. a chaldron on the coal trade, maintaining that they had not yet recovered the purchase price of the Grand Lease and that their profits were not excessive in relation to 'the charges in getting and wynning of [coal]'.[79] Now, however, they prudently gave way. The deal was struck, and its provisions were included in a further new charter for Newcastle granted in 1600. Henceforward, within the limitations agreed in 1599, the oligarchical practices of the Newcastle hostmen had legal sanction and the blessing of the Crown. In 1604 their charmed circle was widened somewhat by the establishment of the right of any Newcastle burgess who could pay the entrance fee to join the hostmen's company.[80] But the essential strength of their position remained. Only hostmen could deal in the coal trade. Hostmen would not buy from non-members, with the result that only hostmen found it profitable to become partners in local mines. Their shrewd concessions permitted them to retain what was close enough to a free hand in the supply of coal to the markets of southern England, as was to be evident on a number of future occasions when in the face of the vicissitudes of the trade they

[78] Tuck, 'Civil Conflict', 14.
[79] BL Lansdowne MS 67, no. 22 (7 April 1591).
[80] Tuck, 'Civil Conflict', 17.

attempted to regulate production, restrict competition among themselves, and keep up prices.[81] While none of these efforts proved to be enduring, they still underline the enormous economic power that was now legally constituted in the hands of the 'Lords of Coal'.

By the exploitation of that power, the leaders of Newcastle's coal-owning oligarchy became prodigiously rich, above all those of them who retained personal shares in the Grand Lease.[82] Thomas Liddell was said to be worth £2,000 per annum. Robert Bewick and his son exported coal worth £4,200 in 1627. Sir Nicholas Cole was described as 'fat and rich, vested in a Sack of Sattin'.[83] Their wealth, derived from the booming fortunes of the coal trade, enabled some of them to buy their way on to the land. The Liddells, for example, purchased both the manor of Farnacres in Whickham and the adjacent Ravensworth Castle estate in Lamesley, establishing themselves as substantial landlords while maintaining their position as major players in colliery. To the historian of Durham's county society, a 'particularly striking' feature of the period was 'the large entry of Newcastle families of coal-owning background. Some dozen of these had settled on estates in Durham by the 1630s. Nowhere else in England, Northumberland included, were there so many landed fortunes founded on this kind of industrial basis. . . .'[84] The Grand Lease was the mainspring of this opulence. Shareholders benefited immensely, and as late as 1662 Bishop Cosin's surveyors reckoned that it was 'worth now above the rent . . . about MM^{li} [£2,000] having bin worth heretofore and may be hereafter 5000^{li} and some times 8000^{li}'.[85]

---

[81] Nef, ii. 111–13; Dendy, *Hostmen*, p. xliv.

[82] Even after the assignment of the Grand Lease to the mayor and burgesses of the city, the personal shares of those who had advanced money in 1583 remained in being. References to shares occur periodically in the wills of prominent citizens, e.g. H. M. Wood (ed.), *Wills and Inventories from the Registry at Durham*, pt. IV, Surtees Soc. no. 142 (Newcastle, 1929), 91, 162. Shares were soon subdivided: e.g. c.1620, 2/3 of a 1/12 share of the Grand Lease was sublet for 21 years at £70 p.a., and c.1637, the same share fetched £260 p.a.: PRO DURH 4/1, 681. In 1646 Sir Frances Bowes of Newcastle's 1/12 share of the Grand Lease for 12 years was valued at £260 p.a.: R. Welford (ed.), *Records of the Committees for Compounding, etc. with Delinquent Royalists . . . 1643–1660*, Surtees Soc. no. 111 (Newcastle, 1905), 123.

[83] R. Howell, *Newcastle-upon-Tyne and the Puritan Revolution: A Study of the Civil War in North England* (Oxford, 1967), 14–15.

[84] M. James, *Family, Lineage and Civil Society: A Study of Society, Politics and Mentality in the Durham Region 1500–1640* (Oxford, 1974), 69.

[85] Durham Cathedral, Dean and Chapter Library, Sharp Coll., no. 167, 'Bishop Cosin's Survey', 170. The estimate of the former value of the lease tallies with the

Investment in land did not mean withdrawal from the coal industry. On the contrary, as in the case of the Liddells, well chosen estates could consolidate a family's industrial strength. More generally, the profits of the coal trade that accrued to the leading Newcastle merchants were used to finance major capital investments. With few exceptions, almost all the capital for the expansion of mining in the seventeenth century seems to have been self-generated from the personal fortunes of the mercantile élite. While there may have been no formal joint-stock companies, there were many short-lived partnerships in which money and resources were pooled. This became all the more necessary because the expansion of the coal trade was built upon the success of a few really large colliery complexes. While it would appear that the 'Lords of Coal' subcontracted the actual business of 'winning' coal and 'leading' it to the river, their capital costs were enormous and required close supervision. They needed to find cash for prospecting to follow the richest seams, for winning, draining, and ventilating their collieries, and for transporting coal from the pit head to the riverside staithes which they had either built themselves or else rented. These costs were neither fixed nor predictable, and at the same time the return was subject to the capricious swings of market forces. Some investors lost badly, sometimes spectacularly; but many did very well, receiving steady and substantial incomes and not infrequent windfall profits.[86]

The heady, buccaneering phase of the trade's expansion between the 1570s and the 1620s witnessed enormous accomplishments in both organization and technology. Large new mines were opened. A substantial labour force was recruited. Technical difficulties were faced and overcome. Production indices doubled and redoubled. A complex transportation infrastructure was brought into being.[87] Moreover, the real cost of a hearthful of coal to the London consumers almost kept pace with wages in this period as a result of the efficiencies of massive scale.[88] Indeed, this very scale

1636 Ship Money assessment of colliery values in which the Whickham part of the colliery was valued at £4,500 and the Gateshead portion at £300: Durham Cathedral, Dean and Chapter Library, Hunter MSS, fo. 22/17.

[86] For a general account of these matters, see Nef, ii. 18, 44 ff.

[87] Nef, i. 21, 25 ff., 241 ff., 351 ff., 383 ff., 435 ff.; ii. 135 ff.

[88] Between 1550 and 1640 the price of coal in London trebled: Nef, ii. 79–80. Although money wages in the south of England also trebled in the period 1500–1640 there was probably some disparity, since during the years 1550–1640 wages rose rather more slowly than before 1550. From c.1625, however, wages were rising while

was perhaps the most distinctive, and to the people of the time astonishing, feature of the Tyneside industry. In seventeenth-century Lancashire collieries were generally small, one-pit affairs, employing only a handful of hewers to win something between 1,000 and 1,500 tons a year. They were also short-lived. Demand was weak, strongly seasonal, and geographically circumscribed as a result of transportation difficulties.[89] Lancashire was perhaps more typical of the English coal industry of the age, but the very importance of the north-eastern industry lay in the fact that it was utterly different. Nef captured vividly this distinctiveness and the drama of its development. 'The traffic in coal', he wrote,

must have absorbed the attention of a spectator seated on one of the hills behind Newcastle, almost to the exclusion of any other sight. Picture the mouth of the muddy, narrow river Tyne, jammed with four or five hundred keels and two or three hundred ships . . . think of the hilly slopes to the north and south covered with hundreds of small carts and wagons, leaving behind them trails of black refuse on the green countryside; and then think of a time when this same countryside was at rest . . . when the only evidence of the coal industry was a few pits at the water's edge . . . [and] masters took on board a lading of coal to ballast their cargoes of fish, or grindstones or jersey cloths. In this comparison you have . . . a view of the change wrought around the town of Newcastle in the century following the accession of Elizabeth.[90]

3. WROUGHT AND GOING PITS: 1570–1652

At the eye of this economic storm were the coal seams that lay beneath the parish of Whickham. They were the principal prize for which the battle over the Grand Lease was fought and won. In our account of those events and their consequences, however, the parish has receded from view. As Galloway, one of the earliest students of the north-eastern coal industry remarked, 'Almost a plethora of information is available regarding the coal trade of the Tyne in this

the price of coal in London was steady, so that it seems that a rough parity with 1550 prices (in real terms) was restored. For wages, see P. Bowden, 'Agricultural Prices, Farm Profits, and Rents', in J. Thirsk (ed.), *The Agrarian History of England and Wales*, iv, *1500–1640* (Cambridge, 1967), 599–600.

[89] Langton, *Geographical Change*, 39, 41, 43, 45–6.

[90] Nef, i. 29–30. The north-east's distinctiveness in the sheer scale of operations is not controversial; cf. Coleman, *Industry*, 49.

era, but the collieries themselves lie somewhat in the background.'[91] Yet restoring them to their proper place is not easy. There survives little evidence of a serial nature on the output of individual collieries in this period which can be compared with the figures recorded in the Newcastle port books. In the following discussion of mining developments in Whickham, therefore, we have been obliged to rely for the most part on the scattered evidence of court cases and taxation documents, fragmentary references in wills and inventories, and casual asides in depositions. The recoverable data can be sometimes almost random in survival. None the less, a careful search of the available sources can reveal a surprising volume of such material, which, as we hope to show, can be reconstituted into a coherent and consistent story.

In Cardinal Wolsey's time, it seems generally agreed, almost all the 'sea-coal' shipped from Newcastle was produced from the seams running beneath the manors of Whickham and Gateshead. Annual production at Whickham in the 1520s may have been in the order of 17,000 tons. Some thirty years later, Bishop Tunstall's lease of 1550 permitted his lessees to work sixteen score corves per pit per day. We do not know how many pits were worked in Tunstall's day; under Bishop Pilkington in the early 1570s, however, we have good evidence that only four pits were working in the manor of Whickham, and there is no evidence that collieries were working in any other part of the parish before the 1570s. If we assume that four pits were working every year in the early part of Elizabeth's reign, and that their stinted production was of a similar order to that permitted by Bishop Tunstall, then we might estimate that their maximum daily production may have been around sixty-four score corves.

This, however, would be a very generous estimate. Such evidence as we have on the output of individual pits in Whickham at a later date suggests that it could vary enormously in accordance with the age and size of the pit, the richness of the seam, and the difficulties encountered in working it on particular days. In the later 1620s the overman of one established pit complained of there being 'onely broken worke . . . sometymes Tenn or Twelve Score [corves] a day and sometymes none attall'.[92] He seems to have regarded twelve score corves as a good day's work. Again, evidence regarding two

[91] Galloway, *Annals*, 129.
[92] PRO E 134 3 Car. I, Ea. 19.

other pits, one working in 1606 and one in 1620, states that they were winning up to six 'tens' of coal per week.[93] A 'ten' was ten Newcastle chaldrons, or ten score corves. A weekly output of six tens would therefore amount to sixty score corves, and if the pits worked a six-day week daily output may have been ten score corves, or ten Newcastle chaldrons (around twenty-one tons at these dates).[94] Given these facts, it might be safer to assume that at best each of the four pits working in Bishop Pilkington's time produced eleven score corves or around twenty-three tons a day, a total daily production for the manorial colliery of around ninety-two tons.

The next difficulty is that of translating such a figure into an estimate of annual production. Clearly, daily output could fluctuate dramatically. Moreover, we lack precise information on the regularity of working at this date and on the length of the seasonal lay-off during the winter dead season of the coal trade. Evidence from a court case of 1611 indicates that work was very slow during the months of December to March, while a further case refers to a contract of 1614 in which two pits were to be worked for an eight-month season running from February to October.[95] Let us assume, then, a working year of some thirty-six weeks. If we make the further assumptions that the pits were worked for six days a week during the working year and that output was steady throughout that period (a distinctly heroic assumption), then the manorial pits of the 1570s may have produced ninety-two tons a day for a total of 216 days: an estimated annual output of close to 20,000 tons on the eve of the first granting of the Grand Lease. These calculations suggest that Whickham's output had risen little from the levels obtaining in the time of Henry VIII.

The petitions and counter-petitions of the 1590s permit us to make a further estimate of the growth of Whickham's production in the immediate aftermath of the Grand Lease. In their 1595

---

[93] PRO STAC 8/53/10, DURH 2/19/137.

[94] The conversion of Newcastle chaldrons into tons is a problem of enormous complexity which has never been resolved satisfactorily. Nef, ii. app. C, suggested that the chaldron gradually increased in size prior to its standardization by statute in 1694. He reckoned that *c.*1616–18 the chaldron contained 43 cwt. Dietz, 'The North-East Coal Trade', 286, challenges Nef's view of the growth of the chaldron, but suggests 42 cwt. as a reasonable standard for the late 16th and 17th c. Dendy, *Hostmen*, 44–5, also suggests 42 cwt. for the early 17th c. For this calculation we have assumed a chaldron of 42 cwt., giving a 'ten' of 21 tons.

[95] PRO DURH 2/10/54, 2/19/211.

submission to the Privy Council, the Newcastle coal-owners indignantly rejected the allegation that in Whickham and Gateshead they were working 'less quantitye of coles . . . than heartofore' in an attempt to 'diet' the trade, confidently declaring that 'the contrary thereof shalbe sufficientlie proved if yor honors desier'. They added, however, that the Grand Lease mines 'ammounte not in quantitye to the vth parte of the Collerye wrought about Newcastell'.[96] Nef suggested that this might mean an output of some 50,000 tons for the Grand Lease collieries at this date.[97] In making this suggestion, however, he used his estimate of the total output of the lower Tyne valley in the *later* 1590s. Since the total Tyneside output was probably less than 200,000 tons in the *early* 1590s, it would seem more plausible that the Grand Lease collieries were producing around 40,000 tons per annum in 1594–5.[98] A proportion of this coal, of course, would have been worked in Gateshead, though this is likely to have been a relatively small fraction of the total output, since our evidence suggests that mining activity in this period was concentrated in Whickham. On the other hand, by the mid-1590s at least one further substantial colliery was operating in Whickham parish: at Gellsfield, on the Blakistons' estate, outside the territories of the Grand Lease. If we assume that this operation offsets the contribution of Gateshead to the Grand Lease output, then for the parish of Whickham as a whole a total output of 40,000 tons may be a reasonable—indeed, a cautious—estimate.[99]

In the space of a decade and a half of unrestricted production,

---

[96] BL Harleian MS 6850, no. 39.   [97] Nef, i. 361.

[98] Nef estimated the total Tyne output on the basis of the seal-sale vend of the later 1590s plus an allowance of 50,000 tons for coal used locally in the salt pans. We have preferred to use his figures for the sea-sale vend of the early 1590s plus a similar allocation of 'pan coal', thus scaling down the estimate of total output to rather less than 200,000 tons. Dietz, 'The North-East Coal Trade', 286, suggests an annual average vend of 160,097 tons in 1593–8. This alternative figure plus a pan coal allowance of 50,000 tons suggests a total Tyneside output of *c*.210,000 tons and a Grand Lease output of 42,000 tons.

[99] In 1636 the Gateshead colliery was valued at 1/15 of the value of Whickham Grand Lease colliery and at less than half the value of the Blakistons' Gellsfield colliery: Durham Cathedral, Dean and Chapter Library, Hunter MSS, fo. 22/17. We cannot be certain of the relative size of the Gateshead and Gellsfield collieries at the earlier date, but this fact makes our offsetting of Gateshead output by that of Gellsfield less arbitrary than might at first appear. Gellsfield was well established in 1595, having been let to Newcastle hostmen as early as 1578: Bourn, *Whickham*, 24; Surtees, *Durham*, ii. 251. Gellsfield may possibly have been in production earlier still, since in 1576 Bishop Pilkington was receiving a £10 p.a. wayleave payment from the Blakistons: BL Lansdowne MS 66, no. 84, fo. 219, no. 87.

therefore, Whickham's output may have doubled after half a century of rough stability. At the same time, it seems likely that its share of the sea-coal market had fallen quite considerably, from a position of dominance in the early sixteenth century to something in the order of a quarter. The new collieries in the neighbouring parish of Ryton—Winlaton, Stella, and Blaydon—all date their take-off from the early years of Elizabeth's reign. Whickham had marked time for too long before the Grand Lease, and it seems possible that even after its acquisition the hostmen of Newcastle, beset by their enemies, did not immediately exploit it to the utmost in competition with other recently established mines. To this extent, there may have been a grain of truth in the allegation that the Grand Lessees had restrained output in Whickham and Gateshead, if only in the sense that production had not risen to the extent expected. Nevertheless, Whickham's potential was soon to be realized in the decades after 1600, as is made clear by the last of the early documents that allows us to estimate the output of the parish: the Ship Money assessment of 1636.

This assessment provides valuations of all the principal collieries situated in the northern parishes of County Durham on the south bank of the Tyne. We have no certainty as to the accuracy of the valuations, but they are not implausible, and it seems reasonable to assume that the two officers responsible for the taxation of the collieries were consistent in their criteria of valuation. That part of the Grand Lease operation situated in Whickham was valued at £4,500, more than twice the value of the next biggest colliery assessed (Blaydon colliery). The five other mining complexes in Whickham parish had a total value of £2,250. Together the six Whickham collieries provided 41.5 per cent of the total valuation of the mines included in the assessment, while Whickham Grand Lease alone accounted for 27.7 per cent of that total.[100]

To translate these figures into an assessment of output, we can begin with Nef's suggestion that the total output of the Tyne valley on the eve of the Civil War 'must have approached 600,000 tons'. About a quarter of the total, however, was probably mined north of the river, and in addition, it seems that smaller land-sale collieries to

---

[100] Durham Cathedral, Dean and Chapter Library, Hunter MSS, fo. 22/17. Plausibility is lent to the Ship Money assessment by the closeness of its valuation of the Grand Lease collieries to that later made by Bishop Cosin's surveyors. See n. 85 above.

the south of the river were not included in the assessment of 1636. Cautiously, Nef reckoned that the combined output of the south bank sea-sale collieries was around 350,000 tons.[101] If we adopt this estimate, the implication of the colliery valuations is that Whickham's total contribution to output was in the order of at least 145,000 tons, of which close to 97,000 tons was dug up in the lands of the manor of Whickham held by the Grand Lease.

We cannot emphasize too strongly that the above account of the changing levels of coal output in Whickham is an exercise in educated guesswork. If its general plausibility is accepted, however, it suggests that production in Whickham rose modestly between the 1520s and the early 1570s, that it doubled between the latter date and 1595, and that thereafter it continued to expand rapidly. In 1636, by which time the Grand Lease colliery may have been already past its greatest days, the output of the parish was still prodigious by the standards of the day and may have stood at something like seven times the level of the 1570s.[102]

Having gained a sense of the scale of overall mining activity in Whickham, we must now turn to the more specific evidence that we have been able to assemble on the development of the industry in the parish. As we shall see, it lends support to the broad picture provided by our output estimates and adds further detail to flesh out our reconstruction.

The most important findings to emerge concern the variations that can be observed in the geography and chronology of

---

[101] Nef, i. 361, n. 2. Dietz, 'The North-East Coal Trade', 281, suggests a sea-sale output of roughly the same order of magnitude in the mid-1630s.

[102] An alternative interpretation is possible. If we assume that the 4 pits of the early 1570s *did* achieve their maximum daily production of 16 score corves each—a total of *c.*134.6 tons a day—and maintained this level of production for a mining season of 216 days, then the total annual output in the 1570s may have reached 29,000 tons. Such an interpretation might derive support from the calculations of Dr Hatcher. In his view, Whickham manor's annual output in the 1520s may have been as low as 12,500 tons, and remained stable until the 1560s. Thereafter colliery rents paid to the bishop suggest to Hatcher an increased output which may have been substantially above 20,000 tons by the 1570s. Estimates based on rental income may be open to the objection that they reflect projected rather than actual output, but in this uncertain field they deserve to be taken seriously as an alternative. Dr Hatcher's further estimates of Tyneside production suggest that Whickham Grand Lease alone had an output of over 50,000 tons in the 1590s and in excess of 100,000 tons by the 1630s. Evaluation of these alternative estimates, for which we are grateful to Dr Hatcher, must await the publication of his study of the early modern industry. What is not in doubt is the prodigious growth in the output of coal in Whickham between the 1570s and 1630s.

exploitation. Most historians of the early coal industry appear to agree with Nef that the mining frontier began on outcropping seams close to the river and then moved inland in the course of the early seventeenth century.[103] One could easily gain this impression from contemporary comments. Our research, however, suggests a rather different reality and leads us to conclusions that are in some respects the opposite of those usually put forward.

Outcrops on the river-bank may indeed have been the very first sites of mining in Whickham at the time of the initial medieval workings in the parish. By the sixteenth century, however, mining seems to have been sited not in the riverside area to the north of Whickham town, but rather on the higher ground to the south of the township, some two or three miles from the river. In a dispute in the 1590s, evidence was given that a coal way had existed across Corn Moor and Cross Moor to Whickham town for some sixty years, indicating the presence of mines well to the south from at least the 1530s.[104] More specifically, the mining leases of the early 1570s refer to pits in Cross Moor and Southfield around one and a half miles from the Tyne, while by 1578 mining was proceeding at Gellsfield, to the south of the manorial boundary, beyond Whickham Fell, some two and a half miles from the river.[105] At the time of the Grand Lease, then, mining seems to have been confined largely to the areas of rough pasture to the south of Whickham town.

Initially, the Grand Lessees appear to have continued this practice. A partnership of six of them was active in South Field in the 1580s, sinking a new pit there in 1589, for example, 'at their equal charges'.[106] Operations were also extended to include 'Hollinbush', beyond Cross Moor on the Blackburn, where Whickham bordered on Lamesley chapelry. A pit was sunk there by another group of Grand Lessees in 1594, perhaps to link up with and extend their workings in land leased nearby at Alydens Close in Lamesley.[107]

As the decade advanced, other hostmen, either individually or in partnership, took the opportunity to consolidate their position in Whickham by acquiring leases of freehold land outside the

---

[103] Nef, i. 26.   [104] GPL Cotesworth MSS CN/1/313.
[105] Galloway, *Annals*, 92; Bourn, *Whickham*, 24; Surtees, *Durham*, ii. 251. For Gellsfield, see n. 99 above.   [106] PRO DURH 2/2/50.
[107] GPL Cotesworth MSS CN/1/313; PRO DURH 2/1/52.

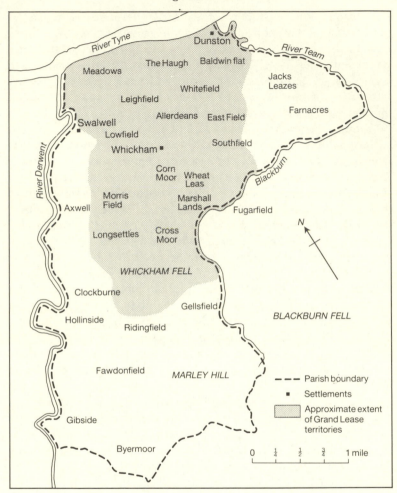

MAP 3. Principal sites of colliery operations in Whickham *c*.1580–*c*.1760
Hatched area indicates approximate extent of Grand Lease territories.

territories of the Grand Lease. Of these acquisitions, the most significant was the lease gained in 1597 from Robert Fawdon of what was to become the Fawdonfield or Greenlaw colliery.[108] Again this land was well to the south, lying in the centre of Fellside quarter, and approximately three miles from the Tyne. Only at the

[108] DRO D/ST 5/13.

very close of the sixteenth century do we find two references to working in the lower-lying northerly parts of the parish. In 1597 the rector's glebe land in Allerdeans was leased to Thomas Liddell, who commenced prospecting there, while in 1599 a lease was acquired by two hostmen of the manor of Axwell Houses.[109]

As the seventeenth century opened, however, workings continued for the most part in the established mines of the southern areas of Whickham. The Grand Lessees sank another new pit in Southfield in 1603, and a year earlier had obtained a lease of a parcel of freehold in the same area, doubtless with a view to extending their operations there.[110] Both the Hollinbush and the Gellsfield mines were still working in 1606 and 1608 respectively, while in Greenlaw–Fawdonfield work expanded and a second pit was sunk in 1606, both pits being described in 1610 as 'wrought and going with full work of coles'.[111]

The major new departure at this date was the opening up of Ridingfield, a section of the Hollinside estate lying between Hollinside, Fawdonfield, Gellsfield, and Whickham Fell. A lease had been acquired by Grand Lessees at some point before 1606, for by that year work was well underway. The Ridingfield pit of 1606 provides an excellent illustration of the nature of mining in Whickham at this date. It was worked on behalf of the owners by an 'overman', John Bainbrigg of Gellsfield, who undertook to 'have the whole charge of working of the said pitt and should at his owne charges worke draw upp and lye above ground at the said pitt evrye weeke five or six tenns of coales or theire abouts'. He was to be paid 22*s.* for every ten wrought and was bound upon pain of a £100 forfeit to perform his side of the agreement. The pit was 30 fathoms deep (180 feet), and at least fourteen named men worked there regularly, the underground workers being let down by what was described as 'a great new rope' suspended from a winding 'lodge' over the pit shaft. Some form of mechanical drainage system was in operation (though its nature was not specified), since it was feared during the period of interrupted work that 'the saide pitte by . . . not workinge at hir would be drowned and loste by abundance of

---

[109] PRO DURH 2/10/54; DRO D/CG 7/1.

[110] PRO DURH 2/2/50, 2/2/63.

[111] PRO DURH 2/2/18, 2/5/141, 2/9/18, 2/11/150; DPD Probate, Will of William Blakiston (1608).

water'.[112] This was a mining operation of considerable depth and sophistication by the standards of the day.

Until the end of the first decade of the seventeenth century, then, there is little evidence of mining on the lower lands of Whickham. The bulk of the activity took place to the south of Whickham town. These findings are consistent with a statement in a later report which, referring specifically to the years before 1610, said that the coal produced in Whickham had 'formerlye bene wrought in divers parts and places of the said moors and wastes' of the parish.[113] The first generation of the Grand Lease appears to have witnessed what was essentially an intensification and extension of operations in those areas of Whickham that were regarded as the traditional sites for mining. The evidence for developments after 1609–10, however, tells a very different story.

In 1610 the Newcastle coal-owners were obliged to write to the Privy Council in response to a new complaint of rising coal prices in London.[114] As was their wont on such occasions, they vigorously rejected the imputation that their pricing policy was responsible, and tartly asked the Council to reflect on whether it was reasonable to expect coal to remain 'at one settled price ... all other commodities beinge uncerten of price according to the difference of Tymes and occasions'. In their view, the root of the problem lay in an expectedly rapid increase in 'the use of Seacoles in London and all other Cost Townes through the Kingdome'. More and larger ships were arriving in the Tyne for coal, and the demand had grown to such a pitch in the previous year that 'the Coleworks which ... formerly were wrought, and were sufficient for the furnishing of the kingdome with that commoditie, is not nowe able to supplie that want by a verye great proportion'. At the close of the previous shipping season (1609), they claimed, 'all men were aground att their pitts, and had very few or no coles upon their staithes at the

---

[112] Our first example of a Ridingfield lease comes from 1612: DRO D/CG 7/12. Clearly there must have been an earlier lease. For the description of the work there in 1606, see PRO STAC 8/53/10. This revealing court case was occasioned by Bainbrigg's failure to work the pit regularly. A new overman was put in, whereupon Bainbrigg allegedly attempted to sabotage the winding gear. Fourteen pitmen were named in the evidence and it was stated that at one point 20 men were working in and about the pit.

[113] PRO DURH 2/20/69.

[114] Dendy, *Hostmen*, 58–9. Dendy was uncertain of the date of this document and ascribed it to the years 1608–10. We feel that it is immediately related to the order that follows it in Dendy's collection and which is dated Nov. 1610.

water syde'. Accordingly the coal-owners, 'seeing the necessitye of a greater quantitye of Coles likely to be vented this yeare then formerly hath bene, did provide to sinke newe pytts and sett on more worke'. This, however, meant working 'both further from the water side and deper, sinkinge to lower Mynes'. Such work necessarily meant significantly higher costs in terms of sinking charges, 'tymberinge of shafts', propping, and drainage, in addition to increased labour costs and the need to pay much more for the carriage of coal to the water. In consequence, it was inevitable that prices had risen.

Whickham certainly participated in this spurt of activity. It was in 1609–10 that the Grand Lessee Lionel Maddison obtained a lease of Marshall Lands, around two miles from the river on the border of Whickham and Lamesley, and commenced work there. The mines were highly successful, yielding 'great quantityes of coles yearly', and the lease was renewed in 1624 for fifteen years at what was called 'a great yearly rent'. By 1632 there were thirteen pits in Marshall Lands and an adjacent part of Lamesley, though by that date some of them were wrought out.[115] In other areas of Whickham distant from the river there was also intensified activity. Greenlaw colliery still had only two pits in 1612, but within a few years there were as many as seven pits working. These must have been working deeper, for by the mid-1620s serious problems were being encountered from what were called 'the falls and aboundance of water'.[116] Gellsfield was still working, though we lack details of the scale of the activity.[117] At Ridingfield, however, described in 1623 as 'all a coale earth and plentifull of coals', there was certainly greatly enhanced activity, signalled by flurries of new leases, and in addition by the 1620s other parts of the Hollinside estate were being worked.[118]

All this is consistent with the pattern of activity described by the Newcastle coal-owners as having been initiated in 1609–10. In the

[115] PRO DURH 2/8/23, 24; PRO Palatinate of Durham, Calendar of Cursitor's Records, Chancery Enrollments, 66/94; DPD Ch. Comm. MS 245007.

[116] PRO DURH 2/10/24; PRO E 134 3 Car. I Ea.19.

[117] DRO D/ST 23/240; Surtees, *Durham*, ii. 251. The Gellsfield colliery may have expanded south, since the lease of 1615 included 'Northbanks' as well as Gellsfield. Northbanks was the later name for the colliery between Gibside and Marley Hill. Later evidence, however, makes it clear that there was little exploitation of the Northbanks area before the 1690s.

[118] DRO D/ST 6/11, 24/33, 24/34, 24/37, 24/38; PRO DURH 2/32/41, 2/32/248; PRO Chancery, C3 336/18; DPD Probate, Will of Dorothy Harding (1626).

Grand Lessees' manor of Whickham, however, developments were
of a different nature. References to the pits in Southfield and Cross
Moor dry up temporarily. The real energy of the two decades after
1610 seems to have been devoted to the bringing into production of
the seams beneath the northern sectors of the manor, between
Whickham town and the river—an area where, according to a
statement of 1620, 'never pits were before'.[119] Evidence given in a
Star Chamber case refers to Grand Lease workings between 1613 and
1618 in the Haugh and Haugh Loning (where three or four pits
were active), the Leigh and Leigh Leazes.[120] East Field was being
worked by 1616–17.[121] A further court case of 1620–1 provides
explicit statements that since 1610 the Grand Lessees had commenced
extensive working in the Leigh, Colewayhaugh, Matfinshaugh,
Westerhaugh, and Allerdean Heads (in the last of which there were
four pits in 1619–20).[122] All these lands were in the northern part of
the manor.

In addition, only after 1610 do we find references to work in
Brinkburne freehold, alias the 'King's Lands'—a collection of
scattered parcels totalling seventeen acres which were located in
Leigh Leazes, the Leigh, the Haugh, Allerdean Heads, and
Dunston. A pit was working in 1611 and activity intensified
thereafter; it was claimed that in 1619–23 these lands yielded 25,000
tons of coal.[123] The manor of Farnacres in Lowhand quarter was
also being brought into production. Before the death of Thomas
Liddell of Newcastle in 1616 Farnacres does not seem to have been
worked; Liddell focused his attention on Blackburn colliery further
inland in Lamesley. His heirs, however, soon commenced the
exploitation of the manor. In Jacks Leazes alone by the mid-1620s
there were four pits working, one of them said to be 'many fathoms'
deep.[124] Meanwhile, to the north of Farnacres towards the mouth of
the Team, pits were being worked in Baldwinflat by 1619.[125] In the
rector's glebe land in Allerdeans a new lease was granted in 1613,

[119] PRO DURH 2/20/69.
[120] PRO STAC 8/245/6. Cf. PRO DURH 2/19/79, which refers to work in the
Leigh in 1620.   [121] PRO DURH 2/19/224.
[122] PRO DURH 2/20/195, 7/18 pts. I and II.
[123] PRO E 134 14 Car. I Mich. 29; PRO DURH 1/19/137, 2/19/163. Cf. Nef,
i. 146–7. Note that not all of these land parcels appear on the accompanying map, as
it is not always possible to locate them with precision; e.g. some are sub-sections of
'the Leigh' or 'the Haugh'.
[124] Wood (ed.), *Wills and Inventories*, iv. 102–3; PRO DURH/2/34/84; PRO
STAC 8/163/18.   [125] PRO DURH 2/7/99.

and this time the lessee appears to have been more fortunate than his predecessor, for by 1617 the work was going well. More than 1,000 chaldrons (over 2,100 tons) of coal were said in June that year to be 'wrought and layd above the ground', while more was worked daily.[126] And finally, over to the west, Axwell Houses was still in production, apparently with some success after a difficult reopening of earlier mines was undertaken in 1609.[127] Overall, we gain a sense of vigorous and increasing activity in the two decades after 1610. This was evident throughout the parish, but was most marked in the northern areas of Whickham manor, where in 1621 alone there were said to be sixteen 'going pits'.[128]

How are we to explain the shifting geography of mining in Whickham? The initial reluctance to mine the lower-lying northern lands of the parish can be explained largely in a single word: water. On much of the higher ground, either there was natural drainage or else underground watercourses could be constructed to draw off water towards lower-lying valleys. If mining penetrated so deep that such methods proved inadequate, however, some form of mechanical pumping became necessary. As we have seen, the first reference to the use of a chain to draw water from a mine in Whickham comes from as early as 1492. We do not know the location of this mine, but it is at least possible that drainage problems in the fifteenth century had dictated the movement of mining to the higher ground of Whickham where most sites were located in the sixteenth century. Seventeenth-century mining operations still used a chain of buckets, driven by men, or horses, or water, or even wind power to draw water from below the levels at which other forms of drainage were practicable.[129] Such drainage, however, was very expensive in materials and labour costs. It demanded the expense of buying and keeping horses, and it involved recurrent maintenance problems.[130] It was also of limited

---

[126] PRO 2/7/99; *Acts of the Privy Council of England, 1616–17* (London, 1927), 271–2.

[127] PRO DURH 2/11/76; DPD Probate, Will of Roger Lumley (1616).

[128] PRO DURH 7/19, pt. I.   [129] Nef, i. 353–9; Galloway, *Annals*, 157–8.

[130] This point was forcefully made in 1667 by the surveyor Stephen Primat, who described how 'in most collieries in the North they make use of chain pumps, and do force the same either by horse wheels, tread wheels, or by water wheels'; J. Thirsk and J. P. Cooper (eds.), *Seventeenth-Century Economic Documents* (Oxford, 1972), 289. The anonymous author of *The Compleat Collier* (London, 1708; 2nd edn. London, 1845), 24, also remarked that 'Were it not for Water, a Collery in these Parts, might be termed a *Golden Mine* . . . for *Dry Colleries* would save several Thousands *per Ann.* which is expended in drawing Water hereabouts.'

effectiveness, and drainage of levels as deep as 240 feet (involving several stages) was regarded as a major technical accomplishment.[131]

Given these facts, the preference of the coal-owners of the late sixteenth century for working the higher ground is readily explicable. Early attempts to mine the lower ground faced great difficulties, as Thomas Liddell found to his cost in the rector's glebe land at Allerdeans, where in more than ten years he claimed to have failed to recover his investment, being forced at one point to lay in the mine for two years, since 'for ditches, dikes, water and other like accidents no worke out of the same [could] be had'.[132] His more fortunate successors were still obliged in 1617 to employ twenty men—ten by day and another ten by night, 'without ceasing'—to keep the mine drained.[133] The mines at Allerdeans, as well as those in the nearby Haugh, Haugh Loning, Leigh, Leigh Leazes, and Leigh Loning, were described a little later as being 'subject to water in the winning or woorking of them which cold or may not without great heade care skill industrie and coste be overcome'.[134] It was the same story in Baldwinflat, where another of the Liddells, Sir Thomas, ran into serious difficulties with water in 1619 and blamed his problems on the adjacent workings of William Sherwood and partners. In rejecting the accusation, Sherwood observed that it was 'the case of mane dealers in Collieries to be at great chardges in sincking and working of pitts and to loose all their chardges by the drowninge of [them]'. The fault was Liddell's, he claimed; Liddell should 'be att chardge' to drain his pits properly.[135]

The problems were clear enough. Yet from 1610 onwards these mines were won. The 'great heade care skill industrie and coste' required were brought into play. In the Allerdeans, as we have seen, the mine was kept dry by continuous human labour. In the Haugh and Leigh areas, in 1613 the Grand Lease employed the experienced mining engineer Thomas Surtees to construct, at considerable cost, an ingenious system involving 'Ingynes' and a 'water milne' which drained much of the area.[136] At Jack Leazes in Farnacres manor, in

---

[131] Galloway, *Annals*, 158. Flinn, *Coal Industry*, 114, suggest that in the early 18th c. 'at depths of between ninety and 150 feet the influx of water almost invariably created problems insoluble by the technology of the day'. As we shall see, Whickham's mines were well ahead of the norm in terms of depth and drainage techniques almost a century earlier.

[132] PRO DURH 2/10/77.

[133] PRO STAC 8/245/6.

[134] Ibid.

[135] PRO DURH 2/7/99.

[136] PRO STAC 8/245/6.

the early 1620s the pithead equipment included five 'horsemills for drawinge of coles and water'. Its owner, Henry Liddell of Farnacres, had no fewer than eight pumps and a pump-chain listed in his inventory when he died twenty years later.[137]

For entrepreneurs to involve themselves in such capital-intensive undertakings in the second and third decades of the seventeenth century, the potential rewards must have appeared to have been very great. The risks remained, and were well known, but at the same time demand was buoyant. The figures derived from the Newcastle port books suggest that there was a near doubling of coal shipments between 1608/9 and 1633/4 from 239,271 to 452,625 tons, while pit-head prices in the early seventeenth century were some three times their mid-sixteenth-century level.[138] Moreover, entrepreneurs already heavily committed to the coal industry may have had little choice other than to reinvest part of their super-profits in much more capital-intensive collieries or else get out of the trade. The easiest workings had already been won by the 1610s, and in all parts of Whickham the complexity of operations and their capital demands were increasing. We have already observed a pit 180 feet deep in Ridingfield in 1606 which required continuous working to keep the water at bay. Such depths were by no means exceptional in Whickham as the seventeenth century advanced—there was another in East Field in 1621 described as 26–30 fathoms deep.[139] At Greenlaw–Fawdonfield colliery in the mid-1620s, deeper working had resulted in serious drainage problems which threatened the loss of part of the mine. An exasperated overman declared later that there was coal enough left to win if the owner 'would have byn att the cost of working them'.[140] The operations at Marshall Lands in the same period required heavy investment too—and received it. Separate pits were sunk 'for working or drawing of coles or water and for the venting of stithe' from the interconnected workings. The pits were constructed to the best standards, being 'well and sufficiently tymbered with wood and tymber to keepe and hinder the ground from thrusting together'.[141] It seems clear that, except for the smallest of pits, there was no longer an easy option in

---

[137] PRO STAC 8/163/18; DPD Probate, Will and Inv. of Henry Liddell (1642).

[138] Nef, ii. 74 and app. E.; Dietz, 'The North-East Coal Trade', 281, 286, modifies Nef's figures but also stresses the rapid growth of the early 17th c.

[139] PRO DURH 7/19. We know of this pit only because an ox grazing nearby fell into it!   [140] PRO E 134 4 Car. I Ea. 19.

[141] DPD Ch. Comm. MS 245007. 'Stithe' was foul air.

coal-mining in Whickham. Knowledge of that fact, together with
the brisk demand and the lack of serious calamities to disturb the
coastal trade, may have made the choice of heavy investment
relatively painless for the big players in colliery. What is certain is
that it was done, above all on the low-lying manorial territories of
the Grand Lease, and it may well have been in these years of heady
expansion that the profits of the Grand Lessees reached '5000[li] and
some times 8000[li]' above the rent.

If so, it could not last, and indeed it did not last. The coal bubble
began to deflate in the second quarter of the seventeenth century
and thereafter the growth of the Tyneside industry slowed. Nef
speaks of glutted markets and cut-throat competition between
mine-owners after 1626, as declining profitability induced a
scramble for the spoils.[142] The Whickham evidence suggests the
continuance of energetic mining. To judge by the Ship Money
assessment of 1636, output was still prodigious, and not only in the
Grand Lease colliery (valued at £4,500) but also at Farnacres (£800),
Gellsfield (£650), Ridingfield (£300), and Fawdonfield–Greenlaw
(£200).[143] None the less, there were signs that the Whickham
industry was faltering. The 1636 assessment makes no mention of
the formerly highly productive Marshall Lands–Fugarfield complex
on the Whickham–Lamesley boundary. Another significant omission
is that of the Brinkburne–King's Lands mines. Other evidence from
1638, in fact, suggests that pits were still worked there but at a low
level of production: five pits were said to have yielded only 600 tens
(perhaps 16,000 tons) in the previous fifteen years.[144] The Allerdeans
glebe mine also passed unnoticed by the assessors, and we have no
other evidence of its working in the 1630s. Perhaps it had finally
succumbed to the chronic drainage problems experienced by its
lessees in the preceding decades. This seems the more likely in that,
shortly after the 1636 assessment, the Grand Lease and Farnacres
collieries experienced a serious reversal in their north Whickham
mines. A statement of 1637–8 declares that 'in the last two years cole
works at Meadowhead, Whickham haugh, some part of Jack Leases

---

[142] Nef, ii. 74–8. Cf. Dietz, 'The North-East Coal Trade', 281.

[143] Durham Cathedral, Dean and Chapter Library, Hunter MSS, fo. 22/17.

[144] PRO E 134 14 Car. I Mich. 29. The tonnage is calculated on the basis of Nef's
suggestion that by the 1630s a Newcastle chaldron contained 52.5 cwt. If we accept
Dietz's suggestion of a standard 42 cwt. chaldron throughout the period, the tonnage
would fall to 12,600 tons. See n. 94 above.

and Allerdeane were drowned, out of which 3000 tens [almost 79,000 tons] were yearly wrought'.[145] The only new colliery of significance to appear in the 1636 assessment was Clockburne, probably an extension of earlier Hollinside operations, which was valued at £300.[146]

The emergence of Clockburne as a colliery in its own right, however, cannot disguise the fact the mining operations in Whickham were undergoing contraction. The pell-mell exploitation of the parish since 1610 had brought many Whickham mines close to the limits of extraction that could be economically achieved at the prevailing levels of technology. In the early 1640s first Scottish invasion and then Civil War brought the coal trade virtually to a standstill.[147]

In the aftermath of the Civil War, as work gradually resumed, a number of reports were prepared on the state of the mines in the parish which provide graphic detail of the consequences of three decades of hectic activity. In 1650 the Commonwealth Church surveyors reported, in valuing the glebe lands of Whickham rectory, that the mines formerly worked in them were 'wrought out and wasted and that the profitts thereof are very uncertayne and doth sometymes render losse'.[148] A survey of Brinkburne–King's Lands in the same year found two pits still working in Lowfield, but another description of these mines from 1649 tells us that they were in fact for the most part 'wrought out' and unlikely to last five years.[149]

The most telling evidence, however, comes from the surveys

---

[145] Nef, ii. 73. Tonnage calculated on Nef's assumptions; on Dietz's assumptions it would be reduced to 63,000 tons.

[146] For the 1636 assessment, see n. 143 above. Macabre confirmation of the somewhat reduced area of operations on the eve of the Civil War is provided by burial registrations of miners killed at work which specify the pits in which men died. In the years 1632–42 the Grand Lease colliery was evidently working pits in Southfield, East Field, Cross Moor, and Lobley Hill. Work was also continuing at Jacks Leazes (Farnacres), Fawdonfield–Greenlaw, Ridingfield, and at Fugarfield and Cocks Close in the Marshall Lands area. According to a Newcastle Corporation account book of 1642, there were 14 working pits in the Grand Lease colliery at that date: Nef, i. 371.

[147] Nef, ii. 282, 285–95. See also Howell, *Newcastle*, 131–3, 135, 154–5, 185, 276 ff. Recovery in the late 1640s was slow, and in 1652 the Anglo-Dutch war brought further dislocation.

[148] Lambeth Palace Library, Comm. XII a/4, fo. 107–9.

[149] DPD Ch. Comm. MS 244145; Welford (ed.), *Committees for Compounding*, 163.

conducted of the manor of Whickham in 1647 and of its collieries in 1652, both occasioned by the Commonwealth's seizure of episcopal property. The surveyors of 1647 found that the Grand Lease colliery was worked on behalf of nine shareholding undertenants and was worth to them a total of £2,500 per annum over and above the rent. Fifteen pits were 'agoing' at the time of the survey, but it was reported that 'those seames and veynes of Cole that are now wrought are farr from the River of Tyne and are wrought near to the utter bounder And in our judgement cannot continue and last to afford Coles to the end of expiration of the present lease'. In their opinion, the future potential of the colliery lay in the exploitation of a deeper seam which was 'already won and wrought near unto the River of Tyne' and 'like to be of Long Continuance'.[150]

The colliery survey of 1652 is a far more detailed document, prepared by the surveyors on the basis of the expert testimony of 'honest judicious and experienced men in collieries who were by us sent underground'.[151] Their brief was apparently to report on the extent to which the coal seams of the manor had been worked and the potential for future operations, and this they did admirably. They are frustratingly silent, however, about where work was currently proceeding at this date—though it may be that little work was actually going on as a result of the stoppage of the Tyne trade occasioned by the Dutch war and the onset of the winter season.[152]

The most obviously striking feature of this report is the surveyors' confirmation of the loss of the lowest-lying mines of the Grand lease. Eastmosthaugh was described as 'wrought out and drowned'. Beneath Matfinshaugh, it was reported, 'all the Colliery here is wrought and drowned', while in Westmosthaugh the coal was mostly wrought and what remained was 'not to be recovered' because of water problems. It is clear enough that the mines in the northernmost parts of Whickham, which had been won at such cost in the orgy of extraction after 1610, had been worked to the limit

---

[150] D. A. Kirby (ed.), *Parliamentary Surveys of the Bishopric of Durham*, ii, Surtees Soc. no. 185 (Gateshead, 1972), 82–3, 105–6. The burgesses of Newcastle must have shared the surveyors' confidence about the future potential of the Grand Lease colliery, for in 1648 the city attempted to buy the manors of Whickham and Gateshead. The scheme failed because London also wanted a share. Newcastle, however, did succeed in holding on to the Grand Lease throughout the Interregnum: Howell, *Newcastle*, 297–8.

[151] Kirby, *Parliamentary Surveys*, 132 ff.

[152] For the effects of the Anglo-Dutch war, see Nef, ii. 297.

and then abandoned. Those that had required constant drainage had subsequently flooded. Moreover, there was abundant evidence elsewhere in the manor of the consequences of forty years of hectic activity. Still in the northern half of the parish, the Main Coal seam had been 'mostly wrought out' in Leighfield, Dunstonfield, and Lowfield. Whitefield and East Field had also been very heavily worked, though both retained considerable potential. Moving south, the surveyors found that in Corn Moor thirty pit rooms had been worked and the Main Coal seam was 'mostly wrought and wasted'. The Main Coal and Top Coal seams had been wrought in Haggdeene on the common. 'Wester Southfield' was 'long since wasted and wrought'. Marshall Lands and Wheat Leas were mostly wrought out, and the common to the south of Marshall Lands was 'very much wrought out'.

Whickham manor might thus be taken to provide a splendid example of the situation described by the Newcastle coal-owners in a petition to Cromwell in 1656, when they complained that 'most of the cole mines which laie neere unto the River of Tyne were worne out and wasted'.[153] There was clearly much truth in this statement. And yet such claims were also the constant refrain of coal-owners on the Tyne, especially when attempting to fend off the demands of central government. In the face of the dramatic evidence of industrial dereliction provided by the 1652 survey, it is too easy to overlook the considerable optimism of the surveyors. Of the four coal seams that they named as having been brought into production, only the Main Coal had been virtually wrought throughout the manor, and in the East Field it was claimed that even in the Main Coal there were twenty-five existing pits that could still yield 'very considerable quantities of good and merchantable coal'. 'Pit rooms' for future exploitation were also identified in Whitefield, where they could 'afford great quantity of coals'; Dunstonfield, where the Five Quarter and Seven Quarter seams could be brought into production; Goose Moor, where little had been wrought as yet; and 'Easter Southfield', where three seams had been reached and were still workable. Moreover, in Lowfield, which was otherwise wrought out, a new seam had been discovered 20 fathoms below the Main Coal which was potentially very rich. Working it might also help to drain the pits in Morrisfield and bring them back into production.

[153] Dendy, *Hostmen*, 110.

This evidence should not be ignored. The mid-century surveys make it clear enough that the great expansive days of the Grand Lease were over. But Whickham was far from finished as a significant centre of coal production. There were pits enough still at work, not only at a variety of scattered locations within the principal manor, but also to the south, in Ridingfield and Gellsfield.[154] And there was coal enough left in Whickham for those to whom it was worth the winning.

4. DOWN THE WAGGONWAYS

The extent to which Whickham's remaining reserves of coal were to be won depended above all upon the market conditions prevailing in the later seventeenth century. Compared with the situation in the first quarter of the century, these were distinctly sluggish. Recovery from the dislocations of the coal trade occasioned by the Civil War was slow, inhibited by further short-term problems such as the Dutch war of 1652–4 and the fiscal demands of the Interregnum governments. It was only in 1655 that social shipments from the Tyne recovered to the levels that had obtained in the later 1630s, and these were not surpassed until 1659.[155] Thereafter, the Tyne coal trade marked time for most of the later seventeenth century. There were further short-term interruptions as a result of maritime warfare or commercial disputes in 1665–7, 1672–3, and 1689–90.[156] Far more serious, however, were those deeper, structural problems which had begun to manifest themselves even before 1640. The industry was over-capitalized, its principal markets were glutted, production costs were rising still, and land transportation charges were sufficiently inelastic to discourage the intensive exploitation of richer inland seams.

There was also a further specific problem. Newcastle's principal rival in the London market—the Wearside industry, exporting coal

---

[154] Registered mining deaths in the years 1647–52 refer to Grand Lease pits in Cross Moor, Southfield, East Field, Lowfield, the Leigh, the Fell, Corn Moor, and on Dunston Hill. These sites were mostly to the south of Whickham town, as might be expected, but the evidence does demonstrate a degree of activity which helps to put the surveys into perspective. For mid-century references to mining at Ridingfield and Gellsfield, we have not only the parish registers but also Surtees, *Durham*, ii. 251; Wood, *Wills and Inventories*, 307; DRO D/ST 6/20.

[155] Nef, ii. 298–9. Cf. Dietz, 'The North-East Coal Trade', 281.

[156] Nef, ii. 74–5.

from Sunderland—was growing vigorously. To quote Nef's account, 'the rate of increase in the Sunderland trade, unlike that in the trade of Newcastle, was scarcely diminished after 1625. In 1609 the shipments of coal from the Wear were less than a twentieth of those from the Tyne, in 1621 they were about a tenth, in 1634 more than an eighth, in 1660 about a fourth, and in 1680 nearly a third.'[157] By 1710 it appears that around a third of all coal shipped from the north-east came from Sunderland and a number of other ports that lay outwith the control of the Newcastle hostmen.[158] To make matters worse, the levy on coal shipments that had been conceded by Newcastle to the Crown in 1600 had the effect of giving the Sunderland merchants an in-built price advantage. In a flat market it could add significantly to the London price of a chaldron of Newcastle coal.

The levels of coal shipments per annum from Newcastle to the other English ports, presented in decadal averages, bring out the sluggishness of the trade in the years 1660–1710, from which year the series is temporarily broken:[159]

1661–70	424,672 tons
1671–80	487,296 tons
1681–90	517,092 tons
1691–1700	469,018 tons
1701–10	462,237 tons

Whatever rise in demand there was in the later seventeenth century was occasioned by continued metropolitan growth, notably after the rebuilding of London, and it appears to have benefited the expanding Wearside industry disproportionately. The Tyne was struggling to retain its market share. Sometimes, however, a period of apparent stagnation can be one of profound structural change, and this is precisely what was in progress in the organization of coal production on Tyneside.

The market conditions of the later seventeenth century might

---

[157] Nef, i. 31.

[158] J. M. Ellis, *A Study of the Business Fortunes of William Cotesworth, c.1668–1726* (New York, 1981), 79.

[159] Ibid. 77. Ellis follows the original source (Cotesworth MSS) in presenting her figures in 'tens'. We have converted them into tons at the 1695 statute rate of 26.5 tons to the ten. Dietz, 'The North-East Coal Trade', 281, 284–5, would prefer a lower conversion rate pre-1695, but agrees that the market for coal was sluggish in the late 17th c.

present acute problems to the Newcastle coal trade, but they could also offer opportunities to the agile entrepreneur. Some inefficient producers were certainly shaken out. Some others voluntarily withdrew. It is no accident that it was in the decades after 1660 that the hostmen of Newcastle, so long the dominant figures in both the production and the sale of sea coal, increasingly abandoned their role as coal-owners to local landlords, not a few of whom were of Newcastle mercantile origin, and confined themselves to trade rather than mining. In the terminology of the industry, they became predominantly 'fitters', the middlemen of the coal trade. They focused their attention upon the safer profits to be made by playing off rival coal-owners, anxious to obtain a vend for their coal, against one another, while keeping a firm grip on their monopoly of the right to trade in coal from Newcastle.[160]

For those who remained involved, coal-mining itself could still be a profitable business, given the possession of coal-bearing land and a willingness to raise and risk the very large sums of capital essential for successful participation. The sluggishness of the Newcastle vend was such, however, that it was possible to establish a highly profitable enterprise only by winning a larger market share for one's own collieries and/or by delivering coals more cheaply to the hostmen–fitters who now stood between the producers and the London market. These twin imperatives were the basis of the fierce competition among coal-owners which contemporaries termed a 'fighting trade'.

Theoretically, of course, there was a third option: to limit production by forming a cartel and thereby guarantee profitable workings by securing a stable return. Contemporaries were certainly not unaware of such a possibility. From the very outset, the basic realities of the coal trade—the small numbers of producers and markets involved and the remoteness of the one from the other which necessitated middlemen—had 'encouraged the development of oligopolistic conditions'.[161] The temptation was always there to exploit the power to control both output and prices. As we have seen, the hostmen were accused as early as the 1590s of abusing their

[160] See Nef, ii. 23, 122 ff., 132. The role of the 'fitters' is also well explained in Ellis, *William Cotesworth*, 95 ff. For their position in the early 18th c. see Flinn, *Coal Industry*, 267–9. The Newcastle hostmen successfully fought off all challenges to their trading monopoly until it was declared illegal by the attorney-general in 1703.

[161] Quoting Flinn, *Coal Industry*, 254.

position as both coal-owners and producers to force up prices, and in the course of the early seventeenth century there were at least six separate attempts by the Newcastle oligarchs to regulate and apportion their vend with a view to enhancing or stabilizing their profits.[162] Success in such schemes, however, depended on the willingness of owners and shippers to stand together and upon the relative balance of power between the Tyneside magnates, the shipmasters of the coastal trade, and the London buyers, not to mention the interventions of a central government sensitive to the importance of keeping London well supplied with coal.

All the early attempts to stint the Newcastle vend foundered on the rock of successful resistance by London customers. In the conditions of the later seventeenth century it was even harder to make such a policy stick, given not only the continued political clout of London, but also the growing separation of mine-ownership and shipping in the north. In 1665, however, an attempt was made. It was provoked by the London authorities' setting of the maximum price of coal at 30s. per chaldron in January of that year, the passage in March of an 'Act for regulating the Measures and Prices of Coales', and conditions of over-supply which left 'a great quantity of coales now wrought and lyinge at pit and staith on the Tyne'. In April, after a meeting of 'the several principle traders in coals', twenty-two mine-owners, several of whom complained of lack of ready money 'to keep on their water charge and other necessary charge for preserving the colliery', agreed that no sea coal should be wrought at their collieries from 1 May until the end of September, by which time it was hoped that present stocks would be sold. The same men and eight other principal traders further agreed to enhance the Tyne price of coal.[163]

This short-term response to pressure from the south, however, was soon overwhelmed by the dislocating effects of the Dutch war upon the coastal trade. In the spring of 1666 the Tyne was still jammed with unsold coal, and the Newcastle hostmen agreed in May that pits should be laid in for three months, later extending their ban until September.[164] What may have begun as a defensive attempt at combination and regulation on Tyneside had turned all

[162] Nef, ii. 110–13; Dendy, *Hostmen*, pp. xliv, 43–7, 56, 63–74.
[163] NEIMME, Bell Coll., vol. 3, 9; Dendy, *Hostmen*, p. xlvii.
[164] Ibid. 131–2. Plague losses in the capital in 1665 may also have reduced demand for Tyneside coal.

too rapidly into a major dislocation of the coal industry which lasted the better part of two years, until the commencement of the rebuilding of London after the fire of 1666 created a buoyant demand, improvements in prices, and a renewed briskness in the trade.[165]

The experience of 1665–7 was not a happy one. The position of the Newcastle men was too exposed, and attempts at combination appear to have been abandoned for a generation. The optimum solution to the difficulties facing the mine-owners of the later seventeenth century lay rather in a lateral expansion of the coalfield. The intensification of operations on the older seams faced unavoidable problems of increasing costs and diminishing returns. If they were not already virtually wrought out, their drainage charges made them very expensive propositions. A shift of the sea coal frontier to the higher, better drained ground in the southernmost reaches of Whickham and Ryton and beyond was the answer.

Such a solution, however, brought its own problems. The costs of carrying coal to the river in 'wains' drawn by oxen and horses was very high. The coalways followed by such traffic swiftly became impassable in wet weather. Rights of 'wayleave' across intervening land were expensive, a source of friction, and a liability that could expose coal-owners to economic blackmail.[166] Stephen Primat, the Restoration estate surveyor, advised potential investors in northern collieries that, even if the coal was plentiful, the mines free from water and easily worked, 'yet if it have not the conveniency to convey the same at a small charge to some river to have the coals exported, they will not be worth the trouble and charge in obtaining them'.[167] It was good advice and long familiar on Tyneside. As we have seen, mines had long been worked quite far to the south of Whickham town; but we have no evidence that the sixteenth and early seventeenth centuries witnessed significant workings more than three miles from the Tyne or its navigable tributaries. The coalfield remained geographically circumscribed by the problem of land carriage. Even at the height of the Jacobean boom, for example, it had been reported of Chopwell colliery, which lay inland in Ryton

[165] Dendy, *Hostmen*, p. xlvii. By June 1667 the London price had risen to £6 per chaldron and trade was back to normal. See Ellis, *William Cotesworth*, 77, for the severe fall in coastal shipments 1665–7.

[166] M. J. T. Lewis, *Early Wooden Railways* (London, 1970), 87–9.

[167] Thirsk and Cooper, *Economic Documents*, 289, 292–3.

parish, that, although the quality of the coal was excellent and its quantity sufficient 'to continue a hundred years', the colliery could not be sufficiently profitable to warrant expansion 'by reason the carriage is far from the water'.[168]

In the later seventeenth century, the answer to the immediate technical problem of inefficient land carriage was found in the construction of wooden waggonways, an innovation observed and admired by Lord Keeper North in 1676:

The manner of the carriage is by laying rails of timber from the colliery down to the river, exactly straight and parallel; and bulky carts are made with four rowlets fitting these rails; whereby the carriage is so easy that one horse will draw down four or five chaldrons of coals and it is an immense benefit to the coal owners.[169]

The waggonways were indeed an 'immense benefit'. They provided a form of bulk transportation that was vastly more efficient and economical than the lumbering coal wains drawn by oxen and horses. They used larger-capacity waggons yet required fewer draught animals, greatly reduced the time needed to 'lead' a load of coal to the water, and at the same time significantly extended the leading season, since they were far less vulnerable to inclement weather. The savings involved could be enormous, as is evidenced by a computation of 1711 that wain transport from the Tanfield Moor colliery south of Whickham parish would permit a profit of only £1. 17s. 6d. per ten of coal, whereas a waggonway would raise profits to £5. 5s. 9d. per ten.[170]

As so often in the coal industry, a technological innovation bred a new occupational group: the waggonway wrights. And as the waggonway wrights grew in experience, so the waggonways they constructed developed in sophistication and efficiency. Prior to 1712 they were usually single-track affairs, perhaps provided with sidings for passing. Later they were double-tracked. As they penetrated deeper into the crumpled landscape of north-west Durham and could no longer rely on a relatively short natural gradient, they came to involve not simply ground-levelling but also massive land preparation. Cuttings were excavated, embankments raised, and bridges built so as to maintain a steady gradient which

[168] PRO E 178 5037 9 Jac. I.
[169] Quoted in C. E. Lee, 'The World's Oldest Railway', *Trans. Newcomen Society*, 25 (1945–7), 143.　　　　　　　　[170] Flinn, *Coal Industry*, 149.

permitted full waggons fitted with a brake to run down by gravity
and empty waggons to be drawn back by a single horse.[171] By the
third decade of the eighteenth century, the waggonways had come
to be civil engineering projects of a scale and ambition that
astounded contemporaries and stirred in Tynesiders a fierce pride in
their own ingenuity and accomplishment. 'Last Munday,' wrote
William Blakiston Bowes of Gibside in 1721,

we begun to lead down ye new Waggon Way, which is ye beginning of my
profitt; it is a work of such great importance and crosses so many
Mountains and Vales, which are all levelled, that I can compare it to nothing
more properly than to ye Via Appia.[172]

William Bowes's brag was echoed in 1736 by Henry Bourne, the
historian of Newcastle, in whose view the waggonways could 'vie
with some of the great Works of the Roman Empire'.[173]

If the waggonways were splendid to behold, however, they were
also phenomenally expensive. Once their potential to increase
profits and extend the area of the working coalfield had been
generally grasped, the fortunate owners of strategically placed
property could wring extremely high wayleave rents from the coal-
owners anxious to cross their land. An outstanding example is that
of Lady Clavering, who obtained no less than 2s. 6d. per ten of coal
led by the owners of the Bucksnook Way (opened in 1712) for the
right to cross only three hundred yards of common on Tanfield
Moor.[174] And wayleaves were only the beginning. The six miles of
the original Bucksnook Way, a relatively unsophisticated waggonway, cost £4,000–£5,000 to construct. Materials alone for a 10,000
yard stretch on the Ravensworth Way cost £500 in 1726, and the
cost of laying it was £2,677.[175] Then there were the costs of constant
maintenance and other operating expenses. The Dunston Way, laid

---

[171] Lewis, *Early Wooden Railways*, 144, 147, *passim*.

[172] BL Add. MS 40747, fo. 184. The waggonway in question was the 'Great
Western Way'. Bowes's comparison was no mere fancy: he had travelled in Italy in
1716.

[173] H. Bourne, *The History of Newcastle-upon-Tyne* (Newcastle, 1736), 159.

[174] Ellis, *William Cotesworth*, 65.

[175] Ibid. 63: E. Hughes, *North Country Life in the Eighteenth Century: The
North-East, 1700–1750* (Oxford, 1952), 154–5. In 1712 James Clavering received a
quotation of £1,000 for laying 6,000 yards of waggonway: 6s. 4d. a yard. He thought
it excessive and said that 2s. to 2s. 8d. was more usual, citing another way 'laid as
strong as possible' which 'had many difficulties to encounter' and cost 3s. a yard:
Ncle. UL MISC MSS 10, 'Clavering Letter Book', 14 Oct. 1712. We are grateful to
Prof. H. T. Dickinson for making available to us his transcript of this letter book.

across Whickham in 1699, was said in 1717 to have cost £6,000 to build and a further £21,000 to maintain 'to this day'.[176] The waggonways revolutionized land transportation in the coal industry, but they also added greatly to the capital costs of colliery operation. Expenditure of this order was justified only because the waggonways could increase both profits and profit margins, while at the same time permitting hitherto inaccessible inland collieries to be worked.[177]

In the early eighteenth century such investment must have seemed worth while, for it was certainly made. By 1739 the partnership of owners known as the Grand Allies had 42 miles of waggonway on Tyneside, said to have involved a capital outlay of £50,000 (an average of £1,190 per mile).[178] Some of these lines penetrated as far as eight miles south of the Tyne.[179] Yet the earliest waggonways were far more modest affairs, and to pass too swiftly from the fragmentary evidence of their inception to the great works of the Augustan age is to omit an important part of our story.

The earliest known English waggonway was that constructed by Huntingdon Beaumont at his Woolaton colliery in Nottinghamshire in 1604. Shortly afterwards Beaumont introduced his ingenious system to the north-east when he laid, at some time between 1605 and 1608, a waggonway linking his workings at Cowpen in Northumberland to the river Blyth.[180] Sadly, Beaumont's inventiveness went unrewarded. He lost his investment, sold out his mining rights in 1614, and returned south to die a debtor in Nottingham gaol ten years later. His invention, however, was not forgotten. William Gray of Newcastle referred in 1649 to Beaumont's introduction of several devices 'not known then in these parts', including 'waggons with one horse to carry down coales, from the pits, to the staithes'.[181]

Gray does not appear to have been particularly familiar with the nature of a waggonway, but by the time he wrote it seems probable that another line was already in operation on Tyneside—in Whickham. On the basis of the registered burials of two children

---

[176] DRO D/ST V.36. For a general discussion of waggonway maintenance, operating expenses, etc., see Lewis, *Early Wooden Railways*, ch. 12.
[177] Ellis, *William Cotesworth*, 63; Flinn, *Coal Industry*, 163.
[178] Ibid. 157.
[179] NEIMME, Buddle Papers, vol. 4, 364.
[180] Lewis, *Early Wooden Railways*, 90–2.
[181] Gray, *Chorographia*, 31.

slain at different dates in 1650 in accidents involving 'a waggon'—as distinct from a wain—and two further references in 1645 and 1650 to a 'waggon gate' and 'the waggon way', it has been argued by M. J. T. Lewis that a waggonway did indeed operate in Whickham at this time. By plotting the recorded incidents on the map, he conjectures that it ran from the pits in East Field through the Leigh and Baldwinflat to the staithes at Dunston, a distance of perhaps rather more than one mile.[182]

Lewis's hypothesis might seem a grandiose speculation on the basis of a handful of glancing references, but there is corroborating evidence that Whickham had at least one operating waggonway in the late 1640s. An agreement of 1647 between the Grand Lessees and the copyhold tenants of Whickham included among its articles the provision that 'the waggon waies should be trenched on either side', that the 'coal gates' should be kept in good repair, and that the copyholders should have the right to nominate the keepers of the gates. Again, the papers of the parliamentary Committee for Compounding relating to the former lord mayor of Newcastle and prominent royalist Sir Thomas Riddell reveal that among his possessions were Baldwinflat in Whickham parish and 'a wayleave through Baldwin Flatt for waggons and horses to carry coals to the waterside'.[183] In the light of these references, we can be confident that a waggonway existed at this date and that it ran across Baldwinflat.

Even this, however, may not have marked the beginning of the Tyneside waggonways, for our research has also brought to light evidence suggesting that waggonways were in use in Whickham at an even earlier date. A deposition taken in a court case of 1621, in which the Grand Lessees were accused of abusing their rights of lordship over the manor of Whickham, included the allegation that they had 'cutt downe and spoild grete store of oak wood within these 10 yeres and have maid 2 waggon waies and built new staithes'. Another witness deposed that they had 'laied waggon waies within ye copiholders pasture grounds', and yet another that they had made 'waggon waies through ye copiholders pastures and meadow field'.[184] These references are quite unambiguous. In the

[182] Lewis, *Early Wooden Railways*, 93–5. A 'waggon gate' was a level crossing.

[183] DRO D/ST 6/32c; Welford, *Committees for Compounding*, 319. Riddell died in 1650.

[184] PRO DURH 7/19, pt. I, Depositions of Cuthbert Reaslie, John Turner, and Nicholas Matfen.

first place, the term 'waggon waies' was a novel one. The routes customarily used for transporting coal to the river were referred to as 'leading ways', 'collways', or most commonly simply 'ways'. Coal was traditionally carried in 'cole wains', not in 'waggons'. The new terminology surely indicates a novel means of transport. Secondly, the deponents spoke of 'waggon waies' in the specific context of complaining about the abuse of timber rights. Thirdly, the 'waggon waies' were described as being 'laied', surely a significant verb. And finally, waggonway construction was clearly associated with the building of new staithes.

It is perhaps significant that these allegations were made at a time when a fierce dispute was raging over wayleave rights and wain carriage costs between the copyholders of Whickham manor and the Grand Lessees, a matter to be explored in greater detail in the next chapter. It seems possible that some of the Grand Lessees, faced with high leading costs and a recalcitrant tenantry, had experimented with the costly alternative of constructing waggonways. If so, they were not alone. At Jacks Leazes in 1622 reference was made to the stables maintained there 'for waggon horses', while two years later a lease of the Farnacres mines included 'all and every the workgeare and colemynes stables waggon wayes waggons [etc.] . . . used about the wynning and leading of the said Colemynes'.[185] Taken together, these references leave little room for doubt that wooden waggonways of some sort were indeed in existence in Whickham in the early 1620s, very possibly in the area of eastern Whickham identified by Lewis where Farnacres and the Grand Lease territories adjoined. They may not have been extensive. They may well have been short-lived, associated in all likelihood with mines that were largely 'wrought out' by mid-century. Nevertheless, they provide a 'missing link' in the development of the Tyneside waggonways, and serve to demonstrate not only that Beaumont's innovation had not gone unremarked, but also that it could be taken up and employed when circumstances justified the expense.

Such circumstances certainly existed after 1650, when the sluggishness of the Tyneside vend and the strengthening competition of Sunderland made it imperative for coal-owners who wished to maintain or to expand their vend to be able to deliver coals to the staithes as cheaply as possible. A short line may have existed from

[185] PRO STAC 8/163/18; PRO DURH 2/34/86.

Fawdon colliery to the Tyne in 1656, though this remains uncertain. By 1663, however, a waggonway was definitely in operation at Crawcrook in Ryton parish, and the 1660s saw a further line opened from Stella colliery in the same parish. The year 1669 saw the building of the 'Old Way' or 'Ravensworth Way' from the Ravensworth and Blackburn collieries to the south-east of Whickham along the Team valley to Team Staithes, an undertaking that was reckoned to make possible a doubling of Sir Thomas Liddell's colliery profits. Finally, the 1670s may have seen a waggonway built at Winlaton colliery, once more in Ryton parish.[186] Thereafter, however, waggonway construction appears to have marked time for almost two decades. The next major venture was the building of the Dunston Way across Whickham in 1699, an event to which we shall return.

Historians of the waggonways have tended, understandably, to move rapidly from the flurry of activity in the 1660s to the early eighteenth-century extension of the waggonway system in north-west Durham which was initiated by the Dunston Way. However, to those more concerned with the general condition of the Tyneside industry in the neglected later seventeenth century, and in particular with the fate of Whickham's collieries, this pause in the development of the waggonways deserves more careful consideration.

For our purposes, two features of the Restoration waggonway system seem to deserve emphasis. First, these waggonways were short, and they served existing collieries set back only a mile or two from the river. The implication is that they were initially undertaken simply as a means of reducing leading costs and not as part of a more ambitious attempt to expand the coalfield itself. The coal-owners of Charles II's reign probably lacked both the resources and the nerve to undertake so radical a project. The early waggonways doubtless helped them to defend or expand their share of the vend, and for the moment, success in achieving that immediate objective seems to have been sufficient for the needs of the day.

Secondly, these waggonways did not serve the collieries of Whickham. There is no evidence that waggonways were used in the parish between 1650 and 1699. Whatever their predecessors had

[186] Lewis, *Early Wooden Railways*, 118–20. Cf. Flinn, *Coal Industry*, 149. For the estimate of the impact of the Ravensworth Way on Liddell's profits, see City of Sheffield Library, Bright Papers, 72/10. We are grateful to Sara Mendelson for this reference.

done, the tenants of the declining Grand Lease colliery do not appear to have regarded continued investment in waggonways as worth their while. Much more importantly, their reluctance was apparently shared by the owners and lessees of the southern collieries of the parish, outside the territories of the Grand Lease. As far as Whickham's industrial history is concerned, the combined effect of these two factors—the spatial containment of the south-bank coalfield for a further generation and the non-involvement of coal-owners to the south-west of Whickham manor in waggonway construction—had an effect of quite considerable significance. They granted a protracted respite to the older mines of the parish, and in particular to the ailing Grand Lease colliery.

In 1662 the Grand Lease of Whickham and Gateshead still had some eighteen years to run and it was valued by Bishop Cosin's surveyors at £2,000 a year over the rent.[187] What this means in terms of output is very difficult to determine, but it was surely far less than the 100,000 tons or more per annum suggested by Nef as the post-1660 production of the Grand Lease.[188] The Bishop's surveyors were aware that the present value of the lease was some two-fifths to one-quarter of its former levels. If their method of valuation was comparable to that used by the Ship Money valuers of 1636, then at £2,000 the Grand Lease would be worth only 41.6 per cent of the £4,800 that had been the combined valuation of Whickham and Gateshead collieries in 1636. Output would surely have fallen by a comparable proportion. We might guess that Whickham manor's production was less than half our 1636 estimate of 97,000 tons. If so, it was far from negligible, but it had fallen back towards the levels that may have obtained in the 1590s.[189]

But this is guesswork. What can be said with confidence is that the Grand Lease was still worked in Whickham. In early 1662 the corporation of Newcastle was letting one-twelfth shares in the Grand Lease on eighteen-year leases and takers had been found for all of them by 1664.[190] As in the past, the shareholders subcontracted the work to overmen, and in the 1670s we find references to going pits in such familiar locations as Lowfield and Southfield.[191] The

---

[187] Durham Cathedral, Dean and Chapter Library, Sharp Coll., no. 167, 170.
[188] Nef, i. 361.   [189] See above, p. 28.
[190] TWA, Newcastle Common Council Books, 589/6, fos. 65, 84.
[191] PRO DURH 4/3, fos. 529ᵛ, 530, 543ᵛ; DPD Probate, Will of George Mathew (1677).

nearest we can come to estimating output in the last decade of the
Grand Lease, however, is a note in the colliery accounts of Sir
George Vane for 1674–5 to the effect that he possessed a twelfth
part of 4,128 tens of coal (109,392 tons) which had been worked
from Whickham Grand Lease and Blackburn freehold.[192] Unfortunately, it is impossible to say how much of this coal was from
Whickham. But even if it was only half, let us say 55,000 tons (a not
unreasonable estimate, given the levels of production known to
have obtained twenty years later), this was not insubstantial. Such
an output would have represented just over 10 per cent of the coal
shipped from Newcastle to other English ports in 1675.[193]

Whatever the case, the Grand Lease was still worth the working,
and it was still worth the having. In 1681 Newcastle's tenure of the
lease expired and it passed to Sir Gilbert and Sir John Gerrard,
grandchildren of Bishop Cosin, who had granted them a reversionary
lease some years earlier at the old, and still scandalous, rent of
£117. 15s. 8d.[194] The Gerrards, acting through an agent in Newcastle, granted licences to win coals in their manors in return for a
specified payment per ten won,[195] and from their accounts, preserved
among the Cotesworth papers, we are at last able to gain a clear sense
of the level of activity at the turn of the seventeenth century.

From references to working pits, it is clear that a good deal of
mining continued in the central areas of the manor of Whickham.[196]
Nevertheless, the overall picture that emerges has been fairly
described as 'a steady process of attrition and elimination'.[197] There
were some substantial operations still; in 1693 Sir Charles and
Captain Phillip Bickerstaffe contracted to lead 250 tens (6,625 tons)
a year.[198] But there were also minuscule undertakings which might

[192] NRO Cookson Papers, ZCO IV/47/2. Tonnage calculated on Nef's assumption
that a late 17th-c. 'ten' was equal to 26.5 tons.
[193] For 1675 shipments see Ellis, *William Cotesworth*, 77 (converted into tons as in
n. 192 above).
[194] GPL Cotesworth MSS CN/1/164; Hughes, *North Country Life*, 164. In 1685
the rent was doubled.
[195] GPL Cotesworth MSS CN/1/373–420, CN/1/60.
[196] For the period 1688–1710, e.g., there are references in the Cotesworth papers
and other sources to working pits in Corn Moor, Goose Moor, Cross Moor,
Longsettles, Newfield, Lowfield, Morrisfield, and at Lobley Hill and Swalwell
Banks. This list is not exhaustive: further named pits cannot be located precisely.
GPL Cotesworth MSS CN/1/200–284; DRO Q/S I/36, 44; DPD Probate, Inv. of
John Barras (1691).   [197] Hughes, *North Country Life*, 162.
[198] Ibid. 162–3. The tonnage conversion rate in this and subsequent references is
the statute rate of 26.5 tons to the ten.

best be described as scavenging; of ten sub-tenants listed in 1693, the five smallest led an average of only 22 tens each (583 tons).[199] Nor did the bigger men find it easy to fulfil their contracted quotas as time went on.[200] The surviving accounts of rents due for coals led paint a depressing picture of the final decline of the once mighty Grand Lease colliery. In six years from the 1690s, production seems to have been reasonably steady, with an annual average of 1,399 tens (around 37,000 tons). In 1700–5, however, the annual average was down to 804 tens (around 21,000 tons) and in 1706–10 it was down again to 676 tens (around 18,000 tons).[201] By this time the output of the surviving mines in the manor of Whickham had fallen close to the estimated levels of the early sixteenth century. It is possible that such work as continued was partly for the provision of low-quality coals sold to local customers for industrial heating. The Grand Lease colliery had been granted a long respite by the constraints that still inhibited the expansion of the coalfield. By the end of the seventeenth century, however, it is hard to disagree with the opinion of two viewers of the colliery in 1697–8 who concluded that to all intents and purposes it was worked out.[202]

A slow decline into relative insignificance seems also to have been the fate of most of the other established collieries in Whickham in the generation after 1660. Brinkburne colliery, already in a parlous state in 1650, staggered on. In the 1660s its lessees were accused of using the Brinkburne pits as a cover for poaching coal from adjacent Grand Lease seams, a situation resolved only when both passed into the same hands in the 1670s.[203] Of twelve separate pits worked in the scattered Brinkburne lands between 1668 and 1679, there were usually only two pits going in any single year and no pit was worked more than three years consecutively. It seems that Brinkburne was working only 'pann coles', sold to the salt pans at

[199] GPL Cotesworth MSS CK/2/5.

[200] See Hughes, *North Country Life*, 162–3. The Bickerstaffes did reasonably well in 1693–5, but thereafter proved unable to meet their agreed quota. Similarly, George Airey, who undertook to lead 250 tens in 1698, was never able to achieve this level: PRO DURH 2/98/61.

[201] GPL Cotesworth MSS CK/2/5–8, 57–69. These are maximum estimates of production. It is not clear whether the tens listed were actually led by those concerned.

[202] Hughes, *North Country Life*, 151.

[203] PRO DURH 4/2, 130–1, 438–9, 4/3, fo. 438ᵛ; PRO E 134 29 Car. II Ea. 20. In 1662/3 they worked so close to the Grand Lease workings that the lessees' pitmen were able to hear 'the noyse of the stroakes' of rival hewers.

Shields, and in the later 1670s it was described once again as 'much wrought out, wasted and consumed'.[204]

Meanwhile at Farnacres the colliery was valued in 1679 at £80 at a rate of 12s. per ten of coals. This suggests an expected output of around 3,500 tons only, around a fifth of the level indicated by the 1636 colliery assessment. It was still working thirty-five years later, when a lease was granted on the basis of an expected yield of 150 tens of sea coal (almost 4,000 tons) per annum. Three years later, however, this lease had to be renegotiated for an output of only 5 tens of sea coal and 145 tens of pan coal. New efforts to extend and improve production were made in 1714–16, but these were clouded by disappointment, and the colliery appears to have continued to survive largely by supplying the salt trade, its output being described in 1717 as 'of an inferior nature—mostly salt pan coal'.[205]

Finally, we have evidence that the established mines to the south of Whickham manor, at Hollinside, Ridingfield, Clockburne, Fawdonfield/Greenlaw, and Gellsfield, were all being worked from the 1660s into the first decades of the eighteenth century, and that coals were led from them by wain down to the Derwent staithes at Swalwell.[206] However, no basis for estimating their production has been found earlier than 1716, when a lease of shares in Fawdonfield, Ridingfield, and Gellsfield was granted to a Newcastle 'Oastman'. His shares amounted to one-sixth of the three collieries and the rent was calculated on the expectation that his shares would bring him at least 120 tens of coal (3,180 tons). The total output of the three collieries, then, may have been in the region of 19,000 tons at this date, somewhat less than the 25,000 tons that can be estimated as

[204] PRO E 134 31 Car. II Mich. 31; PRO DURH 7/43.

[205] Surtees, *Durham*, ii. 244; Bourn, *Whickham*, 90; C. R. Huddleston (ed.), *Durham Recusants' Estates, 1717–1778*, Surtees Soc. no. 173 (Newcastle, 1962), 133–4; J. M. Ellis (ed.), *The Letters of Henry Liddell to William Cotesworth*, Surtees Soc. no. 197 (Durham, 1987), 149, 153, 169, 223, 237, 242, 260; E. Hughes, 'The First Steam Engine in the Durham Coalfield', *Archaeologia Aeliana*, 27 (1949), 34–5. For the estimate of output relative to that of 1636, in 1636 Farnacres was valued at £800 and Whickham Grand Lease at £4,500; if Whickham Grand Lease output was c.97,000 tons, then Farnacres' output in 1636 may have been c.17,244 tons.

[206] DRO D/ST 6/30, 25/131; DPD Probate, Will of Richard Harding (1697); PRO DURH 4/2, 213–14; GPL Cotesworth MSS CK/6/0; DRO Q/S I/17; Huddleston, *Recusants' Estates*, 47; PRO E 134 11 & 12 Anne Hil. 37 (which describes the leading of coal c.1660–1712).

their total production in 1636.[207] Of all Whickham's collieries, it was perhaps these that came closest to holding their own in the later seventeenth century. For the rest, the impression given by the scattered but consistent evidence of mining in the parish is that of an industry gradually settling down and subsiding like the subterranean workings on which its former glories had been based.

But Whickham's industrial fortunes were about to be radically transformed—and in a manner that had consequences for the entire coalfield. For the 1690s witnessed the first really successful attempt to break out of the geographical containment which, despite the advent of the waggonways, continued to straitjacket the Tyneside industry. If this spatial movement can be identified with a particular historical moment, then it is arguable that the crucial date was 30 May 1692. On that day, Sir Francis Blakiston leased mining rights beneath his lands at Gibside, Northbanks, Marley Hill, and elsewhere in the parish of Whickham and the adjacent chapelry of Tanfield to the Hon. Charles Montague. Under the terms of the lease, Montague was to hold the mining rights for a period of thirty-one years. He was to pay a 'certain rent' of £490 per annum for the working of up to 700 tens of coal (18,550 tons), 'during ye time of ye leading and carrying away of ye said coales with carts and waines', plus an additional 'tentale' rent of 14s. for each ten worked over and above the 'certain' total. Furthermore, he was granted wayleave over the Blakiston lands to the Derwent and Tyne for his coal wains, and liberty and licence to lay a waggonway—on condition that if a waggonway was built the certain rent would rise to £630 for the working of 900 tens (23,850 tons).[208] It was an agreement that was to have profound consequences.

Hitherto the Gibside estate has scarcely figured in our account of the coal industry in Whickham. It lay at the south-western extremity of the parish, beyond Hollinside, Fawdonfield, and Gellsfield, some three and a half to four miles as the crow flies from the staithes at the mouths of the Derwent and the Team. While scattered references survive, testifying to the existence of mining in the area from as far back as 1615, there is no reason to suppose that

---

[207] NRO Armstrong Papers, 725 F6, 37. 1636 output estimated on the basis of the total valuation of these collieries relative to that of Whickham Grand Lease; i.e. £1,150: £4,500, therefore 24,789 tons: 97,000 tons.
[208] DRO D/ST V. 36.

work was undertaken on any significant scale before the second half of the seventeenth century. In December 1657 a twenty-one-year lease of the colliery at Northbanks and Marley Hill had been granted by Sir William Blakiston to William Carr, a Newcastle merchant, and by this date the colliery must have been in production, for Carr purchased with the lease a total of 190 tens of coal (around 4,000–5,000 tons).[209] We hear little of this colliery thereafter, but presumably work continued, and meanwhile, at nearby Byermoor, Sir James Clavering established a colliery that is known to have led coals by wain to Swalwell between the 1660s and 1700.[210]

This was not virgin territory, then, but it had witnessed relatively modest exploitation prior to the 1690s, a fact confirmed by a 1716 map of the Gibside/Northbanks colliery on which only the northernmost tip is marked 'wrought before the Hon. Charles Montague entered'.[211] Doubtless the expansion of mining in the area was inhibited by the distance from the river and the continued existence of profitable workings further north in Gellsfield, Ridingfield, and Hollinside. In addition, the Blakistons themselves were in no position to undertake significant investment in colliery. They had suffered badly in the Interregnum, having been heavily fined for both delinquency and recusancy, and for a time their lands had been sequestered. Sir Ralph Blakiston died heavily in debt in 1651, and his heir Sir William faced fines totalling £1,390 in 1652–3 at a time when his estate was valued at only £700 a year.[212] Asset-rich but cash-poor, the Blakistons also seem not to have perceived the full potential of their collieries. Charles Montague was to write with scorn not only of Sir Francis's pride, but also of 'Our Landlord's Ignorance'.[213] All in all, the Blakistons, of whom Sir

---

[209] DRO D/ST 23/240, 23/53a, 54. Estimated tonnage based on a ten of either 21 or 26.5 tons.

[210] PRO E 134 11 & 12 Anne Hil. 37. Clavering's Byermoor colliery was probably an extension of his workings at Fawdonfield in the same period.

[211] DRO D/ST 72/27.

[212] Welford, *Committees for Compounding*, 22, 37, 65, 73, 119–23. For the effects of fines and sequestrations on other landlords in the area, see P. Brassley, 'Northumberland and Durham', in J. Thirsk (ed.), *The Agrarian History of England and Wales*, v, *1640–1750*, 2 pts. (Cambridge, 1985), pt. 1, 44–5. It was perhaps the financial pressure of these years that led William Blakiston to let ¼ of Gellsfield colliery to a Durham gentleman in 1650 for a term of 1,000 years: Inner Temple Library, Barrington MSS, no. 27, 14–16. We are grateful to Marcus Knight for this reference.

[213] Ncle. UL, MISC MSS 85, Montague Papers, I. 231–2.

Francis was the last of the male line, seem to have lacked both ready money and entrepreneurial imagination. Nor had they previously fallen prey to a lessee who had both.

Charles Montague's intervention was crucial. In most accounts of the Tyne coal trade in the early eighteenth century, it is Charles's older brother, Sydney Wortley Montague, who grabs all the attention. But it was Charles who brought his family, and its money, into the coal trade. The fifth son of Edward Montagu, Earl of Sandwich and Samuel Pepys's patron at the Admiralty, Charles has been described as having had 'a career of no particular distinction' in comparison with his brothers and his cousin and namesake Charles Montagu, Earl of Halifax and founder of the Bank of England.[214] He is, none the less, a crucial figure in our story. His mother's brother was Nathaniel Crewe, bishop of Durham 1674–1722, and this connection was obviously central to Charles Montague's northern career. He was a member of Parliament for Durham (1685–7 and 1695–1702), chancellor of the Diocese (1686–9), and high sheriff of the county (1687–1705), in addition to holding a string of minor offices, most of them in the gift of his uncle.[215] He was rich. He was well connected. He had entrepreneurial vision, for it is clear from the very terms of his lease that he already knew full well how best to exploit Gibside's potential. And finally, he was a talented opportunist, an essential prerequisite of success in the buccaneering world of the coal trade. 'I am now such a Trader in the World', he wrote soon after acquiring the Gibside lease, 'as to know all profits depend on Trade and Trade on Chance.'[216]

Montague took his chances when they came, and exploited them to the full. He professed himself shocked, on his first entry into the trade, that 'in Colliery you will find more lying and tricking than in any dealings you have ever yet had'. But he learned quickly, and in particular he grasped the fact that in colliery 'It was impossible for

---

[214] F. R. Harris, *The Life of Edward Montagu, K.G. First Earl of Sandwich (1625–1672)*, 2 vols. (London, 1912), ii. 289–90. The spelling of the family name varies, and in the northern documents it is most frequently spelt 'Montague'. With the exception of this reference to members of the family better known as 'Montagu', we have followed the contemporary northern practice.

[215] A brief note of Montague's career and of that of his more prominent elder brother can be found in R. Sedgwick (ed.), *The History of Parliament: The House of Commons 1715–1754*, 2 vols. (London, 1970), ii. 266, 557. For further details of Charles's career we are indebted to Prof. Eveline Cruickshanks of the History of Parliament Trust.   [216] Ncle. UL MISC MSS 85, I. 24.

the landlord to come to a strict knowledge without a Charge in Attending more valluable than the Coals', so that 'In Generall the Tenants have ye Advantage of ye Landlord.'[217]

Montague was to demonstrate the truth of his adage only too well. He worked his colliery, which was variously described as Gibside, Northbanks, or Marley Hill,[218] vigorously, and at the end none too scrupulously. Among the Strathmore Papers is a substantial bundle of documents describing Montague's operations almost throughout the duration of his lease. First, they provide details of the total output of the Gibside colliery for the full period of the Montague tenancy. Second, they bring out the chronology of development and allow it to be correlated with the major developments of the Tyneside industry during this period—waggon-way construction and incipient combination. Third, they provide some idea of the working practices of the colliery and in particular the geographical spread of mining in southern Whickham during these years.

In an appendix to this chapter, we have set out the full details of mining output at Gibside 1692–1723 alongside the available figures for the Tyneside coastal vend in the same period. At the beginning of the lease these figures show that the Gibside operation was still a relatively minor one, producing rather less than 4 per cent of the Tyneside coastal vend. At the turn of the century, however, its scale increased tremendously, and very suddenly. By 1701 Gibside provided about 10 per cent of the coal shipped coastwise from Newcastle, and over the next decade its market share usually hovered between 10 and 13 per cent. The turning point in the growth of Montague's operation can be very precisely identified. It came with the opening in 1699 of the 'Dunston Way'.

From the very granting of his lease, Montague had clearly borne in mind the possibility of laying a waggonway. In the early years of

---

[217] Ncle. UL MISC MSS 85, I. 102, 233.

[218] The different names given to the Gibside colliery can be a source of confusion. They derive from the different sectors of the leased territory that were worked at particular times. A map of 1716, described as 'A Mapp or Plann of Gibside als. Northbanks als. Marley Hill Collieries', shows pits that are frequently identical to those shown on a 1706 plan of 'Gibside' colliery and described in a 1717 'view' of 'Northbanks' colliery: DRO D/ST 72/27 (1716), 72/32 (1706), 21/11 (1717). There were no well-defined boundaries within what was in reality a single, gradually expanding, colliery enterprise. To add to the confusion, in the early 18th c. the colliery was occasionally described as 'Hutton', probably because much of the coal was worked from the thick Hutton seam that lay above the Main Coal in this area.

his operation, his letters show this possibility hardening into a settled plan. Things went well almost from the outset, for he rapidly discovered that the Gibside coal was establishing an excellent reputation among London consumers. In 1697 he wrote enthusiastically of his coals, *'They are now when they come dry moderately round, but wett melts them extreamely* and then they fall small.' Nevertheless, 'wett or dry, round or small, they are the *best coales in London,* and sought for; if known to be pure or unmixed; and if round, my Customers hope to sell them *Twelve pence dearer* than any coals here'.[219] It would appear that the superior quality of the Gibside coal gave the colliery a decisive advantage in the fickle London market, a crucial edge in a time of sluggish demand.

It was probably this advantage that spurred Montague to invest heavily in a waggonway. On 21 June 1697 he drew up an account that reckoned his recent profits to have been £600 on sales of around 26,000 tons. In April of the following year he estimated that it could be possible to raise his profits to £2,000 per annum by a sale of around 52,000 tons. Perhaps the additional profit per ton in his second calculation reflected the premium price Gibside coal could command in the market-place and the savings on leading his vend which he hoped to achieve.[220] Whatever the basis of his projection, Montague was firmly set on carving a bigger size of the market for Gibside coals. Even when the coal won was not of the optimum 'bigness' and 'roundness', he wrote in 1697, *'by Gret Quantity we may gett Money Enough'*, and the best way to reap the profits of 'Gret Quantity' was clear. At a time when his annual vend hovered around 700 tens, he was dreaming of better things: 'I hope to vend 1500 tenns per Anno: so soon as the waggonway is finished.'[221]

In 1699 the Dunston Way was completed, winding a total distance of around four and a half miles across Whickham Fell and down to the staithes at Dunston.[222] It had involved formidable capital outlay: 'I was out of pock in the North 4000^{l} last year, and this yeare will require 2 or 3000^{l} more', wrote Montague in November 1700.[223] But the effect was almost immediate. The output figures show quite clearly that the opening of the Dunston Way coincided with a dramatic increase in Gibside's level of

---

[219] Ncle. UL, MISC MSS 85, I 245; emphasis in original. London consumers preferred large, 'round' chunks of coal.

[220] Ibid. I. 218, 424.   [221] Ibid. I. 230–1; emphasis in original.

[222] Lewis, *Early Wooden Railways*, 113, 120.

[223] Ncl. UL, MISC MSS 85, II. 714.

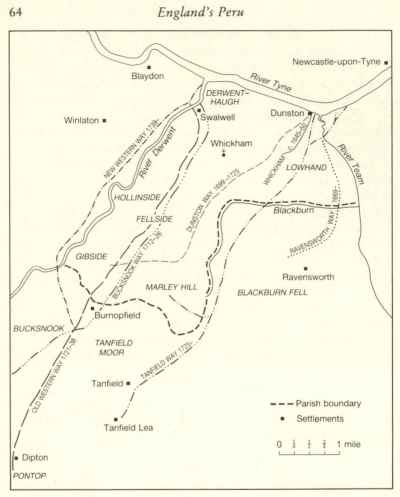

MAP 4. Whickham and environs with routes of waggonways

production. In the space of three years the colliery trebled its
market share. By 1702, after a year in which 2,541 tens were led
(67,337 tons), Montague was dreaming of an output of 4,000 tens a
year (106,000 tons).[224] That level was never in fact reached, though
in the last ten years of the lease production topped 80,000 tons.

The expansion of the Gibside colliery workings necessary to
achieve such levels of production can easily be imagined. A series of

[224] Ncle. UL, MISC MSS 85, II. 754.

accounts from the 1690s, when production was around 18,000–19,000 tons a year, mentions thirteen working pits, yet no more than five of them were noted as going in any one year, not one of them was going every year, and some were worked only a few weeks at a time.[225] An estate survey of 1706, following a year when output was 56,021 tons, indicates that by this time the colliery occupied 770 of the 1,516 acres of the Gibside estate, while a colliery map of the same year shows fifty-seven pits scattered over the landscape.[226] Another map of 1716, with output in 1715–16 of just over 66,000 tons, shows forty-eight pits, many of them identical to those marked on the 1706 map.[227]

Work was therefore geographically extensive, creeping across the colliery as new pits were sunk to extend existing workings and reduce the distances that coal needed to be dragged underground to reach the eye of a pit.[228] It was also, in all probability, increasingly intensive. Seasonality was still evident, to be sure, for it does not appear that coals were led to the staithes between the end of November and early April. But work at the colliery does not seem to have been entirely at a standstill during the four winter months, since at the beginning of the leading season in April the weekly totals were among the highest recorded for the year.[229]

The intensiveness of work underground was brought out only too clearly by a viewers' report of 1717 prepared on the orders of Lady Elizabeth Bowes, the formidable mother of William Blakiston Bowes, who had inherited the Gibside estate as an infant in 1699. Lady Bowes suspected that the colliery was being worked 'disorderly', and the viewers confirmed her fears. In their inspection of nine Northbanks pits they found that in all of them there was 'a great quantity of coal taken away out of ye walles and pillars'. Such 'robbing' of the walls and pillars was a dangerous practice, and indeed it was feared that a 'thrust' or collapse was to be expected in these pits. Worse, in one place 'they did worke a 150 yards in length and 70 yards in breadth leaving nothing but props which is all fallen

---

[225] DRO D/ST V. 36.
[226] DRO D/ST 52/162, 72/32.   [227] DRO D/ST 72/27.
[228] The author of *The Compleat Collier*, 31, stressed that when one pit was sunk and ready to work it was advisable to begin sinking another, so as to have it 'sunk and ready to set to work against the time you have Wrought out your Coaled Working Pit; that so you lose no Time, or Charges of the Water-drawing, by Coal Work standing some time before you Coal another Pit'.
[229] DRO D/ST V. 36.

now'. Such malpractice, said the viewers, was 'a great advantage to the Lessee', but a loss to the owner. There was enough coal left, they maintained, to have continued working the colliery in a proper manner had the lessees been willing to sink deeper rather than going for the immediate gains obtainable by robbing the pillars in existing workings.[230]

Additional papers relating to this dispute reveal that in fact the malpractices of the Montagues were of fairly recent date. Though suspicions of impropriety had been aroused as early as 1710, it was generally accepted that the colliery had usually been worked 'orderly' until 1715, when a programme of systematic pillar-robbing had been introduced. In Lady Bowes's view, the Montagues' motivation was one of ruthless greed, stimulated by the impending expiry of their lease, for it was alleged that they 'did not work away the pillars till they had no hopes of having their lease renewed'. In defence, the Montagues claimed that they had been compelled to work the pillars since otherwise the quality of the coal won would have deteriorated and the colliery would have lost its competitive advantage and become uneconomical.

That there was a measure of truth in both claims is indicated by a letter secretly written to Lady Bowes in December 1716 by Anthony Leaton, the Montagues' chief viewer at Gibside. Leaton was attempting to act as a mediator. He maintained that 'the Colliery may be a topp Colliery for many years to come' if a strategy were followed of both working the pillars and bringing the lower-lying Main Coal seam into full production. If pillar-robbing alone continued, he argued, 'the Colliery will be Ruined in a very few Years'. Yet it was essential that the practice be continued until the Main Coal was won, since 'if the Pillars is Not Wrought at all then the Reputation of the Colliery is Sunk and if once the Colliery be Laid a Side and other Collieryes Brought in to Supply the trade it will be imposable to Retrieve that Loss'.

The Montagues' policy was thus dictated by the demands of the highly competitive 'fighting trade'. At the same time, however, Leaton confessed that his masters had rejected his own advice to win the Main Coal. The reasons for this may be indicated partly by a note on the 1716 colliery map to the effect that some £1,400 had

---

[230] DRO D/ST 21/11. Lady Bowes's mounting indignation as she became aware of her lessees' practices is chronicled in Henry Liddell's letters to William Cotesworth in 1714–16: see Ellis, *Letters of Henry Liddell*, 164–6, 167, 231, 245.

been spent by Mr Wortley Montague on an attempt to extend the drainage system at Gibside, but that this project had proved so 'full of troubles that he was forced to give all over and losse all that money and severall men lost their lifes in the tryall'. 'Orderly' extension of the colliery was perhaps proving too difficult and costly for lessees whose own interest in Gibside was shortly to expire.[231]

As the lease of 1692 approached its end, then, the Montagues chose to maximize Gibside's output of quality coal at the cost of leaving a depleted inheritance to the owner: a sorry story, if a familiar one on Tyneside. Nevertheless, the effects of the Montague lease had been momentous. Charles Montague's vision, enterprise, resourcefulness, opportunism, cunning, greed—call it what you will—had enhanced the wealth of his family and carved out for his heirs, the Wortley Montagues, a place of enormous influence in the entrepreneurial politics of the region.[232] But Montague had done much more in the process. He had restored Whickham to a central place in the development of the mining industry by bringing the waggonways to the south-western extremity of the parish. In so doing, he had opened the way for expansion into what became known as 'the western collieries', the rich unexploited seams beneath the high ground between the watersheds of the Derwent and the Team. It was a breakthrough that proved to have a transforming influence on the whole Tyneside industry.

Charles Montague, it will be remembered, was shocked (or fascinated) by the 'lying and tricking' that were the order of the day in the coal trade which he entered in the 1690s. It was a theme to which he repeatedly returned; 'few are to be believed, much less relyed on in Colliery', he opined in 1697; and again in 1699, 'nothing is too much to be beware of in colliery'.[233] It was, in his

---

[231] BL Add. MS 40747, fo. 72; DRO D/ST V. 36, D/ST 21/38, 72/27. The Wortley Montagues were also guilty of 'disorderly' working practices at their Benwell colliery. In the early 1720s, working the walls and pillars there led to an extensive roof collapse, and in 1726 the colliery had to be closed: Ellis, *William Cotesworth*, 75. In the Gibside case their conduct was eventually restrained by an order of Chancery.

[232] The ultimate beneficiary of the family's business acumen was John Stuart, 3rd Earl of Bute, the favourite of the young King George III. Bute's father-in-law, Edward Wortley Montague, died in 1761 leaving Lady Bute a staggering inheritance of approximately £1 million: Sedgwick (ed.), *History of Parliament: The House of Commons 1715–1754*, ii. 554–6.

[233] Ncle. UL MISC MSS 85, I. 102, 291, 625.

experience, a business environment characterized by sharp practice, malice, spite, and sheer bloody-mindedness, in which the devil took the hindmost.

There were good reasons why it was so. As we have seen, the market for sea coal remained sluggish. The volume of coal shipped coastwise from Newcastle had peaked in 1688 at 23,126 tens (612,839 tons), a level that was not normally surpassed until the 1720s. In fact, up to 1710, after which the statistics suffer a frustrating twelve-year break, shipments were to exceed 20,000 tens (530,000 tons) in only two years, 1699 and 1701.[234] The entre-preneurial logic of the situation has been described succinctly by Dr Ellis. Given the state of the market, it was in every individual coal-owner's interest to sell as much coal as possible, for 'the high proportion of fixed capital costs compelled proprietors to increase production in order to reduce marginal costs'. This being so, 'the profit margins on each chaldron as well as the net annual return on the investment were crucially dependent on the quantity sold'.[235]

These were the imperatives that gave meaning to Charles Montague's dictum that in colliery 'A Quick Vend is the Only Article.'[236] Proprietors anxious to obtain a 'Quick Vend' were forced to suffer as best they could the depredations of the hostmen 'fitters' of Newcastle, who played one off against another with almost proverbial ruthlessness. And behind the Tyneside fitters lay yet another group of merchants whose interests were best served by the continuance of the fervid competition among the producers: the inner ring of London dealers who controlled the prices in the metropolitan market.[237] Predictably, the urgent need to sell coal in an overstocked market bred constant anxiety and periodically provoked sharp price wars, catching up the coal-owners in 'a seemingly inescapable spiral of rising costs, over-production, and static or falling prices'.[238] Only those owners fortunate enough to be producing unusually high-quality coal were in a position to sell as much as they chose, and their very success could be ruinous to their neighbours. To the major players in colliery, however, the

---

[234] Ellis, *William Cotesworth*, 77. Cf. Hughes, *North Country Life*, 160.

[235] Ellis, *William Cotesworth*, 76.

[236] Ncle. UL MISC MSS 85, I. 259.

[237] Ellis, *William Cotesworth*, ch. 4, provides an excellent account of the marketing of coal from the Tyne. For a recent account of marketing in London, see Flinn, *Coal Industry*, ch. 8. sec. iii.

[238] Quoting Ellis, *William Cotesworth*, 80.

search for new sources of high-quality coal seemed the only way to swim with the tide.[239]

Charles Montague's entry into the coal trade served to exacerbate these circumstances. The years 1690–2 had been grim ones in the coal trade, so bad that owners had been compelled to fall over themselves to offer the coy fitters such sweeteners as substantial quantities of 'gift coal' in order to obtain a vend for their stocks.[240] Montague was able to enter the market and participate profitably by virtue of the exceptional quality of his Gibside coal. With the opening of the Dunston Way, he dramatically increased his market share by unleashing a torrent of high-quality coal which swept away the vend of his weaker competitors. Two consequences of his success were to reverberate throughout the next three decades. First, he had demonstrated the possibility of bringing into profitable production the high-quality coal seams to the south-west of Whickham by the use of waggonways, thereby indicating a way forward for those who sought to win in the 'fighting trade'. Secondly, his intervention so exacerbated the existing internecine warfare among the coal-owners as to raise again the desirability of some form of combination and regulation that might stabilize the situation.

Expansion to the western collieries with the aid of waggonways, combination, and a regulated vend: these are the contrapuntal themes that run through the history of the Tyneside industry in the reigns of Anne and George I. And Whickham played a vital part in both. In January 1712 a new lease of Whickham and Gateshead was granted to Alderman Ramsay of Newcastle. This lease had been negotiated by Ramsay's brother-in-law William Cotesworth. Cotesworth was a Teesdale yeoman's son who had made good as a tallow chandler in Gateshead and was by this date emerging as a man to be reckoned with in the coal trade.[241] The new lease, which was to pass to Cotesworth himself on the death of his sleeping partner in 1716, placed Cotesworth in a position of vital importance in the politics of colliery. For by virtue of his lordship of the two manors, and in particular that of Whickham, he was able to control wayleave access

---

[239] Ibid. 80–1. For examples of the owners' awareness of the importance of coal quality, see Ellis, *Letters of Henry Liddell*, 10, 19–20, 78–9.

[240] Hughes, *North Country Life*, 160.

[241] Ibid. 114; J. Ellis, 'A Bold Adventurer, the Business Fortunes of William Cotesworth, *c.*1668–1726', *Northern History*, 17 (1981), 118–23.

to the rich collieries to the south-west of the parish. Without Cotesworth's grant of wayleave, no new waggonway could be constructed across the manorial lands by those proprietors who wished to expand. Without his willing co-operation, no inhibition could be placed on such expansion by those whose interests lay in the establishment of a regulation that could protect their vend from unwanted competition. Much depended, then, upon the extent to which Cotesworth's strategically vital wayleave powers could be either employed to advantage or evaded.

Cotesworth, in fact, appears to have been fairly consistent in his appreciation of the advantages of a regulated vend—though he also knew how to swim with the tide in a fighting trade. In 1708 he had been a prime mover in negotiating what had become known as 'the Regulation', a series of annual agreements between a group of major proprietors and hostmen–fitters to control output in accordance with a rough and ready apportionment of the vend. (In this, incidentally, the largest single portion went to the Montague collieries, of which Gibside, described in 1712 as 'ye chiefest colliery in either river', was the jewel in the crown.[242]) It has been suggested that the new lease of Whickham and Gateshead was in fact a project of the Regulation, masterminded by Cotesworth under the protective cover of Ramsay's name. This may well have been so, for the directors of the Regulation immediately took exclusive leases of the Whickham wayleaves and a common purse was formed to challenge at law wayleave rights that had been granted collusively by the previous holders of the lease.[243] But whatever the case, Cotesworth's involvement in the Regulation, and his willingness to use his power over wayleaves to hamper the operations of non-participants, meant that any subsequent attempts at lateral expansion of the coalfield would necessarily involve either his co-operation or the circumvention of his control.

The first successful attempt to break free followed swiftly, with the construction in 1712 of the Bucksnook Way. Sir John Clavering,

[242] Ellis, *William Cotesworth*, 115 ff.; GPL Cotesworth MSS CR/3/135; Hughes, *North Country Life*, 167–71. The owners' combination was declared illegal by an Act of 1711, but continued clandestinely: see Ellis, *Letters of Henry Liddell*, 35–6, 88, 112, 118, 251, and *passim*.

[243] Ellis, *William Cotesworth*, 123–4. Further evidence for this view can be found in the guarded references to the negotiations for the lease in the letters of Henry Liddell to Cotesworth in 1710–11: see Ellis, *Letters of Henry Liddell*, 3, 6, 8–9, 12, 14, 22–8, 31, 62, 63, 67.

George Pitt, and Thomas Brummell, chafing at the restrictions imposed upon them by the chief participants in the Regulation, were anxious to increase the output of high-quality house coal from their collieries at Byermoor, Lintz, Bucksnook, and Tanfield Moor. They were debarred from using the Dunston Way by the Montagues. Nor could they obtain wayleave over Lady Bowes's Gibside lands or the manor of Whickham, since the interests of both the Bowes family and William Cotesworth coincided with those of the Montagues. They therefore determined to undertake the expense of laying their own waggonway along a route that avoided both, passing eventually through Byermoor (between Gibside and Marley Hill) and then hugging the east side of the Derwent down to the Swalwell and Derwenthaugh staithes. This project was successfully completed in June 1712, after some extraordinarily intensive competition for and conflict over wayleave rights, attempts to incite the tenantry of Whickham to tear up the track, and the actual destruction of the line at one point by Lady Bowes's men.[244]

About much of this, as Edward Hughes remarked, there was 'a distinct sixteenth century flavour', though James Clavering of Lamesley thought it smacked more of farce than neo-feudalism. 'I would gladly have a ballad made of all this', he wrote exultantly after witnessing the panic after the formal opening of the line, when cattle straying on to the way were mistaken by guests 'in the midst of their jollity and cups' for hostile horsemen, an error that occasioned an impromptu counter-attack and 'such riding and tumbling as the like has not been known'. A few months later, as the subsequent court cases and machinations continued, he returned to the theme, declaring that 'this famous waggon way occasions such variety of proceedings and adventures that really could we have its history writ by a good pen would outdo Don Quixot'.[245]

The outcome was serious enough. Henry Liddell's amusement at the events of 1712 was tempered with apprehension; for, as he explained, 'the . . . coals were a much more vendible commodity which would be ledd down that way at a much cheaper rate than usuall and in vast quantitys, and consequently must lessen the vend of those that had a meaner sort'. The hard-won success of the Bucksnook projectors spelled the beginning of the end of the

---

[244] Ellis, *William Cotesworth*, 125; Lewis, *Early Wooden Railways*, 113, 121; Hughes, *North Country Life*, 17–18, 155, 174, 185, 196.
[245] Ibid. 18; Ncle. UL MISC MSS 10, 8 June 1712, 3 Feb. 1713.

Regulation of 1708, which was to fade away by 1715 as hard-pressed members defected or resorted to 'over-vending'.[246] It also, of course, initiated the elaboration of the waggonway network within Whickham parish.

The details of the tortuous politics of the coal trade in the ensuing decade need not detain us. The rivalries, jealousies, and personal hostilities of the chief players in the drama intensified. Both leases of collieries and rights of wayleave in the western colliery area were anxiously sought and bought up, sometimes for use, sometimes merely to be held at 'dead rents' so as to exclude competitors. At the staithes and in the counting houses of the Tyne, the terms of the fighting trade were hammered out.[247] The situation was admirably and succinctly summed up by James Clavering of Lamesley, when he remarked in 1712 that it 'fulfills the old proverb, every man for himself but God for us all'.[248]

Cotesworth, who had originally stood by Lady Bowes in her opposition to the Bucksnook Way (until she left him in the lurch in the ensuing welter of lawsuits), knew when he was beaten. He eventually acquired a share of the Bucksnook colliery himself and used the new waggonway to carry his own coals—much to the chagrin of Sir John Clavering, who hated him.[249] Meanwhile, as undisputed lord of the manors of Whickham and Gateshead, he was able to comfort himself in 1719 by granting wayleave to the Wortley Montagues for coal from their Gibside and Blackburn collieries at a 'tentale' rent of 5s. per ten.[250] This would have brought him upwards of £700 a year from Gibside alone. Cotesworth's position remained enviable. The next major development came when the Claverings and the Boweses, who resented that position, got together to dish him.

In 1720 Cotesworth's quarrel with the Claverings over the

[246] Ellis, *Letters of Henry Liddell*, 69–71, 73–4, 75, 76–7, 78–9; Ellis, *William Cotesworth*, 125–6; Hughes, *North Country Life*, 193–6.

[247] For the general tone of the period, see P. Cromar, 'The Coal Industry on Tyneside, 1715–1750', *Northern History*, 14 (1978); and Ellis, 'Bold Adventurer', *passim*.

[248] Ncle. UL MISC MSS 10, 14 Nov. 1712.

[249] Lewis, *Early Wooden Railways*, 121; P. Cromar, 'Economic Power and Organization: The Development of the Coal Industry on Tyneside 1700–1828', Ph.D. Thesis (Cambridge, 1975), 75; Ellis, *William Cotesworth*, 71–2. By 1717 some nine lawsuits were being fought over the Bucksnook wayleaves. They were bitterly fought and enormously expensive.

[250] Cromar, 'Coal Industry', 197.

disputed wayleave, rights erupted again, and Lady Clavering, another of the tough matriarchs of the coal trade, found an unlikely ally in William Blakiston Bowes of Gibside. Bowes, who had recently attained his majority, was an ambitious youth. In addition to holding other colliery interests, he was eagerly anticipating the demise of the Montague lease of his Gibside collieries. Together with Richard Ridley of the adjacent Burnopfield colliery, he and Lady Clavering conceived the plan of building yet another new waggonway to circumvent Cotesworth's lands and rival the Bucksnook Way. In April 1721 the Western Way was opened, running parallel to the Bucksnook Way through western Whickham, but closer still to the Derwent. It took much of the traffic from the Bucksnook Way and was eventually extended south to Dipton to serve the colliery of John Simpson.[251]

The pride of William Blakiston Bowes in the considerable engineering achievement represented by the Western Way has already been quoted, though he did not live long to exploit it, for in October 1721 he died aged only twenty-four. His brother and heir George Bowes, however, did so. When the Gibside lease fell in he took over his colliery and transferred its coal to the Western Way, thereby rendering redundant the upper sections of the old Dunston Way over Whickham Fell. Moreover, he agreed to allow his partners to lead unlimited quantities of coal over his lands for thirty years.[252]

Cotesworth, having been outmanœuvred, appears to have responded by moving closer still to the Worthley Montagues. Having been ousted from Gibside, they were now co-operating with the Liddell family in working the collieries of Stella Grand Lease in Ryton parish and Blackburn in Lamesley. In 1723 the two families agreed to hold all their collieries in partnership and to build at their joint charges (and with Cotesworth's blessing) yet another new waggonway—this time from Blackburn colliery to the staithes at

[251] Ellis, *William Cotesworth*, 131; Lewis, *Early Wooden Railways*, 113, 121. Bowes describes himself as 'a professed enemy to old Will', whom he accused of 'covetousness and endeavouring to engrosse all ye Coall Trade to himself'. He expected the new waggonway to improve his own colliery revenues by 'above 3000l. per annum': BL Add. MS 40747, fos. 181, 184, 186.

[252] Ellis, *William Cotesworth*, 131–2. The Claverings did so well from the wayleaves granted for the Western Way that in 1726 Sir Francis Clavering, who was also a partner in the Bucksnook Way, closed the latter. This action may have been a last thrust at his old enemy Cotesworth: Lewis, *Early Wooden Railways*, 122.

Dunston and Redheugh in Whickham and Gateshead, respectively. This was achieved in 1724–5 and the line was then rapidly extended south, via the famous Causey Arch, to the Wortley Montague collieries at Causey and Tanfield, almost six miles from the Tyne.[253] With the opening of this Tanfield Way, the old Dunston Way was finally abandoned.

The successive openings of the Bucksnook, Western, and Tanfield Ways had the cumulative effect of flooding the Newcastle market with high-quality coal from the western collieries. The resulting competition enabled Cotesworth to play his master stroke. Since the early 1720s he had been advocating the need for a new regulation. In 1726, having survived an attempt to remove him from the game by poisoning his cup of chocolate, he was able at last to bring the rival proprietors together—not least by skilful use of the leverage given him by his wayleave rights, which had been challenged by his enemies but triumphantly vindicated by a legal decision of 1725.[254] First, in April 1726 he and George Bowes settled their outstanding differences. Next, in the summer of the same year articles were agreed between Bowes, the Wortley Montagues, and the Liddells for the formation of a partnership, the 'Grand Allies', of which Cotesworth was named secretary. The proprietors agreed to hold all their collieries above Newcastle bridge in thirds (with a number of exceptions, including Gibside), and to produce agreed quantities, while continuing to sell separately. Wayleave rights and waggonways were to be shared. No more wayleaves were to be granted to non-members. The costs of 'dead rents' were to be borne jointly. Cotesworth's magnificent pay-off was that he was to receive 5s. per ten on all coals led from the partnership's collieries. In return, he undertook to grant hence-forward neither wayleaves over, nor mining rights for sea coal collieries under, his manors of Whickham and Gateshead.[255] Cotesworth had little indeed to lose by this concession. His assured income would be enormous, and he would forgo little by closing Whickham manor to sea coal mining. Surviving accounts show that output from the Grand Lease colliery in Whickham was still

---

[253] Cromar, 'Coal Industry', 198; Lewis, *Early Wooden Railways*, 113, 122.

[254] Ellis, *William Cotesworth*, 134. For the attempted poisoning, see J. Ellis, 'The Poisoning of William Cotesworth, 1725', *History Today*, 28 (1978), 752–7.

[255] NEIMME, Watson Collection, Shelf 5, no. 5, 7–9; DRO D/CG 16/1076–8; Hughes, *North Country Life*, 233–5; Ellis, *William Cotesworth*, 132–5; Cromar, 'Coal Industry', 199; Lewis, *Early Wooden Railways*, 122.

declining. In 1712–13 production at the remaining pits was around 17,500 tons, in 1718–19 it was down to around 11,000 tons, and in 1720 only 14,000 tons were led—and not all of this can have been sea coal.[256] However, within months Cotesworth was dead, cut off in his moment of triumph, and in 1729–30 Whickham manor passed from his heirs to George Liddell, one of the Grand Allies.[257]

In the quarter-century that followed their formation in 1726, the Grand Allies did their best to exert control over the coal trade. From 1723, figures for the Newcastle vend are again available, and the annual averages of shipments for each decade thereafter bring out clearly the extent to which the opening up of the western collieries in the first quarter of the century had enabled the Tyneside industry to expand its share of the market for coal since 1710:[258]

1701–10	486,368 tons
1711–22	(no data)
1723–30	716,443 tons
1731–40	763,418 tons
1741–50	747,266 tons

It is equally evident, however, that after the 1720s the market was once again sluggish. Accordingly, the Grand Allies, who had controlled around 60 per cent of the capacity of the Tyneside coalfield at the time of their formation, focused their attention on keeping the lion's share of the trade to themselves. They 'vigorously

[256] GPL Cotesworth MSS CN/1/421 (account of 770 tens led in 14 mos. of 1712/13: 770 tens = 20,405 tons in 14 mos.; therefore 17,490 tons in 12 mos.); CN/1/423 (411.5 tens led in 12 mos. 1718–19 = 10,904 tons; 527 tens led in 1720 = 13,965 tons).

[257] GPL Ellison MSS C/37/2, A/33/18. The manor remained with the Liddells for the remainder of our period. In 1737 the minutes of the partnership reveal that 'the usual allowance made for the lying-in of Whickham colliery' was £500: DRO D/ST 49/19.

[258] The figures quoted are derived from those given in J. Ellis, 'Combinations in the Newcastle Coal Trade in the Early Eighteenth Century' (unpubl. paper, n.d.). We are grateful to Dr Ellis for her generosity in providing us with a copy of her paper. In the figures cited here, Newcastle chaldrons have been converted into tons at the statute rate. It should be noted that these figures refer to *all* coal shipped from Newcastle and not merely to coal shipped to other English ports. The figures given here for 1701–10 thus differ from those quoted earlier in this chapter, which refer to coastal shipments only. For our purposes Ellis's figures are preferable to those presented for the coastal trade in Flinn, *Coal Industry*, 218, for two reasons. First, Flinn's figures include shipments from all north-eastern ports, including Sunderland. Second, Flinn's figures for coastal shipments are frequently estimated, a procedure forced upon him by the difficulty of distinguishing coastal shipments from the total 'sea sale' in this period.

and ruthlessly' brought up colliery leases and wayleaves 'for the sole
purpose of denying them to others', and used their collective power
with a will to beggar their neighbours.[259] By 1750 they controlled,
either by ownership or lease, sixteen of the twenty-seven sea-sale
collieries south of the Tyne, and a waggonway network extending
up to eight miles from the river.[260] They never achieved total
domination of the industry, and their coherence as a combination
was periodically dislocated by temporary defections and renewals
of the fighting trade among themselves—as in 1730, when George
Bowes unilaterally cut his prices in order to secure a better vend.
Nevertheless, there seems little doubt that, having played a leading
role in the colliery development that had expanded the Tyneside
vend up to the 1720s, they succeeded in keeping up prices at the
expense of the Newcastle fitters and channelled into their own long
purses the better part of the profits to be made from the coal that
travelled down the waggonways.[261]

5. AN INDUSTRIAL SOCIETY IN A 'PRE-INDUSTRIAL' WORLD

In 1738 the Grand Allies closed the Western Way south of Gibside.
Workings on the Bowes estate were now concentrated in the Marley
Hill area, and these could be served conveniently by the construction
of a new branch-line to the Tanfield Way. Moreover, closure of the
Western Way had the added advantage of denying access to the river
to four of the Grand Allies' competitors in the western collieries.
These unfortunates were obliged to undertake the expense of
constructing a waggonway of their own—the 'New Western Way'
of 1739—which was routed down the western bank of the Derwent,
in Ryton parish, so as to escape the stranglehold on Whickham
wayleaves now exercised by George Bowes and the Liddells.[262]

The closure of the old Western Way provides a convenient point

[259] Cromar, 'Economic Power and Organization', 78; Flinn, *Coal Industry*, 41,
161.
[260] Ibid. 40–1; Lewis, *Early Wooden Railways*, 122.
[261] Cromar, 'Coal Industry', 202–6.
[262] Lewis, *Early Wooden Railways*, 122–3. Bowes had by this time acquired
Axwell Houses colliery and Hollinside, greatly extending his control of the eastern
bank of the Derwent: DRO D/ST 4/75, 23/104, 47/19. In 1742 he also acquired
Brinkburne freehold, further consolidating his position in Whickham: DRO D/ST
23/113, 128, 129.

at which to pause and take stock; for it can be said to have marked the conclusion of the second phase of Whickham's industrial development. In the forty years that separated the opening of Charles Montague's Dunston Way from the closure of William Blakiston Bowes's Western Way, Whickham had re-emerged as one of the most significant centres of coal production on Tyneside. Additionally, it had acquired an altogether new role as the geographical focus of the network of waggonways that had opened up the western collieries and revitalized the Tyneside coal trade.

After 1740 all this was to change. Whickham no longer funnelled the greatest of the waggonways down to the Tyne. The Dunston Way, as we have seen, had been superseded and was taken up between 1723 and 1725. The Bucksnook Way had been closed by Sir Francis Clavering in 1726 in order to enhance his wayleave income from the rival Western Way. Now the Western Way itself was gone. Only the branch-line from Marley Hill and the lower stretches of the Tanfield Way to Dunston remained.[263] Again, Whickham was no longer a major centre of coal production. In the later 1710s, it seems probable that the working collieries of the parish were again producing something over 100,000 tons of sea coal annually, while in 1721–2 Gibside alone yielded over 87,000 tons of prime sea coal.[264] By the mid-eighteenth century, however, output was very much lower. Work continued at Marley Hill and Byermoor (and elsewhere), but such figures as are available do not suggest a total output much greater 25,000 tons a year. Indeed, by 1760 Marley Hill, largest of the remaining collieries, was producing coal at something close to the levels that had obtained at the

---

[263] Lewis, *Early Wooden Railways*, 122–3.

[264] The estimate of total Whickham production in the later 1710s is based upon the average Gibside output 1715/16–1719/20 of *c.*66,000 tons p.a., our estimate for Fawdonfield, Ridingfield, and Gellsfield collieries of 19,000 tons produced in 1716, and the Byermoor allowance of 550 tens in the regulation of 1708, which suggests an output of *c.*14,500 tons for that colliery. These figures provide a total of *c.*99,500 tons. Since it is likely that Byermoor production was substantially higher after the opening of the Bucksnook Way, we suggest a grand total of 'something over 100,000 tons of sea coal' produced annually. Sources: DRO D/ST V. 36; NRO Armstrong Papers, 725 F6, 37; GPL Cotesworth MSS CR/3/135. Since the Grand Lease colliery produced *c.*17,500 tons in 1712/13 and *c.*11,000 tons in 1718/19 (part of which must have been sea coal), this is a conservative estimate. It will be remembered that in 1714–17 the Farnacres colliery was also producing *c.*4,000 tons p.a., most of it pan coal. The total production of both sea and pan coal by all Whickham's working collieries at this date may well have reached 120,000 tons or more. In addition, some very small land-sale operations existed for which no estimate can be attempted.

beginning of the Montague lease.[265] George Bowes of Gibside remained a great coal magnate, said to have had an income from coal of £7,000 a year to add to his landed rental of £5,000.[266] But as Gibside production declined, he probably derived the bulk of his income from colliery interests elsewhere. Whickham remained a mining parish for the rest of the eighteenth century. It was embraced still by the Tanfield and New Western waggonways, which continued to bring coal down to the extensive staithes at the mouths of the Derwent and the Team. But the coal frontier had shifted again, first to the most distant of the Western collieries and then, after 1750, to the new mines to the east of Newcastle, which were now able to work the previously inaccessible deep seams of that area with the aid of steam-driven pumps and novel techniques of ventilation.[267]

Yet all this must be understood in context. Whickham in the mid-eighteenth century was not undergoing a process of de-industrialization. On the contrary, it was being incorporated more deeply into an increasingly complex industrial economy. The Tyneside region was one of the first areas of England to be 'rendered geographically distinctive by industrial activity', one of 'the archetypes of large scale, capitalist, and geographically concentrated industrial organization'.[268] From the later sixteenth century it had witnessed the emergence of industrial undertakings of striking scale and complex organization, of 'specialized and distinctively industrial settlements', and a hitherto unknown concentration of industrial workers.[269] The mining and transportation of coal were, of course, the driving force of this development, the heartbeat of a nascent industrial order. 'This country all about is full of this coale,'

---

[265] In the two years 1758–9 Marley Hill colliery yielded 1,279 tens (33,893 tons), an annual average of *c.*17,000 tons. Byermoor was working in the late 1740s when its viewer estimated output at 300 tens (7,950 tons). Gellsfield was also still working, but probably at a very low level of production; in a parish rate of 1749 its rental value and rating assessment were less than half that of Byermoor. Sources: DRO D/ST 72/21, 338/9; NEIMME, Watson Coll., Shelf 8, no. 4, 'Journal of John Watson 1745–50', 28, 33, 29, 40; DRO EP/Wh 19. Small land-sale collieries, of course, continued to operate, and there were some new developments. In 1759 Norwood colliery, near Dunston, advertised for pitmen and in 1764 for wainmen, our first references to the existence of this colliery: *Newcastle Courant*, 15 Sept. 1759 and 19 May 1764.

[266] Ellis, 'Bold Adventurer', 125.

[267] Smailes, *North England*, 141; P. Cromar, 'The Coal Industry of Tyneside 1771–1800: Oligarchy and Spatial Change', *Economic Geography* 53 (1977); Flinn, *Coal Industry*, 21–2.

[268] Smailes, *North England*, 5–6.　　　　　　　　　　　　　　[269] Ibid. 131.

observed Celia Fiennes in 1698, 'the sulphur of it taints the aire and it smells strongly to strangers; upon a high hill 2 mile from Newcastle I could see all about the country which was full of coal pits.'[270] 'It is observable in this place', remarked Henry Bourne, that 'when the Coal Trade is brisk all other Business is so too . . . It is the Money arising from the Coal Trade that almost entirely circulates in this great Town and adjacent Country.'[271] Increasingly, however, it was not just coal. There was also salt, glass and lime, shipbuilding, copper, and iron; the proliferating industrial undertakings that used the 'small coal' which was unsaleable to the choosy markets of the south; and the myriad subsidiary activities spawned by the needs of the coal industry itself.[272]

In all this, Whickham shared. The coal frontier moved on beyond the parish, but its people, as we shall see, became ever more firmly embedded in an industrial economy and an industrial culture. To take only the most outstanding example, we can point to the Winlaton ironworks established in 1691 by Sir Ambrose Crowley, greatest of the Augustan ironmasters, and their extension in 1707 when Crowley bought out the manufactory and slitting mill of his rival Edward Harrison of Swalwell. By the time of the death of Sir Ambrose's son, John, in 1728, the Crowley factory at Swalwell was a massive manufacturing complex by the standards of the day, comprising forges, mills, furnaces, warehouses, and numerous workshops. 'It is hard to believe', concluded the historian of the Crowley firm, 'that there can have been any larger industrial unit in the country at this time apart from the naval dockyards.' It was to become a place of pilgrimage for admirers of England's growing industrial muscle—and, more to our point, it provided employment for hundreds of men at Swalwell and in the surrounding area and exerted a substantial demand for locally produced 'pan cole'.[273]

As Edward Hughes observed, 'already by 1750 the predominant industrial and social character of the north-east was set as in a mould'.[274] It was a development that astounded contemporaries

---

[270] C. Morris (ed.), *The Illustrated Journeys of Celia Fiennes 1685–c.1712* (London and Exeter, 1982), 176.

[271] Bourne, *History of Newcastle*, 158.

[272] J. Ellis, 'A Dynamic Society: Social Relations in Newcastle-upon-Tyne 1660–1760', in P. Clark (ed.), *The Transformation of English Provincial Towns, 1600–1800* (London, 1984), 193; Brassley, 'Northumberland and Durham', 41–2.

[273] M W. Flinn, *Men of Iron: The Crowleys in the Early Iron Industry* (Edinburgh, 1962), 41, 52–4, 75.   [274] Hughes, *North Country Life*, 467.

whose expectations were formed in a predominantly agrarian society. And it had massive repercussions for national economic development.[275] Daniel Defoe was a man familiar enough with the world of trade and manufacture, but his wonder is almost palpable in his description of the scene as he rode up to Newcastle in 1724:

> Whereas when we are at London and see the prodigious fleets of ships which come constantly in with coals for this encreasing city, we are apt to wonder whence they come and that they do not bring the whole country away; so on the contrary, when in this country we see the prodigious heaps, I may say mountains of coals which are dug up at every pitt, and how many of these pitts there are, we are filled with equal wonder to consider where the people live that can consume them.[276]

In this elegantly balanced sentence, Defoe underscored the symbolic complementarity of London and Tyneside, producer and consumer, and his words capture the essence of the story that we have tried to tell in this chapter. For almost three centuries, the rise of the Tyneside coal industry in general and the supply of the London market in particular were intimately intertwined with the history of Whickham. Whickham lay at the very heart of the extraordinary industrial precocity of Tyneside; the parish was a focal point in an industrial society thrusting towards maturity in a still largely 'pre-industrial' world.

A century after Defoe rode through the thickly scattered pits on his way to Newcastle, much of this early industrial history had been forgotten. The lessees of Whickham whom we have seen sinking their pit in 1836 cannot have been entirely ignorant of the former history of the area—the earliest ordnance survey maps show clearly the numerous 'old shafts' that remained. But they had no detailed knowledge of the accomplishments of their predecessors. Since then, much has been done to correct such ignorance. Historians of the coal industry have recognized the importance of Whickham in

---

[275] Nef's view of the significance of the growth of the coal industry in the 16th and 17th c., expressed in vol. II of *The Rise of the British Coal Industry*, is now generally regarded as overstated. Nevertheless, the broader significance of Tyneside's development has continued to excite comment. See, e.g., E. A. Wrigley's discussion of the Tyneside–London relationship in 'A Simple Model of London's Importance in Changing English Society and Economy, 1650–1750', *Past and Present*, 37 (1967), 58–60. The significance of the complex, long-term influence of the coal industry on British economic development has recently been powerfully reaffirmed in Flinn, *Coal Industry*, ch. 13.

[276] D. Defoe, *A Tour Through the Whole Island of Great Britain*, Everyman edn., 2 vols. (London, 1962), ii. 250.

its development, and in this chapter we have tried to elaborate and extend that generalized appreciation by providing a more sharply focused inside view.

As yet, however, the social history of the early industrialization of Tyneside remains largely unwritten. More than thirty years ago, one of the pioneers of the social history of the north-east wrote that 'the Industrial Revolution occurred here much earlier and its social consequences strike deeper than anywhere else . . . Here at any rate, is a standing challenge to the social historian.'[277] That challenge remains. However detailed our knowledge, and however sophisticated our understanding of the economic history of the coal industry between the sixteenth and early eighteenth centuries, the social transformations that accompanied industrial growth have been expunged from historical consciousness, drowned and lost in time like the waterside pits of Whickham. But that history is not beyond recovery. Our purpose in the chapters that follow is to contribute to the overcoming of that historical amnesia, by exploring the contours of a forgotten social landscape and recovering, in so far as we are able, the textures and the dynamics of the social experience of some of those who lived and died in England's Peru.

[277] Hughes, *North Country Life*, p. xiv.

APPENDIX

Coal Led from the Gibside/Northbanks/Marley Hill Colliery, 1692–1723

Leading year	Tens	Tons[a]	Tyneside coastal vend[b] (in tens)	
1692/3	533	14,125	1692	15,629.9
1693/4	696	18,444	1693	17,965.0
1694/5	663	17,570	1694	16,041.3
1695/6	684	18,126	1695	17,097.0
1696/7	682	18,073	1696	15,109.6
1697/8	712	18,948	1697	18,128.0
1698/9	726	19,239	1698	19,584.4
1699/1700	1,252	33,178	1699	20,700.6
1700/1	1,721	45,607	1700	19,005.1
1701/2	2,541	67,337	1701	21,479.5
1702/3	1,589	42,109	1702	18,297.6
1703/4	1,486	39,379	1703	15,217.0
1704/5	2,205	58,433	1704	19,114.6
1705/6	2,114	56,021	1705	17,437.9
1706/7	1,890	50,085	1706	15,581.5
1707/8	1,430	37,895	1707	14,142.9
1708/9	1,885	49,953	1708	17,878.6
1709/10	2,639	69,934	1709	19,567.5
1710/11	1,262	33,443	1710	15,771.9
1711/12	1,870	49,555		
1712/13	1,965	52,073		
1713/14	2,044	54,166		
1714/15	2,401	63,627		
1715/16	2,492	66,038		
1716/17	2,419	64,104		
1717/18	2,514	66,621		
1718/19	2,438	64,607		
1719/20	2,688	71,232		
1720/1	2,891	76,612		
1721/2	3,295	87,318		
1722/3	3,067	81,276		

[a] Tens converted to tons at the 1695 statutory rate of 26.5 tons to the ten.
[b] No data available from 1710 onwards.
Source: Coals led, DRO D/ST V. 36; Tyneside vend, Ellis, 'William Cotesworth', 77.

2

A World Turned Inside Out: Industrial Development and Agrarian Change

Rich meadows and full crops are elsewhere found
We can reape Harvest from our barren ground.

William Ellis, *News from Newcastle* (1651)

BY 1583, when the Grand Lease of Whickham and Gateshead passed into the hands of the hostmen of Newcastle-upon-Tyne, the manor of Whickham had been a significant centre of coal production for more than two centuries. It was still, however, a predominantly agricultural community. More than a generation later, a report on the state of the manor in 1620, which attempted to depict the conditions that had prevailed prior to the expansion of the Grand Lease colliery, was to insist upon this fact. The manor was described as consisting of 'very large and spacious fields and territories'. Its lands were said to have been 'very fruitfull and fertile', well watered by a score of springs and wells 'contynually at all tymes of the yeare flowing with wholesome and swete water whereby both thinhabitants there themselves with there famylies and there cattle were relieved and nourished'. Moreover, the township had been 'very populous, consisting of Copihold tenants and Copiholders' who were both 'many in number' and prosperous, for, 'by reason of the fertilitie of there said copihold land', they had 'heretofore lived in good estate, able to do service both to there sovraign . . . and to the lords of the said manor'.[1]

Elizabethan Whickham, then, was remembered as a primarily agricultural settlement—well favoured, populous, and well-to-do. Undoubtedly, this was a recollection coloured with the warm tints of nostalgia. Yet such nostalgia was fuelled by the knowledge that

[1] PRO DURH 2/20/69.

by 1620 the world of the copyhold tenants of Whickham was threatened with imminent dissolution. For if the industrialization of Whickham was the harbinger of a new economy and society, it was also the nemesis of an older social formation. In this chapter we shall be concerned with the impact of industrial development upon the copyholders of Whickham, the opportunities it presented and the dislocation it entailed. We can begin by examining the manor of Whickham and the way of life of its tenants in the last third of the sixteenth century.

1. THE COPYHOLDERS OF WHICKHAM

The manor of Whickham was indeed spacious. Its fields and territories occupied the northern and central areas of the parish of Whickham, accounting in all for between a third and two-fifths of its entire acreage. The manor was unenclosed, but highly complex in its field pattern. A survey of 1647 listed no fewer than 19 'townefields' of 'meadow grounds arrable land and pasture' in addition to eight distinguishable areas of open 'common or moore'.[2] Within the town fields, the arable and much of the meadow was divided into 14 'cavells' of copyhold land, each cavell save one containing 5 'oxgangs', and each oxgang comprising 12 acres (a total of 69 oxgangs or 828 acres of copyhold). In addition, the town fields contained 5–6 oxgangs of freehold land (up to 72 acres), some 45 acres of glebe land belonging to the rector of Whickham, and demesne meadows totalling almost 50 acres.[3] The remainder of the town fields (at least 730 acres) consisted of pasture land which appears to have been held in allocations proportionable to the arable and meadow holdings of the tenants, the pastures being divided into notional 'beastgaits' or 'pasture gates', entitlement to which passed with a copyhold tenancy.[4] Finally, beyond the town fields lay upwards of 500 acres of rough pasture, the 'great moores or comons' of Whickham Fell, over which the copyholders, together with the owners of adjoining freeholds, enjoyed 'over Rake and free

    [2] Kirby, *Parliamentary Surveys*, 81–2.
    [3] DPD DDR, HC III F 19, fo. 15; DPD Halmote Court Rentals, Box 11, Bundle 5, no. 193324; PRO DURH 7/19, pt. I; Fordyce, *Durham*, ii. 689–90; Kirby, *Parliamentary Surveys*, 80–1, 107–8.
    [4] Such arrangements are made clear in a case of 1613 in PRO DURH 2/11/182.

libertye of comon and pasture for theire goods commonable to goe and depasture in and uppon'.[5]

Whickham manor was also relatively populous. A rental of the manor which can be dated to the early 1560s lists the names and holdings of 59 tenants.[6] According to the ecclesiastical census of 1563, the parish of Whickham had a total of 93 households.[7] At this point, then, in the first decade of Elizabeth's reign, close to two-thirds of the householders of the parish were copyholders of the principal manor. The remainder were presumably either freeholders or tenants of the smaller manors of Farnacres, Axwell-cum-Swalwell, Hollinside, and Gibside–Marley Hill, which adjoined the manor of Whickham to the east, west, and south-west.

Of the 59 tenants listed in the rental, 16 were apparently cottagers, holding only a dwelling house or cottage together with a garden, a 'garth', or tiny parcel of land or less than one acre; 9 more held 1–6 acres of copyhold land; 24 held 10–29 acres, most of them falling in the 18–24 acre range, and a further 9 held 30–50 acres. Only one tenant held more than that, his holding amounting to some 62 acres.

This document, of course, provides only a partial, unrealistically static, picture of the structure of landholding on the manor. It was a record of land tenure and tenant liability rather than of actual possession, and we have no warrant for assuming that the lands of the manor were actually farmed in the individual units described in the rental. The great majority of the tenants were probably owner-occupiers of their lands, for they were certainly residents of Whickham, but at the same time there is evidence enough in the Halmote Court books of the manor that temporary sub-tenancy agreements were commonplace.[8] At any one time some tenants may have farmed larger or smaller acreages than those specified in the rental. Moreover, some of the copyholders may have held land

---

[5] PRO DURH 2/2/20; Kirby, *Parliamentary Surveys*, 81; DPD DDR, Halmote Court M 6 (Whickham Enclosure), 46.

[6] DPD Ch. Comm. MS 189721. The rental is undated, but identification of the persons listed and comparison with wills dates it firmly to the early 1560s, probably 1563–5.

[7] DPD, 'Returns made by James Pilkington, bishop of Durham . . . 1563' (photocopy of BL Harleian MS 594, fos. 186–95), fo. 188[v].

[8] The Halmote Court was the manorial court of the bishop. Whickham's tenants owed suit to the Chester division court, meeting at Chester-le-Street. From 1585 separate courts were held and court books kept for Whickham itself by virtue of the rights of lordship granted by the Grand Lease.

outside the manor, either in their own right or as sub-tenants. Nevertheless, on the basis of this admittedly imperfect guide to the anatomy of rural society in Whickham manor, it seems reasonable to suggest that the copyholders could be divided into two broad groups. On the one hand, there was the minority of tenants who can best be described as cottagers or smallholders—the word employed in Whickham was 'coteman'. On the other hand, there were those who held small- to middle-sized family farms, generally of more than one and a half oxgangs of copyhold land plus pasture rights within the town fields. Beyond this basic distinction, however, it can be said that while the distribution of copyhold land on the manor was far from egalitarian, the copyholders were not very markedly differentiated from one another in terms of landholding. There were no giants among Whickham's copyhold tenants and the range of differentiation was narrow. For the most part, differences in the acreages held were relatively small, certainly small enough to be easily bridged by a sub-tenancy agreement or by the fortunes of marriage and inheritance, and in this sense the majority of the copyholders of Whickham can be said to have enjoyed a rough and ready parity.[9]

In addition, all copyholders of Whickham held certain advantages in common. All had the right to depasture their beasts on the fell. All enjoyed rights of intercommoning on the town fields between St Cuthbert's day in September and the spring.[10] Their tenure was exceptionally secure, for by the custom of the manor a copyhold in Whickham was 'an estate in fee simple'. Rights of inheritance were guaranteed. Rents and fines were both small and fixed.[11] In an age of

---

[9] R. H. Tawney commented on the relative lack of economic differentiation among north-eastern tenants in *The Agrarian Problem in the Sixteenth Century* (London, 1912), 63–6. We should add that we make no assumptions about the nature of earlier realities (e.g. those of the early 14th c.), which may have been different. Our own account must begin with the known situation of the mid-16th c., which formed the immediate background to subsequent developments.

[10] PRO DURH 7/12.

[11] The phrase 'an estate in fee simple' was used by a Whickham copyholder in PRO DURH 2/27/78. Such an estate was the strongest and most secure form of copyhold tenure, giving the tenant full rights to dispose of his or her land as he or she saw fit: see E. Kerridge, *Agrarian Problems in the Sixteenth Century and After* (London, 1969), 60 ff. Rents were stable throughout the period of this study. For fines, see Kirby, *Parliamentary Surveys*, 84. These advantages were also enjoyed elsewhere on the bishopric estates: James, *Family, Lineage and Civil Society*, 39; P. H. Horton, 'The Administrative, Social and Economic Structure of the Durham Bishopric Estates, 1500–1640', M.Litt. thesis (Durham, 1975), 225–8.

inflation in which many English villagers elsewhere faced landlords anxious to extinguish customary tenancies and to enhance rents and fines, the copyholders of Whickham were fortunate indeed.

The agriculture practised on these lands was predominantly pastoral. Durham, like most of north-east England, endures a climate characterized by cool summers and raw, cold winters, with frequent damaging frosts and snowfalls even at low altitudes. Much of the higher land is of poor quality, while even in the lowlands the prevailing weather conditions entail a short growing season in which the very winning of the hay crop can be a difficult and protracted process. All in all, the area presents 'a generally unkind prospect for agriculture, especially for arable farming'.[12] As might be expected in such a region, the husbandry practised in the sixteenth and seventeenth centuries was everywhere based upon the production of livestock, primarily cattle. This was most markedly so in the highland zone of the Pennine uplands, which lay some miles to the west and south-west of Whickham. Yet even in the intermediate foothills and the eastern lowland zone, where crops of oats, rye, barley, wheat, and peas were grown, animal husbandry remained the mainstay of the rural economy.[13]

Whickham, which lay on the edge of the intermediate and lowland zones of Durham, provided no exception to this general picture. A survey of the surviving farming inventories of the parish for the period 1557–89 reveals very much what might be expected: a pattern of small to middling farms, in which livestock generally accounted for 70–80 per cent of the total valuation of farm goods, variegated by the occasional inventories of poorer cottagers, whose agricultural wealth, such as it was, lay entirely in their stock.[14]

Cattle-raising was clearly the principal activity. Even the cottagers had a young beast or two, while the more substantial farmers all owned oxen, cows, and small herds of 'stotts', 'stirks', 'whies', and calves in varied combination. Horses were kept by all save the cottagers. Sheep featured less regularly in the inventories. They

---

[12] Smailes, *North England*, 52–3; R. I. Hodgson, 'The Progress of Enclosure in County Durham, 1550–1870', in H. S. A. Fox and R. A. Butlin (eds.), *Change in the Countryside* (London, 1978), 84.

[13] Brassley, 'Northumberland and Durham', *passim*, esp. 35, 37–9; Hodgson, 'Progress of Enclosure', 85.

[14] Sixteen farming inventories survive for the period 1557–89. Most of the people involved are identifiable as middle-range copyholders (*c*.12–40 acres).

appear to have been kept in small flocks by only the bigger- and smaller-than-average farmers, and were very much the animal of the poor: all cottagers owned sheep. The principal crops grown appear to have been oats and rye. There is some uncertainty here, for, though every farming inventory contained a valuation of 'corne and hay', the nature of the grain crop was not always specified. Where particular grains are named, oats and rye occur in the largest quantities, with wheat coming a poor third. Barley is never mentioned. None of these crops, however, appears to have been grown in very large quantities. The impression given by the inventories is that grain was produced primarily as a contribution to subsistence needs. Rye was probably the principal bread corn. Oats might serve humans and horses alike. It seems unlikely, however, that Whickham was self-sufficient in grain production. The secondary nature of arable farming in Whickham is further demonstrated by the fact that, where the inventories are sufficiently detailed to permit comparison, the inventoried value of corn is almost equalled on average by that of hay grown for fodder.

These generalizations can be rendered more concrete by provision of a number of examples. A fairly typical Whickham farming inventory of this period was that of John Merreman, taken in early November 1574. Merreman had held 18 acres of copyhold land on the manor of Whickham. At the time of his death he had 20 'thranes' of oats, 10 thranes of 'hard corne' (probably rye), and 6 'fothers' of hay, to a total value of £3. 1s. 4d. The bulk of his farming wealth, however, lay in his 3 'naggs', 6 oxen, 3 cows, and 7 young beasts, which were valued at £15. 18s 0d. in all. He also kept 3 geese, 1 cock, and 3 hens (value 1s. 8d.), presumably for domestic use, while his husbandry gear consisted of one long wain, two short wains, and a plough (total value 13s. 4d.). Essentially similar was the inventory of Margaret Hirst, who was holding her dead husband's 24 acre copyhold in 'widowright' at the time of her death in 1576. In June that year, when her will was made, she bequeathed to each of her brothers 'one bowll of rye so sonn as god shall send my corne of the earth'. By November, when her inventory was taken, the harvest was in, for it included 18 bowls of 'hard corn' and 'haver' worth £2. 17s. 6d. More impressive, however, were her 3 mares, 4 oxen, 1 'fat ox', 5 cows, 4 'stotts', 1 'whye', and 1 calf, which amounted in value to £29. 7s. 0d. She also had 2 sheep, 2 lambs, an 'old goose', and 8 hens, as well as 40 shillings' worth of husbandry gear in the form of the ubiquitous wains (one long and two short), a plough, a yoke, and a soame.

John Merreman and Margaret Hirst may stand as examples of the average copyholders of Whickham. The cottagers, who appear more rarely in probate records, can be represented by John Whitfield, a young married man who in December 1583 left one young 'stirk' and 34 sheep, or Christopher Cooke, who in August 1586 owned 5 geese, 4 swine, 1 'whie', and a flock of 14 sheep which he left to his son and daughter 'equally to be devided betwixt them'.[15]

In sum, the wealth of the copyholders of Whickham lay primarily in their modest herds and flocks. By the standards of the north country their land may have been fertile enough, but they were essentially pastoralists. Their well-being depended upon the higher-quality pastures and meadow lands contained within the town fields of Whickham and upon the extensive rough grazing on the fell. Even the landless could benefit from these resources, and clearly they did so. To be sure, it must have been a hard life for many, and for some a constant struggle to piece together a living in an unpropitious environment. Yet there is good reason to suppose that the majority of the copyholders enjoyed a tolerable economic security. And what they had was securely theirs. They were all well defended by their customs from seigneurial exploitation, and they were free to pass their lands, their goods, and their rights to their children. To this extent, they may well be said to have lived in 'good estate'.

This impression of modest well-being is reinforced if we turn to consider the copyholders' 'howshold stuffe', the domestic goods listed in their inventories, which can be employed, albeit with caution, to gain an impression of their living standards. Inventories of household goods are peculiarly prone to the problems that beset the historian in using probate inventories: patchiness of survival, inconsistency of form, casual or deliberate omissions, unreliable valuations, and variations according to the life-cycle stage of the deceased person.[16] Used with discretion, however, they remain an

---

[15] DPD Probate, Wills and Invs. of John Merreman (1574), Margaret Hirst (1576), John Whitfield (1583), Christopher Cooke (1586). Holding sizes from DPD Ch. Comm. MS 189721.

[16] There is an extensive literature dealing with the problems and potentialities of probate inventories as historical sources. For a useful brief discussion of the pitfalls (which principally affect historians attempting to use these documents with statistical rigour), see U. Priestley and P. Corfield, 'Rooms and Room use in Norwich

invaluable guide to the domestic interiors of the period and provide one of the few opportunities open to the historian to reconstruct the material culture of the age.

In this instance use will be made of the thirteen inventories surviving from the years 1562–1588 which were kept in sufficient detail to give some confidence in their credibility. Eight of these inventories were those of middling to substantial copyholders (holding 18–46 acres), who for the most part died in middle life if we are to judge by the numbers of children mentioned in their wills. A ninth was a smallholder who held at least 4 acres, while the remainder appear to have been cottagers, two of whom, perhaps significantly, were almost certainly young men. To avoid problems of comparability, no attention will be paid to the total valuations of household goods. Instead, attention will be focused upon the types of goods possessed as a means of ascertaining the general level of living standards and the extent to which they can be said to have varied.

Some goods were ubiquitous, most notably those related to the basic necessities of warmth, cooking, eating, and sleeping. Every inventory included fire-irons. Almost all mentioned pots and pans of brass or iron and kettles and/or cauldrons, the essential utensils for cooking porridge, soups, and stews. Only six, however, all of them belonging to copyholders of some substance, mentioned spits. Again, every inventory included pewter vessels for eating and drinking, though only a minority mentioned wooden platters; the latter were perhaps largely ignored as of little value or else were lumped together with other 'wooden vessels'. Similarly, eating implements seem to have been ignored: only two inventories listed them, the implements in both cases being horn spoons. Bedding, however, warranted greater attention. Sometimes there was a single valuation of all 'bedding', and it was always a substantial proportion of the total domestic inventory, but more commonly sheets (linen or harden), pillows or 'codds', and blankets or coverlets were specified in detail. These comforts were general. Not one inventory, however, included a bedstead, and feather beds were also entirely

Housing, 1580–1730', *Post-Medieval Archaeology*, 16 (1982), 94–6. Keith Wrightson is grateful to Dr Lorna Weatherill of the University of Newcastle for her advice on the use of inventories. As will be evident, her work has greatly influenced the manner in which Whickham's inventories are employed, both here and in subsequent sections of this book.

absent. Of the remaining furnishings in general use, almost all inventories included an 'almerye' for storage and at least one chest; a board or 'meat board', doubtless supported on trestles, which served in place of a table; at least one chair, and a form or forms for seating.

As will be evident, these goods indicate a domestic life-style of considerable simplicity and their possession constituted the general pattern. Clearly, the copyholders of Whickham participated to only a very limited degree in the improvement in living standards that has been documented for southern England in the mid to late sixteenth century. They had their pewter, but for the rest they enjoyed few of the improved furnishings beginning to make their way into the wills and inventories of the yeomen and husbandmen of the south.[17] Only a minority appear to have possessed goods implying a greater sophistication in domestic life. Some had candlesticks of pewter, five had 'window cloths', four had linen towels and napkins, and three had tables as well as boards. Three owned an iron 'chimney' as well as their fire-irons. Three had 'painted cloths' or hangings on their walls. One—the most substantial of the copyholders—owned a single cushion. With the exception of the three tables, these items were not novelties appearing only in the later inventories; they could be found from the start. They indicate the variation that could exist in domestic interiors, and it cannot be without significance that for the most part they occur in the inventories of the more substantial landholders.

For the most part, however, the copyholders of Whickham and their poorer neighbours appear to have been little differentiated in terms of the types of goods that they possessed. The differences among them lay largely in the quantity. John Jackson, a cottager, had six pewter dishes, one brass pot, one iron pot, and a pan. Robert Boutflower, a copyholder of some substance, had sixteen pewter

---

[17] For contemporary comment on improved living standards in the south, see F. J. Furnivall (ed.), *Harrison's Description of England*, Pt. I, New Shakspere Soc., 6th ser., 1 (London, 1877), 239–42. Historical studies include W. G. Hoskins, 'The Rebuilding of Rural England, 1570–1640', in *Provincial England* (London, 1965), ch. 7; id., *The Midland Peasant: The Economic and Social History of a Leicestershire Village* (London, 1957), 288–99; K. Wrightson and D. Levine, *Poverty and Piety in an English Village: Terling, 1525–1700* (New York, San Francisco, London, 1979), 26–9; M. Campbell, *The English Yeoman under Elizabeth and the Early Stuarts* (New Haven, Conn., 1942), chs. 5–7. Unfortunately, the Whickham inventories yield little evidence of housing standards at this date beyond references to the 'hall' or 'hall house' as the principal room.

dishes, two pots, four pans, a kettle, and a spit. Jackson owned one chest; Boutflower had three. Jackson's family sat round their 'bord' on 'ii litle forms'; Boutflower's had a 'meat bord', two forms, two stools, and a chair. Jackson had 'one bed of clothes'; Boutflower had several. And so we might continue. Such differences certainly mattered; yet in terms of material culture, the Jacksons and the Boutflowers were essentially at one.[18]

We have, then, a sense of an agricultural settlement that was populous, well favoured by the standards of the north, and modestly prosperous, in which economic and social differentiation was certainly real, but at the same time relatively muted. Finally, it must be observed that the copyholders of Whickham not only shared a way of life and a common material culture, but also possessed a distinct and powerful sense of collective identity. They enjoyed vital tenurial rights in common. They had a collective interest in the good management of their fields and pastures. They acted together in their Halmote Court, taking decisions that were enforced by their annually elected officers, the Grieve and Sworn Men. Moreover, they were accustomed to the collective defence of their rights through the agency of their officers, above all in fending off encroachments upon the pastures which were both crucial to their well-being and jealousy guarded.[19] Had it not been so, they would not have responded as they did to the very real changes that were to come to Whickham in the wake of the granting of the Grand Lease.

2. COALWAYS AND COAL WAINS

At the death of Bishop Pilkington in 1576, there were only four working pits in the manor of Whickham.[20] To the copyholders of the manor, mining must have seemed an ancient and familiar but essentially peripheral activity. It was confined to the pasture in Southfield and to the waste on Cross Moor.

---

[18] DPD Probate, Registers of Wills, II. fos. 30–30ᵛ (Robert Boutflower, 1562), 178ᵛ (John Jackson, 1565).
[19] For the election of the grieve, see PRO DURH 2/1/16. For examples of the officers' defence of customary rights, see PRO DURH 2/2/20, 2/5/46, 2/27/77, DURH 7/12.
[20] BL Lansdowne MS 66, no. 84, fo. 219.

In the first quarter-century following the acquisition of the Grand Lease by the Newcastle hostmen, this situation does not seem to have altered dramatically. Exploitation of the advantages conferred by the lease appears to have been relatively restrained. There was not the urgent rush to pillage the coal seams lying beneath Whickham that has sometimes been assumed. To be sure, mining activity increased. By 1594–5 it seems likely that the output of the pits worked by the Grand Lease colliery within the manorial lands had come close to doubling. Yet evidence of new sinkings remains relatively sparse as compared with what was to follow in the early seventeenth century. Nor did the Grand Lessees begin by attacking the seams closest to the river Tyne and then work inland, as has often been stated—a strategy that would have involved the sinking of pits within the best meadow and arable land of the manor. On the contrary, they appear initially to have expanded operations within the traditional areas allocated to mining, in the grazing lands to the south of Whickham town, while at the same time consolidating their position by acquiring additional mining leases in the freehold lands and lesser manors adjacent to Whickham Fell.

There are several possible reasons for the exercise of such restraint. In the first place, the Grand Lessees may have been cautious in delaying heavy investment in an acquisition that for a decade and a half remained insecure, contested, and the object of political conflict. They may indeed have been short of investment capital in the wake of the substantial outlays that had proved necessary for both the purchase price and the defence of the lease. It is possible that they had acquired Whickham and Gateshead in a moment of opportunism, with a view primarily to the long-term potential of the Grand Lease, rather than as a means of meeting immediate needs. They owned other recently established collieries in neighbouring parishes, and it is arguable that these were largely sufficient to meet present demand. The lessees may have been genuine in their contention of 1595 that the significance of the Whickham and Gateshead mines had been exaggerated by their opponents. Again, there may well have been initial difficulty in recruiting the skilled labour necessary for rapid expansion. In nearby Winlaton colliery in the 1580s the pits were on occasion laid in 'for lack of workmen'. Women were apparently employed there, an expedient regarded as both unusual and undesirable, and the owners were also said to have sent into Scotland in the hope of attracting immigrant miners.[21]

With regard to the siting of their pits, there were of course good technical reasons for working pits on the higher ground in order to evade the trouble and expense of major drainage undertakings. All of these factors may have played their part. In addition, however, it may well be that the Grand Lessees were to some extent inhibited by the need to avoid disruptive conflict with the interests of the copyholders of Whickham, some of whom appear to have been less than enchanted with the uncertain prospects conjured up by the transference of lordship over their lands from a complacent bishop to first a courtier and then a mercantile oligarchy.[22]

For whatever reasons, or combinations of reasons, the Grand Lessees appear to have proved remarkably careful of the Whickham copyholders' susceptibilities during the first generation of their tenure of the manor. They apparently paid compensation for every rigg of ground damaged by mining operations or carriage at the rate of five nobles and ten groats 'for the ground of evrie pitt of the grand lease where coles were layed upp', four shillings 'for overgate of evrie coppiholder rigg that was corne land', and two shillings 'for evrie lay rigg'.[23] There was no strict legal necessity for them to do so, for the Grand Lease gave them untrammelled rights as lords of the soil, but it had been the custom since at least the fourteenth century for mining lessees to compensate the tenants in this manner, and the Grand Lessees complied.[24] Similarly, they observed customary practice in fencing in all 'going pits' as a safety precaution, while 'wasted' pits were filled up after their abandonment, 'to cleanse and ridd the ground of all thill metall and rubbishe that were cast out of them', in order that the copyholders 'might use

---

[21] PRO E 134 29 Eliz. Ea. 4. The Grand Lessees Anderson and Selby were themselves among the proprietors of Winlaton colliery: PRO Palatinate of Durham, Calendar of Cursitors Records, Chancery Enrollments, 57 (85), Roll 2 of Bishop Barnes, Membrane 2, 20 Eliz.

[22] See below for early challenges to the Grand Lessees' rights. There is also evidence of the copyholders' withholding of rents in the early 1590s: PRO DURH 2/1/16, 34.

[23] PRO DURH 7/18, pt. I: testimony of William Hodgson, taken in 1620 but describing practices of 'about 40 or 50 yeres since'. Cf. testimony of Nicholas Arnold in PRO DURH 2/20/195.

[24] See e.g. the conditions of Bishop Hatfield's lease of 1356: Page (ed.), *Victoria County History . . . Durham*, ii. 322.

and have there common and eatage whereof they were hindered by working of the same pits'.[25]

As for the leading of coal from the pits down to the river, prior to the 1610s the lessees or their agents apparently approached the Grieve and Sworn Men of Whickham whenever the sinking of a new pit required the establishment of a new coalway, and the officers then 'dowled and sett forth' some 'competent way' which would be least prejudicial to the copyholders' interests.[26] Moreover, the copyholders of Whickham were given preference in the task of carrying the coal to the river in their wains, such employment being regarded as their due, 'both in respect that they had hurt by such cariage in there corne and medow as also they would have most care to do the least hurt'.[27] In general it appears that few 'straingers', 'foraners', or 'outdwellers that had no interest in the soile' were involved in this work in the early years. William Hall, who drove a coal wain in the years 1600–10, said that at that time 'there were no strangers permitted but the Towne had all the caryages for then there were but few pitts and few wayes'.[28] At the peak of the shipping season, when fleets of colliers lay in the Tyne waiting to be served and 'the cole owners stood need of more cariages then they of Whickham were able to furnish', 'they sent to the greve and other officers . . . to pray leave that straingers might come to carrie to supplie there wants which was done according and when there fleet of shipps were gone and the cariages grew less then the straingers were debarred'.[29]

All this may well appear a model of industrial responsibility and good public relations. It was not without friction and incident, as we shall see; but in general the *modus vivendi* established between the copyholders and the coal-owners seems to have been maintained well enough with the help of the manorial officers. For their part, the copyholders made sure that the principal coalways were kept open, the Halmote ordering more than once that 'everie man shall repaire the cole way leding over ther several grounds'.[30] At the same

---

[25] PRO DURH 2/20/69. Cf. Bourn, *Whickham*, 26.

[26] PRO DURH 2/20/195, confirmed by several deponents in DURH 7/18, pt. I.

[27] PRO DURH 7/18, pt. I, testimony of Thomas Gamesby. Cf. testimony of William Hodgson and George Watson jun. The latter claimed that the Whickham men were given preference 'by reason they might best prevent hurt from their corn and grass'.   [28] PRO DURH 7/18, pt. I.

[29] PRO DURH 7/18, pt. I, testimony of George Watson jun.

[30] DPD DDR, HC III F 18, fos. 14^v (1590), 64^v (1603).

time, they clearly insisted upon proper consultation, and they acted vigorously to maintain their interests. Carriage of coal was prohibited by the officers in unseasonable weather, and offenders against this rule were liable to have their wains unloaded and their teams impounded. 'Forreners' were actively prevented from leading coal when they appeared. Copyholders making unauthorized coalways were prosecuted in the Halmote. They could also be dealt with summarily; Andrew Rodham recalled that 'when he was a boy and dwelt with his father . . . and by his commaundement did drive a cole wain, if he had gone out of the way dowled or lede coles without the greve approvement the said greve would have put him of and given him some strokes'.[31] Those with 'an interest in the soile' were anxious to preserve it.

If the copyholders needed to keep a wary eye on the development of the Grand Lease colliery, however, it seems that they had relatively little cause for complaint in these early years. Their new lords were not remotely interested in agricultural estate management. At no time was the security of their tenures challenged. Rents and fines remained small and stable. There was no attempt to enclose the manor. An examination of copyhold landholdings up to 1600, based on the comparison of rentals of 1591 and 1600 with that of the early 1560s, reveals a great deal of stability and continuity in the landholding structure of Whickham.[32] More than half of the tenant families of the 1560s still retained their holdings 'in the name'. Where the tenancy had changed hands as a result of sale, marriage, or inheritance, the individual holdings largely retained their integrity as units: there had been little 'engrossing' or subdivision of holdings. Much as in the 1560s, there were 10 copyholders who held smallholdings of 1–7 acres. Whereas 24 had held 10–29 acres in the 1560s, in 1600 there were 22 who held 9–29 acres, most of them still in the 18–24 acre range. There were still 9 tenants holding 30–49

---

[31] PRO DURH 7/18, pt. I. For Halmote action, see e.g. DPD DDR, HC III F 18, fa 55ᵛ (1601).

[32] DPD DDR, HC III F 19, fos. 173–174ᵛ; DPD Halmote Court Rentals, Box 11, Bundle 5, no. 193323. These rentals provide the names of tenants and rents payable, but not acreages. It is possible, however, to match the holdings of 1591 and 1600 with those detailed in the survey of the early 1560s through tenant continuity, the naming of holdings, or the identical rent paid. As a result, a 'survey' of landholding for 1591 and 1600 can be reconstructed. The accuracy of this reconstruction has been confirmed by tracing the descent of individual holdings in the Halmote Court records of land transfers.

acres. Change, where it had come, was most noticeable at the top and the bottom of the manorial hierarchy. One new accumulation of over 70 acres had emerged as the result of the bringing together of holdings of the Shafto family which had been separately held in the 1560s. Meanwhile the number of cottage holdings had increased from 16 to 26. These modifications of the landholding pattern are certainly worthy of note, especially in the light of subsequent developments in the course of the early seventeenth century. Up to 1600, however, change is far less striking than continuity on the manor of Whickham.

The surviving agricultural inventories of Whickham copyholders for the period 1593–1618 also suggest a considerable degree of stability. The pattern revealed remains one of small to middling pastoral farms in which the value of livestock generally accounted for upwards of 70 per cent of the valued farm goods. Oats and 'hardcorne' (usually rye when specified) were still the principal crops. Hay, when separately valued, continued to provide a substantial proportion of the total valuation of 'corn and hay'. The inventories were not without change as compared with those of the period before 1590, as we shall see, and their novel features can be attributed directly to the expansion of the coal industry. In terms of agricultural practice, however, it is abundantly clear that the established patterns of farming in Whickham persisted.[33]

These indicators suggest that, from the point of view of the manorial tenantry of Whickham, things were well enough during the early decades of the Grand Lease. Indeed, not only did the copyholders have little reason for complaint, they also had good cause to welcome industrial expansion, for it brought income to Whickham in a number of ways. One of these was direct employment in the pits, either as pitmen or supervisory overmen. Of the twenty-seven pitmen whose names are recoverable from Whickham records between 1587 and 1607, only three were definitely members of copyholder families. As overmen, however, the copyholder families were more prominently represented. Six of the fifteen known overmen in 1600–18 were copyholders or members of their families, most of them drawn from the ranks of the cottagers and smallholders. Perhaps local men provided the

---

[33] This discussion is based on 14 copyholder farm inventories surviving for the years 1593–1618. Most were middle-range copyholders, a few were cottagers.

nucleus of skilled labour required by the Grand Lease colliery.[34]

Again, property could be sublet to the coal-owners or their work-people. Anthony Barras owned a parcel of freehold in addition to his copyhold lands and he let it for mining on terms that brought him both a regular supply of 'fiar coles' and a cash income sufficient to provide substantial legacies for his younger children. He also rented a house to a pitman.[35] Ann and Richard Hedworth sublet a parcel of copyhold for use by a staitheman.[36] Some of the new cottages that had appeared by 1600 were held by existing copyholder families and were presumably sublet. If so, they were not inhibited by the Elizabethan statute against the erecting of cottages without four acres of land attached, for it explicitly exempted the cottages erected for miners and quarrymen within one mile of their place of work.[37]

There was money to be made too from the supply of victuals and drink to the growing industrial work-force. It is probably no accident that at the turn of the sixteenth century the copyholders appear to have kept rather more cows than had their predecessors. Half a dozen of them also figure prominently on a list of unlicensed butchers, 'brousters', and 'tipleres' presented to the Durham assizes by a common informer at the end of Elizabeth's reign.[38]

Above all, however, the copyholders of Whickham stood to benefit from the privileged position that they enjoyed in the matter of wain carriage. Coal was carried from the pits to the riverside staithes in small wains holding a *fother* (which in Whickham at this date appears to have meant around 10½ hundredweight), and drawn by a yoke of oxen and a pair of horses.[39] They were distinctive and specialized vehicles, unsuitable for other uses by

[34] There is no single source for this information. Names of pitmen and overmen were drawn from a name index based on all available Whickham sources. Those who were from copyholder families were identified from Halmote Court records, parish registers, and probate records.

[35] DPD Probate, Will and Inv. of Anthony Barras (1594).

[36] PRO DURH 2/19/10.   [37] 31 Eliz. c 7 (1589).

[38] PRO DURH 17/1, pt. I, undated 'information' c.1599–1602. The informer covered several parishes in the coalfield area, which clearly provided rich pickings for an informer on offences in the victualling trade.

[39] Lewis, *Early Wooden Railways*, 87, defines a 'fother' as 17½ cwt. However, this was the late 17th-c. measurement. A case of 1619, referring to a coal contract of 1613–14 at Blackburn colliery, near Whickham, states the practice of 'accounting forty usuall fothers to every tenne': PRO DURH 2/19/211. Nef, Dendy, and Dietz suggest that at this date a 'ten' (ten chaldrons) amounted to c.420–430 cwt. (see ch. 1, n. 94). A fother can thus be regarded as approx. 10½ cwt. at this date.

virtue of their impregnation with coal dust, and described by Celia Fiennes in the late seventeenth century as 'a little sort of dung potts'.[40] Initially, the hostmen of Newcastle appear to have experienced some difficulty in obtaining sufficient carriage for the coals wrought at their pits. At Winlaton in the 1580s 'there was always when some carriage was done more coles left at the pitte then they were able to lead', while in 1595 the coal-owners made a general complaint that 'ther ar now for thes last three or fower yeares more Colles wrought then could be gotten carried to the water'. They claimed that the costs of carriage had risen in recent years from 3*d.* or 4*d.* to as much as 12*d.* a fother, and put this forward as one of the prime causes of the increased price of coal.[41]

Ultimately the coal industry was to call into being a substantial army of semi-independent wainmen, such as the seven who described themselves in a court case of 1611 as 'servants for . . . Mr Thomas Liddell makinge caryage of . . . coles for ordinarie wags as usuallie they do from other pitts nere to the said River of Tyne'.[42] In the early years of the Grand Lease, however, when carriage was at a premium, there may very well have been solid economic reasons for the special relationship that came into being between the Grand Lessees and the copyholders of Whickham. During this initial period, the copyholders were allowed preference in the supply of wains and the leading of coal from the Grand Lease colliery, and their involvement in this work rapidly became very substantial. Of the surviving inventories of Whickham copyholders from the period 1557–89, not one makes mention of a coal wain. Of those taken between 1590 and 1619, in contrast, almost three-fifths contain valuations of a 'colewaine' or of 'cole waynes', together with the oxen and horses necessary to draw them, alongside their agricultural goods.[43] For example, Thomas Harrison, a young man whose goods were inventoried in October 1603, held nine acres of copyhold land and another five acres elsewhere in Whickham. He had 'hard corne' and 'oates' harvested and laid up in his 'stagarth'

[40] Morris, *Celia Fiennes*, 175–6. Fiennes saw an 'abundance' of these 'litle carriages' as she approached the river.
[41] PRO E 134 29 Eliz. Ea. 4; BL Harleian MMS 6850, no. 39.
[42] PRO DURH 2/10/54, 2/10/77. They were carrying coal from the Allerdeans glebe-land pits. Several were Whickham men. None were copyholders.
[43] Coal wains are listed in 8 of the 14 copyholder farm inventories for 1593–1618. They are also mentioned in the inventories of some men who were not copyholders of the manor of Whickham: e.g. DPD Probate, Wills and Invs. of Thomas Wigham of Swalwell (1590), William Whetston (1599).

and other 'corne sown on the ground'. His stock consisted of four oxen, two horses, and a cow; his 'gear' of a plough, a long wain, and 'two coale waines'.[44]

Coal wains were relatively inexpensive vehicles. Where they were separately valued, they ranged from the 13*s*. valuation of John Harrison's coal wain recorded in 1594, through the £1 valuation of two coal wains of George Dalton in 1610, to the mere 3*s*. 8*d*. entered in Thomas Pearson's 1604 inventory as the value of 'one coal waine with the implements'.[45] Doubtless a great deal depended on their age and condition. They could be drawn by the oxen and horses which had always been part of the farm stock of Whickham copyholders. Involvement in wain carriage therefore cost the copyholders little in terms of equipment and draught animals. Nor, for that matter, was it particularly costly in time.

Wain carriage was not a continuous activity. It peaked in the early spring in anticipation of the arrival of the first collier fleet of the shipping season, and thereafter whenever a fleet lay in the Tyne ready to be served. Wainmen, as the hostmen of Newcastle stated in 1603, were 'ymployed more or lesse, as the yeare falleth oute'.[46] Small pastoralist farmers, who were in all likelihood underemployed for parts of the year, could well afford such periodic bursts of intense activity. And if they could not give the time on particular occasions, they had children and servants who could act for them. We have already seen Andrew Rodham driving a wain as a boy at his father's 'commaundement'. William Hall, Whickham's black-smith, was another who drove a wain as a young man. He later hired William Gibson to do the job for him, Gibson in his turn having had two years of experience in leading coal when he was a servant of Widow Robson.[47] The on–off nature of involvement and the life-cycle-related element in wain carriage are both illustrated by a deposition made in an ecclesiastical court case of 1607 by one John Hedley. Hedley, who was aged twenty-six, and his young brother worked their widowed mother's farm. He began his evidence by stating that on the date in question he had 'all the daie beene

---

[44] DPD Probate, Will and Inv. of Thomas Harrison (1603).

[45] DPD Probate, Will and Inv. of John Harrison (1594), Invs. of George Dalton (1610), Thomas Pearson (1604).

[46] Dendy, *Hostmen*, 22.

[47] PRO DURH 7/18, pt. I, testimony of Andrew Rodham, William Hall, William Gibson.

working in the feilds'. He must have remembered better, however, and corrected himself, for the scribe struck out these words and substituted 'all the daie bene fetching coales from the pitts'.[48]

In return for a modest outlay on a wain and some intermittent, though doubtless backbreaking, work, the copyholders were well paid. In the 1590s, according to the coal-owners, 3*d*. or 4*d*. a fother was the going rate for wain carriage, though the wages paid could be pushed as high as 12*d*. a fother. In the early seventeenth century, however, 4*d*. or 5*d*. a fother was the rate usually paid to Whickham copyholders.[49] Let us assume that 4*d*. a fother was the general rate of pay. At that rate, if a Whickham fother was approximately 10½ hundredweight, and if the output of the Grand Lease colliery in Whickham was in the region of 40,000 tons a year at the turn of the sixteenth century, then the wainmen of Whickham, most of them copyholders, must have earned almost £1,270 a year between them.[50] This might be expressed as a supplement of over £18 a year for each of the sixty-eight copyholders on the rental of 1600, though it is highly unlikely that the money was so evenly distributed. It was true enough, as the yeoman James Harper of Swalwell later put it, that 'the leading of coles there are very beneficiall to the leaders thereof, and especialy to the Towne of Whickham'.[51] As output rose, so too did the potential benefit.

Given these circumstances, it is scarcely surprising that the analysis of the surviving inventories of the copyholders suggests that living standards in Whickham were rising significantly at the turn of the century.[52] Unfortunately, the evidence relating to domestic buildings, rooms, and room use in the period 1590–1619 is still too sparse to permit an assessment of whether or not the copyholders were able to extend and improve their housing. Such

---

[48] DPD DR v/8 fo. 221ᵛ.

[49] BL Harleian MS 6850, no. 39, fo. 163; PRO DURH 7/18, pt. I, testimony of George Watson, Thomas Rodham, James Younge, William Gibson, Thomas Wilkinson.

[50] We offer this calculation simply as a means of giving a rough indication of the earning potential of involvement in wain carriage. It is, of course, possible that the fother in use may have been larger, though, equally, wages were sometimes higher, 5*d*. a fother being not uncommon.

[51] PRO DURH 7/19, pt. I, testimony of James Harper.

[52] What follows is based on 20 copyholder household inventories for the period 1590–1619. It is worth noting that the inventories of other Whickham residents who were not copyholders tell much the same story.

references as we have are principally to the 'halle' or 'hall house', with occasional mention of service rooms such as the 'kitchinge' or 'brewhouse', or of an upper 'chamber' or 'loft' used for sleeping. Perhaps the housing of Whickham's copyholders remained largely at one with other parts of the north in exhibiting 'a simplicity comparable only with houses of a century earlier in the south-east'.[53] If this was so, however, the evidence relating to the 'househowld geyre' of the copyholders tells a fuller and different story.

In general, the copyholders of early Elizabethan Whickham had lived well enough, if simply. When we examine the inventories of the period 1590–1619, there are certainly continuities with this earlier time, but there are also marked changes. The copyholders still had their accustomed fire-irons, but almost half the inventories now included the iron 'chimnies' previously possessed only by the few. Their cooking and eating utensils continued to be much as before, but in the 1590s the 'meat bord' began to be replaced by the 'frame table', and after 1600 ownership of at least one table was virtually universal. The bedding of the earlier copyholders had been far from primitive, but not one had possessed either a bedstead or a feather bed. Bedsteads, like tables, began to appear in the 1590s, and were ubiquitous after 1600. Feather beds became commonplace in the same period, taking their place alongside the more familiar sheets, blankets, coverlets, and pillows.

Turning to other furnishings, cupboards made their first appearance alongside the more traditional storage 'almeryes' and after 1603 displaced them entirely. Candlesticks became more common. In the earlier period only one inventory included a cushion; half the later inventories mention at least one cushion and some people had several. The frontier of domestic comfort was shifting and was now represented by the handful of copyholders who owned settles in addition to their forms, stools, and occasional chairs, the three who had acquired chamber-pots, and the one whose best tables were graced with two 'carpetes'. Finally, while there was clearly a distinct improvement in the quality and sophistication of the commonly owned domestic goods, it is also evident that furnishings of all sorts were possessed in larger quantities. Middling to substantial copy-

[53] M. W. Barley, 'Rural Housing in England', in J. Thirsk (ed.), *The Agrarian History of England and Wales*, iv *1500–1640* (Cambridge, 1967), 756–7.

holder households of the earlier period, for example, tended to have between ten and twenty pieces of 'pewter vessel', and two or three pairs of sheets; their successors usually had twenty to forty pieces of pewter and five to eight pairs of sheets. Even the newer types of furniture were frequently possessed in multiples—two or three bedsteads, several feather beds, two or three tables, half a dozen cushions, two cupboards, and so on.

There were, as might be expected, occasional holders of decent-sized copyhold farms who appear to have continued to live very simply, in a manner close to that of their parents and grandparents. The difference of scale in the inventoried possessions of substantial copyholders as compared with cottagers also remained. It may even have grown—we have too few cottagers' inventories to make a rigorous comparison. Yet even cottagers were not excluded from the changes we have tried to describe. The domestic living standards of a man like Edward Robinson, 'laborer', who held a copyhold cottage and owned six sheep, a cow, a whie, and two hens when he died in 1607, were not to be compared with those of even a moderately well-equipped smallholder like Thomas Pearson, who died in 1604. Pearson held little enough land, at least directly, but he had six cows, two 'stirks', nineteen sheep, three horses, two oxen, and a good stock of hay. He also had a coal wain. He slept on one of his three bedsteads, between one of his six pairs of sheets, comforted no doubt by his feather bed and laying his head on one of his six pillows. He ate at one of his three tables, doubtless from one of his twenty-eight pewter dishes and by the light of one of his six candlesticks. Robinson, by contrast, had only two pewter dishes and a single candlestick. He and his wife Agnes may well have eaten directly from their 'pottage pot'. Nevertheless, they too had acquired a bedstead (though no feather bed), a table, and three 'old chairs', and they had two 'litle cupboards'.[54]

The overall impression given by Whickham inventories at the turn of the century is of a limited but nevertheless significant enhancement of living standards among the copyholders. Predictably, the most expensive and sophisticated items belonged only to the few, but if this was so it was also the case that a range of desirable furnishings had become more generally available. The

---

[54] DPD Probate, Wills and Invs. of Thomas Pearson (1604), Edward Robinson (1607).

poorer may have been obliged to acquire them second-hand. Those of moderate prosperity and above, however, were clearly in a position to purchase goods of some quality in considerable quantities. The basic floor of domestic comfort in Whickham was rising. And so, it would appear, was the standard of individual clothing. The average valuation of personal apparel in the inventories of late Elizabethan and Jacobean Whickham was almost treble that of the preceding period.[55] It is impossible to say exactly how much of this growing material prosperity can be attributed directly to the growth of the coal industry, but it is at the least a reasonable supposition that income derived from coal had paid for a considerable part of the new domestic trappings of the copyholders of Whickham.

All in all, it would appear that in the first quarter-century of its operation the Grand Lease colliery brought few disadvantages and many benefits to the copyholders of Whickham. Of course it was not all plain sailing. Some copyholders became more deeply involved in the industry than they could easily afford, and the unwary or the unlucky could get their fingers badly burned.

Mathew Harrison was a case in point. In 1607, 'beinge a yonge man and a newe beginner in the trade of Collyerye', he undertook to work a pit at the Longsettles pasture as both overman and farmer, renting two-twelfth shares of the pit from the Grand Lessees. He rapidly ran into financial difficulties and in consequence he applied to Samuel Rawling, a Newcastle hostman, 'and made a great moone unto him for money'. In November 1607 Rawling agreed to advance him £30 for his 'present use', in return for which Harrison undertook to deliver 400 fothers of coal to Rawling at the Derwent staithes—forty fothers to be there by 1 March 1608 in readiness for the spring fleet and forty fothers to be led weekly thereafter until the debt was paid. As was usual in such deals, Harrison gave a bond with a penalty of £60 for non-performance of his contract, two of his kinsmen supporting him as sureties. Scarcely had the initial delivery been made, however, than Harrison died. His widow, Ann, was left with insufficient assets to pay the debt. To make matters

---

[55] In the 12 inventories providing a separate valuation of apparel 1557–89, the average valuation was 12s. In the 17 inventories giving comparable information 1590–1619, the average valuation was 32s. Despite the uncertainties surrounding valuation, the contrast seems too great to be meaningless. Unfortunately, very little detail is provided as to the nature of the clothing valued.

worse, before she could obtain administration of his goods, his share of the coals won at Longsettles pit, which had been laid up above ground in a separate heap (as was customary in mining partnerships), was carried off and sold by his former partners. His widow claimed that she and her children were 'utterly impoverished' as a result. Nor did matters end there, for Samuel Rawling attempted to recover his losses by suing Harrison's sureties Nicholas Arnold and George Dalton, an action that dragged them into a morass of attempted composition with Rawling, a further bond for payment of the debt in instalments, renewed default, and yet more litigation, cost, and grief.[56]

Harrison's was not an isolated case. Nicholas Whelpdon was sued for failure to deliver twenty-two tens of coal contracted to a Grand Lessee in 1609. In the same year John Startforth got into financial difficulties and fled the area, leaving his sureties to face the music and precipitating thereby a flurry of debt litigation as the consequences of his collapse rippled out through the community.[57] Nicholas Arnold, who was singularly unfortunate in these matters, got into trouble again when he joined with the overman Thomas Wakefield to work a pit for Robert Shafto of Newcastle. Wakefield, 'who was better acquainted with the workes and reckonings of the said coles' than Arnold, died in 1612, leaving Arnold burdened with a debt of £23. 6s. 8d. to the coal-owner.[58]

Clearly, involvement in the coal industry could be exceedingly risky for those whose ambitions outran their experience and their means. Given the practice of demanding bonds and sureties for the performance of contracts, those who failed could all too easily drag their friends and kinsmen down with them when the penalties for default were enforced. Most of the copyholders of Whickham, however, appear to have been content to be paid by the fother for their seasonal contributions to the task of keeping London's fires burning. As wainmen they could do well enough, and for the rest they had their farms to attend to. A new economy and society was slowly growing up in Whickham, but as yet the old was able to adapt to innovation with relative ease and benefit besides.

[56] PRO DURH 2/6/21, 2/6/71, 2/6/151, 2/7/91, 2/8/35, 2/8/43.
[57] PRO DURH 2/6/2, 2/6/22, 2/6/30, 2/6/49, 2/6/51, 2/6/55, 2/6/68, 2/6/79, 2/6/80, 2/9/82.
[58] PRO DURH 2/11/86, 2/12/2. Cf. 2/9/49 for yet another similar case.

3. THE COPYHOLDERS OF WHICKHAM AND
THE LORDS OF COAL

The balance of advantages and disadvantages in the relationships of the copyholders of Whickham and the Grand Lease colliery was to change, and change dramatically, in the course of the second decade of the seventeenth century. Indeed, we can date the shift in the situation quite precisely to the shipping seasons of 1609–10. Late in 1610, the coal-owners of Newcastle wrote to the Privy Council to explain that 'the cole workes which the last yeare and formerly were wrought' were no longer able to supply southern demand for coal 'by a verye great proportion'. Accordingly, they had taken steps in 1610 'to sinke newe pytts and sett on more worke'. This, however, involved either deeper sinking to work lower seams or the opening of pits further from the river. Deeper sinking meant greater capital expenditure, rising drainage costs, and higher wages for the pitmen. More extensive working entailed higher carriage costs, in terms of both payments to wainmen and payments for wayleave. The result was a rise in the price of coal, which had brought howls of protest from London.[59]

The coal-owners, then, had a double problem. They needed more working pits on good coal seams, and they needed to keep down their escalating production and transportation costs. Both problems had to be solved if they were to keep London supplied at reasonable prices and avoid the displeasure of the royal government upon whose favour their own privileged position in the coal trade depended. It may well have been the case that, of the various options open to them, the least problematical was to initiate much more intensive exploitation of the Grand Lease colliery in Whickham.

Before the introduction of the waggonways, the opportunities for economically viable workings more than a few miles from the river were extremely limited. More and deeper pits were therefore needed close to the water, and the cost of drainage operations would have to be faced. Biting on that bullet made it the more desirable that the other principal charges of colliery—rents for mining leases, and wayleave and carriage costs—should be kept down. This consideration in turn made the manorial lands of Whickham the more

[59] Dendy, *Hostmen*, 58–9.

attractive as a sphere of operations. The Grand Lease placed no limitations of the rights of the lessees to mine the demesne, copyholds, pastures, and wastes of the manor. More pits could therefore be sunk without incurring new rental charges. At the same time, it accorded the coal-owners unrestricted wayleave over the manorial territories—an advantage that could be utilized not only with regard to pits within the manor but also for the leading of coal from mines in adjacent lands. Thus far the Grand Lessees had operated with restraint and even consideration in Whickham. To do so had cost them little. Now, however, they had powerful reasons to exploit the uniquely generous terms of the Grand Lease to the utmost. They knew it, and they acted accordingly.

The years after 1610 witnessed a remarkable intensification of mining activity in Whickham as a whole. The collieries to the south and south-west of the manor of Whickham were expanded and extended. Farnacres was brought into production by the Liddells. The Brinkburne colliery was established on islands of freehold land within the town fields. Above all, mining commenced in the northern sectors of the manor of Whickham itself, in the fields of the Haugh and the Leigh, in Allerdeans, East Field, and Lowfield—the best arable, meadow, and pasture lands of the manor, where 'never pits were before'. The massive expansion was under way which by the 1630s was to make the Grand Lease and its satellite collieries by far the greatest mining complex in Britain.[60]

Something of the atmosphere of this period of heady expansion can be recaptured in the frequent disputes that broke out among the rival owners of Whickham's mines. For them this was a time of heavy investment, undertaken in the hope of winning massive profits. The prizes were great. Yet their pursuit was fraught with anxiety, for in colliery the risks of catastrophic losses were constantly present. These circumstances appear to have bred an entrepreneurial climate that has been well described as one of 'ruthless opportunism and obsession with gain'.[61]

[60] The reasons for the allegedly increased demand for coal after 1610 remain obscure. Dietz, 'The North-East Coal Trade', 286, confirms that output increased sharply on the Tyne after 1610 and suggests that it may have been linked to intensified competition between Tyne and Wear coal-owners following the withdrawal in 1610 of the imposition formerly levied on coal shipped from Sunderland. A more fundamental cause may have been the demand exerted by the massive suburban growth of London in 1600–20, recently charted in closer detail in Finlay and Shearer, 'Population Growth and Suburban Expansion', 42.

[61] James, *Family, Lineage and Civil Society*, 90–1.

Certainly, the coal-owners' behaviour in defence or advancement of their interests was, to say the least, uninhibited. As early as 1595, the Grand Lessees had been accused of deliberately directing their workings so as to sabotage the pits of those owners who had had mining leases in being at the time of the granting of the Grand Lease, 'causing their mines to be choked and drowned under the ground, whereby the said tenants were at last obliged to turn over to them the state of their leases'.[62] If this was indeed true, it succeeded in keeping rival workings at arm's length for a decade and a half. After 1610, however, as they moved into the northern fields of the manor, the Grand Lessees found themselves once again working cheek by jowl with competitors, notably the lessees of the rector's glebe in Allerdeans and of Brinkburne freehold.

The fierce possessiveness of these coal-owners is amply illustrated by Thomas Liddell's threat in 1611 that, if the new rector persisted in his attempts to cancel the Allerdeans lease granted to Liddell by his senile and insouciant predecessor, Liddell would 'drowne and surrounde the said pitts and overthrow the whole worke and collyerie'.[63] Men who had invested heavily in the winning of mines were anxious to grab what they could when they could, while the lack of well established mining laws, coupled with the delays attending test cases in the courts, did not breed scrupulosity.[64] Boundaries were neither easy to recognize nor easy to defend underground, and in Whickham there was the added complication that by custom it was 'lawfull for the occupiers of any colliery to digg, or myne into or through the freehold of any other person unless hee or they shall by a pitt sunck in his or their owne ground countermine, or thurle into their works and thereby let or hinder them'.[65] Given the urgency of the desire to follow a good seam, this was nothing if not a recipe for trouble.

Mining operations were subcontracted to overmen who were

---

[62] Dendy, *Hostmen*, 8.

[63] PRO DURH 2/10/77. In 1610 Mr Ferniside had been described as 'a man not capable of perfectt reason and understandinge to Rule or governe himself or to respectt his owne estaite', all this 'by reason of his aige and longe continuance of sickness'. He had not exercised his office for 14 years: DPD DR v/9 (unfol.), 20 Apr. 1610.

[64] On the slow development of the law relating to mining, see Nef, i. 289 ff., 338–9.

[65] DPD Ch. Comm. MS, 244145 (Parliamentary Survey of Brinkburne Colliery, 1650).

paid by results. It seems clear that the actual owners exercised little supervision and asked no questions of their employees so long as the coal was won. William Sherwood, for example, whose men were accused of 'unorderly working' in his Allerdeans mine on several occasions in the 1610s, admitted that he 'was never personally under any of the grounds' in dispute. He denied instructing his workmen to work in a manner detrimental to neighbouring mines in Grand Lease territory, but his general attitude is perhaps best revealed by the fact that his own overman testified that his master had authorized him to work 'at his pleasure'.

Sherwood and his partner Francis Liddell were accused of permitting the undermining of Grand Lease workings in 1614, the extraction from them of £300 worth of coal, and the subsequent flooding of the wasted seam to camouflage their incursion. In subsequent years they allegedly repeated this exercise, and in addition not only robbed the walls and pillars of their mine, which rendered it dangerous both to their own men and to those working neighbouring pits, but also deliberately directed their own drainage channels into the Grand Lease workings. This was certainly one way of reducing drainage costs, but the result was that Thomas Surtees's elaborate drainage system was overburdened to the point of collapse. Sherwood denied everything and counter-charged the Grand Lessees with having initiated the trouble by trying to drown his mine.

In fact, the whole catalogue of malpractice may well have been the result of the independent initiatives of overmen anxious to keep up output and keep down the drainage costs for which they were responsible in the Allerdeans mines.[66] If so, the coal-owners did little enough to restrain their overmen, and the 'unorderly' practices described above were to be frequently adopted both in the course of the Jacobean expansion of Whickham's collieries and thereafter. William Sherwood was later accused of drowning Sir Thomas Liddell's mines, which lay lower than his own. He primly responded that Liddell should drain his mines better and that it was unreasonable of him to try 'to force others nott to use their own for

---

[66] PRO STAC 8/245/6. Coal was apparently paid for weekly, at a previously agreed rate, when it was delivered. This put pressure on the overman to keep output up and working costs down. For an example of such arrangements and a further case of an overman engaged in disorderly working on his own initiative, see PRO DURH 2/19/211, 2/39/125.

their best benefitt without prejudice to the Common wealth, the benefitt and profitt of evrie particular subject being equall in the eie of the lawe'.[67]

In addition, there were repeated accusations of poaching on the preserves of the Grand Lease from pits in Brinkburne freehold and the Allerdeans.[68] The Liddells, who were well to the fore in all of this, added new twists by exploiting their control of wayleaves in Farnacres and of the staithes on the Team to harass the Grand Lessees' operations in the Fugarfield/Marshall Lands area.[69] They were also not above intimidating the workmen of two sub-tenants whose contract they had come to regard as 'too profitable and gainefull'. This was done 'to the end and purpose that neyther they nor either of them should find any workmen that would or durst undertake to worke in anye of those pitts for feare', and that they would consequently be obliged to relinquish the pits. (All this was accomplished with the assistance of the rector of Whickham, who abused his powers as a JP to commit several recalcitrant miners to Durham gaol.[70])

In sum, the accusations and counter-accusations arising from the coal-owners' quarrels give a cumulative impression of a Hobbesian war of all against all beneath the fields of Whickham. It was a world of 'greedie disposicon, envyinge and grudginge' as the rivals fought it out with, as one aggrieved complainant put it, 'a covetous and insatiable desire of wynning and getting whatsoever to themselves though to the hurt and peradventure the undoinge of others'.[71]

In much of this, the Grand Lessees appear as complainants, victims of the malice of their neighbours. But they were far from blameless themselves in the manner in which they conducted their operations within the town fields of Whickham. By 1620 the consequences of a decade of breakneck expansion were only too apparent, and it was to become clear that the hostility that constantly simmered between the Grand Lessees and their coal-owning peers was as nothing compared with the resentment that their activities had engendered among the copyholders of Whickham.

In April 1620 a submission was prepared by Robert Cooper, attorney to the bishop of Durham, for consideration by the

---

[67] PRO DURH 2/7/99.
[68] PRO DURH 2/19/136, 2/19/163, 2/39/160.
[69] PRO DURH 2/32/71.   [70] PRO STAC 8/163/18.
[71] Quoting PRO STAC 8/163/18 and 8/245/6.

Chancery Court of the Palatinate, in which Cooper detailed developments within the manor of Whickham in the preceding decade.[72] It presents an appalling catalogue of industrial pollution and devastation. 'Within these ten yeares last past', charged Cooper, the Grand Lessees had 'wrought sunck and digged above the number of one hundred and fiftie cole pitts' in the territories of the manor of Whickham. Pits had been sunk not only in the wastes and commons, but also 'in ther cornfields of the said copiholders and upon there severall and known copihold lands being arable and in tillage'. Of the pits sunk, over 120 were now 'wasted' and had been for several years. Others were still 'going pits', and new pits were being sunk constantly. Neither the working pits nor those now wasted were fenced in. Waste pits had not been filled up, and 'thill rubbishe and metall' cast up from them remained covering the surrounding land. As a result, the copyholders had lost 'the eatage and profitt of the same grounds', while the pits themselves, especially those situated near the highways, constituted a perennial hazard. People had fallen into pits 'casually and at unawares in the dark'. Some had been killed by the fall or drowned in flooded pits. Elsewhere, oxen and sheep grazing near open pits had been lost.

There was more. The 'digging of sluces and trenches within the same township under ground' had had the effect of draining and destroying the manor's twenty springs and wells and had 'not left so much as one well or spring within the wholl said townshippe' to serve its numerous inhabitants and their animals. Dwelling houses and even the parish church itself had been 'undermyned', with the result that some houses were 'ruynated and falne downe', while the church and churchyard were in present danger of the effects of subsidence.

Meanwhile, the consequences of unrestrained mining had been compounded by the damage inflicted by surface works and the indiscriminate driving of new coalways. The Grand Lessees' workmen, it was alleged 'do daylye cutt wyde trenches and make ways with carts and caryags over and throughe the cornfields and the most fertile and best meadowes and pastures within the said whole townshippe'. All restraint had been cast off. The Grand Lessees acted 'against the mynds and without the consent of the said copiholders and without giving or paying any recompense for the same'. All in all, it was claimed, these and other unspecified 'losses

[72] PRO DURH 2/20/69.

and damage' meant that 'more than a full third part of the said towne is laid quite waste and yelds not nor cannot yeald any profitt at all by reason of the said pitts and rubbishe lying about them and of the said trenches and wayning of the said grounds'. If such exploitation were to continue, it would be to the great loss of the inhabitants and the disinheriting of the bishop. Ultimately Whickham would be rendered uninhabitable and 'quite depopulated'.

Faced with these sweeping charges, our first response must be to ask whether they were justified. The Grand Lessees, as might be expected, rejected the principal charges against them. They denied that so many pits had been sunk or that those near to the highways had been left unfenced and unfilled. Some pits had been left open of necessity, 'to give ayere to the workers of theire mynes underground who would otherwyse be stifled'. They further claimed never to have sunk pits in the cornfields without consent, 'unless in some cases of rare necessitye . . . when for the prevention of the losse of theire myne they were forced to sinck some one pitt'. The springs and wells in Whickham were as numerous as ever. No house had been undermined, still less the church. Wayleave to and from their pits was necessary, and the lessees' legal right. Drainage works were inevitable if coal was to be won. Where the copyholders' interests had been damaged, they had been compensated by the coal-owners, who claimed to have 'used all due respect and conscience' in dealing with them and maintained that 'they had no just cause of complaynte'.[73]

The Grand Lessees were able to furnish witnesses enough from among their employees to support their version of events—and they were well-briefed witnesses, giving almost identical testimony in response to the interrogatories of the court.[74] Robert Cooper, however, persisted in pressing his charges on the copyholders' behalf, and threw in for good measure the further point that 'two hundred acres and above' of good meadow land had been 'quyte spoiled and cankered with the water that issueth out of the colewaists'.[75]

There is evidence enough in the records of the ensuing inquiry to show that Cooper was justified in his persistence. That the Grand Lessees had painted a distinctly rosy picture of their activities is suggested by the statements of one of their own witnesses, John

---

[73] PRO DURH 2/20/68.   [74] PRO DURH 7/19, pt. I.
[75] PRO DURH 2/21/74.

Dover, whose replies came to take an unusually independent tack. He agreed with the Lessees' other witnesses that only six or seven pits a year had been sunk in copyhold land in recent years and that the copyholders had received compensation, for he had paid it to them on his masters' behalf. At the same time, however, he acknowledged that 'he knoweth that there are many old waister pits in Whickham Lordship' of which 'some are opened and not filled up', albeit a number were required for ventilation. Moreover, he offered the opinion 'that there is a great waist made of the grounds belonging to Whickham by reason of the Grandleasseses getting and handling of coles and other freeholders in and through the said grounds. And that he thinketh the said waisted ground will not be fertyle againe for a long time.'[76] The copyholders themselves were to add a great deal more in their answers, and did so in convincing detail.

The copyholders were in a truculent mood when they appeared to give evidence against the Grand Lessees.[77] Unlike the coal-owners' witnesses, however, they do not appear to have concerted or rehearsed their testimony, for it varied considerably in specifics. Nevertheless, it all tended the same way and the variance lay primarily in the particular examples with which individuals supported their general assertions.[78] It is immediately apparent that, although Robert Cooper had almost certainly exaggerated the number of pits actually sunk by the Grand Lessees in the last ten years, he had presented an essentially accurate view of the pockmarked and waste-bestrewn landscape of the manor. The Grand Lessees themselves were said to 'have wrought and now doe usuallie work 10 pitts yerelie', while additional pits were working on the freehold lands of the manor. Estimates of the total number of pits visible, regardless of the precise date of their sinking, varied

[76] PRO DURH 7/19, pt. I, testimony of John Dover. Dover was in a rather ambivalent position. Though currently employed by Henry Maddison, and twice called to give evidence on the Grand Lessees' behalf, he had formerly been a servant of Mr Ferniside and had served as parish clerk. He was also an established inhabitant of Whickham and later became a copyholder himself.

[77] One witness, Cuthbert Reaslie, aged 63, answered several questions put on the copyholders' behalf, but on being confronted with a further list of counter-interrogatories on the Grand Lessees' behalf declared that he 'doth refuse to be examined except he have his charges first given him for his abode here': PRO DURH 7/19, pt. I.

[78] The copyholders' depositions are all to be found in PRO DURH 7/19, pt. I. The following discussion is based upon this source, except where separately referenced.

from a vague 'manie' to 'one hundred', 'one hundred att the least', 'c
and odd', and 'towards the number of one hundred and fiftie'. All
were agreed, however, that the sinking of pits in the cornfields was a
recent and unwelcome innovation. Of the numerous pits scattered
over the landscape, fifteen or sixteen were apparently 'going' and
the remainder were wasted. Most of the wasted pits were unfenced,
and of those recently worked few had been filled in. One witness
knew of thirteen still surrounded by 'unclensed' rubbish; another
cited twenty of his 'certaine knowledge'; while yet another merely
said there were 'a great manie'.

The danger presented by open or partially filled pits, especially
those lying close to paths and highways, was well attested. Different
witnesses named a total of five persons actually killed by falling into
pits, while in addition losses of oxen, horses, and sheep were
exemplified in specific detail.[79] The alleged loss of water supplies
was also well supported by testimony. Of the numerous springs and
wells that had formerly existed, only two remained. One lay behind
Nicholas Arnold's home in Whickham town; the other lay 'a
quarter of a mile or more distant of the said towne whereat most of
the said towne do wash their said clothes'. For the rest, the
inhabitants were obliged to rely upon the Derwent, the Blackburn,
and 'day water that cometh from Teame', all of which involved
considerable inconvenience.[80] With regard to subsidence, only one
witness agreed that the church and churchyard were threatened 'by
reason pitts are sunck hard by the said church'. There were
numerous specific cases, however, of houses 'falne downe to the
ground', 'rent through the walles', or held up by props 'for feare
they should fall downe'.

The witnesses were at one in maintaining that ways to and from
the pits were now driven indiscriminately through arable, meadow,
and pasture alike, 'both by carrying of coles and working men that
worke thereat', with consequent losses to corn, hay, and pasture.

---

[79] In addition to this evidence, a quite separate case of 1619 concerns a claim for
compensation for the loss of an ox in a pit in East Field: PRO DURH 2/19/224. The
unusually detailed parish register burial entries for the 1630s provide further
examples of people accidentally killed by falling into pits. Clearly, it was a very real
hazard.

[80] The dislocation of water supplies is independently revealed in the later
reduction of the rating assessment of Farnacres Mill because of 'the water of the
water corne mill there being diverted by the workinge of the Collyerye of the said
Grand Lessees': DRO Q/S OB 4, 290.

Evidence given in a parallel case of 1620 elaborates our knowledge of this grievance. According to the grieve of the manor, the coal-owners had in recent years abandoned their former practice. They now led coal from their pits 'without ever calling the owners of the said ground or the Grieve . . . to have a way sett and dowelled furthe to the least hurte and spoil of the owners grounds through which the way should pass'. Coal was also led in 'unseasonable and wett weather'; and when the ways became 'so deepe rutted that waynes could not contynye', the wainmen drove 'over new unbroken swarthe grounde till it was as ill as the first'. In addition, as others testified, 'now of late when cariages want coles to lead from anie pitts they goe to other pitts within the same pasture over the swarth and unbroken ground and so make wayes over all'.[81]

The combined result of these practices was not only severe damage to pasture land but also the spoiling of corn and hay growing by the coalways with coal dust. Hay was doubly threatened. It could be so badly polluted with dust that copyholders were 'manie tymes forced to shake and thresh the dust out of it before there beasts can eat it'. But even this was preferable to a meadow sodden with the 'unwholesome', 'cankered', or 'infectious' water that flowed from the drainage channels of the mines. Some meadow land was so affected that 'there groweth no grass thereon'; elsewhere animals refused either to drink the filthy water or to eat the grass affected by it.[82]

There were other grievances to add which had not been part of Cooper's formal submission: the erection of houses, sheds, and smithies on the copyholders' lands; the despoiling of the woodlands on a massive scale to provide timber for pits, staithes, and 'waggon waies'. But enough has been said. The copyholders variously estimated the lands 'layed waste and spoiled' as amounting to between a quarter and a third of the entire area of the manor, and their detailed testimony carries a conviction that can scarcely be gainsaid. It is true, as the Grand Lessees claimed, that they were offered compensation in the form of 'composition' for heap room, wayleave, and spoil. But such payments as were made were apparently small and irregular. They amounted to 'Twenty markes

---

[81] PRO DURH 2/20/195, DURH 7/18, pt. I, testimony of James Younge, Thomas Gamesby, George Watson. George Watson jun. added that coal wains now had 'yron bun wheles' which 'much cutt and spoile the ground', especially in wet weather. [82] PRO DURH 7/19, pt. I.

yerely' (£13 6s 8d.), in the judgment of the agent who paid the copyholders on behalf of the coal-owners. As for their regularity, one of the recipients remarked dismissively that 'those compositions are sometymes paied and sometymes not paied', while another contemptuously deposed 'that the Cole owners make composition as it pleaseth them and giveth good words but maketh noe performance'.[83] There can be little doubt that by 1620 the benefits initially brought to the copyholders of Whickham by the expansion of the coal industry were being progressively offset by the devastation of the physical environment and the threatened dislocation of the agrarian economy that such spreading desolation entailed.

Inexorable as the process might seem to historians blessed with the benefits of hindsight, the devastation of the manor of Whickham had not been allowed to proceed without a struggle. We have already suggested that the initial restraint and consideration displayed by the Grand Lessees in other dealings with the copyholders of Whickham may have owed something to an awareness of the need to avoid the local political problems that might arise from the alienation of the manorial tenantry. In their reply to Robert Cooper's allegations, the Grand Lessees referred to a decision of the Council of the North of 1585 which had apparently confirmed their right to 'free libertye of ingres, egres and regres' within the manor.[84] No records of the Council survive, and we can discover nothing more directly of this early case. It seems likely, however, that the decree of 1585 and its confirmation in 1602 were the outcome of two 'suitts held at York', which the Grand Lessees cited elsewhere as evidence of the legality of the privileges they claimed in Whickham. If so, the decree was said to have accorded them 'free passage with draughts and carriages for the Coles from all the Cole pitts digged or to be digged within that Lordshipp to any staithes at the water of Derwent or to be made within the said Lordshipp through all and everye the Coppiehold lands . . . of Whickham lyeinge betwixt the said pitts and staithes'. At the request of the Lord President of the Council, however, the coal-owners had agreed 'for the sake of quiet' to negotiate an annual

[83] PRO DURH 7/19, pt. I, testimony of John Dover, John Turner; DURH 7/18, pt. I, testimony of Andrew Rodham.
[84] PRO DURH 2/20/68. This decision was apparently confirmed in 1602.

recompense payable to the copyholders for spoil of their soil, corn, or grass.[85] From the outset, then, the copyholders had apparently been prepared to test and challenge the unprecedented privileges granted to the holders of the Grand Lease. The good behaviour of the coal-owners in general, and the particular care and favour displayed towards the copyholders in the matter of coalways and wain carriage, had not been freely granted; it was the outcome of action at law and authoritative mediation.

The *modus vivendi* arrived at with the Grand Lessees appears to have held up tolerably well in general up to the 1610s, with the help of the careful policing of the manorial officers. Nevertheless, the potential of the copyholders for harassing the coal-owners remained and was not infrequently demonstrated. In March 1594 a group of copyholders had stopped the carriage of coal over their land on the grounds that a field of growing corn was being excessively damaged. The coal-owners brought and won a case at Durham over this incident and their wayleave right was upheld, but only with regard to a specified traditional coalway. Moreover, it was laid down that if that way proved impassable the copyholders should be further compensated for the additional waying of their ground—a not insignificant gain for the Whickham tenants, and a demonstration that further concessions might be wrung from the Grand Lessees by well-timed action.[86]

The fact that this stoppage of wain traffic took place in March, at the beginning of the shipping season, is significant. The copyholders knew very well that the best time to bring pressure to bear on the coal-owners was whenever a fleet lay ready to be served. The pattern was repeated in July 1605, when John Hedworth and Andrew Man stopped a number of wains in Southfield and 'unloaden and cast out' the coal, 'well perceyving and knowing', as the owners complained, 'that yor orators can make no profitt at all of theire coales . . . unless they furthwith and in this somer season doe lead and carry the same'.[87] Almost exactly a year later yet another copyholder, John Hall, followed suit. The aggrieved hostman protested that he could not 'lead or utter' his coals 'but att this instant time'. A twelve-day stoppage had already cost him £30 and he was like to lose more, for he was 'bounden by sundrie great bonds in divers sumes of monie for the delivery of many tens and

[85] DPD Ch. Comm. MS 244231.
[86] GPL Cotesworth MSS CN/1/313. [87] PRO DURH 2/2/50, 2/2/63.

chalders of coals at London'.[88] A 'quick vend' was 'the only article in colliery' in 1606 no less than in the 1690s, and stoppages of this kind could cause not only the loss of an immediate sale but also the diminution of eventual profits, for the coal stockpiled at the pitheads was notoriously liable to deteriorate. Hence Thomas Liddell's frustration when his quarrel with the rector in the spring of 1611 kept over 1,600 tons of coal tied up at his pits, 'all which said coals the tyme of yeare now serveing for venting of the same, wold both be much worse and impared by lyinge ther'.[89] Little wonder that each stoppage tended to give rise to court action in Durham within days and that speedy accommodations were the usual outcome.

These early disputes and interruptions of wain carriage appear to have resulted from the actions of aggrieved individuals among Whickham's tenantry. The rapid expansion of mining operations after 1609–10 certainly multiplied the occasions of such grievance. But, initially at least, the manorial officers seem to have observed the terms of the settlement mediated by the Council of the North.[90] In April 1611, for example, the jury of the Halmote supported the interests of the Grand Lessees by ordering 'that none of the Inhabitants of Whickham shall take any coles from the cole waynes in their passage from the pitt [to] the staithe' on pain of a 6s. fine for every default.[91] Such co-operation, however, was soon to be rendered redundant as the coal-owners themselves abdicated their responsibilities by what the grieve called their 'unreasonable and carelesse' actions.[92] The turning point may have been the Grand Lessees' failure, after 1613, to apply to the grieve and sworn men for the dowelling out of approved coalways, for it was about this time that prosecutions for the making of illicit coalways became a regular

---

[88] PRO DURH 2/2/18, 2/5/42. In this case Hall seems to have been attempting not only to prevent carriage across his land but also to put a stop to mining on a parcel of freehold land which he had leased to John Barker of Newcastle to his subsequent regret.

[89] PRO DURH 2/10/54. The rector, it will be remembered, was trying to extract a new and more favourable lease for the colliery in his glebe land in Allerdeans.

[90] This is not to say that the council's decree was quite as the Grand Lessees described it. In 1620 the copyholders were to deny that it gave the coal-owners the rights they claimed: PRO DURH 2/14/137. In the absence of the original decree, we cannot judge the validity of these claims and counter-claims.

[91] DPD DDR HC iii F 18, fo. 86.

[92] PRO DURH 2/20/195.

feature of the business of the Halmote.[93] Individual stoppages of wain traffic recurred unopposed by the manorial officers.[94] Most seriously of all from the point of view of the coal-owners, from the mid-1610s the copyholders 'privately combined themselves together' under the leadership of their elected officers to commence regular harassment of the leading of coal.[95]

Matters finally came to a head in 1619 with an incident that provoked an eruption of litigation in the course of which the festering resentment of the copyholders and the means they had adopted to defend their interests were fully revealed. At some point in that year, the workmen of four of the Grand Lessees 'took upon them to sett downe and digg a colepitt' in a two-acre parcel of copyhold land in Allerdean Heads which belonged to John Hindmers. In doing so they were following the Main Coal seam from adjacent workings. They did not, however, trouble to seek Hindmers's consent before moving in their men. Nor did they apply for an authorized coalway when they commenced leading their coal.[96]

All this was imprudent. Hindmers was one of the principal copyholders of Whickham, a sixty-three-year-old village elder who had long served on the Halmote jury. He was a sworn man and was to be elected grieve early in 1620.[97] He was also an associate in manorial and other affairs of Nicholas Arnold, the grieve for 1619. Arnold was another man to be reckoned with, a sixty-eight-year-old who had served frequently as grieve since 1602. He had considerable experience of litigation, both as an officer and on his own behalf, and had had his fingers burnt more than once in his dealings with the coal-owners—a fact that may have done something to colour his attitudes.[98]

---

[93] Thomas Gamesby dated the change to 1613 or thereabouts: PRO DURH 7/18, pt. I. For Halmote prosecutions, see DPD DDR HC III F 18, fos. 86ᵛ, 94ᵛ, 103, 103ᵛ.

[94] GPL Cotesworth MSS CN/1/315; *Acts of the Privy Council of England, 1616–17*, 271.

[95] In 1619 the Grand Lessees claimed that such action had been frequent in the preceding four years: PRO DURH 2/19/183.

[96] PRO DURH 2/20/195.

[97] Hindmers's age was given as 65 in his deposition of 1621 in PRO DURH 7/19, pt. I. He marked his deposition with a clear 'H' and may have been partially literate. His manorial career can be traced in DPD DDR HC III F 18, *passim*.

[98] Arnold gave his age as 70 in 1621: PRO DURH 7/19, pt. I. He may have been a little younger, for he described himself as 50 years old in 1603: DPD DR V/7 (unfol.). For his manorial career, see DPD DDR HC III F 18, *passim*. For his

When the leading of coal began, Hindmers and Arnold acted. On 3 November 1619, they prevented carriage over their own copyholds. Then Arnold, on his authority as grieve, forbade the carriage of coal by the wains employed by Henry Maddison, the principal coal-owner involved, a prohibition subsequently extended to all Grand Lease carriage. It was not the optimum time for action, since the shipping season was nearing its close, but it served well enough. For the remainder of November the Grand Lessees 'could gett but verie litle carriage' despite offering increased wages, which was to their 'great losse and damage'. Maddison claimed to have lost the leading of at least 50 tens of coal a week that month, a loss that ultimately proved worse still, since 'by reason of the said stoppage the coles laie all the winter unled', for 'bad weather came in and would not suffer them to lead any tyme after that'.[99]

On 1 December 1619, Maddison and his partners brought a case against Arnold and Hindmers in the Palatinate Chancery of Durham. The two copyholders were charged as individuals, but it was already clear that the case was intended to settle once and for all the troubled relationship between the Grand Lessees and Whickham's manorial tenantry. The Grand Lessees accused Arnold, Hindmers, and other copyholders of having wronged them repeatedly in the previous four years by hindering wain carriage. In their 'Answer' of February 1620, Arnold and Hindmers took the opportunity to present a general indictment of the Grand Lessees' activities in recent years. A month later, the Lessees 'Replication' ignored the immediate occasion of the quarrel to mount a general defence of their rights and privileges, citing the 1585 decision of the Council of the North and accusing the copyholders of further abuses. Arnold and Hindmers replied in kind on 7 April in a 'Rejoinder', which challenged the Lessees' version of the York decree. By then matters had further escalated, for on 1 April 1620 Robert Cooper had

frequent engagement in litigation as grieve or on his own behalf, see PRO DURH 2/2/50, 2/5/57, 2/6/71, 2/7/91, 2/11/14, 2/11/86. For his chastening experiences of the coal trade, see notes 56 and 58 above. Arnold invariably made his mark on documents to which he put his name, and was almost certainly illiterate.

[99] PRO DURH 2/19/183, 2/20/195, DURH 7/18, pt. II. It is possible that the copyholders also tried to prevent carriage of coal at the start of the spring season in 1620, since the quarter sessions records for April 1620 include a number of indictments laid against Nicholas Arnold, his wife Jane, and other copyholders for riotous assault. Sadly, no further information is available on the exact nature of these cases: DRO Q/S OP 1, 19–20.

entered his submission on the copyholders' behalf, triggering a further round of accusations and counter-accusations which was to drag on into 1621.[100]

These interconnected cases fully revealed the situation in Whickham as it had developed since the granting of the Grand Lease to the hostmen of Newcastle, with particular emphasis on the events of the 1610s. The documents that were generated as they proceeded show the lines of conflict very clearly drawn. The copyholders complained bitterly of their recent usage at the hands of the Grand Lessees, expressing themselves roundly in submissions and testimony crackling with resentment and indignation.

Equally striking is the manner in which the copyholders placed their specific grievances within a framework of principle which expressed their conception of the proper relationship that should exist between them and their manorial lords. As might be expected, they placed great emphasis upon *custom*, appealing both to the customary usages of the episcopal 'Halmote and Manor of Chester' to which they had formerly owed suit and to the more recently established practices which had been observed by the Grand Lessees at the turn of the century. Custom was not held to be unchangeable or inviolate, but it was clearly regarded as the stoutest bulwark they possessed against exploitation. They also made considerable play of the *unreasonableness* of the Grand Lessees' dealings in recent years. The unrestricted driving of ways over their land was 'unreasonable'. The unrestrained mining rights claimed by the Grand Lease within the manorial territories were 'utterly against reason'. A further principle frequently asserted was that of *consent*. John Hindmers's copyhold had been entered and mined 'without his consent and privitie'. Consent was no longer sought from the manorial officers for the laying out of new coalways. The sinking of pits in the cornfields was 'against the mynds and without the consents' of the copyholders.

Most striking of all are the terms in which the copyholders challenged the coal-owners' right to proceed 'att their pleasures', for they explicitly accused them of arrogating to themselves an

---

[100] The records of the case of Maddison and partners *v.* Arnold and Hindmers are found in PRO DURH 2/14/37, 2/19/83, 2/20/195, DURH 7/18, pts. I and II and in DPD Ch. Comm. MS 244231. The records of the parallel case brought by Robert Cooper are in PRO DURH 2/14/16, 2/20/68, 2/20/69, 2/21/74, DURH 7/19, pts. I and II. The following account of the litigation of 1619–21 is based upon these sources, unless otherwise specified.

extra-legal *absolute power*. George Watson and Thomas Gamesby rejected the Lessees' claim to 'absolute power' to make ways freely. Nicholas Arnold stated that 'the cole owners never had and as he verelie thinketh oughte to have absolute power to way all copiholders grounds'. John Hindmers himself denied them 'such absolute power interest and authoritie to sinck for digg and carrye away coles in and through all the copihold lands and grounds of the said townshippe'. Of the twelve copyholders who made submissions or gave evidence in the initial case of Maddison and partners against Arnold and Hindmers, only two could sign their names to their depositions. But they were articulate enough, and their opposition arose from a core of principle that shaped their interpretation of their experiences. The issues, as they emerge from their indignant statements, were those of custom, consent, reasonable dealing, and hostility to the exercise of an arbitrary absolute power. These were village Hampdens indeed.

The position of the Grand Lessees was diametrically opposed to that of the copyholders. They asserted their rights to all mines 'as well opened as nott opened' within the demesne and copyhold lands of the manor, together with 'free libertye to gett and winn the coles . . . by sincking or workinge any newe or old pitts in the same', emphasizing that, with regard to copyhold land, 'they may digg in the same without the consent of the copieholders'. In addition, they claimed 'heape roome way leave egresse and regresse outt of into and through all the said demesnes and coppihoulds', and the authority to make ways 'to their best advantage', a right that their witnesses said they had exercised 'att their wills and pleasures without contradiccon' hitherto. These privileges, they argued, were theirs by virtue of the terms of the Grand Lease and had been confirmed by the Council of the North. Moreover, since the mineral rights were vested 'in the Lords of the soile by lawe', the right both to mine and to enjoy access and wayleave should be theirs by customary law. For, 'though there were no custome' of a specific nature, these rights were customarily acknowledged as belonging to the lords of the soil, 'which custom is grounds enough for reason in Coppihold estates which have all theire being onely by custom'. Having cleverly tried to outflank the copyholders' appeal to custom in this way, the Lessees subsequently denied that the customs and practices observed prior to the 1610s were material to the issue.

These points of principle asserted, the Lessees rejected the allegations that their conduct had been irresponsible or unreasonable, pointed out that they had freely paid compensation and mended their coalways annually 'uppon hope to have had the carriages quietly', and argued that the copyholders themselves, as wainmen, had been responsible for much of the waying damage of which they complained. With regard to compensation, the Lessees were of course correct—though its inadequacy and the regularity of its payment would seem to have left much to be desired. And there must have been more than a little force in their final thrust against the copyholders, though as we have seen the Halmote court was not slow to fine those who had made illicit ways.

By 1619–20, however, the issues were much more fundamental than any quarrel over responsibility for particular acts of negligence. It was a head-on collision between the rights claimed by the coal-owners and those defended by the copyholders. This might be interpreted as a conflict between the prescriptive legal rights of the former and the customary usages of the latter: a straightforward case of law against custom. But, as E. P. Thompson has recently argued, it is unwise to posit too sharp a distinction between law and custom.[101] Custom had formal recognition in English law whether it was established by ancient usage, continuance, or recognition. Moreover, the 'reasonableness' to which the copyholders appealed was a concept with legal force in manorial law. 'Reasonable' and 'unreasonable' in this context were 'legal terms of art', which meant ' "consonant", "consistent", "reconcileable" or their opposites'. A 'reasonable' custom was one that could be reconciled with other customs of the manor. A custom that threatened the preservation and maintenance of holdings was 'unreasonable'.[102]

In this instance we have a conflict between two interpretations of customary law. The Lessees appealed to what they claimed were the customary rights of the lord of the soil, though they were unwilling to acknowledge the 'lived-in environment' of established practice in Whickham.[103] The copyholders regarded these rights as

---

[101] This discussion of law and custom is influenced by points made by E. P. Thompson in his Past and Present Lecture, 'Law, Use Rights and Property in Land', delivered at the University of London on 24 March 1986.

[102] Kerridge, *Agrarian Problems*, 67–8.

[103] The phrase is E. P. Thompson's. In their evidence and submissions, the coal-owners carefully avoided acknowledging the customary practices described by the copyholders, while at the same time claiming that their own rights had been enjoyed 'time out of mind'.

'unreasonable' because of their manifest consequences for the manor. They therefore regarded their own actions as perfectly justified 'in lawe and equitie', as Nicholas Arnold put it. It was perhaps the very strength of the copyholders' case in customary law that led the coal-owners to place the greater emphasis upon their lease and its legal confirmation.[104] And it was perhaps the copyholders' knowledge of the unambiguous nature of the Grand Lease (and of the political influence that the Lords of Coal could summon up to defend it) that prompted them to introduce the pejorative concept of 'absolute power' in their efforts to defend their manor and its customs. By doing so, they added a distinctive dimension to a situation which, with its clash between rival conceptions of law and incompatible definitions of property rights, was in many ways comparable to the numerous conflicts between lords and tenants that accompanied agrarian change in this period.[105]

The copyholders of Whickham, however, were not simply small farmers defending their fields and commons. By 1619–20 it may already have been too late for that, and perhaps they knew it. Real as their purely agrarian grievances were, they were also part-time industrial employees. Far from remaining passive in the face of change, they had adapted themselves with some willingness to the opportunities provided by the growth of the coal industry.

Moreover, as the industrial exploitation of their lands proceeded, such involvement had probably become unavoidable. By the 1610s, earnings from wain carriage may have been assuming an increasingly important role in the domestic economies of at least some of the copyholders. One of the features of the agricultural inventories of the copyholders in the first two decades of the seventeenth century

---

[104] In fact, the rights of the lords of the soil varied considerably in their implications: Nef, i. 305 ff.; Flinn, *Coal Industry*, 36.

[105] The copyholders probably had good legal advice in presenting their case, perhaps from Robert Cooper himself. In Cooper's case against the Grand Lessees, one of the counter-interrogatories put to the copyholder witnesses on the Lessees' behalf asked, 'Have you solicitted this suite or borne any part of the chardge thereof?'. Most answered 'Yes'. There is no need to assume, however, that the copyholders were wholly dependent on an astute lawyer in the formulation of their grievances. They would have been perfectly familiar with manorial law. Moreover, they may have been aware of struggles in Newcastle against the privileges of the hostmen and of discontent within the bishopric regarding the bishop's extensive powers. Dr C. W. Brooks of Durham University, for whose advice on this point we are grateful, is of the opinion that 'there is a good deal of scattered evidence that people in the north-east were well aware of the dangers of excessive "legal" powers' (private communication).

is a shift from the raising of young beef cattle towards the keeping of large numbers of draught animals in the form of oxen and horses. Inventories are, of course, problematic sources, and we are dealing with small numbers, but a gradual shift of this kind is discernible. As the seventeenth century advanced, some copyholders may have been drawn deeper into the business of either providing wain carriage or raising oxen and horses for sale to wainmen and overmen, or both. Alongside this development, there is the possibility that the loss of agricultural land itself undermined the traditional subsistence balance of the copyholder families most directly affected, edging them gradually towards a greater dependence upon industrial wages. Whereas these had been initially a welcome supplement to pastoral farming, by the later 1610s they may often have become a substitute for farming income.

Part of the complexity of the dispute between the copyholders and the coal-owners, and a good deal of the bitterness with which it was fought out, derived from these circumstances of gradual accommodation to an emerging industrial order. For the conflict of 1619–21 was not occasioned solely by agrarian grievances. Underlying the quarrel over the devastation of the manor of Whickham was a sub-plot of industrial conflict which at times came to assume a prominence so great as to suggest that, for some at least of those involved, it was the major issue. This concerned the employment of 'stranger' wainmen.

The copyholders of Whickham quite clearly regarded themselves as entitled to a favoured position in the provision of wain carriage 'before any other out dwellers that were not interested in the said towne'.[106] According to Nicholas Arnold, the carriage of coal had been interrupted in November 1619 not only because of the arbitrary mining of John Hindmers's copyhold, but also because the coal-owners had brought in strangers to lead their coal. This had been done despite the facts that there were copyholders 'ready and as willing to have ledd . . . as the strangers did if they had been spoken to', and that some of the Whickham men were 'idle at that tyme for want of worke or were driven to goe lead from farre of from other pitts forth of the said towne'.[107]

---

[106] PRO DURH 2/20/195.

[107] PRO DURH 2/20/195 (Nicholas Arnold's reply), DURH 7/18, pt. i, testimony of George Watson. The testimony regarding the enforced idleness of Whickham men is further evidence of a growing dependence on wain carriage.

The Grand Lessees countered this complaint by asserting that they had the right to employ whoever they chose as wainmen and that this point had long been established by the decree of the Council of the North.[108] This seems to have been so, but the fact remains that strangers appear to have been employed rarely before the 1610s. The coal-owners themselves admitted that until around 1615 they had been content to use the copyholders as their principal wainmen, provided 'they were as reasonable in their prices as others'.[109] When strangers were needed, they were brought in with the consent of the manorial officers; at other times they were customarily 'barred and not suffered to lead anie coles so long as the inhabitants . . . could lead them'.[110] These arrangements seem to have worked well enough in the first decade of the seventeenth century, when according to William Hall 'there were no strangers permitted but the town had all the caryages for then there were but few pitts and few wayes'.[111] The changing situation as the 1610s advanced was succinctly described by William Hodgson: 'there being more pitts and much more cariages then the townsmen could undertake, the cole owners [brought] in strangers'.[112]

An attempt was apparently made to pre-empt the conflict that might flow from this development by the payment to the copyholders of an additional compensation over and above their 'composition' for heap room, wayleave, and spoil. This took the form of a levy of 2s. per annum for every 'stranger' wain employed.[113] One of the copyholders claimed that the townsmen had an 'order' to this effect, and it is possible that the arrangement dated back in part to the mediation of the Council of the North in either 1585 or 1602. What is certain is that it did not work well. 'Stranger' wainmen were a transitory and elusive band of men. John Turner complained that, despite the copyholders' 'order' for 2s. per wain, 'that same monie was not paied accordinglie for some would pay and other some went away before the time of payment came'.[114] At some point in the later 1610s, the copyholders apparently agreed

[108] DPD Ch. Comm. MS 244231.
[109] PRO DURH 2/19/183. The copyholders agreed about the 'reasonable prices' issue and claimed that they had been reasonable: DURH 7/18, pt. I.
[110] PRO DURH 7/18, pt. I, testimony of Thomas Rodham.
[111] Ibid., testimony of William Hall.
[112] Ibid., testimony of William Hodgson.
[113] PRO DURH 7/19, pt. I, testimony of William Bunting and James Harper.
[114] Ibid., testimony of John Turner.

'to keepe a generall booke for the receyving of a yearely rent of two shillings for every wayne', the task being entrusted to John Dover, who was the agent of the Grand Lease colliery responsible for the payment of the copyholders' annual 'composition'.[115] But this too failed as a means of enforcing payment from the strangers, for, as Nicholas Arnold ruefelly testified, 'manie tymes they cannot get half of it paid for they will carrie some litle tyme and long ere the yere end they are gone'.[116]

It was probably this situation that prompted the copyholders to introduce what the Grand Lessees called 'new customs and exactions' with a view to re-establishing full control over wain carriage. From around 1615 they had apparently taken to forbidding wains driven by strangers to cross their land unless the strangers agreed to pay to them 'a certain somme of monye which they call catches'.[117] The aptly named 'catches' payments were regarded as licensing a 'foreign' wain to operate for the season, and they could be considerable. Archibald Gibson reckoned he had paid sometimes a noble, sometimes ten shillings and sometimes a mark yearly 'for a catch'. Thomas Haddock claimed he had paid 10s. one year, while in 1619 he had been forced to part with 26s. 8d. for two catches.[118] The levying of these catches payments was very likely a device of the resourceful Nicholas Arnold, for he was the manorial grieve in 1614–15 and in 1617–19.[119] Clearly, it was in part a method of enforcing extra compensatory payments for the copyholders. But it may also have been a way of forcing up the leading costs of strangers in such a manner as to secure for the copyholders the lion's share of the work and the income it provided in the face of an increasing propensity of the coal-owners to bring in wainmen of their own.

If this was so, it seems to have worked temporarily. The Grand Lessees said that in recent times they had taken once more to employing mainly copyholders.[120] Having done so, however, they had found themselves almost entirely in the power of the

---

[115] PRO DURH 7/18, pt. II, testimony of John Dover.

[116] PRO DURH 7/19, pt. I, testimony of Nicholas Arnold.

[117] PRO DURH 2/19/183. The dating of this practice from the mid-1610s is confirmed by Edward Bellerbie's testimony in DURH 7/18, pt. II.

[118] Ibid., testimony of Archibald Gibson and Thomas Haddock. Cf. the evidence of Thomas Maddison, William Cragg, and others.

[119] DPD DDR HC III F 18, fos. 93, 120, 136.

[120] DPD Ch. Comm. MS 244231.

Whickham men. The copyholders, they claimed, had abused their position 'to raise the prices of the carriages', of coal, seeking an 'excessive gaine'.[121] On occasion the copyholders would deny carriage to the Grand Lessees in 'tymes of need', 'when shippes and meanes are best to vent coles and thereby exact unreasonable prices out of the necessitye of the tyme when they yield to goe'. They had succeeded in driving up their wages from 4*d*. to 4½*d*. or even 5*d*. a fother by such action. Worse, they had gone so far as to refuse to carry coal for the Grand Lessees while actually carrying it for rival coal-owners, even in unseasonable weather, with the result that the lessees 'could not gett new ledd coles to serve their hostmen withall whearby theire hostmen went awaie from them to be loaden'. On one occasion they 'were hindered the leading of nyne hundred fothers of coles in one weeke'.[122]

It is therefore scarcely surprising that the Grand Lessees had apparently begun to experiment with the construction of waggon-ways. Such expensive undertakings might well seem worth the cost if they could free the coal-owners from their vulnerability to the interventions of a work-force that clearly detested them, and was capable of harassing their operations at every turn. Conversely, awareness of the potential competition from the waggonways perhaps prompted the copyholders to complain of the Grand Lessees' despoiling of the manorial woods, since it was this timber that provided the materials for waggonway construction.[123] But this would appear to have been secondary matter in 1619. Much more prominent in the copyholders' testimony was the complaint that the Grand Lessees had once more bought in substantial numbers of 'forraners' to lead their coal. Several coal-owners were named who had done so, who paid the strangers the unprecedented wages of 6*d*. a fother (doubtless to overcome any reluctance on their part), and who 'would not intertaine the copiholders of Whickham to lead'.[124] They were out to break the hold of the Whickham tenants once and for all.

These, then, were the issues that underlay the showdown of

---

[121] PRO DURH 2/19/183.

[122] PRO DURH 7/18, pt. II provides much evidence on all this. See esp. testimony of Thomas Rand, William Cragg, Archibald Gibson, Thomas Palmer.

[123] For the complaints regarding waggonways, see p. 52 above.

[124] PRO DURH 7/18, pt. I, testimony of George Watson, Thomas Rodham, William Hall, James Younge, and others. The offending coal-owners were said to include Henry Maddison, Robert Bewicke, Robert Shafto, and Mr Bonner.

1619–21. It was triggered by the incident of John Hindmers's copyhold, but it involved every aspect of the process of industrialization in Whickham. However amicable their relationship in times past, the intensified pace of industrial expansion since 1610 had brought the copyholders of Whickham and the Grand Lessees into full-blown confrontation. The devastating effect of pell-mell mining expansion on the manorial lands was a deep and rankling grievance to those who saw their accustomed way of life threatened with dissolution.

But if the copyholders as small farmers were anxious to arrest this spreading desolation of waste and spoil, they were also vitally concerned to defend their interests as an industrial work-force. One of them was quoted in August 1620 as having declared that, 'if the coppie holders of Whickham might have their wills, theire should no Coles be ledd theare but onely by themselves and that theire should not be any suffered to come theare but only themselves and that they would have such prices as they themselves would desire and thought good'.[125] If this was true, and it has a credible ring, then yesterday's peasants were after the erection of a kind of manorial closed shop. The owners replied with a lock-out, and if that failed them they had a new technology in reserve. In their view, the copyholders of Whickham, 'haveing had so greate a taste of . . . mildness', were seeking 'more and more to incroach upon them'. They protested that, if an end was not put to this now, the Grand Lease colliery would not be able to operate save with the permission and at the whim of the copyholders of Whickham.[126] That was precisely the point.

On 6 September 1621 Sir Richard Hutton, Justice of the Common Pleas and Chancellor of the County Palatine of Durham, delivered his judgement in the case of Nicholas Arnold and John Hindmers *v.* Henry Maddison and partners, the farmers of the Grand Lease. The court had clearly been swayed to a considerable extent by the intervention of Robert Cooper on the copyholders' behalf. The judgement rehearsed Cooper's complaints against the recent proceedings of the Grand Lessees in considerable detail and accepted their general validity, finding 'the sayd losse hurt and damage' to be 'as is affirmed farr greater then was in former tymes by reason of the increase in pitts and workes of Collyerie now of

---

[125] Ibid., testimony of Thomas Rand, quoting 'one Blenkinsopp'.
[126] DPD Ch. Comm. MS 244231.

late found owte and sett on worke within the said lordship'.
Nevertheless, the Chancellor also found that 'the uttering and
venting of coles from thence is become a matter of great necessitie
and much concerninge the generall good of the kingdome'. The
'getting wynning and working of coles' and their transportation 'to
London and to the most porte Townes and parts of this kingdome
. . . and lykewyse into forren parts beyond the seaes' was of 'great
benefitt and commoditie' both to his majesty the King and to many
of his subjects. Valid as the grievances of the copyholders of
Whickham might appear, the national interest must take priority.

Accordingly, the Grand Lessees were granted 'full and fre libertie
at all times hereafter . . . to sinke digg wynne worke and gett coles
within all or any of the coppiholders landes and groundes parcell of
the manor of Whickham' for the duration of their lease, together
with 'convenient and necessarie wayes and wayleaves for the leading
and carrying of ther coles' from pits to staithes. As for the
copyholders, steps were to be taken hereafter to meet some of their
grievances. The sinkers of pits were to consult with the grieve and
sworn men and to 'sett forth and dole out' agreed coalways. A
'reasonable and competent recompense' was to be paid the
copyholders for the losses and damage occasioned by colliery
operations. They were also to receive fire coal for their homes at a
price of a 1*d.* per bowl. Those wasted pits that were adjudged
unnecessary for ventilation purposes were to be filled in, and those
that must of necessity lie open were to be hedged or fenced 'with all
convenient speed'. Care was to be taken in future to avoid the
undermining of houses and the parish church. No houses were to be
erected on copyhold land without the consent of the copyholder
concerned. A commission of 'men indifferent and of good
judgement and understanding in these kinds of busynesses' was
nominated, with the consent of the parties, to arbitrate future
disputes over the siting of coalways and levels of compensation, to
determine which wasted pits should be filled in, and to make
recommendations as to 'how water may be brought to the said
towne'.

At the same time, the copyholders were ordered not to hinder the
mining and carriage of the Grand Lessees. They were required to
abandon the exaction of 'catches' from strangers. They were
forbidden to enter into any 'agreement or combination amongst
themselves not to leade but at such and such Rates as themselves

shall agree', and if they and the Lessees could not agree, the commission was to set wage rates. Preference was to be given to them over strangers in the provision of wain carriage, but no machinery was created for enforcing this requirement, and it was ordered that, if they should 'refuse or neglect to leade the said coles at such tymes as they shalbe required or be not able to lead the same or yf they refuse to lead the same at such rates as the forriners would lead the same, then the coleowners to be at libertie to sett on strangers and outdwellers to lead the same and the coleowners to be alwayes at libertye to lead their coles with their owne proper draughts at ther pleasure'.[127]

The copyholders thus did not come away from Durham empty-handed. But on all essentials, they had lost. They appear to have been unable to agree on the level of compensation due to them from the Grand Lessees, and this was eventually set by the commissioners appointed by the court at £40 per annum. This money was paid over in instalments at the feasts of Martinmas and Pentecost 'to the head man of every Cavill of land in Whickham aforesaid to be by him distributed to every man within that Cavill accordinge to the proportion of land'. It was almost three times the level of compensation paid before 1619, but it was little enough, and there was no guarantee that it would go to those most directly affected by the coal works. The smaller tenants cannot have received more than a pittance.[128]

In effect, the decision of 1621 meant that the fate of the copyholders of Whickham was sealed.[129] This is not to say that they were entirely cowed, or that they lost their appetite for defending and advancing their interests when occasion arose. The year 1625

---

[127] PRO DURH 5/7/100–4. There is a nice historical irony in the fact that the same Sir Richard Hutton was later to find for John Hampden in the famous Ship Money case. (We are grateful to Dr D. J. V. Fisher of Jesus College, Cambridge, for pointing out this connection.)

[128] For the compensation paid, see PRO DURH 4/1, 205–6, 209. Pre-1619 levels of compensation are described by John Dover in DURH 7/19, pt. I.

[129] Its later importance as a precedent is testified to by the fact that in 1720–1 William Cotesworth employed an agent to search the Durham Chancery Office for precedents concerning wayleaves in Whickham, and that (probably as a result) copies of some of the case papers survive in the papers of his heirs: GPL Cotesworth MSS CN/1/158, 165; Ellison MSS C/15/1, C/15/2, C/15/4. Certified copies of the principal documents were also prepared for the Church Commissioners in 1886, including one document which we have been unable to locate in the original files now held in the PRO: DPD Ch. Comm. MSS 244227–244239.

brought a further limited attempt to prevent Grand Lease carriage, though it was swiftly scotched by the Lessees' appeal to the Privy Council.[130] At about the same time, additional wayleave compensation of five marks per pit was obtained from the farmers of Brinkburne freehold.[131] In 1630–2 a number of men took it upon themselves to fill up wasted pits in the Marshall Lands/Fugarfield complex on the Lamesley border, to the fury of the owners, who claimed that some of them needed to be reopened.[132] A year later seven copyholders, including the grieve, seized six wains carrying coal across Whickham Leigh to the Team staiths for Thomas Liddell of Ravensworth. They claimed that Liddell had broken the terms of a separate agreement made with the manorial officers in 1619 by leading coals from more pits than had been specified at the time and by allowing his men to widen the agreed coalway from 7 to 24 yards. This action succeeded in winning both a more favourable wayleave deal and Liddell's agreement that henceforward he would use only wains that were either his own property or supplied by the Whickham copyholders.[133]

Finally, as the coal trade revived in the aftermath of the Civil War stoppage, the copyholders succeeded in renegotiating to a limited extent the terms of the 1621 settlement with the Grand Lessees. The provisions regarding coalways, wasted pits, wain carriage employment, fire coal, and water supplies remained much as before, but the copyholders' compensation was raised to £70 a year, with small additional payments for the sinking of new pits and the spoiling of meadow and arable land. The Lessees further agreed to trench either side of their 'waggon waies' for safety and to allow the copyholders to nominate the keepers of the 'coalgates' or level crossings.[134]

---

[130] *Acts of the Privy Council of England, 1625–6*, 91–2.

[131] PRO E 134 29 Car. II Ea. 20. This case of 1677 states that the payment had been made for 52 years.

[132] DPD Ch. Comm. MSS 245007–245008.

[133] PRO DURH 2/39/98, DURH 4/1, 107–10. Liddell's wains, leading from Ravensworth colliery, were said to raise 'such great quantityes of dust . . . that the pasture arrable adioyning to those wayes are much spoiled'. A commission investigated the grievance and in 1635 it was agreed to pay £7 p.a. for the wayleave and an additional £3 p.a. per pit if the pits at Blackburn colliery also used the way. The previous level of compensation had been £7 p.a., plus 2s. per wain in use. The fact that the earlier agreement had been made in 1619 raises the possibility that the copyholders may have been hoping to force upon the Grand Lessees a compensation deal similar to that recently arrived at with Liddell. Liddell was still paying £7 p.a. compensation in 1676: DRO D/ST 6/32b.

[134] DRO D/ST 6/32c.

All this showed that the spirit of 1619–21 was far from dead. But these were sallies and skirmishes, even though some of them resulted in modest gains. The copyholders remained punctilious in collecting the mess of pottage that had been awarded them, and retained the temerity to ask for more; but the fact remained that in 1621 they had lost the battle to exercise significant control over the exploitation of the land that was their birthright. As for the Grand Lessees, the confirmation of their rights and the hamstringing of copyholder resistance that they had achieved in 1621 cleared the way for what was probably the most intensive period of coal extraction in the history of the manor of Whickham.

What the judgement of 1621 could mean in practice is nicely illustrated by the experience of Robert Harding more than a decade later. On 9 September 1634 Harding apparently discovered Grand Lease workmen on part of his freehold land at Clockburne, 'where they had sett on worke to sinke down a staple pit'. Harding approached 'and did discharge them from working there and told them they should not worke there'. Only a day later, the Grand Lessees laid a complaint against him at Durham, claiming that the land was copyhold of the manor of Whickham and was covered by the decision of 1621. On 15 September the court ordered Harding to cease his interference and to appear before it, authorizing the Grand Lessees in the meantime to continue sinking their pit 'and what other pitt or pitts they shall think fit to sincke within the grounds aforesaid'.

When Harding appeared he protested that his land was not copyhold of the manor of Whickham, but freehold of the manor of Hollinside, and on 26 August 1635, almost a year after the initial incursion, the Grand Lessees were ordered to cease work pending a decision in the common-law courts. They were permitted to have the coal that they had wrought already, but Harding was promised compensation if his case was proved. In the end he did prove his case, though it took him almost four years to get a decision at common law. His eventual compensation order of March 1640 revealed that, in the period of their working, the Grand Lessees had won a total of 720 tens of coal from his land, 'worthe in clear value all the charges in workeinge and leadinge deducted twentie shillings a Tenn'. Four pits had been worked in Clockburne and a further 'eleeven severall staples' had been sunk. Harding was awarded £720 damages for the coal taken and £500 damages for the spoil of his ground, which had been reduced in rental value from 40s. to 10s–12s. a year.[135]

Much the same scenario was almost certainly being played out throughout the best lands of the manor of Whickham. The crucial difference was that the copyholders were unable to claim compensation on the scale obtained by a freeholder like Harding. The results of such breakneck exploitation of the most accessible seams were to become clear with the parliamentary surveys of 1647 and 1652. The demesne meadows by the river were 'for the most parte imployed for stayths to lay Coles on', together with 'houses for the Staythmen to dwell in'. The Fell was speckled with 'diverse Intacks houses and Lodges taken of and builded . . . for the use of the Grand Lease Coalworks which the Grandlessees pretend they may do by virtue of their lease without Impeachment of waste'.

The extent of the workings in the town fields has already been indicated. In all, 16 out of 19 had been mined, some to exhaustion. Where the surveyors were specific, we learn that in East Field 25 pits had been worked in the main coal, 14 in the 'top coal', 9 in the 'five-quarter' coal, and 6 in the 'seven-quarter' coal. Moreover, 30 'pit roomes' had been worked in Corn Moor, 12 in Goose Moor, 6 in Whitefield, and 3 in 'Blinkensop' close. Most of the areas worked since 1610 were simply dismissed as 'wrought' or 'wrought out', and no attempt was made to count the numerous pits that must have been sunk. As for the eight distinguishable areas of 'comon or moore', the surveyors of 1647 listed them and continued: 'All which with cole carriages and other carriages are totally spoyled with great beaten and worne ways' excepting only Talbot Green, an area of around one hundred acres.[136] The worst fears of the copyholders in 1619–20 had been realized. Whickham had not been depopulated: far from it. But the fields and territories of the copyholders had been turned inside out.

4. GENTLEMEN COPYHOLDERS

The surveys of 1647 and 1652 provide graphic evidence of the most obvious and visible physical consequences of the tidal wave of intensive industrial activity that swept over the manor of Whickham

[135] PRO DURH 4/1, 205–6, 209, 458–9, 634; DPD Ch. Comm. MS 244891–4; DRO D/ST 25/74, 25/75.
[136] Kirby, *Parliamentary Surveys*, 81, 82, 84, 107–8, 135 ff.

in the second, third, and fourth decades of the seventeenth century. Less immediately manifest, but no less significant, were the effects that both the generation of vigorous exploitation and the slow ebb of mining operations thereafter had on the restructuring of copyholder society.

In the short term, the peaking of the Grand Lease colliery's operations in Whickham appears to have brought about a severe, if temporary, dislocation of agriculture in the manor. For the decades 1620–49 remarkably few farming inventories survive for the parish of Whickham as a whole, despite the fact that the total numbers of surviving inventories of all sorts is close to that of the preceding thirty years.[137] Moreover, those that do survive belong for the most part to farmers whose lands lay in the southern reaches of the parish, the area least affected by colliery operations at this date. At Byermoor, for example, on the southern extremity of the parish, Lionel Harrison, a gentleman of modest means, had a well-stocked farm with oxen, cows, young beef cattle, rye, and oats growing and husbandry gear of various sorts, in addition to his coal wain.[138]

Within the manor itself, there were certainly some who continued to practise the familiar patterns of agriculture. In November 1634 George Lee had 11 oxen, 14 head of other cattle, 9 horses, 7 sheep, pigs and poultry, 7 fothers of hay, a stack of rye harvested, 40 thrane of oats, 6 thrane of bigg, and 8 bowls of seed rye ready for sowing. Two and a half years later. Richard Hodgson had 6 oxen, 9 other cattle, 4 horses, and 15 sheep, besides a substantial quantity of 'hard corne' and oats sown, his husbandry gear, and 2 coal wains. All this sounds familiar. But these men were exceptional, in two ways. First, they farmed on an unusually large scale by earlier copyholder standards. Second, theirs are the only true farming inventories to survive for copyholders of the manor of Whickham in this period.[139] The more typical copyholder inventories of these

---

[137] In all, 22 inventories survive for the period 1620–49. Of these, 17 contain references to 'agricultural' goods, but only 7 can really be called farm inventories of the earlier type, listing stock, corn and hay, husbandry gear, etc.

[138] DPD Probate, Will and Inv. of Lionel Harrison (1646).

[139] DPD Probate, Wills and Invs. of George Lee (1634), Richard Hodgson (1636). Lee held at least 60 acres of copyhold, to judge by what his widow held in 1647, in addition to which we know that he frequently leased land as a sub-tenant from other copyholders. He was a grieve of the manor. Hodgson had at least 45 acres of copyhold and an unspecified amount of freehold land: Kirby, *Parliamentary Surveys*, 91–4, 96–7; PRO DURH 2/11/182, 2/19/23, 2/20/8, 2/21/90, 2/27/107, 2/27/134.

years are those of cottagers and smallholders who possessed only a few head of stock. John Swan had an 'old cow', some hay, two geese, hens, and a cock in November 1633. John Shafto, who was also the miller at Swalwell, had a horse, a mare, six cows (of which four were apparently wretched creatures grazing loose in 'the hye land'), and three pigs. William Rutherford had a single cow and a small stock of hay.[140]

Though it is inevitably an argument based on silence, and one that must remain tentative, our impression is that the traditional pattern of mixed agriculture in the manor had been disrupted by the mining of the best arable land. There were problems with pasture, too. These years witnessed unusually large numbers of prosecutions in the Halmote for 'overstinting' the manorial grazing lands. Shortage of pasture is scarcely surprising, given the testimony of the surveyors of 1647 and 1652 on the mining of the town field pastures and the waying of the common. If the 1647 surveyors' estimate of the undamaged common is reliable, then around four-fifths of the fell pasture had been 'spoyled', and they were equally emphatic in their statement that what remained was 'straight and little'.[141]

This situation was not, of course, permanent. Back in 1621, one of the witnesses for the Grand Lessees' defence against Robert Cooper's allegations had remarked, complacently enough, that 'the same grounds which are waisted in tyme will prove fertyle againe both for grasse and corne'. He was right; though, as another witness correctly predicted, 'the said waisted ground will not be fertyle againe for a long tyme'.[142] By the 1660s and 1670s, however, inventories of Whickham's copyholders are once more extant in fair numbers which reveal the classic local pattern of a mixed, though predominantly pastoral, agriculture.[143] On average, the oxen and other cattle are there in numbers comparable with those owned by their predecessors two generations earlier. They kept more horses

---

[140] DPD Probate, Wills and Invs. of John Swan (1633), John Shafto (1635), William Rutherford (1637).

[141] DPD DDR HC III F 18, fos. 147, 212, 217, HC III F 19, fos. 16, 97, and *passim*; Kirby, *Parliamentary Surveys*, 82.

[142] PRO DURH 7/19, pt. I, testimony of James Harper, John Dover.

[143] Based on 17 copyholder farm inventories 1660–79, of which 14 indicate the practice of mixed farming. These form part of a total of 46 inventories for the parish as a whole, of which 27 contain 'agricultural' items, however marginal these were.

and fewer sheep. They grew oats, rye, and wheat. Most of them owned at least one coal wain.

But if the older pattern of agriculture had been re-established, this emphatically did not mean that there had been a comparable restoration of the copyholder society of the years before the 1610s. Averaging the agricultural goods listed in these inventories, as a means of assessing the general pattern of farming, conceals the fact that a substantial minority of the copyholders of the third quarter of the seventeenth century appear to have been farming on a scale that had been rare at the turn of the sixteenth century. Moreover, seven of them were, or called themselves, gentlemen, and an eighth used that designation elsewhere. These were copyholders with interests, and sources of income, that extended beyond the manorial territories of Whickham, and their presence is an indication of the extent to which the copyholder community had been transformed.

When we turn to the surveys of landholding on the manor in the mid to late seventeenth century, this impression of a restructured copyholder society is both confirmed and elaborated. We have seen that up to 1600 the basic structure of landholding on the manor of Whickham had remained essentially stable, despite the inevitable changes that had taken place in the identity of the individual tenants. The situation captured in the parliamentary survey of 1647 was very different. This was an unusually detailed survey. The copyholders appeared before the parliamentary commissioners and 'showed their coppies', which were duly recorded. The eighteen tenants who failed to appear were listed, and their holdings can all be identified with the aid of a partial rental of the manor drawn up 'about the yeare 1638'.[144]

Analysis of the 1647 survey reveals that, in the course of the early seventeenth century, the pattern of copyhold tenancy had changed radically. Three points of contrast can be noted. First, the number of copyhold tenants had risen quite substantially. Second, there had been a marked redistribution of the copyhold lands. Third, the social identity of Whickham's copyholders had been transformed. Let us consider each of these developments.

In 1600 there had been some sixty-eight copyhold tenants. This

---

[144] Kirby, *Parliamentary Surveys*, 80–109; DPD Halmote Court Rentals, Box 11, Bundle 5, no. 193324. The latter document can be dated from a copy of 1723 which is dated 'about the yeare 1638': GPL Cotesworth MSS CN/1/304 (A). The following discussion is based upon these documents.

number may have remained fairly stable for some years thereafter, for in 1621 Nicholas Arnold, who as grieve must have known the tenants well, deposed that there were sixty copyholders in the lordship 'at the least'.[145] By 1647 there were 101 copyhold tenants.

As the absolute numbers of manorial tenants increased, the distribution of landholdings among them underwent significant change. Whereas in 1600 there had been twenty-two holdings of 9–29 acres (most of them in the 18–24 acre range), by 1647 there were only nine such holdings, most of them of less than 20 acres. In 1600 there had been nine holdings of 30–49 acres; in 1647 only three remained in this category. The middle-range holdings of 1–3 oxgangs of land which had retained their integrity up to 1600 had largely disappeared as separate units and their lands had been redistributed. John Dalton's 2½ oxgang holding, for example, was now held partly by Richard Jackson's widow Susan and partly by James Clavering. The Hindmers and Merriman families retained only 6 and 7½ acres, respectively, of their former holdings of 24 and 18 acres. The rest had passed into other hands. Such transfers of land as can be traced were by no means always direct, for portions of former holdings not infrequently passed through several hands between 1600 and 1647. But the end result was the same. The characteristic middle-range copyholdings had undergone a process of dismemberment, and with their demise the relatively narrow range of differentiation that had been a feature of the landholding structure of the sixteenth century became a thing of the past.

Meanwhile, a number of very large accumulations had emerged. In 1600 only two copyholders held more than 50 acres and the largest had only around 70 acres. By 1647 there were five holdings of more than 50 acres, two of them falling in the 80–100 acre range and one being of no less than 170 acres. These major holdings had sometimes been built up by families already notable in 1600. The Shaftoes had held 70 acres at the earlier date and now held 92. George Lee, whose inventory we have already discussed, built up from a family holding of 3 oxgangs to a total of over 60 acres at his death, most of which remained in his widow's hands in 1647. The Matfen family similarly expanded their holdings. Others had established themselves in Whickham during the early seventeenth century and acquired land piecemeal as it became available. Susan Jackson, widow of Richard Jackson, held 89 acres in 1647 which

[145] PRO DURH 7/19, pt. I.

had been acquired from seven other copyholders at various dates between 1623 and 1647, most of it before 1640. John Clavering, the new giant among Whickham's copyholders, owned land amassed in the 1630s from the holdings of nine earlier tenants of the manor.

The emergence of a larger number of very substantial copyholders, however, was more than matched by change at the other extreme of the tenant hierarchy. In 1647 there were 18 smallholdings of 1–7½ acres, compared with ten such holdings in 1600. Moreover, the number of tenants who held only a house or cottage and/or gardens, garths, and tiny parcels of land of less than one acre had swollen from twenty-six to sixty-six. Some of these new dwarf- or cottage-holdings had emerged from the dismemberment of the traditional oxgangs of the manor; others were new cottages and houses erected on plots of hived-off land. Most appear to have been tiny encroachments upon the commons of the manor and were described as such in 1638.

A third point of change remains to be discussed: the changed social identity of the Whickham copyholders. In 1600 over three-fifths of Whickham's tenants had held at least one acre of land and close to half had more than nine acres. The great majority of the copyholders appear to have been residents of Whickham, small- to medium-sized farmers and cottagers who derived their living from their lands and commons and supplemented it with their earnings from by-employment in the coal trade. Only a handful had any claim to gentility by virtue of family connections to the lesser gentry of the surrounding area or substantial interests outside the manor.[146] Those who can be said to have had such claims were less than one-ninth of the landholding tenantry, and their total holdings amounted only to around a quarter of the town fields.

Of the copyholders of 1647, little over one-third held more than one acre and only one-sixth had more than ten acres. No fewer than sixteen can be identified as of gentle status, and these gentlemen copyholders comprised one-quarter of the landed tenantry and held in all close to half the copyhold land in the town fields. They accounted for most of the holdings of over fifty acres, as might be expected, but their interests in Whickham were not confined to the accumulation of substantial landholdings. Some had more modest holdings and others held only small parcels of land, houses, or

---

[146] These and subsequent identifications of copyholders discussed below are based upon the information contained in our full name index.

groups of cottages. A few had emerged from among the ranks of the 'yeoman' copyholder families long established in Whickham. Most had bought their way in from outside—like John Clavering, a member of one of Durham's principal land- and coal-owning families.[147] Some of these gentlemen copyholders certainly farmed their lands in Whickham and occupied their houses. Others appear to have been non-resident and must have sublet their property.

This 'gentrification' of Whickham's copyholders was one aspect of the changing social composition of the manorial tenantry. The other was the sheer numerical dominance of those whose connection with the land was marginal at best. Almost two-thirds of the copyhold tenants of 1647 had little if any land of their own. A number may have worked the land of others as sub-tenants or labourers. Rights of common were doubtless valued by all. But of those landless copyholders who can be identified, it is clear enough that many had little connection with agriculture beyond the possession of a cow or two, some pigs, or poultry. They included, for example, overmen and pitmen, staithemen, wainmen, smiths, and victuallers. Their livings were tied to the coal industry and to the numerous ancillary activities that it had spawned.

Such people can scarcely be regarded as copyholders at all in the sixteenth-century sense. Indeed, there is reason to think that contemporaries themselves took this view. No share in the compensation paid by the Grand Lessees was due to those who had no interest in the cavills of lands within the town fields.[148] The rental of 1638 listed separately the rents paid by 'the 14 Cavells belonging to the Coppyholders of the Towne of Whickham' and the 'Small-Rents' payable on copyhold houses, cottages, and encroachments.[149] The surveyors of 1647, in their prefatory description of the manor, distinguished on the one hand the landholding 'copyholders' and on the other hand those cottage holdings 'called the Smalls'.[150]

By 1647, then, the copyhold tenantry of Whickham was more numerous, more sharply differentiated, and more socially diverse

---

[147] John Clavering of Newcastle, alderman, and his son James acquired the manor of Axwell cum Swalwell in 1629 from William Smith of Durham and began building up their holdings in the area: Bourn, *Whickham*, 91.

[148] This is clear in a description of the distribution of this money in proportion to the amount of land held in PRO DURH 4/1, 205–6, 209.

[149] DPD Halmote Court Rentals, Box 11, Bundle 5, no. 193324.

[150] Kirby, *Parliamentary Surveys*, 84.

than half a century before. Nor were these processes of change complete. The proliferation of houses and cottages on the manorial territories continued, as is evident from the eighty-eight 'small rents' paid for such properties in 1692.[151] Among the landholding copyholders, the tendencies towards the accumulation of land in fewer hands and the greater prominence of gentleman copyholders observable in 1647 continued apace until 1678, when the town fields of Whickham were enclosed.

In February 1678, when the landholding tenants surrendered their copyholds in the Halmote, in anticipation of the 'resurrender' of their allocations under the enclosure award, such tenants numbered only twenty-four, as compared with the thirty-five of 1647. Of the holdings surrendered, the largest (Sir James Clavering's) now amounted to around 245 acres. There was another accumulation of 130 acres and two more in the 50–100 acre range. The number of holdings of 10–29 acres had remained stable since 1647 at nine, but the smallest holdings, of 1–9 acres, had been snapped up by engrossers and were reduced in number from eighteen to only four. Conversely, holdings in the 30–49 acre range had been augmented; there were seven of these in 1678, as opposed to three in 1647.[152] Clearly, the processes of accumulation and redistribution had continued, recasting yet again the profile of landholding on the manor.

As for the social composition of the tenantry, of the twenty-four landholding copyholders of 1678, two were baronets and a further fourteen were gentlemen, one of them a Doctor of Physic. Two-thirds were of gentle status, and they held between them 89 per cent of the copyhold land surrendered. As in 1647, some were socially promoted heirs of earlier copyholders who had prospered in the intervening years; for example, Thomas Jackson, heir to 130 acres in 1678, was the first of his line to call himself a gentleman. Others were newcomers, like Thomas Brignall, originally from Lambton, or Sir Thomas Liddell of Ravensworth, a great coal-owner and a man of county stature, a baronet who was not above snapping up a mere 35 acres of copyhold land in Whickham.[153]

---

[151] GPL Cotesworth MSS CN/1/2 (Mich. 1692); cf. CN/1/420 (May 1695).

[152] DPD DDR HC III F 20, fo. 104 ff.

[153] Thomas Jackson's grandfather, Richard, as well as being a 'yeoman' copyholder, had been a subcontracting overman working pits near 'Fugar houses' in Lamesley for Lord Lumley's farmers: PRO DURH 2/39/125. Thomas Brignall,

That the restructuring of the profile of landholding on the manor and the accompanying transformation of the social identity of the copyholders were processes intimately connected with the development of the coal industry can scarcely be doubted. The proliferation of cottage holdings, houses, and tiny encroachments on the commons was clearly related to the demands of the coal industry for labour of all sorts and to the complementary development of a larger service sector. This process had begun before 1600 and had accelerated thereafter as the industry expanded. Of course, not all of Whickham's growing industrial and commercial population was accommodated in copyhold property. But there were copyholders willing to hive off cottages, houses, and building plots, and the manorial lords had good reason to be complacent in the face of encroachments on the common.

The occupants of the numerically predominant 'smalls' had come to Whickham either to work in the coal industry or to supply the needs of those who did so. Among those of the landed population of the manor who had either expanded existing holdings or brought their way in, motivation was probably more complex. Some of those established copyholders who endeavoured successfully to accumulate land in the early seventeenth century may have done so largely with a view to maintaining viable farms in an increasingly adverse physical environment. The industrial workings in the town fields and the accompanying pollution cannot but have threatened the viability of family farms. In this situation the more substantial copyholders, and perhaps those in particular like the Matfens and the Shaftoes who also held freehold land, may have been in the best position to take on more land as a way of keeping their heads above water. George Lee, for instance, whose farming inventory of 1634 revealed continued heavy involvement in both arable and pastoral husbandry, appears to have been extremely active, not only in acquiring copyhold land when occasion arose, but also in taking out sub-tenancies from his neighbours.[154] Nicholas Hodgson behaved similarly, acquiring land both within and outside the manor and involving himself in colliery undertakings to boot. His heir Richard

'yeoman', of Lambton came to Whickham around 1656 as a sub-tenant of the Grand Lease for pits in Southfield. By the time of his death he was Thomas Brignall of Gellsfield, gentleman: Welford, *Committees for Compounding*, 136 n; DPD Probate, Will of Thomas Brignall (1685).

[154] See n. 139 above.

clearly maintained a substantial farm until his death in 1636.[155]

There were, after all, good commercial reasons for farming in Whickham if it could be done on land not totally devastated by the colliery. The dense population of the coalfield area provided a ready market for grain, meat, and dairy produce. Horses and oxen, oats, and hay could be produced for sale to the coalmasters. Opportunities of this kind had considerable influence on agricultural development throughout the region, and doubtless played their part in stimulating demand for land in Whickham.[156] As former agricultural land was brought back into production in the third quarter of the seventeenth century, the farmers' influence must have grown. Such considerations may well have been uppermost in the minds of those copyholder families that piloted their way through the maelstrom of the early seventeenth century and emerged with enhanced holdings into the calmer waters of the Restoration period. Nor can they have been ignored by the gentlemen who acquired land on the manor both before and after 1647, several of whom were certainly farming in their own right.

The peculiar attraction of copyhold land in Whickham, however, was of a different nature. It derived rather from the opportunities provided to benefit directly from the industrial and commercial development of the manor. Land prices in Whickham were apparently high; according to one witness for the Grand Lessees in 1620, they had been significantly enhanced by the advent of the Grand Lease colliery.[157] It is not difficult to imagine why. Houses and cottages could be erected and rented. On holdings near the river, staithes and 'staitherooms' could be profitably let.[158] Despite their defeat in 1621, the copyholders and their assigns retained the right to preferential treatment in wain carriage for the Grand

---

[155] For Richard Hodgson, see n. 139 above. For his father Nicholas Hodgson's activities as an engrosser, sub-tenant and lessee of land, partner in colliery undertakings, and staith owner, see PRO DURH 2/19/10, 2/19/33, 2/19/46, 2/22/202, 2/32/71. It is striking that, quite apart from major coal-owners such as the Claverings and Liddells, several lesser figures engaged in accumulating copyhold land are known to have derived some of their income from direct involvement in the coal industry, e.g. Thomas Brignall, Richard Jackson, Nicholas Hodgson, Mathew Matfen.

[156] Brassley, 'Northumberland and Durham', 41 ff.

[157] PRO DURH 7/19, pt. I, testimony of James Harper.

[158] The Hedworth family received £10 p.a. for a 21-year lease of a parcel of copyhold land 82 by 30 yards in extent 'lying nere or adioyning to the water of Darwent' and known as 'Crosse Weelde staith': PRO DURH 2/29/10.

Lessees, and in 1635 they won a similar concession for the Liddell collieries at Ravensworth and Blackburn. The extent of their continued involvement in this activity is indicated by the fact that three-fifths of the copyholder inventories of the period 1650–79 included coal wains; indeed, it was not unusual to possess two.[159] The copyholders might not be able to dominate wain carriage totally in the manner some had envisaged in 1619, but they could still profit by it—and not simply as wainmen, for there was also the vital question of wayleave.

The judgement of 1621 had established the right of the Grand Lessees to wayleave throughout the manor, and the compensation they paid was paltry enough even when improved in 1647. But the crucial point was that this decision applied only to Grand Lease operations within the manor of Whickham. As early as 1621, the manor was surrounded by other colliery operations. It also contained, interspersed among its lands, the freehold collieries that lay outside the jurisdiction of the Grand Lease. There was something to be gained here, and we know that the copyholders negotiated payment for the wayleaves granted across their land to the owners of both the Brinkburne freehold pits and the Liddell operations at Ravensworth and Blackburn.[160] Moreover, as the Grand Lease colliery entered its long decline and the coal frontier once more shifted south and south-west of the manor, opportunities to profit from the charging of wayleave to the staithes at the mouths of the Team and the Derwent were greatly enhanced.

Despite the prohibition in 1621 of the levying of 'catches' payments on the 'foreign' wains employed by the Grand Lessees, the copyholders do not seem to have abandoned the practice of charging catch money on strangers leading the coal from other collieries. During the 1620s, a charge of 2s. per wain was apparently levied, by agreement, on the Liddells' wains from Ravensworth.[161] In 1678, as part of the enclosure settlement, it was ordered by the Halmote 'that noe Coppiholder within the said Manor (cottagers excepted) shall pay Two shillings for catch carriage'.[162] This was clearly meant to safeguard existing rights (which did not extend to

[159] Based on 17 copyholder inventories 1650–79.
[160] The Brinkburne agreement yielded £3. 6s. 8d. in 1649–50: DPD Ch. Comm. MS 244145. It was still in being up to 1678: PRO E 134 29 Car. II Ea. 20. For the Liddell agreement, see n. 133 above.
[161] See n. 133 above.
[162] DPD DDR HC III F 20, fo. 147.

cottagers) in the post-enclosure world, and it indicates that the levying of a 'catch' charge was still prevalent.[163] The practice of the manor was fully described in a later court case of 1712 which provided evidence of wayleave arrangements stretching back to the 1660s. According to a wainman who had considerable experience of catch money,

the copyholders of Whickham do usually take from all persons not being copyholders within that Manor a certain rent of two shillings a year for every foreign cart or wain that commonly go in the Coleways over any part of the said manor, which is paid by the person to whom such carts belong to the staithman where they deliver their Coles who accounts over the same to the Grieve or Balyffe of Whickham.

One staitheman claimed that he alone had regularly paid £8–£12 a year in this way.[164]

Clearly, the recognized coalways were subject to an organized system of toll collection. What copyholders were able to gain individually from wains that left the coalways and crossed their personal holdings can only be guessed at. Witnesses in a dispute occasioned by the opening of the Bucksnook waggonway recalled that in the 1660s George Shafto had been paid 40s. a year by Sir James Clavering for wayleave for wains from Clockburne colliery. In addition, Shafto was in the habit of stopping wains from any other colliery if they strayed from the coalway when it was congested or impassable; he charged them 1s. per wain for passage across his land.[165] In the 1690s there were said to be 'upwards of 600 wains' leading coals to the Derwent staiths alone.[166] Practices such as Shafto's could yield a welcome income.

Given Whickham's strategic position with regard to access to the Tyne and the approaching demise of the Grand Lease, it is surely no accident that its copyhold land was attractive to buyers and that several of the gentlemen who acquired land on the manor were either coal-owners or Newcastle hostmen. The outstanding case was of course that of the Claverings, who had amassed 170 acres by 1647 and 245 by 1678. An active market in land, however, requires

---

[163] The levying of 'catches' is also indicated by evidence given in a case concerning the wayleave from Brinkburne freehold in 1678: PRO E 134 29 Car. II Ea.20.

[164] PRO E 134 11 & 12 Anne Hil. 37, testimony of George Taylor and John Laverick. This describes the situation c.1700, but the evidence presented implied that it was a far older practice.

[165] Ibid. *passim.*   [166] NEIMME, Bell Collection, vol. 20/373.

sellers as well as would-be buyers. If the advantages of copyholding
were so great, it may seem surprising that the tenants of the
manorial lands were willing to sell their holdings on a scale
sufficient to bring about so far-reaching a restructuring of landholding on the manor. Both their tenures and rights of inheritance,
after all, were exceptionally secure.[167] Sub-tenancy agreements for
periods of years provided a frequently adopted alternative to the
permanent alienation of land for those faced with financial
difficulties.[168]

Of course, the existence of a market in land was no novelty in
Whickham, and yet the developments of the seventeenth century
went far beyond the modifications of holding size that had formerly
resulted from the 'normal' contingencies of mortality, inheritance,
marriage, and the waxing and waning of individual fortunes. There
are perhaps three interconnected explanations. First, the dismemberment of so many of the middle-range holdings may have
owed much to the specific impact of the despoliation of the town
fields of Whickham after 1610. We have no detailed map either of
the location of individual holdings or of the siting of the pits, heaps,
and ways of the Grand Lease colliery. If such charts existed and
could be compared, however, they might do much to explain the
pressures that persuaded some copyholders or their heirs to alienate
part or all of their holdings in the town fields. It seems more than
coincidental, for example, that one of the dismembered holdings
was that of John Hindmers, whose copyhold arable land we know
to have been mined in 1619 and thereafter. At the least, the specific
pattern of industrial devastation may have weakened the inhibitions
of tenants with regard to the piecemeal alienation of land.

Secondly, the prices offered for copyhold land in Whickham were
apparently very good, and not a few of the would-be accumulators
had long purses. This must inevitably have meant that when land

---

[167] The extent of this security is evidenced, for example, in Nicholas Hodgson's
reluctance to proceed with a planned purchase of 18 acres of copyhold from Nicholas
Matfen on the grounds that Matfen's 18-year-old son had an interest in the land as
heir and might subsequently challenge the validity of its alienation. Hodgson agreed
to pay the purchase price only on condition that he was given additional land as
security in the meantime and that on his majority the son would join with his father
in transferring their rights: PRO DURH 2/19/46.
[168] e.g., in 1612 one copyholder who was heavily in debt, and was ultimately to be
imprisoned, sublet two parcels of land for 9 and 11 yrs. respectively, later renewing
the agreement for a further 13 yrs.: PRO DURH 2/11/182, 2/27/107, 2/27/134.

came on to the market in the normal course of events it was likely to pass into the hands of those able to pay such inflated prices and perhaps willing to bid very high. Moreover, if there was pressure on some copyholders or their heirs to alienate their rights to their land, exceptionally high land values may equally have provided a strong incentive for others to do so voluntarily. A small parcel of land of diminished agricultural value, and a small share of the copyholders' compensation and wayleave payments could be exchanged for a fairly substantial immediate payment. Such considerations may have weighed much both before 1647, when the middle-range holdings were broken down, and in the years thereafter, when the dwarf-holdings of 1647 were snapped up assiduously whenever they became available.

Thirdly, the very existence of alternative sources of income in the form of wain carriage payments, colliery work, and the servicing of the industrial population may have made such decisions the easier to make. The devastation of the landscape may have diminished the copyholders' attachment to the land, but it did not necessarily entail their impoverishment. The inventories of household goods surviving for the copyholders and their neighbours in the period 1620–49 indicate that the gains that had been made in living standards in the preceding generation were maintained and even modestly improved. Such minor luxuries as cushions, carpet-cloths, and chamber-pots, for example, became widespread possessions. Among the household linen, tablecloths were more frequently specified as separate, specialized items, and towels appeared more commonly.

The non-gentle inhabitants, to be sure, did not share the sophisticated living standards that had now emerged among the gentry of Whickham, whose houses exhibited a new standard of elaboration in their construction and a new level of comfort in their furnishings. But they had not slipped back.[169] They held their own

---

[169] Only 6 copyholder household inventories survive for this period, but the picture they present is clear and is confirmed by 14 additional non-copyholder inventories. The sophisticated living standards now available to the lesser gentry of the parish are indicated by the inventory of Henry Liddell of Farnacres (1642). His house had 14 named rooms and a gallery and contained such luxurious furnishings as 'chaires covered with velvet', a 'cabanet with drawers', a screen and a clock, as well as much plate. Inventories of non-gentle inhabitants now provided more details of rooms—usually a hall, parlour, chambers, and service rooms such as a kitchen and brewhouse: e.g. DPD Probate, Wills and Invs. of John Lancaster (1635), George Lee (1634), Henry Harrison (1624).

because of their continued capacity to cope with the pressures and to respond to the opportunities of their situation. Such adaptation, influenced, in various combinations, by some or all of the factors discussed above, underlay the restructuring of the pattern of landholding on the manor. Inevitably, however, it ultimately involved the demise of the copyholder community in its sixteenth-century form. This was already apparent in 1647, and more so by 1678. There was little middle ground remaining between Whick-ham's new gentlemen copyholders and the occupants of the 'smalls'.

The enclosure of 1678 can be said to have effectively completed this process, and, like the recasting of copyhold landholding in the preceding two generations, it was deeply influenced by the imperatives of the coal trade. Throughout County Durham there was a powerful trend towards the enclosure of town fields, and it has been argued that this was stimulated above all by the desire to improve agricultural efficiency and output so as to meet the demands of the growing industrial population.[170] Whickham was not exempt from this regional trend, and there is evidence of piecemeal enclosure within the town fields from the 1620s and the 1650s.[171] None the less, a petition of the grieve and sworn men to divide their lands, which was submitted to their manorial lords the mayor and burgesses of Newcastle in 1649, was apparently rejected.[172] At this point, it was perhaps still in the interests of the Grand Lease colliery to keep the town fields open. By the 1670s, however, things had changed. The end of the Grand Lease was imminent. The town fields were largely worked out. In their renewed pressure for enclosure, Whickham's gentleman copyholders, not a few of them coal-owners or hostmen, may well have had in mind the desirability of easing future wayleave problems and enhancing future wayleave income by consolidating their land-holdings within the manor.

Whatever the case, in April 1672 the decision to enclose was taken, with the blessing of the Newcastle oligarchy. The enclosure division was published in 1673, and quarrels over the allocation of particular lands were settled in the following years. In February 1678 the formal process of surrender and resurrender was enacted in

[170] Hodgson, 'Progress of Enclosure', 90; Brassley, 'Northumberland and Durham', 47 ff.
[171] PRO DURH 2/34/14; DPD DDR HC III F 18, fo. 220ᵛ, HC III F 19, fo. 84.
[172] TWA, Calendar of Newcastle Common Council Book 489/4, fo. 590.

the Halmote. The copyholders surrendered their titles to their lands and beast-gates and received compact holdings enhanced by their shares of the pasture fields. Sir James Clavering, for example, surrendered holdings of just over 245 acres and was regranted 463. Mr Mathew Matfen of Newcastle surrendered 56 acres and received 133. Whickham now had five copyholders with consolidated holdings of over 100 acres and another seven with 50–700 acres. Four had 30–49 acres, six had 10–29 acres, and the remaining two had 4 and 6 acres, respectively.[173] The tenants of the 'smalls', of course, were not included, though presumably they retained their rights on the unenclosed waste of Whickham Fell.[174]

With the enclosure division of 1678, a new stability descended upon the copyhold lands of the manor of Whickham. Most of the allocations of 1678 retained their integrity as units, and many their continuity of ownership, well into the eighteenth century.[175] On the enclosed lands the familiar pattern of agriculture continued to be practised until the early years of the eighteenth century, from which time the inventories fail us.[176] Thereafter there was apparently a further shift towards an agriculture directly related to the needs of the coal industry, for the rector was shortly to complain that some of his parishioners had taken to depasturing their grounds 'with Horses imployed in leading Coals along ye waggon-ways (and so called waggon-horses)', while others raised horses and cattle 'which are not imployed in Husbandry, nor intended to be'. It was usual to pay 40s. for the pasturing of a waggon horse from May Day to Michaelmas, and the result was that 'more than half of the Ground in the said Parish that lately grew either Corn or Hay is converted

---

[173] DRO D/ST 25/107; PRO DURH 4/3, fo. 370; DPD Halmote Court M6 (Whickham enclosure); DPD DDR HC III F 20, fo. 104 ff. For a subsequent challenge on behalf of an aggrieved tenant whose allocated lands contained pits belonging to Sir James Clavering, (the colliery rights being reserved to Sir James), see PRO DURH 4/3, fos. 518, 529–530ᵛ, 546–547ᵛ, 580–580ᵛ. Cf. DRO D/ST 6/25.

[174] Some 500 acres of Whickham Fell remained unenclosed until 1821. In 1713, however, it was described as 'not sufficient for feeding and depasturing one half of the goods and cattle of and belonging to all the several Coppyholders within the said Manor who are interested therein and intitled thereunto': PRO E 134 12 Anne Trin. 10.

[175] Holdings can be traced on subsequent rentals of 1692–1727: GPL Cotesworth MSS, CN/1/2, CN/1/420, CP/5/90. The early 18th c. saw yet more 'gentrification' of the copyholders and a degree of further consolidation of holdings.

[176] Farm inventories are rare after 1700 and only one survives for the years 1710–60. Fewer inventories of any kind survive post-1720.

into Pasture', with a consequent detrimental effect on the rector's tithe income.[177]

However, the new stability enjoyed by the manor at the turn of the seventeenth century was the calm that followed a great storm. And such continuities as existed with the world that had preceded the rapid industrialization of the manor were at best superficial. The whole context had changed. For the owners of most of Whickham's copyhold land, their copyhold tenancy was, in Hughes' striking phrase, 'no more than the proverbial egg-cup holding up the crust in the pie of colliery way-leaves and staith rooms'.[178] With the coming of the waggonways after 1699, these copyholders profited handsomely from their prescience in the acquisition of such strategically vital wayleave rights.[179] Their sub-tenants and the tenants of the smalls lived for the most part in a quasi-urbanized environment in which such agricultural interest as they had were a mere supplement to their industrial and commercial activities.[180] The institutions of the manor were now all but defunct. From the mid-1630s the presentment of offences against manorial regulations had become intermittent, and such activity ceased altogether after 1666. Thereafter the Halmote was a mere land registry, and one that copyholders did not greatly trouble to attend.[181]

To be sure, the copyholders of Whickham still retained a degree of institutional identity. In 1709 they came to an agreement with the Montagues whereby they received £50 a year as compensation for any inconveniences arising from the waggonway over Whickham Fell.[182] But both the parties to the agreement and the manner in

---

[177] DRO EP/Wh 33.   [178] Hughes, *North Country Life*, 129.

[179] Thomas Shafto was said to enjoy £80 p.a. from waggonway wayleave rents, a sum that came close to equalling the rental value of his copyhold and freehold lands: PRO DURH 4/4, fo. 282. In 1737 George Bowes's costs included £2,350 for 'Hardings wayleave rent', presumably for the right to cross Hollinside manor and other Harding land: DRO D/ST 47/19. For payments made by the Wortley Montagues to other Whickham copyholders from 1723, see Cromar, 'Economic Power and Organization', 82. These included £56 p.a. to Mr Shafto, and £50 p.a. to John Carr.

[180] Of 32 inventories that list agricultural goods 1680–1709, only 9 can be regarded as true farm inventories. The others indicate no more than the possession of livestock as a domestic supplement.

[181] The demise of the Halmote's role and authority is evident in DPD DDR HC III F 19 (1633–63), F 20 (1663–81), and F 21 (1681–1718), *passim*. In 1647 it was complained by the surveyors that some tenants 'never yet came to take up [their] said lands by Coppy in Court', while in 1727 only 8 of 20 tenants troubled to attend the Halmote: Kirby, *Parliamentary Surveys*, 106; GPL Cotesworth MSS CP/5/90.

[182] DPD Durham Chancery Records. Chancery Decree Award no. 10.

which the money was spent are a measure of the extent to which the copyhold tenantry of Whickham had been transformed. Only gentlemen copyholders were named. The money received by the grieve was used partly to pay the copyhold rents, which were still fixed at their sixteenth-century level, and partly to meet 'publick charges and expenses'. What remained was employed 'every Candlemas Day when he makes up and starts his account with the said Copyholders [to entertain] them with a Dinner the expense and charge whereof is payd out of the publick stock'.[183]

The gentlemen copyholders who sat down to table in the reign of Queen Anne were a world removed from their predecessors of the reign of Elizabeth. In the late sixteenth century the manor of Whickham had been an agricultural community partially involved in industrial activity; by the early eighteenth century the copyholders of Whickham were simply a peculiarly privileged group within an industrial society, deriving specific benefits from their antique rights. In essence, this had already been so for half a century. The Elizabethan agrarian community had been submerged within a larger industrial and commercial order. An old world had gone. A new world had been created. It is with that new world, with its own distinctive structures, identities, and forms of community, that we must now concern ourselves.

[183] GPL Ellison MSS C/15/5 (1712). Copyhold rents remained at their 16th-c. level in 1791: NEIMME, Buddle Papers, vol. 20/3.

3

Living by the Benefit of Coales:
The Anatomy of Industrial Society
in Whickham

To all Defects the Cole heape brings a Cure
Gives life to Age, and Rayment to the Poore
William Ellis, *News from Newcastle* (1651)

IN the century after 1563, the world of the copyholders of the manor of Whickham was utterly transformed by industrial development. Long before the mid-seventeenth century, however, most of the inhabitants of Whickham were not copyholders, and never had been. While one outstanding social consequence of industrial growth had been the dissolution of the agrarian community of the sixteenth century, there are two others that also demand our attention: the emergence of a new industrial population, and the creation of a new social structure.

Both of these processes were in train by the turn of the sixteenth century and they proceeded alongside, and were influenced by, the struggles of the copyholders to adapt to the dynamic of economic change. It is only in the 1660s, however, that we are able to take stock of these developments in the parish as a whole—our opportunity being provided by the hearth-tax returns of the Restoration era. It is appropriate, therefore, that we should preface our account of industrial society in Whickham by presenting an anatomy of the population of the parish in the reign of Charles II—a population that had emerged in the course of three generations of drastic change and which lived, in William Gray's telling phrase, 'by the benefit of coales'.[1]

---

[1] Gray, *Chorographia*, 29.

1. THE HOUSEHOLDERS OF WHICKHAM IN 1666

Five hearth-tax listings of householders survive for Whickham between Lady Day 1663 and Lady Day 1674, each of them independently drawn up by the sheriffs, receivers, or farmers who variously administered the tax in the period covered by the returns.[2] Of these listings, the first, for Lady Day 1663, is inadequate for our purposes, providing only the totals of taxable hearths and the names of householders exempted from the tax in the Whickham, Lowhand, and Fellside quarters of the parish. The second, for Lady Day 1664, is even more disappointing, being so damaged as to be virtually illegible save for the list of taxpaying householders from Swalwell quarter. The fifth, for Lady Day 1674, lists taxpayers in all four quarters of the parish, but includes householders exempt from the tax for Swalwell quarter only. The third and fourth lists, however, contain listings of both taxpaying and exempted householders for each quarter of the parish. Moreover, they have the additional value of having been separately drawn up only six months apart; the former at Michaelmas 1665 for the Crown's receivers, the latter for the tax farmers collecting the tax for Lady Day (25 March) 1666.[3]

The most immediately striking feature of the returns of 1665 and 1666 is that they include uncorrected totals of 252 and 390 names, respectively. This disparity between the two totals of householders listed just six months apart demands explanation. It is tempting to suggest that the difference between them is real and that it may reflect the laying-in of sea-sale collieries initiated by the Tyneside coal-owners in April 1665. Conceivably, the cessation at work in the summer of 1665 might have occasioned a flight of coal-workers to the nearby mines of the river Wear and an actual fall in the number of Whickham's residents by Michaelmas 1665, subsequently reversed in the late winter of 1665/6 as miners returned in anticipation of a resumption of work.[4] Such a possibility is not beyond the bounds of credibility and should not be ruled out

[2] For the administrative history of the tax, see T. Arkell, 'A Student's Guide to the Hearth Tax: Some Truths, Half-Truths and Untruths', in N. Alldridge (ed.), *The Hearth Tax: Problems and Possibilities* (Humberside College of Higher Education, Hull, 1983), 5.

[3] PRO E 179 106/21 (1663), 106/27 (1664), 106/25 (1674), 106/28 (1666), 245/27 (1665). A microfilm of these records is available at the DRO.

[4] For this stoppage, see sect. 1.4 above. Work did not, of course, resume as anticipated and the stoppage was prolonged into the summer of 1666.

arbitrarily; but another, more cautious, explanation might be found in the administrative history of the hearth tax. While the receivers of 1665 are generally regarded as having been more efficient than their predecessors in compiling their assessments and returns, the tax farmers of 1666 might have had an added incentive to proceed efficiently when listing householders, since it was in their direct, personal interests to maximize the yield of the tax.[5] We will return to these possible interpretations in due course. For the moment, however, we will focus our attention on the tax list of 1666, the fullest of those available to us.

The return of 1666 has been carefully scrutinized for possible duplication of householders, a not infrequent phenomenon in listings of this type. Where identical names occur twice or more, they have been checked against the family reconstitution forms for the parish and against a name index based on the supplementary records available for Whickham in order to determine whether or not the parish did contain more than one householder of the same name at this period. As a result, two categories of duplication emerged. In a small number of cases individuals appear to have been listed twice, either through scribal error or because they owned two properties in different areas of Whickham.[6] Somewhat more numerous were cases in which, within a single quarter of the parish, individuals appear to have been listed first as taxpayers and subsequently as exempted householders. These cases presumably reflect the anxiety of the tax farmers to maximize the number of payers, with the result that particular individuals were included who later established a right to exemption.[7] In all, this exercise reduced

---

[5] Arkell, 'Student's Guide', 5, argues that administration of the tax became stricter under the receivers of 1664–5, and that under the tax farmers of 1666–7 'popular hatred of the tax reached its peak'. In a private communication Dr Arkell has suggested to us that the list of Michaelmas 1665 might possibly be an earlier list, drawn up by the receivers at Michaelmas 1664 or in the spring of 1665 and subsequently re-used. Unfortunately, we have no way of testing this possibility since no Durham lists for Michaelmas 1664 or Lady Day 1665 survive. However, close examination of the persons listed indicates, as we will see, that the list was compiled in the year 1665.

[6] In such cases individuals have been counted under the quarter of the parish in which they are first listed. The list proceeds through the quarters in the order Whickham, Lowhand, Fellside, Swalwell.

[7] Some householders may have been reduced from the status of taxpayers to that of exemption by the hardships of the stoppage of 1665–6. It seems unlikely that this temporary crisis seriously inflated the level of exemption, however; for, where they can be identified on earlier tax lists, most of the individuals concerned were already exempted. Those appearing as both taxpayers and exempted have therefore been counted as exempt.

the total number of individual householders in Whickham from 390 to 367. It is on this corrected list of householders that the subsequent analysis is founded.

In 1666, Whickham's corrected total of 367 households represented a quadrupling of the 93 households resident in the parish in 1563. Whereas there is good reason to believe that at the earlier date population had been concentrated in the township of Whickham itself, and supplemented by the riverside hamlets of Swalwell and Dunston and by outlying houses and farms, the picture for 1666 is one of augmented population density in the existing settlements, supplemented by a very substantial number of new cottages which had been erected in the Lowhand and Fellside quarters, i.e. in the Team Valley and on Whickham Fell. The distribution of households by quarter and by the number of hearths attributed to householders is represented in Table 3.1.

TABLE 3.1. *Hearth Tax 1666: Distribution of Householders*

No. of hearths	No. of householders									
	Whole parish		Whickham		Lowhand		Fellside		Swalwell	
	No.	%	No.	%	No.	%	No.	%	No.	%
1 Exempt	274	74.7	69	70.4	103	83.1	73	76.0	29	59.2
1 Chargeable	17	4.6	1	1.0	8	6.5	—	—	8	16.3
2 Exempt	15	4.1	—	—	2	1.6	10	10.4	3	6.1
2 Chargeable	27	7.4	8	8.2	7	5.6	4	4.2	8	16.3
3	12	3.3	5	5.1	2	1.6	4	4.2	1	2.0
4	8	2.2	7	7.1	—	—	1	1.0	—	—
5	4	1.1	4	4.1	—	—	—	—	—	—
6	2	0.5	2	2.0	—	—	—	—	—	
7	2	0.5	1	1.0	—	—	1	1.0	—	
8	1	0.3	—	—	1	0.8	—	—	—	—
9	2	0.5	1	1.0	1	0.8	—	—	—	—
10	2	0.5	—	—	—	—	2	2.1		
11	1	0.3	—	—	—	—	1	1.0	—	—
Total	367	100	98	99.9	124	100	96	99.9	49	99.9
% of parish total		100		26.7		33.8		26.2		13.4

The figures presented in the table provide a first approximation of the social profile of Whickham in 1666, a distribution of households based solely upon the categories of the tax listing itself and involving no further interpretative intervention. The outstanding features of this distribution are the very high proportion of Whickham householders who lived in one-hearth dwellings (79.3 per cent), and the almost equally large proportion (78.8 per cent) who were exempted from the tax. These characteristics emerge with particular clarity when we compare the Whickham figures with some of those assembled for a range of other areas of England.[8]

In comparison with most of the rural areas included in Table 3.2, Whickham is distinguished by having a larger proportion of one-hearth households, a smaller middle range of two- to five-hearth households, and a sharper, narrower pinnacle of very substantial households with six or more hearths. As compared with the sample of major urban centres, Whickham again stands out as having an exceptionally large base of one-hearth households, few middle-range households, and very few households' in the 6+ hearth categories. Of the three industrial areas included in the table, Whickham's peculiar features emerge once again in comparison with metalworking Birmingham and the Essex cloth town of Coggeshall, though Whickham had much in common with the coalfield parishes of north-eastern Warwickshire. In one respect, however, Whickham stands out from all the areas and communities included in this comparison: none had a level of exemption from the tax that came close to Whickham's 78.8 per cent. Indeed, of the published hearth-tax figures available to us for comparison, only two communities appear to have shared Whickham's experience in this respect: one was the nearby coal-producing parish of Chester-le-Street, Co. Durham, with an exemption rate of 78 per cent; the other was the Sandgate ward of Newcastle-upon-Tyne (79 per cent), the riverside home of the keelmen who rowed Whickham's coal to the collier fleets at the mouth of the Tyne.[9]

   [8] T. Arkell, 'The Problem of Establishing Regional Variations in England's Hearth Tax Household Structure during the Later Seventeenth Century', in R. Smith (ed.), *Regional and Spatial Demographic Patterns in the Past* (Oxford, 1990). For the purpose of comparison we have adopted the analytical categories suggested by Dr Arkell as those most appropriate for the detection of regional variations. We are grateful to Dr Arkell for allowing us to use his paper in advance of publication.
   [9] R. I. Hodgson, 'Demographic Trends in County Durham, 1560–1801: Data Sources and Preliminary Findings with Particular Reference to North Durham',

TABLE 3.2. *Hearth Tax: Comparative Analysis of Household Distribution*

	% housholders assessed on: (No. of hearths)					% NL[a]	Total no. of house- holds
	1	2	3–5	6–9	10+		
Rural							
Essex 1669–70	48.0	18.5	25.3	6.3	2.1	33.8	20,897
Cambs. (Part) 1674	50.0	29.9	16.5	2.7	1.0	19.0	5,377
Beds. 1669–70	62.1	17.7	16.2	2.8	1.2	29.8	7,730
Warwicks. 1669–70	68.9	16.2	11.9	2.2	0.9	36.1	14,509
Herefords. 1664	73.9	13.2	10.3	2.0	0.6	38.6	11,034
Cheshire (part) 1664	74.4	14.9	7.8	2.0	1.0	22.4	1,548
Urban							
York 1672	33.6	22.0	29.8	10.6	4.0	20.6	2,124
Chester 1664–5	45.9	21.6	22.0	8.2	2.4	40.4	1,675
Colchester 1669–70	45.5	25.0	21.9	5.9	1.7	52.8	2,190
Coventry 1666	44.5	23.9	23.2	6.5	1.9	41.4	1.435
Newcastle 1665	61.8	14.1	17.8	5.0	1.1	41.4	2,510
Industrial							
Birmingham 1673–4	51.9	24.3	19.2	3.6	1.0	46.8	786
Coggeshall 1669–70	59.6	20.8	14.1	4.7	0.7	59.8	458
Warwicks. coal- field 1669–70	76.6	14.1	7.3	1.2	0.7	49.8	1,704
Whickham 1666	79.3	11.5	6.6	1.8	0.8	78.8	367

[a] NL = non-liable, i.e. exempted.

Source: all comparative figures from Arkell, 'Regional Variations'.

Comparisons of this type help to emphasize the distinctive features of Whickham's social profile as evidenced in the hearth-tax distribution of households. But this exercise carries us only so far.

Univ. of Manchester School of Geography Research Papers, no. 5 (1978), 18; Ellis, 'A Dynamic Society', 197. Ellis describes Newcastle's social structure as being markedly polarized between 'an unusually restricted elite' and 'the vast quasi-proletarian multitude of the poor'.

We must also ask ourselves what these statistical categories actually mean in the specific case of Whickham. In order to answer this question, we have attempted to identify the householders of 1666 in socioeconomic terms, employing for this purpose the family reconstitution forms for the parish, our principal name index, and also a separate name index of both ratepayers and paupers on parish relief derived from the detailed overseers of the poor accounts for the years 1677–1714. The results present a surprisingly clear picture of Whickham's social structure in the first decade of the Restoration.

Whickham's three households with ten or more hearths are immediately identifiable as the seats of the principal gentry families of the parish: the coal-owning Claverings, Blakistons, and Liddells. Their owners were all baronets. The eleven households with between five and nine hearths were, with two exceptions, those of the lesser gentry families of the parish, ranging from the rector of Whickham, Dr Thomas Wood, through Robert Harding of Hollinside, to the cadet branches of the Liddells. Several of these men were minor coal-owners; others were principal copyholders at the time of the enclosure division of 1678. For four of these families inventories of goods survive dating from 1671–8. Total valuations ranged from £51 to £171, with an average of approximately £116, while valuations of household goods (perhaps a better indication of relative living standards than total inventory valuations) averaged approximately £39. All had stock, indicating an active concern with farming in their own right, and two possessed coal wains.

Thus far, the hearth-tax categories appear to provide a generally reliable, though not entirely predictable, guide to the relative position of individuals within Whickham's social hierarchy. But for the exceptions noted, households with five or more hearths were those of the wealthiest and most prominent members of parish society.[10] Those with ten or more hearths were a distinctive élite, men of weight not only in parish but also in county society.

---

[10] Of the two exceptions, one was the widow of a yeoman copyholder whose son subsequently received sixteen acres at the enclosure of 1678; the other, 'Thomas Grobs', was probably the Thomas Grubb, tailor, who died in 1690, and whose inventory listed only household goods to the value of £5. 11s. 2d. Grubb may have been living in reduced circumstances at the time of his death, however, for his widow's will of 1691 and supplementary papers indicate that her late husband had been owed debts of £50 which had not been paid. She also complained of the 'unkindnesse' of a son-in-law who 'did not allow her sufficient maintenance'. Grubb may have been a man of some substance in earlier life whose circumstances had been

This general correspondence between hearth-tax categories and relative social position continues to hold good as we descend the tax list. With four-hearth householders we appear to enter a borderland between the lesser gentry and the principal farmers of the parish. Thomas Brignall of Gellsfield, who had begun life as a yeoman and a sub-tenant of the Grand Lease pits in Southfield, called himself a 'gentleman' as early as 1664. He received an allocation of 56 acres of copyhold land at the enclosure of 1678. At his death in 1685 his inventory amply justified his claims, totalling over £131, with household goods to the value of £57, plus stock, husbandry gear, and coal wains.[11] Given that he owned two houses in 1666, both of four hearths, it might be more appropriate to regard him as in effect an eight-hearth householder. Thomas Pescod was another man who claimed gentility. His inventory of 1671 totalled over £98 and included ample stock, grain, and a couple of coal wains, though his household goods were valued at only £18. He was the son of Mr Bartholomew Pescod, curate of Whickham during the Interregnum and a copyholder in 1647.[12]

The remaining four-hearth householders called themselves yeomen. One, Robert Harrison, received 24 acres in 1678. The inventories of three others, taken between 1666 and 1682, had total valuations in the £60–£69 range, with household goods valued at £14–£21, together with the stock, grain, and hay (and on occasion coal wains) which provide a clear indication of their economic activities. Though the term 'yeoman' cannot be assumed in north-eastern England to imply that a man was a substantial farmer, for it was used indiscriminately for all landowners below gentry status, there can be no doubt that these men were the principal farmers of Whickham and the leading non-gentle parishioners. All who survived to 1677 and beyond paid the parish poor-rate, usually at the superior assessment of 2*d*. per week.

The three-hearth householders were more varied occupationally. They included several yeomen, but also an overman, a staithe-owner, and a Newcastle hostman–fitter whose father had been a Whickham copyholder. Occupationally, these householders had

reduced by age, imprudent loans, and transfers of property to his daughter's husband: DPD Probate, Inv. of Thomas Grubb (1690), Will and Inv. of Isabella Grubb (1691).

[11] For Brignall's career see ch. 2, n. 153.

[12] DPD Probate, Inv. of Thomas Pescod (1671); Lambeth Palace Library Comm. XII a/4, fos. 107–9.

much in common with the larger group of taxpaying two-hearth householders, whose identifiable members included yeomen in addition to overmen, staithemen, a carpenter, and a blacksmith. With the three- and two-hearth householders, then, we have entered the world of the superior employees and semi-independent middlemen of the coal trade, those who held responsibility as overmen or staithemen, or who acted as fitters to the coal-owners.

Of the yeomen, two at least enjoyed property that would have placed them on a par with the four-hearth yeomen of Whickham discussed above. Thomas Jackson had inherited 89 acres of copyhold land built up by his yeoman/overman father Richard. His own son, another Thomas, was to surrender it for an allocation of 130 acres in 1678 and was to be the first of the Jacksons to style himself 'gentleman'.[13] William Lonsdale left an inventory totalling over £77 in 1668, with household goods valued at over £18.[14] The remainder, however, were lesser folk, to judge by the available evidence—in particular, those without land to their names. Inventories relating to eleven of these two- and three-hearth taxpayers survive for the period up to 1695. Some may be depressed in value by reason of their late date, though it would be equally possible to argue that householders who survived to the late 1680s or early 1690s had had the opportunity to accumulate as well as to disburse wealth as they aged. At any rate, they ranged from £3 to £37 in total valuation, averaging just under £12. Household goods ranged in value from £2 to £15, averaging just over £6. One further unifying characteristic of the two- and three-hearth taxpayers should be noted. One-third of those with three hearths and one-quarter of those with two hearths (or their widows) are known to have contributed to the poor-rate after 1677, usually at the rate of 1*d*. per week. Given the fact that these are minimum figures, including only those who survived or remained in the parish after 1677, they offer convincing testimony to the modest prosperity of this group.

Of the seventeen chargeable one-hearth householders, far fewer can be identified readily—a fact that is of some significance. George Hebron, described as a 'yeoman' at the time of his death in 1686, was a ratepayer and enjoyed modest prosperity.[15] Charles Jordan was a staitheman and a brewer or victualler when he died in 1688.

[13] For Richard Jackson, see ch. 2, n. 153. Thomas Jackson sen. died in 1667.
[14] DPD Probate, Inv. of William Lonsdale (1668).
[15] DPD Probate, Inv. of George Hebron (1686).

He possessed a very substantial quantity of household equipment, draught animals, three coal wains, and two 'colle botes' or keels, and lived in a house far larger than the one-hearth dwelling on which he had been taxed in 1666. His actual occupation in 1666 is unknown, though he had recently married the daughter and heir of a yeoman and staithe-owner, which may help to explain his subsequent success.[16]

Occupation of a one-hearth house could be a starting point in adult life; but it could also be a persisting condition or a conclusion, as we shall see. Other evidence relating to the one-hearth taxpayers of 1666 suggests that the gently descending socioeconomic hierarchy of Whickham was approaching another borderline with these householders. Hebron and Jordan apart, only two of the individuals concerned were to pay the parish poor-rate after 1677. The widows of two others, however, are known to have ended their lives on parish relief.

In coming to those householders actually exempted from taxation in 1666 (78.8 per cent of the total), it is as well to remind ourselves of the technical criteria for exemption from the hearth tax. Officially, exemption should have been granted automatically to all those whose 'poverty or smallness of estate' meant that they were unable to pay the church or poor-rates of their parish. In addition, exemption could be claimed by the occupiers of houses worth 20s. per annum or less 'upon the full improved rent', and by persons with land, tenements, or goods valued at less than £10. From 1664, no exemption was to be allowed to persons with more than two hearths.[17]

Given these criteria, it is now clear that exempted householders cannot simply be categorized as paupers—an assumption sometimes made by early students of the hearth tax. At the same time, it is equally apparent that the exempted were likely to include the least prosperous members of any given parish—the smallholders, cottagers, labourers, widows, and single women who, while not necessarily in receipt of parish relief, were those to whom contemporaries referred broadly as 'the poor' or 'the labouring poor'.[18] Identifying the exempt in Whickham assumes particular importance inasmuch as it was Whickham's astonishingly high

[16] DPD Probate, Inv. of Charles Jordan (1688).
[17] T. Arkell, 'The Incidence of Poverty in England in the Later Seventeenth Century', *Social History*, 12 (1987), 32–3.   [18] Ibid. 33–47, *passim*.

proportion of exempted householders that so markedly differentiated the parish even from those other rural areas known to have had comparably high proportions of one-hearth households.

We can begin by considering the fifteen householders living in two-hearth dwellings who were granted exemption from the tax by the Whickham assessors. These householders can be said to represent an extension deeper into that shadowy area between modest well-being and the risk of poverty which we have already observed in discussing the one-hearth taxpayers. Occupationally, they included the widow of a smith, the widow of an overman, a middle-aged yeoman also known to have been a colliery worker, a wain driver, and a labourer. The others remain obscure, but three of them had been classified as one-hearth exempt in 1663, while three more had a subsequent Poor Law history which may be instructive. Thomas Laybourne was later to be a contributor to the poor-rate. The widow of Thomas Watson was, in contrast, to be a recipient of relief. Thomas Holyday was to pay the rate in 1677–81, but in the last three years of his life, 1691–4, he received relief, as did his widow following his death.

In some ways, it would make good sense to regard the one-hearth taxpayers and the two-hearth exempt as belonging to essentially the same stratum in Whickham's social hierarchy, artificially divided by the assessor's decisions regarding their relative circumstances in 1666. They appear to have straddled a socioeconomic borderline. They might or might not qualify to pay the poor-rate, but they were unlikely, on the whole, to find themselves or their widows among those in receipt of parish aims.

The one-hearth exempted householders, on the other hand, seem to have belonged more firmly to the labouring poor of the parish. Once again, of course, there are exceptions that must be recognized and that can be explained in life-cycle terms. Thomas Nixon, a young married man in 1666, was to die eleven years later described as a yeoman and with good claim to that title. His inventory totalled almost £58 and included stock, grain, a couple of coal wains, and over £9 worth of household goods. Conversely, Widow Thompson of Swalwell had lived well earlier in life. Her husband Ralph, a smith, had left an inventory in 1662 which listed his tools, four oxen, two cows and their 'followers', five horses, poultry, 'big' and hay growing, and a well-furnished house of at least four rooms: a man of apparent prosperity. It was probably his massive debts, also specified in the inventory, that reduced his widow to the status of a one-hearth exempted householder.[19]

We have only two other inventories for householders in this category, both taken thirteen years later in 1679. Richard Wright, of Team Staith, had goods totalling £7. 19s. 0d., including 'one hogg pigg', a quantity of 'smale cole', and simple household goods to the value of just over £4. George Frame, of Whickham Lowhand, had goods to the value of only £4. 15s. 5d., over half that total being accounted for by 'one little old cowe', 'a little pigg', and his purse and apparel.[20] The remaining householders in this category are not to be found among the inventoried population. We have occupational designations for only thirty-six of them—or for their former husbands, for forty-nine (17.8 per cent) of the householders in this category were widows. Nevertheless, these tell a consistent story. Some were described as yeomen, though they can scarcely have been more than smallholding sub-tenants, given their absence from all surveys of landholding. The vast majority, however, were coal-workers of one description or another—pitmen, overmen, colliery labourers, wain drivers, a colliery smith, a chandler supplying candles for the pits. Their means of livelihood enter the historical record only because of their untimely deaths in the pits or their peripheral involvements in disputes relating to collieries. How many of the other exempted householders were also wage-workers in the coal industry we cannot know, but it is reasonable to assume a great many.

We have one other means, however, of indicating the socio-economic identity of the one-hearth exempted householders: the records of Poor Law administration.[21] Of the 274 householders in this category, only four are known to have paid the poor-rate after 1677. No fewer than eighty-eight of these householders, however, were to appear themselves, or to be represented in the persons of their widows, among the lists of those in receipt of relief after 1677. That almost a third of these households came to be dependent on parish alms is a startling finding—especially in view of the fact that this can be only a minimum estimate, since some householders and their widows were dead before the commencement of detailed overseers' records in 1677. Indeed, their vulnerability to actual

---

[19] DPD Probate, Invs. of Thomas Nixon (1677), Ralph Thompson (1662).
[20] DPD Probate, Invs. of Richard Wright (1679), George Frame (1679).
[21] DRO EP/Wh 22, 'Poor Rate Book', 1677–1715.

destitution can be represented even more graphically. In order to appear in the Poor Law records, a man or his widow needed not only to survive until 1677, but also to remain resident in Whickham. That many of the one-hearth exempted householders were not resident in Whickham for any length of time is indicated by the fact that almost a third of them do not have a family reconstitution form in the reconstitution study of the parish. The 185 one-hearth exempted householders for whom a family reconstitution form could be compiled (however patchy and incomplete its contents) were the relatively stable. And of these, no less than 43.2 per cent were subsequently represented among Whickham's paupers on relief—another minimum estimate, but a telling one. In sum, the one-hearth exempted householders, whose presence in such large numbers was a distinctive feature of early industrial society in Whickham, appear to have been predominantly wage-earning coal-workers who seem to have eked out a reasonably adequate living in most years but were greatly at risk of actual impoverishment in the later stages of the life-cycle.

We would argue, therefore, that in Whickham at least the hearth-tax listing of 1666 provides an admirable basis for an exploration of the social structure of the parish—though only when supplementary records can be deployed in a manner that can establish, first, the social meaning of the crude hearth-tax categories and, second, the exceptions and anomalies that they can conceal. Having established the nature of the principal socioeconomic strata in Whickham, we might go on to transfer specific individuals from group to group, modifying the statistics derived directly from the tax listing.[22] But our object is not to produce a fixed, numerically precise account of Whickham's social structure; for it was not a fixed reality. More important is the sense that we have gained of the structure of society in Whickham and of the socioeconomic distance between its component groups.

Society in Whickham in 1666 was composed of five principal groupings. At the top was a tiny élite of three coal-owning baronets. Next came a small group of lesser gentlemen. Below them was a further small group of substantial farmers. Only with the fourth group—the lesser yeomen, holders of middle-rank places in the coal trade, and some modestly prosperous craftsmen—did the social

---

[22] In fact, the resulting statistics would differ very little from those already presented. Individuals transferred from category to category largely cancel one another out.

pyramid begin to broaden significantly. This group of 'lesser ratepayers'—if we can adopt that term to give some overall identity to an occupationally varied stratum—was supplemented from below by a further group of householders who occupied a social–structural borderland between the lesser ratepayers and our fifth clear category: the great mass of coal-workers and cottagers which included over three-quarters of the households of the parish.

Such a structure might be taken to imply a subtle gradation of wealth and living standards from top to bottom, and so in one sense it did. Yet, given the relative size of the different groups concerned, it was more likely to be experienced in terms of the stark contrast between the gentlemen and principal parishioners of Whickham and the massive industrial work-force that surrounded them. There was relatively little middle ground in the social structure of Whickham, and those who occupied it seem often to have been closer in their experience to the labouring poor than to the major farmers and gentlemen of the parish.

There was a topographical element in this, too, which can be discerned if we re-examine Table 3.1 in the light of our account of Whickham's householders. Those families constituting the pinnacle of Whickham society resided on the periphery of the parish in the great households of Fellside quarter. The lesser gentry were concentrated in Whickham town, with outposts in Lowhand quarter where the Liddells of Farnacres held sway. The greater farmers again tended to live in Whickham town. In contrast, the 'lesser ratepayers' were spread across all four quarters of the parish. (They were the leading inhabitants of Swalwell.) Finally, almost two-thirds of the labouring poor lived in the Fellside and Lowhand quarters. How far such intra-parochial variation may have affected individual perception of the structure of Whickham society we can only conjecture.

The pattern of social stratification was not the only distinctive feature of industrial society in Whickham to be revealed by our examination of the hearth tax. As we have seen, a substantial proportion of the one-hearth exempted householders of the 1666 list were found to have no family reconstitution form in the reconstitution study based upon Whickham's parish registers. Their impact upon the parochial registration system was either fleeting or non-existent. This phenomenon, however, was not confined to householders in the one-hearth exempt category. In all, a total of

120 of the 367 householders listed in 1666 were found to have no family reconstitution form. The possible implications of this fact are that some of the householders of Whickham were only briefly resident in the parish, that some may have been long-term residents but remained unmarried, that some were married householders who had spent much of their lives (including the child-bearing stage) elsewhere, or that extensive religious dissidence existed in the parish, resulting in widespread failure to conform to the ritual requirements of the Church of England.

To begin with the last of these possibilities, we have no reason to believe that religious nonconformity was widespread in Whickham at this date. Indeed, we can be quite positive about this, for in November 1662 Bishop Cosin of Durham conducted a searching visitation of his diocese which was particularly concerned with the identification of religious noncomformity. This resulted in the presentment from Whickham of nine 'popish recusants', one 'Anabaptist' who was also guilty of 'keeping her children unbaptized', and eight 'separatists', two of whom were likewise said to be 'keeping their children unbaptized'.[23] Of the Catholics, some were the wives of householders, and others were not included among the list of householders in 1666. (Some of them may have been servants in Catholic households.) Of those who were included, one had a family reconstitution form, though with no entry after 1645. Three other 1666 householders, however, all of them gentlemen, almost certainly left no trace in parochial registration because they were Catholics. With regard to the Protestant dissenters, the visitation book tells us that all but two had conformed by 1663. These sturdy souls were present in 1666, and we have family reconstitution forms for both of them, though one contained no entry later than 1642. Of those who conformed, one died in 1665 and another was not present in 1666. Of those present, four have family reconstitution forms and two do not. Protestant dissent appears to have cost the reconstitution study only two families.[24]

In all, religious dissidence seems to have had only a marginal influence on the registration history of Whickham's householders. As for the other possibilities, some of the 1666 householders were

---

[23] DPD DR II/3, fo. 103.

[24] All those said to be keeping their children unbaptized have family reconstitution forms, though that of Isabel Emminson, who did not conform, contains no entry after 1642.

definitely unmarried. A few certainly lived on in the parish unwed, as we shall see. Most of those whom we know to have been unmarried in 1666, however, either married later and left registration records or else vanished from Whickham records. Others among the 1666 householders may have been both unmarried *and* temporary residents. Finally, there were some householders who had spent, or were to spend, much of their lives elsewhere. This was true of the great gentry, of course, but also of some lesser inhabitants. George Hodgson appears to have spent his early adult life in Newcastle.[25] Michael Wheatley, a Fellside householder in 1666, would be entirely absent from Whickham's records thereafter were it not for the chance survival which tells us that in 1690 he was living across the parish boundary on Tanfield Moor.[26]

We are left with a strong impression of the mobility, indeed transience, of a substantial minority of Whickham's householders. It is an impression that is greatly reinforced if we turn from the householders for whom we have no family record to those for whom we have reconstitution forms. Examination of these reveals that very few of the Whickham householders included were baptized, married, *and* buried in the parish. More appear to have arrived as young people, married, baptized their children, and subsequently found burial in Whickham. Many, indeed most, arrived already married, entering the registration record only with the baptism of their children.

Permanence of settlement among these two categories of immigrants, however, is not to be assumed; for, of all those who spent at least part of the child-rearing phase of the family cycle in Whickham, most were not recorded as having been buried in the parish. To be more precise, of the 247 householders of 1666 who left sufficient registration evidence to permit reconstitution, 43 (17.4 per cent) had been baptized in Whickham, 116 (46.9 per cent) married in Whickham for the first time, and 113 (45.7 per cent) were ultimately buried there. As regards generational continuity, 111 (44.9 per cent) had at least one child who eventually married in Whickham and continued the family line in the parish into the next generation.[27]

[25] In 1634 he was prosecuted for not attending Whickham parish church, but pleaded successfully 'that he liveth at Newcastle where he usuallie repaireth to Church': DPD Prior's Kitchen, Fragments of Durham Chancellor's Visitations c.1634–7.   [26] DPD Probate, Inv. of Joan Wheatley (1690).

[27] Some householders, of course, appear in more than one of these categories.

There was a degree of social variation in all this. Householders identifiable as substantial farmers were somewhat more likely than others to have been baptized in Whickham, and both they and the lesser gentry were considerably more likely than others to be buried in the parish. They can be said to have formed the stable core of parish society. But the overall picture is essentially one of considerable turnover of families at all social levels. In short, while a substantial minority of the householders of 1666 appear to have been temporary residents at best, an even larger number spent only part of their adult lives in the parish.

The mounting impression of the high mobility of Whickham's inhabitants becomes one almost of volatility when we compare the hearth-tax listing of 1666 with that returned for Michaelmas 1665. The list of 1666 is, of course, much longer, and for this reason it is scarcely surprising that a large number of the 1666 householders do not appear on the 1665 list. They may have been present, but omitted. What is more perplexing is the fact that a very substantial number of the 1665 householders cannot be located on the 1666 list drawn up only six months later.[28] On closer scrutiny, some of the missing householders of 1665 can be accounted for easily enough by the accidents of death, heirship, and succession. George Walton died early in 1666 and was represented on the 1666 list by his son and heir Thomas. Similarly, the Alice Bellamy of the 1666 list was the widow of the Thomas Bellamy of the 1665 list. Yet even after discounting such cases, we are left with a total of 121 householders in 1665 who had apparently vanished by March 1666!

The disparity between the two lists is most marked in the cases of the exempted householders (especially those of the Lowhand and Fellside quarters) and the lower reaches of the taxpaying population. Of those who paid tax in Whickham in 1666, three-quarters had also been listed in 1665 (including all the principal householders of the parish). Those who did not appear in 1665 were overwhelmingly householders charged on one, two, or three hearths. Of the exempted population of 1666, only a quarter had been listed in 1665. Conversely, the 1665 list provides the names of thirty-seven taxpayers who did not appear in 1666—all but two paying tax on

---

[28] We are assuming here that the listing was indeed drawn up at Michaelmas 1665 and was not a re-used receivers' list of Michaelmas 1664 or Lady Day 1665. Even if this was not so and the lists were separated by 12–18 ms., the turnover of householders would remain remarkable.

one or two hearths—and a further eighty-four exempted house-holders who were missing in 1666. Given these disparities, the central question becomes whether they represent a very high degree of population turnover among what we have termed the 'lesser ratepayers' and the industrial work-force of Whickham, or are simply to be explained in terms of the inefficient listing of these same groups in 1665 and perhaps also in 1666.

This question can best be approached by attempting to trace the 121 'missing' householders of 1665 in the family reconstitution forms and supplementary documents. Four categories emerge. First, there are seventy-one householders for whom no family reconstitution form could be compiled. On occasion we know something of these individuals. Mathew Matfen owned copyhold land in Whickham but was absent from the tax lists after 1665, and we know that in later life he lived in Newcastle;[29] he may well have moved there in 1665/6. Robert Horsley and William Craggs were both children of Whickham families and young unmarried house-holders in 1665, their parents being dead. Neither was married or buried in Whickham and neither is traceable thereafter; they may well have moved. For the great majority of these householders, however, we have no supplementary information. They left no trace in Whickham's records save their presence in 1665, and were probably temporary residents.

A second group of thirteen householders have family re-constitution forms, but these include no events later than 1665. Two were certainly dead. The possessions of William Newby and John Leash were inventoried in May and June 1666, respectively.[30] When they had died or where, however, is uncertain, for neither was buried in Whickham. John Todd and his wife baptized children in Whickham in 1661 and 1663, but the register tells us that they were 'of Lamesley'; they may have returned there. Others simply had no registration events or other references after 1665. Christopher Horner and his wife, for example, were neither baptized nor married in Whickham. They baptized four children there in 1655–62, but neither they nor their children can be traced thereafter.

A third category consists of thirty-three householders whose family reconstitution forms include events before 1665 and later

---

[29] He was described as 'of Newcastle, gent.' in a list of freeholders of 1684: Surtees, *Durham*, ii. 239.

[30] DPD Probate, Invs. of William Newby (1666), John Leash (1666).

than 1666, but contain registration gaps sufficiently large to make it possible that they were absent from the parish in 1666. Richard and Elizabeth Simpson were newcomers to Whickham when they married in 1645. They baptized nine children between 1645 and 1668, but with a four-year registration gap between 1664 and 1668. Mathew and Margaret Blacket were neither baptized nor married in Whickham, but had two children baptized there in 1659 and 1661; thereafter we have no record of them except her burial in 1681. These families may or may not have left Whickham for some years and subsequently returned. John and Isabel Trumble certainly did. Like so many others, they entered registration only with the baptism of a child in March 1664. Another child was baptized in August 1668—a posthumous child for John, who had 'died at Beamis[h]' the month before. Isabel stayed on and was buried in Whickham.

Our fourth and final category consists of four householders whose family reconstitution forms contain events before and after 1665/6 and for whom there is positive evidence that they may have been resident in Whickham during 1666. Robert and Jane Foster baptized children in Whickham in November 1665 and October 1666; they may well have been omitted from the 1666 tax list. Francis and Isabel Purdy baptized children in September 1665 and February 1667; if they were absent in March 1666, it can scarcely have been for long. George and Elizabeth Shafto had a child baptized in January 1666 and George helped appraise an inventory the following August; he was certainly around Whickham. The only possibility that he was not actually dwelling there in 1666 lies in the fact that in his will of 1668 he refers to his 'Aunt Dodds' who was living in his 'messuage' in Whickham. She is identifiable as the Anna Dodds, widowed in 1665, who was listed in 1666. Finally, James Young had a child baptized in Whickham in August 1666; his will and inventory were made in January 1667, and give his place of residence as Whickham (though intriguingly, he was not buried there).[31]

To sum up the results of this analysis, it seems reasonable to argue that, of the 121 'missing' householders, 4 had probably been omitted from the 1666 tax list, for they were very possibly present in Whickham; a further 33 may have been omitted, but may equally

---

[31] DPD Probate, Will of George Shafto (1668), Will and Inv. of James Young (1667).

well have been temporarily absent from the parish; the remaining 84 had probably left the parish between Michaelmas 1665 and Lady Day 1666, for they were certainly not settled inhabitants thereafter.

If this was indeed the case, then the equivalent of at least a quarter of the total number of householders of the parish listed in 1666 had moved out over a six-month period. And they had been replaced. For if we perform a similar exercise on the 240 householders of 1666 who were *not* listed in 1665, we find that, while a substantial number had almost certainly, or very possibly, been present in 1665 and had been omitted from the earlier list, there were many more who were probably newcomers. To be specific, the family reconstitution forms of 42 of the 1666 householders make it virtually certain that they were present in Whickham in 1665, while those of a further 95 contain events before 1665 and after 1666, though no certain evidence of presence in that year. Together, these householders would more than make up the shortfall between the tax lists of 1666 and 1665. At the same time, however, 17 of the 'missing' 1666 householders have family reconstitution forms that included events only after 1666, while a further 86 have no reconstitution forms at all; any, or even all, of these householders may have been new arrivals in Whickham in the spring of 1666.

We might juggle these figures to arrive at a revised total of households for Whickham in 1665/6 and a revised estimate of the social composition of the parish. But to do so would be an exercise in educated guesswork. If anything, it would mean that the total number of households was somewhat larger than is indicated by the 1666 list, and that the proportion of one-hearth and exempted householders was even higher than we have already calculated. The whole point of our findings, however, is that in a parish like Whickham it is impossible to be so precise. Whickham's population was mobile to a degree far exceeding the norms of population mobility in pre-industrial England. Many of the exempted house-holders, in particular those belonging to the industrial work-force, appear to have been essentially transient inhabitants. Yet it seems unlikely that the industrial stoppage of 1665–6 had caused a massive flight of coal-workers from Whickham to the pits of the Wear valley. It may be more significant that the great turnover of householders occurred in the off-season of the coal trade, between the conclusion of one mining and shipping year and the commence-ment of the next. This seasonal layoff, it would seem, was also the time to move on. The fluidity of Whickham's population, like the structure of parish society as presented in the frozen moment of 1666, was doubtless a direct product of the demands of an economy built upon coal.

To conclude, in our analysis of the householders of Whickham in 1666, three prominent features stand out. First, there is the massive growth in the number of Whickham's inhabitants between the ecclesiastical census of 1563 and the hearth tax listing of 1666. Second, the older manorial community of Whickham, itself in the process of dissolution, had been eclipsed by a new industrial population composed of a thin stratum of managerial and supervisory employees and a much greater body of work-people directly engaged in the winning and transportation of coal. Third, Whickham's householders exhibited an extraordinary degree of geographical mobility, with all the consequences that this could bring for both the social structure of the parish and the social identities of its inhabitants. For many of those who lived by the working of coal, their community, and the locus of their social bonds, may have been not any single parish or manor, but rather the entire coalfield and the industrial society that had developed upon it in the three generations before 1666.

2. 'SERVANTS AND WORKMEN', 1580–1660

The prodigious increase in the number of recorded households that accompanied the first century of industrial development in Whickham was not an isolated phenomenon. In the parishes of northern County Durham the number of households increased by 137.7 per cent between 1563 and 1674, as compared with a figure of only 71.4 per cent for the county as a whole.[32] This leaves no room for doubt that the demographic growth centres of County Durham in this period were those Tyneside and Wearside parishes known to have been the principal centres of mining operations—notably, Whickham, Gateshead, Ryton, and Chester-le-Street—supplemented by the river-mouth parishes, which thrived on the coal trade.[33] Even among Durham's mining parishes, however, Whickham's growth was outstanding. The number of households in

---

[32] Hodgson, 'Demographic Trends', 29.
[33] Ibid. 21 (Table II), 27.

Ryton and Gateshead more than doubled; in Chester-le-Street growth was in the order of 20 per cent; but in Whickham the number of householders in 1666 represented at least a four-fold increase on the total of 1563.[34]

The precise chronology of Whickham's population growth is much more difficult to establish. The manorial rentals that survive from the turn of the sixteenth century deal with the manor of Whickham only, as distinct from the parish as a whole. Even within that restricted area, they provide evidence of the numbers of manorial tenants rather than the entire population.

From 1620–1, however, comes some indication of the scale of growth up to that date in the form of statements made in the course of the litigation between the copyholders of Whickham and the Grand Lessees. In April 1620 the bishop of Durham's attorney, Robert Cooper, claimed that the manor of Whickham was 'very populous', the inhabitants numbering 'above one thousand men women and children'.[35] His witnesses, unfortunately, were far from consistent in their estimates when they gave evidence over a year later. Nicholas Arnold put the number of copyholders at more than sixty, which was near enough correct, but estimated the town's inhabitants at only 'about 100 and a halfe of people'. Cuthbert Reaslie suggested '100 christned people', as did John Turner. George Watson reckoned 'there are 200 men women and children inhabiting within ye towne'. John Leash put it at 'above 500 in men women and children', while John Dover (a former parish clerk and a Grand Lease agent) came close to Cooper with his estimate of 'a thousand persons that are inhabitants within the said towne'.[36] Clearly, no formal count had taken place. The witnesses, like Cooper himself, were seizing on round numbers which, in the context of complaints over the destruction of Whickham's fresh-water supplies, were generally meant to indicate 'a lot'. There is uncertainty as to whether some may have thought in terms of householders rather than total population. Again, some may have been thinking strictly of the settlement of Whickham town while others may have meant to include the manorial lands as a whole.

---

[34] Ibid. 21 (Table II). Hodgson, in fact, underestimates Whickham's growth by employing the 1674 hearth tax. For a detailed discussion of Chester-le-Street, see C. Issa, 'Obligation and Choice: Aspects of Family and Kinship in Seventeenth-Century County Durham', Ph.D. thesis (St Andrews, 1987), 44.

[35] PRO DURH 2/20/69.   [36] PRO DURH 7/19, pt. I.

Nevertheless, it would not be implausible to think in terms of a parish population as high as 1,000 or more by 1620, the greater part of it concentrated within the manor of Whickham. The growth of Whickham's population was clearly linked to the growth of the coal industry. Coal output had probably doubled between the 1570s and 1600, and thereafter we know that mining operations expanded rapidly in the 1610s. If the 93 householders of 1563 represented a total population of perhaps 400 or so, then a population of around 1,000 in 1620 seems entirely reasonable.[37]

Our inclination to accept the general plausibility of the highest estimates made in 1620–1 is further supported by consideration of the next source of information on Whickham's population: the Protestation return of 1642. In Feburary 1641/2 a total of 773 male inhabitants of Whickham parish, 'both Householders and others, being of Eighteen Years of Age and upwards', presented themselves and duly swore to maintain and defend 'the true, reformed, Protestant Religion', 'the Power and Privilege of Parliament', and 'the lawful Rights and Liberties of the Subjects'. A further nine men, most of them known Roman Catholics, were listed as having failed to take the oath.[38] In a 'normal' English parish at this date, according to the estimates of Wrigley and Schofield, such adult men might be expected to comprise some 36 per cent of the total population.[39] Given Whickham's listed adult male population of 782, the total population of the parish may have been in the order of 2,200 at this date!

Such an estimate seems startlingly high when we consider that on conventional assumptions the 367 households listed in 1666 suggests a total population of around 1,600.[40] It is not beyond the realms of possibility that Whickham's population had peaked on the eve of the Civil War and fallen back thereafter. Coal production in Whickham reached its seventeenth-century pinnacle in the mid-1630s, after which it dropped somewhat, was dislocated during the war years, and resumed at a lower level thereafter. However, even if

---

[37] Using the multiplier 4.3 to convert households into total population, as suggested by T. Arkell, 'Multiplying Factors for Estimating Population Totals from the Hearth Tax', *Local Population Studies*, 28 (1982).

[38] H. M. Wood (ed.), *Durham Protestations*, Surtees Soc. no. 135 (Durham, 1922), 2, 47–53.

[39] Wrigley and Schofield, *Population History of England*, app. 3, data for 1641. We assume in the following calculation a sex ratio of 100 for the population over 18 yrs. old.   [40] See n. 37 above.

some loss of population did take place after 1642, there is further reason to suppose that a population estimate of 2,200 at that date is unrealistically high. Our calculation is based upon the assumption that Whickham was a 'normal' parish in its age and sex structure; yet, clearly, Whickham was nothing if not abnormal in its economic structure. It is perfectly possible, indeed probable, that the parish contained disproportionately large numbers of able-bodied young men, many of them unmarried and living in lodgings or in cottages erected by the coal-owners.[41] This supposition derives much support from the fact that, of the 782 men listed in 1642, no fewer than 273 (34.9 per cent) could not be identified in the reconstitution study either as heads of families or as unmarried children of reconstituted families—a far larger proportion than the group of unmarried male servants that one would expect to find in a 'normal' English parish.[42]

Given such realities, the conventional means of transforming the Protestation return of 1642 into a total population estimate are simply inapplicable in the case of Whickham. Moreover, the possibility that Whickham included a substantial number of young men dwelling as lodgers or living in non-familial situations raises the further question of the applicability of the multipliers conventionally used to transform totals of householders into overall population totals in the parishes of 'pre-industrial' England. Whickham was not a 'pre-industrial' parish: it was an industrial parish in a 'pre-industrial' age. We cannot state with any confidence what the total population of the parish may have been in either 1642 or 1666; what we can say is that the population of Whickham had risen dramatically since 1563, its growth far outstripping both local and national norms. By the central decades of the seventeenth century, both the Protestation and the hearth-tax returns indicate that Whickham was the most densely populated rural parish in

[41] A similar conclusion was arrived at independently by D. A. Kirby in 'Population Density and Land Values in County Durham during the Mid-Seventeenth Century', *Trans. Institute of British Geographers*, 57 (1972), 90–1. Kirby's figures differ from ours by reason of his different assumptions concerning the multiplier for households and the proportion of the population aged over 18, and his employment of the 1666 hearth tax listing without correction. The essential point, however, remains the same.

[42] In Laslett's sample of 100 parish listings 1574–1821, servants (male and female) made up 13.4% of the population. The sex ratio of servants was 106.6: P. Laslett, 'Mean Household Size in England since the Sixteenth Century', in P. Laslett and R. Wall (eds.), *Household and Family in Past Time* (Cambridge, 1972), 152.

County Durham.[43] Moreover, we can add that Whickham's population growth, whatever its precise magnitude, had owed comparatively little to natural increase. This issue can be approached in the first instance by considering the results of the family reconstitution study of Whickham for the first half of the seventeenth century.[44]

Whickham presents peculiar problems for demographic analysis by family reconstitution. These arise not so much from deficiencies in the parish registers of Whickham (though there are occasional gaps in the record) as from the historical fact that the population of the parish was so highly mobile. As a result, many of the family reconstitution forms generated in the course of the analysis of Whickham's population are seriously incomplete, and the 'reconstitutable minority' of families that forms the usable sample for some crucial calculations is much smaller than would normally be expected in a parish of this size. Undoubtedly, the results are biased towards the experience of the more stable, settled families within the parish. This is the case in all family reconstitution studies. It does not usually mean that these stable families are unrepresentative of the demographic realities of the population as a whole; but in the specific case of Whickham, it presents the likelihood that all calculations requiring both the date of baptism of an individual and long-term residence thereafter are likely to be based disproportionately upon the family histories of the landholding section of the population.

Our examination of the family reconstitution forms of the householders of 1666 would suggest that this was so. The experience of other groups within the population is certainly not excluded, and looms large in the figures for infant and child mortality. But in other respects it is in all probability masked. With these reservations, the results of the study are presented in Table 3.3, where they are compared with the figures calculated from reconstitutions of twelve other English parishes held by the

[43] Kirby, 'Population Density', 89.
[44] Family reconstitution based on DRO EP/Wh 1–3, 7, Whickham Parish Registers 1576–1773. A microfilm of the registers is available at the DRO and a transcript is at Newcastle-upon-Tyne Central Library. The commencement of the registers in the late 1570s means that no reconstitution results can be given pre-1600, since essential data are lacking on many family reconstitution forms for couples married in the late 16th c.

TABLE 3.3. *Family Reconstitution Results, 1600–1649*

	Whickham	Cambridge Twelve
Mean age at first marriage		
Men	27.5 (90)[a]	28.0
Women	25.5 (80)[a]	26.0
Age-specific fertility rates		
(per 1,000 woman-years lived)		
20–24	368	384
25–29	331	346
30–34	265	303
35–39	277	245
40–44	267	127
Cumulative 20–44	7.54	7.03
Infant and child mortality (MF)[b]		
0–1	169	137
1–4	112	87
5–9	42	37
0–9	293	241
Adult mortality		
(life expectation at age 30)		
Men	25.5	29.8
Women	29.1	29.6

[a] Numbers are in parentheses.
[b] MF = male and female.

Cambridge Group for the History of Population and Social Structure.[45]

In considering the first two sections of this table, the most striking feature is the close similarity of the Whickham figures to those of the Cambridge Twelve. Both men and women married somewhat earlier on average in Whickham, but the difference was miniscule. Clearly, the availability of industrial employment or by-employment had no significant effect on the age at first marriage in Whickham—at least, not for that section of the population most

[45] Figures presented in Wrigley and Schofield, *Population History of England*, 248–57.

prominently represented in these figures. As regards age-specific marital fertility, Whickham women proved somewhat less fertile in the earlier age groups considered, but distinctly more fertile in the later age groups. The overall outcome was that slightly more children were born in completed families in Whickham than in the Cambridge Twelve parishes.

The relevant demographic evidence therefore, indicates that the reproductive experience of the settled core of Whickham's population did not differ significantly from the English norm. The remaining two sets of figures relating to mortality, however, tell another story. Infant and child mortality was high in Whickham, and adult mortality also showed a distinctive pattern. The life expectation of women at age thirty was only marginally lower than that of women in the Cambridge Twelve parishes, but male life expectation in Whickham was distinctly lower than the English norm: a sex-specificity in mortality that was entirely absent in the Cambridge Twelve parishes. Clearly, the material environment in Whickham was highly deleterious to the health of the inhabitants of the parish—sufficiently so, it would seem, to cancel out the slight demographic advantage that the parishioners derived from their lower mean age at first marriage and higher marital fertility.

The suggestions contained within the figures produced by the sophisticated technique of family reconstitution can be elaborated and confirmed by consideration of the crude totals of vital events recorded in the parish registers of Whickham. These figures have the advantages of enabling us to extend the discussion back to the final decades of the sixteenth century, and of including events relating to all persons who married, baptized children, died, and found burial in Whickham. They provide chronological perspective and can be said to reflect more adequately the overall experience of the inhabitants.

Four notable features emerge from our consideration of these figures. First, between the 1580s and the first decade of the seventeenth century, the annual average of marriages celebrated in Whickham doubled—much as might be expected in a population undergoing rapid growth. Thereafter, however, it remained fairly stable through to the 1670s. Since we have every reason to believe that the population continued to grow rapidly in the early seventeenth century, the implication is that nuptiality levels in Whickham's new population were low. Secondly, the annual average of baptisms in the parish shows a similar trend—a doubling over the first three decades from 1580 and relative stabilization thereafter. The suggestion of these figures is that, within Whickham's total population growth, child-bearing couples formed only a limited proportion of the overall total. Thirdly, during the period 1577–1606, burials in Whickham significantly outnumbered baptisms, while in the succeeding decades the baptismal surplus over burials was small. For the whole period 1577–1659, there were 5,350 children baptized in Whickham to offset 5,264 burials.

Finally, examination of the sex ratio of burials in the parish reveals that, whereas in the decades 1580–1609 it was close to the 'normal' level of a little over 100 male for every 100 female burials, thereafter it became chronically unbalanced. In the three decades 1610–39 the sex ratio at burial leapt to 142, 140, and 135, before plummeting to 100 in the 1640s, shooting up again to 149 in the 1650s, and then returning to normal levels of 100–14 for the remaining decades before 1690. These figures provide conclusive proof of the predominance of men in Whickham's population during much of the early seventeenth century.

Drawing together the implications of these findings, it would appear that, whatever the fertility of the more stable core of Whickham families represented in the family reconstitution study, nuptiality levels among Whickham's enhanced population were surprisingly low and mortality levels were disastrously high. The overall result was that in terms of natural increase the population of Whickham could scarcely replace itself in the long term. In order both to replace losses and to grow as it did, Whickham needed a constant flow of immigrants, most of whom were clearly men. Some of these newcomers subsequently married in the parish; some came already married and bore children there. A substantial number seem neither to have married nor to have remained permanently in Whickham, except when they died and were buried there. To this extent, the recoverable demographic experience of Whickham is less reminiscent of the rural parishes of early modern England, be they agricultural or 'proto-industrial', than of the growing cities of the period, those 'devourers of mankind'.[46]

---

[46] For the principal features of urban demography, see Clark and Slack, *English Towns in Transition*, ch. 6. The demographic experience of London is explored in detail in R. Finlay, *Population and Metropolis: The Demography of London 1580–1650* (Cambridge, 1981), and summarized in Finlay and Shearer, 'Population Growth and Suburban Expansion', 46–51.

Migration to Whickham may well have come in a series of waves, the most prominent of which, to judge by the sharp rise in the numbers of events recorded in the parish registers, and the chronically unbalanced sex ratios thereafter, probably occurred in the first and second decades of the reign of James I. But it was a continuing process. An analysis of the surnames recorded in Whickham's baptismal registers from 1577 to 1758 found that in the period 1603–28 some 58.5 per cent of all surnames were new to the parish—a striking confirmation of the nature of the Jacobean surge of population. In the succeeding period 1629–54, the process continued. Of all surnames recorded during those years, 50.4 per cent were new to Whickham, 43 per cent were found also in the period 1603–28, and only 6.6 per cent could be found in Whickham before 1603. Calculation of the 'coefficient of relationship by isonymy' (a measurement of the degree of genetic relationship among parishioners as indicated by surnames) revealed that the years 1603–54 witnessed the greatest drop in genetic relationship to be found within the entire period 1577–1758.[47]

The authors of the above study were concerned with genetics rather than with economic and social history. Their selection of Whickham for analysis was fortuitous. Lacking detailed knowledge of the economic history of the parish, they regarded the movement that they discovered in Whickham's population as having predated the 'industrial revolution' by some seventy-five years. In fact, as we now know, it coincided, like the transformation of Whickham's sex ratio at burial, with the most intensive period of exploitation of the Grand Lease and the surrounding collieries in Whickham. Substantial immigration and continuous population mobility were intimately connected with the industrialization of the parish and in particular with the structure of employment in the coal industry.

Coal mining is conventionally distinguished from most other industries in early modern England not only by the fact that it involved substantial capital investment, but also by the associated fact that it demanded a large and geographically concentrated labour force. There were the sinkers who opened new shafts, the hewers who drove the headways and cut the coal, the putters who dragged

---

[47] G. W. Lasker and D. F. Roberts, 'Secular Trends in Relationship as Estimated by Surnames: A Study of a Tyneside Parish', *Annals of Human Biology*, 9 (1982), 301, 305.

full corves of coal to the eye of the pit, the fillers who attached the corves to the ropes, the banksmen who unloaded and checked them at the surface, the horse drivers who saw to the powering of winding-gear and pumps, and the overmen who supervised the entire operation.

As early as 1607, we know of one pit in Ridingfield which 'usuallie' employed fourteen named men and an unspecified number of unnamed others.[48] At an Allerdeans pit in 1617, twenty men were employed on drainage operations alone, to say nothing of the overman, hewers, putters, and the rest.[49] If the average number employed per pit in the actual winning of coal was around twenty—which was typical of Whickham pits working in the early eighteenth century—then when Whickham had four pits operating in the later 1570s there was work for some eighty men and youths; with fifteen pits, three hundred would be needed; with thirty pits, six hundred; and so forth. We cannot know exactly how many pits were working in Whickham at any given time, but in 1621 there were sixteen 'going' within the manor of Whickham alone, and there were probably almost as many again in other parts of the parish.[50]

These estimates provide some idea of the scale of the work-force needed for the winning of coal. In addition, there were the wealers or wailers, who screened the coal at the pithead (the only task usually given to women in the northern coalfield); the labourers who shovelled coal; the wainmen who led it to the river; the staithemen and their labourers who transferred it to the keels, and the keelmen who rowed it to the collier ships. Finally, each working pit drew on the services of corvers to weave its corves, chandlers to supply its tallow candles, smiths to sharpen tools, carpenters and

---

[48] PRO STAC 8/53/10.

[49] PRO STAC 8/245/6. Double shifts could also be worked, which would increase the number of men employed per unit. At least one Grand Lease pit was working 'two shifts (that is to say) night and day' in 1662: PRO DURH 4/2, 130–1.

[50] PRO DURH 7/19, pt. I. Nef, ii. 137–8, suggests that the average output per miner (by which he appears to mean not only hewers but all those engaged in winning coal) was *c*.200 tons. If so, then some 100 miners may have been employed in Whickham in the 1570s (output *c*.20,000 tons), 200 in the early 1590s (output *c*.40,000 tons), and 725 in 1636 (output *c*.145,000 tons). The last of these figures certainly seems excessive given an adult male population of 773 in 1642, yet on the other hand not all miners were adults, and in addition it is likely that some of Whickham's work-force came in daily from adjacent parishes. All such estimates are inevitably highly speculative; nevertheless, they provide an indication of the range of possibility.

wrights to line shafts and maintain wooden plant, and in some instances masons to wall parts of the workings.

Some of these tasks would be performed by independent craftsmen working for any pit that required their services—like Robert Lawson, a chandler, who in 1630 had so much demand for his candles from Whickham pits that he had severe difficulties in obtaining sufficient supplies of tallow from local butchers.[51] The greater part of the mining work-force, however, tended to be described as the 'servants and workmen' of a particular owner.[52] This conventional terminology expressed an important distinction among them; for in context it is clear that the term 'servant' usually implied an overman, while the term 'workmen' was applied to the pitmen who laboured under his supervision. In 1618, for example, an overman at the Liddells' colliery in the Allerdeans was described as 'a principall servant and director of the said workes'. A year later a group of miners working in a pit of Sherwood and partners excused themselves from culpability in a dispute over their workings by pleading 'that they have bin onlie workemen paid to worck in the pitts . . . for their wages'.[53]

How much occupational differentiation was observed among the underground workmen is uncertain. There may have been a life-cycle progression from putter to hewer and back again, as was later to be the case. Youths may have learned their mining skills by acting as putters for their fathers. On 30 November 1632, for example, the parish register notes the burial of Thomas Surrett and his son James, both 'Slaine in a pitt in Jacks Leazes'. James's baptism was the first evidence of the Surretts' presence in Whickham. He was fourteen when he died. For the most part, however, we have no direct evidence of how work was conducted underground. The records provide only occasional glimpses of the pitmen at work. We can see with the mind's eye the men of another pit in Jacks Leazes, ten years before the Surretts died, who, being 'called up' by their overmen from their work-place 'many fathoms downe under the ground', came up the rope to the surface with their 'hackes' in their hands. We can hear in the imagination 'the noyse of the stoakes' which

[51] PRO DURH 2/32/43.
[52] e.g. PRO STAC 8/53/10, 8/163/18; DURH 2/27/73; E 134 29 Eliz. Ea. 4, 14 Car. I Mich. 29.
[53] PRO STAC 8/245/6; DURH 2/7/99.

alerted a group of Grand Lease workmen to the encroachment of rival hewers.[54] But the rest is silence.

Whatever the division of labour underground, that between 'servant' and 'workman' was vital to the structure of the Elizabethan and early Stuart industry. In the Whickham collieries the general managerial role of the colliery 'viewer' does not appear to have emerged before the late seventeenth century. The only example we have of such a figure is Thomas Surtees, 'a gentleman expert and skilfull in Mineralls', who directed the Grand Lease workings during the 1610s and constructed the drainage system which brought the waterlogged Haugh and Leigh pits into production.[55] In the general absence of such officials, the crucial link between the coal-owners and the mining work-force in early seventeenth-century Whickham was the contracting overman.

Overmen were experienced miners who contracted with a coal-owner to work a specific pit or pits for a season in return for an agreed sum of money per ten of coal wrought. They generally put in a conditional bond with financial penalties to guarantee performance of their agreement, accounted weekly for the coal produced, and were paid accordingly. In return, each overman was to work his pit 'at his own charge', without troubling the owners further.[56] To quote a particularly detailed example of such an agreement, William Emmison and Arthur Robinson contracted with Henry Liddell in 1623 to undertake 'the workeing and sinkeinge of the said pitt or pitts . . . and the winninge and getting of coles . . . and the payment of all workmen dealinge in and about the same' for a specified sum per ten. All costs were to be 'att there owne chardge', and the contract specifically stated that Liddell was not 'to be trobled with the providinge of sinckers hewers or any such like workmen'.[57]

The recruitment and payment of the labour force, therefore, was a matter delegated to the overmen. That the workmen were regarded as their responsibility is graphically illustrated by the fact

[54] Burial Register 30 Nov. 1632; PRO STAC 8/163/18; PRO DURH 4/2, 130–1. Langton observes that Lancashire patterns of work varied greatly and underground workers did not usually perform a single task only. At Haigh, however, hewers (all of them men) confined themselves to hewing, while women dragged the sleds of coal: Langton, *Geographical Change*, 68–9.

[55] PRO STAC 8/245/6. Cf. Nef, i. 417. Surtees was certainly a forerunner of such men as John Buddle, the great viewer of the early 19th-c. coalfield, and like Buddle he made his fortune. He was, however, an exceptional figure.

[56] e.g. PRO STAC 8/53/10, 8/163/18.   [57] PRO DURH 2/27/73.

that, when a working pitman was killed in Whickham, the name of the overman in charge of the pit was generally entered in the parish register alongside the registration of burial. However, while the overmen were bound to their masters by rigorous legal instruments to work their pits for an agreed season, their relationships with their workmen appear to have been far more casual. When Thomas Wakefield took over the working of a pit in 1607 he was approached by a group of former workmen there 'with their worke loumes or worke geare' who 'did entreat [him] that they might be sett on worke'. He took them on, but the nature of his relationship with them is perhaps reflected in the fact that shortly afterwards he confessed himself unable to remember the names of more than four of them.[58] Another hiring occurred when Robert Crawforth approached Archibald Gibson, a chandler who supplied him with candles for his pits, and asked him to 'let him have' his son and his servant to work 'in drawing of water'. Gibson agreed on condition that the youths were paid 'such wages . . . for there worke as was given to other laborers then in that kinde', and in the event they worked at the pits for four months.[59] When John Hedworth and Michael Hall fell out with the owner of the pits they operated over the terms of their agreement, some of their 'workfolkes' abruptly left them, unwilling to be involved. They quickly took on others without any apparent difficulty.[60]

These are rare glimpses of the actual process of hiring men and boys in the early seventeenth century. Wages were clearly agreed beforehand in at least one case. But for the rest, there is no hint of either the terms and conditions or the fixed period of hiring which were to be central features of the miners' hiring bond of the eighteenth century. The workmen of the early seventeenth century seem to have come and gone almost casually, their names scarcely remembered by the men who hired them, directed their work, and paid them.

The very casualness of hiring, and the lack of restrictions imposed upon the men hired, suggests that labour was readily available. It had not always been in such ready supply. In the demographic conditions of the late fourteenth century, the Bishop of Durham had found it necessary to authorize the seizure of workmen and coal-bearers within the liberty of Durham to supply the labour

[58] PRO STAC 8/53/10.   [59] PRO DURH 2/17/123 (1617).
[60] PRO STAC 8/163/18 (1623).

needs of the mines of Whickham and Gateshead.[61] Two centuries later, around the time of the granting of the Grand Lease, there is evidence of a local shortage of labour from nearby Winlaton. Pits were laid in 'for lack of workmen'. Women were employed, and there was talk of sending to Scotland for men.[62] Thereafter, however, there are few hints of more than temporary difficulty in recruiting labour. There was no need to bind miners to their masters for life in the manner adopted in Scotland.[63] Nor were women employed in the Tyneside mines, in contrast to the practice in other coalfields.[64]

If both 'servants' and 'workmen' were available to the coal-owners, however, their origins are largely obscure. Doubtless there was a local pool of skilled labour within Whickham which could be drawn upon in the initial expansion under the Grand Lease. We have seen that six of fifteen early overmen whose names are known were sons of Whickham copyholder families.[65] Again, of ten coal workers required to give evidence in church court cases in 1586–9, eight declared that they had known the Whickham people involved in these cases for between sixteen and twenty-five years. In most instances, that meant from childhood or adolescence.[66] Very soon, however, the labour requirements of the pits must have outgrown what could easily be supplied by those of Whickham's people who were familiar with colliery work. Some local men were clearly promoted overman—or promoted themselves, as when Thomas Gamesby approached Mathew George of Hollinside and paid him 40s. to put in a good word for him with the owners as George's successor as overman.[67] But others, both overmen and workmen, needed to be drawn from further afield.

It has been suggested that many of these recruits came from

---

[61] Page (ed.), *Victoria County History, Durham*, ii. 322. This was in 1373–4.

[62] PRO E 134 29 Eliz. Ea. 4. It is not clear whether men actually were recruited from Scotland.

[63] T. C. Smout, *A History of the Scottish People, 1560–1830* (Glasgow, 1969), 168–70.

[64] Nef, ii. 167, found no reference to the employment of women underground in the northern coalfield other than the Winlaton case cited above. It is clear even in the Winlaton evidence that this expedient was regarded as unusual and undesirable. Women were, however, employed underground in Lancashire and elsewhere: Langton, *Geographical Change*, 69.   [65] See p. 97 above.

[66] DPD DR v/3, fos. 54, 54ᵛ, 122–123ᵛ; DR v/5, fos. 76, 78.

[67] PRO DURH 2/6/31. On this occasion (late 16th c., undated) Gamesby's ploy failed, but he was later to become a prominent Whickham overman.

Scotland and the border dales, on the basis of the Winlaton case and subsequent statements that many Scots and borderers were employed in the Tyneside industry and represented a security risk at the time of the Bishops' Wars and the later hostilities between the Commonwealth and Scotland.[68] That there were many Scots on Tyneside was undoubtedly true. They were particularly associated with seasonal work as keelmen, and were long to remain so.[69] Some may also have come to find work in the mines. The parish registers of Whickham have their complement of distinctively Scottish names, and a number of known miners have names that may betray their origins: Andrew Leslie, John Lindsay, William Wallace, Edward Maxwell, William and Robert Dagleish. There are border surnames too: Armstrong, Graham, Nixon, and Robson. Of course, many families of border or Scottish origin may have been on Tyneside for generations, but it is a reasonable assumption that many more were attracted by the opportunities afforded by the boom conditions in the coal industry.

The bulk of Whickham's work-force, however, appears to have been recruited locally. Most of the surnames recorded in Whickham's parish register are English and often of distinctly North Country provenance. Identifiable coal-workers were called Atkinson, Bainbridge, Cleugh, Dobson, Emerson, Foster, Harrison, Liddell, Milburn, Richardson, Stephenson, and Wilkinson, to list but a few distinctive regional surnames. A survey of the whole range of references to the connections of Whickham people with other settlements in the century from 1560 reveals that the 'social area' of the parishioners was focused on Newcastle, Gateshead, and the parishes of north-west Durham, but also extended south-westwards to Weardale, south-eastward to the lower Wear valley and beyond, and northwards to include parts of south Northumberland adjacent to the Tyne.

It is within this broad region, among a population many of whom may have had some acquaintance with coal work at small land-scale collieries, that we must look for the origins of Whickham's migrant population. Thomas Wakefield, we know, came from Pelton, where his father held some land.[70] Ralph Gibson, working in Whickham in

[68] Nef, i. 148; *CSPD, 1640*, 81–2; *CSPD, 1650*, 299.
[69] J. M. Fewster, 'The Keelmen of Tyneside in the Eighteenth Century, Part I', *Durham University Journal*, N.S. 19 (1957), 27–8.
[70] PRO DURH 2/64/106.

1592, came from Wolsingham, probably brought in by his employer Cuthbert Pearson who had 'two or three cole pitts at Whickham and two pits at Wolsingham'. He was 'commonly evill thought of' in his parish of origin, remembered as 'of bad and noughty behavor' and 'reported runne way for theft'. He was only nineteen.[71] Other workmen in the Whickham collieries are known to have come from Birtley, Eighton, Gainford, Blaydon, Hartlepool, and Newcastle.

In all likelihood Whickham, in common with the other coal-mining parishes of the county, attracted the surplus population of both upland and lowland Durham. Migrants from Northumberland must have come too, either directly, or via Newcastle and the mining parishes on the north bank of the Tyne across the river from Whickham. Population was apparently buoyant in the palatinate as a whole, and yet the baptismal surpluses of parishes outside the coalfield do not seem to have been translated into localized population growth of the kind that might have been anticipated. Sedgefield's population grew by only 30 per cent between 1563 and 1666. The vast upland parish of Stanhope-in-Weardale actually saw a 25 per cent decline in households in 1563–1674 despite the baptismal surplus evident in the registers.[72] It seems probable that the disproportionate population growth of the mining parishes, and of Whickham above all, drew upon the surplus young people of such parishes and upon those commoners in the uplands who saw a better living elsewhere.[73]

Migrants may have been attracted by the prospect of good wages, but it is exceedingly difficult to establish whether or not such expectations were justified. In 1603 the hostmen of Newcastle were accused of *cutting* the wages of 'poore Collyers', a charge that they vigorously rejected, maintaining that 'as concerninge the wages of suche poore Laborers as Doe Woorke in the Coale Mynes, . . . theire wages are not abridged but inlarged'. Seven years later, they once more maintained that the need to expand operations rapidly and to work deeper since 1609 meant that the miners had 'had their wages much increased, a fowerth pennye at the least'.[74]

What those wages were, however, and how they compared with those of agricultural labourers or the wage-workers of Newcastle,

[71] DPD DR v/3, fos. 157ᵛ, 159, DR v/5, fo. 61ᵛ.
[72] Issa, 'Obligation and Choice', 66, 85.
[73] Hodgson, 'Demographic Trends', 32 suggests that migration to the coalfield was largely local and regional.   [74] Dendy, *Hostmen*, 19–20, 22, 58.

are matters almost entirely hidden from us in the available sources. One overman in 1610, who was in the apparently unusual position of being paid a fixed wage by his masters, got 'for his fee every weeke five shillings'.[75] That was not a princely living by any standards, but it is roughly comparable to the £4. 6s. 8d. a year plus meat and drink which the Durham justices of the 1670s regarded as the proper wage for 'a bayliffe in husbandry . . . called an overman that is hired with a Gentleman or such yeoman that doth not labour himselfe, but putteth his whole Charge to his servant'.[76] Overmen paid by the ten might make much more (though they could also lose out badly if their charges in winning coal proved excessive); but most pitmen were not overmen and never would be. What they earned at this date we simply do not know. We do not even know whether they were paid piece-rates or by the day, or both (according to task), as was later the case. The wages of 'common labourers' in County Durham were assessed in the 1670s at 6d. a day in winter, 7d. a day in spring, and 8d. a day in summer, all without meat and drink.[77] It is doubtful whether miners in Whickham in the early seventeenth century earned any more than the highest of those rates. Had they done so, they would have been on a par with our salaried overman.[78]

The one clear fact is that throughout the area the colliery work-force was regarded by contemporaries as poor, in the broad usage of that term. There is no hint of the status of labour aristocrat that was attributed to miners from the eighteenth century. In 1595, on the eve of the great dearth of the 1590s, they were described as 'those pore men who worke the colles under the grounde', and said to be scarcely able to 'sustaine their lives' on their wages. In 1603 they were 'the poore labourers', and in 1666 'pore workpeople'. The migrants recruited for the pits of Chester-le-Street in 1619–22 were called 'the incoming poor'. William Dodds was described in 1624 as

---

[75] PRO DURH 7/8, deposition of Mathew George.

[76] DRO Q/R/W 1–6 (Wage-rate assessments 1672–9). Meat and drink allowances were generally assessed at 4d. a day. If an agricultural 'overman' was fed for the entire year, his wage in cash and kind would be the equivalent of £10. 8s. 4d. The colliery overman in this case would have had to work a 46-week season to earn the same. Such a rough comparison, of course, makes no allowance for price differentials between the 1610s and the 1670s.   [77] DRO Q/R/W 1–6, *passim*.

[78] Nef also found information on wages frustratingly thin. He regarded it as unlikely that 17th-c. colliers were significantly better paid than other labouring people—in marked contrast to the situation obtaining in the 18th and 19th c.; Nef, i. 182; ii. 195–6.

'a poor labouring man and worketh at the cole pits and hath nothing to live on but that he doth earn by dailie labour'. George Carmichael was 'a poor man . . . and for such a one commonlie reputed where he dwells . . . being a poor collier'.[79]

Many of those who migrated to the coalfield in the late sixteenth and early seventeenth centuries may have done so less in expectation of betterment than as 'subsistence migrants', in search of a living of any kind. If they had no settled place in agrarian society, the north-east offered them few alternatives, for, as a report of 1605 put it, 'in the countyes of Durham and Northumberland there be no great trades as clothing and suchlike used by which the poorer sort are sett on worke and relieved from begary, saving only the trades of colyery and salting'.[80]

To the young, male migrants the trade of 'colyery' offered not only wages but also lodging, at least temporarily. The provision of shelter in the form of, at the least, the temporary erections described as 'lodges' or 'hovels' was part of the starting costs of any colliery. In 1597 three of the Grand Lessees erected 'certain newe cottages' near the Blackburn and placed in them coal-workers described in a complaint as 'ill disposed persons alyens and forinners'.[81] In 1609 the lease of Axwell Houses colliery empowered the lessee 'to build and erect howses lodges or hovells in and upon the premises'.[82] At Jacks Leazes in 1622 the works around the four pits included 'lodges' and 'houses'.[83] A year earlier, the taking of liberty by the Grand Lessees to erect 'dyvers houses for there workmen' on the manorial territories was one of the grievances raised by the copyholders of Whickham.[84] But although the copyholders were disposed to make an issue of this in 1621, there is every reason to think that they themselves (or some of them) had benefited from the opportunity to erect and let cottages or to hive off patches of land for that purpose, thus facilitating the growth of the cottage holdings

[79] BL Harleian MS 6850, no. 39; Welbourne, *The Miner's Unions of Northumberland and Durham* (Cambridge, 1923), 4; Issa, 'Obligation and Choice', 56; DPD DR v/11, 15 Jul. 1624, DR v/12, 12 Mar. 1629/30.

[80] Quoted in Brassley, 'Northumberland and Durham', 57.

[81] PRO DURH 2/1/52.   [82] PRO DURH 2/11/76.

[83] PRO STAC 8/163/18. The temporary nature of colliery housing is indicated not only by the frequent use of such terms as 'lodges' and 'hovels', but also by an order of Durham quarter sessions in 1620 that cottages erected for coal-workers in an unnamed township were only to 'continue so long as the tennte within the same houses shall continue in the said cole work': DRO Q/S OB 1, 99.

[84] PRO DURH 7/19, pt. i, testimony of John Turner and Cuthbert Reaslie.

subsequently described as the 'smalls' in the manorial rentals. It was the same story in Chester-le-Street, where no formal restriction was imposed upon the subdivision or subletting of holdings, despite periodic complaints by the manorial jury against the activities of tenants 'who have cottages to let and doe take in undertenants', or who 'doe entertaine into their houses tenants and undersettlers'.[85]

It is in any case doubtful whether the copyholders could have inhibited the mushroom growth of lodges, hovels, and cottages on the manorial waste; for some of the incoming coal-workers themselves appear to have taken the initiative in erecting dwellings, and the lords of the manor can hardly have been disposed to prevent them. Despite his personal grievance against the Grand Lessees, John Hindmers admitted in 1621 that 'there are manie litle howses built . . . but whether these defendants or there workmen did build them he cannot depose'.[86] There were presentments of encroachments on the waste in the Halmote Court of 1635, some of them explicitly involving dwellings, and these were doubtless some of the 'diverse and severall Intacks houses and lodges taken of and builded on the comon and waists of this Mannor' remarked upon by the surveyors of 1647.[87] After 1635, however, no notice was taken of these encroachments by the Halmote jury until the later 1650s, when a brief period of regular presentment ensued. The jurors may have determined then to tax, by periodic fines, a process that they could do nothing to arrest.[88]

With the proliferation of cottages, lodges, and hovels, by the mid-seventeenth century Whickham had taken on not only the physical aspect described by the parliamentary surveyors of 1647 and 1652, but also the pattern of settlement implied by the hearth-tax listing of 1666. The face of the parish was pockmarked with pits and thickly littered with the cabins of those whose living depended on them. Yet, although the landscape created by their coming endured, the

---

[85] Issa, 'Obligation and Choice', 57–61. A similar proliferation of cottages also took place in Ryton, Winlaton, and Gateshead parishes: R. Hodgson, 'Agricultural Improvement and Changing Regional Economies in the Eighteenth Century', in A. R. H. Baker and J. B. Harley (eds.), *Man Made The Land: Essays in English Historical Geography* (Newton Abbot, Devon, 1973), 148.

[86] PRO DURH 7/19, pt. I, testimony of John Hindmers.

[87] DPD DDR HC III F 19, fo. 25 ff.; Kirby, *Parliamentary Surveys*, 84.

[88] DPD DDR HC III F 19, fos. 84, 97, 111, 122, 129, 145, 169; DDR HC III F 20, fos. 25–41. Our earlier discussion of shifts in the sex ratio at burial suggests that the 1650s saw a new wave of immigration following the recovery of the coal trade from wartime dislocation.

roots of many of the workmen of Whickham were as insubstantial, and their residence in the parish as temporary, as the wretched dwellings they inhabited.

In part, the perennially high degree of population mobility in Whickham is to be explained in terms of the realities of coal-mining and the coal trade and the extent to which the people of the parish depended upon both. For some, work in the mines may have been a life-cycle-related activity, a phase through which they passed in adolescence or early manhood, comparable to the institution of service in husbandry which was so characteristic of English rural society. This was certainly the case for some of the wainmen who transported Whickham's coal. But we have no evidence that it was generally true of the mineworkers themselves.

Some overmen, of course, came from landholding families, and others did well enough in the coal industry to acquire land in due course. The same could be said of some of the staithemen, who occupied positions comparable to those of overmen at the riverside staithes. Our records provide no instances, however, of by-employed pitmen. Most of the workmen at the pits, so far as can be seen, appear to have lived in a condition of permanent rather than temporary or partial proletarianization. The best that they could hope for would be to acquire the reputation that might win them an overman's place, and that was an opportunity open to relatively few. Contemporary comment consistently presents them as poor. It is also consistent in describing their total wage dependency. In 1591 they were called 'people that have not anie other liveing than they gett by . . . coales'; in 1595, 'men . . . having no other meanes to sustaine the necessaries of them selves and families then ther owne laboures'.[89] The stoppage of the Tyne coal trade in 1637–8 meant that 'greate number of those poore men who formerly gott theire liveings by diging of coales and were imployed in the venting of them are now like to perish for want'.[90]

It was this situation that exposed the colliery workmen to numerous uncertainties and insecurities which directly affected their ability to make a living. They were employed by a specific overman to work a particular pit, but they were guaranteed neither work nor wages if their pit, for whatever reason, ceased production.

[89] BL Lansdowne MS 67, no. 22; Harleian MS 6850, no. 39.
[90] Quoted in Nef, ii. 75. Nef also reckoned that by the early 17th c. mining (as distinct from transportation work) was no longer a by-employment: ii. 143.

At best, they might have steady work for a whole season. What they did at the end of the season, as winter approached, is almost completely obscure. Some were certainly kept on to maintain drainage operations through the winter. Others may have lived on money put by, or credit. The unmarried might perhaps return to their families of origin. Those with families to support might perhaps seek work elsewhere, possibly at a land-sale colliery less tied to the seasonality of east-coast shipping. Some of these options might involve temporary or permanent removal from the parish.

These were the best of times. But colliery was an uncertain trade. If work at a pit proved 'broken', or if an overman found his costs exceeding the productive capacity of his pit, men might be discharged. Pits might also be worked out before work became available at another sinking. Any of these circumstances might encourage, or force, a man to move. Then there were the stoppages of trade which periodically brought the Tyne industry to a halt, like that of 1637–8 cited above. In such circumstances, men facing total loss of income might head for the Wear or the inland collieries.

The mobility of Whickham's population is therefore scarcely surprising. Fortunate men, or men with a high reputation for skill and industry, might be able to pursue almost an entire working life in Whickham. It was not unusual for overmen to be long-term residents. Some worked for many years for a single owner, like Archibald Gibson, who served twenty-seven years at Greenlaw colliery, or George Young, who served for twenty years at Langeyfield near Ravensworth, presumably walking to his work from Whickham.[91] There were also pitmen who appear to have been continuously resident in Whickham for considerable periods, like Robert Daglesh, who arrived already married sometime before 1651 and stayed until he died in a pit in 1674.[92] But such stability among the workmen was not the norm. We would do better to regard most of them less as the work-force of Whickham than as members of a free-floating body of labour who had good reason to regard the whole coalfield rather than a single territorial unit as their work-place.

One further factor needs to be discussed in explaining the volatility of Whickham's population: mortality. The family reconstitution results indicate that Whickham's demographic experience

---

[91] PRO E 134 3 Car. I Ea. 19; DURH 7/31.
[92] His death is noted in the burial register for 20 Mar. 1673/4.

was distinguished above all by the high mortality of its parishioners. Consideration of the burial statistics over time emphasizes still more powerfully the disastrous nature of Whickham's mortality regime. Figure 1 provides an annual series of burials in Whickham for the century after the onset of registration in 1577, presenting the data in 'raw' form in order to capture the annual variability that would be smoothed out by use of a moving average. The outstanding characteristic of this graph is the explosive annual variation of burials in the parish.

Wrigley and Schofield's reconstruction of the population history of England has made it clear that, while dramatic year-to-year and even month-to-month swings are to be expected in parish register burial statistics, recurrent crisis-level mortality was not the usual experience of English rural parishes in this period.[93] What was remarkable about Whickham's experience was the profound impact of repetitive crisis years.[94] The jagged peaks of the burial series are most evident at the turn of the sixteenth century, but these harrowing decades were not the only times when crisis-level mortality touched Whickham's population. If we define 'crisis' to mean years when annual burials were more than double the surrounding, 'background', level, there were no fewer than seventeen identifiable mortality crises in Whickham during the first century of parochial registration.[95]

Determining the causes of these explosions of mortality involves the combination of quantitative and qualitative evidence. The seventeenth-century crises would appear to have been invariably the result of outbreaks of epidemic disease, above all bubonic plague. The parish register is quite definite in describing the cause of death as 'plague' in 1604, 1610, and during the repeated crises of the 1640s

[93] Wrigley and Schofield, *Population History of England*, app. 10.

[94] The north-east, like northern England in general, was more prone to serious mortality crises than southern England. Whickham, however, was outstanding in this respect even among the parishes of Co. Durham: A. B. Appleby, *Famine in Tudor and Stuart England* (Stanford and Liverpool, 1978), 134, 147; Hodgson, 'Demographic Trends', 31.

[95] In *Population History of England*, app. 10, Wrigley and Schofield use rather different measurements and consider mortality crises on a monthly basis by means of a computer-assisted algorithm. Our measurement of annual mortality is much less sophisticated. We also face the problem in the Whickham case that some 'normal' years used to establish levels of 'background' mortality witnessed burial rates that would be considered relatively high by the standards of the day (e.g. 1590–2). Nevertheless, both the severity of Whickham's mortality regime and the frequency of years of particularly heavy mortality remain clear.

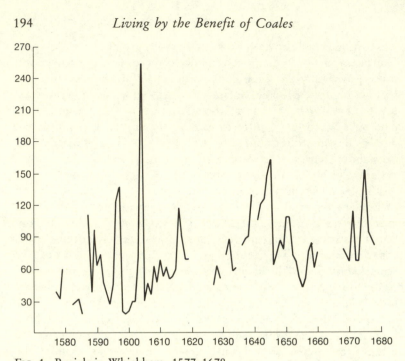

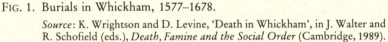

FIG. 1. Burials in Whickham, 1577–1678.

Source: K. Wrightson and D. Levine, 'Death in Whickham', in J. Walter and R. Schofield (eds.), *Death, Famine and the Social Order* (Cambridge, 1989).

(above all 1645). This testimony is supported by additional references in the records of Whickham to households 'visited with the infection of the plague', or 'clensed and made safe' after epidemics, and to the flight of householders from Whickham town to 'lodges' on the fell in a vain attempt to escape the pestilence.[96]

Moreover, both parish registers and county records indicate the presence of plague even in years when mortality in Whickham is not known to have reached crisis proportions. In April and July 1626, for example, the Durham quarter sessions order book refers to plague in Gateshead, South Shields, and Whickham, while in July 1638 the justices ordered the payment of £18 for the relief of 'the towne of Whickham, lately infected with the plague'.[97]

[96] PRO DURH 2/2/51, 2/9/73; DPD DR v/8, fos. 31–32ᵛ; DPD Probate, Inv. of Thomas Pearson (1604).

[97] DRO Q/S OB 1, 242, 261; Q/S OB 2, 276. In the case of the 1626 outbreak, the parish register seems deficient and we cannot confidently assess the dimensions of the mortality, which may have been severe.

Closer analysis of the major crises of the early seventeenth century certainly reveals the demographic 'footprint' of the plague. In 1604, most catastrophic of the crisis years, 254 inhabitants of Whickham were buried in only five months, perhaps a quarter or more of the entire population. Burials were at their peak in July to September, declining thereafter as winter approached—a seasonal pattern of mortality characteristic of the plague. Moreover, many deaths were bunched in family units, another familiar feature of epidemic mortality.[98] Of the fifty-one victims of the plague who could be 'placed' in reconstituted families, more than half occurred in family clusters, with mortality worst among infants and young children.[99] While some of Whickham's relatively settled families suffered drastically, however, the culling of the parish population seems to have been at its worst among the floating population of sojourners and short-term residents attracted to Whickham by the labour needs of the coal industry. Clearly, the isolated individuals of the migrant population suffered dreadfully.

Examination of the epidemic of 1645 produces an essentially similar picture. Of the 161 burials in that year, 98 were of people stated to have died of the plague. The seasonal distribution of burials was less clear-cut than in 1604, but the register is quite specific on the cause of death. Deaths occurred in family clusters, and within those families children were hardest hit. The one significant difference between 1604 and 1645, however, was that in the latter year almost three-quarters of the victims of the plague could be linked to reconstituted families.[100] Perhaps the disparity in the ratio of successful linkages between the reconstituted populations of 1604 and 1645 provides further testimony to the extraordinary upheaval in Whickham's population at the turn of the sixteenth century, and to the relative stabilization of the 1640s.

The crises of the early seventeenth century can thus be attributed confidently to plague outbreaks. Plague may well have been

---

[98] R. S. Schofield, 'An Anatomy of an Epidemic: Colyton, November 1645 to November 1646', in L. Bradley (ed.), *The Plague Reconsidered*, supplement to *Local Population Studies* (1977), 95–126. Cf. P. Slack, *The Impact of Plague in Tudor and Stuart England* (London, 1985), 177 ff.

[99] Of those traceable in the reconstitution, 28 of 51 (55%) were in family clusters, and 39 of 51 (76%) were infants or children.

[100] Of the 98 plague victims of 1645, 72 (73%) could be traced in the reconstitution, 58 (59%) were in family clusters, and 48 (49%) were infants or children.

endemic on Tyneside by this date.[101] Those of the late sixteenth century, however, are more problematic. The mortality of 1587–8 involved inflated numbers of burials between July 1587 and March 1588, with burials at their highest between September and December 1587. Although 1586–7 is known to have been a year of harvest deficiency and widespread dearth, it seems unlikely that famine underlay the winter deaths of 1587, since the inventories of two of the victims record well-stocked farms and supplies of grain.[102] The pattern of mortality, however, was remarkably similar to that found in Cumberland and Westmorland in the same year. It has been argued that the mortality in the Lake Counties was most probably occasioned by an epidemic of typhus, perhaps attacking a population already weakened by malnutrition. This interpretation was influenced by the distinctive age-pattern of deaths in the north-west, a matter that cannot be explored in Whickham, given the very laconic nature of the relevant parish register entries.[103] Typhus, however, may very well have been the villain of the piece, a supposition strengthened by the fact that crisis mortality was found elsewhere in County Durham in 1587 and that it was attributed in the south of the county to 'fevers'.[104]

Whatever the precise nature of the 1587 crisis, that of 1589 was clearly occasioned by a plague outbreak: 53 burials out of an annual total of 101 were recorded in the eight weeks from late August to early October. The mortality of 1596–7, however, was of an altogether different nature. The seasonal pattern of burials in these

---

[101] For the frequency of plague outbreaks on Tyneside, see Howell, *Newcastle-upon-Tyne*, 7, 319–20; James, *Family, Lineage and Civil Society*, 8–10; Hodgson, 'Demographic Trends', 24–30; Slack, *Impact of Plague*, 62. Of course, we cannot be certain that plague was *constantly* present, as distinct from being frequently introduced via trading contacts with London.

[102] DPD Probate, Invs. of Richard Arnold (1587), Robert Donkin (1587).

[103] Appleby, *Famine*, 102–8. Parish registers can be used to explore the age incidence of mortality only if they record details of family relationships implying minor status (e.g. A son of B), or cover a time-frame sufficient to permit family reconstitution. The Whickham register offers neither advantage with regard to the 1587 crisis.

[104] Personal communication from John Smith of Durham University. For the widespread nature of the crisis of 1587 in Co. Durham, see the graphs in Hodgson, 'Demographic Trends', 23–5. A further possibility is that the crisis of 1587 was a 'mixed' crisis involving both hunger and epidemic disease. For such crises, see P. Slack, 'Mortality Crises and Epidemic Disease in England, 1485–1610', in C. Webster (ed.), *Health, Medicine and Mortality in the Sixteenth Century* (Cambridge, 1979).

years was quite distinct from those of both earlier and later crises. Heavy mortality was concentrated in the five winter months of November 1596 to March 1597, which together accounted for more than three-fifths of the burials in the parish for the two years affected (164 of 261). This monthly pattern would seem to suggest a classic 'crisis of subsistence' precipitated by food shortage.

There is other evidence to support such an interpretation. It is well established that the mid- to late 1590s witnessed a succession of disastrous harvests throughout northern Europe. Indisputable evidence of famine has been found in north-west England, and similar conditions have been uncovered for other upland areas in these years, though in the main, England appears to have suffered the privations of 'dearth' rather than the horrors of outright famine.[105] The north-east, like the north-west, was an essentially pastoral, grain-poor region, dependent to a large extent on supplies of bread corn from southern England and abroad, and it is scarcely surprising that by 1596 there were anxious reports of serious food shortage in both Durham and Northumberland.[106]

Under normal conditions, however, a parish such as Whickham, with its proximity to the port of Newcastle and therefore to relief shipments, might have expected to be spared the extreme consequences of food shortage. Indeed, in January 1597 some grain shipments did reach Newcastle, and were said to have saved thousands from starvation.[107] The crucial difference in 1596–7 seems to have been that for the most part vessels bearing foodstuffs were unable to reach the north-eastern ports. Throughout the winter the commander of the garrison at Berwick, which also depended on imported supplies, wrote graphic accounts of shortage to the council in Westminster. In March 1597 it was said that only one-fifth of the usual winter supplies had reached that port. Some had been withheld from shipment by local authorities in Yorkshire and Lincolnshire anxious about the scarcity in their own counties. Some ships that had sailed laden with food had been unable to reach the north-east because of many weeks of adverse weather. In July 1597 rye was being sold at the astounding price of 96s. a quarter in Newcastle, despite the arrival of three grain ships. As late as

---

[105] Appleby, *Famine*, 109–21, 133–45. Cf. Slack, *Impact of Plague*, 73–4.
[106] S. J. and S. J. Watts, *From Border to Middle Shire: Northunberland, 1586–1625* (Leicester, 1975), 49; James, *Family, Lineage and Civil Society*, 8.
[107] *CSPD, 1595–7*, 348.

September, further shipments had brought prices down only to 36s. a quarter, and the records of the Corporation of Newcastle spoke of 'poor folks who died for want in the streets'.[108]

In view of such well-documented conditions, it seems probable that the crisis of 1596–7 in Whickham was occasioned by hunger and the associated diseases of malnutrition. Perhaps the swelling population of the parish had suffered the terrible consequences of a dependence upon regular food imports which had been dislocated by a combination of shortage elsewhere and adverse weather. As early as December 1595, the coal-owners of Newcastle had reported that their workers, in the face of 'the darthe of . . . victuales', were unable to 'sustaine ther lyves' without a wage increase. In the winter of 1596–7 things were far worse, and the industrial workers of Whickham may have faced rocketing food prices at the very time of the year when their wages were at their lowest, since the mortality coincided with the dead season of the coal trade.[109] Against such an interpretation can be placed only the facts that conceptions were not markedly lowered in Whickham during the months of highest mortality, and that plague was reported in Whickham in July 1597.[110] There was indeed a flurry of burials in the summer of 1597 which might be attributed to the plague; but these came well after the main period of crisis mortality.[111] As for conceptions, it is perfectly possible that these were little inhibited in Whickham because the effects of malnutrition were concentrated largely among particular sections of the population—notably the poor and the young, unmarried migrants.

[108] *Cal. of Border Papers, 1595–1603*, 128, 138–9, 185–6, 200, 231, 273, 281–2; *HMC*, VII. 295–6. Cf. Appleby, *Famine*, 113. We are grateful to Dr R. B. Outhwaite of Gonville and Caius College, Cambridge, for making available to us his file on the crisis years of the late 1590s.

[109] BL Harleian MS 6850, no. 39, fo. 163. For a comparable situation, see Slack's account of the listing of the poor of Crompton, Lancs., in 1597. The vast majority of those listed were not the usual 'impotent' poor but members of labouring families, some of them headed by colliers who were unable to earn enough to maintain their families in this dearth year: P. Slack, *Poverty and Policy in Tudor and Stuart England* (London, 1988), 66.

[110] Conceptions averaged 3 per month during the crisis as against 4.5 per month for the remaining 19 months of 1596 and 1597. For the report of plague, see M. A. Richardson, *The Local Historian's Table Book of Remarkable Occurrences*, 2 vols. (Newcastle, 1841), i. 231. Plague was also reported in Newcastle in the late spring and summer of 1597: *CSPD, 1595–7*, 420.

[111] Slack felt unable to attribute the heavy mortality of 1596–7 in Newcastle to plague alone. See also his general discussion of the relative significance of famine and disease in the mortalities of the later 1590s: *Impact of Plague*, 62, 73–4.

That there was such a bias in mortality, we can be sure. Eight copyholders of the manor of Whickham died in the crisis months of 1596–7: the copyholder population was literally decimated. Yet of those who died, only one held as much as six acres of land. Most of the rest held only houses and gardens, or tiny holdings nibbled from the waste of the manor.[112] The copyholder victims of the crisis were drawn almost exclusively from the very lowest stratum of the manorial hierarchy. If this could be the fate even of those with a toehold on the land and rights of pasture, how much more starkly must the crisis have affected the landless, wage-dependent migrants who appear to have provided the bulk of the dead?

In reviewing this evidence of Whickham's disastrous record of crisis mortality, it would appear that the chronic vulnerability of the parishioners to plague outbreaks after 1589 and their experience of famine in 1596–7 were both intimately connected with the industrialization of lower Tyneside in general and with the social environment that this process produced in Whickham in particular. The consequences of Tyneside's industrial growth and closer incorporation into networks of national and international trade were double-edged. Whickham benefited from an industrial expansion and trading ties which created work, generated income, and kept the inhabitants well supplied with food in most years. Yet it witnessed also the growth of a large, dense, squalidly housed, wage-dependent population of workmen and cottagers who were chronically vulnerable both to the exceptional circumstances of an interruption of their food supplies and to the perennial ravages of infectious disease. The catastrophe of 1596–7, which was experienced also in the other Tyneside parishes of County Durham and in the industrializing Wearside parish of Chester-le-Street, may have been the outcome of a unique combination of circumstances involving the pre-existing weaknesses of the local agrarian economy, rapid recent population growth in the industrial areas, and the interruption of shipping.

We have no reason to believe that Whickham ever again suffered the horrors of famine (though we would be more confident in making that judgement if burial registration survived for 1622–3, the last year of widespread famine in northern England and one that saw enhanced mortality in some Durham parishes). By the

---

[112] Based on the rental of 1591 and the recorded land transfers during and after the crisis: DPD DDR HC III F 18, fos. 25–49ᵛ, HC III F 19, fos. 173–174ᵛ.

mid-seventeenth century, the local economy appears to have adjusted to the necessity of regularly supplying a large industrial population. Newcastle was known as a major receiving port for grain not only from southern England, but also from the Baltic. In 1649 it was described as 'an Aegypt to all the shires of the north (in time of famine)'.[113] Yet Whickham's vulnerability to epidemic disease appears to have been constant throughout the early seventeenth century. For the parish had been incorporated not only into a larger trading pattern, but also into a unified system of disease transmission focused on London. If its mortality regime had features more like those of a city than of a rural parish, this was because it was, in effect, an extension of the demographic experience of urban and metropolitan England.

But it also had at least one peculiarity of its own, and this can be explored if we consider once more, and in greater detail, the family reconstitution figures relating to mortality in Whickham. In Table 3.4 these are set out alongside comparable figures from Terling in Essex and Colyton in Devon. The figures in the first part of the table serve to remind us of the severity of infant mortality in Whickham. Life expectation at birth was in the order of four years less than in Terling, a community broadly representative of the average of the 'Cambridge Twelve' parishes referred to above. Similarly, adult male life expectation at age 25–9 was some four years less than in Colyton. Male life expectation remained significantly lower in Whickham than in the Devon parish up to the age group 40–4. In contrast, Whickham women had a better life expectation than their Devonshire counterparts at all ages. As in Table 3.3, the exceptional result of the Whickham family reconstitution study is the severity of male mortality and the marked disparity between male and female mortality. We can now see that excess male mortality was particularly notable in the early years of marriage, the very years when, owing to the risks associated with child-bearing, we could normally expect excess *female* mortality. If, as in Whickham, this period was actually one of excess male

[113] Gray, *Chorographia*, 33. Though the burial register is frustratingly broken for the early 1620s, there are no indications of unusually high mortality in either the probate records or the Halmote records. There is also no evidence of exceptional mortality in the dearth years of 1630–1 and 1647–50. For high mortality in other Co. Durham parishes in 1596–7 and 1623, see Hodgson, 'Demographic Trends', 23–5, and Issa, 'Obligation and Choice', 47–8.

TABLE 3.4. *Mortality in Whickham, Terling and Colyton*

(i) Infant and Child Mortality

	At risk	Dying	Rate/000	Life expectation at birth[a]	Corresponding Rate/000
Whickham 1600–24					
0–	1,917	325	169	42.78	168
1–4	1,052	118	113		118
5–9	553	23	42		28
10–14	360	13	36		17
Terling 1550–1624					
0–	1,059	136	128	46.61	137
1–4	665	48	72		95
5–9	338	14	36		27
10–14	241	10	41		19

(ii) *Adult Mortality: Life Expectation at Various Ages*

	25–29	30–34	35–39	40–44	45–49	50–54	55–59
Whickham 1600–49[b]							
Male	27.6	25.5	23.4	21.5	18.9	16.8	14.7
Female	31.4	29.1	26.7	24.2	21.2	18.4	15.8
Colyton 1600–49							
Male	31.3	27.8	25.1	22.0	19.5	17.0	13.9
Female	29.1	26.1	22.5	19.7	17.1	15.1	12.4

[a] Figures for life expectation at birth derived from S. Ledermann, *Nouvelles Tables—Types de Mortalité* (Paris, 1969: 134).
[b] The Whickham statistics are derived from combining 'optimistic' and 'pessimistic' assumptions about age-specific mortality. This procedure was required because so few of the adult parishioners actually remained 'in observation' long enough to be traced through to their burials. This method was devised to allocate death dates to these birds of passage. We must stress, however, that the Whickham people whose burials *were* registered form the parameters within which these other deaths were allocated.

mortality, then the impression is that Whickham men were engaged in an activity considerably more dangerous to their lives than childbirth was to Whickham women.

The parish register confirms our suspicion as to the nature of that activity. Between November 1630 and April 1652 it was kept with unusual care, and the more specific registration of those years tells us of fifty working miners killed in Whickham's pits. In addition, the register provides details of a further nine industrially related deaths which did not involve underground workers.[114] In all, during the period of exceptionally detailed registration 1630–52, the fifty-nine burials that were either directly or indirectly attributable to coal-mining represented 3.2 per cent of all burials registered. Of those who died in the pits, eight are known to have been youths, the youngest of them ten years old; five were unmarried adults; and twenty-four were married men. Of those adults whose ages are known, most were under thirty-five years of age, and this was probably true also of those married men with young families whose precise ages are unknown. The impact of industrial deaths within the population of Whickham was therefore likely to be far more focused than is suggested by the global figure of industrial deaths as a proportion of all burials. The reconstitution results, in their description of excess male mortality, bear out this surmise only too well.

While the development of the coal trade did much to enhance the general level of mortality in Whickham, the activity of mining coal thus made its own specific contribution. Taken as a whole, Whickham's distinctive mortality regime, with its high level of 'background' mortality, periodic crises, and steady trickle of deaths by industrial accident, had a further impact on the social structure of the parish in that it contributed to the high level of population turnover. There was a constant need for replenishment among the industrial population of Whickham, comparable to that observable in the cities of the period. Like the plague that ravaged the metropolis of London, Whickham's mortality regime was both symptomatic of the social and economic environment that sustained it and an independent variable aggravating the instability of that

---

[114] The precise cause of deaths of working miners is rarely specified. The other industrially related deaths included children killed by coal wains or waggons or by falling into disused pits, and men slain by industrial machinery or in transportation accidents.

environment.[115] The migrant workers who flowed into the parish came as isolated individuals and families. They were attracted and held primarily by the prospect of wage work in and around the pits and staithes. Mortality crises, accidental deaths, and the perennial haemorrhage of life in a squalid and unwholesome environment could obliterate such isolated individuals and loosely rooted families. Acting alongside the fluctuations in employment opportunities which could stimulate renewed movement, the harsh realities of death were in themselves a significant influence on the shaping of the social world of the early industrial work-force of Tyneside.

By the third decade of the seventeenth century at the latest, the essential characteristics of that new world had congealed. Whereas in 1591 the coal-owners of Newcastle could speak of a relatively finite group of 'above 500 people' who were 'mainteyned in worke' about their pits, by 1618 they had abandoned all effort at specificity and spoke of 'multitudes of people who are daylie set on worke'. By 1656 this had become 'many Thousand poore families dependinge thereupon'.[116] Clearly, they thought in terms of a coalfield-wide work-force, and the evidence reviewed above supports the validity of that perception.

Whickham's new population was part of all this. From the point of view of the remaining representatives of the older copyholder families of the parish, the advent of the mining population must have seemed 'less like the polarisation of the old traditional society than the rising in their midst of a wholly new and mobile society'.[117] Yet we have no reason to suppose that in Whickham this massive transformation bred conflict between the copyholders and the coal-workers. The copyholders' quarrel was with the coal-owners rather than their workmen, and, as we have seen, it was at least as much a battle to secure and expand their own role in the coal industry as an attempt to resist its advance. The workmen of the collieries seem to have been almost outside all this. One, called to give evidence in

---

[115] Paraphrasing Slack's characterization of the influence of the plague in London: 'plague was both a symptom of urban instability and an independent variable which aggravated it, raising death rates which were already abnormally high and accelerating a turnover of population which was already rapid': *Impact of Plague*, 161.

[116] BL Lansdowne MS 67, no. 22; PRO STAC 8/245/6; Dendy, *Hostmen*, 10.

[117] Quoting Issa's characterization of similar developments in Chester-le-Street in 'Obligation and Choice', 56.

1620, could speak confidently of current practice in the wain carriage of coal, but declared himself ignorant of, and therefore unable to comment upon, such matters as land tenure in Whickham, former customs concerning the dowelling of coalways, the history of coal-mining in the manor over the last generation, and the levels of compensation formerly paid to copyholders. Another said of such matters, 'he cann saie nothing to them being but a coteman', and yet another that he could not depose 'by reason he is no copiholder nor farmer but onlie liveth by his own industrie and paines'.[118]

So, as the older copyholder community underwent dissolution in the first half of the seventeenth century, a new social order grew up in its place. A man's place in this new world was determined not so much by land, by the rights that accompanied it, or by participation in the institutions of manorial Whickham, as by his role in the exploitation of Whickham's mineral wealth. For, if anything gave overall coherence to the social order that had emerged in Whickham and can be anatomized in the hearth tax listing of 1666, it was coal. As Gray wrote in his *Chorographia* of 1649, 'most of the people that liveth in those parts lives by the benefit of coales'.[119] Coal had brought wealth to the great gentry families of Whickham, two of which had come to their estates via success in the coal trade. Coal underpinned the gentility of most of the lesser gentry of the parish. Coal supplemented the incomes of the farmers. Coal provided the occupations of the staithemen, overmen, and fitters. In the winning and transportation of coal, the labouring poor earned their bread. One historian has described the society of Whickham as represented in the manorial survey of 1647 as 'a traditional order blurred and distorted by the impact of coal production'.[120] So it might seem from that manorially structured document, with its emphasis on copyhold tenures and acreages. But the fuller record of the hearth tax, once explicated, tells a different story. The social order of Whickham that was in place by 1666 was 'traditional' only in the limited sense that landownership and copyhold tenures provided the legal basis of mineral and wayleave rights. This was an industrial society, reflecting in its social composition the structure of the coal industry that had created it: owners, lessees, wayleave rentiers,

[118] PRO DURH 7/18, pt. I, testimony of Christopher Robson; 7/19, pt. I, testimony of Ralph Kenetye, John Dover.   [119] Gray, *Chorographia*, 29.
[120] James, *Family, Lineage and Civil Society*, 96.

overmen, staithemen, transportation workers, colliery craftsmen, and Whickham's temporary complement of those 'many thousand' people who lived by the winning of coal.

3. PEOPLE AND WORK, *c.*1660–1760

The hearth-tax listing of 1666 provides a unique opportunity to take stock of Whickham's social development after a century of momentous change. Yet our analysis of the householders of the parish in 1666 represents only a moment in time—an artificially frozen moment in an essentially dynamic process. The social order described had no fixed internal structure. It had come into being in response to the industrial development of Whickham, and it would shift with the changing patterns of industrial activity.

In the century after 1666, Whickham's economic history fell into three distinguishable phases. First came the gradual decline of the Grand Lease and its neighbouring collieries, a process already under way in 1666. By the early 1690s Whickham's output of sea coal had probably been reduced to the levels that had obtained at the beginning of the seventeenth century. A new burst of industrial expansion began in the 1690s with the development of the Gibside–Northbanks colliery, the laying of the waggonways, and the establishment of the Crowley ironworks at Swalwell. The first three decades of the eighteenth century saw Whickham restored to its pre-eminence as a centre of high-quality coal production, in addition to which the parish became the focal point of the waggonway network which was opening up the 'Western collieries', and the site of Augustan England's most significant vertically integrated manufactory.

By the 1730s this new wave of expansion had broken. Whickham's collieries, though not insignificant, entered another phase of slow decline, and the waggonway network within the parish was largely dismantled by 1740. Nevertheless, the greatest of the Tyneside waggonways still embraced the boundaries of the parish. The riverside staithes of Dunston and Swalwell remained vitally important in the transhipment of coal from newer colliery complexes situated within an hour's walk of the Fellside quarter. The Crowley ironworks entered their second generation of flourishing activity. Even the farmers of the parish were orientated primarily towards the supplying of industrial needs. In short, Whickham was embedded more deeply than ever within an increasingly complex industrial economy. All of this, inevitably, had its consequences for both the parish and its people.

In the seventy years that followed 1666, a period of demographic stability in England as a whole, Whickham's population continued to grow. Sadly, we lack any documentary basis for a population estimate at the turn of the seventeenth century which might enable us to assess more precisely the impact of renewed industrial expansion. In 1736, however, Bishop Chandler's parochial survey of Durham placed the population of Whickham at 700 families.[121] In terms of households or families, therefore, the population of the parish had almost doubled since 1666.

For reasons already explained, we have hesitated hitherto to translate numbers of households into estimates of a total population for Whickham. By the mid-eighteenth century, however, Whickham's household structure may have been less abnormal than we suspect to have been the case in the earlier seventeenth century. An enumeration of able-bodied men drawn up in the later 1750s, probably in response to the Militia Act, gives a total of 712 men for the whole parish.[122] This number did not include men who were regarded as aged or infirm, but it none the less compares interestingly with the 782 adult men listed in the Protestation return of 1642 at a time when the number of families in Whickham was almost certainly far fewer. It is probable that Whickham's population of young male coal-workers, housed in lodges and hovels, had been higher on the eve of the Civil Wars than it was ever to be again. If the household structure of the mid-eighteenth century was somewhat closer to the English norm, then the 700 families of 1736 might represent a population of around 3,000.[123] The general plausibility of this estimate is supported by the fact that, according to Joseph Grainger, the total population of the parish in the year 1780 was 2,790.[124]

---

[121] DPD 'Bishop Chandler's Parochial Remarks on his Visitation' (photocopy of the original in Newcastle-upon-Tyne Central Library).

[122] DRO D/ST 301. The Fellside men are fully listed. Only totals are given for Whickham, Lowhand, and Swalwell quarters.

[123] See n. 37 above.

[124] J. Grainger, *General View of the Agriculture of the County of Durham* (London, 1794), 73. The 'Diocese Book' of 1793 says of Whickham, 'about 800 Houses—a populous Parish'. In the 1801 Census Whickham's population was found to be 3,659. DPD DR XVII/1; Page (ed.), *Victoria County History, Durham*, ii. 265.

As in the later sixteenth and earlier seventeenth centuries, Whickham's population growth was not an isolated phenomenon, but was shared by the other industrial parishes of northern County Durham. Whereas the population of the county as a whole rose by some 60 per cent in the period 1666–1736, the bulk of this increase was concentrated in the industrial areas—notably the mining parishes of the expanding Wearside coalfield and in the area affected by the opening up of the 'western collieries'. The population of Chester Ward, the north-western division of the county and the principal area of coalfield expansion, increased by no less than 142 per cent, and the inferred link between mining development and population growth was made explicit in the parish of Washington, where the families numbered in Bishop Chandler's survey were described as 'Many of them Colliers new come in'.[125]

Population growth in post-Restoration Whickham was primarily the result of immigration, largely occurring after 1700. The family reconstitution results for the parish, presented in Table 3.5, reveal that mean age at first marriage remained stable in the later seventeenth century. Marital fertility likewise remained stable before 1700, rising thereafter. In all, the indicators of fertility suggest a somewhat greater demographic buoyancy in Whickham than was the case in the 'Cambridge Twelve' parishes, notably in the early eighteenth century. But this was offset by a continued history of high infant and child mortality, which was actually worsening in Whickham over time, and by an adult mortality pattern that retained its peculiar sex-specificity in the lower life expectation of Whickham's men.

This was not a recipe for significant natural increase in Whickham's population, and the parishioners remained scarcely able to replace their numbers in the long term. A small baptismal surplus in the quarter-century from 1650 became a small deficit in the final twenty-five years of the seventeenth century. In the first quarter of the eighteenth century a baptismal surplus provided Whickham's best phase of natural increase in the entire period under study. But again, it was modest enough, and was reversed in 1726–50, a period that witnessed Whickham's worst baptismal deficit since the disastrous years at the end of the sixteenth century.

[125] P. W. Brassley, 'The Agricultural Economy of Northumberland and Durham in the Period 1640–1750', B.Litt. thesis (Oxford, 1974), 20, 22, 26; id., 'Northumberland and Durham', 42; Hodgson, 'Demographic Trends', 27–8.

TABLE 3.5. *Family Reconstitution Results, 1600–1749*

	1600–49		1650–99		1700–49	
	Whick- ham	Camb. 12	Whick- ham	Camb. 12	Whick- ham	Camb. 12
Mean age at first marriage[a]						
Men	27.5 (90)	28.0	27.3 (194)	27.8	26.9 (352)	27.5
Women	25.5 (80)	26.0	25.3 (157)	26.5	25.5 (248)	26.2
Age-specific fertility rates						
(per 1,000 woman-years lived)						
20–24	368	384	356	376	431	382
25–29	331	346	332	347	382	352
30–34	265	303	332	295	364	287
35–39	277	245	272	241	311	224
40–44	267	127	135	129	101	108
Cumulative						
20–44	7.54	7.03	7.14	6.92	7.94	6.77
Infant and child mortality (MF)						
0–1	169	137	153	148	164	132
1–4	112	87	129	102	171	89
5–9	42	37	47	43	61	31
0–9	293	241	297	268	349	234
Adult mortality						
(life expectation at age 30)						
Men	25.5	29.8	26.9	28.4	26.3	30.4
Women	29.1	29.6	29.3	28.9	28.2	30.2

[a] Numbers given in parentheses.

In fact, Whickham remained outstanding among the parishes of the area in the severity of its mortality regime. The disappearance of the plague had brought a degree of stability to the burial graph of the parish as compared with the years before 1650, and those mortality crises that can be detected in Whickham—in the mid-1670s, the late 1720s, and the early 1740s—were shared by other parishes in the region. What made Whickham different was the perennially high 'background' mortality of its quasi-urban demographic regime.[126]

[126] Hodgson, 'Demographic Trends', 23–6.

All this points to a new phase of heavy immigration as the source of Whickham's population growth in the early eighteenth century. It is a supposition that receives support both from our own analysis of the sex ratio at burial and from an analysis of the surnames recorded in the parish. Whickham's sex ratio at burial, which had normalized after 1660, began to rise once again in the 1690s and peaked at 149 male for every 100 female burials in the decade 1700–9, gradually subsiding thereafter to reach conventional levels by the 1730s. This trend is mirrored in the fact that there was a considerable fall in the proportion of new surnames in the Whickham baptismal register in the later seventeenth century, suggesting a degree of stabilization after the upheaval of the early century; thereafter, however, the incidence of new surnames rose (though never to the levels obtaining before 1654), only to stabilize once more from the 1730s.[127]

Both sets of findings tally perfectly with the industrial history of the parish. The 1692 Montague lease of the Gibside colliery included the right to build 'Houses, Stables, Hovells, Lodges or Sheds ... for the standing Lodgeing Laying and placing of the Workmen, Workehorses and Workegeare to be used or Imployed' in the new colliery. The Crowley firm recruited men widely for its Derwent valley works, promising 'constant employment and their wages every week punctually paid', and provided them with housing both at Winlaton in Ryton parish and at Swalwell.[128] The effects are discernible in the distribution of able-bodied men among the quarters of the parish in the late 1750s as compared with the distribution of householders in 1666. Some three-fifths of Whickham's able-bodied men now lived in the Swalwell and Fellside quarters, as compared with two-fifths of the householders of 1666. Moreover, Swalwell, formerly a large hamlet, now had the greatest concentration of population in the parish.[129]

The linking of Whickham's demographic development between 1666 and 1736 to the phases of its industrial history had consequences for the occupational and social structures of the parish. It is possible that the later seventeenth century saw some decline in the number of pitmen and colliery workers resident in Whickham. At

[127] Lasker and Roberts, 'Secular Trends in Relationship', 301.
[128] DRO D/ST V. 36; Flinn, *Men of Iron*, 233–6, 240; Bourn, *Whickham*, 92–3.
[129] DRO D/ST 301. The distribution of men by quarter was: Swalwell 250, Fellside 162; Lowhand 150; Whickham 150.

the same time, however, it should not be forgotten that many pits were still working both in the Grand Lease territories and in neighbouring collieries. While their output is exceedingly difficult to assess at this period, it would be foolish to underestimate the level of employment that they and other collieries just outside the parish boundaries could still provide.

The continued significance of coal extraction is reflected in the numerous surviving inventories of parishioners taken in the later seventeenth century that include, for the first time, accounts of the possessions of men engaged wholly, or primarily, in coal mining. Some of these men were clearly overmen. George Mathew, for example, left six 'trams', six shovels, and a set of 'swingell trees belonging to horse gear' among his possessions, as well as eleven tens of coal wrought and laid up at his Lowfield pit. Robert Ellett left 'pit geare' valued at only £1. 1s. 0d. but 'Coales at Pitt' to the value of £115. Even more impressive in its detail, John Barras's inventory included 'Three mells thre wedges one paire of Hookes and Chines with Horse Geere and one iron bolt', 'Three Trams Three Shovells and one sled', 'one paire of Man Rowle stands', and 'Two pit ropes' to a total value of £2. 17s. 0d., as well as 'One Cole Ginne standing upon his Goose Moore pitt' (value £10) and almost seventeen tens of wrought coal ready at pit and staithes, valued at close to £50. Barras also left notes of money he had disbursed 'For sinkeing the Goose moore pitt from the Top Cole to the maine Cole', 'For sheths and dales and fure wood to secure her', and 'For smith worke at the said pitt'.[130]

In addition, there are specialists like the borer John Rawling, with his 'one [h]acke' and 'Boreing rods', the corvemaker Thomas Sanders, with his 'Two hundred bunch of corve rods' and '12 dozen of corffe bows' (total value £2. 16s. 6d.), and the colliery carpenter Mathew Watson, who in addition to his 'great saw, ax and . . . other work tools' had 'Coggs, Rongs with trimnell heads, four old shovells and old Ropes, two tramms', and 'Two hookes with chaines and a paire of horse geare', valued in all at £1. 14s. 0d.[131] The actual pitmen, however, are missing, with the single possible exception of Gabriel Rice, whose tiny inventory, taken in 1689,

---

[130] DPD Probate, Invs. of George Mathew (1677), Robert Ellett (1698), John Barras (1691).
[131] DPD Probate, Invs. of John Rawling (1685), Thomas Sanders (1686), Mathew Watson (1676/7).

included '2 cole trames', '6 pitt catts', and a pair of 'hose pads'. We know that he had worked at Greenlaw twenty-five years before, for he was knowledgeable of 'the Colliery, Mynes and seames of Cole' there, but whether as a pitman or an overman, or both, remains uncertain.[132]

Although the inventories of the parish did not usually include the pitmen, they none the less remind us of their continued presence. And in addition, they provide abundant evidence of Whickham's growing importance as a centre for the transportation of coal won from both its own pits and those of neighbouring parishes. From 1669 the 'Old' or 'Ravensworth' waggonway, constructed to serve Sir Thomas Liddell's collieries at Ravensworth and Blackburn, ran down to the Team staithes on Whickham's eastern boundary.[133] Moreover, heavy wain traffic continued to traverse the parish, notably on the western coalways which converged on the Derwent staithes near Swalwell. A wayleave dispute of 1712 generated the testimony of numerous witnesses who recalled driving coal wains from pits at Ridingfield, Fawdonfield, Clockburn, Byermoor, Marley Hill, Northbanks, Tanfield, and elsewhere to Derwent staithes at various dates between the 1660s and the 1690s.[134] In 1690, it was said, 'upwards of 600 wains were employed in leading the coals to Derwent Gut'.[135]

The inventories bear witness to the continuing involvement of Whickham men in this traffic. Of the 89 inventoried inhabitants of the period 1660–99, 24 had coal wains and the draught animals which drew them; 12 possessed two, three, four, or more wains. Some of the owners of a single wain were smallholders or sub-tenants who doubtless drove their own wains on a seasonal basis. The owners of two or more wains, however, must have employed men to conduct carriage on their behalf, and there is plenty of evidence that this was so. Richard Harding of Hollinside, a minor coal-owner in his own right, referred to one of his wains as the one 'that William Stubbs leads or drives with'.[136]

Other minor gentlemen or substantial farmers doubtless had their

[132] DPD Probate, Inv. of Gabriel Rice (1689); PRO DURH 7/43, pt. I. He was 70 years old at his death.

[133] City of Sheffield Library, Bright Papers 72/10, 19. Liddell's colliery complex was described as 'the best in the North of England' in 1669. We owe this reference to Dr Sara Mendelson.   [134] PRO E 134 11 & 12 Anne Hil. 37.

[135] NEIMME, Bell Collection, vol. 20/373.

[136] DPD Probate, Will of Richard Harding (1698).

hired men too, and this is confirmed by the testimony taken from wain drivers and former wain drivers in 1712. Most of these men described themselves as having been 'servants' of one or another of Whickham's coal-owning gentlemen—notably Sir James Clavering. George Stoker of Axwell Wood, for example, was for thirty-two years 'a servant at Axwells to Sir James Clavering . . . to doe and work husband-labour and to drive his coale waines'.[137] By the later seventeenth century, if not before, the personal involvement of by-employed copyholders in wain carriage that had obtained at the beginning of the century would appear to have given way to a more highly organized traffic conducted by employees of wain-owners and coal-owners. In all probability, this activity provided wages for hundreds during a substantial part of the year.

Nor should we forget the men employed at the riverside, unloading coal and transferring it to the keels. Particularly prominent among Whickham inventories of the late seventeenth century are those of the staithemen of Team staithes, Dunston, and Swalwell. These men appear to have emerged into the inventoried population by virtue of a growing prosperity based upon their vital role in the transportation network. Thomas Hindmers of Swalwell was a man of solid middling prosperity by Whickham standards. He appears to have combined the running of his staithes with the provision of beer and entertainment for the waindrivers and keelmen who frequented the riverside. He had a well stocked brewhouse and a pair of 'old virginals' set up in a hall well provided with a form, stools, and chairs for seating and decorated with 'five old pictures'. Hindmers was doing well, and indeed some of his fellows among the staithemen of Team and Dunston were passing rich by the standards of the time. Of the four whose inventories survive, three owned several coal wains and teams of draught animals and two owned keels. Two were brewing and perhaps victualling on some scale, and like Thomas Hindmers had sets of virginals in their halls.[138]

As befitted busy men, the staithemen of Team were also among those few inhabitants of Whickham who possessed clocks. Their movable property and household possessions placed them on a par

---

[137] PRO E 134 11 & 12 Anne Hil. 37, testimony of George Stoker.
[138] DPD Probate, Invs. of Thomas Hindmers (1694), James Johnson (1681), Charles Jordan (1688), James Emerson (1691), Will and Inv. of Lancelot Turner (1696).

with the principal farmers and minor landed gentry of the parish, but neither their working world nor their sense of time was that of agricultural society. Rather, they linked the activity of coalways and waggonways to the bustle of the river. Lancelot Turner handled Liddell coal and supplied waggon horses for the Ravensworth Way, and he also had property in Sandgate and Newcastle, owned two keels, and employed two 'skippers' to operate them. One of the 'Trustie and Loveing friends' appointed as guardians for his children was the staitheman of Stella in Ryton parish. If Whickham's coal began its journey with men like Gabriel Rice, working by candlelight in his 'hose pads', it ended with men like Turner, who passed it on to the fitters of Newcastle, including such a man as John Watson, owner of part of the Team staithe complex, and of eight waggons, seven keels, and shares in six collier ships.[139] And it provided employment and income all the way.

All this serves as a reminder that the later seventeenth century should not be written off as a period of stagnation or relative decline. Nevertheless, the period after 1690 did see a new expansion and elaboration of the working world in Whickham. Following the Montague lease of 1692, the growth of the Gibside–Northbanks–Marley Hill colliery alone must have constituted a major increase in employment opportunities for pitmen and ancillary workers, to say nothing of the important workings at nearby Byermoor. How many men were drawn into Whickham by this development we can never know, but the scale of the activity can be judged by the fact that fifty-seven pits had been sunk by 1706, and that ten years later there were forty-eight pits still standing open in the colliery.[140] Only a minority of these would be working at any one time, of course. In December 1716, at the close of the working year, only five were in production.[141] The remainder were described as being 'wrought out'; but this can have meant only at the existing levels, for many of them are known to have been in production some years later. In November 1723 and January–April 1723/4 ten different pits are known to have been worked, though not all at once; in March 1724, for example, seven pits were producing coal, one of

---

[139] DPD Probate. Inv. of John Watson of Newcastle (1688). His keels lay at Jarrow and his waggons were at Stella colliery in Ryton parish. He had acquired a staithe and 'keelroom' at Dunston and Team in Whickham in 1666: PRO DURH 2/63/unnumbered.
[140] DRO D/ST 72/27, 32. [141] DRO D/ST 72/27.

them working a double shift.[142] Again, in the season January–November 1725 nine different shifts were worked in the colliery.[143]

As to the numbers employed per pit, we have no evidence of the complement of underground workers before the 1740s. In 1742, however, we know that 31 men worked at hewing and putting at two of the pits during one fortnightly pay period.[144] At the Bowes pit during one month early in 1751, 40 men were employed in winning coal, up to 33 of them on any one day.[145] In 1752 paybills for three pits indicate that 18 underground workers plus an overman, a banksman, and a 'gin-horse driver' was a fairly typical complement for a working pit at any one time. In the course of the year (incompletely) covered by those bills, however, no fewer than 94 men worked at these pits for at least part of the year.[146] Earlier, in 1723/4, summary paybills indicate that three pit-head officials were normally employed at a working pit, in addition to which four to seven 'wealers' would be employed per pit screening the coal, and a handful of 'heap sho[v]ellers' would be labouring nearby.[147] Two years later, fortnightly payments also included charges for chandling, corving, smith work, walling shafts, leading pit props, and 'casting stones'.[148]

Putting together this scattered information, it might be concluded that in the second quarter of the eighteenth century a single pit provided work for a total of around 30 people at any one time. In March 1724, then, with seven pits at work, one on a double shift, perhaps 240 people were employed daily at the Gibside colliery. To approach this problem from another direction, Flinn's estimate of an annual output of 200–250 tons per head for the whole colliery labour force (as distinct from face-workers alone) suggests that the new colliery may have employed 72–90 people in the late 1690s (output *c*.18,000 tons), and 260–325 in the late 1710s (output *c*.65,000 tons), subsequently declining to perhaps 68–85 (output *c*.17,000 tons) by the later 1750s.[149]

Whereas colliery expansion created greater work opportunities of a familiar kind, the coming of the waggonways introduced a wholly new world of work. Flinn has commented that 'we know virtually

[142] DRO D/ST 220, 246.   [143] DRO D/ST 298.
[144] DRO D/ST 233.   [145] DRO D/ST 243.
[146] DRO D/ST 277.   [147] DRO D/ST 246.
[148] DRO D/ST 298.
[149] Flinn, *Coal Industry*, 365. For the colliery output, see App. to ch. 1 above.

nothing about the numbers employed on the waggonways',[150] but it is possible to gain at least a sense of the scale and variety of the employment that they brought. The initial construction of a waggonway was a massive undertaking, involving levelling, cutting, the building of embankments and bridges, and the laying of rails, and employing numerous labourers and wrights. We have no detailed accounts for these great projects, but we know that one work gang of 32 men was indicted in the course of the dispute attending the construction of the Bucksnook Way in 1712, that 24 labourers were employed levelling a stretch of ground for George Bowes in 1722, and that 41 labourers were employed during the spring and summer of 1764 levelling ground for a branch of the Tanfield Way—some of them for a few days only, but 23 for more than thirty days each and a core of seven men for up to six months continuously. Even laying a minor extension to serve a pit at Northbanks could involve the work of thirteen men and boys— wrights and labourers—for up to three weeks.[151]

Once laid, a waggonway required constant maintenance, and this was a task that provided employment for wrights, smiths, and labourers laying and renewing rails, shovelling cinders on to the track to reduce the risk of slippage, or clearing snow. On the short Marley Hill–Northbanks branch-line of the Tanfield Way in 1763–4, no fewer than 78 men and boys were employed in maintenance work. A core of 21 men, grouped into regular work-crews, worked for all or most of the year and were supplemented by others taken on at peak periods of activity, notably in the winter months when carriage was suspended and track renewal could proceed un- hindered.[152] The numbers involved in such work when the Dunston, Bucksnook, and Western Ways were in their heyday can easily be imagined.

The building and maintenance of the waggonways thus created new occupations that became a permanent feature of coalfield life. Their operation, in contrast, could be said to have destroyed one occupation: that of wainman. George Stoker testified that, after a lifetime driving his master's coal wains, the opening of the Bucksnook Way in 1712 meant that thereafter he was 'employed to drive his waines and carts with Manure, Hay, Corn, and other

[150] Flinn, *Coal Industry*, 365.
[151] DRO Q/S OB 8, 171–2; D/ST 243; D/ST 355/12.
[152] Based on analysis of pay bills in DRO D/ST 355/12.

things': a sad declension, it would seem.[153] Coal wains, in fact, disappear entirely from the inventories of Whickham people after 1700. But the waggonways provided alternatives. The farmers who had supplied wains and servant drivers under the old dispensation could provide horses and drivers for the new means of transportation, and some were indeed required by their leases to do so. George Bowes insisted on the provision of horses by the tenant of Parkhead Farm in 1726, while Lady Windsor's leases of land in Whickham included such clauses as 'that the said John Taylor will set on and keep constantly employed yearly . . . during the Leading Season twenty able Horses and Twenty Drivers for the Leading of Coals . . . after the same Rates and Prices that she shall pay to other Carriagemen'.[154]

Other drivers were employed directly by the coal-owners and the total numbers involved were considerable. There were 85 waggons on the Dunston Way in 1711 and 109 in 1723. In 1727 the Tanfield Way had 490 waggons in operation, passing down to the Tyne, it has been estimated, at a rate of one waggon every forty-five seconds. Eleven years later George Bowes paid 61 waggon men who were responsible for 119 waggons. Each of these presumably had its driver, to judge by the terms of a waggonmen's bond of 1766, in which 77 men undertook to provide a total of 195 horses, each of which was to have 'an able and sufficient man' who was both to drive the horse and load and unload his waggon.[155] Finally, the waggonways employed gatekeepers who watched over the level-crossings where the ways traversed the roads of the parish: a light task, generally given to the elderly or the widowed, like Elizabeth Carr of Swalwell, who kept the gate at Morrisfield Lane and dwelt in a cottage there built for the purpose.[156]

With the expansion of mining in the south of the parish, waggonway construction, and the eventual flood of coal not only from Gibside and Byermoor but also from the western collieries, activity at Whickham's staithes was also vastly enhanced. In 1721 the Western Way to the Derwent ended in two adjoining staithes, almost half a mile in length overall, which provided berths for fifty

---

[153] PRO E 134 11 & 12 Anne Hil. 37, testimony of George Stoker.
[154] DRO D/ST 356/20; NEIMME, Johnson Collection, Shelf 4, vol. 1, 195. Cf. Shelf 4, vol. 1, 208.
[155] Lewis, *Early Wooden Railways*, 204–6; DRO D/ST 317, 348/41.
[156] PRO E 134 11 & 12 Anne Hil. 37, testimony of Elizabeth Carr.

keels at a time.[157] The staithemen, who had already emerged into prominence, found their responsibilities and their status increased both at the waterfront, where they dealt with keelmen and fitters, and in the supervision of waggonmen placed under their authority. They were key men in the transportation network, and their value was known. 'A Good Staithman is the Key of our whole Business', opined Charles Montague, 'But a hundred Inconveniences follow when A Staithmen is Knave and fool, or either.' In 1700 his staitheman at Dunston, Thomas Denham, threatened to leave his employment as a protest against his inadequate housing, prompting Montague to urge his cousin to find him 'some house to his satisfaction at Whickham or anywhere, whatever it costs'.[158] Under the supervision of Denham and his like, coal was received, warehoused, loaded on to keels, and dispatched down river—all tasks creating yet more employment.

The growth of Swalwell as Whickham's principal centre of population was doubtless initiated by its proximity to the Derwenthaugh staithes. But it was of course greatly accelerated by the establishment there in 1707 of the Crowley factory. Sir Ambrose Crowley's move to Swalwell was precipitated by the need to buy out his rivals Edward Harrison and partners, who had established a small ironworks in the township in 1702–4. However, it represented also an extension of his thriving works at Winlaton and Winlaton Mill, built up between 1691 and 1703. Between 1707 and 1728 the Swalwell factory grew, under the management of Sir Ambrose and (from 1713) his heir John, into the chief centre of manufacture in the Crowleys' extraordinarily integrated business empire.[159]

This was a manufactory of prodigious scale and complexity by the standards of the day. At Swalwell two forges were employed in the conversion of pig to bar iron; rolling and slitting mills produced rod iron and plate for Crowley's nailers and oddware makers; a foundry turned out a variety of cast iron goods; two furnaces were devoted to steel production; three specialized forges produced anchors and chains for the navy, and twenty-nine workshops were

---

[157] Lewis, *Early Wooden Railways*, 161, 208. Cf. Galloway, *Annals*, 248.

[158] Ncle. UL MISC MSS 85, II. 533, 637, 708. In 1723 the staitheman's house at Coleway Haugh was occupied by Thomas Denham. In his will of 1725, Denham called himself 'gentleman'. By that time he was a staitheowner in his own right: NRO Armstrong Papers, 725 F1, 4; DPD Probate, Will of Thomas Denham (1725).

[159] Flinn, *Men of Iron*, 48–54, 79. Further works at Team were added to the Crowley complex in 1735.

occupied by master craftsmen, 'hammermen', and 'boys' who manufactured hoes, frying pans, and other miscellaneous 'oddware'. The forges, mills, and furnaces employed water-driven bellows, hammers, and rollers, while vast quantities of coal were consumed in the hearths of the firm's smiths.[160]

Crowley's employees were recruited both locally and from the metalworking areas of Yorkshire and the Midlands and represented a substantial addition to the population of Whickham. They included officials, clerks and warehousemen, operators of the heavy equipment of the factory, the mass of oddware makers, and casual employees of all sorts. The loss of the records of registration of new employees means that no precise figures can be given.[161] Nevertheless, it is known that in 1728, at John Crowley's death, 157 Swalwell workmen were listed as owing debts to the company, and Flinn estimated that in the period 1725–50 the Swalwell factory probably employed around 250 people at any one time.[162] If so, the Crowley factory in itself can be regarded as approximately equivalent in its creation of employment to the development of the Gibside colliery. It represented a massive intervention in the economy of the parish of Whickham and added new dimensions to its industrial base and occupational structure.

The Gibside colliery, the waggonways, and the Crowley factory together constituted the second major phase of Whickham's industrial development. Of course, not all of those involved in these enterprises were Whickham people; some were inhabitants of adjacent parishes. However, they undoubtedly increased employment opportunities within Whickham and attracted new workers to it. The consequences for the occupational structure of Whickham itself can partly be seen in two detailed occupational listings which survive from the 1750s. The first, a listing of householders in Whickham quarter, was drawn up in June 1750; the second, detailing the names and occupations of the adult men of Fellside, was part of the survey of able-bodied men and was probably prepared in 1757 or shortly thereafter.[163]

The lack of comparable material for the Lowhand and Swalwell quarters necessarily limits the conclusions that can be drawn from

---

[160] Flinn, *Men of Iron*, 184–91.

[161] Ibid. 205, 239.

[162] Ibid. 75. Crowley also employed an estimated 650 or more people elsewhere in the area.   [163] DRO D/ST 22 (Whickham), 301 (Fellside).

these lists. None the less, they provide a revealing picture of the distribution of occupations among close to half the adult males of the parish in the mid-eighteenth century. The various occupational categories that emerge and the numbers involved are presented in Table 3.6. The overwhelming impression gained from these listings in their 'raw' form is that of an industrial community in which male occupations were geared to the production and transportation of coal. Despite the relative decline of Whickham's collieries by the 1750s, the overman, banksmen, borers, sinkers, pitmen, corvers, and the single wailer directly involved in coal production formed the largest single occupational grouping in both quarters of the parish, involving 19.7 per cent of the male householders of Whickham and 25.6 per cent of the adult men of Fellside. Those employed in the transportation of coal (waggonmen, keelmen, a gatekeeper, and a sailor) provided a further 13.1 and 16.1 per cent respectively of the men listed.

The influence of coal, however, went deeper still. Two of the gentlemen of Fellside quarter were Anthony and John Leaton, the 'viewers' or general managers of the Gibside colliery under the Montagues and Boweses. Again, many of the craftsmen and tradesmen of Whickham, notably the wrights, smiths, masons, joiners, carpenters, and farriers, were in all likelihood employed for at least part of their time in maintenance work at the pits and on the waggonways. If we add these trades (involving 13.9 and 18.3 per cent of men respectively) to the colliery and transportation workers, we find that in all 46.7 per cent of male Whickham householders and 60 per cent of Fellside men were engaged in 'coal-related occupations'. The further addition of the labourers who may well have found some work at pits, waggonways, or staithes would raise these proportions to 50.8 and 75.6 per cent in the separate quarters.

Nor did industrial involvement end there. Seven of the Whickham metalworking householders were probably employees at the Crowley works, while Fellside had an anchor-maker who can scarcely have worked elsewhere. Some of the smiths, of course, may also have been Crowley men. As for the six paper-makers, they were employed in a small manufactory at Gibside which appears fleetingly in the estate accounts.

We have, then, a powerful impression of a working world dominated by industrial employment. Had similar lists survived for the Swalwell and Lowhand quarters, this conclusion would

TABLE 3.6. *Male Occupations c.1750–1757*

Occupation	Whickham householders, 1750[a]	Fellside men, c.1757[b]
Gentlemen	6	3
Professions	2 (1 doctor, 1 schoolmaster)	1 (1 schoolmaster/land tax collector)
Agriculture/horticulture	17 (9 farmers, 5 husbandmen, 3 gardeners)	10 (9 farmers, 1 gardener)
Food trades	4 (1 miller, 1 baker, 1 butcher, 1 brewer)	1 (1 brewer)
Clothing trades	13 (4 weavers, 4 tailors, 1 breeches maker, 4 shoemakers)	5 (2 weavers, 2 tailors, 1 shoemaker)
Metalwork trades	10 (1 file-cutter, 1 nailer, 2 hammermen, 1 turner for Crowley, 1 steel-maker, 1 smith for Crowley, 2 smiths, 1 farrier)	13 (11 smiths, 1 anchor-maker, 1 farrier)
Stonework trades	8 (8 masons)	7 (6 masons, 1 stone-cutter)
Woodwork trades	7 (1 joiner, 6 wrights)	13 (6 joiners, 6 carpenters, 1 wright)
Miscellaneous trades	4 (2 coopers, 1 glazier, 1 barber)	6 (6 paper-makers)
Transportation	16 (13 waggonmen, 2 keelmen, 1 sailor)	29 (28 waggonmen, 1 gatekeeper)
Coal production	24 (1 banksman, 19 pitmen, 3 corvers, 1 wailer)	46 (1 overman, 1 banksman, 2 borers, 2 sinkers 36 pitmen, 4 corvers)
Household servants	—	11 (4 servants, 4 footmen, 1 coachman, 1 postillion, 1 groom)
Labourers	5	28
Occupation unstated	6	7
Totals	122	180

[a] The Whickham list also included 27 female householders: of these, 19 were stated to be widows, 4 were called 'Mrs' (i.e. gentry), and one (a widow) was also described as a farmer. The occupants of the poorhouse were not listed.
[b] The figures for Fellside included aged and infirm men subsequently excluded.

certainly be reinforced and elaborated. A set of long, annotated lists of 'old decayed Work People and Poor Widows' in Whickham, Lowhand, and Swalwell which survives among the Gibside accounts for 1764 gives a taste of what may be missing.[164] Alongside the predictable references to pitmen and waggonmen, or their widows, the lists provide numerous instances of keelmen and staithe workers in Lowhand quarter, a former 'Foundry Man', and a couple of labourers said to have been employed 'at Swalwell'. Even here, however, the scores of Crowley workers remain obscure; they had their own welfare provision. They must be imagined as a large, permanent, but surprisingly poorly documented division of Whickham's army of 'work people'.

Against all this, those involved in supplying Whickham's people with food and clothing were a smaller group than might be anticipated. Victuallers are particularly notable by their absence— there had been forty-six licensed victuallers in the parish in 1718, twenty-six of them in Whickham and Fellside quarters.[165] A minority were women, and therefore excluded from our lists. Many of the others may have been by-employed in victualling, like the staithemen already noted. Indeed, the licensees of 1718 included men also known to us as craftsmen, waggonmen, or labourers. As for agriculture, if we exclude the gentlemen-landowners, only 13.9 per cent of Whickham's male householders and 5.5 per cent of Fellside's men were given agricultural or horticultural designations. Those described as 'labourer', of course, must have included men engaged primarily in agriculture. But equally, Whickham's farmers included men whose principal activity was supplying horses to the coal trade.

Such problematic cases raise the broader question of occupational complexity and mobility in Whickham. The economic activities of individual householders in early modern England were frequently diverse. In particular, forms of industrial employment were commonly combined with agricultural work in a mesh so tight as to make it more accurate to speak of involvement in a 'dual economy' rather than a single employment, and this was so not only of workers engaged in the 'putting out' system of textile and metalworking regions, but also of the miners and transportation employees of the Cumbrian coalfield and the lead-mining dales of

---

[164] DRO D/ST 336/7.
[165] DRO Q/R LV/1.

the Pennines.[166] Given such realities, our occupational analysis might be regarded as implying a rigidity of categorization that is spurious and misleading.

There was, in fact, a strong element of the 'dual economy' in Whickham and a degree of life-cycle-related occupational mobility. Wain carriage, of course, began as a by-employment for the copyholders of Whickham, and it remained a seasonal employment for small farmers to the very end. Many of the former wainmen who gave evidence in 1712 described themselves as yeomen or, less commonly, husbandmen. Moreover, some of them were explicit in declaring that they had driven wains in their youth, the presumption being that they subsequently concentrated on their agricultural tasks or crafts. Charles Montague assumed the dual employment of his wainmen when he remarked in a letter of July 1697 that 'Tho the leading be great at present, yet the Harvest coming on and at the autumn, you see the Carriage declining apace.'[167]

This situation certainly continued to some extent even after the building of the waggonways, for the leases of farms sometimes included the obligation to provide both waggon horses and drivers. Again, the surviving inventories of the later seventeenth and early eighteenth centuries indicate that an interest in agriculture was retained by many householders over and above the familiar yeomen–wainmen of Whickham. Several of the staithemen of Team, Dunston, and Swalwell clearly farmed on some scale in addition to their involvement at the staithes, in leading coal, and in victualling.[168] Similarly, the viewer Anthony Leaton combined his managerial activities in 1716 with both tenancy of a Bowes farm and brewing.[169] The goods of one smith inventoried in 1662 included oxen, cows, horses, poultry, hay and bigg growing, and the valuation of a lease of two riggs of land, as well as his 'workgear with other iron in the shop'. That of another just over a century later mentions not only his workshop but also a horse, a mare, a

[166] R. W. Malcolmson, *Life and Labour in England 1700–1780* (London, 1981), 24–5, 38–9; J. V. Beckett, *Coal and Tobacco: The Lowthers and the Economic Development of West Cumberland, 1640–1760* (Cambridge, 1981), 64–6; C. J. Hunt, *The Lead Miners of the Northern Pennines in the Eighteenth and Nineteenth Centuries* (Manchester, 1970), 110, 145–52.

[167] PRO E 134 11 & 12 Anne Hil. 37; Ncle. UL MISC MSS 85, I. 214.

[168] See e.g. the inventories cited in n. 138 above.

[169] DRO D/ST 21/8. In this letter of 1716 Leaton refers to his 'coarne and Hay', his byre and 'oxfould', as well as discussing his new brewhouse.

filly, and a cow, as well as a stack of hay and an acre of oats.[170] Then there were the many who had at least a horse, a cow or two, some poultry, or all three, like the corvers Thomas Sanders and Ralph Peverley, the overmen Mathew Watson and Robert Ellett, the cordwainer John Stenton, or the weaver Robert Wilkinson.[171]

Occupational complexity is thus a well-documented reality in Whickham, and there is also evidence of occupational mobility. John Lonsdale, a wheelwright in 1712, had driven a coal wain as a Clavering servant in his mid-teens. Henry Bainbridge, a keelman at the age of forty-three, had spent his youth on his father's small farm (now in the occupation of his brother) and had worked as a hired man on Mr Thomas Shafto's land before going to the keels at Swalwell.[172]

Nevertheless, we should pause in assessing the occupational structure of Whickham before coming to the conclusion that a 'dual economy' model has broad applicability. It is certainly true that 'many Durham families were prosperously involved in a variety of occupations both industrial and agricultural';[173] the inventories of the late seventeenth and early eighteenth centuries provide examples enough of such people. Yet the agricultural interests of most of the inventoried population suggest less dual employment than the small-scale supplementing of family income by the keeping of at least a few head of stock. No doubt the opportunity to graze an animal or two on a rented close, or on the unenclosed stretches of Whickham Fell, mattered. But it did not necessarily constitute a 'dual economy'. And how far even such minor engagement in animal husbandry extended beyond the inventoried population is a matter for conjecture.

Again, the farmer–waggonmen who supplied draught horses for the waggonways also undertook to provide a 'sufficient man' for every horse to load, lead, and unload coal. Were these waggonmen a discrete occupational grouping? Were they partly or fully employed in such work? The same question can be asked of the other industrial employees of the parish, and above all of the pitmen. The

---

[170] DPD Probate, Inv. of Ralph Tomson (1662); DRO D/ST 341/8 (inv. of James Walker, 1765). A James Walker also supplied a waggon horse for the Bowes's use.

[171] DPD Probate, Invs. of Thomas Sanders (1686), Mathew Watson (1677), Robert Ellett (1698), John Stenton (1690), Robert Wilkinson (1698), Will of Ralph Peverley (1748).

[172] PRO E 134 11 & 12 Anne Hil. 37, 12 Anne Trin. 10.

[173] Hodgson, 'Agricultural Improvement', 148.

author of the *Compleat Collier* wrote of those engaged in sinking pits that 'it is not every Labourer who has been (by chance) in a Coal Pit, or at Labor in other sort of digging above Ground, that is fit to be imployed in this Work, but it should be one that understands the Nature of Stone and Styth and Surfet by some Experience had before.' Only skilled men would do 'for their own security sake, as also for the Benefit of the Owner'.[174] Was this equally true of the pitmen in general, or did they merge at times with the labour force of the waggonways and the farms?

Happily, the Whickham evidence permits us to pursue these questions to at least a limited extent. We have done so by cross-checking the individuals named and ascribed an occupation on the lists of the 1750s against more than a score of other lists providing occupational information and evidence of employment in a variety of tasks in the period 1725–66.[175] The results of this survey indicate that the working life of Whickham was dominated by the coal industry even more than is suggested by the 1750s listings already analysed, and that the principal groups of industrial workers were engaged almost wholly in their stated occupations.

Consideration of those listed as farmers or husbandmen in the 1750s confirms immediately our earlier surmise concerning their industrial involvement. There are some who are known to the records only as farmers. Most, however, also appear as waggonmen, bonded to provide horses and drivers, signatories to an agreement regarding compensation for killed or injured horses, or paid for coals led on the waggonways by themselves or their men. Ephraim Fenwick, for example, was a Bowes tenant who supplied a single horse in 1738, two in 1740, two in 1762, and three in 1766. Francis Jackson was responsible for the provision of two horses continually from 1738 to 1766. A similar story could be told of John Bland, Thomas Brown, Lovel Jackson, George Hall, Isaac Smiles, and others. In fact it was the norm, and such activity may have extended beyond the farmers identifiable as contracting waggonmen, for our evidence relates largely to tenants of the Bowes family. Others who

---

[174] *Compleat Collier*, 22–3.

[175] These include estate, colliery, and waggonway paybills; the bonds of pitmen and waggonmen; lists of keelmen, waggonmen, people in receipt of fire coal, recipients of charity and aged and decayed work-people, and a rating assessment specifying the tenants of lands. We have also drawn upon our general name index. DRO EP/Wh 24; DRO D/ST 233, 243, 246, 252, 277, 298, 301, 317, 322, 323, 336, 344/22, 348/41, 355/12; TWA Keelman's Papers, 394/1, 12.

are known to have been Clavering tenants, for example, may also have been involved but escape notice in the surviving records.

Nor were those stated to be farmers and husbandmen the only ones to be engaged in coal transportation. Mr John Barras of the Whaggs supplied six to eight waggon horses in the 1740s and 1750s; John Leaton, viewer, Bowes tenant, and brewer, supplied two in 1751; Mr Thomas Rawling provided four in 1766. Others involved included men described on the 1750s lists as smiths, a tailor, a weaver, a servant, and a labourer, some of these lesser figures also being men known to be tenants of small parcels of land (where they presumably grazed their animals), and most of them providing only one, or occasionally two, horses. In documents relating to leading coal, all of these men were described as 'waggonmen'. Some may have driven waggons themselves for much of the year; others may simply have enjoyed a supplementary income as middlemen. In more than a few cases, however, it seems likely that the waggonways provided a substantial part of their living.[176]

Turning to those stated to be waggonmen on the 1750s lists, we find that they can be divided into two categories. On the one hand, there were those who, like the farmers, undertook to provide a horse or horses and were paid accordingly, not a few of whom were also tenants of small parcels of land. Such men may have been distinguished from those described as farmers or husbandmen only in that the compilers of the 1750s lists regarded them as being wholly or principally employed on the waggonways. Perhaps they always drove themselves.

On the other hand, there were those (the majority) who do not appear on the documents listing the names of the principal waggonmen. Presumably these men either worked for other coal-owners or, more likely, were simply drivers. Occasionally they turn up doing other work, generally of a coal-related nature. Edward Hall and Thomas Mason, for example, found work as waggonway labourers in 1764, the former for only fourteen days, the latter for just over a month. John Burn was a staithe labourer briefly in the winter months of 1764. William Coats and George Sumerson appear regularly on pit paybills in 1764. John Rain, also a waggonman in 1757, had been a Gibside estate labourer in 1752. We

---

[176] This confirms Lewis's suggestion in *Early Wooden Railways*, 211, that, while many Tyneside waggonmen were drawn from local farms and also worked smallholdings, industrial employment was often their principal activity.

have, then, some evidence of occupational shifts and some of supplementary labouring work, generally in the months when leading was suspended. Most of these men, however, are known to us only as waggonmen. The evidence suggests that, if leading coal on the waggonways provided income supplements and/or dual employment for most farmers and some craftsmen, it was also the exclusive occupation of some minor contractors and many wage-earning drivers.

Waggonway maintenance and construction also involved a core of fully employed specialists, though of course they are not described as such on the 1750s lists. Of those who were engaged in such work for the entire year 1764, for example, Joseph Hopper was described as a smith, Thomas Robson as a waggonman, and Thomas Foster as a labourer. These men and others worked in regular gangs which can be seen performing specific tasks in particular pay-periods of the year covered by the surviving paybills.

The waggonways also, however, offered work for non-specialists for periods of the year. The husbandman George Richardson cleared snow, alongside many others, in January 1764. The farmers John and Thomas Brown, both of whom were also waggonmen, worked for twenty-two and twenty-nine days respectively at the beginning and again towards the end of the year. Another farmer, Anthony Newton, who is not known to have provided waggon horses, did a few days' work in April and then laboured continuously from May to December 1764, levelling ground on part of Tanfield Moor. Then there was the joiner Edward Elliott, who worked seventy-eight days in all, mostly between March and July; the labourer John Foster; the pitman John Emerson, who picked up two days' work in the autumn; and the waggonmen already noted who found temporary work maintaining the wooden railways that they normally traversed. Once again, we have some elements of multiple employment, including multiple industrial employment, but it involved men engaged largely as a casual supplement to a body of specialized workers.

Some of these workers were of course skilled craftsmen, and our evidence brings out still more fully the nature of their involvement in industrial work. Of the handful of known or surmised Crowley workers, none was found engaged in any other employment. For the rest, wrights like John Harbottle, Thomas Smart, and William Allen were paid for work at Northbanks colliery in 1752, 1763, and

1764, as were the carpenter Hugh Pallaster and the smith John Nicholson. The masons of the 1750s lists appear more frequently in the 1752 accounts of the Gibside estate, engaged for part of the year in George Bowes's ambitious programme of building. But at least one of them, John Laburn, did masonry work at one of George Bowes's pits as well as on his parkland follies, while Thomas Shields and two assistants spent more than seventy days walling pits at Northbanks in the later months of 1752.

Many of the other craftsmen of Whickham must also have been employed regularly at the pits without leaving a record; for the surviving paybills, while invariably including payments made for smith work and wright work, and not infrequently for masonry work, rarely reveal the names of the men involved. Such people doubtless plied their specialized trades in whatever context was required of them, though we can at least confirm that it was frequently in an industrial context.[177] And just as the craftsmen worked at whatever task required their particular skills, so the labourers of the 1750s lists worked wherever their more diffuse skills and muscle power were needed. Some are identifiable as regular employees at Gibside, engaged primarily in husbandry, wood-cutting, and the like; others flit intermittently through the records, now at Gibside, now on a waggonway gang, now shovelling at the staithes, now helping to erect a colliery gin. At least one, Thomas Ramshaw, had become a regular pitman by the early 1760s, compensating for another, John Semar, who appears to have left the pits in 1752 and worked as a day-labourer thereafter.

With Ramshaw and Semer we come at last to the pitmen, and with the pitmen we find an occupational discreteness that amply bears out the implications of the opinions expressed by the anonymous author of the *Compleat Collier*. Of the sixty men described as overman, borer, sinker, banksman, or pitman on the 1750s lists, and the two more who were given no occupational designation but can in fact be identified as pitmen, only one is known to have engaged in any other form of work during the period when he was working in the pits: John Emerson, who did

---

[177] Only those tradesmen engaged in the food and clothing trades seem rarely to appear in the records of industrial employment, though as shown above at least one tailor and one weaver supplied waggon horses, while we know of a further weaver who worked briefly as a staithe labourer in 1763–4 and of a shoemaker who later became a pitman.

two days as a waggonway labourer in 1764. The vast majority of these men were pitmen only, and in a sizeable minority of cases we can say that they spent most of their adult lives as such. Ralph Crawhall, a sinker in 1757, can be found working at the Northbanks pits from 1725 to 1764. Robert Bainbridge, William Chapman, Robert Cockburn, and Anthony Maddison are traceable from 1740 to 1764, and Francis Pigg, James Jopling, Samuel Crozier, and others from 1750 until 1764.

Nor is there more than a modicum of evidence of occupational mobility among the pitmen. As might be expected, some men can be traced entering the industry. Robert Chapman, a pitman in 1757, had appeared as a waggonman in a list of 1740. He was bonded as a pitman in 1741 and appears as such in every reference we have to him thereafter. John Maddison was a shoemaker in 1750, a pitman thereafter. William Coates was a waggonman and Thomas Ramshaw a labourer in 1757, but both were pitmen by the early 1760s and appear as such in several sources. However, although men can be found entering the pits, only a handful can be identified as having left for other occupations. John Semer was called a labourer on the 1757 list and had been one since 1752; but from at least 1748 until 1752 he had been a pitman. Robert Brown was a pitman in 1757 and 1763, but in 1764 he worked all year as a member of a waggonway gang and in 1766 he was a waggonman. Had these men been injured? Were they ageing? All we can say is that, among those pitmen who remained 'in observation' for a decade or more, Semer and Brown were exceptions to the general rule.

We cannot be absolutely certain of the exclusive claims of mining as an occupation, since most of the men described on the 1750s lists as directly employed in winning coal did not remain in observation. Of the sixty-two who appear on the occupational listings, three-fifths are known to us only from those lists or from independent evidence of colliery work for dates very close to those of the listings. They were probably present in the parish for only a few years at most. In addition, the surviving pit paybills, miners' bond, lists of pitmen receiving fire coal, and the rest provide us with the names of many miners between 1741 and 1764 who did not appear on the Whickham and Fellside listings either as miners or in any other occupation. Presumably they either passed through the parish briefly or lived in Swalwell or Lowhand quarters, or else they came in to work from neighbouring parishes, just as some Whickham pitmen certainly worked in collieries beyond the parish bounds. We have one further means, however, of testing whether this larger body of mineworkers engaged in a supplementary occupation, during at least one year: 1752.

For the year 1752 we are fortunate in having the best surviving series of paybills for the Northbanks colliery, covering the Bowes pit for forty-eight weeks and the Dike and Fortune/Gate pits for thirty-two and thirty-eight weeks respectively. To judge by the full records of the Bowes pit, the seasonal layoff in coal mining had been much reduced at Northbanks by the mid-eighteenth century, a fact that may be of some significance in explaining the occupational stability of pitmen that we have already observed. None the less, work could fluctuate considerably at all these pits, and in slack periods, as well as in the weeks of closure after Christmas, individual pitmen may have looked for temporary work elsewhere. If so, one of the best sources for such employment was the Gibside estate, which lay close to Northbanks, was owned by the miners' employer George Bowes, and required a considerable labour force in husbandry, maintenance work, quarrying, and building. By good fortune, a complete year's set of labourers' paybills survives for Gibside for the year beginning in mid-December 1751, detailing the work done by 148 estate workers. These paybills offer an altogether exceptional opportunity to learn how many of the 94 pitmen employed at the Bowes, Fortune/Gate, and Dike pits in 1752 also found work at their master's estate that year.

The answer is, only two. The first of these is already known to us. John Semer had been a pitman since at least 1748. He worked at the Bowes pit from January to March 1752. Thereafter he disappears from the pit paybills only to reappear in September and October 1752 as a labourer at Gibside. He seems not to have returned to the pits, for he was listed in Fellside as a labourer in 1757 and does not figure on any list of pitmen after 1752. George Selby had been bonded as a pitman at Northbanks in 1741 and was certainly working there in 1742. From December 1751 until March 1752, however, he worked intermittently at Gibside for a total of twenty-one days. From May until December 1752 he appears regularly on the pit paybills. He seems to have left the area by 1757. In all, then, our survey of work at Northbanks and Gibside in 1752 yields a single instance of occupational mobility involving a pitman and a further example of casual labour performed by a pitman during the winter. The precise circumstances underlying the changing activities of these men can never be known to us. None the less, it is clear that their experience was exceptional. Pitmen, it would seem, were pitmen.

To summarize this investigation of occupations, occupational complexity, and occupational mobility in Whickham in the mid-eighteenth century, it is evident that the working lives of the men of Whickham and Fellside were heavily dominated by the availability of industrial employment—more completely so than is apparent even in the raw figures of the distribution of male occupations which can be derived from the listings of the 1750s. For some, notably the farmers, such work offered a supplement to their livings—though on occasion that 'supplement' was very likely the tail that wagged the dog. For others, notably the craftsmen and day-labourers, it provided an unusually broad range of opportunities for the practice of their trades or the piecing together of a patchwork living. At the same time, it is clear that Whickham was peopled in the main by full-time, specialized, industrial workers: the waggon-men proper, the waggonway crews, the numerous but frustratingly ill-documented Crowley workers, and above all the pitmen.

Despite the quality of some of the records available to us, the picture inevitably remains incomplete. We can say little of any value about the keelmen or the staithe workers, save that they too were present, like the Crowley men, elsewhere in the parish. Among the more historically visible groups of industrial workers, however, occupational complexity appears to have been very limited and occupational mobility slight. Geographical mobility, in contrast, could be considerable. This was less so for the waggonmen, whose living was tied to the wooden railways that stretched inland from the mouths of the Team and the Derwent, serving many collieries, and who might also be held by the tenancy of land. But it was emphatically the case for the pitmen, among whom the presence of a stable core of long-term employees at Northbanks only serves to highlight the perennial coming and going of the 'marras' with whom they worked.

We now have a sense of the elaborate structure of the working world of Whickham as it developed in the century after 1660, and of the manner in which the people of the parish made their living. The question remains: what kind of a living did their work afford them?

4. GOODS

Up to now, we have attempted to assess some of the economic consequences of industrial growth for individual families by examining the evidence provided by the inventories of household goods of the copyholders of the manor of Whickham.[178] We saw that the generation of copyholders caught up in the initial expansion of the Grand Lease colliery experienced a general rise in living standards as reflected in domestic possessions. Bedsteads, feather beds, tables, and cupboards became commonplace in their inventories; candlesticks and cushions became more widespread; pewter and bed-linen were possessed in greater quantities. While clear differentials existed in the quantity (and presumably also in the quality) of the domestic goods owned by copyholders of different wealth, there was a general shift in the material culture of the household, away from the relative simplicity of the mid-Elizabethan period and towards an enhanced comfort and amenity. Though fewer inventories survive for the period 1620–49, those extant are consistent in indicating that these developments were consolidated and maintained in the second quarter of the seventeenth century. In addition, during the same period the clergymen and lesser gentry of the parish began to enjoy an altogether new degree of luxury in their domestic lives, as indicated by both the quantity and the sophistication of their furnishings, and by the appearance in their inventories of such novel items as glassware, looking-glasses, clocks, books, and decorative maps.

These trends, of course, were observable principally among the copyholders and other landed members of the population: the great majority of those for whom inventories survive prior to 1650. Although they also involved the cottagers of the manor to a degree, we have no way of knowing to what extent industrial work brought comparable changes in the living standards of Whickham's growing population of workmen and labourers. Such evidence as we have of their condition suggests rather their relative poverty and their dependence upon wages that were hard won and unexceptional by the standards of rural society. Save during the dreadful year 1596–7, these appear to have been sufficient to provide a basic living, but it seems unlikely that they afforded any degree of comfort beyond

[178] See ch. 2 above.

food and warmth—the more so for those who dwelt in the insubstantial 'hovels' and 'lodges' scattered across the parish.

For the later seventeenth and early eighteenth centuries, the evidence enables us to extend our knowledge a good deal. In the first place, inventories of goods survive in far greater quantities for the decades between 1660 and 1720 than for the earlier period. Moreover, those that survive extend across the social scale of the parish, from the minor gentry through the substantial farmers and the 'lesser ratepayers' of the parish to that marginal area on the borderland between modest prosperity and the threat of poverty. These inventories include neither the apex of Whickham society in the late seventeenth and early eighteenth centuries—the great gentry—nor the mass of the work-people of the parish. Nevertheless, they can be supplemented in various ways in the second quarter of the eighteenth century so as to provide more than a little evidence of the economic fortunes even of the labouring poor. Let us begin by considering the record provided by inventories of household goods.

Seventy-six inventories of household goods survive for the period 1660–1719. In terms of the basic domestic requirements of warmth, food preparation, eating, sleeping, and storage, they indicate an essential continuity with the household interiors that had become the norm in Whickham in the first quarter of the seventeenth century. Fire-irons are listed for most households, and almost half also had at least one iron 'chimney'. Bedsteads or occasionally a 'close bed' appear in almost every inventory, together with substantial quantities of bedding which were frequently itemized into sheets, blankets, pillows, and coverlets. Almost three-quarters of the inventories listed one or more feather beds, though only one (that of Thomas Liddell of Farnacres) included a mattress.

The detail with which kitchen utensils were specified varied, but the basic items of pots and pans were ubiquitous, while spits were mentioned in more than half the inventories and frying pans in more than a third. People ate from wooden trenchers and pewter dishes, employing spoons (which were generally of pewter where such detail was provided), and they drank from pewter pots and tankards, all of these items being commonplace at every social level. Tables and chairs were also ubiquitous, though as might be expected the richer households had more chairs, and finer ones at that. Stools and forms provided additional seating in most households. Storage was in cupboards. Lighting was provided by candlesticks of wood, pewter, brass, or iron. Personal cleanliness entailed the use of the numerous napkins listed (sometimes together with towels). Of the relative luxuries of the early seventeenth century, cushions, carpets, and chamber-pots were now quite widely used, all of these items occurring in a third to two-fifths of the inventories.

So much for basic items. There were also novelties. Some inventories now included a desk or a 'pair', 'chest', or 'case' of drawers. Window curtains and rugs made their appearance. Drinking glasses, known only in the households of the rectors and the Liddells of Farnacres in the earlier seventeenth century, were more widely owned. By the 1660s ceramics, very rarely mentioned in the inventories of earlier generations, appear regularly and are prominent thereafter in the form of 'stone' dishes and pots, 'earthern' dishes, plates, and porringers, or more rarely 'painted earthern dishes' or even 'cheney' or 'chieny' dishes and a 'cheney posset cup'. Only the rectors are known to have possessed a looking-glass, pictures, or maps in the early seventeenth century, but in later-Stuart Whickham both looking- or 'seeinge' glasses and pictures of one sort or another were more widespread. Clocks were found in only two inventories before 1650 but in ten after 1660. Books, which had previously been found only among the possessions of the rector and the Liddells, now occurred in twelve inventories. Items of silver plate, formerly the preserve of the richer gentry, were now to be found in almost one-third of inventories in the form of cups, 'tasters', spoons, and the like. Finally, musical instruments made their first appearance in the parish in the sets of virginals listed in fifteen inventories.

The frontier of domestic consumption had evidently moved forward once more in Whickham. This can be inferred in part by the acquisition of novel forms of what have been termed 'back stage' goods, items for daily use. But more significant were the trends towards the elaboration of the 'frontstage' goods of a household—those intended for display as well as use—and towards the more widespread ownership of 'information goods'—books, pictures, maps, clocks, even the 'seeinge glasse'.[179]

However, this generalized picture of advances in domestic

---

[179] For these terms, and for a general discussion of consumer behaviour in this period which examines the experience of the north-east alongside that of other regions, see L. Weatherill, *Consumer Behaviour and Material Culture in Britain, 1660–1760* (London, 1988), 9–11, 28, and *passim*.

consumption among the households of Whickham must not be allowed to mask the very real differentials that existed between the householders of the parish, differentials which can be explored more fully after 1660 as a result of the larger and more socially varied nature of the evidence. The inventories, in fact, fall into three broad categories. First come those belonging to the minor gentry, the more substantial farmers, and the richer staithemen of the parish. Among these householders, domestic goods invariably totalled more than £15 in value and not infrequently amounted to much more. The wealthiest of these people, with household goods valued at upwards of £20, could indeed be said to have formed a subcategory of their own, but for present purposes it is more convenient to regard all of these substantial inhabitants as a single broad group. A second category in terms of household goods embraces the lesser yeomen, a variety of craftsmen and tradesmen, and some of the middle-rank employees in mining and the coal trade (some overmen, a borer, a corfmaker, staithemen of lesser means). This group corresponds very largely to those designated the 'lesser ratepayers' in our analysis of the hearth tax. Their inventories of household possessions ranged in value from £6 or £7 to £12 or £13. Finally, there remains a minority of inventories of household goods valued at less, usually substantially less, than £5, including those of a weaver, a smith, a cottager, a carpenter, an overman, and a number of poor widows.

In putting forward these categories, we do not wish to imply any rigidity of categorization. We are not talking of discrete social entities; nor are we arbitrarily dividing up the inventoried households on the basis of valuations of household goods. Rather, these groupings emerged from the analysis of domestic goods as it proceeded, and were found to correspond in general with certain occupational and status groups and broad bands of inventoried wealth. We are perfectly aware of the deficiencies of inventories as historical sources and of the need to avoid putting too much strain upon the evidence. But at the same time, we are satisfied that the 'consumption groups' identifiable in the evidence had an undoubted reality, and one that demands discussion if the nature of the process of enhancement of living standards in the later seventeenth and earlier eighteenth centuries is to be properly comprehended.

The key to understanding that process lies in a simple awareness of distinctions, of crucial differentials which can be found even in equipment relating to the most basic dimensions of domestic life.

Fire-irons, for example, were near universal possessions, but iron chimneys or leaden grates were very rarely to be found in the poorer households. Around three-quarters of inventories included feather beds. Those that did not were usually those of the poorer householders, who might have a 'flockbed' or a 'chaff bed', or simply a bedstead, sheets, and blankets. Cooking pots and pans were universal. Spits and frying pans might be specified in the inventories of rich and poor alike. Yet only kitchen inventories of relatively high value bore witness to a proliferation of specialized culinary equipment: chafing dishes, fish steamers, pudding pans, saucers, mortars and pestles, spice boxes, toasting-irons, iron or brass scales, and the like. Some of the inventories of lowest value lacked cupboards. Others are reminiscent of the copyholder inventories of a century earlier in that seating was provided by a form and stools rather than chairs.

Such variations can be found also with respect to those items that had become more widespread from the second quarter of the seventeenth century. Cushions occur principally in household inventories of £6 or more; carpets and chamber-pots, with few exceptions, in inventories totalling more than £15. Of the novelties of the later seventeenth century, earthenware could be found throughout the inventoried population, possessed by the relatively wealthy, the modestly prosperous, and the relatively poor alike. Yet there was a pattern to the recorded possession of most of the other new consumer items of the period. China, glassware, looking-glasses, pictures or mounted wall decorations of other kinds, and sets of drawers and desks were largely, though not exclusively, confined to household inventories valued at more than £15. Only in the early eighteenth century do we find such goods filtering down in any significant degree to the middle range of inventories. Clocks, musical instruments, and silverware were even more socially restricted; they were found, with few exceptions, in the inventories of gentlemen, the richer yeomen, and staithemen of comparable substance. Of the goods that might be regarded as relative luxuries, books alone appear to have escaped such social confinement; only a sixth of inventories mention them at all, but they can be found at all social levels.

Awareness of these differentials provides a clearer sense of the varying social depth of participation in the new world of domestic goods in later seventeenth- and early eighteenth-century Whickham.

Among the inventoried population, there were significant, though by no means totally rigorous, distinctions between those who headed the localized consumption hierarchy (the minor gentry, wealthier yeomen, and leading staithemen) and their neighbours. We have already glimpsed some of the household goods of the staithemen. Alongside them can be placed a minor gentleman like William Jackson, who died in 1671. His seven-room house was crowded with furnishings, which included two wainscot tables, an oval table, and three smaller tables; two armchairs, twenty-four leather chairs, and 'one childs high chaire'; two curtained and vallanced bedsteads (one with 'silke fringe') and two other beds; a case of drawers; a wainscot presser; a pair of virginals; three carpets; green and yellow rugs; 'a large seeinge glasse', 'nine hanging pictures'; and a set of 'window curtings'. He possessed mountains of linen of all sorts and his kitchen was elaborately stocked with pewter, iron, and brass utensils. The household goods of the wealthy yeoman James Liddell were no less numerous and elaborate. At his death in 1690 he had a 'Brass Clocke', two chests of drawers and 'a nest of small drawers', and a colour-coordinated parlour which contained an 'elbow chair covered with green', 'eight thrum wrought chairs with green coverings', and four stools 'covered with green'. There was a choice of bed curtains too, 'one of housewife plains ye other of stript linnen and woollen'.[180]

In comparison, the lesser yeomen and average craftsmen and tradesmen of the parish can be said to have maintained the living standards achieved by the copyholders of the early seventeenth century, while also enjoying some of the newer goods of the post-Restoration world. The craftsman George Davison, whose goods were inventoried in 1682, had a couple of bedsteads and plentiful bedding, two cupboards, three tables, two chairs, a form, and two stools. He had candlesticks and eight cushions, two of them 'work quishens'; but no carpets or chamber-pots were listed. Finally, he had plenty of pewter and kitchenware of a simple kind. His was a domestic setting that would have been familiar enough to his grandfather, save for his possession of a set of 'chieny dishes'. Almost twenty years later, the yeoman Christopher Harrison's inventory showed rather more signs of the novelties of the age. His goods were similar enough to Davison's in basic essentials, but also

[180] DPD Probate, Invs. of William Jackson (1671), James Liddell (1690).

included some 'old drawers' in the kitchen, a 'case of drawers' in the chamber, a desk, and some 'paper picters' on the walls.[181]

The inventories of the poorer households, however, rarely include any of the novel consumer goods of the age. Indeed, in a fair number of instances such people can scarcely be said to have achieved the living standards reached by the average copyholder in the reign of James I. Their inventories are commonly so meagre that examples can be quoted almost in their entirety. George Frame, who died in 1679, had two 'little old close bedsteads', a feather bed, a bolster, two blankets, four pillows, and two pairs of sheets, all described as 'old', 'little', or 'coarse'. He also possessed one 'little old cubbart', a 'little old table', two 'little' stools, a 'little' form, an 'old' chair, three 'little' pewter dishes, a 'little' candlestick, twelve wooden trenchers, and seven earthenware plates. Even his few pots and his frying pan were called 'old' and 'small'.

The frequent repetition by the appraisers of the disparaging adjectives 'old' and 'little' only serves to enhance the sense of bareness that attends the list of Frame's goods. But his range of possessions was typical enough of the poorer inventories, and the manner of description was not unique either. Cuthbert Whitfield's goods were fairly similar, except that he had only one 'old close beddstead with very ordinary bedding', no pewter (only earthern dishes and cups and wooden 'vessells'), and 'a peace of an old cubbert bottom with a few old peacess of rotten dalls and a little stoule'. He did, however, possess two cushions. The only clue we have to his occupation is his possession of 'one old shovell'. Thomas Emerson was a carpenter and a little better off. He had two 'close bedsteads', two 'chaff beds', two bolsters, and three pairs of sheets; a table, two chairs, two forms, and a cupboard; a little pewter and a few 'old' pans and 'iron girr' in the 'low house' where the cooking was done. The widow Margaret Lonsdale owned two bedsteads and their bedding, which together constituted almost half the value of her household possessions, two tables (one of them 'little'), a chair, a form, two cupboards, some pewter and brass, a pot, and three pans. The interior of the coal-worker Gabriel Rice's cottage must have been dominated by his bedstead and his 'case bed', in addition to which his furniture consisted only of a table, two forms, and two chests. His was the inventory of an elderly man living alone. He had

---

[181] DPD Probate, Invs. of George Davison (1682), Christopher Harrison (1701).

little bedding and only minimal cooking equipment, but he did possess, listed alongside the coal mining equipment already quoted, 'one great bybell'.[182]

Careful consideration of the inventory evidence can thus confirm the trend towards enhanced domestic comfort which has been noted by a number of historians in recent years. At the same time, however, it reinforces the need to guard against exaggerating the extent of plebeian participation in the new 'consumerism' of the seventeenth and early eighteenth centuries.[183] In Whickham new patterns of consumption were pioneered by the lesser gentry, substantial farmers, and the more prosperous participants in commerce and industry—groups that clearly overlapped a good deal in the case of this coalfield parish. They extended only slowly and unevenly, however, to the modestly comfortable 'lesser ratepayers' of the parish, and there is very little evidence that they were of more than peripheral significance in the domestic lives of the great bulk of the householders of the parish.

Awareness of these limitations is vital to any appreciation of the social distribution of the prosperity afforded by industrial and commercial development. Equally, such awareness provides the essential context for an understanding of the social meaning of new developments in domestic consumption among those who were able and willing to invest resources in the acquisition of the 'decencies' and minor luxuries that the age afforded.

The status-enhancing and status-defining functions of household possessions can be sensed in the very location and arrangements of goods described in the more elaborate inventories. Housing was still relatively simple in Whickham. Inventories of modest or low value frequently failed to distinguish rooms in a dwelling, or else mention only 'forehouse', parlour, and 'backhouse'. Among the more prosperous, a typical house consisted of hall or forehouse, parlour, kitchen, and two or three upper rooms described as chambers, lofts, or garrets, with occasionally a buttery or brewhouse to complete the scene. Nor was room use marked by highly developed differentiation of functions beyond the kitchen and service rooms, to judge by the physical distribution of furnishings. Bedsteads were still commonly found in the hall and parlour as well as in upper

---

[182] DPD Probate, Invs. of George Frame (1679), Cuthbert Whitfield (1677), Thomas Emerson (1694), Margaret Lonsdale (1693), Gabriel Rice (1689).

[183] Weatherill, *Consumer Behaviour*, chs. 8–9, discusses this issue fully.

rooms, while few of the latter seem to have been regarded purely as bedchambers. Nevertheless, the inventories of Whickham's wealthier inhabitants do provide evidence of a degree of 'front-of-house display' in the discernible arrangements of possessions by room.

The prosperous yeoman and wain-owner Thomas Johnson had a bed in his parlour, but that principal room also contained his oak table and chairs, his set of virginals, his books, 'one seeing glasse', all his cushions, and '10 old pictures and one glass case'. Others among the minor gentry and wealthier farming and commercial families had begun to reserve their main room for eating, reception, and display. George Shafto and William Jackson, for example, kept their more sophisticated furnishings in their halls alongside their best tables and sets of virginals. A few even had a room that appears specifically devoted to seating and entertainment. James Liddell's household seem to have cooked and eaten in the forehouse; the parlour had only two 'small' tables, but it also contained his best chairs, two chests of drawers, a looking-glass, pictures, glasses, his clock, and his items of silver plate.[184] In the light of such evidence of domestic display, it is worth considering that, in a local society in which traditional foci of social identity and traditional criteria of social status had been so thoroughly disturbed by industrial and commercial development, domestic living standards (and in particular the possession of specific novelties) may have acquired a significance of an altogether new order. The common enjoyment of a certain material environment may have done much both to encourage a sense of social identity among the occupationally varied leading inhabitants of the parish and to differentiate them from both plain parishioners and the labouring poor.

By the second decade of the eighteenth century, detailed inventories of household goods begin to fail us. They are rare thereafter, but the process of gradual change that they reveal certainly continued among Whickham's principal parishioners, and the social significance of the acquisition of new and finer goods finds expression in evidence of another kind. James Clavering of Lamesley, who frequently enjoyed the society of his peers in nearby Whickham, very commonly requested luxury items of one sort or another when writing on coal-trade matters to his agent in London, and was generally well satisfied with their arrival, via the collier

[184] DPD Probate, Invs. of Thomas Johnson (1674), George Shafto (1668), William Jackson (1671), James Liddell (1690).

fleets, in what he called 'my box'. In the winter of 1712–13, while engaged in the removal of his household to Newcastle, his letters prove particularly revealing. He asked for a set of 'prints and pictures for my staircase', leaving the choice to his agent's discretion, though reminding him, 'I am a subscriber for Raphael's cartoons, therefore you must not be extravagant.' For his parlour, however, he had more specific intentions and a distinct social and political message to convey. In December 1712 he ordered portraits of political message to convey. In December 1712 he ordered portraits of the Archbishop of Canterbury and the Bishop of St Asaph, and pictures of three 'patriots' to be selected at discretion. By February 1713 these were on his walls, 'and I assure you', he wrote, 'add much to the beauty [and] lustre of my parlour'. (He was so satisfied that he sent for another bishop and a few more 'true Brittains' for the empty spaces that remained.) Meanwhile, he had also ordered a set of fine chairs for his best dining room and conveyed his wife's request for a new bed. His agent was authorized to spend up to £21 on these items and was advised to consult his friend Lady Liddell, then resident in London, on the choice of colours for the bed.[185]

James Clavering was as anxious as his wife to secure furnishings appropriate to their standing on their entry into Newcastle society, though he was more preoccupied with the impact upon his guests of his parlour portrait gallery and dining room than with the details of the bedchamber. The vital female role in the selection and arrangement of domestic goods is more visible in the planning of the furnishing of Dr Robert Thomlinson's new rectory at Whickham in 1717. 'Aunt would have 50l. to furnish her drawing room', wrote the Thomlinsons' nephew John in his diary, '20l. for silver tea kettle, lamp and table; 5l. in glasses and sconces; 10 or 15l. in hangings, and the rest in chairs, cushions and curtains etc.—may buy a good and cheap buro in Cambridge and have it brought by Lynn.'[186] Clearly the subject fascinated him—as became a young curate on the make.

As these examples indicate, the leading inhabitants of the parishes of industrial Tyneside were conscious of both the range of goods available to the prosperous of Augustan England and the status-confirming and status-enhancing role of domestic furnishings. For

---

[185] Ncle. UL MISC MSS 10, 29 Nov. 1712, 5/6 Dec. 1712, 3 Feb 1712/13.

[186] 'The Diary of the Rev. John Thomlinson', in J. C. Hodgson (ed.), *Six North Country Diaries*, Surtees Soc. no. 118 (Durham, 1910), 85.

them, this consumerism provided the framework of a developing milieu of polite sociability, a genteel world of lustrous parlours, tea, and table talk.

Nor were the Claverings and Thomlinsons exceptional in the sophistication of their tastes, if we are to judge by the inventory of Mrs Isabel Barras taken in 1742. She had twenty-seven pictures on her staircase. Her two fine bedchambers, the 'blew' and 'yellow' rooms, were furnished in the appropriate colours and graced with dressing tables and mirrors. Her dining room had a 'Mahogany Skreen Table', 'black kane' chairs, a 'Tea Table', and 'China and Glasses in the Bowfoot', while her parlour was set with small cabinets, wainscot tables, more 'kane' chairs, a fine winged mirror, an 'Eight Day Clock', and a 'Tea Chest and Cannisters'. In such a setting Mrs Barras could well receive the local 'quality', including no doubt her kinswoman Mrs Thomlinson; and, to judge by her kitchen equipment, she could entertain them royally to tea, coffee, chocolate, and fine meals served on 'Delf' dinner plates.[187] For the principal households of Hanoverian Whickham, the accoutrements of private domesticity and genteel sociability were well within the range of a purchasing power that had been enhanced by their involvement in the coal trade. Such goods could be obtained either directly from the shops of nearby Newcastle or from the metropolis itself, via the regular commercial contracts that the coal trade ensured.[188] Commercial and cultural incorporation marched hand in hand.

5. WAGES

For the majority of Whickham's householders, continued industrial and commercial development brought not so much a new urbanity as a more abundant supply of the old essentials of work, shelter, and food. As we have seen, the inventories of the relatively poor do not suggest that they shared to any significant extent in the accumulation

[187] DPD Probate, Inv. of Isabel Barras (1742). She also had a coffee pot and a copper chocolate pot in the kitchen.

[188] Bishop Pococke wrote of Newcastle in 1760 that the city imported 'every thing for the use of Northumberland, Durham, Westmoreland and part of Cumberland, so that they have great shops of all kinds': 'The Northern Journeys of Bishop Richard Pococke', in J. C. Hodgson (ed.), *North Country Diaries*, 2nd ser., Surtees Soc. no. 124 (Durham 1915), 244.

of minor 'decencies' apparent among their modestly prosperous neighbours at the turn of the seventeenth century. The paucity of inventory evidence thereafter precludes direct comparison of their fortunes with those of the other 'consumption groups' evident in the inventoried population of the parish. But the lack of such evidence is compensated for by the survival, from the second quarter of the eighteenth century onwards, of our first detailed and reliable evidence of their earnings.

This evidence comes in two forms. On the one hand, we have a variety of sources of information on the rates of pay current in Whickham in particular years (generally in the form of statements of rates contained in summary accounts and employment agreements or sums paid for specified tasks). On the other hand, we have information on the actual wages paid over considerable periods of individual years to particular work-people, material that is sometimes of sufficient quality to permit calculation of the annual earnings of workers in a variety of occupations. Let us begin by considering the evidence of wage rates.

Table 3.7 sets out in summary form the information on the wage-rates for certain sectors of the work-force of the parish in the years 1722–66, alongside the minimum wage-rates assessed by the justices of the peace for County Durham in 1672–9 and the statements on wage levels in the coal industry made by the author of the *Compleat Collier* in 1708. As will be evident, these rates require a degree of explanation.

In the case of agricultural wage-rates, the Durham justices followed the customary practice of assessing maximum rates, which varied both seasonally (with lowest rates in the winter season), and according to whether or not the worker received 'meat and drink' from the employer. The wages actually paid on the Gibside estate in 1752 also varied seasonally and according to task, but appear to have been paid on a 'without meat and drink' basis. If the justices' assessments provide a reliable guide to the wage levels current in the county towards the end of Charles II's reign, it is clear that in 1752 the wages paid at Gibside represented a significant advance of those of the later seventeenth century, generally in the order of a 20–25 per cent improvement. This rise in wages may have been relatively recent in 1752, for it has been argued that agricultural wages in the county were fairly stable in the late seventeenth and early eighteenth centuries; wages of 6*d*.–8*d*. a day were still the norm on the

TABLE 3.7. *Adult Male Wage-Rates, Durham Region and Whickham*

(i) *Agricultural labour, 1672–1752*

	Q/S assessed maxima 1672–9		Gibside Estate 1752	according to season
	With	Without		
Haymaker	6d. p.d.	11d. p.d.		10d. p.d.
Shearer of corn	4d. p.d.	8d. p.d.		10d. p.d.
Common labourer	2d.–4d. p.d. (according to season)	6d.–8d. p.d.	Trenching, planting, hedging, clearing drains, clearing coach road	} 8d.–10d. p.d.
			Ploughing, sowing, harrowing, liming, threshing, carting, dunging and general labour	
			Felling/lopping trees, railing, piling wood	} 10d.–16d. p.d.
			Fencing, sawing, snow shovelling	} 12d.–18d. p.d. / 8d. p.d.

TABLE 3.7 (*cont.*)

(ii) *Masons and carpenters, 1672–1752*

	Q/S assessed maxima 1672–9		Gibside 1752	Northbanks colliery 1752
	With	Without		
Mason	12*d.* p.d.	18*d.* p.d.	16*d.*–18*d.* p.d.	18*d.*–24*d.* p.d. 'walling pits'
Carpenter	12*d.* p.d.	18*d.* p.d.	12*d.* p.d.	14*d.* p.d. scaffolding at pits

(iii) *Waggonway work, 1722–66*

	Northbanks 1722	Northbanks/Tanfield 1764	Marley Hill 1766
Leading coal	—	—	14*d.*–17*d.* per 'gate'
Construction/maintenance			
General labour	10*d.*–12*d.* p.d.	8*d.*–12*d.* p.d.	—
Skilled labour	—	14*d.*–20*d.* p.d.	—

(iv) *Colliery work, 1708–52*

	Compleat Collier (1708)	1725 (2 pits)	1741 (Bond)	1742 (2 pits)	1751 (1 pit)	1752 (3 pits)
Overman	16*d.* p.d.–8*s.* per wk. 1*d.* p.s.c.	—	—	—	—	—
Banksman	14*d.* p.d.	2½*d.*–3*d.* p.s.c.	2½*d.*–3*d.* p.s.c.	—	—	—

Gin horse-driver	—	—	—	12d. p.d.	8d. p.d.	8d.–9d. p.d.
Hewer	10d.–12d. p.s.c.	6d. p.s.c.	10d., 12d., 17d. p.s.c	9d.–10d. p.s.c.	14d. p.s.c.	10d.–14d. p.s.c.
Putter	20d.–22d. p.d.	22d. p.d.	22d. p.d.	22d. p.d.	22d. p.d.	22d.–24d. p.d.
Horse-drawing	—	6d.–8½d. p.s.c.	12d. p.d.	12d. p.d.	—	9d. p.s.c.
Corving	—	2s.6d.–3s. p. 21 s.c.	—	—	2½d. p.s.c.	3d. p.s.c.
Smithwork	—	6d. p. 21s.c.	—	—	1d. p.s.c.	1d. p.s.c.
Wrightwork	—	—	—	—	4d. p.10s.c.	4d. p.10s.c.
Wailing*	—	—	—	5d. p.d.	4d. p.d.	4d. p.d.
Shovelling*	—	—	—	—	—	6d. p.d.
Snow shovelling	—	—	—	—	8d. p.d.	10d. p.d.
Pit watchman	—	—	—	—	—	14d. per night
Horse-keeper	—	—	—	—	—	13s. per fortnight

Notes: p.21s.c. = per 21 score corves   p.10s.c. = per 10 score corves
p.d. = per day
p.s.c. = per score corves
* commonly a woman's task

Sources: DRO Q/R/W 1–6; DRO D/ST 233, 243, 277, 298, 317, 322, 344/22, 355/12.

Gateshead estate of William Cotesworth in the early eighteenth century.[189] Unfortunately, we have no way of testing this possibility in the case of Whickham. Our only reliable evidence for agricultural wage-rates before 1752 is a statement made in 1686 that a particular labourer was accustomed to work for 8*d.* a day.[190]

In the case of two groups of craftsmen, masons and carpenters, we have the assessed maxima for master craftsmen of the 1670s, and also the rates paid for masonry and carpentry work, both at the Gibside estate and at the Northbanks Colliery in 1752. As might be expected, these men were paid more than was usual for most categories of agricultural labour. Carpentry work, however, was paid for at rates below those assessed in the 1670s, while masonry work brought wages close to or above the maxima set by the justices some eighty years earlier. Clearly, work at the colliery was better paid than at the estate, this being particularly evident in the case of master masons.

Smith work and wright work at the pits cannot easily be compared with the daily rates paid to masons and carpenters, since both smiths and wrights in attendance at the colliery were paid not by the day, but according to the number of scores of corves won at the pits they served. The same was true of the corvers who made and maintained the corves of a pit. Corvers would appear to have been considerably better paid than smiths, and smiths better than wrights, in the early 1750s in terms of rates per score of corves won. In the case of corvers and smiths, it is also evident that their rates of pay had advanced markedly since the 1720s, almost doubling for corvers and more than trebling for smiths. This escalation of the wage rates for smiths naturally raises the possibility of competition for skilled labour with the nearby Crowley works. Unfortunately, no hard information is available on the wages paid at the Crowley factory, except that some men were paid weekly wages and some piece-rates, and that in the 1750s the anchor-makers of Swalwell were reported to be the best paid of the Crowley men on wages of 12*s.*–14*s.* a week (somewhat more than could be earned by a colliery mason working a six-day week).[191]

---

[189] Brassley, 'Northumberland and Durham', 42.

[190] DPD Probate, Letter accompanying inv. of Adam Rochester (1686).

[191] Flinn, *Men of Iron*, 190, 205. In 1771 Arthur Young reported that the Crowley workmen earned 1*s.*–2*s.* 6*d.* a day. This suggests an enhancement of wages since the 1750s. A. Young, *A Six Months Tour Through the North of England*, 3 vols. (London, 1771), iii. 9.

Turning to work on the waggonways, paybills for maintenance and construction work survive from both 1722 and 1764. These indicate that general labour on the waggonways was paid at rates comparable to those current for agricultural labourers, and that, as in agriculture, the daily rate varied with the season. Most of the men paid were actually remunerated at the lower rates specified in the table. Skilled men were consistently paid more, at daily rates comparable to those paid for skilled labour at Gibside and the colliery. That variation existed both seasonally and according to task is evident from the sums paid to individuals, but unfortunately, the paybills do not specify the exact nature of the work performed by particular skilled men. Some were doubtless wrights, some smiths, and so forth.

As regards the waggonmen who actually led the coal, we have only one statement of the rate of pay per 'gate' (the return journey between the pithead and the staithes). This varied from pit to pit, and those cited are the rates current for the various pits working at Northbanks/Marley Hill in 1766. The waggonmen were paid by the 'gate' at rates calculated to be around 3*d*. or 4*d*. per mile of the downward journey. On the Bucksnook Way in 1716, three-fifths of the money paid was due to the horse-owner and two-fifths to the driver of the waggon, a practice that seems to have been regarded as usual on Tyneside. Most drivers apparently completed two gates a day.[192] On these assumptions, a waggonman serving the Northbanks pits would earn around 28*d*.–34*d*. a day if he drove his own horse (though he would need also to pay for his horse's feed and harness). A contracting horse supplier would earn 16¾*d*.–20½*d*. per horse per day, gross. A driver employed by a contracting waggonman would earn around 11¼*d*.–13½*d*. per day, a daily income comparable to that of the better paid forms of agricultural labour. Drivers, of course, would probably serve different pits and even different collieries on different days or at particular times of year, and their pay would vary accordingly.

Finally, we come to work at the collieries other than that performed by craftsmen. The rates of pay quoted are taken from the *Compleat Collier*, from the Northbanks miners' bond of 1742, and from overmen's 'presentments' or paybills for a variety of Northbanks pits between 1725 and 1752. Most of the latter are for individual fortnightly pay-periods; only the material for 1752

---

[192] Lewis, *Early Wooden Railways*, 208.

extends across the whole working year. The system of payment in mining was exceedingly complex, and the figures quoted express some of this complexity. There was no single characteristic 'miner' in terms of the payment system, which reflected the complicated differentiation of the labour process and the managerial system at the colliery.

From the beginning of the eighteenth century, and perhaps from the very outset of the Montague lease, the colliery at Gibside/ Northbanks had been under the general supervision of a viewer, one of those men 'very well acquainted with collieries and the managing and working thereof' who were now emerging as key figures in the managerial hierarchy of the coal industry.[193] The viewers of Northbanks during this period were first Anthony Leaton and then his son John. Both regarded themselves, and were regarded by their neighbours, as gentlemen, and both had many irons in the fire economically, but the precise nature of their remuneration for their colliery duties remains obscure.

Under the Leatons' direction, the overmen of the colliery seem to have lost something of the status of semi-independent sub-contractors which they had enjoyed as principal 'servants' of the coal-owners in the early seventeenth century. 'Undertakers' could still contract to work a pit or group of pits for a year 'at their own proper costs and charges' in return for an agreed sum per ten of coal won—as we know from a surviving contract of 1725 and a further reference to this practice in 1732.[194] Even in such cases, however, the working of the pits was to be firmly under the direction of the viewer. In the 1725 instance, for example, Leaton was not only to check that the working was done 'fairly and orderly' and that the coals were 'round, Dry and Clean', but also to specify the target output for particular weeks. In addition, he was to examine and approve a presentment of work done fortnightly.[195]

Whether such contracting 'undertakers' should properly be

---

[193] For viewers in the 18th c., see Flinn, *Coal Industry*, 52 ff. The passage quoted is a self-description by the viewer John Fenwick in 1712: PRO E 134 11 & 12 Anne Hil. 37. For a contemporary account of a viewer's duties, see *Compleat Collier*, 32 ff.

[194] DRO D/ST 344/35, 47/35. The 'undertaker' in the second of these cases was not a working miner, but Mr William Barras, former husband of Mrs Isobel Barras, whose 1742 inventory is discussed above. His anticipated profit was in the region of £800 p.a.

[195] DRO D/ST 344/35. The later agreement (D/ST 47/35) specified that 'everything necessary [is] to be done according to the direction of the Viewer'.

regarded as overmen by this period is open to doubt. By the second quarter of the century, most of the Northbanks overmen appear to have been straightforward employees.[196] Each was responsible for the operation of a pit, or for a single shift at a pit working two shifts. They made fortnightly presentments of the work done, the charges incurred, and the wages due to their men. They themselves were paid according to output, their wages being supplemented on occasion by 'considerations' of one kind or another. The actual rate of the overman's pay per score of corves is stated only in the paybills of 1725 (1*d*. per score of corves), though the sums paid in 1752 suggest rates of at least 1½*d*. per score of corves, a significant rise in the remuneration of these men over the second quarter of the eighteenth century.[197]

As for those who worked under the overmen's supervision, hewers were paid according to the number of scores of corves won individually at the coal-face, each man's personal output being checked by means of a system of tallies placed in his corves. Hewing rates, however, varied from pit to pit and seam to seam, 'according to the tenderness or hardness of the coal', as the *Compleat Collier* put it. Inevitably, this meant that a single hewer might work for different rates of pay at different times of the working year.[198] Putters were paid by the day, though the rate could vary according to the distance coal was dragged to the eye of the pit. Underground horse-drawing of coal was paid at a daily rate substantially lower than the rate paid to putters, though it could also be paid on a per-score-of-corves basis. Meanwhile, at the surface, banksmen at Northbanks received a sum per score of corves drawn to the surface, rather than the daily rates suggested by the *Compleat Collier*. Wailing of the coal and heap shovelling was paid for by the day at very low rates. (Both were often women's tasks.) Other work was paid on a daily or nightly basis, the horsekeeper alone receiving a fortnightly wage.

In terms of daily pay-rates, the putters were clearly very well paid by the standards of the day, earning daily wages higher than those

[196] Nef, ii. 425–7, suggested a trend towards salaried status for the overman in the later 17th c.

[197] It is difficult to be certain, because of the problem of separating the wage paid per score of corves in 1752 from additional payments which were not always separately specified. There is little doubt, however, that overmen's wages were rising.

[198] *Compleat Collier*, 35. The variation in the rates at which individual miners were paid is very evident in the 1752 paybills.

paid to skilled men at Gibside or on the waggonways. Underground horse-drawing was paid at day rates somewhat higher than those earned by most agricultural workers and similar to those paid to waggon drivers. Male surface workers engaged in such activities as snow shovelling were paid wages similar to those of agricultural labourers. Comparison of the rates of pay of those paid per score of corves is impossible without knowledge of the numbers of corves hewn or drawn. Over time, however, while putters' wages were stable, those of hewers appear to have been rising, even if we allow for the fact that our first set of pit bills from 1725 may represent pits with rather low wage-rates for hewers.

Consideration of the rates of pay current in Whickham thus gives us an initial sense of the earning capacity of the work-people of Whickham and of the differentials that existed among them. In particular, it indicates that work in the coal industry was well paid, sometimes very well paid, by the standards current for agricultural labourers in the area. As compared with the vast bulk of England's rural proletariat, the industrial workers of Whickham, and above all the pitmen, would appear to have enjoyed considerable advantages. The validity of such a conclusion, however, depends upon a further question which we have scarcely explored as yet—the problem of what these rates of pay (especially rates per score of corves in the coal industry) actually meant in practice.

The translation of rates of pay into estimates of the annual earnings of wage-workers in the eighteenth century is no simple matter. In the case of men paid by the day or week, we need to know just how many days or weeks they actually worked in a given year. Seasonal employment or underemployment was a besetting problem for the agricultural labourer, and this was no less so in the Whickham area than elsewhere. 'You have done well in discharging useless hands and reducing wages at the proper time', wrote William Cotesworth to his steward in October 1723, an opinion that was unlikely to be shared by the men concerned.[199]

Industrial employment was also affected by seasonality. Though the shipping season in the coal trade was gradually extended as the eighteenth century advanced, initially to a February start and a December closure,[200] the remaining weeks of the midwinter dead season posed problems for those whose living was tied to the trade,

---

[199] Quoted in Hughes, *North Country Life*, 139.
[200] Ellis, *William Cotesworth*, 93–4.

problems that were no less severe because they were expected. The keelmen were among the worst hit. 'What must become of the poor keelmen?' protested George Liddell in 1729 when it was proposed to delay the start of the shipping season until mid-March:

They give over work the beginning of November and many of them had not then a shilling before hand. They live upon Credit and a little labouring work till they get their binding money at Christmas. That money goes to their Creditors and they borrow of their fitters to buy provisions . . . and so they put off till trade begins. Now if they are not to begin till about Ladyday, half of them will be starved, for as their time of working will be so much shorter trades people will not trust them . . .[201]

They were not alone. The waggonmen also attracted Liddell's concern, for their leading too was closely tied to the shipping season.[202] In 1751 on the Tanfield Way waggonmen were paid for a season extending only from April until late December, the December coal presumably being stockpiled at the staithes to await the first fleets of spring. This might be a matter of little concern for the farmer–waggonman, but it had profound implications for the full-time driver's earning capacity. Nor were the Crowley workers exempt from the problem of intermittent work. Heavy dependence upon naval orders at Swalwell meant a pattern of periodic boom and slump, exacerbated by stoppages when supplies of imported raw materials ran low or when there was insufficient water to drive the mills. Key workers were kept on at retaining wages when work was short, but no such consideration was extended to day-labourers or piece-workers, and for most of the Crowley men there can have been little regularity of employment except in wartime.[203]

While there are general problems in determining the length of the working year and the degree of regularity of employment, the mining industry provides peculiar problems of its own. All those employed in and around the pits, of course, faced the realities of seasonality in their work—although in a less severe form than was the case for transportation workers in the coal trade and in a manner that was diminishing over time. In 1734 an account of the coals won at Northbanks indicates that the two longest working pits were 'going' from 1 March until 21 December, leaving the men idle after their customary Christmas break for two full months. By 1752,

[201] Quoted in Fewster, 'Keelmen', 27.
[202] Lewis, *Early Wooden Railways*, 210.
[203] Flinn, *Men of Iron*, 205, 242–4.

however, the best of the Northbanks pits were at work from the third week of January until 22/3 December, with a layoff (including Christmas) of only four weeks.[204]

A more serious problem than the diminishing seasonal stoppage was the intermittent nature of work even at 'going' pits. Ideally, the pits should have worked a six-day week, and the standardized fortnightly presentment accounts drawn up by pit overmen were set out in a form designed to represent each man's work over twelve days. It was comparatively rare, however, for the pit to be at work for a full twelve days. Of the six pits detailed in a bundle of daily presentments covering the period 6–18 March 1724, two were at work for only eight days, two for ten, and one for eleven, while the sixth pit was out of production for the entire fortnight. The reasons for such stoppages varied. On 7 March five pits were described as not working 'by reason of raine'. The day before, the West pit was idle while 'making ready for topp Coale'. On 9 March Fellside pit was 'not working for want of deales', while after the rain of 7 March the East Brow pit remained out of commission 'not working 3 Men Mending Shaft and will not be finished the fortnight'.[205] Such circumstances make it exceedingly difficult to estimate the number of days pitmen actually worked in a given colliery season, and of course played havoc with the earnings expectations not only of men paid by the day, but also of those paid by the score of corves hewn or drawn.

Output, as might be expected, varied enormously, and not only from pit to pit—the basis of the wages of overmen, banksmen, and pit craftsmen—but from man to man. The author of the *Compleat Collier* reckoned that, in a pit of sixty fathoms' depth, 'about 21 Scores of Corves of Coals wrought and drawn *per* Day, is a good Days work, and as much as most Collieries of that depth, can, or do constantly work'.[206] He was optimistic. At Northbanks on 12 March 1724 only one of five working pits produced twenty-one score corves. The others won nineteen and a quarter, thirteen and a quarter, seven, and three score corves respectively. Over the fortnight from which this day was randomly selected, daily output at a single pit could vary from three to more than thirty score corves, while fortnightly output ranged from 96 to more than 187 score corves, averaging 138.[207] As for the individual miners, on whose output depended not only their own wages but also those of

204 DRO D/ST 322, 277.   205 DRO D/ST 246.
206 *Compleat Collier*, 32.   207 DRO D/ST 246.

their banksman and overman, at the Corne pit in May 1742 six of the eight hewers cut more than twelve score corves in one fortnight, the best of them winning seventeen score and ten corves. Yet at Graham's pit in the same fortnight only three of eleven hewers achieved the twelve score corves level, though the 'big hewer' of the pit managed almost nineteen score.[208]

Clearly, a hewer's wages depended both on his own strength and skill and on his luck in working a good 'bord' in a good pit at the right time. According to the *Compleat Collier*, it was customary for the hewer to agree with the overman as to 'what Quantity he will work dayly', though it was not always possible to complete this 'intended Days work or Quantity'.[209] Once he had completed his agreed quota or stint, the hewer was apparently free to leave the pit or to work on to increase his output and earnings. Many apparently left, and it was commonly reported that hewers worked far fewer hours than the putters, who were required to remove whatever coal had been cut on a particular day in return for their day's wages.[210]

Another form of personal influence over output and earnings was voluntary absenteeism. This was certainly known, as at Graham's pit at Northbanks on 6 March 1724 which was 'not working because men did not come afeild in time', or at Fellside pit four days later, when 'Men Sleeped the Caller' who roused them daily from their cottages.[211] It might also be inferred from the sporadic attendance records of individual pitmen, visible in the most detailed fortnightly presentments. But it would be a mistake to interpret such simple realities as evidence of a systematic 'leisure preference' among pitmen, a tendency to give over work once a certain level of earnings was assured in a particular pay-period. Most attendance records appear to have been good. There were too many intangibles involved in a miner's work for a man to be able to calculate in advance his likely wages even after the best of days, and there could be many reasons for periodic absence other than a preference for leisure. The most obvious of these were illness and minor injuries, perennial hazards of the pitman's life which find only occasional mention in the records. In June and July 1752, for example, Dr Alexander Cockburn submitted bills to George Bowes for treating

[208] DRO D/ST 233.   [209] *Compleat Collier*, 36.
[210] T. S. Ashton and J. Sykes, *The Coal Industry of the Eighteenth Century*, 2nd edn. (Manchester, 1964), 163; Flinn, *Coal Industry*, 368.
[211] DRO D/ST 246.

'one of Northbanks Lads his hand crushed and his thumb split in Anthony Leaton's pit', and another 'his Hand and finger crush'd in the Pitt'.[212]

In addition, the extent to which a man could anticipate, or exert some personal control over, his earnings was greatly hampered by the fact that the division of labour among pitmen was by no means rigid at this period. At Graham's pit in May 1742 only one man was a hewer only; eleven others were paid for hewing, putting, 'ridding stones', leading pit props, and propping underground in a variety of combinations. Nearby at Corn pit, seven men (or youths) did horse driving only, but the remaining eight underground workers were employed in a combination of hewing, driving headways at a fixed price per yard, leading props, propping, and 'laving watter'.[213] Few assumptions could be made about a miner's earnings, and even fewer can be safely employed by historians seeking to estimate them. For all these reasons, scholars attempting to do so have generally been obliged either to declare the impossibility of the task or to fall back upon estimates of hewers' earnings alone, based on known rates of pay, contemporary suggestions as to a hewer's daily output, and guesstimates of the numbers of days worked in a year.[214] Given the realities we have described, such calculations are likely to be very approximate at best.

Fortunately, the unusually high quality of some of the records relating to pay on the Bowes estate that survive among the Strathmore papers means that we can do a little better in the case of Whickham. These documents permit a fairly full reconstruction of the actual earnings not only of the pitmen, but also of some other work-people of the parish. We can begin by considering the evidence provided by the Gibside estate paybills for the year commencing in late December 1751.[215]

In all, 140 men and 8 women found employment on the Gibside estate during the year covered by the paybills. Just over one-fifth of these people worked for fewer than twelve days, some two-thirds worked fewer than a hundred days, and only one-fifth can be said to have found relatively full employment at Gibside in that they worked there for two hundred days or more. How those who worked only for a few days or a few months pieced together the rest of their living, we do not know. Consideration of the regularly

[212] DRO D/ST 277.
[214] See e.g. Flinn, *Coal Industry*, 386 ff.

[213] DRO D/ST 233.
[215] DRO D/ST 277.

employed minority, however, can reveal a good- deal about the earning capacity of the most fortunate members of the labouring class of Whickham. We can best illustrate their experience by drawing upon examples of men who appear not only on the Gibside paybills but also on the occupational listings of the 1750s.

William Cragmill was singularly fortunate. In 1757 he was to be described as a gardener, but in 1752 he performed all kinds of work at Gibside: trenching and planting, shovelling snow, cleaning the coach road, and working on the construction of George Bowes's column, as well as assisting with haymaking and corn harvest. In winter, after the Christmas break, he also found work about the gardens, perhaps establishing a skill that led to more specialized future employment. In the course of the year he was paid for 290 days' work, receiving a total of £12. 1s. 4d., and in addition it can be observed that his fortnightly income was fairly regular: a fortunate man indeed.

Others who appear on the lists of the 1750s as labourers and who can be identified working regularly at Gibside in 1752 were somewhat less well-off. Joseph Richey put in 242 days' work at a variety of tasks akin to Cragmill's and appeared in almost every paybill save those of early February and early June. He earned £9. 8s. 9½d. in all. John Craggs worked for 215½ days between 15 February and 9 December 1752, earning £8. 10s. 9d. in all. What he did in late December, January, and early February we do not know, though eleven years later he turned up as a staithe labourer during a single week in December 1763. If he was able to earn 8d. a day for much of the time that he did not work at Gibside in 1751–2, he might have been able to raise his income to between £9 and £10 for the year, though this seems unlikely. William Thurlaway, William Raine, John Foster, and Thomas Foster all worked between 191 and 231½ days at Gibside and were paid between £6. 15s. 7½d. for 204 days to £8. 19s. 7d. for 231½ days' work. Raine and John Foster were somewhat more specialized as labourers in husbandry than the others, but all were clearly prepared to turn their hands to any task offered to them. The differences in their earnings derived from the number of days they worked and the going rates of pay in the seasons in which they found most of their employment. Overall, the working histories of these men suggest that an individual adult male agricultural labourer who enjoyed pretty full employment by the standards of the time might hope to earn between £7 and £12 in a year. Those with thinner work records at Gibside may or may not have been able to supplement their earnings to this level.

The Gibside paybills also provide evidence of the actual earnings of some craftsmen, notably the masons who worked on George Bowes's follies. George Reay was described as a mason in 1757, and he worked as such in 1752 at Gibside, mostly 'scalping stones' at the quarry, but also doing some plastering and repairs about the house and constructing a drainage channel. In addition, he worked as a haymaker for twelve days. Reay was usually paid at rates well above those paid to general estate labourers, and for his ninety-five days of work, scattered across the year from January to October, he received £5. 5s. 4d. Doubtless he also looked for work elsewhere, especially during a gap in his Gibside work in April and May and after October. If he found it, he might have doubled his income; but then again, he might not. Another mason, John Labren, worked fewer days than Reay (eighty-three in all between 13 June and 9 October), but was better paid. His work was all on the column, perhaps performing highly skilled tasks. He received £6. 16s. 5d. for his four months of more-or-less continuous work. Yet another, Richard Ellett, worked at the quarry only between 27 June and 6 October and got £3. 1s. 7d. for three months of well-remunerated work.

Turning these certain earnings into estimates of the year's income is clearly very difficult. We do not know how much work there actually was for masons away from the Gibside building programme, though in the same year at least one, Thomas Shields, worked for seventy-three days between 1 September and 23 December walling pits at Northbanks and was paid £5. 9s. 6d. for his labour. Perhaps a mason could earn between £10 and £20 in a year, depending on his skill, experience, and good fortune in finding jobs, but it seems probable that for most their annual income would be nearer to the lower end of this range.

The paybills for waggonway maintenance and construction that survive for 1764 provide further evidence of the annual earnings of both labourers and skilled craftsmen.[216] As at Gibside, only a minority of the men and boys employed found work in every pay-period of the year, but the records of those who were regularly employed are revealing. Of those who worked almost all year as labourers, Ralph Wild, Anthony Scott, and Thomas Robson all put

[216] DRO D/ST 355/12.

in 299 days' work and earned between £11. 17s. 7d. and £12. 5s. 4d. Their incomes were comparable to the best paid of the Gibside labourers, and it is obvious that they were able to achieve this level of earnings primarily because of the greater regularity of employment which the waggonways afforded members of established maintenance crews. Anthony Newton, who had been listed as a farmer in 1750, worked only 212 days from late April to December and received £10. 3s. 4d. The frequency with which he did labouring work during more than eight months of the year suggests that this may have been his principal source of income in 1764.

As for the waggonway craftsmen, Joseph Hopper, a smith according to the 1757 listing, did 303 days' work at skilled men's wages and earned an impressive £23. 2s. 0d. He was exceptional, however. Other skilled men who found regular work throughout the year included John Kendal, John Eltringham, and Thomas Foster, who worked between 223 and 300 days in all and were paid between £14. 18s. 0d. and £18. Of those who did not work so regularly, Edward Elliot, listed earlier as a joiner, found seventy-seven days' work in January and between April and July. He was clearly prepared to do general labour as well as plying his skill, to judge by the rates of pay he received at various times, and his income from waggonway work totalled £3. 10s. 0d. Perhaps with work elsewhere he might have tripled this sum in the course of the year; perhaps not. All in all, the waggonway evidence suggests that, of those who enjoyed upwards of 200 days' work, a labourer could clear £10–£12 and a skilled man £14–£20 or even more. This was not so dissimilar from the experience of the Gibside labourers and craftsmen, save in the vital respect that for a fortunate minority industrially related work offered a greater regularity of employment.

The best-off of the waggonway maintenance crews, then, could hope to earn significantly more than their peers in more 'traditional' forms of work. As for the waggonmen who led the coal from pit to staithe, an excellent series of paybills for the leading seasons 1751 and 1760 reveal that the contracting waggonmen of Whickham who led coal all season (not only from Northbanks but also from other 'partnership' pits) earned between £25. 9s. 1d. and £31. 3s. 1d. per horse in 1751 and between £19. 10s. 7½d. and £23. 12s. 5d. per horse in 1760.[217] Some of these men provided only one horse and may have driven it themselves; others provided several horses

[217] DRO D/ST 252, 301, 317.

and their total earnings have been divided accordingly. Earnings averaged £27. 8s. 0d. per horse in 1751 and £21. 6s. 0d. per horse in 1760, which was clearly a rather poor season for these men.

We may therefore calculate that a waggonman who was an owner-operator might expect to earn £21–£27 a year gross, before deducting the costs of his horse and harness. A horse-owner among Whickham's farmers and gentlemen who did not drive himself might receive £13–£16. 10s. per horse gross, if as Lewis suggests he took three-fifths of the money paid. A driver employed by such a contracting waggonman might earn £8. 6s.–£11 for the season's work. The earnings of the driver-waggonman were thus broadly comparable to those of an estate or waggonway labourer. Those of an owner-driver might place him on a par with a craftsman, and his income would increase with every additional horse he was able to supply. Farmers and minor gentlemen who supplied horses in addition to running a viable mixed farm clearly stood to gain a handsome income supplement from the waggonways.

We can now turn to the pitmen. A considerable number of fortnightly pit presentments survive from the Northbanks colliery between the 1720s and 1764. Most, however, cover only a brief period of work at any given pit. The presentments for the year 1752 are exceptionally valuable in that they provide details of work done at the Bowes pit for the whole working year from late January to late December, at the Dike pit from February to August, and at the Fortune and Gate pits (which employed the same basic crew) from April to December.[218] These documents provide evidence of the working lives of no fewer than ninety-four men and youths, of whom twenty-four underground workers remained 'in observation' for every pay-period of the year, either at the Bowes pit or at a combination of pits. Before providing details of their actual earnings, however, we must pause to consider what these records reveal about those aspects of the working life of a pitman that bore so heavily upon their earning capacity.

All the features that we might expect to find are borne out by the evidence of the presentments. In the first place, the output of individual pits varied dramatically from fortnight to fortnight. Fortnightly output at the Bowes pit averaged 108 score corves but ranged from 62 to 179 score corves. The Fortune and Gate pits both averaged 107 score corves a fortnight, ranging from 63 to 138, while

[218] DRO D/ST 277.

the Dike pit produced an average of only 83 score corves a fortnight, with a range of 15 to 111 score corves. At best, this was poorish output by the standards of the *Compleat Collier*.[219]

Variation in output was most obviously influenced by the number of days that a pit was actually in production. The Bowes pit worked a full twelve days in only seven of the twenty-four pay-periods of the year. In all, of a maximum of 290 working days,[220] there were 31 when the pit was idle (10.7 per cent), and in the worst fortnight the closure lasted 5 days. We do not know the reasons for such closures, though the fact that a number of men who generally worked as hewers were employed to shovel snow at the pit on one February day gives us an idea of the circumstances on at least one such occasion. The Dike pit never worked more than eleven days in a fortnight and often only nine or ten, though at the Fortune and Gate pits between April and December things were better, with only 13 of a possible 230 working days lost through closure (5.7 per cent). Even when a pit was going, however, output was clearly affected by the quality of the workings, to judge by the numerous days or weeks of lower-than-average winnings. Once again, we do not know why, though there were problems with water at the Dike pit in late March and at the Gate pit in mid-November.

Factors such as these inevitably placed limits upon the earning capacity of the pitmen. But even when a pit was going and working was good, there were considerable variations in fortnightly income from man to man. This depended partly on the tasks that a man was called upon to perform, and on whether he was paid by the day or per score of corves, and partly on individual strength and skill. In a pit where horses were employed for underground haulage, such as the Fortune pit, a fairly strict division of labour appears to have been observed. Some men were hewers only; some men and youths drove horses only. Where horses were not employed, however, as at the Dike and Bowes pits, most pitmen appear to have done some hewing and some putting, though many did far more of one task than the other. Again, a man's principal activity underground might

---

[219] The *Compleat Collier*, 32 reckoned 21 score corves a good day's work. A good fortnight of 12 days' work at this rate of production might therefore see 252 score corves won. Comparison of this estimate with the actualities at Northbanks in 1752 amply demonstrates the risks of basing output estimates on such sources and the even greater risks involved in estimating the men's earnings in like manner.

[220] i.e. 23 × 12 days + one 'long' fortnight of 14 working days before the Christmas closure.

change if, as not infrequently occurred, he was moved from one pit to another and came under the direction of a different overman. In all, of the ninety-four pitmen identifiable in the presentments, sixty-three hewed some coal (67 per cent), though it could be as little 21 *corves* in the year or as much as 280 *score* corves. In general, it is certainly unwise to make too rigorous a distinction between the hewer and the putter.[221]

As for strength and skill, there were men at Northbanks who wielded their picks with artistry as well as power and who would qualify in the jargon of the coalfield as 'big hewers'. Robert Curry could cut thirty-five corves of coal on a good day, and he was not alone. In terms of regular high output, William Pickering was an archetypal big hewer. He never cut fewer than seven score corves in a fortnight, he could manage nearly fifteen score at best, and his fortnightly average was around twelve score. Fifteen of the thirty-seven men who hewed coal at the Dike pit and twelve of the twenty-six hewers at the Bowes managed to cut ten score corves or more in at least one pay-period. They had the skill to do so. Our impression is that the workings did not sufficiently often provide them with the opportunity. And when working was poor, putting could actually provide a surer income than hewing.

Finally, if the men had the skill to win coal, they also had the will, for the records provide precious little evidence of voluntary underemployment or 'leisure preference'. The working histories of many of these pitmen are intermittent by virtue of the patchiness of coverage of the working year. No man or youth who worked only at the Dike or Fortune and Gate pits can be traced for the whole year, and still others are lost for parts of the year. Nevertheless, there was a high degree of regularity of attendance among most of the men, and absence for a pay-period or two could as easily be explained by sickness or injury as by voluntary absenteeism. If we focus on the twenty-four pitmen who can be traced across the whole working year, we find that the best attender among them worked for 256 out of a possible 259 days, and the worst for 223 out of 259. The average attendance at work was 239 days (and in some cases the maximum that they could have worked was less than 259 days).

Absenteeism, then, was not common. Work was regular when the

---

[221] This, of course, also has implications for estimates of earnings that are based on either hewers' or putters' wage rates and assume a rigorous division of labour.

pit was working. Nor is a preference for leisure once a customary income had been assured suggested by the fact that some of the highest earners among these men were also very good attenders at work. Robert Curry, the highest earner of all, who was paid more than £1 in seven fortnights of the year and whose nearest rival achieved this only twice, showed no pattern of absenteeism after his big paydays other than on one occasion. In the fortnight following his receipt of £1. 5s. 6d. on 10 June, he worked only five out of a possible eleven days. Those five days, however, came not at the beginning of the period, when he was flush with silver, but at the end. And he lost another four days at the start of the next fortnight. It as at least as likely that he was sick or injured at this time as that he was drunk or idle. The overwhelming impression given by the employment histories of the Northbanks pitmen is not one of voluntary underemployment but rather of how hard they worked when work was available. Even the biggest hewers dragged pit-props or shovelled snow if there was nothing else for them to do.

What, then, did they actually earn in 1752? Of the twenty-four underground workers for whom we have a complete year's pay record at the Northbanks pits, five were youths who earned between £6. 8s. 4d. and £7. 10s. 6d. in the course of the year, averaging £7. 0s. 11d. for an average working year of 242 days. A youth in the pits, then, could earn three-quarters of the annual earnings of an adult Gibside labourer like Joseph Ridley, who also worked 242 days. As for the nineteen men, their wages ranged from £11. 9s. 10½d. to £21. 4s. 5¼d., averaging £16. 5s. 4½d. for an average working year of 238 days.[222] The highest earners were those who worked principally as hewers, the lowest, those who were engaged primarily in putting. An adult pitman, then, earned wages comparable to those of a skilled craftsman engaged in waggonway maintenance.[223] On average, such men could bring home about a quarter as much again as the very best paid estate labourer at Gibside in 1752.

The basic problem for the pitman was not the level of his wages,

[222] Cf. Langton, *Geographical Change*, 117, where earnings of £12–£17 for a full working year are suggested for the Lancashire coalfield in the early 18th c.

[223] In 1797 Sir Frederick Eden's investigation of the northern poor suggested that a Newcastle pitman's earnings were on a par with those of Tyneside masons and joiners. Our study bears this out—though by 1797 wages were higher, at about 15s. a week: R. Colls, *The Pitmen of the Northern Coalfield: Work, Culture and Protest, 1790–1850* (Manchester, 1987), 68.

which was very good by contemporary standards, but their unpredictability from fortnight to fortnight. Robert Curry's best fortnight, for example, brought him £1. 5s. 6d., his worst only 3s. 8d.; Percival Pickering was paid £1. 0s. 9½d. on 23 December, but only 10s. 2d. on 4 March; Lancelot Trotter got 18s.–8½d. on 24 June, but 2s. 1d. on 5 February; and so we could go on. All things being equal, the pitmen at Northbanks could do very well indeed. But as we have seen, all things were rarely equal. As among their contemporaries in the coalfields of south Lancashire, the unpredictability of labour demand and working conditions must have meant that their working lives guaranteed only a meagre fortnightly income which was, to be sure, punctuated throughout the year by 'irregular but frequent large cash surpluses' at those times when the hewer had the opportunity to demonstrate his skills to the full.[224]

Before leaving the colliery, something can be said of the surface and supervisory employees. Where the wages of overmen are specified on the fortnightly presentments, they commonly received upwards of £1 per fortnight. Their wages clearly varied with output, though not so predictably as those of the face-workers, for they were liable to receive other payments and 'considerations' which are unexplained in the records. At the Bowes pit, William Pickering senior received £23. 7s. 3d. for the twenty pay-periods in which his exact wage is stated. Estimating his income for the remaining four fortnights of the year on the basis of output suggests an annual total of around £28. 5s. 0d., an income that placed him well ahead not only of the best paid of his workmen, but also of the craftsmen of the parish.

In contrast, the gin-horse driver at the pithead received only £8. 11s. 10d., earnings comparable to those of a driver on the waggonways in a poorish year. The earnings of the colliery craftsmen remain uncertain, since we cannot be sure, in the absence of names, whether payments for smith work, wright work, or corving went to a single person or several men, and whether such craftsmen were in constant attendance or moved from pit to pit. At the Bowes pit wright work cost £5. 1s. 8½d. for the full year, which seems unlikely to have been the total income of one skilled man. Smith work cost £10. 16s. 1d. and corving £27. 4s. 1½d. Whether these sums were paid to single individuals or to a variety of men at different times we do not know, though in the case of corving it

---

[224] Langton, *Geographical Change*, 211.

seems probable that a single master craftsman was at work. The Dike pit presentments refer to payments to 'the corfer', while an agreement to work two pits at Northbanks in 1725 had specified by name the corver to be employed in making and maintaining the corves.[225] If a single man performed this task at the Bowes pit, then he was very well paid, earning almost as much as the overman. Such potential earning capacity may do something to explain why, of all colliery workers, only overmen and corvers tended to appear with any frequency in the inventoried population of Whickham.

This survey of actual earnings among Whickham's wage-workers inevitably leaves much to be desired. But it establishes at least the range of actual incomes that can be shown to have prevailed among wage-earners who enjoyed something approaching full employment in the mid-eighteenth century. Clearly, there could be considerable variation even among men with the same occupation, and marked differentials between workers of different kinds. None the less, the evidence suggests that Whickham's work-force can be divided, on the basis of earning potential, into two broad groups. On the one hand, there were those whose labour was likely to earn them between £8 and £12 for a working year of 220 or more days: the estate labourers, the waggonway labourers, waggonmen who did not own a horse of their own, the less well paid craftsmen, a gin-horse driver at the colliery. On the other hand, there were those who might reasonably expect around £15–£20 for a comparable year's work: the adult underground workers at the pits, the better paid master craftsmen at Gibside, on the waggonways, and at the pits. A small minority of the work-force might be said to form a third category of élite workers: the overmen, perhaps also the corvers, who could earn upwards of £25. If the best paid Crowley workmen, the anchor-makers, did earn 12s.–14s. a week in the 1750s, then they too might have shared the pinnacle of the wage-earning pyramid for a comparable working year.

These figures, of course, are optimistic. They are derived from proven earnings, but they relate to men who enjoyed very regular employment, and it certainly cannot be assumed that a working year of 220 or more days was typical. Nevertheless, they help us to establish the upper dimensions of expectation for wage-workers in the period and the extent to which they varied from group to group. Before proceeding to translate them into an estimate of living

[225] DRO D/ST 277, 344/35.

standards among Whickham's work-people, however, we must pause to consider a further factor that must be taken into account in any attempt to establish the income of working people: that of the 'family wage'.

As has been increasingly recognized in recent economic and social history, the incomes of the labouring families of early modern England cannot be assumed to have depended solely on the earnings of the husband. Women and children earned too. Whereas it was formerly argued that the emergence of a proletarianized labour force in both agriculture and industry deprived women of the productive role that they had enjoyed on small farms and in independent craft workshops, it is now accepted that these developments led less to an abrogation than to a restructuring of the working life of women.[226] Similarly, children had always worked, often from around the age of seven, and they continued to do so wherever suitable opportunities presented themselves in both agriculture and industry.[227] If, as has been argued, 'the efficiency of the family economy continued to be the compelling priority in plebeian life', and if that efficiency potentially involved the contributions of every member of the domestic group able to participate, then we must take account of the opportunities for such participation that existed in Whickham.[228]

It can be readily recognized that women had work enough to do about the small farms of the parish, and that, among those families in the parish whose incomes were supplemented by the keeping of a cow or two or some poultry, the care of these animals was part of a woman's domestic tasks. We get a small glimpse of such activity in 1721 when the gardener John Wilkinson established the time of an incident he was called upon to describe in court by recalling that it was just after his wife 'came from milking the cows in the evening'.[229] Similarly, it is to be expected that both women and

---

[226] See e.g. A. Clark, *The Working Life of Women in the Seventeenth Century* (London, 1919); L. Charles and L. Duffin (eds.), *Women and Work in Pre-Industrial England* (London, 1985); Malcolmson, *Life and Labour*, 42–3; J. Rule, *The Experience of Labour in Eighteenth Century Industry* (London, 1981), 11, 15–16, 42. For a stimulating discussion of recent work in this field, see J. M. Bennett, ' "History that Stands Still": Women's Work in the European Past', *Feminist Studies*, 14 (1988).

[227] M. Spufford, 'First Steps in Literacy: The Reading and Writing Experience of the Humblest Seventeenth-Century Spiritual Autobiographers', *Social History*, 4 (1979), 413 ff.; Malcolmson, *Life and Labour*, 42–3, 57–8, 61; Rule, *Experience of Labour*, 15–16, 42.   [228] Quoting Malcolmson, *Life and Labour*, 57.

[229] PRO DURH 17/2.

children had significant roles to play in some of the craft workshops of the parish, in the running of victualling establishments and the like. Another deposition, for example, provides a glimpse of Elizabeth Armstrong keeping shop for her husband Robert, a Swalwell grocer, in 1742.[230] For the wives and daughters of landless wage-workers, however, the possibilities of making a significant contribution to the family budget appear to have been distinctly straitened by the lack of employment opportunities in the parish.

It has been argued with some plausibility that the demands of industry for workers created a labour shortage in agriculture on Tyneside which led to the employment of much female labour.[231] The Whickham evidence, however, does not suggest that the demand for female labour was great. It is true that on the Gibside estate in October 1759 thirteen women and girls were employed at up to 8*d.* a day as reapers and root gatherers on the 'Fallow Ground'. The few days' work thus recorded might be taken to be indicative of a general situation; yet the estate labourers' paybills of 1752 tell a different story. Only 8 of the 148 persons employed were women. Four of them worked regularly, at a variety of tasks much like those performed by male labourers, for between 156 and 188 days in the months from March to November, and they earned between £3. 18*s.* and £4. 14*s.*—welcome additions to any family's income. But these women were exceptional. The others found only eleven, eight, two, and one day's work respectively, and if the Gibside estate displayed so little need for female labour, it is hardly to be expected that women agricultural workers were regularly employed elsewhere in the parish.[232]

Nor did industry provide many alternatives. In 1702 Ambrose Crowley, having 'oft found that ye want of having Employment for Girls and Women hath not onely born hard on their parents, but hath lead them into a slothful and lazy life', determined to encourage the young women of Winlaton to learn to make nails as 'in Staffordshire and ye adjacent countryes'. He offered cash 'encouragements' for the achievement of particular levels of skill. Yet Flinn could find little evidence in the records of the Crowley company that this scheme came to anything at Winlaton, and there

---

[230] DPD Consistory Cause Papers, Box 4.
[231] Brassley, 'Northumberland and Durham', 57.
[232] DRO D/ST 352/35, 277.

is no evidence that women were employed at the Swalwell works.[233] As for the coal industry, women seem very rarely, if ever, to have been employed underground on Tyneside. Where they did find work it was in wailing the coal and in heap shovelling at the pithead. In 1752 at the Dike pit, two named women were paid 6*d*. a day (as compared with 10*d*. for men) for heap shovelling, one of them fairly regularly, the other occasionally. At the Bowes pit in the same year a total of £12. 15*s*. 6*d*. was paid for a year's wailing. Four wailers seem usually to have been at work, but no names are given. If the same women worked all year, then their earnings would have averaged £3. 3*s*. 11*d*.[234]

Once again, these sums represent welcome contributions to the incomes of a number of families, but at the same time, it is evident that work for a handful of wailers and shovellers per pit can have absorbed only a small proportion of the potential female labour force of the parish. Again, the waggonways provided no work for women save as gatekeepers, as when the fifty-seven-year-old widow, Elizabeth Carr, was established in a gatekeeper's cottage by one minor coal-owner on condition that she 'shovell up and take Care of three pitts of his coals . . . and . . . take care of the said gate in lieu of rent'.[235] Only at the staithes were more women to be found working, once more as wailers, to judge by the 1764 listing of the aged poor and widows for the Lowhand quarter, which includes seven female 'wealers', three of them more than sixty years old and one of them, Phyllis Denham, said to be eighty. The same set of listings provides many instances of poor widows or single women said to be 'industrious', but the nature of their work is specified only occasionally. Other than those engaged in wailing coal, the female occupations mentioned included two spinners, two washer-women, a schoolmistress, a 'fishcadger', a breadbaker, and a seller of bread.[236]

While the area offered little other than casual employment for women or girls, however, there was certainly work for boys and youths. They can be identified working at Gibside, with the waggonway gangs and in the Northbanks pits, on occasion alongside their fathers. They were employed at the Crowley factory

---

[233] NRO ZAN M13/D30, 27 Jan. 1701/2; Flinn, *Men of Iron*, 237–8.
[234] DRO D/ST 277.
[235] PRO E 134 11 & 12 Anne Hil. 37, testimony of Elizabeth Carr.
[236] DRO D/ST 336/7.

at Winlaton and presumably at Swalwell too.[237] Moreover, the 1764 listing of the Lowhand poor mentions several boy keelmen, the youngest of them twelve years old.[238]

What all this could mean for the income of a family can be imagined easily enough. A regularly employed female agricultural labourer with wages of around £4, or a wailer earning something over £3 a year, could add very significantly to the income of any labouring family. Elizabeth Borren, who shovelled coal at the Dike pit for thirty-five days in late September and October 1752, can provide an example. She was twenty-seven years old and the unmarried daughter of a pitman. In the six weeks for which her working life is documented she brought home 17s. 6d. to set beside the 39s. that her father earned in the same period: a 45 per cent boost to the family income. There were certainly others like her, and their wages may have made an even greater contribution to the domestic economies of families headed by men less well paid or less regularly in work. Given the employment situation in Whickham, however, most of our evidence of additional family income relates to the earnings of sons. Anthony Scott earned £11. 19s. 8d. on the waggonways in 1764 and his son Anthony junior earned £7. 11s. 10d., which appears to have been paid directly to the father. John Brabbon senior was paid £18. 15s. 11½d. for his work as a hewer at Northbanks in 1752; his son John, aged ten, brought home a further £7. 17s. 2d. as a horse-driver in the same pits.

These examples illustrate the optimum situation for a labouring family, that phase of the family cycle when earnings could be maximized by the combined earning power of a man in his prime and children who were of an age to contribute significantly to the family budget. Unfortunately, we have no way of determining just how representative such a situation was. Perhaps most families passed through such a phase. At the same time, however, it seems probable, given the observable structure of employment in Whickham, that only a minority of families can have enjoyed such a situation at any one point in time. Work for women was in relatively short supply. Boys had more opportunity, and an early commencement of paid work was part of their expectations. Yet the evidence of 1752 and 1764 does not suggest that they contributed

---

[237] In 1702, 29 of the 195 Crowley workmen listed at Winlaton were boys, presumably apprentices: NRO ZAN M13/D30, Feb. 1701/2.
[238] DRO D/ST 336/7.

more than a small proportion of the work-force at Gibside, at Northbanks, or on the waggonways in any one year. While some families reaped the benefit, for a few years at least, of multiple incomes, others would be wholly or largely dependent upon a single male wage by virtue of their occupation of earlier or later stages in the family cycle. Yet others might be sustained by what women or children could earn in the absence of an adult male breadwinner.

The lists of the aged, decayed work-people and widows drawn up in 1764 illustrate these alternative realities only too well. Michael Cook and Robert Miller were both waggonmen and each had a wife and five small children to support. The former was described as 'painstaking and very deserving', the latter as 'sober, industrious'; both were also 'very poor'. Barbara Farmer's son was a keelman supporting both his widowed mother and his own family of 'seven or eight' small children. Thomas Richardson was 'a widdower and waggonman with 4 children, eldest about 8 or 9: sober and careful and very deserving', but poor. Their cases could be paralleled by the waggonmen Peter Hopper, George Averick, and Thomas Newton, and the labourers Ralph Whitfield and Edward Thompson. Then there were the ageing men like Thomas Foster, who had 'brought up a very large family with great credit, being pitman', but was now reduced to poverty; William Reed, able now to find work only as 'a Carman in Summer'; or the weaver James Bigby, 'scarce able to work any' but somehow surviving with his wife and one child. John Usher had lost his senses and 'his wife is about 50 and supports him by washing'.

Other women struggled as widows to maintain themselves and their families with the aid of the older children. Ann Daglish was 'a spinster, her son lives with her, is a keelman and is only 14'. Mary Herbert had '2 boys, the eldest 14, both work at the pit. They are her chief support.' Nanny Wall was 'a spinster that is supported by her spinning together with a small assistance from her daughter a servant'. Mary Greaves lived 'with her Grandson about 14; he has 8*d*. a day and ys her chief support'. The Peverley children, '3 of them very small', had neither father nor mother, but were 'supported by an elder Brother a labourer at Swalwell'.

These were not, for the most part, parish paupers supported by alms, but work-people struggling through the most difficult stages of the life-cycle. The officers who listed them and noted their particulars were well aware of the significance of the 'family economy'. They noted the ages of children in a manner that clearly implied that those under nine years old were unlikely to be able to contribute economically, and the absence of children to provide support was occasionally cited as a sufficient explanation in itself of an aged widow's poverty. Barbara Arkles's case was summed up as 'all her children are dead'; Hannah Mitchison's with 'All her children, which perhaps may be two or three are about London . . . she has no relief from them.'[239]

The point is simple. The 'family economy' was a vital reality in the lives of the labouring poor. The 'family wage' could dramatically raise the earnings ceiling of a family. But it was subject to both short-term fluctuations and a long-term cycle, and an awareness of the high collective earnings that it *could* entail must be balanced by an appreciation of the broader context within which those times of feast were located. Family earnings could mean temporary affluence by the standards of the labouring population, but they might also mean simple survival to those for whom they constituted not a supplement to a living, but the living itself.

Having considered these issues, we can now turn to an assessment of the level of living afforded by their earnings to the work-people of Whickham. In order to do so, we must first establish what it cost a labouring family to live in Whickham in the central decades of the eighteenth century. Two sources of information are available for this purpose, both of them derived from the Poor Law records of the parish. First, in June 1756 the parish vestrymen of Whickham agreed that the master of the parish workhouse should be paid 21*d*. per week for each 'poor person' in his care. From this he was to furnish them with 'proper and sufficient victuals' according to an agreed 'Bill of Fare' (which unfortunately does not survive), to provide and mend their clothing, to purchase coal for heating the workhouse, and to 'wash and keep clean and doe every other thing necessary and convenient for the comfortable support of the Poor in the said Workhouse'.[240] At this rate, keeping a single pauper in this manner would cost £4. 11*s*. 0*d*. per annum. If we assume that two children would cost roughly the same as one adult, then the cost of keeping a family of man and wife and two children would be £13. 13*s*. 0*d*.

An alternative means of estimating the living costs of a labouring

---

[239] All examples drawn from DRO D/ST 336/7.
[240] DRO EP/Wh 19, 118–20.

family is provided by the detailed accounts of specific payments made by the overseers of the poor to the 'out poor' in the years 1751–8 and recorded in their account books.[241] These include payments made to, or on behalf of, individuals for their support over periods of up to one year, and sums disbursed to provide specific items of clothing or clothing materials, rent, and fuel. According to their accounts, keeping a child for a year cost the overseers between £3. 18s. and £5. 4s. An adult woman cost £3–£4. 4s. a year. Men were rarely given support for more than a few months, at a cost of around 6s.–8s. a month, which can be translated into an annual cost of £3. 12s.–£4. 16s. Finally, in one instance the support of a widow and her unspecified number of children cost £2. 2s. 4d. a quarter, or £8. 9s. 4d. a year. If we err on the side of caution and base our estimate on the lowest possible combination of these sums (i.e. on the lowest annual rate for a man plus the payment made to the widow and her children), then we can suggest that the basic maintenance of a man, wife, and dependent children at the level considered appropriate by the overseers for 'out poor' would cost at least £12. 1s. 4d. To this we can add allowances of 13s. 6d. for rent, 6s. 3d. for fuel, £1. 4s. 1d. for clothing, and 11s. 2d. for replacement of essential household goods, to reach a grand total of £14. 16s. 4d. a year as the basic living costs of a hypothetical labouring family.[242]

We are dealing here, of course, with estimated living costs. In reality, families may have been able to live more cheaply. Some labourers may have provided part of their own foodstuffs, or bought them cheaply from their employers. Most pitmen and some regular labourers and waggonmen received fire coal free of charge, and the pitmen often lived in housing provided free or at a nominal

[241] DRO EP/Wh 19, *passim*.

[242] Estimated as follows: *Rent*: 13s. 6d. paid for the rent of a pauper couple. *Fuel*: 6s. 3d. as the recorded price of 2½ fothers of fire coal, this being the minimum quantity given by Mrs Bowes to her pitmen in 1763 firecoal accounts. *Clothing*: actual costs to the overseers in outfitting a boy (10s. 6d.), a girl (3s.), a man (hat 1s.; coat 10s. 6d.; shirt 2s.; breeches 2s. 6d.), and a woman (4 yards jersey for a gown, 5s.; 2 yards flannel for under-petticoat, 2s.; hat 1s.; thread and buttons 1s.), plus 3s. for two pairs of stockings each and 6s. 8d. for 5 pairs of second-hand shoes. The total was divided by two on the assumption that a new outfit might last two years. *Household goods*: payment of £1. 3s. 6d. for household goods made to a woman discharged from the workhouse, divided by three on assumption of a 3-year replacement cycle. The overall estimate is of course conjectural, but has the virtue at least of being based on actual payments made to the poor for the items specified.

rent by the coalmasters. Clothing was distributed annually by Mrs Bowes in the 1760s to deserving poor women. Household goods could be inherited or acquired second-hand, and may have required infrequent replacement. Nevertheless, our estimates are based upon actual payments made to or on behalf of the poor of Whickham in the 1750s, and it should be emphasized that they are cautious estimates. At the very least, they provide a rough and ready yardstick which enables us to give meaning to the data on earnings that we have assembled. Put simply, most of the labouring families and driver-waggonmen of Whickham would have been unable to subsist at such levels unless the wages of the male breadwinner were supplemented by the earnings of others in his family. When such supplements were not available, they must have lived poorly indeed. Pitmen working underground, horse-owning waggonmen, and master craftsmen, in contrast, could expect to live above, and sometimes comfortably above, these levels from the wages of the household head alone.

It is perhaps in these simple realities that we can find the origins of the pride in high earnings among the industrial work-force which was to find expression in the early industrial songs of Tyneside, collected and published at the turn of the eighteenth and nineteenth centuries—the waggonman coming down the waggonway, 'His pocket full of money and his poke full of hay'; the 'bonny pit laddie' that 'sits on his cracket and hews in his jacket, And brings the white siller to me'.[243] By the general standards of the labouring poor, the high earners of the industrial labour force had money indeed, and the fact was celebrated in doggerel which, significantly, was usually couched in the form of the admiring comments of a satisfied woman.

To be sure, it was singularly unlikely that the average pitman was able to participate to any significant degree in the acquisition of the domestic comforts and sophisticated consumer goods that we have traced emerging in the inventories of parishioners whose means depended upon more than strength, skill, and a good seam. It has been suggested that even an income of £20 a year left little margin for consumer spending on any significant scale.[244] Nevertheless,

---

[243] J. Bell (ed.), *Rhymes of the Northern Bards: Being a Curious Collection of Old and New Songs and Poems peculiar to the Counties of Newcastle-upon-Tyne, Northumberland and Durham* (Newcastle, 1812), 36, 300. A 'cracket' was a small, low, stool.   [244] Weatherhill, *Consumer Behaviour*, 194.

what they could afford was food, clothing, modest domestic goods, and minor personal indulgences on a scale denied to most of their neighbours. The inventory of the Crowley factory warehouse, taken in 1727, provides an indication of the types of goods on which the wage-workers of the period were likely to spend their surplus. There were no clocks and no portraits of Whig bishops. But there was cloth in abundance—broadcloth, plaincloth, jersey, cotton, harden, shalloon, and callamanco—and the thread with which to sew it. There were ready-made breeches, stockings (coarse or jersey), and shoes. There were fire-irons and pans, candles, bread, and tobacco.[245] And the man with money to spare in Whickham did not need to look far for beer.

The big wage-earner could enjoy a modest affluence which distinguished him and his family among their peers. But it was a precarious affluence, uncertain from fortnight to fortnight and concentrated within particular phases of the life-cycle. In short, it was enjoyed against a background of perennial insecurity and in the almost certain knowledge that advancing age would bring descent into the status of what the parish officers termed an 'object of charity'.

Ralph Crawhall was the biggest hewer at Graham's pit in the fortnight ending 26 May 1742. He was paid for winning almost nineteen score corves of coal, in addition to his earnings from putting on several days, and brought home £1. 11s. 3d. Yet in 1764 he was one of the decayed work-people of Fellside, 'at sundry times sick and wife and children starving'.[246] Thomas Foster, John Chapman, Robert Cockburn, Thomas Stokoe, William Shevill, and James Davison were other pitmen (some of them big earners in 1752), who were listed among the deserving poor of 1764, and the lists included also the widows of a good many more of their fellows. In all, the surveys of decayed work-people, the aged poor, and widows conducted in 1764, together with a separate enumeration of the poor of Fellside quarter, included 241 named individuals (not counting children). Most of them were householders overburdened with family responsibilities, disabled by sickness, or facing the almost inevitable consequences of old age and widowhood for members of their class.

The comments of the enumerator provide a depressing litany:

[245] Suffolk Record Office (Ipswich) HA/GD/4/14, 25 ff.
[246] DRO D/ST 233, 336/7.

'poor and deserving'; 'a great object of charity'; 'careful but makes a very bad Fend in the world'; 'very ragged'; 'in great necessitie'; 'lamentably poor'; 'extremely poor'; 'miserably poor'; 'excessively poor'.[247] Such was the general tone of the comment of an informed observer upon approximately one-third of the householders of Whickham. While the admiring descriptions of visitors to the pits, the waggonways, and the Crowley factory provide eloquent testimony to the achievements of industrial Tyneside, and the inventories and paybills of Whickham stand witness to some of the real benefits of industrial enterprise, the laconic judgements of the compiler of the 1764 lists serve to remind us of the severely limited extent to which those benefits were shared by the proletarianized population of the coalfield.

[247] DRO D/ST 336/7.

4

Sooty Faces and Elysian Shades:
Social Identities and Social Relations

A most tumultuous, sturdy set of people, greatly impatient of
controul

Arthur Young, *A Six Months Tour Through the North of
England* (1771)

True liberty takes way noe mans right, or hinders no mans right.
That indeed . . . is true liberty that defends every man's right.

Inscription placed upon the Tyne Bridge, 1651

SOME twenty years after the compilation of the survey of Whickham's 'deserving poor', the antiquarian and topographer William
Hutchinson travelled through the parish on his way to Gibside
Hall. Passing along the riverside, he observed the bustle and activity
at the staithes of Dunston and Derwenthaugh. On the hilltop above
he paused to take in the splendid view of the Tyne valley, and in
Whickham town he noted with approval that the 'chief buildings'
were 'many of them modern and handsome'. Turning south-west
across the enclosed town fields towards Hollinside, Whickham Fell,
and the interior of the parish, however, he found that 'the adjacent
countryside wears an unpleasant aspect to the traveller'. Here the
land was 'cut and harrowed up with loaded carriages' and 'scattered
over with mean cottages, from whence swarm forth innumerable
inhabitants, maintained by working in the mines'. In this district, he
remarked, 'many a sooty face is seen by every hedge-way side'. And
yet, he reflected, 'the workmen earn great wages, which recompense
every other evil'. Moreover, there was an aesthetic dividend to be
derived from the squalor of the scene, for 'the meagreness of the
tract by which you pass the environs of Gibside, renders the scene
more striking, and enhances the beauty of the pass which leads
immediately to those Elysian shades'. At last he came to Gibside
park itself and waxed lyrical on the splendours of George Bowes's

carefully created environment, a monument to the most elevated taste of the age, watched over from the pinnacle of its 150-foot column by a gilded statue of 'British Liberty, in whose service the person who erected the work was enthusiastically virtuous'.[1]

Hutchinson's perception of the coalfield and its inhabitants—alien, unpleasant, mildly threatening—expressed in metaphors of violence and disorder, was one that was widely shared by his contemporaries, and one that has exercised a pervasive influence on the historiographical image of the mining areas of the north-east. For it can be said with little exaggeration that we do not have a social history of the early coalfield. Instead, we have inherited an historiographical stereotype which persistently depicts the people of the colliery districts as 'a race apart', a type of people physically and culturally separated from the generality of humankind.

The roots of this stereotype may go deep (an issue that we cannot pursue in detail here).[2] What is certain, however, is that it was given increasing currency and elaboration in the later eighteenth and early nineteenth centuries, notably in the observations of visitors of evangelical or reforming bent engaged in what they regarded virtually as the cultural colonization of the coalfield. Such commentators brought their preconceptions and their prejudices with them to the mining communities, and, given the selectiveness of their vision, it is scarcely to be wondered at that they found them amply confirmed. To John Wesley, the colliers of Plessey in Northumberland stood (at least prior to their conversion), 'in the first rank of savage ignorance and wickedness of every kind'. Arthur Young found northern miners in general 'a most tumultuous, sturdy set of people, greatly impatient of controul [and] very insolent'. A later visitor to the northern coalfield described its inhabitants as 'a rude, bold, savage set of beings, apparently cut off from their fellow men in their interests and feelings', while in 1817 the Newcastle

---

[1] Hutchinson, *Durham*, ii. 447–51.

[2] Its roots may lie in the suspicions harboured against the inhabitants of areas of heath, forest, and fell by the authorities of Tudor and Stuart England. Such districts were regarded as lying outside the effective control of the agencies of both Church and State. They were also the principal areas of industrial development in the 16th and 17th c. See the discussions of this issue in K. Wrightson, *English Society 1580–1680* (London, 1982), 171–2 and R. W. Malcolmson, '"A Set of Ungovernable People": The Kingswood Colliers in the Eighteenth Century', in J. Brewer and J. Styles (eds.), *An Ungovernable People: The English and Their Law in the Seventeenth and Eighteenth Centuries* (London, 1980), 85–9, together with the references cited there.

Religious Tract Society deemed them 'yet enwrapt in moral darkness, as profound and opake, as if they had been reared in a heathen or pagan country'.[3]

By the mid-nineteenth century this convention of moralistic rhetoric had achieved the status of unquestioned historical fact, and the people of the colliery districts could be described to a parliamentary commission as 'just emerging from the greatest possible moral and intellectual darkness', a condition that could largely be explained by the fact that 'for generations they had lived beyond the control of their social superiors' civilizing influences'.[4] Early historians of the pitmen and their unions, though far more sympathetic to their subjects and apt to attribute their deplorable condition to their deprivation, were also prone to accept the testimony of such 'keen and honest observers' as the Methodist evangelists. Accordingly, the miners of the eighteenth century and before were depicted as men with 'minds as dark as their work', 'neglected, wretched and degraded', illiterate, ignorant, 'drunken, dissolute and brutalized', lacking exposure to 'civilizing influences' and 'tyrannized over by their employers'; a people walking in darkness and awaiting still the transforming power of what Sidney Webb called the 'two inspiring influences, Religion and Trade Unionism'.[5]

More recent historians have proved less ready either to take at face value the allegations of the moralists, or to subscribe to the teleology of the older school of labour history. The impact of an evangelical mentality, however, still reverberates in the historiography. The coalfield population continues to be described, albeit less judgementally and in a more fashionable sociological garb, as 'a

---

[3] Quoted in Flinn, *Coal Industry*, 435; J. L. Hammond and B. Hammond, *The Skilled Labourer 1760–1832* (London, 1919), 19; R. N. Boyd, *Coal Pits and Pitmen: A Short History of the Coal Trade and the Legislation Affecting It*, 2nd edn. (London, 1895), 25; Colls, *Pitmen*, 1.

[4] *Parliamentary Papers, 1842*, XVI, 744, 747.

[5] Quoting from Boyd, *Coal Pits and Pitmen*, 7, 21, 23; R. Fynes, *The Miners of Northumberland and Durham: A History of their Social and Political Progress* (Newcastle, 1873; reprinted Wakefield, 1971), 9; S. Webb, *The Story of the Durham Miners* (London, 1921), 16–21. For the currency of this view of the previous century in late 19th-c. Whickham, see Bourn, *Whickham*, 105: 'If tradition can be depended upon, the moral darkness which prevailed was almost impenetrable.' Since Bourn made this point in the context of discussing the lack of provision of a place of worship in Swalwell before the initiatives of the Presbyterians and Methodists, we might hazard a guess at whose traditions he was drawing upon.

race apart', inhabiting 'communities apart', often physically and always culturally isolated, a separated and a separate society, and one curiously static until galvanized by forces of change which came late and from outside.[6]

That this should still be so is perhaps the more surprising in that for several years both historians of the Victorian mining industry and contemporary sociologists have expressed dissatisfaction with an interpretative tradition based on prior expectations which have their historical roots in the moralistic rhetoric of the late eighteenth and early nineteenth centuries. The 'ideal type' of miner and mining society has been challenged as a conceptual model which 'closes the mind rather than opens it'. Emphasis has been laid upon the variability of mining society and upon the myriad factors that can influence its nature and development. Above all, it has been argued that the sociological image of coalfield society fails to explore the dynamics of mining communities, the mutability of the relationships that bound their inhabitants together, and the variety and historical specificity of their patterns of social relations; it has ignored, in short, 'the grand fact that History itself is a "variable"'.[7]

In this chapter we will attempt to respond to this critical challenge by exploring those aspects of Whickham's social develop-ment that up to now have been pushed to the margins of our story. For the industrial development of Whickham and its environs involved not only economic, technological, demographic, and social–structural change, but also a reshaping of social identities and

[6] See e.g. Nef, i. 428; ii. 150–2, 175–6; Ashton and Sykes, *Coal Industry*, 70, 150; Buxton, *British Coal Industry*, 121–2; Rule, *Experience of Labour*, 18, 207; Malcolmson, *Life and Labour*, 53–4; Flinn, *Coal Industry*, 434–6; Colls, *Pitmen*, 55. The general tendency is to quote moralistic accounts of the coalfield population with a degree of scepticism and some sympathy for the denigrated miners, while at the same time insisting upon their attributes of isolation and cultural separateness (though for Scottish miners Rab Houston has challenged the 'race apart' stereotype in his 'Coal, Class and Culture: Labour Relations in a Scottish Mining Community 1650–1750', *Social History*, 8 (1983), esp. 13–14.) Change is rarely discussed before the early 19th-c. advent of methodism and trade unionism, the one implanted and the other a response to initiatives by the coal-owners which threatened the status, independence, and wages of the men. Colls's recent work is essentially a powerful and eloquent restatement of this theme.

[7] R. Harrison, 'Introduction', in id. (ed.), *Independent Collier: The Coal Miner as Archetypal Proletarian Reconsidered* (Hassocks, Sx, 1978), 2–7, 13–14; R. Church *et al.*, *The History of the British Coal Industry*, iii, *1830–1913: Victorian Pre-eminence* (Oxford, 1986), 611–37. Cf. M. I. A. Bulmer, 'Sociological Models of the Mining Community', *Sociological Review*, 23 (1975); B. Williamson, *Class, Culture and Community: A Biographical Study of Social Change in Mining* (London, 1982), 229.

shifts in the patterns of social relationships. Change of this kind was no simple and mechanical response to the imperatives of industrial development. It was a complex and uneven process, a continuing interaction between inherited traditions and novel circumstances. Our aim, therefore, is to capture something of the dynamism and historical contingency of that process as the identities of the people of Whickham, and of the emerging industrial society of Tyneside to which they belonged, were forged and reforged between the anvil of established ways and the insistent beating of the hammers of change.

1. THE ELIZABETHAN COMMUNITY

Although William Hutchinson's Whickham appeared to conform in large part to the stereotypical image of an early coalfield settlement, two centuries earlier the situation had been utterly different. Elizabethan Whickham, as we have seen, was an essentially agrarian community, based on the land and structured and defined by a set of overlapping territorial jurisdictions. Its inhabitants thought of themselves as the people of a parish, the tenants of manors, members of the households of a township and its associated hamlets, neighbours. More broadly, they were subjects of the bishop of Durham and the queen of England, and also participants in the mesh of economic and social ties that constituted the hinterland of the city of Newcastle-upon-Tyne. Such common identity as they possessed was a composite of all these elements. Nevertheless, at the level of the parish, the whole was something greater than the sum of its parts.

The territorial jurisdictions that defined Whickham geographically also granted rights to the inhabitants, imposed obligations upon them, and provided institutions which focused their interactions one with another. The parish, for example, was not only a unit of ecclesiastical jurisdiction, but also one of moral and ritual obligation. In the parish church of St Mary the Virgin, the people of Whickham were required by law to meet together in worship, to participate in the rituals of marriage, baptism, and burial, and to join (if they were 'in charity' with their neighbours) in communion. There also they stood witness to the public penances of those presented by the churchwardens to the ecclesiastical courts at Durham for moral delinquencies or failures in their religious duties, and heard sentence of excommunication read out against the obdurate and contumacious individuals who ignored those sanctions.

The manors, most notably the principal Manor of Whickham, similarly conferred rights, required participation, and enforced obligations. At the meetings of the Halmote Court titles were recognized and transactions were recorded. Men were elected to offices that were both positions of trust and responsibility and marks of advancement in the *cursus honorum* of local life. Breaches of custom and nuisances 'contrary to neighbourhood' were presented and disciplined. Disputes between tenants were heard and adjudicated. Within the broader society of the parish, the tenants of the Manor of Whickham—some two-thirds of the householders of the parish in the 1560s—formed a distinctive group. Shared interest in the town fields and in the commons of Whickham Fell gave them a formally constituted collective identity, and their attachment to their land, at least in the later sixteenth century, provided a core of relative stability within the population of the parish.[8] Rights in the land encouraged persistence among established families, and the institutions that recognized and defended those rights also served to incorporate newcomers. By definition, no tenant was a 'stranger' or a 'forinner'.

Out of such ties, and out of those other less formal arenas of participation that leave scant record to the historian, grew neighbourhood. The neighbourhood, of course, was in no sense a corporate body; it had no formal identity and no defined geographical boundaries, though it was at least to some extent moulded by the institutional structures of parish and manor. It is to be envisaged rather as a dense tangle of intersecting social networks. None the less, neighbourhood, here as elsewhere in early modern England, was a social bond of immense importance and one that involved rights and duties of its own. Economic and social differentiation certainly existed in Elizabethan Whickham, but as we have seen it was relatively limited in extent, and muted in its

---

[8] Of the 59 copyhold holdings of the early 1560s, 30 remained 'in the name' up to 1600 in the sense that they were still held by the original tenant, his widow (by widowright), or a direct male heir; 12 others had passed into the hands of men who were members of copyholder families already established in the 1560s. One was acquired by marriage to a copyholder's widow. Only 16 passed to newcomers with no known previous connection with the manor. DPD Ch. Comm. MS 189721; Halmote Court Rentals, Box 11, Bundle 5, no. 193323; DDR HC III F 18, *passim*, HC III F 19, fos. 173–174ᵛ.

nature.[9] In such a context the canons of neighbourhood governed the relations between effective if not actual equals, and when people spoke of their neighbours, or still more '*the* neighbours', they used the term in an inclusive sense to describe a single community of settled residents.

The neighbours constituted a support network, most visible historically in the myriad relationships of small-scale debt and credit recorded in the wills and inventories of the parishioners.[10] But if such transactions leave the most tangible evidence to the historian, the neighbourhood was no less significant in the spheres of personal recognition and emotional support. From a casual aside in a court deposition taken in 1589, we learn how John Whelton, busy in the street, saw Thomas Watson open his door 'to sit him downe on the threshold'. Doubtless they nodded to one another. At about the same time, Thomas Wakefield, 'walking through the street in Whickham towne by the window of Margaret Jackson . . . did heare a child wepe very sore and took occasion to call and know what the cause was of the childe weeping'.[11] Such unremarkable scenes might stand in general for the manner in which neighbourhood bridged the gap between the relative privacy of the individual household and the openness of the public street. But it was a gap far narrower in Elizabethan England than would be the case today. For the neighbourhood was not only a support network, but also a reference group and a moral community, founded upon the expectation of adherence to conventional standards of both public and private behaviour.

Within a context of personal familiarity, individual standing and reputation—matters of no small practical as well as psychological significance—were constantly assessed and reassessed. When Cuthbert Pearson's marital difficulties led to litigation in the Consistory Court at Durham, nineteen of the witnesses called could attest to a total of 293 years of knowledge and experience of the man on which to base their assessment of the rumours concerning his demeanour.[12] Thomas Pearson, one of a group of gossips who sat in Elizabeth Harrison's alehouse in 1589 appraising the conduct of John Dobson, found himself the subject of public reproof for his quarrelsomeness several years later when he was left a legacy

[9] See sect. 2.1 above.   [10] See below pp. 286–7 and nn. 29–30.
[11] DPD DR v/5, fo. 75ᵛ, DR v/7 unfol.
[12] DPD DR v/3, fos. 54–54ᵛ, 122ᵛ–123ᵛ, 158, DR v/5, fos. 62, 73ᵛ–78.

conditionally on his henceforward 'behavinge himself honestlie and neighbourlie as a christian should and ought to doo'.[13] To be reputed 'honest' by the neighbours mattered. Hence the willingness of those who found themselves defamed by gossip to go to law in defence of their 'honestie' and 'good name and fame', lest, as Elizabeth Ranson complained in 1603, these be 'impaired and diminished and she worse thought of amongst her neighbours who thought well on her before'.[14] In the ties of neighbourhood, private life and public conversation met, and both were scrutinized and judged for good or ill. The neighbourhood was inclusive. It was intimate and supportive. It could also be narrow, constrictive, and highly demanding.

Perhaps the most revealing evidence of the complex of institutional and personal ties that bound together the inhabitants of Elizabethan Whickham is to be found in the surviving records of the way the people of the parish handled the individual trauma and the 'social disturbance' occasioned by death. Death came untimely to all too many of the parishioners of Elizabethan Whickham; and, faced with the imminence of death, the necessity of settling their affairs, and above all the need to provide for their dependants by an orderly transmission of the property upon which their future well-being would depend, it is scarcely surprising that they drew on all the resources available to them to cope as best they could with this most drastic of transitions.

For the copyholders, vital institutional support was provided by the manor. In law, copyhold property could not normally be devised by will.[15] Instead, on the death of a tenant the heirs of the holding were recognized and admitted to the land by the jurors and steward of the Halmote Court.[16] If the heirs or heirs to a holding

---

[13] DPD DR v/7 unfol.; DPD Probate, Will of Robert Fawdon (1603).

[14] DPD DR v/8, fo. 28ᵛ. Cf. DR v/3, fos. 122ᵛ, 157ᵛ, 163ᵛ, DR v/5, fos. 73ᵛ, 77–8 for other cases. P. Rushton, 'Women, Witchcraft, and Slander in Early Modern England: Cases from the Church Courts at Durham, 1560–1675', *Northern History*, 18 (1982), 131, finds that defamation cases in Durham were predominantly brought by women against other women, and were commonly motivated by a desire to defend their reputations against allegations of sexual misconduct. 'Honestie' and 'good name', however, clearly involved more than just chaste conduct, and they were qualities valued by men also—as the Thomas Pearson case suggests.

[15] E. Gibson, *Codex Juris Ecclesiastici Anglicani*, 2nd edn. (Oxford, 1761), 462.

[16] Some tenants sought to anticipate this process by making transfers during their lifetimes, such transfers being not infrequently connected with the marriage of heirs. Most tenants, however, appear to have been content to allow the custom of the manor to operate after their own deaths, even when their heirs were already of age.

were minors, the widow of a male tenant would be admitted to hold in 'widowright' until the coming of age of the heir.[17] If the heir was already of age, the holding descended by primogeniture to the eldest son. In the absence of sons, it either passed to a single daughter as sole heir or was divided between surviving daughters as co-heirs. In the absence of a widow or direct heirs of the tenant, the court recognized the rights of the next of kin—perhaps a brother or sister, or on occasion a more distantly related person—adjudicating where necessary between rival claimants. Clearly, the jurors were expected to know, or to acquaint themselves with, such family connections.[18] Finally, the manor court lent its authority to register arrangements that had been privately arrived at within families, the commonest of such circumstances being the continued provision for a widow after the transfer of a holding to an adult heir.[19]

The manor, then, was the vital mediating institution in the transference of copyhold property from generation to generation. The custom of the manor was the crucial determinant and guarantor of the rights of the members of copyholder families. Moreover, this role was central to the activities of the Halmote Court—of more than two hundred transfers recorded in the court book for the period 1585–1607, close to half were occasioned by the death of a tenant.[20]

While the laconic entries of the Halmote Court book provide telling evidence of the centrality of the manor in the lives of a substantial proportion of the households of Elizabethan Whickham, testamentary records relating to the disposition of the moveable

[17] e.g. when Alexander Barley died in 1583 his messuage and 12 acres were granted to his widow Janet and held by her in widowright until 1590 when her son Richard was admitted to his inheritance: DPD DDR HC III F 18, fos. 7, 11. For similar cases involving the Scott and Brod families, see ibid. fos. 11ᵛ, 37ᵛ (Brods), 15ᵛ, 76ᵛ, 91ᵛ (Scotts).

[18] For examples of the recognition of more distant kin by the jurors, see ibid. fos. 70ᵛ, 93ᵛ, 102.

[19] e.g. Michael Blacket died in 1568. His widow held the family land in widowright until 1587 when her son Nicholas was admitted as heir. He promptly transferred part of the holding back to his mother for her natural life, and sublet the rest. William Thompson, James Jackson, and Richard Hedworth were among others who similarly provided for elderly mothers by transfers for life of part of their inherited land: DPD DDR HC III F 18, fos. 10ᵛ, 24ᵛ, 26, 31ᵛ, 67ᵛ. Another form of family agreement must have underlain William Watson's action in 1598 of transferring his newly inherited holding to his brother George: ibid. fo. 31.

[20] Ibid. fos. 1–71, *passim*. Actual figures, 91 of 204. The remainder were either transfers for a period of years, or permanent alienations of holdings.

goods of the parishioners offer still richer insights into the matrix of personal and institutional ties within which they lived their lives. Of course, not every parishioner made a will. Only a small minority did so. For those who died intestate, an administrator (usually the widow or the next of kin) could be appointed by the ecclesiastical courts at Durham and charged with the payment of the outstanding debts and funeral expenses of the deceased and the division of the remainder of the estate between surviving dependants in accordance with the custom of the Province of York.[21] By the same custom, the freedom of action of even those who made a will was severely constrained. Only an unmarried and childless person could devise goods by will with complete freedom. A man who had either a wife *or* children could dispose freely of only half his goods, while a man who had both a wife *and* children could devise only a third of his goods by will, the remaining thirds being due to his wife and children respectively. The rights of widows and children to their shares of the family's moveable goods were therefore guaranteed in law, each child in particular being entitled to a 'filiall and childes portion' by equal division. No will could override these rights, and the only exceptions permitted were in those cases in which an elder child was debarred by virtue of being already the heir to freehold lands, or in which a particular child had been 'advanced' earlier in the father's lifetime—advancement being defined as the provision of 'a competent portion whereon to live'.[22]

Given such provision for the families of intestates and the restrictions placed upon testators, it is scarcely surprising that so many Whickham householders did not trouble to make a will. Nevertheless, last wills and testaments were made by some parishioners of all social levels from cottager to substantial yeoman, and in choosing to make their wills the individuals concerned appear to have been impelled by a variety of discernible motives. One such was the desire to appoint a specific 'tutor' to look after the

---

[21] For the law of intestacy, see Gibson, *Codex*, 477 ff. Where minor children were involved the administrator was in effect appointed their 'tutor' or 'tutrix' and the administration bond included undertakings to bring up the child or children and to pay them their portions in due course. For the duties of tutors under the custom of the northern province, see H. Swinburne, *A Treatise of Testaments and Last Wills* (London, 1635), 168 ff. Actual Whickham examples of such arrangements can be found in DPD Probate Bonds: 1576, bonds 75, 80; 1583, bonds 219, 226; 1587, bonds 64, 463; 1603, bonds 55, 97, 116, 191, 277.

[22] Swinburne, *Treatise of Testaments*, 182 ff; Gibson, *Codex*, 475 ff.

interests of young children, a procedure permitted under the custom of the northern province.[23] Another was the wish to name a supervisor (commonly a brother-in-law), to assist in the settlement of the estate, a provision that may have been linked to anxieties concerning the competence or trustworthiness of potential administrators.[24] More generally, however, the making of a will represented a resolution on the part of an individual facing death to make a formal acknowledgement of his or her obligations and affections and to undertake a personal settlement of the estate. The will was a last act of social recognition and a final exercising of personal authority, and it is as such that wills are most revealing.

For the majority of testators who faced death in the midst of the family cycle, their first obligations were of course to their wives and children. These they met as they were bound to do by the custom of York. Some of them took the opportunity to specify with minute precision the exact nature of each child's portion of goods or money; others simply devised the residue of their estates, after the payment of their debts and funeral expenses, to their immediate dependants. More than a few, however, were also concerned to use such freedom of action as the law allowed them to make small legacies to others beyond their own nuclear families as tokens of affection and regard—to brothers or sisters, nephews or nieces, and very occasionally to more distant kin, or to godchildren, servants, or unrelated neighbours.

John Whitfield, for example, who died in 1583, left the bulk of his goods to his wife and child, but also provided for small legacies in kind to his father, mother, brother, and three sisters. Similarly, Thomas Wigham left animals or small sums of money to his half-brother, four sisters, brother-in-law, four nephews, and two nieces. Alexander Barlow included among his beneficiaries the sister of his son-in-law, his goddaughter, and the 'poore widows' of Whickham. John Yawton remembered his brother-in-law, to whom he gave a blue coat, and Roger Watson (described as 'Sander Barlaies man'),

---

[23] See n. 21 above. For examples of testators naming tutors: DPD Probate, Wills of Margaret Hirst (1576), Richard Harrison (1587).

[24] DPD Probate, Wills of Robert Boutflower (1562), Richard Hedworth (1565), John Yawton (1581). That estates were incompetently or dishonestly administered on occasion is evident in such court cases as PRO DURH 2/6/81, DURH 4/3, 281–3.

to whom he bequeathed 'thre shepe skinns which are at John Stobbes to make him a dublett of'.[25]

Those testators who were widowed and in the final stage of the family cycle, and those who were unmarried and had neither wife nor child to provide for, were permitted greater freedom of action under the law. But they used it circumspectly. The former, who included all female testators, concentrated their bequests upon their children, grandchildren, and sons- and daughters-in-law, sometimes explicitly adjusting legacies to take account of prior 'advancement', as when Robert Donkin left a small token sum to one of his sons-in-law 'over and besides the childes portion which he hath receaved of me with my daughter Christabell his wyfe'. They were more likely than married testators to include token legacies to such close relatives as brothers, sisters, nephews, nieces, and sisters-in-law, but they rarely extended their concern deeper into the universe of kin.[26] Youthful will-makers, lacking immediate dependants, were entirely free, but tended to distribute their possessions among their parents, siblings, and nephews and nieces.

The recognition of bonds of personal obligation and sentiment enshrined in the wills of the parishioners thus indicates both the centrality and the limits of family ties in the lives of Whickham's inhabitants. Testators concentrated in the first instance, as we might expect and as the custom of York insisted, on their duty to attend to the well-being of their wives and children. They were certainly sensible of a somewhat broader set of kinship ties, and in all some 72 per cent of testators in the period 1550–1603 left at least tokens of their regard to kinsfolk beyond their own immediate dependants. Yet recognition of broader family relationships was restricted in genealogical range; it very rarely extended beyond parents, grand-children, siblings and their families, and a comparable range of affinal kin. The impression given is that kinship sentiments and obligations were focused within a cluster of households linked by close ties of consanguinity and affinity and geographical proximity; that range of effective kin described in contemporary parlance as 'friends'.[27] The relative freedom of action permitted to some

[25] DPD Probate, Wills of John Whitfield (1583), Thomas Wigham (1590), Alexander Barlow (1583); Regr. IV, fo. 172 (John Yawton, 1581).
[26] DPD Probate, Will of Robert Donkin (1587). There was no significant difference in the behaviour of male and female testators.
[27] Our findings regarding kinship recognition in Whickham wills are almost identical to those of Dr Issa's analysis of the wills of three other Durham parishes—

testators by their life-cycle stage and economic resources meant in practice that they enjoyed more room to exercise personal discretion in recognizing individuals selected from within that limited range of kinsfolk. John Merriman, for example, who died in 1574, left legacies only to his wife, three sons, one daughter, and a single grandchild; in contrast, his widow Jennet, who died six years later, included alongside her sons, daughters, and three grandchildren, token legacies to a son-in-law, a daughter-in-law, two sisters, and a sister-in-law.[28]

Jennet Merriman was also among that minority of testators who extended their consideration to embrace unrelated neighbours. She left tokens of regard in the form of items of clothing to four female neighours, including Elizabeth Harrison 'the mittwyfe', who received a cap and Jennet's second-best kerchief. The neighbours, however, were much more likely to make their appearance in testamentary records either as witnesses to the making of a will, or in the lists of outstanding debts and credits appended to wills and inventories. It is clear that these lists were often dictated by the

upland Stanhope, lowland Sedgefield, and industrial Chester-le-Street: Issa, 'Obligation and Choice', ch. 2, esp. 125. They are also compatible with the actual evidence of effective kinship ties beyond the nuclear family presented by Miranda Chaytor in her study of Ryton, Co. Durham, Whickham's neighbour: M. Chaytor, 'Household and Kinship: Ryton in the Late 16th and early 17th Centuries', *History Workshop Journal*, 10 (1980), 36 ff. They are not compatible, however, with Chaytor's interpretative emphasis on the significance of the extended kinship group. In our view, Chaytor is right to criticize the excessive preoccupation of English social historians with the nuclear family household, but in demonstrating the significance of kinship relations beyond the individual household she pays too little attention to the narrow genealogical range of the kinship ties involved. More recently, David Cressy has also criticized the 'fixation' of English historians on the nuclear family and 'individualism', and has challenged the significance of testamentary evidence as a guide to the range of effective kinship ties: D. Cressy, 'Kinship and Kin Interaction in Early Modern England', *Past and Present*, 113 (1986), esp. 53 ff. We entirely accept his general argument that a broader network of 'latent' kin existed which could be drawn upon when occasion demanded, and that the English kinship system might be better characterized as 'contextual', 'fluid and flexible', than as narrow and restricted. We will explore these issues further in sec. 4 below. Nevertheless, we remain persuaded, like Issa, that wills provide a useful indicator of the range of kin with whom close ties of obligation and sentiment were maintained, and we find most plausible the view that the range of effective kin on a day-to-day basis was relatively circumscribed.

[28] DPD Probate, Will of John Merriman (1574); Regr. IV, fo. 163ᵛ (Will of Jennet Merriman, 1580). As in this example, what might appear to be gender differences in kinship recognition existed; however, they were slight and can usually be explained by differences in life-cycle stage and in the nature of the immediate responsibilities faced by married men and widowed women.

testator upon his or her deathbed—as for example in the tally of Richard Arnold's debtors, which commences: 'Impr. Nicolas Blaket oweth me . . . '—and they reveal a web of economic interconnectedness within the neighbourhood which a dying person did well to clarify as a prologomenon to the settlement of his or her estate.[29]

The seventeen Whickham testators who left a record of both their debts and their credits between 1557 and 1603 recorded such relationships with no fewer than 310 named individuals. Some arose from dealings with the farmers of adjoining parishes, or with merchants and tradesmen in Gateshead and Newcastle. Most, however, recorded the economic dimension of neighbourhood, the bargains struck and the assistance extended and received in the normal course of the year among a group of known and presumably trusted individuals: payments owed, or owing, 'for a cow', 'for flyche', 'for a bushell of rye', 'for haye', 'for wintering of two oxen', or simply small sums listed as 'lent money'. On the deathbed such obligations among neighbours were publicly recognized and declared with the intention that they be honoured, and the fact that in some cases they involved also a degree of personal warmth is on occasion attested to by testators directing that particular debts be 'forgiven' by their executors.[30]

The precise terms of a will and the range of social recognition recorded in such documents could thus vary according to the personal circumstances of individual testators, the life-cyle stage at which a person died, and the degree of individual freedom in the disposal of goods that he or she enjoyed. Taken together, however, the Whickham wills bring out clearly the extent to which the dying person was faced not only with the responsibilities of transferring property, but also with the management of what could be very

[29] DPD Probate, Will and Inv. of Richard Arnold (1587). There are many other examples of the use of the first-person and present tense in lists of debts and credits, indicating dictation. The duty of declaring debts and credits may have been a further factor in encouraging people to make a will. In 1644 one Whickham man reportedly formed 'a firme and settled resolution to make his will after he had begun to compute and reckon up such debts as was due and oweing unto him': DPD Probate, Will of John Nixon (1644).

[30] e.g. DPD Probate, Wills of Robert Donkin (1587), Thomas Wigham (1590), Anthony Grundie (1600), Robert Fawdon (1603). For a close analysis of the web of debt and credit in three other Durham parishes, which examines the relative importance of kinsfolk and neighbours in such relationships, see Issa, 'Obligation and Choice', 207 ff., esp. 212–13.

complex webs of personal relationships, with their attendant obligations and competing demands. Such management involved the exercise of authority in the making of decisions, and the familial tensions and anxieties that underlay decision-making sometimes left their mark in the terms of wills. Thomas Watson directed his brothers and executors to 'be good unto my father'. Ralph Hall left a legacy to his brother George 'if that he will kepe himself of good conversation'. Anthony Grundie commanded his daughter Mary 'to be obedient and dutifull in following her mothers good counsell', and Anthony Barras warned that his son Ralph should have nothing if he 'by sute or otherwise' chose to 'vex or molest' his brother Gregory, the principal heir and executor.[31]

Surviving accounts of the process of will-making, usually in the form of the testimony given at the proving of a nuncupative (non-written) will, vividly illuminate these realities. They show that the deathbed could be a public place, that making a will was often a participatory process involving a broad range of those among whom the testator had spent his or her life, and that, though the eventual will represented a formal settlement of the material and emotional obligations contracted in life, it could also be the outcome of a complex round of familial diplomacy.

Thomas Harrison, for example, lay dying at the beginning of August 1603. He was an unmarried man and during his sickness was kept in the house of his mother Jane and his stepfather, the formidable Nicholas Arnold (who was to lead the copyholders sixteen years later in their struggle against the Grand Lessees). There he was nursed and attended in the fortnight preceding his death by his sister Ann Watson, a young married woman who had travelled from her home in Weardale to be by his side, and by Elizabeth Pearson, a 'cosen' of the Harrisons. All these people were present, together with Agnes Harrison, widow, a relative by marriage, when he declared his wishes concerning the disposition of his estate early on the morning of the Saturday preceding his death. His will, however, was not committed to writing. On the following Thursday evening he was visited by two more relatives, George and Dorothy Dalton, and by Elizabeth Pearson's husband Thomas. Thomas Pearson later described how the visitors 'found him lyinge sicke in Bedd', and how, 'after they had asked him howe he did and

---

[31] DPD Probate, Wills of Thomas Watson (1569), Ralph Hall (1581), Anthony Grundie (1600), Anthony Barrass (1594).

staied there a litle', the conversation turned to his will. George Dalton promptly attempted to persuade him to leave his nine acres of land to his brother Mathew rather than his brother Henry. Dorothy Dalton urged him to give a certain cow to Ann Watson, rather than to his mother. According to Pearson, the dying man resisted both suggestions, saying of the cow that 'he would not geve her from his mother who had disirved more of his goods'. George Dalton told a different story. According to him, Thomas took him by the hands and complained 'that he would faine have made his will and disposed of his goods but his mother and father and other his friends would not lett him'. Though his true desires had been thwarted, he was prepared to acquiesce, saying 'they would not be contented and therefore let them do with it what they will'. At this point Nicholas and Jane Arnold allegedly interrupted and prevented further discussion of the matter. Exactly what transpired around Thomas Harrison's deathbed can never be known, but the terms of the nuncupative will eventually accepted by the probate court have an air of compromise. Brother Henry was named heir to the nine acres; brother Mathew, however, was to have Thomas's stock, corn, wains, and husbandry gear and was to be granted a lease of the land for a term of twenty-one years. Agnes Harrison's fatherless son was remembered, as was Thomas Pearson. Nicholas Arnold got Thomas's best hat, and Thomas's mother got her cow.[32]

Such deathbed diplomacy was not unique and could involve a variety of people who were far from backward in voicing their opinions as to how a testator should act. William Marshall, a plague victim, was attended by his son-in-law Adam Hogg, Helen Henderson, a widow who had been hired to look after him, John Dobson, who had known him for fifty years, and another longstanding neighbour, William Bainbrigg. Marshall was unwilling to make a will, saying 'that he would not whilst he lived give and dispose his goods to anye'. But he was won over by William Bainbrigg, who argued that he should

consider of the great paines and charges that Adam Hogg his sonne in lawe had and was like to bestowe upon him in the tyme of his visitacon and to consider of the same in giving to him his goods as he had proved a good sonne in lawe to him so herein to shew himself a kind father.

[32] DPD DR v/7, unfol. 22 Oct. 1603; DPD Probate, Will of Thomas Harrison (1603).

Marshall left everything to Adam, 'saving one pott and one pann which he wold give unto his sister for a remembrance'.[33]

Nor was the testator always treated with great deference or sensitivity. Martin Wilson was also dying of the plague, which did not prevent several of his friends and neighbours being present when he told his wife Alice, 'Honye I wold thou would remember thy sister . . . she hath taken pains for us, I wold thou would give her two kyne.' Back came the retort, 'I have rewarded her, we are not so far behind with her as you trow, if you give her two kyne what shall I have to bring up my child.' Martin took the point. 'Nay, said he, take you all during yor life to bring up my child and at your death consider of yor sister', adding only that he wished her to pay all his debts, especially that due to John Bainbridge, 'saying that he had done much for them'. No will was drawn up in this case 'for want of pen and inke'. We know of this discussion only because Martin's death from plague was rapidly followed by those of his wife and child, and settlement of the claims on his small estate involved the taking of depositions from witnesses to his dying wishes.[34]

The deathbed, then, was a public place, even a public forum for debate. Its principal concerns were those of settlement. The material and emotional obligations of an individual's lifetime were recognized. Provision was made for the discharge of the responsibilities that weighed heavily on the minds of the dying. Efforts were made, with the participation of family, 'friends', and neighbours, to minimize the social disturbance that might be occasioned by imminent death. Through examination of the bequests made by Whickham's testators and the decision-making that lay behind them, we are able to approach these matters and to assess their social–structural implications. But wills were not solely concerned with the disposition of material goods, and there are two further ways in which the testamentary records of the parish can cast light upon both the complexes of communal ties within which the people of Elizabethan Whickham lived their lives and the identities that they derived from them.

In the first place, every surviving will from 1547 began with the bequest of the testator's soul to god. The terms in which these clauses were couched, of course, were usually devised by the scribes who wrote the wills—generally the rector or curate of the parish.

---

[33] DPD DR v/8, fos. 31ᵛ–32. Marshall's will does not survive.
[34] DPD DR v/8, fo. 32ᵛ; PRO DURH 2/2/51.

They were at least tacitly approved by the testators concerned at the reading aloud of the completed will, but they tell us little of the personal faith of the individual man or woman. At best, they can be employed to trace the transition from the conventional catholicism of a bequest of the soul 'to god almyghtye to our blessed ladey sanet Maii and to all the holy company of heven' in the last year of Mary's reign, to the equally conventional protestantism of a surrender of the soul 'into the hands of almyghtie god my maker beleving onlie to be saved by the death of Christ my only saviour and redeemer', which was the norm by the third decade of Elizabeth.[35] Neverthe-less, whatever their precise theological implications, all such bequests of the soul shared the same basic concept of the spiritual significance of death. Death was a calling upon the individual soul by god, a belief reflected also in the manner in which testators described the possibility of the premature deaths of their children— 'if it please allmightie god to call of my daughter'; 'if it happen that god call my child'; 'if God take him before he be of lawfull years'— and also in William Bainbrigg's advice to William Marshall to settle his goods on Adam Hogg 'yf it please god to call upon him'.[36]

Wills commencing in such a manner and couched in such terms convey an impression of dignified resignation in the face of death and of firm confidence in an afterlife to come. They imply that Whickham's testators died calmly and devoutly, in accordance with the contemporary ideal of a 'good death'. This impression, of course, is inevitably coloured by the very formal nature of these documents. Not all can have died well. There must have been pain and mental anguish, fear and squalor. William Marshall, as we have seen, was not reconciled to the inevitability of death. Nor is piety and repentance to be assumed. Yet the very public nature of the deathbed may have provided both emotional support for the dying and a social pressure to conform themselves to shared expectations of an appropriate comportment in the face of death. Part of that

[35] Quoting from DPD Probate, Wills of Richard Lowson (1557), Robert Robinson (1584). In Whickham the Elizabethan settlement brought an immediate switch to the perfunctory bequest of the soul, 'to almightie god'. Only two 'catholic' bequests can be found thereafter, in 1565 and 1575. The latter was that of Claude Rent, rector 1558–75. Interestingly, Rent appears not to have acted as scribe for the wills of his flock, leaving that task to his curate. More elaborately Protestant bequests of the soul commence in the 1580s, during the ministry of Rent's successor Mr Ferniside, who frequently wrote his parishioners' wills.

[36] DPD Probate, Regr. II, fo. 30 (Will of Robert Boutflower, 1562), Wills of John Whitfield (1583), Robert Donkin (1587); DPD DR v/8, fos. 31ᵛ–32.

support came from the clergy of the parish, who were witnesses to two-thirds of the wills drawn up in Elizabethan Whickham—a sufficient testimony to their assiduousness in their duty of ministering to the dying. And part of that comportment was the making of a settlement with God as well as man. Thomas Harrison, after declaring his will, 'did for the most part of all the daie perfectly readd praiers in a Booke' and then awaited death in the company of his 'friends', 'and did well knowe them after he had lost the sight of one of his eyes'.[37] He died well, and others may have done as much, 'in sure and certain hope' of the salvation promised them by their church.

Secondly, while Whickham's testators were concerned with the meeting of their material, emotional, and spiritual obligations, they were also deeply preoccupied with the fate of their earthly remains and with the funeral rites that would mark their passage from the world. Elizabethan testators almost invariably specified that they wished to be buried in Whickham church or Whickham churchyard, while close to half the surviving wills contain even more specific instructions. Some wished to be buried 'at the east end of the church', 'at the queer [choir] end', 'in the queyre', or 'near the quere door'—a preference quite commonly expressed up to the 1580s and perhaps indicative of a desire to lie near the altar, at the 'holier' end of the church or churchyard. A few asked to be interred 'nighe unto my owne stall', 'near unto my stall', or 'under the pewe where I did sitt', a more personal expression of attachment to a specific place within the parish church and perhaps, by implication, within the social order of the parish.[38] Rather more (a quarter of all testators) wished to lie not so much in particular places as by particular people—'as near unto the grave of my father as possible may be': 'nere to my brother Nicholas'; 'as neare unto my late wyfe as maye be'; 'nere unto my husbande'; 'as ner unto my sister and by those of my friends deceased as canne'; or 'neer unto the burials of my auncestoures.'[39] Such requests, which are entirely individual and unrelated to the identity of the scribes of wills, surely indicate both

[37] DPD DR v/7 unfol. 22 Oct. 1603.

[38] e.g. DPD Probate, Wills of Richard Lowson (1557), Richard Hedworth (1565), John Yawton (1581), Alexander Barlow (1582), Robert Robinson (1584), Richard Harrison (1587), Anthony Grundie (1600).

[39] e.g. DPD Probate, Wills of Ralph Hall (1581), Eleanor Watson (1585), Robert Donkin (1587), Richard Arnold (1587), Anthony Barrass (1594), Effam Hall (1598), John Harrison (1594), Robert Fawdon (1603).

the continued power of family ties sundered by death and a sense of belonging to a community that embraced both the living and the dead in Whickham.[40]

In addition, testators expressed firm views about the appropriate manner of their burial, and here above all the place of the individual within the neighbourhood was emphasized. They frequently specified that they should 'be honestlye brought forth', or enjoined their executors to 'bringe me honestlye forth', a phrase repeated with small modifications in many wills.[41] The actual costs of funerals, which are sometimes recoverable from inventories, varied considerably, both as absolute sums and as a proportion of the total value of a deceased person's inventoried goods. It is clear enough, however, that each family had a good notion of what constituted an 'honest' funeral, and that an appropriate degree of ceremony mattered greatly both to the testator and to his or her survivors. One heir, William Thompson, actually went into debt to the tune of 40s. in the midst of the dearth crisis of 1596 to see his father, a modest yeoman, buried in the manner that he had requested.[42]

Detailed funeral expenses indicate that certain items of expenditure were more or less fixed and that the overall costs of a funeral tended to depend upon the amount spent on the 'forthbringing' itself. This was the bringing of the corpse from the house of the deceased to the parish church, a ceremony that included the dispensing of food and drink among the neighbours present. In the 1560s this might cost only 5s. for a cottager like Thomas Turner, or could run to 13s. 4d. for a yeoman like Lawrence Sotheron. Nevertheless, each received one final act of social recognition in that 'ritual of inclusion' which Eleanor Watson later described as 'my outbringing honestilie amonge my neighbours'.[43]

---

[40] The individual nature of such requests is indicated by an account of the deathbed of Richard Hedworth. He desired to alter his will 'and add to it, namely saieing that he would be buried in Whickham church as nere unto his father and mother as conveniently might be': DPD DR v/9, unfol. 17 Oct. 1607. For the frequency of the desire to be buried in a specific place or near particular people elsewhere in early modern England, see C. Gittings, *Death, Burial and the Individual in Early Modern England* (London, 1984), 86–7.

[41] e.g. DPD Probate, Wills of Lionel Watson (1548), Elizabeth Matfen (1563), William Smith (1568), Thomas Watson (1569), Eleanor Watson (1585), Edmund Dobbinson (1589).

[42] DPD Probate, Will and Inv. of Cuthbert Tompson (1596).

[43] DPD Probate, Invs. of Thomas Turner (1569), Lawrence Sotheron (1562), Will of Eleanor Watson (1585). Cf. Gittings, *Death*, 60 ff., 89 ff., and 151 ff., for

Taken together, the various ways in which the inhabitants of Whickham confronted the perennial reality of death serve to highlight the complex of institutional and personal ties that bound them together. The forthbringing, culminating in burial at a specified place, even near named individuals, provided the final ritual expression of the communal identity of the inhabitants of the parish. Elizabethan Whickham can be described as a community that was based on the land, defined and structured by the institutions of the manor and the parish, constructed and maintained as a local social system by the interrelationships and regular interactions of individuals and groups as members of families, kinsfolk, and neighbours, and expressed in such symbolically significant occasions as the manorial transfer, the deathbed, the will-making, and the forthbringing—events that both represented and reinforced a particular socially constructed reality.

We have dwelt on all this at some length for the simple reason that, if we are to understand the subsequent development of local society in Whickham, we must begin from a firmly delineated context of preceding realities. In attempting to provide such a context we have endeavoured to avoid sentimentality, and in describing Whickham in the later sixteenth century as a 'community', we have used the term advisedly. We do not mean to imply that the social world of the inhabitants of Elizabethan Whickham was essentially 'pre-modern', small-scale, geographically bounded, economically simple, introverted, deeply rooted, warm, personal, intimate, homogeneous in values, and above all stable—though in varying degrees it may have possessed some or all of these qualities. Still less do we wish to conjure up a nostalgic vision of a pristine agrarian past, a cool sequestered vale of life in which the rude forefathers of the parish engaged in useful toil and homely joys, far from the madding crowd; a sentimentally conceived 'before' to which the subsequent experience of the parish and its people can be juxtaposed as an 'after' of declension and dissolution. It should be apparent enough that Elizathan Whickham was no rustic paradise. Yet its people constituted a community of a particular kind in the limited and specific sense that they shared in a complex of

discussions of the intensity of the desire for proper burial, the mounting of funerals commensurate with the standing of the deceased, the large attendance at funerals, and the hospitality provided. The phrase 'ritual of inclusion' is from T. Laqueur, 'Bodies, Death and Pauper Funerals', *Representations*, 1 (1983), 112.

interactions and reciprocities. They were involved in certain arenas of participation focused within, though not rigidly bounded by, a specific geographical location and expressed and structured by particular institutions. Moreover, they possessed a demonstrable sense of local identity.

We have tried to illustrate the nature of these realities so that we can better appreciate the discontinuities of Whickham's subsequent history. For Whickham's experience, in social structure, social relations, and social identities no less than in economic life, was to be dominated by discontinuity. To be sure, it was not a discontinuity as radical as that which was to obtain in what have been termed the 'constructed communities' of the nineteenth-century coalfield. There was no element of the *tabula rasa* in Whickham's development comparable to that of those artificially established collectivities of migrant workers housed in colliery rows.[44] On the contrary, Whickham had a pre-existing identity which played no small part in determining the possibilities of subsequent development.

Nevertheless, in the course of the seventeenth and early eighteenth centuries Whickham was to witness the emergence of a local society of a novel and distinctive type. Its people lived, in a sense, in a liminal space between the late-medieval agrarian world and the industrial Tyneside of the nineteenth century. Part of that experience was that, while some of the institutions and behavioural paradigms that had structured the social relations of the past endured, others were rendered redundant or called into question. The inhabitants of the parish, like others who shared their experience, were forced to construct an alternative social system, new forms of community, and novel understandings of their world within the limits of the possibilities apparent to them in their particular social and historical situation. It is to these processes of adaptation and change, to the uncertainties of social construction and their halting and uneven resolution, that we must now turn.

2. SOCIAL DISLOCATION?

In the first half of the seventeenth century Whickham passed through a maelstrom of rapid industrial expansion which had

---

[44] For 'constructed communities', see Williamson, *Class, Culture and Community*, 6.

profound consequences for the social structure of the parish. There were three developments of particular note. In the first place, this period witnessed the gradual demise of the existing copyholder community of the manor of Whickham and the recasting of copyholder society. Secondly, industrial development involved the emergence of a large new population of industrial workers characterized by wage dependency and by a startling degree of population mobility. Thirdly, these developments together produced a further consequence: the emergence by the mid-seventeenth century of a new social structure, one that reflected in its composition the coal industry that had brought it into being. Whickham's population by the time of the hearth-tax listings of the 1660s was not only larger and more mobile, but also more socially differentiated. It was on the one hand a more gentrified local society than the copyholder world of the later sixteenth century, while on the other hand it contained a larger reservoir of poverty.

In the light of these relatively rapid transformations, we are bound to ask whether the processes of social change in Whickham involved any degree of social dislocation. Did they produce a local society lacking in social cohesion, prone to disorder, or bereft of 'controlling influences', as was so often implied in later descriptions of early coalfield settlements?

If such conditions were indeed part of Whickham's experience of industrialization, we might reasonably expect that they would be particularly intense in the earlier part of the seventeenth century, during the initial decades of upheaval occasioned by the expansion of mining activity. This was, after all, a period that saw mounting antagonism between the copyholders of Whickham and the Grand Lessees, culminating in the copyholders' defeat in 1620/1. Is there any further evidence that might indicate the existence of a more general situation of disequilibrium, incoherence, or social dislocation?

The surviving records of the secular and ecclesiastical courts do not suggest that this was so. Cases arising from Whickham present a catalogue of petty disorders familiar enough to any student of social regulation in this period. The act books of the episcopal consistory court and of the court of the archdeacon of Durham, which together provide full coverage of ecclesiastical court prosecutions between 1600 and 1619, reveal that the churchwardens of Whickham presented parishioners to the church courts for sexual mis-demeanours (usually fornication), for laxity in their religious obligations, or for profaning the sabbath by such activities as drinking and playing cards or 'nineholes' in church-service time.[45] The indictment rolls and process book of the court of quarter sessions, which permit a full reconstruction of prosecutions between 1598 and 1636, add their complement of constabular presentments for such misdemeanours as keeping a greyhound illegally, drunkenness, rescuing impounded animals, or running an unlicensed or disorderly alehouse, together with occasional privately brought prosecutions for theft or assault.[46] In addition, the Halmote Court dealt regularly with tenants presented for the breach of agrarian by-laws and occasionally with matters as serious as an affray between quarrelling copyholders.[47]

In all this, known coal-workers not infrequently found themselves the objects of the disciplinary attentions of the parish officers, the ecclesiastical judges, and the justices of the peace—as would be expected, given their growing presence in the local population. But they were very far from being exclusively responsible for Whickham's minor disorders, and they exhibited no peculiar prominence among those knots of individuals who found themselves repeatedly in trouble. The court records relating to early seventeenth-century Whickham, in fact, indicate little in the misbehaviour of the inhabitants of the parish that would not be equally evident in the records of an agricultural parish of comparable size in this period. Gaming in church-service time was perhaps more frequently singled out as one of the disorders permitted by delinquent alehousekeepers, which may relate to the leisure habits of a large and mobile population of regularly paid, young, male, wage-workers. Again, occasional group assaults and affrays were a not uncommon feature of disputes between parties in the 1620s and early 1630s. These generally arose, however, from quarrels between parish notables, occasioned, where the source of friction can be discovered or inferred, by disputes over land or debts. Whickham's rapid

---

[45] The surviving records of ecclesiastical court prosecutions prior to the Civil War are as follows. Consistory Court: DPD DR ii/1–2 (1577–87), DR iii/12 (1632–33), DR iv/1–7 (1579–1618); DPD Prior's Kitchen, 'Consistory Court Book of Acts Ex Officio, 1619–21', 'Fragments of Durham Chancellor's Visitations c.1634–7'. Archdeacon's Court: DDR DR viii/1 (1600–19). Together they provide full coverage of this side of ecclesiastical justice only for the period 1600–19.

[46] DRO Q/S I/1–15 (Indictments, 1595–1636); Q/S OP 1 (Process Book, 1619–36); Q/S OB/1–3 (Orders, 1616–44). Only fragments of the assize records of the late 16th and early 17th c. survive in PRO DURH 17/1.

[47] DPD DDR HC iii F 18, F 19.

economic development may have provided more occasion for such conflicts of interest, but in themselves they were far from distinctive in their nature.

In short, Whickham's disorders were conventional enough, and the situation does not appear to have occasioned any discernible alarm among the officers of parish and township. With the exception of a brief period at the very beginning of the century when the curate Richard Dereham seems to have taken the initiative in prosecuting neglect of religious duties and service-time offences, there appears to have been no *sustained* effort at the establishment of a tighter or more demanding regime of moral and social regulation in Whickham. Nor does Dereham's brief initiative appear to have won him any friends. It is perhaps unsurprising that he should have aroused the hostility of one John Cooke, presented in May 1602 for being 'a carder and for speakinge verie opprobrious wordes in the Church against Mr. Dearham'. More significant may be the fact that Dereham's own churchwardens presented him in September 1601 'for not wearinge his surpless in tyme of divine service', and that the churchwardens in the following year refused to be sworn 'by their minister (as he informeth) and so not being sworne doe not present falts'. Clearly, the parish officers shared neither their young minister's enthusiasm for reformation of manners in the parish, nor his scruples regarding ritual conformity.[48]

As these events indicate, local officers could be negligent in prosecuting or wilfully indifferent to the petty disorders of local life, and court records, of course, reveal only what was reported to the courts. Yet the record of Whickham's officers was not generally one of inactivity or gross negligence. The conflict of the churchwardens with Mr Dereham was a brief phenomenon which may

[48] DPD DR v/5 (unfol.), 15 May 1602, 12 & 26 Sept. 1601, DR viii/1, fo. 117. Dereham is first mentioned in Whickham's records in 1593 as 'minister at Whickham'. He was curate to the aged and infirm rector Mr Ferniside. He was a regular preacher, described on one occasion as 'the preacher at Whickham', and the surplice incident suggests that he may have been inclined to nonconformity. On the other hand, the church was said in 1600 to lack both a decent surplice and the prescribed books, and he was at loggerheads with the churchwardens in 1601–3 over the state of its fabric and furniture. Their presentment of him for implied nonconformity may have been malicious. Richard Dereham, 'preacher', was buried on 17 Nov. 1603, towards the end of the plague outbreak of that year. After his death, prosecutions for failure to attend church or to take communion declined abruptly, though in other respects the churchwardens made their presentments as usual. DPD DR v/5 and DR viii/1, *passim*; DPD Probate, Wills of John Harding (1593), Robert Fawdon (1603), Inv. of John Middleton (1603).

have reflected simply their distaste for the disruptive enthusiasm of an over-precise curate. In general, the court records indicate that they did their duty well enough for the most part. Sexual offences were presented to the church courts regularly and other mis-demeanours were reported to the authorities intermittently, most probably when they were the occasion of public scandal or could no longer be ignored. Like many of their fellows across the kingdom, Whickham's officers appear to have held the line against unaccept-able disorders without feeling any compelling desire to tighten the boundaries of the permissible. And the one instance of a form of offence on which we have a source of information that allows us to supplement and test the records of the courts—the bearing of illegitimate children—does not suggest that they faced a peculiarly threatening situation.

Illegitimacy was high in Whickham in the reign of James I. The baptismal register of the parish reveals that the illegitimacy ratio (the proportion of all children baptized who were registered as bastards) rose from 0.24 per cent in the decade 1585–94 to 3.47 per cent in 1595–1604 and peaked at 7.12 per cent in the decade 1605–14. These figures might appear to provide alarming evidence of a breakdown of conventional sexual morality in the parish, but it must be remembered that rising illegitimacy ratios were by no means uncommon in rural England at the turn of the sixteenth century. A national sample of ninety-eight parishes reveals an early peak of the illegitimacy ratio of 3.2 per cent in the decade 1600–9, while the levels of registered illegitimacy in individual parishes were often much higher than the national norm. Illegitimate children made up 5.1 per cent of all registered baptisms in both Colyton (Devon) and Hawkshead (Lancashire) in the years 1601–10, while in the entirely rural parish of Terling (Essex) the ratio exceeded 9 per cent in the same decade. Whickham's experience, then, was by no means exceptional, even though the parish must be numbered among those that experienced higher than average levels of illegitimacy in the early decades of the seventeenth century.[49]

[49] Comparative figures from P. Laslett, 'Introduction: Comparing Illegitimacy Over Time and Between Cultures', and D. Levine and K. Wrightson, 'The Social Context of Illegitimacy in Early Modern England', both in P. Laslett, K. Oosterveen, and R. M. Smith (eds.), *Bastardy and its Comparative History* (London, 1980), 14 (recalculated by decade), 18, 165. In the case of Whickham it could be said that it was less the early 17th-c. peak in illegitimacy ratios that was unusual than the very low level of illegitimate births in the late 16th c.

Whickham was also far from unique in the social circumstances surrounding illegitimacy in so far as these can be recovered. The parents of illegitimate children in the peak decades 1600–19 were for the most part socially obscure. This was especially true of the mothers of bastard children, who can rarely be traced in the parish records with any confidence. As for the fathers, close to two-thirds remain totally obscure in the records of the parish—an indication in all likelihood of their low social standing and/or transience. Of those who can be identified, three-fifths are known to have been coal-workers. A handful of these men and women are known to have borne, or to have fathered, illegitimate children upon more than one occasion. Several others appear in the records of the secular or ecclesiastical courts accused of other misdemeanours (generally associated with drink or alehouse disorders). Such evidence of repeated sexual delinquency or of other forms of 'bad conversation', however, was less common in Whickham than in the Essex parish of Terling.[50] Much more prominent in the circumstances leading to illegitimate births in Whickham, as in Terling and in other parishes in which this phenomenon has been closely studied, were the difficulties and uncertainties surrounding the process of marriage among the labouring poor. Close to half the illegitimate children registered in Whickham between 1600 and 1619 are known to have been the outcome of liaisons that were 'marriage-related' in that their parents either declared in court that they intended, or had intended, to marry, or else subsequently did marry. (And this was a circumstance equally true of couples accused of fornication who did not subsequently produce an illegitimate child.[51])

Clearly, in Whickham, as elsewhere in early modern England, the sexual anticipation of an imminent marriage was a common and socially acceptable feature of serious courtship. Equally clearly, the marital expectations of the labouring poor were highly vulnerable to

[50] Cf. Levine and Wrightson, 'Social Context', 168. This was conceivably because Terling was a more rigorously controlled parish. A high level of recorded delinquency (other than sexual) may have been 'created' among the individuals concerned by the activities of vigorous parish officers pursuing minor offences which might have gone unprosecuted elsewhere.

[51] This is of course a minimum estimate, dependent on those concerned either appearing in court to state their intentions or remaining and marrying in Whickham. In some cases the laconic parish register entries do not even provide us with the names of the parents. For the 'marriage-related' interpretation of trends in illegitimacy, see n. 54 below.

dislocating circumstances which could result in either a delay in the establishment of an independent household or the total abandonment of a prospective marriage. That this was so almost certainly derived from the fact that the courtships of the migrant poor were less closely supervised than those of settled, propertied families because the couples concerned were more dependent on their own resources in finding the wherewithal to marry and set up house independently.

In a study of marital litigation in the Durham courts, it has been argued that, while parents rarely initiated the matches of their children, both parents and close kin took a very active role in the approval and furtherance of their children's courtships. They were particularly concerned with the economic viability of prospective marriages, and their support could be of vital significance in the successful conclusion of a match.[52] That this was also true among the copyholder families of Whickham is suggested by the consent and practical support indicated by land transfers associated with marriage. Thus Roland Harrison transferred three parcels of land to his son Peter at the first meeting of the Halmote Court following the latter's marriage in 1605. Nicholas Harrison transferred land to his daughter Jane in September 1607, and Jane transferred it in turn to Anthony Kirsop whom she married on the first of November that year. John West had his son William's name inserted into his lease of land held from Sir William Blakiston in 1623 on the occasion of William's marriage, and in addition provided houseroom for William and his bride for most of the first year of their marriage on the understanding that William would 'bear and defraye there half of the charges and expenses of housekeepinge'.[53] Migrant wage-workers, in contrast, were probably both free of such supervision and bereft of such support. The successful accomplishment of their matches depended not only on personal fidelity to their promises, but also on the availability of work, wages, and housing. They belonged to a social group whose propensity to marry was heavily subject to the vicissitudes of fortune. To this extent there was an opportunistic element in their marital plans which could render them highly vulnerable to dislocation.

[52] Issa, 'Obligation and Choice', 428 ff. Cf. P. Rushton's discussion of Durham evidence of the opposition of parents and 'friends' to unsatisfactory matches in his 'Property, Power and Family Networks: The Problem of Disputed Marriage in Early Modern England', *J. Family History*, 11 (1986), 205–19.

[53] DPD DDR HC III F 18, fos. 68, 84ᵛ, 85; DR V/11 (unfol.) 24 July 1623.

Such vulnerability was equally true, of course, of England's growing population of agricultural labourers, cottagers, and workers in domestic industry, and the national peak in illegitimacy ratios at the turn of the sixteenth century has been explained as a consequence of the disastrous economic crisis of the 1590s, followed by a prolonged period of uncertain marital opportunity in the hard times of the early decades of the seventeenth century. As expectations adjusted to this less propitious climate of marital opportunity, levels of illegitimacy fell (this adjustment being assisted by punitive action against the parents of illegitimate children and preventative action against pauper marriages on the part of parish officers anxious to avoid additional charges upon the poor rate). Only from the mid-eighteenth century did illegitimacy ratios begin to rise again in a context of economic expansion and of improving (though still highly insecure) marital opportunities for a labouring population that was once more expanding.[54]

The principal distinctiveness of Whickham's experience may have lain not so much in the fact that illegitimacy ratios were high in the Jacobean period, as in the possibility that the circumstances underlying the rise in illegitimacy were more akin to those operating nationally in the later eighteenth century than to those afflicting more typical rural parishes of the early seventeenth century. In both cases, the key to the situation lay in the insecurities attending the decision-making of the labouring poor. But in Whickham those insecurities were part and parcel of a process of swift economic expansion. The higher-than-average levels of illegitimacy in the parish may have resulted from the sheer size of the labouring population most at risk, whose courtships were pursued in a context of heavy in-migration and an exceptionally high degree of population turnover, which was in turn the consequence of short-term, highly volatile employment opportunities.

[54] D. Levine, *Family Formation in an Age of Nascent Capitalism* (London, 1977), ch. 9; Laslett, 'Introduction', Levine and Wrightson, 'Social Context', and K. Wrightson, 'The Nadir of English Illegitimacy in the Seventeenth Century', all in Laslett, Oosterveen and Smith, *Bastardy*, 53 ff., 170 ff., 186 ff. For long-term trends in nuptiality and the relationship between these and illegitimacy, see Wrigley and Schofield, *Population History of England*, 257–69, and E. A. Wrigley, 'Marriage, Fertility and Population Growth in Eighteenth-Century England', in R. B. Outhwaite (ed.), *Marriage and Society: Studies in the Social History of Marriage* (London, 1981), esp. 155 ff.

A further distinctive feature of the Whickham situation seems to have been the presence of a proportion of couples who were actually cohabiting in anticipation of eventual marriages. George Mallaburn was presented for 'kepinge house' with Alice Foster 'and having had two children in fornication with her' in the year prior to their marriage in February 1595, though neither of these children had been registered in Whickham. Similarly, Henry Humble was presented since he had 'kept house an whole year with Agnes Jesoppe and ar unmaryed'. Nothing more is discoverable of this couple in the Whickham records: presumably they moved on.[55] More stable was Emat Barker, who was presented with her partner John Burne in 1600 'for dwellinge together not being maried'. They pleaded their intention to marry and the court subsequently noted that they had done so, though the marriage did not take place in Whickham. By 1615 she was a widow, resident in Whickham, and in that year and the next she bore two illegitimate children by Henry Dixon, a pitman with whom she was now living. They were prosecuted in the consistory court in 1615 and again in 1618, and were excommunicated for their contumacy. The next spring however they sought absolution, declaring their intention to marry, and they were subsequently married in Whickham in May 1619.[56]

The relative frequency of such stable, though illicit, liaisons in Whickham may be indicated by the fact that it was not unusual for the churchwardens of Whickham to present a named man for fornication along with 'eius concubin'—an indication not only of the nature of the relationship but also of the fact that they did not know the woman's name. (Names were filled in later as the case proceeded.[57]) To take a specific example, 'one Gilchrist et eius concub' were prosecuted for fornication in June and October 1605. They were in fact George Gilchrist and Ann Clark, whose bastard child was baptized in September 1605. They eventually appeared before the ecclesiastical judge in January 1606/7, declaring their intention to marry, and were married early in the next month. George Gilchrist's occupation is unknown, but his son became a pitman.[58] William Hutchinson was an overman working in Allerdeans

[55] DPD DR v/3, fos. 130, 171.

[56] DPD DR viii/1, fo. 5ᵛ, DR iv/7, fos. 291ᵛ, 394; DPD Prior's Kitchen, 'Consistory Court Book of Acts Ex Officio, 1619–21' (unfol.), 8 Apr. 1619.

[57] e.g. DPD DR iv/6 (unfol.), 26 Oct. 1605, 2 Nov. 1605, 28 Mar. 1607, DR iv/7, fos. 49, 124, 202ᵛ.

[58] DPD DR viii/1, fo. 171, DR iv/6 (unfol.) 26 Oct. 1605, 17 Jan. 1606/7.

pit for the Liddells in 1614. He and Lucy Swadell 'eius conc'
were first presented for fornication in March 1608, and were represented almost exactly two years later. Their bastard child was
baptized on 23 September 1610 and they eventually married a
month afterwards.[59]

Some such couples, however, did not subsequently marry—at
least, not during their years in Whickham. William 'Morrow' or
Murray 'et eius concubin', subsequently identified as Elinor
Dobson, were presented for fornication every year from 1605 to
1608 but are not known ever to have married. The pitman James
Fawside and his partner Alice Johnson were first prosecuted in
January 1606, baptized a base child a month later, and were
repeatedly prosecuted for fornication in the years up to 1610. They
remained stubbornly excommunicate and did not marry in Whickham.[60]

The precise reasons why these couples chose to live together
before their marriages, delayed so long before marrying, or were
content to remain unwed are beyond recovery. The existence of a
substantial minority of such couples, however (for the most part
drawn from the ranks of the immigrant coal-workers, it would
seem), provides another reason for Whickham's relatively high
incidence of illegitimacy in these decades. Nevertheless, this was
scarcely a situation of unchecked licence, for the churchwardens
busied themselves in keeping a careful eye on such behaviour. Half
of those who baptized illegitimate children in Whickham in the first
decade of the century were prosecuted in the ecclesiastical courts
and in the second decade the score rose to more than three-fifths,
the presentments usually being made before the birth of the child in
question.

Similarly, of those couples accused of fornication who did not
produce bastard children but who subsequently married, almost all
were prosecuted prior to their marriages. The churchwardens of
Jacobean Whickham were not concerned with retrospective prosecutions for pre-nuptial fornication, unlike many of their counterparts elsewhere.[61] But they were very much concerned to clarify the

---

[59] DPD DR IV/6 (unfol.), 30 Mar. 1608, DR IV/7, fos. 49, 51ᵛ, 52, 54ᵛ, 57, 78ᵛ.

[60] DPD DR IV/6 (unfol.), 26 Oct. 1605, 17 Jan. 1605/6, 11 Oct. 1606, 28 Mar.
1607, 30 Mar. 1608, DR IV/7, fo. 52, DR VIII/1, fos. 205ᵛ, 236ᵛ.

[61] M. Ingram, *Church Courts, Sex and Marriage in England, 1570–1640*
(Cambridge, 1987), ch. 7; Wrightson and Levine, *Poverty and Piety*, 132–3.

intentions of suspected couples and to identify the parents of prospective bastard children. Whether their activity had much of an inhibiting influence upon the behaviour of Whickham's growing population is open to doubt, for their coercive power was small and the parishioners were highly mobile. But at the least, they probably hastened along a number of marriages, while their regular present-ments reaffirmed the boundaries of conventional morality.

Whickham, then, had its share of minor disorders in the early decades of the seventeenth century, and the evidence generated by the institutions of social regulation suggests that the parish had some distinctive features of its own. Yet far more striking is Whickham's conventionality in these matters, the degree to which it shared the experience of other English parishes. Certainly there is nothing here to suggest the existence of any serious threat to order or social stability. Moreover, the illegitimacy ratio fell gradually after 1615, reached a nadir of under 1 per cent per decade between the 1650s and the 1680s, and then stabilized at around 1 per cent until the later 1730s. In short, the parish conformed to the national trend, being distinctive only in that, before the later 1590s and after the 1650s, its illegitimacy ratio was actually *below* the national average. Whatever uncertainties had plagued the marital oppor-tunities of the poor in the early years of the century, they appear to have been resolved by mid-century.

A gap in the records of the ecclesiastical courts after 1619 prohibits systematic examination of the problems faced by the churchwardens in the remaining years before the Civil War, though a surviving visitation of 1635 indicates that they were still active. They presented the usual handful of sexual offenders, drunkards, and gamblers in service time, several popish recusants, two men accused of 'barbing upon the sunday', a woman who refused 'to sitt in her owne pew', and two elderly men 'liveing apart from there wives', who appeared and pleaded 'that they are willinge to live with ther wives, but they [i.e. their wives] refuse to live with them'.[62] The Restoration brought an ecclesiastical survey of religious dissidents in 1662. Thereafter, however, regular annual presentment of moral or religious delinquencies to the church courts seems to have ceased—though occasional fornicators found themselves cited to

[62] DPD Prior's Kitchen, 'Fragments of Durham Chancellor's Visitations *c.*1634–7' (unfol.). A few more Whickham presentments for 1632–4 can be found in DPD DR III/2, *passim.*

appear at Durham and enjoined to do penance as late as 1740.[63]

As for the secular courts, no quarter sessions indictment rolls survive between 1636 and 1664 and only two-fifths of the original rolls have survived for the period 1664–99. In the years for which records survive, Whickham provided only a handful of cases of theft, assault, or closebreaking, a record of sporadic minor offences only briefly enlivened in the later 1680s by a spate of group assaults led by prominent parishioners and apparently occasioned by quarrels over boundaries in the newly enclosed town fields and disputed mining rights on the former territories of the Grand Lease. Between 1700 and 1740 barely 15 per cent of the quarter-sessions rolls survive, and they yield only one Whickham case.[64] The Assize records of the Palatinate, however, which are patchy for the seventeenth century and include no Whickham cases, survive very fully for the earlier eighteenth century. In the years 1700–66, Whickham produced only one assault case, nine prosecutions for theft, a case of counterfeiting, two infanticides, and three homicides. Of the most serious of these offences, the infanticides involved servant girls sufficiently terrified by the prospect of bearing an illegitimate child to conceal their pregnancies and subsequently dispose of their children after traumatic secret births. The homicides involved the accidental death of a child, one purely formal indictment occasioned by the discovery of an unidentified skeleton, and the slaying of a member of a naval press-gang by a Swalwell barber resisting impressment (who was subsequently acquitted).[65]

None of this suggests that Whickham was a sink of disorder or the habitat of a savage and brutalized plebeian population which had slipped the bridle of control. Unlike the inhabitants of

---

[63] For the 1662 presentment of catholics and dissenters, see ch. 3 above, p. 166. The surviving evidence of ecclesiastical court prosecutions post-1660 is as follows: Consistory Court: DPD DR II/3 (1662–70), 'Boxes of Visitation Papers (fragments) 1668–1770', DR III/15–26 (1662–1772); DPD Prior's Kitchen, 'Consistory Court Book of Acts Ex Officio, 1662–72'. Archdeacon's Court: DPD Prior's Kitchen, Durham Dean and Chapter Muniments, 'Archdeacon of Durham Act Book 1685–1705'; Durham Cathedral, Dean and Chapter Library, Raine MSS 81, Archdeacon of Durham's visitation, 1697.

[64] DRO Q/S I/17–73, Q/S OP 2. The rolls are fragmentary 1740–56, and the series is broken thereafter. A full series of quarter sessions order books survives for 1649–1774, and these do not indicate any Whickham criminality of note; Q/S OB 4–13.

[65] PRO DURH 16/1, 17/1–10, 19/1–3. It can be added that the local newspapers of the early 18th c., which reported some crimes, do not indicate an unusually serious problem of law and order. All the Whickham cases reported can also be located in the Assizes and quarter sessions records.

Kingswood Forest—whose reputation for disorder was disproportionately influential in shaping the expectations of the early Methodist missionaries to the coalfields and the stereotype of mining society that they publicized—the people of Whickham could scarcely be described by contemporaries as 'living without government or conformity in idleness and dissoluteness', or as not 'responsible to any Civil Officer or Minister for their behaviour or Religion'. Nor can we describe them, like the historian of the Kingswood colliers, as 'a group of men very much withdrawn from the normal means of social discipline'.[66] Indeed, to the best of our knowledge, no such allegation was made about the coalfield parishes of Durham and their inhabitants prior to the evangelical mission of the mid-eighteenth century.

This was not because the local authorities of the area were indifferent to the problem of order, or unreceptive to calls for greater vigilance in the defence of conventional morality. In 1656 the justices of Durham, perhaps stimulated by the presence on the bench of Cromwell's Deputy Major-General Lilburne, issued a general order for the restraint of alehouse-haunting, tippling, drunkenness, swearing, sabbath-breaking, the keeping of unlicensed or disorderly alehouses, bloodshedding, and affrays. In 1691, 'taking into serious consideration the great prophanation of the Lords day, the too much common practices of cursing and swearing, excess of drinking and the impudent committing of leudnesse and debauchery which they are convinced have of late increased', they issued a similar general order and provided for its publication. Nine years later they gave their endorsement to the royal 'Proclamation against Immorality and Prophaneness', ordering local officers to take action against the usual list of petty disorders, while in 1715 they rehearsed the contents of another proclamation 'for the Encouragement of Piety and Vertue and for preventing and punishing of Vice, Prophaneness and immorality' and declared their 'fixed resolution' to root out 'dissolute, immoral or disorderly practices', exhorting all persons 'who have a sense of God's honour and desire to promote his Glory and the welfare of their Country' to do likewise.[67]

As these orders indicate, Durham was in no way insulated from the call for a reformation of manners, either during the Interregnum

---

[66] Malcolmson, 'A Set of Ungovernable People', 91.
[67] DRO Q/S OB 4, 351, OB 7, 287–8, 601, OB 8, 227.

or at the turn of the seventeenth century. Indeed, in the latter period it has been suggested that the county was an area of particular success for the Societies for the Reformation of Manners, not least because the extensive jurisdiction of the bishop facilitated the co-operation of the civil and ecclesiastical authorities.[68] What is striking, however, is that none of these initiatives singled out the colliery districts as requiring any special attention. The vices and disorders attacked were the traditional fare of moralistic indignation, and they were regarded as offences to which the common people were equally prone in all places. The colliery people had not yet, it seems, acquired any peculiar reputation for wickedness. And the evidence from Whickham, incomplete as it often is, does not suggest that such a reputation was justified.

3. MARRIAGE AND THE FAMILY

The records of the courts provide little support for the suggestion that Whickham's industrialization involved a degree of social dislocation such as to breed an unusual level of disorder by the standards of the day. None the less, local society in Whickham was subject to profound and relatively rapid change. Given this fact, we might reformulate our initial question and ask: what gave structure, cohesion, and identity to the dynamic industrial society that had emerged in Whickham by the mid-seventeenth century?

At the most basic, individual level, of course, personal bonds of family and kinship, friendship, and neighbourhood continued to exert their force in a transformed environment. Such relationships retained their centrality in the lives of individuals, establishing spheres of interdependence and networks of practical and emotional support, and providing the touchstones of personal identity. Indeed, they may have been the more significant in the larger, more diverse, and more differentiated society of industrial Whickham.

Marriage clearly remained central in the life-cycles of rich and poor, landowner and labourer, alike. It was the crucial point of transition from the relative dependency of youth to the responsi-bilities of adult life. The initiation of courtship appears to have been a matter that was usually left to the young people concerned, as in

---

[68] J. A. Sharpe, *Crime in Early Modern England 1500–1750* (London, 1984), 155.

the case of Isabel Blackett and John Kirtley, who were said to 'have borne good will love and affection thone to thother in waie of marriage for about six years together' before they moved towards 'a conclusion touchinge their longe affection'.[69] The successful conclusion of a match, however, involved not only personal attractiveness on the part of the couple, but what contemporaries termed a satisfactory 'parity' of economic and social standing and what has been called the 'multilateral consent' of all interested parties.[70]

'Multilateral consent' is of course a flexible concept, and the nature of the actual involvement of parents and 'friends' in the making of a match could vary considerably. Among the great gentry, for example, the proposed marriage of Sir Thomas Liddell's heir to the daughter of a Yorkshire family in 1669 was essentially a matter of parental arrangement, subject to the ultimate consent of the young people. It was a measured and discreet affair, which involved careful enquiry on the part of the prospective bride's family into both the character and upbringing of the young man and the wealth of his father.[71] At the other extreme, Sir James Clavering of Axwell declared in his will of 1702 that his orphaned granddaughter had 'without my consent, nay contrary to my expresse advice married below her selfe'. He did not, however, exclude her from his will on this account, and, 'considering that shee will require maintenance', he settled £300 on her and her children, provided that her husband and his relations gave surety that the sum would be for her use only and relinquished any claim on her father's estate.[72]

The wills of the heads of lesser gentry families in Whickham also make clear the significance accorded to the consent of parents, 'friends', and trustees in the conditions laid down regarding the inheritances of their daughters. If sons seem not to have been subjected to such sanctions, the evidence of hard bargaining between what one document refers to as 'the friends on either side' provides sufficient testimony to the imperative of familial involvement for all persons of property, be it in the form of the complex marriage settlements of the Blakistons, Boweses, and Liddells or the

[69] DPD DR v/11 (unfol.), 13 Jan. 1624/5.
[70] For 'parity', see Wrightson, *English Society*, 79–80. The concept of 'multilateral consent' is discussed in Ingram, *Church Courts, Sex and Marriage*, 134–6.
[71] City of Sheffield Library, Bright Papers 72/1–19. We are grateful to Sara Mendelson for this reference.
[72] DPD Probate, Will of Sir James Clavering (1702).

less legally formalized provisions hammered out by yeoman families like the Harrisons and the Wakefields.[73]

The circumstances that lay behind such eventual negotiations are well enough revealed in the diary of the young curate of Rothbury, John Thomlinson, who spent a good deal of his time visiting his uncle Robert, the rector of Whickham. John was in his mid-twenties at the time he kept his diary in 1717–18 and was acutely conscious of the need to secure his future by providing himself with a stock of fifty-two sermons, a living, and a wife. Among these concerns, however, his marital prospects were perhaps his principal pre-occupation. His senior uncle, the rector of Rothbury, had indicated that 'he would give me leave to please myself in choice of a wife and he thought I might please him too', but persistently nudged John firmly in approved directions and embarrassed him by making public his search for a wife during dinner-table conversation. Uncle Robert, on the other hand, was more sensitive, but he too advised John frequently on his courtships, urging him to look further than Dolly Collingwood, whom he regarded as a 'Flanders Mare', for one who might bring a 'greater fortune' and be a 'genteeler woman'. He suggested, for example, the daughter of a Newcastle attorney whom he regarded as 'well educated, religious and 2 or 3000l. fortune'.[74]

John himself was confused. He had romantic impulses enough, recording the story of Robert Wrightson and Emma Railton of Bowes, who had allegedly died of grief in the face of parental opposition to their marriage, and detailing the less apocryphal love affair of one of his friends (in which he himself acted as a mediator) who was driven almost to despair by the uncertainty of his beloved—a condition of romantic distraction that eventually prevailed upon her to promise marriage to him 'if he could gett her friends consent.'[75] At the same time, however, he was not above

---

[73] For wills including marital consent conditions, see e.g. Wood (ed.), *Wills and Inventories*, iv. 307; DPD Probate, Wills of John Juett (1738), Thomas Shafto (1746). Such conditions usually applied only in the case of daughters seeking to marry before the age of majority, or a stated age. For other evidence of property transactions at marriage see e.g. the marriage settlements of the greater gentry: DRO D/ST 6/69, 8/7, 8/8, 9/2a & b, 17/9, 17/26, 23/59. For the arrangements of lesser folk, see e.g. PRO DURH 2/64/106, 4/3, fo. 207ᵛ; DPD Probate, Will of Thomas Crawforth (1709). Remarriage could also involve hard bargaining to secure a widow's independent property rights: e.g. DPD Probate, Wills of Rebecca Liddell (1677), William Barras (1739), Isobel Barras (1742).

[74] Hodgson, 'John Thomlinson', 72, 73–4, 82, 90, 121.

[75] Ibid. 74, 132.

noting down the going rates for bridal portions in marriage settlements, though he later observed, after reading William Secker's *A Wedding Ring fit for the Finger* (1658), that 'some think any wives good enough, who have but goods enough—But take heed for sometimes the bag and baggage go together', and told uncle Robert on a subsequent visit to Whickham that he 'thought we did not manage well in affairs of courtship—looked mercenary'.[76]

For John Thomlinson, the community of minor gentry and urban professionals through which he moved socially was virtually mapped in terms of prospective marriage partners. Whether it was so in their own sphere for the young work-people of Whickham we cannot say, for we have no comparable evidence. Pitmen were later said to marry young, and there were good reasons for them to do so, since their earnings would usually peak during their youthful years of health and strength in early manhood. Unfortunately, we cannot test this proposition, since their very mobility across the coalfield renders it virtually impossible to reconstitute their families. Of more than ninety pitmen employed at Northbanks colliery in 1752, the age at first marriage can be established for only three.[77]

Nevertheless, at whatever age they married, marriage was a fundamental transitional step for labouring people also. It required the earning power to set up an independent household and to provide for a wife and children who would be able to make only limited contributions to the family budget, while the economic help that such couples might expect from their families was inevitably very limited.[78] Their 'portions' were unlikely to be greater than those indicated by the will of Alice Gibson, an overman's widow. In 1681 she distributed her meagre goods among her five children, two unmarried sons receiving small sums of money, items of furniture, and 'a complete beding of cloaths' each, her two daughters receiving

[76] Ibid. 86–7, 116, 145. William Blakiston Bowes was frankly mercenary in his consideration of potential matches. In May 1721 he confided that he was temperamentally indisposed to fall in love and determined that, 'if I can find a Young Lady whose Fortune will keep herself and pay ye childrens Fortunes, of a modest discreet behavior, not deformed, I shall make my addresses to such a one': BL Add. MS 40747, fo. 186. He died unmarried later that year.

[77] NEIMME, Tracts vol. 29, 'Queries Concerning the State of the Pitmen' (*c.*1800). Langton, *Geographical Change*, 119, also found reconstitution of the families of Lancashire miners an impossible task.

[78] Pitmen at Hartley, Northumberland, in 1757 lived in independent nuclear family households: Flinn, *Coal Industry*, 433. Such a situation is also implied in the 1750s lists of householders and men in Whickham and Fellside and in the accounts of 'decayed workpeople' in the lists of 1764 discussed in ch. 3 above.

equal shares of the remainder of her bedding and 'half of all my iron materials belonging to huswiferee' each, while an already independent son inherited the residue of her goods. For many they might be as bare as that of the servant girl who deposed in 1760 that she 'had one half of her Mother's child bed linen in her possession for some time past, the whole of which her mother had divided and given the one Half to her sister who had married about Four years ago and the other half to herself'.[79]

Within the context of such restraints, however, young workpeople had the right to choose their prospective spouses in a manner less constrained than that of their social superiors, to judge by Edward Chicken's *The Collier's Wedding*. This celebratory, if somewhat condescending, dialect poem, first published in 1727, purported to describe courtship and marriage among the colliery folk of Benwell, just across the Tyne from Whickham, and has been described as 'a classic in accuracy and record'.[80] According to Chicken, colliers 'always marry'd one thro' other' and were likely to meet their prospective spouses at the periodic sports and 'hoppings' that punctuated the working year and at which they appeared 'drest Genteel and in their very best', endeavouring to 'look smart, be clean from top to toe, As all that wou'd be married do'. His heroine Jenny's 'name was up' for her winning combination of domestic virtue, modesty, and good looks. She was 'brisk and clean', 'loved to spin but blush'd to kiss', and had 'music in her heels'. His hero Tommy, having been attracted to her at Benwell hopping, pressed his suit over a drink between dances in a manner that indicated his conception of the companionate ends of marriage and of a good husband's qualities:

> My comely Jenny
> I love thee better far than any
> If thou'll have me, faith I'll have thee
> And love thee till the day I dee.
> I'll work my bones to make thee easy
> Do everything in life to please thee
> Both day and night I'll do my duty
> Come speak, I cannot live without thee.

---

[79] DPD Probate, Will and Inv. of Alice Gibson (1681); PRO DURH 17/8.

[80] For Chicken and his poem, see R. Colls, *The Collier's Rant: Song and Culture in the Industrial Village* (London, 1977), 58–9. Chicken was a local schoolmaster and vestry clerk and in a good position to observe the behaviour he described.

Having won her consent, subject to the proviso that 'I must wed to please my mother', Tommy sought that of her mother and received it readily enough when she was assured of Jenny's contentment. This being accomplished, the wedding was subsequently celebrated with the full ritual circumstances of the fetching of the bride, procession to the church by the couple's friends, scrambling for the bride's garters after the ceremony, a race home by the young men, supper, dancing, the drinking of a 'posset', the bedding of the couple, and 'throwing the stocking'.[81]

All this was apparently characteristic of a proletarian wedding in the relatively good times of the early eighteenth century. The local antiquarian John Brand later maintained that such customs were to his knowledge typical of 'vulgar Northern Weddings about Half a Century ago'. If so, then the centrality of marriage in the life-cycles of the work-people of the area was accorded appropriate recognition within their own communities of workmates and neighbours.[82]

Whether or not Chicken's account of plebeian courtship and marriage can be accepted as entirely typical, marriage was un-doubtedly a vital event in that it established the set of personal relationships that would be central to the adult lives of individuals of both sexes: relationships between husband and wife, between parents and children, and between households linked by ties of affinity and consanguinity. Of the actual quality of those relation-ships, the sentiments and values that informed them, and the consolations that they offered, all too little can be recovered. The records of the area, however, provide at least some insight into those private experiences that existed alongside the world of public affairs which leave more record to the historian.

According to a moralistic pamphlet by Bishop Synge, which was apparently distributed among the parishioners of Whickham in the 1760s, 'Husbands must love their wives with a most tender Affection; of which they must give all the proof they can in all their Actions: And Wives must in like Manner love and also be obedient to their Husbands, and each of them must be strictly just and faithfull to the other in all Things.'[83] This was traditional enough

---

[81] E. Chicken, *The Collier's Wedding*, 10th edn. (Liverpool, 1779), *passim*.

[82] J. Brand, *Observations on Popular Antiquities* (Newcastle, 1777), 334–6. Some of the details are also confirmed by John Thomlinson; e.g., he himself scrambled for a bride's garters at a wedding in 1718: Hodgson, 'John Thomlinson', 103.

[83] E. Synge, *An Essay Towards Making the Knowledge of Religion Easy to the Meanest Capacity* (London, 1760), 24. Eleven copies of this cheap pamphlet, 'Price

moral advice, and might be taken as representative of the prescriptive norms governing conjugal relations in the period. That reality was infinitely more complex and variable is clear enough from the diary entries of John Thomlinson.

Preoccupied as he was with marriage, and engaged as he was in pastoral duties, John was aware of both its rewards and its tragedies. Within a few months of 1718 he set down with evident disapproval instances of two men who were 'hen-pecked, cannot rule the house' and of another who 'beats his wife sometimes—and has been surly with her a long time'. He also recorded the distraught reaction of a loving husband whose young wife died in a riding accident on her way to fetch 'babes cloths' from her mother and who, 'being told God might have sent greater afflictions', replied 'hardly'. Thomlinson assumed a world of male primacy and female subordination, tempered by a high ideal of marital companionship and devotion. But he knew well that such norms were fragile in the face of reality. One of his fellow ministers, he noted with amusement, 'was marrying a couple, and the man would say obedient. At another time the woman would not say obedient.' And he concluded his most prolonged reflection on the subject with the adage that 'Husbands and wives are like locks and keys, that rather break than open, except the wards be answerable.'[84]

John Thomlinson's ideal of marital best practice may have been influenced by the example of his uncle Robert and aunt Martha. Clearly, he found the atmosphere of their household agreeable, and the references to Martha Thomlinson in her husband's letter-book suggest that the rector of Whickham was a concerned and attentive spouse.[85] The letters of James Clavering and his first wife Catherine (alias 'Dowey'), provide a deeper insight into an individual marriage, but they reveal an altogether less comfortable situation.

Clavering appears to have been a somewhat testy, combative, and demanding man, and he seems not to have found in his wife the spirited competence and self-reliance that he so much admired in his cousin Ann Clavering, the wife of Henry Liddell, governor of the Hostman's Company, with whom he frequently corresponded. In

2d. or 2s. per Hundred', were found among the Gibside estate papers for the early 1760s in DRO D/ST 341/36. They were almost certainly part of a batch bought for distribution.

[84] Hodgson, 'John Thomlinson', 116, 119, 123, 141, 142.
[85] NRO ZAN M13/C7. See e.g. lettes of 26 Sept., 5 Nov., and 17 Nov. 1741, written during Mrs Thomlinson's illness.

1712, at the age of thirty-two, he could write to a friend wishing him 'all the pleasure and satisfaction the married state can afford', but his references to his wife in his letters suggest that his own marriage offered little lasting satisfaction. His attitudes towards her varied from the fondly condescending to outright irritation. During her pregnancy that summer he showed little sympathy with her anxieties about her coming confinement, which he dismissed as 'so many chimeras', and was at best prepared to indulge the whims of 'my big-bellied Dowey', 'my grumbling Dowey', 'for peace and quietness sake, which at present I believe never was more wanted'. Nor did he postpone his annual shooting trip to the Pennine moors as her term approached, though he knew he would be criticized 'for leaving my Dowey in her condition', and he set off expecting 'to have a bairn fathered on me' before his return.

He did, in fact, return before her confinement, and the birth of their child (after a difficult labour which more than justified Catherine's anxieties) seems to have mollified him somewhat. 'Poor woman, she had a hard bout of it', he observed, and he took pains to secure a replacement for a 'canary bird' she had much admired which had been neglected and had died during her confinement. But by November he was irritated again by her anxieties over the removal of their household to Newcastle—'she crys day and night'; 'her uneasiness I cannot express, which makes my life not very comfortable and the affairs of the family proceed not with the pleasantness I could wish and desire'. And within a year he could write to her brother, 'Poor woman, her mind and judgement is as variable and fickel as the weather.'[86]

That such tensions were by no means unusual in this marriage is evident from Catherine's earlier letters to her husband during his absences on business. They bring out both her love for her husband—she longed to see her 'Dearest Jewell' and anticipated eagerly 'that happy minet we shall meet'—and her apprehension that her affection was not fully reciprocated—'Tis you I fear thats loth to leave London as you're free of poor me.' They are couched in a tone of submissive, self-deprecating anxiety and provide evidence in abundance of her dependence upon his approval, her frequent failure to secure it, and her resulting 'mallingcolly drouping spirits'—'[I] will take all your reproves and reflections

[86] Ncle. UL, MISC MSS 10. Quoting letters of 30 May, 6 June, 13 June, 20 June, 30 June, 11 July, 13 July, 12 Oct., 14 Nov. and 28 Nov. 1712, and 27 Aug. 1713.

upon me with patiens'; 'I am never better pleas'd than when I have yor abriabation in all things'; 'it is my wholle indeavor to do what is most exceptable to you'. Only occasionally is there a flash of resistance: 'I assure you, let my ill natur be what it will, you are the first that ever accus'd me of it.'[87]

This was a marriage rendered unquiet by fundamental differences of temperament and overshadowed by misfortune—the Claverings lost four sons and two daughers in infancy and childhood, and their eldest son was the victim of a paralysing disease. And so, it would seem, it continued. 'Dowey's' last surviving letter to James, written in 1718, five years before her death, reveals her apologizing to him once more for words spoken 'undeysignedly' which had given him offence, and 'under all the trouble and concerne that a poor creature can be under at your going away in so much pashon and anger, and especially so sad a rainy dark night'. 'My care', she assured him, 'shall allwaies be to performe my duty', which she hoped would win his 'favours and affection and that we might live happily and comfortable together'.[88]

Whether or not the majority of couples who left behind them neither diaries nor letter-books lived 'happily and comfortable' is of course impossible to say. What can be said is that for most of them marriage was a practical partnership in the maintenance of a household, that the day-to-day performance of their respective roles in that sphere of interdependence must have dominated their waking hours, and that for most wives the qualities required of them were probably considerably sturdier than Catherine Clavering's genteel submissiveness. Among the upper gentry it was perhaps less so, and their womenfolk may have been socialized accordingly. The sole surviving letter of George Bowes's first wife to her husband, written at '12 at night' and occasioned by his failure to return home, is another note of abject apology. It expresses her 'fears and uneasinesses' at having caused his displeasure, the alacrity with which she intends to perform his instructions, and her resolution 'to make it my whole study to convince you that your happiness shall be ye constant care of . . . your dutifull and affectionate wife'. This suggests a temperament and marital experience similar to that of Catherine Clavering, and serves as a

[87] H. T. Dickinson (ed.), *The Correspondence of Sir James Clavering*, Surtees Soc. no. 178 (Durham, 1967), 208, 209–11, 212, 213, 219, 220, 222, 223.
[88] Ibid. 224.

reminder that the Claverings' marital difficulties were as much a product of the conventional gender roles of the period as of individual character and circumstances.[89]

The fundamental paradox of those roles was that wives were expected to display not only deference and obedience to their husbands, but also a high degree of personal capacity in the performance of their duties, a competence that was both defined and assessed by a spouse whose authority could not be questioned. A more successful example of the negotiation of the intricacies of the role required of women in great gentry families is provided by Ann Liddell (née Clavering). She was a sharp, spirited woman who took a very active interest not only in family matters, on which she was rather conservative (she thought that for a woman to initiate a proposal of marriage went 'beyond the rules of decency'), but also in politics, and above all in the affairs of the coal trade. 'The prospect of a new seam', she wrote 'has given me new life.' Ann acted as her busy husband's intermediary in coal trade matters with James Clavering, and her imperious cousin seems to have found nothing inappropriate about discussing such issues with her. On the contrary, he seems to have warmed to her strength of personality and assumed her knowledge, capacity, and good judgement.

The frustrations inherent in Ann Liddell's situation, however, become apparent from her remarks to him following a visit to her London house of the redoubtable William Cotesworth. Cotesworth was in the south to safeguard the coal trade from the unwelcome attention of Parliament, but he had declined to discuss these affairs with her. 'No,' she fumed, 'I'm a female and consequently not capable of understanding further than that some one day betwixt this and Monday morn, he leaves the Town!' Nevertheless, she knew her own worth: 'I desire to manage for my son a little; and a virago I know I shall be called, but I care not . . . and fancy I could understand my trade as well as many coal owners Mr Cot[esworth] has been with.'[90] It was a justified boast, and one that could have been echoed by Lady Elizabeth Bowes, Cotesworth's doughty

[89] BL Add. MS 40747, fo. 191. Bowles later endorsed the note 'My Dear Wife's letter'.

[90] Dickinson, *Clavering Correspondence*, 43, 46, 121–2. See also James Clavering's letters to her in Ncle. UL, MISC MSS 10, *passim*. For a stimulating discussion of gender roles and socialization among the gentry, see L. Pollock, ' "Teach Her to Live Under Obedience": The Making of Women in the Upper Ranks of Early Modern England', *Continuity and Change*, 4 (1989), esp. 233, 247, 250.

opponent on Tyneside. (Nor, incidentally, should we forget that Mary Astell was the daughter of a Newcastle hostman.)

Lower in the social scale, near constant activity was expected of women about the household and, when required, in the byre, fields, and shop. The nature of a woman's daily round can be inferred from the items listed in inventories of household goods. Here, alongside the farm stock, craftsmen's tools, shop goods, or coal at pit and staithes, were the ubiquitous cooking implements—those 'iron materials belonging to huswiferee'—and in larger households the brewing vessels. Here also can be found the milk bowls, churns, and pails, the yards of linen cloth for sewing into sheets and under-garments, the 'washing tubbs' and 'rubbing brushes', and in the fuller inventories of the later seventeenth century the 'smouthin' irons, spinning wheels, and hanks of 'harden' yard. These laconic listings of domestic equipment bear witness to the female input into the support and maintenance of a household; and if there was comparatively little paid work for women available in Whickham, it is perfectly evident that their hands were rarely idle.

The complementary activity of husband and wife could doubtless breed at the very least a sense of shared endeavour and a dogged companionship in facing and surmounting the insecurities of existence. Obviously it cannot always have been so, and although among the propertied an unsatisfactory marriage had to be borne until death brought release, there is evidence that among the labouring poor, who were less tied to the parish and less socially prominent, a shorter way out could be taken. Margaret Robson's husband, a Crowley employee, deserted her twice, and after his second disappearance in 1717, when he left her pregnant, she never saw him again (though it was rumoured that he had been seen at Prestonpans in Scotland). Again, the lists of the deserving poor drawn up in 1764 included several women brought to poverty by desertion, such as Jane Hobson of Swalwell, 'her husband a bad and wicked man who came from Windy Hill; He run away and left her'. We might recall also the two Whickham women who refused to live with their husbands in 1635.[91]

Nevertheless, there is good reason to believe that for many, marriage was an effective partnership within the boundaries established by the expectations of the day. It would perhaps be

[91] PRO DURH 17/2, evidence of Margaret Robson; DRO D/ST 336/7. For the 1635 case, see n. 62 above.

unwise to make too much of the fact that by the later seventeenth century it had become customary for the minor gentlemen, yeomen, and tradesmen of the parish to refer in their wills to 'my lovinge wife', 'my welbeloved wife', 'my deare and loveing wife', 'my tenderly and dearly Beloved wife'. The significance of such a convention might be as open to question as Edward Chicken's assertion that colliers and their wives were always 'very fond of one another'.[92] But it was the convention all the same. And it was backed by continued careful provision for widows which reflected, in the changed context of the seventeenth and eighteenth centuries, the same sense of responsibility for a partner's well-being that had distinguished the wills of the sixteenth century and had been enshrined in the customs of the manor and of the northern province.

Moreover, the trust reposed in the competence of their wives to manage family affairs was evidenced in the fact that, at all social levels represented, widows were almost without exception named as the sole executor of an estate.[93] Some testators, indeed, went further. A few desired, like their Elizabethan predecessors, to be buried close by a deceased wife or husband, and there were a handful whose nuncupative wills broke through the usual restrictions of a formal testament to reveal a simply expressed depth of feeling which is usually hidden from us. John Nixon, a labourer, apparently declared on his deathbed in 1644 that 'all my goods and chattells, debts and creditts whatsoever they be I doe give and bequeath the same unto my wife Margaret Nixon who hath taken very greate paines for my profitt and benefitt and saved me from many a sore dayes worke'. Edward Newby, a small yeoman (he had six acres) and pit overman, stated even more strikingly in 1659, 'That what estate he had, he together with his wife Jane had got it by their industry and therefore he gave and bequeathed all his whole

---

[92] For variants of such phraseology, see e.g. DPD Probate, Wills of George Lee (1635), Henry Winship (1649), George Shafto (1668), Tristram Fenwick (1674), George Pescod (1684), William Robson (1708), Thomas Denham (1725), Nathan Wetherall (1750); Chicken, *Collier's Wedding*, 5.

[93] The custom of the manor no longer applied to most of the inhabitants and the custom of the northern province was abolished in 1692. Nevertheless, it remained usual for a widow to be left the remainder of an estate after allowance for the children's portions. Where real property was involved, the widow very commonly received a life interest in house and/or land. In the 16th c. executorship had usually been vested in the widow and a son jointly; in the 17th and 18th c. the widow was usually sole executor.

estate to his loveing wife, to be at her disposall, and that if it were more, his said wife deserved it well.' Close to a century later, John Thompson, a Swalwell victualler, simply left everything in the competent hands of 'my Dear and loving wife Eleanor . . . with whom I have liv'd very Happily for many years'.[94] Such instances are in their very nature rare, but they provide arresting evidence of the expectations and realities of some marriages in early industrial Whickham. In these cases, at least, to use John Thomlinson's phrase, 'the wards' were 'answerable'.

While marital relationships can be conveniently isolated for the purposes of discussion, we must immediately add that the development of the conjugal bond, and of the domestic roles of husbands and above all wives, was for the most part inseparably linked with the bearing and rearing of children. This was a process that began soon after the celebration of a marriage and continued thereafter until the completion of a wife's childbearing age—if, that is, it was not interrupted by premature death.

In this vitally important particular, the developmental cycle of the early modern family was radically different from that of its twentieth-century counterpart, a point well worth remembering when we are tempted to over-modernize our conceptions of family life in the past. Many of the emotions involved may be instantly recognizable, establishing a bond between past and present experience. But the *context* was different, ideologically, materially, and demographically. A married woman in seventeenth- and eighteenth-century Whickham who survived to the age of forty-four was likely to have spent close to a quarter of her married life pregnant and a good deal more engaged in the care of young children. Neither child-bearing nor child-rearing was a distinct and bounded stage of the family cycle, concentrated in time. Despite the ravages of infant mortality and the departure of some children into service at an early age, child-rearing commonly continued up to and often beyond the sundering of the marital partnership by death.

Children, in short, were usually a perpetual presence in the household, and their needs were an immediate and continuing preoccupation. This much is obvious in the family reconstitution forms on which the demographic histories of individual families are reconstructed. It is witnessed too in the contents of the inventories

[94] DPD Probate, Wills of John Nixon (1644), Edward Newby (1659), John Thompson (1744).

of Whickham's householders. Roger Lumley, for example, had 'a broken cradell' among his household goods, and Thomas Wakefield both a cradle and 'one litle chare ioynt for a child'. William Jackson's appraisers found 'one child's high chaire' in the hall and a 'little bed' in the 'Lytle Room' above, while those of the Dunston staithman James Emerson listed 'a childes chair' in the hall, 'a cradle' in the parlour chamber, and in the parlour itself 'a childes table chair' and 'a childes whistle and corrall'.[95]

These realities can be readily recognized. Yet much of the experience of childhood and child-rearing in these often physically crowded households remains hopelessly obscure. From scraps of surviving evidence, we can infer that children were much prized and desired. The Clavering letters, for example, reveal that among the gentry pregnancy was an occasion for congratulation, sometimes accompanied by appropriate gifts, and that while childbirth aroused justifiable anxiety, a successful birth was a source of private satisfaction and public celebration.[96] James Clavering was delighted at the birth of his new son, 'a fine boy', in July 1712, and he expressed a swaggering satisfaction at the growth of what he called 'the little flock': 'on Monday night my spouse fathered another lad on me, so on my part I support the family bravely'.[97]

That such feelings were by no means confined to gentlemen preoccupied with the continuance of an ancient lineage is indicated by a letter of William Cotesworth's steward to his master. One of the estate workers, Harry Potts, had 'gott a son of which he's very fond': 'he got it in his armes the morning it was born, which was yesterday and said "Honny thou's my Darlin and shalt want for nothing as long as I am able to worke for thee".'[98] Again, John Brand later reported the lavishness of northern christening celebrations even among those of the labouring poor 'unfortunate enough to provide more *Mouths* than they find *Meat* for' (the costs being defrayed by the gifts of guests), and the local custom of

---

[95] DPD Probate, Invs. of Roger Lumley (1666), Thomas Wakefield (1665), William Jackson (1670), James Emerson (1691). Cf. those of William Emerson (1666), William Newby (1666), Thomas Jackson (1675), Katherine Witty (1684), Robert Stoker (1709).

[96] Dickinson, *Clavering Correspondence*, 8, 22; Ncle. UL MISC MSS 10, 28 Jul. 1712, 3 Aug. 1712.

[97] Ibid. 8 Jul., 11 Jul., and 9 Sept. 1712. His neighbour Col. Liddell referred to his own children fondly as 'the barns' (bairns), and 'the infantry': Hughes, *North Country Life*, 35.   [98] Ibid. 36–7.

presenting a newborn child on its first visit with gifts of an egg, salt, or bread to welcome the infant and wish it well.[99]

Successful childbirth, then, was an event to be celebrated. But at the same time, frequent childbirth was almost inevitable, and it could be both physically and emotionally devastating. Catherine Clavering's experience seems to have undermined her early willingness to please her husband (and herself) by bearing 'those great blessings ever so much desired by hus both', and by 1712 James was not at all confident that she shared his enthusiasm to 'venture for a 4th son'.[100] Moreover, it brought with it heavy responsibilities. The basic duties of child-rearing were pithily summed up in the usual obligations imposed by a bond of tutorship in the northern province: to 'honestly or vertuouslye educate and bringe uppe the said [child] with meate drincke clothes and all the necessaries fitt and convenient for such a manes child to have', and to see to the securing of its 'filiall or childs portion' at its coming of age or marriage. These were confirmed and elaborated upon by Bishop Synge's pamphlet of 1760, which enjoined those of the parents of Whickham who read it to

honestly endeavour to provide for their children, and to teach and breed them up in such a Manner as may be best, both for their Souls and Bodies, diligently and tenderly watching over them, to keep them from all Harm, countenancing and encouraging them in every thing that is good, and reproving them, and sometimes correcting them, but without Bitterness or Passion, when they find them given to anything that is evil.[101]

The fundamental task of making adequate physical provision for their children must have loomed large in the daily thoughts of many fathers in what was already mainly a male-breadwinner economy—men like Harry Potts, whose child would want for nothing while he could work, or the waggonwright father of Anthony Errington of Felling, who in the 1780s 'wrought at waggons and waggonery all day, and 3 or 4 nights a week . . . was down the pit, Erning to get money to bring up his family'. Then there was Henry Beamson, who described himself to George Bowes in 1759 as 'having a wife and four children to endeavour for and none to assist him but his hard labour', or again, the aged and decayed work-people of the

[99] Brand, *Observations*, 339 n., 403–4.
[100] Dickinson, *Clavering Correspondence*, 212; Ncle. UL MISC MSS 10, 20 Jul. 1712.   [101] PRO DURH 2/6/81; Synge, *Essay*, 24–5.

Whickham lists of 1764 who had laboured in their day, or laboured still, to bring up their families.[102]

The records, however, also provide glimpses of parental efforts at the 'honest' upbringing of their children. Small children were apparently heavily indulged. Brand refers to the fond 'dandling' of their infants by the wives of the keelmen, to the accompaniment of the traditional song, 'A you a hinny'. Thomas Bewick, brought up in a yeoman/overman family at nearby Wylam in the 1750s, recalled being made 'a great "pet"' by the womenfolk of the family: 'I was not to be "snubbed" (as it was called), do what I would.'[103]

As they grew older, the children's socialization proceeded by precept and example, reinforced on occasion by severe paternal discipline. Thomas Bewick described how 'the winter evenings were often spent in listening to the traditionary tales and songs, relating to men who had been eminent for their prowess and bravery in the Border Wars, and of others who had been esteemed for better and milder qualities, such as their having been good landlords, kind neighbours, and otherwise in every respect bold, independent and honest men'. (We might wonder what role models were held up for the girls.) Thomas's mother, who was 'of a religious turn', also endeavoured to instil her values in her son, 'but as I did not clearly understand her well-intentioned lectures, they made little impression. My father's pithy illustrations [i.e. beatings] . . . were much more forcibly and clearly made out: I understood them well, and they operated powerfully upon me.' Such, no doubt, was also the case for the child-workers of the Crowley firm whose parents were obliged either to pay fines occasioned by their misdemeanours or to inflict appropriate punishment upon them. Anthony Errington, however, recalled no beatings, writing of his father that 'he gave us all a Education so as to make us fit for business. And his Law was to us all to be honest, to be Charatable, to shun bad Company, and to keep the Comandments in a Christin life. And to love each other was the Charge from our parents.'[104]

---

[102] P. E. H. Hair (ed.), 'Coals and Rails: The Autobiography of Anthony Errington' (unpubl. typescript), 4. We are grateful to Professor Hair for making available to us his unpublished edition of Errington's MS. Anthony's father lived 1732–1818. For Beamson, see DRO D/ST 262.

[103] Brand, *Observations*, 184 n.; T. Bewick, *Memoir of Thomas Bewick Written By Himself 1822–1828* (London, 1961), 5.

[104] Ibid. 12, 46; M. W. Flinn (ed.), *The Law Book of the Crowley Ironworks*, Surtees Soc. no. 167 (Durham, 1957), 6–7; Hair, 'Anthony Errington', 4.

For some children this process also involved formal schooling. Catherine Clavering wrote to her husband in 1705 of their son Jemmy's early school experiences: 'My little sweet harte wente to scoull of tusday to his greate greive.' She was worried about his slowness in reading, occasioned in her view by the fact that 'His master never herse him but wons a week read.' 'I make him read wons a day,' she reported, and it seems she used the Bible as her primer: 'can't read one verse without miscalling his letters and puting in words of his own, nor can turne to a Chapter. A great deale of pains must be taken with hime to come to it right.'[105]

Jemmy Clavering's experience of the acquisition of basic literacy was in all probability shared by only a minority of Whickham's children, but it was none the less an aspect of a child's education that was growing in significance in the seventeenth and eighteenth centuries. A survey of more than fifty individuals who appended their signatures or marks to documents in late sixteenth-century Whickham reveals that very few indeed were able to sign their names.[106] This was a local society of heavily restricted literacy in which only the clergy, a single gentleman, and a handful of the more substantial copyholders could pen their signatures. The vast majority of wills were of necessity written by the clergy. Nuncupative wills needed to be reported orally 'for want of pen and inke', or in the absence of a skilled hand to use them. Even an action so simple as the reading over of a bill of sale could require the sending of 'a little wench' post haste to locate and bring back the curate who had gone 'fishinge in Darwen water a little beneath Ebchester'.[107]

The sheer inconvenience of such circumstances in a local economy increasingly penetrated by complex commercial dealings was in all probability the principal reason for the subsequent growth in the provision for schooling the children of the parish—an incentive reinforced by the manifest risks of illiteracy, as when in 1606 one 'simple unlearned man' put his mark to a coal contract which seemed 'to his understanding and hearing onelie articles of

---

[105] Dickinson, *Clavering Correspondence*, 211, 214–15, 215.

[106] We have adopted the usual (albeit imperfect) conventions for the measurement of literacy, as proposed in R. S. Schofield, 'The Measurement of Literacy in Pre-Industrial England', in J. Goody (ed.), *Literacy in Traditional Societies* (Cambridge, 1968). Survey of ability to sign based on name index to all available sources. Men were 76% illiterate overall on this criterion. All women included made marks.

[107] DPD DR v/8, fos. 33, 61–61ᵛ.

covenant', and later found himself 'subtilie deceived' by the onerous terms to which he had agreed.[108]

The earliest reference to the presence of a schoolmaster in the parish comes from 1601, when it was reported to the church courts that Christopher Watson 'teacheth children not licensed'. By the mid-1630s, however, no fewer than six people, including the curate and three women, could be presented for the same offence.[109] The intermittent activity of such teachers was probably the principal source of formal education throughout the seventeenth century, save for a brief period in the Interregnum when funds were provided by the state to maintain a schoolmaster in Whickham.[110]

In the early eighteenth century more settled provision was made. Following the establishment of his Winlaton factory, Ambrose Crowley provided for a schoolmaster for his workers' children, who was paid from a fund to which both employer and employees contributed, and schoolmasters were subsequently maintained also at his Swalwell and Winlaton Mill works. According to Crowley's 'Laws', the schoolmaster was 'carefully to teach and instruct the workmen's children', to correct lying, swearing, and other 'horrid crimes', and 'to carry it with an even hand to all his scholars, and not despise any for their poverty, but to encourage ingenuity and virtue in all of them and not discourage any by shewing more than ordinary favour or care to such children whose parents may be able to be grateful'. He was also to show the governors of the factory samples of the writing of the workmen's children from time to time.[111] Meanwhile, Robert Thomlinson, who was an active supporter of the SPCK, founded a parish school in 1714 with the aid of a large bequest from Mrs Jane Blakiston which made possible the regular maintenance of a schoolmaster who, among other duties, was 'obliged to teach 36 poor children'. By mid-century Mr Bowes was also maintaining a schoolmaster at Marley Hill, thus completing a local network of schools which, while far from providing

[108] PRO STAC 8/53/10.

[109] DPD DR IV/5 (unfol.) 12 Sept. 1601; Priors Kitchen, 'Fragments of Durham Chancellor's Visitations *c.*1634–7'.

[110] Howell, *Newcastle-upon-Tyne*, 329. Finance came from the Committee for the Propagation of the Gospel in the Northern Counties. In the late 17th c. the principal schoolmaster in Whickham was probably George Walton. He was described in 1721 as a schoolmaster who had lived in his present house for 60 years: PRO DURH 17/2. He was also the scribe of many late 17th-c. wills and inventories.

[111] Flinn, *Men of Iron*, 227; id., *Law Book*, 154–5.

universal opportunity for basic education, was fairly generous by the standards of the day.[112]

The results of these varied initiatives over a century and a half were not unimpressive. For the period 1600–1749, examples of the signatures or marks of more than six hundred individuals survive, and these indicate a very substantial reduction in levels of illiteracy in the parish.[113] Illiteracy among the minor gentry of the parish was virtually wiped out in the course of the early seventeenth century, and by the later seventeenth century most of the women of these families could also sign their names. Among yeomen and farmers, a group including many smallholders, tenants, and part-time wain or waggon-drivers, male illiteracy was also reduced, from 83 per cent in the late sixteenth century to 63 per cent in the early seventeenth century; it was down to some 18 per cent by the late seventeenth and early eighteenth centuries. The illiteracy of craftsmen and tradesmen also fell markedly at this time; by the early eighteenth century around three-quarters of such men in our sample were able to sign their names. Less progress was observable, however, among the womenfolk of these two groups, most of whom continued to make their marks. Outside the families of the gentry and professionals of the parish, girls do not seem to have benefited significantly from the educational opportunities now being extended to their brothers. They were not alone, however, in their relative exclusion, for prospective occupation was clearly as significant a factor as gender roles in influencing the parental decision to put a child to school. Of the score of agricultural day-labourers who enter our sample, only a handful could sign their names.

Finally, workers in the coal industry remained overwhelmingly illiterate as late as the mid-eighteenth century. There were a few significant exceptions to this generalization. Staithemen and viewers

---

[112] Bourn, *Whickham*, 20, 22, 41; NRO ZAN M13/C7, 28 Apr. 1721, 28 Apr. 1742; DRO D/ST 277, 322. Both the Whickham and Marley Hill schoolmasters appear on the occupational listings of the 1750s discussed in sec 3.3 above.

[113] Collected from all available sources and consolidated in our name index. The evidence is biased towards the middling and upper ranks of parish society. Rather than provide figures for overall male illiteracy, which would be seriously biased as a result, we have broken the evidence down by occupational and status groups and by sex. For the broader context of illiteracy in the area, see D. Cressy, 'Social Status and Literacy in North-east England, 1560–1630', *Local Population Studies*, 21 (1978), and R. A. Houston, 'Illiteracy in the Diocese of Durham, 1663–89 and 1750–62: The Evidence of Marriage Bonds', *Northern History*, 18 (1982).

were almost invariably literate; nineteen of the thirty pit overmen included in our sample could also sign their names. The actual pitmen, however, with few exceptions, were unable to do so. Of the thirty-eight men who put their names to the Northbanks colliery bond in 1741, for example, thirty-five did so by inscribing their marks.[114] Pitmen, it might be thought, would have had earnings sufficient to be able to send their sons to school, for they could enjoy incomes comparable to those of many craftsmen and tradesmen. They might also have had the motivation to do so, for it was already the case, as a later report put it, that 'such of the workmen who have a knowledge of reading writing and arithmetic . . . are often advanced from Pitmen to Overmen . . . [and] from this they are sometimes advanced to a Viewer'. But this appears to have been an insufficient incentive, even where opportunities were available. Perhaps the frequent mobility of the colliery work-force tended to disincline them from sending their children to school at an age when they might be set to work. More probably, however, they simply failed to perceive any compelling need to do so.[115]

Formal schooling thus had a growing place in the experience of childhood in industrial Whickham. By the later seventeenth century, the parish was participating fully in England's general progress towards the creation of a society in which basic literacy was widespread, though unevenly distributed between social and occupational groups. For the majority of the children of the parish, however, such schooling as they obtained can have represented at most a relatively brief interlude in their development towards adult life, and a limited aspect of their education in the fuller sense of that word. Most girls must have received their education for their future roles in the setting of the household, initially at their mothers' sides, later perhaps as domestic or farm servants. And most boys, whether or not they were taught to read and write, would have begun at an early age to acquire appropriate skills from their fathers and older brothers, perhaps later being taught specific trades as apprentices to local master craftsmen or tradesmen.

Of all this, we have little direct evidence in the parish beyond the known apprenticeships of Whickham boys to some of the Newcastle companies, or the known occupations of some boys and youths

[114] DRO D/ST 344/22.   [115] NEIMME, Tracts vol. 29, 'Queries'.

indicated in the paybills of the eighteenth century or the lists of the poor of 1764.[116] Some must have shared the experiences of Thomas Bewick. As a child he learned to help with the sheep, to 'muck' the byre, and to care for the horses, as well as being engaged in such tasks as levelling the molehills in his father's pasture, until it was eventually decided to apprentice him, at the age of fourteen, to a Newcastle engraver.[117] Others, like Anthony Errington, must have learned early to face the darkness and hazards of the pits. 'I did not like going down', he remembered, and for a while his father let him try his hand at farmwork. But at fourteen he came back to the colliery: 'I started to clean the way for 8*d.* per day, and going with my father and brother John, in a short time the fear of the pit left me.' Anthony was becoming what was later called 'pit hardened', and thereafter, 'I was taut the pit language and got on with my trade very well.'[118]

Of childhood we can say very little more. Much of it must have passed in play, or in such escapades as Anthony Errington recalled—bird nesting, slinging stones with his garters, swimming, and scrambling over the 'adventure playground' of the coalfield with the other boys. He remembered childhood as a time of relative freedom, enjoyed against the background of the protective shadow of his parents—a context sufficiently summed up in Thomas Bewick's memory of 'my father's well-known whistle which called me home'.[119]

As for the parents, children could be a source both of delight and emotional satisfaction and of desperate anxiety and grief. 'Your little son is very well', wrote Catherine Clavering of Jemmy in 1705, 'He's my bedfellow . . . He calls me "Mamay"'; or again, 'He is a very good boy . . . He and his sisters entertained hus with being dres'd in boys close and him in gerlles.' 'I really dread the consequences', wrote her husband eight years later of the early signs of Jemmy's illness, a preoccupation that dominated his letters that years as the sickness progressed until, after 'many melancholy hours and more thoughts', he determined to attempt to 'submit to what

---

[116] e.g. lists of enrolled apprentices in Dendy, *Hostmen*, 285 ff. and id., *Extracts from the Records of the Merchant Adventurers of Newcastle-upon-Tyne*, ii, Surtees Soc. no. 101 (Durham, 1899), 184 ff. For the evidence of paybills and lists of the poor, see sect. 3.5 above.   [117] Bewick, *Memoir*, 10–11, 12, 13, 15, 44.

[118] Hair, 'Anthony Errington', 12, 13.

[119] Ibid. 5–8, 9, 12; Bewick, *Memoir*, 5–6, 15. We have no comparable information on the play of girls.

Providence shall order', 'being satisfied in my own mind that everything has been done that's possible and that to make his life comfortable and easy while in this world is what only remaines'.[120]

Whatever the fortunes of individual families, and however inadequate our evidence of the inner thoughts and feelings of their members, it seems reasonable to conclude that raising a family was the dominant preoccupation in the lives of most of Whickham's householders. The demands of that responsibility must have been central to the partnership of marriage. The working lives of husbands and wives alike were directed towards maintaining their families in the present and towards the accumulation, if it was possible, of the wherewithal to provide eventual portions for their children. For many, such long-term accumulation can never have been attainable because of the life-cycle variation of their earning capacity. Moreover, industrialization inevitably involved an increase in that proportion of the population of Whickham for whom the death or incapacity of the male breadwinner left his dependants compelled either to 'shift for themselves' or to fall upon the parish.[121] Among those who were able to do so, however, the wills of the seventeenth and early eighteenth centuries demonstrate a striking continuity with those of Elizabethan Whickham in the priorities and concerns of the testators. The economic context had changed in that few any longer possessed copyhold land to pass on according to the custom of the manor, and the portions of their children were now much more likely to be expressed in terms of cash sums to be raised or distributed rather than in terms of farm stock or household goods. Nevertheless, the fundamental obligations with which they were concerned and the attitudes and values that informed their decisions remained essentially the same.

4. KIN, 'FRIENDS', AND NEIGHBOURS

The wills of Whickham's parishioners reinforce our impression that relationships within the nuclear family were central in their lives.

---

[120] Dickinson, *Clavering Correspondence*, 212, 214–15; Ncle. UL, MISC MSS 10, 9 Jan. and 27 Jan. 1712/13, 11 Sept., 30 Oct., and 25 Dec., 1713. Jemmy lingered on as a chronic invalid and died in London in 1726.

[121] The phrase is that of the curate of Whickham, used in 1686 to describe the circumstances of the children of a recently deceased labourer: DPD Probate, Letter with Will of Adam Rochester (1686).

These same documents also provide a reminder of the fact that family life was conducted within a broader context of relationships with kinsfolk and neighbours. As in Elizabethan Whickham, between 70 and 80 per cent of all testators in each of the three sub-periods 1600–49, 1650–99, and 1700–60 recognized kinsfolk beyond their own nuclear families in their wills. In terms of the range of kin mentioned, there was again a remarkable stability. Married men were those least likely to include relations beyond their wives and children in their wills, though more than half of them did so (generally by leaving token bequests to grandchildren, siblings, or nephews and nieces). Unmarried or widowed men and women were much more likely to recognize a greater number of relatives. The unmarried focused their attention on their siblings, nephews and nieces, parents (if living), brothers- and sisters-in-law, and very occasionally cousins. The widowed distributed their goods and tokens of regard (once their children and grandchildren had been provided for) to sons- and daughters-in-law, siblings, nephews, and nieces. Once again, no significant difference could be found in the behaviour of testators of different sex once allowance had been made for the different life-cycle stages of male and female testators. All in all, kinship recognition in wills seems to have been genealogically narrow and shallow; nevertheless, it is clear that within that circumscribed range testators could attach considerable significance to relationships with members of other households closely related by blood or marriage. These were what they called their 'friends'.[122]

To assume that such emotional closeness meant that the householders of industrial Whickham generally spent their adult lives in constant interaction with their brothers, sisters, and other members of their respective families, however, would be mistaken. Undoubtedly this was sometimes the case. During the first year of their marriage William West and his wife shared William's father's

---

[122] There are a few instances of testators who ranged more widely in naming kinfolk in their wills. The outstanding example was the childless widower Nathan Wetherall, gentleman. His will of 1750 mentioned 47 nephews or great-nephews and nieces and 14 cousins and/or their children. He also left money to provide for unspecified (and perhaps individually unknown) descendants of his aunts and uncles, who might fall into need in the future. Wetherall was aware of a vast cousinage and took leave of it in style. His behaviour demonstrates the possibilities inherent in the flexible and permissive English kinship system. But it was utterly untypical. Even those testators who named a relatively large number of kin usually remained within a narrow genealogical range. See also n. 27 above.

house, and there they saw much of William's married sister, who was 'dwelling hard by and soe very often at her fathers house', and of his new sister-in-law Katherine Appleby, who lived a short walk away at Byermoor and 'was verie often seing her sister'.[123] Another court deponent declared in 1626 that he was familiar with the affairs of Christabel Colson, 'being brother in law to the said Christabel and living neare unto her at the tyme of her death'.[124]

Far less edifying as an example of frequent kinship interaction was the series of events beginning in July 1618 when Barbara Scott of Swalwell received simultaneous visits from her two daughters-in-law Elizabeth and Deborah Scott, her niece Jane Patterson, and Jane's sister-in-law Ann Cooper. Jane Patterson and Elizabeth Scott had apparently 'beene att some variance theretofore', and the conversation rapidly degenerated into 'hote and chollerick speeches', culminating in Jane declaring that Elizabeth was an 'unsoncye read headed fox and that she was ill to meet withall first in a morninge and that she was a witch and a bitch'. This quarrel, however, did not prevent Jane, on her way to Newcastle to market three weeks later, from following Elizabeth into David Taler's alehouse in Swalwell 'to know . . . when she would goe so as she might have her companye'. To her chagrin, she was pre-empted by overhearing Elizabeth describe Ann Copper as 'Thomas Currey's whore' and she retreated to Darwin staithe where she promptly reported the slander to Ann Cooper herself, who was standing there awaiting a boat to Newcastle. The result, shortly afterwards, was the public spectacle of Ann Cooper and Elizabeth Scott 'chidinge together' on the staithe. Elizabeth called Ann an 'arrant stinking whore', and being challenged by Ann's father John Patterson (who had also appeared on the scene) to repeat to him 'what she had called his daughter', she demonstrated her command of defamatory language by coming up with the choice epithet 'Janye open before'. All this resulted in two court cases in which, perhaps predictably, Barbara Scott, her daughter Isabell, and Deborah Scott all sided with Elizabeth, while Ann Cooper, Jane Patterson, and John Patterson also stood together.[125]

[123] DPD DR v/11 (unfol.), 24 Jul. 1623.

[124] DPD DR v/12 (unfol.), 8 Dec. 1626.

[125] DPD DR v/10B, fols. 338^v, 392^v, 393, 403, 403^v, 407, 407^v, 408, DR v/11 (unfol.), 13 Nov. 1618. Jane Patterson was the wife of a pitman later killed at Brinkburne colliery.

Such examples might give the impression that parish society in Whickham was in effect a mesh of kinship ties, reinforced perhaps by the legendary tendency towards marital endogamy of a group of workers regarded as a 'race apart'. In fact, it was not so. In order to test the realities of kinship linkage among the householders of Whickham, we have attempted to reconstruct as far as possible the kinship networks of each of the householders of Whickham in the hearth-tax listing of 1666 and to establish the degree of interlinkage that existed among them. The results of this exercise are set out in Table 4.1, where they are compared with similar figures for the agricultural parish of Terling, Essex, in 1671.[126] As will be evident, the proportion of Whickham householders known to have been linked by relationships of blood or marriage to other householders was very low as compared with Terling. The absolute density of the kinship network in Whickham—calculated as the average number of kinship links of the householders—was similarly very low. Relative kinship density—the known kinship links as a proportion of the total number of possible kinship links among the householders—was exceedingly low as compared with the Essex parish. This was a consequence of Whickham's lower degree of interlinkage and much larger population. In fact, the only points of similarity between the two parishes were that most of the linkages traceable were very close ties of blood or marriage, and that links established between people of different generations predominated over links between householders of the same generation.[127] If the kinship network of the householders of Terling could be described as 'relatively loose', that of the householders of Whickham was exceedingly so.

It must be acknowledged that these figures are certainly an underestimate of the degree of kinship linkage in Whickham. In

[126] The Terling figures are from Wrightson and Levine, *Poverty and Piety*, 87, and are also discussed in K. Wrightson, 'Kinship in an English Village: Terling, Essex 1550–1700', in R. M. Smith (ed.), *Land, Kinship and Life-Cycle* (Cambridge, 1984). As in the Terling study, we have used the family reconstitution forms and all other evidence of ties of kinship contained in our name index to attempt to trace the kin of each householder back for two generations and forward to the date of the listing. Uncles, aunts, cousins and second cousins, siblings, nephews, and nieces were all included where possible. If the householder was, or had been, married, affinal links were also traced.

[127] The commonest forms of linkage in Whickham were parent–child, uncle/aunt–nephew/niece, brother–sister, sister-in-law–brother-in-law and mother/father-in-law–son/daughter-in-law.

TABLE 4.1. *Kinship Links between Householders in Whickham and Terling*

	Whickham 1666		Terling 1671	
	No.	%	No.	%
Total no. of householders	367	100%	122	100%
Unrelated to others	317	86.4	74	60.7
Related to 1	30	8.2	32	26.2
Related to 2	12	3.2	10	8.2
Related to 3	8	2.2	4	3.3
Related to 4	—	—	2	1.6
Total related to other householders	50	13.6	48	39.3
Absolute kinship density		0.21		0.59
Relative kinship density		0.06%		0.5%

reconstructing the kinship networks of the householders, the greatest problem was that many householders had not been baptized and/or married in Whickham, so that other possible family relationships may be concealed from us. This problem also existed in the Terling study, though in less severe form. Again, studies of this kind can deal only with links *between* households; links that may have existed *within* households, by virtue of the presence of co-resident kinsfolk, are hidden from view in both parishes, though on occasion they may be suspected. John Hutchinson's household provides an example. His father had died in 1661 but his mother was still alive in 1666, though not a listed householder: was she now living with her son?[128]

[128] Occasional examples of co-resident adult kin can be found. In addition to the case of William West, cited above, the will of Archibald Bell explicitly describes a 'stem family' household: DPD Probate, Will of Archibald Bell (1733). More commonly, close examination of the family reconstruction forms reveals instances of daughters who were baptized in Whickham and subsequently buried as unmarried adults but who are not known ever to have been independent householders. Presumably they remained at home until their parents died and may subsequently have lived with relatives, e.g. with a married brother or sister. We are not suggesting that such co-residence was common, but it certainly occurred sometimes and is hidden in our calculations.

Even were we to double the degree of kinship linkage of Whickham, however, it would remain low. One extreme inter-pretative possibility would be to regard all householders with a common surname as potentially related, and this would indeed produce a different result. The proportion of householders with kinship links to other householders would rise to 58 per cent, some of them having as many as seven kinsmen. Absolute kinship density would rise to 1.5 and relative kinship density to 0.4. But such an exercise in maximizing potential linkage would be nonsensical. We know a great deal about the six Bainbridge households, including the fact that two of them were related; it is exceedingly unlikely that *all* were so linked. Again, there were seven Watsons, spread over all four quarters of the parish and approximate contemporaries in age. There may have been some bonds of kinship between them, hidden by the fact that one has no family reconstitution form at all, none were baptized in Whickham, and only three were married in the parish; but it seems improbable that all, or even most, were linked. Nor is it likely that Margaret Liddell, an exempted householder living in a one-hearth cottage, was a close kinswoman of Henry Liddell of Farnacres. With such surname groups, we are dealing with common surnames widespread throughout the Tyneside region, and recognizable kinship linkage cannot be assumed.[129]

The looseness of Whickham's kinship network as presented in Table 4.1 is doubtless exaggerated. It must be remembered, however, that the frustration and doubt that attends an attempted analysis of this kind derives above all from the fact that the genealogical records of individual families are obscured by their geographical mobility. Frustrating as it may be for genealogical purposes, the realities of both massive immigration and a continued high degree of geographical mobility were essential aspects of the historical experience of industrialization in Whickham. It is clear that they must have had profound consequences for the kinship networks of the parishioners. Whether or not Elizabethan Whickham

---

[129] The use of surname sets as a guide to kinship linkage has its value where circumstances prohibit family reconstitution and the systematic collation of other evidence of linkage. See e.g. the cautious and ingenious use of such evidence (excluding common surnames and focusing on the unusual) in J. Boulton, *Neighbourhood and Society: A London Suburb in the Seventeenth Century* (Cambridge, 1987), 249–53. In terms of proportions of related householders, Whickham's experience appears closer to that of Boulton's Southwark than to that of Terling.

had exhibited a higher degree of kinship interlinkage than that of 1666 is impossible to say, for we lack the records necessary to test the question properly.[130] It is our impression that it probably did. Though the Elizabethan population was certainly not bounded or immobile, there was a considerable degree of stability among the large core of copyholding families.

To this extent, industrialization and the emergence of a much larger and more volatile population may well have altered significantly the structural context within which kinship relations were conducted. But we cannot be certain. Much clearer is the fact that Whickham was most certainly not a tightly knit, densely interrelated mining community of the familiar stereotype. The conditions of the coal industry as it developed in the seventeenth century were not conducive to the establishment and maintenance of communities of that type.

All this should not be taken to imply that relationships among kinsfolk were of little significance. The wills of the parishioners have already indicated that close relatives certainly were part of the emotional universe of the testators of Whickham, and there is evidence enough that they could also play significant roles in the lives of the parishioners. In 1616, for example, Thomas Nixon deposed that he and John Hunter, the miller of Swalwell, had been 'for the space of divers yeares very familiar and stood in great kindnesse and friendshippe', so much so that he had laid out close to £80 on Hunter's behalf 'your orator and he being in great kindnesse together, he being brother to your orators wife'.[131] And there were many more examples of the operation of such 'kindnesse'. Mathew Matfen helped out his brother, who was greatly in debt, by permitting the use of a parcel of his own land as security, his motive being 'the love and affection he beareth to his said brother'. William Parmerley and his wife maintained her aged mother in the two years prior to her death. Martha Bonner nursed her staitheman brother George in his final illness in 1648, and Christopher Whitfield similarly took in his sick brother Thomas in 1664. Jane Rochester came to the aid of her granddaughter Margaret, the wife of a Fellside

---

[130] No list of all householders survives for the 16th c. and the inadequacy of the genealogical links provided in the manorial evidence limits the possibility of reconstructing kinship linkages even for lists of tenants. The late commencement of registration means that the early family reconstitution forms can do little to compensate for this deficiency in the evidence.
[131] PRO DURH 2/15/58.

waller, in 1708 when her husband's improvidence threatened to reduce the family 'into poverty and want'. In 1725 Thomas Denham confidently turned to his brother John to help his wife and daughter 'in the management of their affairs' after his own imminent death.[132]

Kinship relations were not always warm and supportive, however. Some of the instances of assistance cited above left a record only because they ended in disappointed expectations, conflict, and even litigation. Isabella Grubb, a tailor's widow, complained bitterly on her deathbed in 1690 of the 'unkindnesse and hardship towards her' shown by her son-in-law John, who 'did not allow her sufficient maintenance but she was like to be starved'. Elizabeth Hall accused her brother Henry of attempting 'by surprize, circumvention . . . indirect practices or contrivancy' to get her to sign away her property to him. William Pearson insisted vehemently in 1676 that his brother Thomas and sister-in-law Margaret 'nor either of them . . . should have any thing to do with, or be in the least concerned with the education of his . . . daughter Alice, or of his goods and chattels'.

These cases convey a sense of bitterness occasioned by betrayed expectations. But it is equally significant that Elizabeth Hall left her estate to her 'loveing sister' Grace, while William Pearson's daughter was entrusted to the care of another sister-in-law, Katherine, an obligation 'which the sayd Katherine was very willing to imbrace and accept of, and then and there she . . . told the same William . . . that she would (god willing) to the uttermost of her power endeavour well and truly to performe and fulfill such his sayd request'.[133] It was no doubt knowledge of the potential support of 'trusty and welbeloved friends', as well as a desire to avoid dissension among a network of people whose relationship should be characterized by 'kindnesse', which led several testators to state explicity that they had drawn up their wills, as John Blakiston put it in 1645, 'to avoid all future discords among my alliance and friends', or, as his neighbour Thomas Brignall of Gellsfield put it twenty years later 'for the prevention of future

[132] PRO DURH 2/19/46, 7/43; DPD DR v/2 (unfol.), 8 Dec. 1626; DPD Probate, Inv. of George Bonner (1648), Wills of Jane Rochester (1708), Thomas Denham (1725).
[133] DPD Probate, Wills of Isobel Grubb (1691), Elizabeth Hall (1697), William Pearson (1676).

trouble which after my decease might happen among my children'.[134]

To return to the householders of 1666, the quality of the relationships that existed among those of them who were linked by blood or marriage cannot be known with certainty, but it is at least likely that such relationships were of some significance to those involved. Ann Cooper, who had been so colourfully slandered fifty years before, was still dwelling in Whickham, as Widow Cooper, and she numbered among her neighbours in the parish a brother, a nephew, and her now widowed sister-in-law Jane Patterson—the same Jane who had been her ally in 1616. Charles Jordan, a young married man in 1666, very possibly owed his future advancement as a staitheman to his staithe-owning father-in-law and neighbour James Harrison.

In addition, loose as Whickham's kinship network was, it must be remembered that kinship networks, like the families that sustain them, pass through cycles. The situation in 1666 is an artificially frozen moment in a dynamic process. Elizabeth Dodds, for example, was a widow with no known adult kin in Whickham in 1666. Yet as a young married woman in 1647 she had been living near her widowed father and her married elder sister Susanna. Her father was killed in a pit in 1647 and her sister's family vanish from the Whickham records after 1651, presumably having moved from the parish. William Daglish had only a widowed cousin among the Whickham householders of 1666. As a child and young man in the 1630s and 1640s, however, he had been surrounded by households headed by a maternal uncle, two cousins, two elder brothers, and a sister. Edward Maxwell had two uncles and a cousin heading households in Whickham during the early years of his married life; in 1666 he had no known relations in the parish outside his own household. Such examples can easily be multiplied by tracing individuals either backwards or forwards in time from 1666. Kinship certainly had its place in the social structure of industrial Whickham, and if the overall network of kinship was indeed loose at any one given moment, from the point of view of the individual it varied markedly over time.

Finally, there was a spatial as well as a chronological dimension to

---

[134] Wood, *Wills and Inventories*, iv. 307; DPD Probate, Will of Thomas Brignall (1685). Cf. the will of Sir James Clavering (1702); he appointed a mediator in case of dispute and enjoined his heirs to 'goe not to law among themselves'.

the developmental cycle of kinship relations, for they were inevitably bound up with the contingencies of geographical mobility: the dispersal of young adults, the subsequent removals of particular households, the arrival of incomers. Some of the householders of 1666 are known to have had kinsfolk living outside Whickham—sometimes in neighbouring Lamesley, Ryton, Gateshead, or Chester-le-Street, or perhaps in Newcastle or further afield. The same was of course true of the numerous testators throughout the period of our study who made reference to close relatives not resident in the parish, and it must certainly have been a general reality. Some such relatives, located across parish boundaries but within easy walking distance, could easily have enjoyed the benefits of close association on a day-to-day basis. Others were out of reach for such purposes, though they must have met or maintained contact periodically.

Such kinsfolk, dispersed across the parishes of the area, clearly constituted a resource: a network of trusted individuals bound by a special obligation, a pool of assistance and support which could be drawn upon when occasion demanded. If Whickham people themselves chose to move residence, as members of the industrial work-force in particular so often did, or if they sought a place for a child reaching adulthood, the resultant mobility might well have been at least partly influenced by the information derived from relatives elsewhere.[135] To this extent individuals and families may have moved into and out of clusters of kinsfolk in the course of a lifetime.

Whether they moved or stayed put, however, it seems likely that the residences of close relatives were important points of reference in the mental maps of the inhabitants of the parish. In this highly mobile society in which dense clusters of locally resident 'friends' were only temporarily part of the immediate context of life—above all a feature of young adulthood, it would seem—a dispersed network of close relatives could serve as one of the integrating mechanisms linking the inhabitants of Whickham with the larger world of industrial Tyneside. It might provide an alternative sense of identity to that derived from tenancy of a manor or habitation within a parish—for some, perhaps, even a stronger one.

---

[135] Langton, *Geographical Change*, 115, suggests that kinship links may have influenced the mobility patterns of Lancashire miners.

Personal relationships between husbands and wives, parents and children, and the members of kinship networks based above all on the nuclear families of origin of man and wife were thus central to the individual lives of the people of industrial Whickham. In reviewing the inevitably sparse evidence of such relationships and their nature, we have suggested an essential continuity, a perdurance of basic values and behaviour. This is not, however, to suggest that there had been no change of significance in these spheres of life, still less to hint at the absurd conclusion that such fundamental human bonds have no history. To be sure, we have depicted a certain stability in conventional values, in individual aspirations, in expectations and modes of conduct, in forms of expression. Yet if we are to apprehend the meaning of these relationships over time, we need also to make certain crucial adjustments. Words and actions often remained the same; the contexts in which words were spoken, however, and in which actions were taken had changed utterly.

Economically, Whickham was transformed in the early seventeenth century, and that economic transformation and its subsequent consolidation and development clearly had profound consequences. It affected the manner in which the people of the parish earned their livings, the likelihood of geographical mobility, the nature and viability of domestic economies, the predictability of marital opportunity, the degree of domestic comfort that could be enjoyed, the extent to which security could be provided against old age or widowhood, and the provision that could be made for the advancement of children. In all of these areas of life, a changing socioeconomic structure can be said to have produced both novel realities and an enhanced diversity of experience which must inevitably have added layers of meaning to the commonplace emotions and activities of daily life. New options had been opened. New constraints were being felt.

The subtler influences of all this can never be documented in detail. We can describe the facts of a changing situation, but we can claim no depth of insight into the fuller ramifications of such developments. None the less, we can at least remain aware of the manner in which contextual influences may have affected the central experiences of individual lives. We can remain alive also to the likelihood that it was in and through the intimately personal experiences of marrying, bringing up a family, interacting with relatives, and facing decisions in all these spheres that the broader historical process of industrial and commercial development was mediated into the subjective consciousness of individuals.

As with the ties of the family, so too with the bonds of neighbourhood, which in themselves constituted yet another of the vital contexts within which family relationships were lived out and personal and social identities were constructed. Here too there was continuity. The inhabitants of industrial Whickham undoubtedly continued to value the virtues of good neighbourliness. They worked together on farms, on staithes, in pits, and in keels. They lent one another money, stood surety for one another's bonds, witnessed one another's wills, and appraised each other's goods. They drank together; played cards, bowls, nineholes, and football; greeted one another in the street, travelled to Newcastle together, knew one another's business; gossiped, quarrelled, and visited each other when sick.

All this and more can be instanced in the records of the parish in the seventeenth and early eighteenth centuries. But these relationships also were being conducted in traditional ways within a new context, a transformed social environment. Over time, the population of the parish was becoming larger, denser, more mobile, more diverse, and more differentiated in occupation and wealth. By the later seventeenth century, parish society was not only more populous and less homogeneous, more complex and more segmented than it had been in the sixteenth century; it was also a local society in which the centrality of the manor as a local institution involving a majority of households in a common nexus of interaction, a common discourse, had been destroyed. In addition, the pattern of settlement had been radically redrawn. This was no longer a local society focused on a single major settlement with satellite hamlets and farms. By the early eighteenth century at the latest, it was three major settlements—Whickham, Dunston, and Swalwell—plus the inchoate sprawl of the Fellside, with each quarter having its own identity—as witness the habit of testators of stating their residence at Swalwell, Team Staithes, and the like—and its own distinctive social structure.

Within this context, neighbourly relations still mattered greatly. But it might well be argued that long before 1750 Whickham was not one community but several overlapping communities, and that relations between its inhabitants were conducted not within '*the* neighbourhood' but within several neighbourhoods—for example the staitheworkers and keelmen of Dunston, the ironworkers of Swalwell, the pitmen of Fellside, the tenants of the major estates, and the genteel inhabitants of Whickham town. Such changing contexts could produce both a certain centrifugality in social relations, and associated shifts in senses of identity.

These suggestions can hardly be documented in full. We are speaking of impressions gained from our reading of the documents, the greater salience of the separate quarters of the parish in the activities of parochial administration, the location of schools, the geographical restrictions on the activities of certain will appraisers, the manner in which individuals were identified by third parties or in entries in the parish registers—of a cumulative sense that a variety of social fields of force had come into existence in Whickham. But such change may perhaps be discerned in at least one tolerably well-documented aspect of personal decision-making and neighbourly relations: the changing burial customs of the parish.

Whickham's burial customs did change in the course of the century and a half after 1580, and they did so in ways that may be significant. In the first place, a new element was added to the ritual of the forthbringing: the distribution of a dole to the poor. Before the 1580s small sums were occasionally donated by testators to the 'poor mans box', but from the later 1580s bequests to the poor became larger and more common, and from the 1590s it was not uncommon to state explicitly that the sums bequeathed were to be distributed at the funeral. This custom persisted into the third quarter of the seventeenth century, but thereafter charitable bequests became both rarer and more directed to specific purposes.[136] This overall trend may reflect both the increased wealth of some of the parishioners and an enhanced awareness of the presence of the labouring poor, which taken together suggest a sharper sense of differentiation within the neighbourhood.

A second development was the decline of the traditional 'forthbringing among the neighbours'. In the sixteenth century the costs of the forthbringing had dominated the funeral expenses of the parishioners. Early in the seventeenth century, however, detailed funeral expenses reveal that some parishioners had begun to have a

---

[136] For examples of instructions regarding funeral doles, see DPD Probate, Wills of Cuthbert Thompson (1596), Anthony Grundie (1600), Robert Fawdon (1603), John Middleton (1603), Thomas Pescod (1671), Tristram Fenwick (1674).

private dinner which eclipsed the costs of the forthbringing. In 1600 Anthony Grundie's executors spent £4. 4s 2d. on 'an arvall dinner', 5s. on a sermon, 30s. for a dole to the poor, and only 20s. 'at his bringing forth to the buriall'. Three years later John Middleton's spent 14s. 'for meate among his frindes being a dinner', 10s. on a sermon, 20s. to the poor, and only 7s. 'at his bring forth for bread and drink'.[137] The forthbringing was being overshadowed on the one hand by a private family dinner, and on the other hand by the dole to the poor. Commensality was giving way to familial privacy and public charity. Thereafter the forthbringing declined rapidly, and our last reference to a 'bringen' comes from 1615, at the burial of the yeoman Henry Hall.[138] Detailed funeral expenses surviving from the later seventeenth and early eighteenth centuries indicate that the sums expended varied considerably. Only one, however, indicates anything comparable to a forthbringing.[139] That ritual of inclusion was effectively dead.

Thirdly, in the course of the seventeenth century Whickham testators appear gradually to have lost interest in the place and manner of their burial. In Elizabethan Whickham it will be remembered, virtually all had specified burial in Whickham church or churchyard and almost half were absolutely specific in requesting burial at a particular place or near a particular person. Both customs declined in the early seventeenth century, and in the years 1660–1760 only twelve of seventy-three testators even requested burial in Whickham, while a mere five asked for interment in a specific place—all but one of them requesting burial near a deceased spouse. The disposal of the corpse was now customarily left 'at the discretion of my executors', and indeed after 1730 it was rarely mentioned at all. Nor did testators show the interest of their forebears in the manner of their burial. The former insistence upon an 'honest' forthbringing gave way first to a conventional request for burial 'in decent manner', occasionally accompanied by specific restrictions on the sum to be spent, and after 1730 to silence, broken

---

[137] DPD Probate, Invs. of Anthony Grundie (1600), John Middleton (1603).

[138] DPD Probate, Will of Henry Hall (1615).

[139] DPD Probate, Inv. of George Lewen (1665), Lewen's executors spent £9. 12s. 10d. for wine, spices, and 'biskett' consumed at Lewen's Newcastle house and a further £2 'Att Whickham for the neighbours disbursed for beere, wine, cakes, tobacco'. The fact that money was also paid to 'those that were employed to invite to the funeral', however, suggests that the gathering, though perhaps large, was also exclusive. Lewen was a minor gentleman.

only by John Thompson's suggestion in 1744 that his wife see to his burial 'with all requisite prudence'.[140] 'Honesty', with all that the word implied in terms of social relations, had given way to 'decency' and 'prudence'.

Such were the changes that overcame the burial customs of those who were for the most part drawn from the core of Whickham's settled society. Developments of this kind were not unique to Whickham. They were part of a general process of cultural change in seventeenth-century England which had been attributed to the influence of a rising sense of individualism.[141] Perhaps so. Our own preference, however, is to emphasize the influence of the changing contexts of social structure and social relations which rendered such shifts in attitudes and behaviour desirable. In late sixteenth-century Whickham, the apparent insouciance and relative privacy that came to characterize the wills and funerals of the Augustan parishioners would have been scarcely intelligible, let alone matters of cultural preference and personal choice. The context had changed, and the alteration in the ways of life of Whickham's people was reflected in their ways of death. Among the leaders of parish society, the 'honest' forthbringing, which had expressed the place of the heads of copyholder families in a neighbourhood restricted in size and closely focused, became redundant because it slowly lost its meaning. As for the others, pitmen were brought in for burial by their overmen;[142] Crowley workers were buried at the expense of the factory poor fund, which paid for a coffin, met the church fees, and laid out a maximum of 9s. on 'drink among the workmen';[143] and paupers were interred by the parish at a standard rate.[144]

The specific nature of Whickham's changing social context was the gradual dissolution of the economic, social, and institutional structures of one kind of community and their replacement by alternative forms. But we do not wish to appear unduly elegiac in

---

[140] DPD Probate, Will of John Thompson (1744).

[141] K. Thomas, *Religion and the Decline of Magic: Studies in Popular Beliefs in Sixteenth and Seventeenth Century England* (London, 1971), 721–3, links this process to the influence of the Reformation. Gittings, *Death*, 13–14 and *passim*, traces change in English burial customs and develops the theme of 'a changing conception of the self and a heightened sense of individuality'. Cressy, 'Kinship', 61–2, presents evidence of the decline of funeral feasts in Essex.

[142] See sect. 3.2 above.   [143] Flinn, *Law Book*, 11–12, 84.

[144] The overseers accounts for 1725–44 (DRO EP/Wh 18) indicate that a standard pauper burial costing 4s. for a coffin and 2s. 6d. for the funeral was usual.

our interpretation of such change. At the level of the individual, those personal ties that were the principal preoccupation of particular lives continued to play their part as reference points of identity and sources of material and emotional security. And more broadly, if one form of community had been dissolved, others were in the making. It is with the broader influences that moulded the structures and identities of local society in industrial Whickham that we must now concern ourselves.

5. THE PARISH, PATERNALISM, AND THE PITMAN'S BOND

One vital influence in the maintenance of a broader social and institutional identity in industrial Whickham was the civil parish. In this, as in so much else, Whickham stood in marked contrast to the Forest of Kingswood, that *locus classicus* of the disorder associated with early coalfield society. Kingswood was a border area in both civil and ecclesiastical jursdiction; it included parts of four adjoining parishes, had no church of its own and no administrative identity, and its inhabitants lived 'relatively unconstrained by the immediate presence of institutional authority'.[145] In Whickham, this was not so. The developing industrial society of Whickham was for long contained within the jurisdictional boundaries of a single large parish, and as the institutional identity of the civil parish was enhanced in the course of the seventeenth century, this important fact created new possibilities in terms of social organization.[146]

While the earlier seventeenth century witnessed the gradual decline into relative insignificance of the manorial institutions that had been at the heart of Whickham's sixteenth-century community, the same period also saw the rise of a novel structure of parochial administration which was to define the rights and obligations of the parishioners in a new way and to create new arenas of participation and interaction. By the 1630s the parish of Whickham was governed by a close vestry of twenty-four men. To judge from the surviving lists of its membership, this was composed of the principal gentlemen and coal-owners of the parish, supplemented by leading farmers and tradesmen. Members appear to have served for life,

[145] Malcolmson, 'A Set of Ungovernable People', 86, 89, 91.
[146] The classic account of the emergence of the civil parish remains S. and B. Webb, *English Local Government from the Revolution to the Municipal Corporations Act*, i, *The Parish and the County* (London, 1906).

adding to their numbers by co-option when occasion arose.[147] By the later seventeenth century the vestry can be said to have replaced the Halmote Court as Whickham's principal agency, and 'the Gentlemen of the Four and Twenty' had acquired that position at the pinnacle of the *cursus honorum* of local life that had once been occupied by the leading copyholders who composed the manorial jury. Upon them and their chosen subordinates fell the many and varied duties of parochial administration, but from the outset their dominant responsibility was the administration of the Poor Laws.[148]

The emergence of an enhanced consciousness of the presence and needs of the poor within the parish found its first expression in the charitable bequests of the parishioners. The Elizabethan neighbourhood, which had been sufficiently restricted in size to be included in the commensality of the 'forthbringing', was first supplemented and then overwhelmed at the turn of the sixteenth century by a new population of inhabitants for whom a more appropriate form of social recognition was the funeral dole. To this extent Whickham's new industrial population stood outside, or more accurately on the periphery of, the traditional neighbourhood. If their way of life rendered them vulnerable to poverty and to the misery of short-term economic crises, their landlessness also placed them outside what has been called the 'customary' Poor Law of manorial provision for the aged, the widowed, and the orphaned.[149]

The consequences of industrial expansion in terms of generating a larger population of wage-workers whose economic security was at best marginal and temporary is well documented in the neighbouring parish of Chester-le-Street, which was deeply involved in the expansion of the Wearside mining industry in the early seventeenth century. As early as 1622, the 'incoming poor' of the parish were

---

[147] The emergence of the vestry remains obscure. The first list of the Four and Twenty is in the parish register for 1633 and thereafter new lists were periodically entered there: DRO EP/Wh 1, 2, 4, 6, 7. Since this register book contains events dating back to 1576, it seems reasonable to assume that the vestry had emerged comparatively recently. Examination of the lists of the Four and Twenty shows that new members were added on the deaths of old. By the 1730s 'the Gentlemen of the Vestry' appear to have been a 16-man sub-committee of 'the Gentlemen of the Four and Twenty'.

[148] In a sense, they were the direct heirs of the Halmote jury, for they were often also the leading copyholders of Whickham. They now held sway, however, not in that capacity but by virtue of their role in the administration of the civil parish.

[149] Slack, *Poverty and Policy*, 63.

being described as 'a great charge and inconvenience to the inhabitants'. In 1616 and 1618 the coal-owner Sir William Lambton had been persuaded to pay 20s. annually to the overseers of the poor for Chester-le-Street 'soe long as [his] said coal mines shalbe wrought and no longer', an arrangement subsequently parelleled by deals with the owners of the collieries of Lumley and Harraton. That this failed adequately to meet the problem, however, and that the mounting burden of relief was resented by the 'inhabitants', is indicated by local orders of 1622 and 1656 stipulating that any inhabitant letting cottages to 'undertenants' or entertaining 'any fforainer or Strainger' should give a bond to the overseers that their tenants would not become 'predudiciall or chargeable' to the parish, and by a complaint of 1661 that the continued influx meant that 'there are many poore people brought and orphans left to the charge of the parish'.[150]

The situation in Whickham was almost certainly similar, though the consequences may possibly have been slower in making themselves felt. Clearly, in Chester-le-Street that crucial innovation of the Elizabethan Poor Laws, the levying of a compulsory poor-rate, had already been instituted by the 1620s, and the 'inhabitants' were feeling the costs of the needs of the incoming poor in their purses. This was by no means always so in the early seventeenth century, for many rural parishes continued to get by, or to make do, with voluntary contributions of the type evidenced in the wills of Whickham.[151] By mid-century, however, Whickham was also participating fully in the statutory system of poor relief, and the emergence of the vestry may have been not unconnected with that process.

Our first reference to the poor-rate comes in November 1643 with the minuting of a vestry decision to raise and disburse 27s. for the use of the poor. Detailed assessments of the parishioners and annual lists of the paupers relieved by the parish survive from 1677.[152] As in Chester-le-Street, the collieries, the very presence of which was a major contributing factor to the levels of indigence in

---

[150] Issa, 'Obligation and Choice', 56, 57, 60, 61. The general nature of the problem posed by colliery development is made clear by the frequency with which the justices were called upon to adjudicate disputes over the poor-rate assessments in affected parishes; e.g. the running battle over whether Rainton Pit Houses should be regarded as in Houghton-le-Spring or in Pittington for poor relief purposes: DRO, Q/S OB 5, 324, OB 7, 259.

[151] Slack, *Poverty and Policy*, 170. 　　　[152] DRO EP/Wh 1, 2; EP/Wh 22.

the parish, were specially assessed. From at least 1677 and probably long before, payments were made on behalf of the Grand Lease colliery and in respect of every 'working freehold pitt' in the parish. In the early eighteenth century, collieries, wayleaves, and staithe-rooms were all subject to special assessment. Of the industrial undertakings in Whickham, only the Crowley firm remained outside the parochial system of poor relief, maintaining its own scheme financed by a combination of employers' and employees' contributions, administered by a group of 'Governors' appointed from among the managers of the works, and offering a wide range of benefits.[153]

In addition to the sums raised from the coal industry, the parish also enjoyed occasional windfall income in the form of sums bequeathed in wills and, from the 1690s, the benefit of a growing number of endowed charities. In 1690 Dr Wood, a former rector who had been elevated to the bishopric of Coventry and Lichfield, bequeathed a substantial sum, the interest from which was employed 'among decayed Workmen chiefly and there Widows and Children'. This was subsequently supplemented by endowments from Mr Ralph Harrison, 'applyed towards binding out Poor Children and Clothing them', and from Lady Jane Clavering, whose charity, established in memory of her son, was distributed annually 'among such workmen and their families as are the greatest objects of charity and are not in the poors books'.[154] Meanwhile, in 1702 Sir James Clavering left an annual rent, part of which was to be used by his heirs to provide each year 'coates, petticoates, or waistcoates' for 'twenty-foure poore men, women or childer borne and liveing within the parish of Whickham', and the rest by the overseers of the poor to distribute 'twenty foure penny loaves of wheaten bread' at twelve noon every Sunday 'to twenty foure poore people of the said parish who shalbe present at Divine service or sermon (if not hindered by age, or sicknes then to be sent to them)'. These, together with subsequent endowments for the clothing of the poor or the education or apprenticeship of their children, completed the array of charitable provision that was at the disposal of, or mediated through, the vestrymen and the officers under their supervision.[155]

---

[153] DRO EP/Wh 18 and 22 *passim*; Flinn, *Men of Iron*, 228 ff.; id., *Law Book*, 154–62, 174 ff.　　　[154] DRO EP/Wh 32, 3; Hutchinson, *Durham*, ii. 449 n.
[155] DPD Probate, Will of Sir James Clavering (1702); Bourn, *Whickham*, 20–2.

In the parish books, which provide the best evidence of their activities, the parish officers' assiduousness in the performance of their duties can easily be appreciated. Yet there was more involved in all of this than simple administration. For in the deliberations and decisions of the 'Gentlemen of the Four and Twenty' and the broader group of officers who participated in the executive roles of parish government, the local society over which they held sway was defined and redefined.

Those regarded as of ability to share the burden of the poor-rate were included in assessments in which they were described as 'the parishioners' or 'the substantiall inhabitants' of Whickham, a definition that carried financial obligations but also differentiated them from the remainder of the population. Conversely, those in regular receipt of parish relief were also listed annually and were designated 'the poore of the Parish of Whickham', 'the Monthly Poor', or the 'Quarterly Poor'. These were terms that, for all their apparent descriptive innocence, both defined their rights—they had been recognized as settled inhabitants to whom relief was due—and imposed upon them a specific public identity. It was an identity, moreover, that was reinforced by the Act of 1697 requiring that parish paupers wear a cloth badge consisting of the initial letter of the parish name.[156] That larger group who might on occasion need temporary relief, or who benefited periodically from the annual disbursements of the parish's charities (principally at Christmas), were also defined thereby, albeit temporarily, as 'the poor', 'poor persons', 'decayed workpeople', or 'objects of charity'. If ultimately they fell wholly upon the parish for maintenance, that definition was confirmed. If they were unfortunate enough to lack a clear settlement, however, they became objects of dispute, grudgingly added to the lists of Whickham's poor if the justices found against Whickham, defined out and removed from the parish if Whickham won.[157]

Nor was this process of definition and redefinition confined to the discrete categorization of Whickham's inhabitants. It also developed a geographical dimension even within the boundaries of the parish. We have suggested that eighteenth-century Whickham

[156] These terms are employed in the overseers' assessments and disbursements in DRO EP/Wh 18 and 22. For the act of 1697, see Slack, *Poverty and Policy*, 193.

[157] Terminology employed in DRO EP/Wh 18 and D/ST 336/7. For settlement disputes involving Whickham, see DRO Q/S OB 7, 544, 598; OB 8, 519, 529, 534; OB 9, 129, 202, 349; OB 10, 251.

might well be regarded as not one community but several, less one than a collection of neighbourhoods within the perimeter of a single parish. The administration of the Poor Laws amply confirms that perception. By an Act of 1673 provision was made for individual townships within large parishes to administer poor relief on a separate basis.[158] This was a legal change eagerly seized upon by some of the industrial parishes of the north-east as a means of confining responsibility for the burden of poverty associated with industrial development to the industrial townships themselves. The potential implications of such decisions were to be seen in Whickham's neighbour, the parish of Ryton, where in 1729 it was complained that the industrial 'constablery' of Ryton Woodside was 'so burthened with poor' that the poor-rate assessment was set at 'twelve pence in the pound at the Rack Rent', whereas in nearby Chopwell township there were only six maintained paupers and the rate was only 2*d.* in the pound.[159]

It was perhaps the prospect of an enhanced burden of poverty as the second major phase of Whickham's industrial growth began with the opening of the Gibside colliery that prompted 'divers Inhabitants within several Villages and Towneshipps in the Parish of Whickham' to consider the same option. If this was so, they may have had some justification, for the average annual number of parish pensioners, which had been 80 in the four years 1687–90, had risen substantially to an average of 106 in the four years 1691–4.[160] Whatever the reason, in January 1694 the inhabitants petitioned the justices 'That they may maintaine the poore within their respective Villages and Towneshipps according to the forme of the Statute . . . without contributing with the whole parish of Whickham'. Their petition was granted, and, no objections having been received, it was confirmed the following year.[161]

This petition certainly reveals both the extent to which the parish authorities were conscious of the increasingly separate identities of the four 'quarters' into which the parish had traditionally been divided, and the limits that existed on their sense of communal responsibility. How far they actually acted upon the justices'

[158] N. McCord, *North-East England: An Economic and Social History* (London, 1979), 87.

[159] DRO Q/S OB 8, 501. Ryton's problems were to continue to trouble the justices for many years: see Q/S OB 10 and 12, *passim.*

[160] Figures based on DRO EP/Wh 22. This increase took place before the onset of the dearth years of 1694–8.   [161] DRO Q/S OB 7, 415, 418, 423.

enabling order, however, remains uncertain. It is clear that from 1694 the disbursements of the overseers of the poor were administered separately, for the parochial accounts thereafter are divided up by quarter. The rating assessment, however, was still set for the parish as a whole, and at a common rate until 1712, after which year a gap ensues in the assessment records.[162] Presumably the sums raised were divided up among the officers of the separate quarters according to some rule of thumb which was never made explicit. Nor indeed was it desirable that it should be made explicit, for in Whickham the object of the exercise seems to have been not the setting of separate township rates, but a more complex strategy which would enable the ratepayers of the riverside quarters (and above all Whickham Town) to benefit from the rating of the new collieries, while at the same time limiting the extent to which they could be held responsible for the growing population of colliery workers in the Fellside quarter.

The vestrymen were certainly anxious to maximize the income that could be raised from the coal-owners, as was evidenced in 1709 when the justices were obliged to hear and determine an appeal regarding the assessment of Gibside colliery.[163] At the same time, they were not averse to using income from the colliery rates, which was essentially Fellside income and which after 1709 more than equalled the total sum raised from the contributions of the individual ratepayers, to subsidize the poor-rates elsewhere in the parish.[164] This was made clear in 1711, when they engaged counsel to plead, successfully, before the justices 'that the Collieries there should contribute to the maintenance of the poor within the . . . Townshipp of Whickham'.[165] What they were seeking to avoid was that the ratepayers of Whickham Town, Lowhand, and Swalwell should in turn be obliged to contribute to the support of Fellside's poor.[166] For, whatever informal arrangements were made to confine the responsibility of the ratepayers of the riverside quarters to the maintenance of their own poor only, in accordance with the order of 1694, it is clear that no such privilege was permitted to the

---

[162] DRO EP/Wh 22, *passim*.   [163] DRO Q/S OB 8, 129.

[164] In 1709 the colliery assessment, most of it raised from collieries in the Fellside quarter, yielded 11s. 4d. a week or £29. 9s. 4d. p.a. In 1712 the private ratepayers' assessments totalled 9s. 1d. a week, or £23. 12s. 4d. p.a. DRO EP/Wh 22, 125, 138.

[165] DRO Q/S OB 8, 156.

[166] The growing industrial population of Swalwell was not a problem, given the Crowley firm's own relief scheme.

Fellsiders: they were to maintain their own poor *and* to contribute to the support of those elsewhere in the parish.

This was an arrangement against which the representatives of Fellside petitioned angrily in 1718, urging that they too should be 'henceforth a Constablery distinct and separated by it selfe from any other place or part of the said parish: and that such poor only as have their proper settlements within the said Townshipp or village of Fell-side shall be maintained thereby and that it shall not bee charged to ye maintenance of any other poor whatsoever'. But they protested in vain, for, though the justices responded sympathetic-ally, by the next sessions a counter-case had been made and the proposal was quashed.[167] Ultimately a compromise emerged, and by the early 1740s the practice was to draw up two rating assessments—one for lands, wayleaves, staitherooms, breweries, and collieries in the parish as a whole, and another at a much lower rate for the domestic ratepayers of the several quarters.[168] By this time, however, the ratepayers of the parish had clearly been long accustomed to thinking of themselves 'in severalty', and the recipients of poor relief had long been categorized as 'Whickham Poor', 'Lowhand Poor', 'Swalwell Poor', and 'Fellside Poor'.

In all these ways, the administration of the civil parish operated to define and redefine both social and communal identities in the conglomerate that was now the parish of Whickham. And it did more. For the Poor Laws also structured and mediated the relationships between those who occupied different positions in the social hierarchy of the parish and its constituent townships. In Whickham, as elsewhere in seventeenth- and early eighteenth-century England, the Poor Laws functioned essentially to provide relief at critical stages in the life-cycles of the labouring poor.[169] The overwhelming majority of those in receipt of regular 'allowances' were women, most of them widows, some of them aged and bereft of support, others left to maintain young children without adequate means. Men figured far less frequently and less regularly among the

---

[167] DRO Q/S OB 8, 270, 276.

[168] DRO EP/Wh 18 (including assessments 1742–4). Later, completely separate assessments by quarter were introduced (see EP/Wh 19, assessments from 1749), but by then the whole system of relief was about to be overhauled.

[169] See e.g. T. Wales, 'Poverty, Poor Relief and the Life-Cycle: Some Evidence from Seventeenth-Century Norfolk' and W. Newman Brown, 'The Receipt of Poor Relief and Family Situation: Aldenham, Hertfordshire 1630–90', both in Smith, *Land, Kinship and Life-Cycle*, esp. 342–3, 360–7, 369 ff., 382 ff., 411–12, 415, 419.

pensioners of the parish, and those who did so were not uncommonly designated 'old', 'lame', 'blind', 'almost blind', or 'sick'. Then there were the children, some of them suffering from special disability, like 'Harrison's lame lass' or 'Peariths lame lad'; some too numerous for their parents to maintain adequately; others simply orphaned and placed, singly or in groups, in the care of householders who often enough were themselves poor.[170]

The profile of those who benefited from the annual disbursements of the parish charities was somewhat different, to judge from the two years for which complete lists of the recipients of Bishop Wood's charity survive. Most of those in receipt of small sums of a shilling or two at Christmas 1715 and 1743 were *not* also regular pensioners of the parish; they were not, in the terminology used, 'in the poor book'. Women, most of them widows, and children, many of them disabled, were of course prominent; but they made up a much smaller proportion of the poor relieved from the charitable endowments. Men, on the other hand, figured far more frequently in these lists, providing in all 42 per cent of those not also in receipt of regular 'allowances' in 1715 and 45 per cent in 1743. As in the lists of 1764, mentioned above, the beneficiaries of the charities could be described as 'the old, decayed Work People and Poor Widows', but they were not regarded as sufficiently destitute to qualify for regular parochial relief.[171]

Of the importance of the system of poor relief in the life-cycles of the labouring poor, there can be no doubt. Of the social and psychological consequences of the system, however, there can be no certainty; for, although the attitudes of the parish officers are occasionally made apparent, we cannot penetrate the minds of those who were in receipt of regular or occasional relief. It would be possible to argue that the system was in the final analysis divisive, that it enshrined a social cleavage between those who paid and administered the rate and those who were at risk of becoming a charge upon it. The relief granted could be mean, and it could be grudging. The 'weekly allowances' granted at the turn of the seventeenth century were small and could scarcely have provided

---

[170] Based on DRO EP/Wh 22 (1677–1715), 18 (1725–44), 19 (1745–75), *passim*.

[171] Lists of disbursements at Christmas 1715 and 1743 can be found in DRO EP/Wh 18. What the parish officers referred to as 'Bishop Wood's' money was by 1715 the consolidated income of the charities founded by Dr Wood, Mr Harrison, and Sir James Clavering.

more than a supplement to the livings of the recipients—how could Jane Grey have maintained herself and her '5 small children' on her 6*d*. a week, or Widow Spencer and her three children have got by on their 4*d*.? Again, the parish officers were clearly anxious to keep down the numbers of those relieved and the costs of the system, and could go to some lengths to do so. In 1737 one of them spent two days riding to Corbridge and 'searching the Redchester' to provide proof of the place of birth and settlement of 'Richard Lues Girl' in order to secure her removal from Whickham.[172]

On the other hand, the system did provide relief, and over time it did become more generous. In the early 1740s those receiving monthly allowances of 12*s*., 16*s*., or 24*s*., which presumably varied according to individual family circumstances, could have lived on the sums granted. Those paid less frequently and less generously— at rates, for examples, of 5*s*.–10*s*. a quarter—were presumably in less need and doubtless welcomed the supplement afforded them. And those 'Poor needful people as was not in the Poor Book' who received 'by payments' at 'Sundry times' in the form of cash, medical expenses, or clothing, or who were given a Christmas shilling or two from Bishop Wood's charity, may well have been grateful for the attention of the overseers. The pregnant Mary Chicken had cause to be thankful that the parish paid Dr Rayne in October 1751 'for pulling in [her] Ancle Joynt' and another fee later that month 'when lying in'.[173] There were also those children for whom the parish provided an education and an apprenticeship. Although it would be going much too far to suggest that the system was essentially 'benevolent and sympathetic' in operation, it would be churlish to ignore the fact that it was sometimes so.[174]

Moreover, the day-to-day administration of relief could involve a recognition of obligations and rights which could lay a bridge of sorts across the realities of social distance—the more so, perhaps, when the overseers, some of them also vestrymen, were personally involved in the investigation of cases and the granting and payment of relief to those in their charge within their respective quarters.[175]

The crucial point is that the system of poor relief, which was at

[172] DRO EP/Wh 18, notes on expenditure in 1737. The girl had been maintained by the parish for 27 weeks at a total cost of £1. 9*s*. 8*d*.

[173] DRO EP/Wh 19, 'by payments' Oct. 1751.

[174] The phrase is W. Newman Brown's, with reference to the tone of relief in Aldenham, Herts., 'Poor Relief and Family Situation', 419–20.

[175] Slack, *Poverty and Policy*, 168–9, 208.

the very centre of the responsibilities of the civil parish, did all of this. For good or ill, it was the principal institutional nexus between the inhabitants of industrial Whickham and its constituent townships. Oligarchical as was the parish vestry, service as an overseer was a circulating office which involved many of the 'substantiall inhabitants' of Whickham—at least thirty-four of them in the two decades after 1677, for example. And the scale of involvement with the system by those in receipt of relief was prodigious indeed.

One-third of the one-hearth exempted households listed on the hearth-tax assessment of 1666, and 43 per cent of those of such households that were sufficiently stable to appear in the family reconstitution study, are known to have received relief at some point in the years 1677–1714. Furthermore, these figures are minimum estimates of the degree of involvement across the life-cycle.[176] For later periods we are unable to attempt such estimates because the overseers' books do not provide a full and continuous series of disbursements. Nevertheless, there are two years for which both a list of regular pensioners and a list of the recipients of aid from the charities survive and the message of these, as presented in Table 4.2, is plain. In 1715 a total of 299 adults, and in 1743 at least 253 adults, received poor relief from the parish in some form. If these adults were separate householders, as can generally be assumed, and if the parish contained approximately seven hundred households, as was reported to Bishop Chandler in 1736, then in 1715 some 43 per cent of households, and in 1743 at least 36 per cent, were beholden to the parish to some degree.[117]

These figures are broadly compatible with, though not directly comparable to, our other estimates of the degree of indigence and marginality in the parish. More to the point, they firmly reinforce our sense of the centrality of the poor relief system in late seventeenth- and early eighteenth-century Whickham. It was the principal source of such institutional coherence as the parish retained. It defined and redefined the rights and obligations of the parishioners and the geographical segmentation of local society. And it provided one of the most salient points of contact between the inhabitants of Whickham and its townships, structuring their public identities and mediating institutionally the interactions of

[176] See pp. 163–4 above.
[177] In 1715, 14% from regular relief + charity; 29% from charity only. In 1743, 17% from regular relief + charity; 19% from charity only.

TABLE 4.2. *Recipients of Poor Relief and/or Charity, 1715 and 1743*

	1715	1743
(i) Regularly relieved		
Men	13	35
Women[a]	83 (64)	82 (59)
Children[b]	13	9
(ii) Bishop Wood's Charity[c]		
Men	94	68
Women[a]	171 (121)	81 (47)
Children[b]	16	3
(iii) Appearing on both lists		
Men	4	4
Women[a]	58 (46)	9 (4)
Children[b]	7	—
(iv) Total individuals[d]		
Men	103	99
Women[a]	196 (139)	153 (102)
Children[b]	22	12
Total adults	299	253[c]

[a] Figures in parentheses pertain to widows.

[b] Children or groups of children listed separately. Some adult recipients also had children, or course.

[c] The 1743 charity list is not wholly specific as to the identities of all recipients. In each quarter the officers concluded their lists of names with a further sum disbursed 'for severall'. At the rates usually paid to recipients, these sums could account for a further 14–35 recipients who cannot be identified and have not therefore been included in the table.

[d] i.e. (i) + (ii) − (iii).

Sources: EP/Wh 18: Bishop Wood's Christmas 1715 and 1743; Disbursement listing 1743; EP/Wh 22: Disbursement listing 1715.

vestrymen, overseers, ratepayers, and that shifting population of work-people who walked the narrow path between sufficiency and dependency.

While the civil parish provided the institutional context of social relations in industrial Whickham, its structuring influence was supplemented by the bonds of paternalism and deference which connected the leading gentry families of the parish and their social subordinates. Paradoxically, industrialized Whickham was a far more gentrified society than the Elizabethan parish had been. The restructuring of copyholder society that accompanied industrialization saw the emergence of a larger number of minor gentry families. Much more important, however, was the fact that industrial interests and land purchases greatly enhanced the salience in parish affairs of the coal-owning squirearchy and baronetcy—the Claverings of Axwell, the Liddells of Ravensworth and Farnacres, and (from the 1720s) the Boweses of Gibside. Again, industrialized Whickham was not only more gentrified, but also a local society in which a far greater proportion of the population was involved in relationships of economic dependence with the local gentry—as tenants, as employees, and often as both.

With the enhanced social–structural significance of the gentry came a denser web of patronage relationships and the emergence of a highly visible paternalistic style. Placed as it was in the early eighteenth century between the principal seats of three powerful families who were increasingly dominant figures in its parish affairs, Whickham was very much a stage for what has been called 'the theatre of the great'.[178]

At the level of the parish, the Claverings and the Boweses, together with several of the minor gentry, were the benefactors of the parochial charities already discussed. They were also supporters of the parish schools. Moreover, the influence of the immense fortunes that they derived above all from their colliery interests could be exerted to signal effect upon other occasions. In the dreadful winter of 1739–40 it was reported in Newcastle that George Bowes had 'ordered his Agents to enquire into the Exigencies of the poor Families in the Parish of Whickham' and to distribute £25 'to feed and to clothe the Necessitous'. In addition he, Edward Wortley, Sir Henry Liddell, and George Liddell had 'jointly ordered a large sum to be distributed to those in Lamesley, Whickham and Tanfield' in like need.[179] A similar scheme was

---

[178] E. P. Thompson, 'Patrician Society Plebeian Culture', *Journal of Social History*, 7 (1974), 389–90.

[179] *Newcastle Journal* 2 Feb. 1740, 23 Feb. 1740. That not all were impressed by the coal-owners' beneficence is illustrated by the following 'EPIGRAM on the Great Charities during the late Frost', also published in the *Newcastle Journal* on 3 May

apparently pursued in Whickham with 'much success' in February 1754, and nine years later the rector of Whickham was again writing to the widowed Mrs Bowes's agent concerning a proposal to be made at the next vestry meeting 'for a Contribution towards the Support of the Poor . . . at this severe season'. He urged him 'to recommend the matter to Mrs Bowes, whose Goodness on this, and all other occasions of this kind, I am certain we may rely on'.[180] That he was not mistaken in his assessment of her character is indicated by the surveys of the deserving poor of Lowhand, Whickham, and Swalwell quarters that survive among her estate papers for 1764, together with accounts of monetary assistance disbursed to 162 of those listed and a separate list of 'money paid the poor' of Fellside quarter in December 1764.[181] And if this were not enough, she also distributed gowns and other clothing annually at Christmas: to twenty-six people in 1764, forty-seven in 1765, and thirty-six in 1766.[182]

At the level of the individual, the gentry also intervened to provide support for clients, dependants, or other deserving petitioners who had fallen upon hard times or found themselves in trouble. Mr Thomas Shafto reduced the rent of a necessitous widow to a single capon per annum, and when she gratefully offered him another bird paid her a shilling for it, she 'being a poor woman'. George Bowes became involved in the case of a keelman and former employee of thirteen years' standing who had been impressed for the navy and had turned in desperation to his former master, urging him 'to consider his case and befriend him'. Mrs Bowes's estate agent, acting on his mistress's behalf, recommended a sick waggon-wright to the governors of Newcastle's recently founded infirmary, intervened in the case of a poor woman threatened with removal from the parish and suffering 'immediate Distress', and threatened to

---

1740: 'Yes, 'tis high time, I cry'd, t'impose the Chain, / Destin'd and due to Wretches self-enslaved; / But when I see such Charity remain, / I half cou'd wish this People might be sav'd; / Faith lost and Hope, our Charity begins, / And 'tis no doubt a wise Design on Heaven, / If this can cover Multitudes of Sins, / To take the only way to be forgiven.'

[180] DRO D/ST 317. [181] DRO D/ST 336/7.

[182] DRO D/ST, 323, 352/37. Mrs Bowes was presumably implementing the provision of her late husband's will regarding clothing for the poor. The recipients were usually women, and to judge by the 1765 list they 'applyd' for clothing. In D/ST 323 a letter survives written by the curate on 24 Dec. 1765 recommending a disabled young woman as 'a most fit object for Mrs Bowes' Charity, which I am informed is given in Cloathing to a number of poor women yearly at this Season'.

take legal action against a constable who had 'vilely treated' a small
debtor by seizing his goods in an irregular manner.[183]

The conventions of paternalistic consideration (and the deference
that was expected in return) are familiar enough to any student of
English landed society in this period. They might be expected to
flourish in a context such as that described by some of Sir John
Clavering's men in 1712. Thomas Maxwell and Robert Cowing,
both of Swalwell and aged sixty-three and fifty-five respectively,
could recall two generations of involvement with the Claverings as
tenants and employees. William Story, also of Swalwell and aged
fifty-five, had been a household servant of the family for four years
and had worked as a wain man for 'old' Sir James Clavering,
'young' Sir James Clavering, and then Sir John over a period of
more than two decades. He may well have been one of those
servants granted 40s. each at 'old' Sir James's death.[184] Such
multigenerational involvement, however, was far from the norm in a
local society as mobile as that of industrial Whickham, and the
extension of paternalism into the sphere of industrial relations, and
in particular into the relationships between the coal-owners of the
parish and their pitmen, was by no means automatic.

This is not to suggest that the coalmasters were utterly indifferent
to the welfare of their work-people. During the trade stoppage of
1666, the hostmen of Newcastle, sensible of the fact that 'by reason
of the laying in of the works as aforesaid, the poore worke people
are like to come to extreme want', laid an assessment on every
member to raise funds which were to be paid 'unto the respective
Cole Owners to be by them distributed to the poore workpeople of
each respective Colliery . . . towards the reliefe of their present
necessities'.[185] In 1698 Charles Montague reflected uneasily that
'The loosing Limbs and Lives are the most Melancholy Circumstances of getting money', and two years later he instructed his
colliery manager: 'I desire no barbaryty nor hardship, nor
Extortion, nor Unnecessary hardship to be put upon the Poor Men,
but lett them live as well as any Labourers in their Condition
doe.'[186] His words echo strikingly the guiding rule regarding

---

[183] PRO E 134 11 & 12 Anne Hil. 37; DRO D/ST 262, 317, 323, 362.
[184] PRO E 134 11 & 12 Anne Hil. 37; DPD Probate, Will of Sir James Clavering
(1702).
[185] Dendy, *Hostmen*, 131.
[186] Ncle. UL MISC MSS 85, I. 522 (25 Oct. 1698); II. 714 (3 Dec. 1700).

landlord–tenant relationships set out in the instructions to the Council of the North in 1538 that 'the poor people be not oppressed, but that they may live after their sorts and qualities'.[187] Montague saw his responsibility as lying primarily in the payment of fair wages. 'It is my Designe and Desire to give as Good Wages for every thing as any Gentleman does, who pays well and has work well done,' he wrote in 1700, and three years earlier he had expressed contempt for coal-owners and overmen who cheated their workmen or paid them in kind (among whom, incidentally, he numbered old Sir James Clavering).[188]

A sense of obligation to look to the interests of their workmen, therefore, was not absent among at least some of the coal-owners in the later seventeenth century. None the less, it appears to have been somewhat limited in its form, and it may have been less an expression of traditional attitudes in the coalfield than a relatively recent development. The coal-owners of the earlier seventeenth century appear to have been somewhat remote from their workers. They were for the most part outsiders, geographically distanced from the men who won their coal. Work was subcontracted to overmen who were not supervised at the point of production. Pitmen were hired by the overmen, who seem to have taken no responsibility for them beyond the payment of wages. Moreover, the pitmen were an exceedingly mobile labour force, constantly changing in composition from season to season. Our sense of the situation is very much that described by a recent historian as one in which neither the traditional personalized relationship of landlord and tenant nor the quasi-familial, patriarchal relations of servant, apprentice, or journeyman and master craftsman prevailed. For most of the seventeenth century, the pitmen of Whickham, like those of the Forest of Kingswood, may have been 'only minimally involved in any relation of clientage with members of the governing class'.[189]

As the coal industry matured on Tyneside, however, and as it entered a new phase of development after 1690, this situation

---

[187] James, *Family, Lineage and Civil Society*, 38.

[188] Ncle. UL MISC MSS 85, II. 714 (3 Dec. 1700); I. 190–1 (8 Mar. 1696/7).

[189] James, *Family, Lineage and Civil Society*, 94. Malcolmson, 'A Set of Ungovernable People', 86. It was in the earlier 17th c. that the organization of production in Whickham, via subcontracting overmen, was most akin to the system that continued to prevail in 18th-c. Kingswood.

gradually changed. Two influences appear to have been vital in this process. First, there was the general passage of control of the production of coal from the merchants of Newcastle to the locally based owners of landed estates, a transition which, as we have seen, was largely accomplished in the second half of the seventeenth century.[190] Secondly, there was the gradual emergence of a stronger, more formal, and at the same time more personalized connection between the coal-owners and their pitmen. In order to appreciate the growth of this greater sense of identification between master and men, we must focus our attention on the developments that took place in managerial strategies and relationships in the coal industry at the turn of the seventeenth century, and in particular on a crucial institutional innovation—the emergence in the early eighteenth century of what became known as 'the pitman's bond'.

The pitman's bond, a legally enforceable conditional bond by which a man undertook to work in a particular colliery for a full mining season of almost one year, and the annual bonding days, those occasions on which pitmen came in to a colliery to hire on and subscribe the bond, were both firmly established features of life in the northern coalfield by the mid-eighteenth century. The origins of the practice of bonding, however, remain obscure, perhaps hopelessly obscure. Early historians of the coal industry tended to regard the bond as having its origins as far back as the fourteenth-century Statute of Labourers, and interpreted it as an application in the industrial context of the annual contracts between masters and servants-in-husbandry that were established at the hiring-fairs of rural England.[191]

There may, indeed, be a grain of truth in such speculations; hiring laws and customs in the world of agriculture could have provided both a context and a model for the development of the pitman's bond. But it would be entirely suppositious to assume that the bond itself had a continuous history stretching back for centuries. It is true that in seventeenth-century Lancashire some colliers signed annual bonds to work for a coalmaster, and that in Scotland a far more onerous form of lifetime servitude was imposed by law upon the colliers and salters of that kingdom in the early seventeenth

---

[190] See sect. 1.4. above.
[191] Boyd, *Coal Pits and Pitmen*, 13; R. Turner, 'The English Coal Industry in the Seventeenth and Eighteenth Centuries', *American Historical Review*, 28 (1921), 12; Ashton and Sykes, *Coal Industry*, 84.

century.[192] It is also true that on Tyneside an annual bonding system was employed industrially, among the salters of Shields who used the 'pan coal' rejected as unfit for sea-sale, and among the keelmen, though from what date such labour contracts were employed remains uncertain.[193]

A variety of precedents therefore existed. Nevertheless, the coal industry grew up outside the traditional framework of labour regulation, and the fact that, despite the abundant documentation of the early coal industry on Tyneside, 'we know nothing of the history of the bonding system during the seventeenth century' suggests that it is highly unlikely that its roots were deep.[194] Indeed, not only is there no direct evidence of the use of the pitman's bond on Tyneside before 1703, but there is also good evidence to the contrary. The Whickham evidence regarding the taking on and discharging of labour in the earlier seventeenth century makes it clear that overmen worked pits for absentee owners 'at their own charges', that they were individually responsible for the finding of labour, and that men appear to have been taken on and discharged in a fairly casual manner.[195]

All this makes it far more plausible to regard the pitman's bond as having been introduced in the northern coalfield in the early eighteenth century, and to locate that innovation within the context of a broader managerial revolution occasioned by the circumstances of the coal trade at the turn of the seventeenth century.[196] To recount those circumstances briefly: the late seventeenth and early eighteenth centuries witnessed a sluggish market for Tyneside coal. This was a period of 'fighting trade' for the coal-owners, among whom the internecine struggle for market share led to a search for

---

[192] Langton, *Geographical Change*, 68; Nef, ii. 165; Ashton and Sykes, *Coal Industry*, 70; Smout, *Scottish People*, 168–70. Conversely, the binding system was entirely unknown in the Cumbrian coalfield and in the lead mines of the northern Pennines: Beckett, *Coal and Tobacco*, 64; Hunt, *Lead Miners*, ch. 2.

[193] DRO Q/S OB 4, 256, provides a case from 1653 of a Shields salter hired 'for the time of one whole yeare' who had broken his contract and hired himself elsewhere; he was ordered to return to his first master. For the keelmen see Fewster, 'Keelmen', 24, 28.

[194] Nef, i. 400–1; ii. 165.   [195] See sect. 3.2 above.

[196] This view of the origin of the bond was hinted at by Nef, first suggested by H. Scott, 'The Miner's Bond in Northumberland and Durham', *Proceedings of the Society of Antiquaries of Newcastle-upon-Tyne*, 4th ser., 11 (1947), 56–8, and is supported by Cromar, 'Economic Power and Organization', 122, and Flinn, *Coal Industry*, 352.

new sources of high-quality coal, lateral extension of the coalfield, and heavy investment in colliery leases, new sinkings, wayleave agreements, and waggonway construction.[197] Owners anxious to defend or to expand their profit margins in this intensely competitive business environment were also increasingly concerned to extend closer supervision and control over the extractive process which had formerly been delegated to their overmen. By this means they hoped to secure a regularity of production that would keep coal flowing, and to facilitate that 'Quick Vend' which was 'the only article' in colliery. This concern in turn led to the emergence of the colliery viewer, a direct colliery manager employed to oversee the work of an entire colliery. It underlay the reduction of the overmen of particular pits to the status of salaried middle-management employees rather than independent subcontractors.[198] In all likelihood, it led also to the introduction of the pitmen's bond as a means of securing the regular services of those skilled pitmen who were so much in demand in an expanding coalfield.[199]

The earliest surviving example of a pitman's bond is dated 26 November 1703 and represents an agreement between the hewers, barrowmen, and boys of Benwell colliery and their employer the Hon. Charles Montague.[200] Benwell was a new, expensive, and highly productive undertaking. The involvement in its management of Charles Montague, who was both a lawyer and a prescient innovator in his colliery undertakings, not least at Gibside, inevitably raises the question of his possible role in the introduction of the bond. What, we might well wonder, lay behind his remark in December 1700, in discussing his workmen's wages, his willingness to pay well for work well done, and his disavowal of oppressive intentions, that 'No doubt the workmen will be against all Improvement. But it is the Part of a manager to persuade and Convince them'? Again, was he thinking of the bond sixteen months later when he issued an instruction to 'Gett a good stock beforehand att pitts; for then you will not depend on your Pitt-men in the Summer and make better bargains with them against next

---

[197] See sect. 1.4 above.
[198] See sect. 3.5 above.
[199] For a discussion of the competition for labour and the advantages of the bond, see Flinn, *Coal Industry*, 340, 343, 350, 353. Colls, *Pitmen*, 55, also stresses the importance of regular working in the 18th c. and its implications for unit costs.
[200] Welbourne, *Miner's Unions*, 13; Scott, 'Miner's Bond', 56; Flinn, *Coal Industry*, 352.

Winter'?[201] Of the presence of a single, highly calculative, business intelligence behind the introduction of the bond we can only speculate. None the less, it is clear that the use of the bond became more common as the eighteenth century advanced.

Few early bonds, in fact, survive. One is known to have existed for Gatherick colliery in 1706, though the original has been lost. Another, for collieries owned by Lady Windsor and Mr Simpson at Lanchester Fell, Harlaw, Pontop Pike, Harperly, and Lintz, has been tentatively dated to 1757 at the earliest. Extant examples become fairly numerous only after 1760.[202]

It would be a serious mistake however, to underplay the growing significance of the bond in the early eighteenth century. In the first place, further research on what is still a relatively neglected period of development in the coal industry will almost certainly yield fresh examples of early bonds; our own investigations of the Strathmore papers, for example, have produced two more to add to the list, one for West Hartford in November 1722 and another for Gibside/Northbanks from December 1741.[203] Again, there is incidental evidence of the use of bonds to secure the services of pitmen for a particular season. At Pittington in 1718 George Dickenson, 'then an unmarried person', was hired by the lessee of the colliery 'to serve for a whole year in working in the said colliery' for stated rates of pay and under agreed conditions, and received 'one shilling in earnest' at his signing on. 'Bond men' are referred to at one of William Cotesworth's collieries in 1722, and 'binding bonds' are alluded to in the Grand Allies' minutes of 1731. On 11 November 1726 the 'retained Hewers and Masters of Horses' agreed with the lessee of the collieries at Tanfield and Causey, 'by Article under Hand and Seal', to work for a full year 'at certain rates and under certain Penalties'. The journal of the viewer John Watson for 20 February 1748/9 contains the entry, 'This morning Bound Byermoor Men.'[204]

---

[201] Ncle. UL MISC MSS 85, II. 714 (3 Dec. 1700), 747 (11 Apr. 1702). He had earlier ruminated on the costs of labour, remarking ruefully in 1697, 'I know no reason my Collyers should not take the same pay others doe': I. 190/1 (8 Mar. 1696/7).

[202] Scott, 'Miner's Bond', 58–9; Colls, *Pitmen*, 45. Colls points out that the evidence of the stamp on the undated Windsor and Simpson bond could date it to any time between July 1757 and Dec. 1772.

[203] DRO D/ST 72/15, 344/22.

[204] DRO Q/S OB 8, 488–9; GPL Cotesworth MSS CP/2/31; NRO Armstrong Papers, 725 F 50, 2; DRO D/ST 298; NEIMME, Watson Collection, Shelf 8, no. 4, 28.

There can be no doubt that the pitman's bond was an increasingly familiar phenomenon in the second, third, and fourth decades of the eighteenth century. Its spread was almost certainly gradual and uneven; there is no mention of the bond in the *Compleat Collier* of 1708, for example, and its absence at Birtley colliery in the 1720s is indicated by the testimony of one Roger Gray, 'Pittman or Hewer'. Gray worked there for three separate periods between 1722 and 1728, being hired by an overman on each occasion and working for periods of only three, six, and five months respectively, with intervals of up to two years during which 'he left working in the said Colliery'.[205] It is possible also that the bond went through developmental stages that as yet remain obscure—on the question of what proportion of the work-force was actually bound, for example.[206] Doubtless the pitman's bond was a flexible instrument with an early history as complex as its later history in the nineteenth century. The fact remains that by the mid-eighteenth century the pitman's bond was very widespread, even general. It extended to the pitmen themselves, or to a significant proportion of them, a contractual agreement of a kind that had previously existed only between the owners of the collieries and their contracting overmen or 'undertakers'. Given the fact that in the same period it became usual also to bind waggonmen to their employer (whether or not they were also bound by the terms of their leases), it might justly be said that contractual 'binding' had become the characteristic form of relationship between the coal-owners and their men in the eighteenth-century industry.[207]

One aspect of this development was a degree of stabilization of the highly mobile colliery work-force. This was certainly so in the short term, over periods of up to one year. It may also have been so in the medium term; for the fact that from the outset men were bound usually in late autumn or early winter, before the end of the mining season and with the winter closure lying ahead, was some

---

[205] DRO D/ST 25/63. Nef, ii. 165, also observes that early 18th-c. pitmen on Wearside were often not year-long employees and that seasonal migrations took place between the Wearside sea-sale and south Durham land-sale pits. Cf. Scott, 'Miner's Bond', 57.

[206] Flinn suggests that only the most skilled grades were bound at some collieries even in the early 19th c.: Flinn, *Coal Industry*, 353.

[207] Lewis, *Early Wooden Railways*, 207. The chronology of this development is also uncertain. A bond of 1766 survives for the Bowes waggonmen in DRO D/ST 317.

incentive for men to sign on for a further year at the same colliery. As we have seen, the colliery work-force at Gibside/Northbanks remained highly mobile in the early eighteenth-century, but it may have been less so than previously.

Whether the pitmen stayed with their masters for one year or several, however, the bond also appears to have been an important contextual influence on the development of a stronger sense of direct connection, even of identification, between particular coal-owners and the men who won their coal. This can be detected in James Clavering's proprietorial choice of phrase when, in discussing his relationships with other coal-owners, he wrote of 'my pit men' and 'theres'.[208] It was also to become increasingly evident, as the eighteenth century advanced, in a developing industrial paternalism on the part of at least some of the coal-owners.

In 1725 the Northbanks paybills include sums paid as 'Charyty' to sick or injured pitmen; Francis Ramsay of the Bowes pit was maintained in this way for sixteen and Robert Byers of the Pee pit for fourteen consecutive weeks. Similarly, in 1728 a sum was paid for the burial of one John Watson's widow. That such acts of charity were not isolated incidents is demonstrated by entries in the minute books of the Grand Allies, which include not only individual notes of pensions granted to the widows of pitmen killed at work, but also the establishment in 1731 of a fund to which all the partnership collieries were expected to contribute 'towards relieving such of the pittmen and their families as shall happen Misfortunes'.[209] In the harsh winter of 1740, when the Tyne was frozen and the coal trade at a standstill, efforts were made to keep the waggonways clear of snow as a means not only of preparing for the reopening of the trade but also of keeping in employment 'great Numbers of poor People', with the result, it was reported, that 'the labouring People in this Neighbourhood have the Happiness to enjoy the Blessings of Plenty'.[210] Again, during the scarce months of the spring of 1757 the coal-owners of the Tyne banded together to arrange for the import of 50,000 bushels of rye 'for the Support of the Worke People employed in their Works'. At Northbanks specifically, the viewer John Leaton reported to George Bowes that after consultation with other agents it had been agreed 'to give the

---

[208] Dickinson, *Clavering Correspondence*, 226.
[209] DRO D/ST 298, 47/32; NRO Armstrong Papers, 725 F 50, 2, 7.
[210] *Newcastle Courant*, 12 Jan. and 19 Jan. 1740; *Newcastle Journal*, 26 Jan. 1740.

Pittmen six pence per week each man and to all his famyly four pence per week each on account of the dearness of meal and corne'.[211] Then there were the medical expenses paid for injured pitmen, the fire coal sold to them cheaply, and myriad minor acts of patronage and assistance to pitmen and their families, such as the efforts made to find an 'easy Employ' in a fire-coal pit at Northbanks for the aged and decayed pitman Ralph Allen.[212]

Nor were relief and assistance the only forms in which industrial paternalism found expression, although they are the most visible in our records. There were the treats too: the 'Coaling-Money' given the sinkers for drink when a shaft was complete; the drinking that accompanied the beginning of production, which might cost 'sometimes 5 to 10 Guineas or more according to the Generosity of the Owner'; the 'Punch Waggon' lined with tin and filled with punch which celebrated the opening of a waggonway (like that which James Clavering saw come down the Bucksnook Way 'in triumph' in 1712, accompanied by a procession of dignitaries and 'fiddlers and pipers intermixt with the whole company' before the punch was 'demolished att Steath'); the plate costing three guineas which John Thomlinson saw 'run for by wain horses or cart horses' at Whickham on 26 July 1717 'for the encouragement of the coal-pittmen'.[213]

In the course of the early eighteenth century, then, industrial paternalism became a prominent feature of the social relations of the coalfield, and one that most certainly made its mark in the lives of many of the inhabitants of Whickham. Nor indeed were such relationships confined to the coal-owners and their workers; for, although industrial paternalism in Whickham's collieries was in large part an application in a different context of the paternalistic manner of the landed estate, it is tempting to speculate that it also

---

[211] *Newcastle Courant*, 7 May 1757; *Newcastle Journal*, 7 May 1757. For the success of the scheme, the arrival of 30,000–40,000 bushels at Newcastle, and its sale 'at a low rate to their Workemen', see *Newcastle Journal*, 6 Aug. 1757. Announcing the Northbanks scheme to Mr Bowes, Leaton grumbled that it was 'a very great tax upon the trade' and that 'it might have been done for less, the sixpence per week for a man is enough, but 4 per week each child is too much': DRO D/ST 322. For the foundation of 'a Society for the Relief of the Industrious Poor' at Durham in January 1757 and its activities on Wearside, see *Newcastle Courant*, 15 Jan.1 757 and *Newcastle Journal*, 5 Feb. 1757.

[212] DRO D/ST 277, 235, 262; NRO Armstrong Papers, 725 F49, 12.

[213] *Compleat Collier*, 31 54–5; Lewis, *Early Wooden Railways*, 225; Ncle. UL MISC MSS 10, 8 June 1712; Hodgson, 'John Thomlinson', 67.

owed something to the example of Sir Ambrose Crowley's ironworks at Winlaton and Swalwell.

Crowley, who has been described as 'one of the formative characters in the evolution of modern industrial society', recognized a paternalistic duty to what he called 'my people' and set about the establishment of conditions that 'would make them quiet and easy amongst themselves and a happy and flourishing people amongst their neighbours'.[214] Accordingly, he and his successors housed them in factory villages, built a school and a chapel for them, employed a chaplain, schoolmasters, and after 1724 a doctor, set up a 'Court of Arbitrators' to hear their grievances and settle their disputes, and ran a private poor relief scheme which by 1749, if not earlier, covered all his employees and meant that none of them were chargeable to the parish of Whickham.[215]

At the same time, in his anxiety to 'have service answerable to the wages I pay', Crowley imposed upon them a rigorous code of labour discipline designed to ensure that his workers showed 'a due regard in doing their duty by labouring to do their utmost in the lawful promoting my interest and answer the end of their being paid'.[216] Penalties were laid down to discourage his workers from brawling, creating disturbances, or raising a 'tumult or mobb', drunkenness, dawdling, betting, swearing, smoking, and 'easing themselves' anywhere other than at appointed places. A Monitor was appointed to 'create an account of time' and ensure that his clerks and officials gave eighty hours a week of 'neat service after all deductions for being at taverns, alehouses, coffee houses, breakfast, dinner, playing, sleeping, smoaking, singing, reading of news history, quarrelling, contention, disputes or anything else foreign to my business'. Each man was to have a time paper recording his movements which was to be used in calculating his pay by the hour. In addition, informers were encouraged 'to discover fraud, vice, negligence and treachery' among his clerks.[217]

Crowley's 'Laws', the collected orders of this benevolently despotic 'man of iron', with their 'characteristic combination of high moral tone and rigorous authority', have been described as embodying a 'comprehensive conception of an industrial society'; and so indeed they do.[218] Crowley was tackling that 'central

---

[214] Flinn, *Men of Iron*, 219, 255.
[215] Ibid. 220–32; Bourn, *Whickham*, 94.   [216] Flinn, *Law Book*, 88–9.
[217] Ibid. 5 ff., 150–1, 89 ff., 26 ff.   [218] Ibid. pp. v, xv.

management problem of the industrial revolution, requiring the fiercest wrench from the past'—the 'rational' and methodical management of labour. He pursued that objective in the context of a comprehensive welfare system which anticipated the industrial paternalism of some nineteenth-century factories.[219] In the process, he created among his workers a 'society' that was both part of and distinct from the parishes of Ryton and Whickham whose borders his works straddled. The pensioners of the works relief scheme wore on their left sleeves not the initial letter of their parish, but a badge bearing the legend 'Crowley's Poor', and by 1740 his men described themselves and were 'commonly distinguished by the name of Crowley's crew'.[220]

Crowley's remarkable example may or may not have influenced the gentlemen coal-owners who supplied his factories' fuel. But they faced the same managerial problems, and something of the same pattern of development can be seen in their relations with their own work-people. Industrial paternalism had come to the northern coalfield, where it was long to exert its influence;[221] and as in the Crowley factory, it both expressed a conservative sense of patriarchal social obligation and served the purpose of legitimizing the enhanced disciplinary authority of management.

Mrs Montagu of Denton expressed the situation perfectly in describing her distribution of a piece of meat to each of the eighty families employed in her colliery on the occasion of her husband's death and her feasting of their children in her courtyard 'on rice pudding and boiled beef'. She was conscious of her obligations to what she called 'my colliery people', 'my black friends', and she intended also to 'bestow some apparel' on the needy and to establish a spinning school for her pitmen's daughters if profits held up. Furthermore, as with Charles Montague three-quarters of a century earlier, attention to the workmen's well-being calmed her personal misgivings: 'I cannot yet reconcile myself to seeing my fellow creatures descend into the dark regions of the earth; tho' to my great comfort, I hear them singing in the pits.' It was also cost-effective: 'It is very pleasant to see how the poor things cram

---

[219] S. Pollard, *The Genesis of Modern Management: A Study of the Industrial Revolution in Great Britain* (London, 1965), 160. Cf. E. P. Thompson, 'Time, Work-Discipline and Industrial Capitalism', *Past and Present*, 38 (1967), 81–2; Flinn, *Men of Iron*, 219.

[220] Bourn, *Whickham*, 95; TWA Keelmen's Papers 394/51.

[221] See e.g. Flinn, *Coal Industry*, 424–6; Buxton, *British Coal Industry*, 133.

themselves, and the expense is not great. We buy rice cheap, and skimmed milk and coarse beef serve the occasion.' Finally, it brought certain tangible results from a managerial perspective: 'Some benefits of this sort and a general kind behaviour gives to the coal owner, as well as to them, a good deal of advantage. Our pitmen are afraid of being turned off, and that fear keeps an order and regularity amongst them that is very uncommon.'[222]

The civil parish, and the paternalism of the gentry and of industrial management, thus served to preserve Whickham's institutional identity, to define particular geographical, social, and industrial subgroups within the parish, and to establish the character of relationships between rich and poor, master and man. One further influence, however, was also at work, not only in sustaining a sense of parochial identity but also in underpinning the conventional structure of values and of social authority in Whickham: the ministrations of the parochial clergy.

By the mid-seventeenth century, it can be said with some confidence that the parish church could scarcely have contained half of Whickham's growing population, had they chosen to attend it at one time.[223] Nevertheless, the Church of England appears to have long maintained an effective spiritual and ideological monopoly in the parish. Bishop Cosin's visitation of 1662 found only a handful of 'popish recusant' households in the parish, headed by Sir William Blakiston and Mr Henry Liddell, one Anabaptist, and a dozen 'seperatists', most of whom were to conform themselves within a year.[224] Thereafter the conservative tone of the religious life of the parish seems to be well represented by the preamble to the will of the rector Thomas Mason in 1681, in which he declared himself proudly 'in all things Conformable to the Rites, discipline and doctrine of the Church of England'.[225]

In the early years of the eighteenth century, the influx of Crowley

[222] Quoted in Hammond and Hammond, *The Skilled Labourer*, 18–19.

[223] Bourn, *Whickham*, 6, states that in 1862 the church had pews to seat 549 people.

[224] DPD DR II/3, fo. 103. For a further presentment of 10 Catholics and dissenters in 1685 'for not coming to ye publick Assembly Prayers and Service of ye Church', see DPD Prior's Kitchen, 'Archdeacon of Durham Act Book 1685–1705', fo. 8.

[225] DPD Probate, Will of Thomas Mason (1681). Hodgson, 'Demographic Trends', 8–10, suggests that Durham had fewer nonconformists than any other English county save Westmorland.

workers into the area apparently threatened to enhance the tiny dissenting presence, but this was forestalled by the erection of a chapel for Crowley's crew at Winlaton in 1705. Robert Thomlinson, the future rector of Whickham, hastened to preach the opening sermon there without awaiting the Bishop's consent, despite the misgivings of fastidious colleagues, since 'it was necessary they should preach before the bishop's answer could be gott—for they would have a meeting-teacher next sunday in town, and the sacrament at which time they would tie by oaths and covenants, and by that means they would lose perhaps 200 souls'. Thereafter the Crowley chapel and most of the work-force were solidly Anglican, the chaplain being enjoined by Crowley's 'Laws' to read common prayer twice every Sunday and on Wednesdays, Fridays, and holy days, to preach twice every Sunday and on other specified occasions, to visit the sick, 'rebuke vice and promote virtue', 'see that his flock neither wanteth spirituall nor temporall assistants', and 'forbear frequenting alehouses or att least not to make any considerable stay there'.[226] As for the parish of Whickham, as late as 1736 Bishop Chandler's survey found that, of seven hundred families, only three were papists, seventeen Presbyterians, and one Quaker in religious affiliation.[227]

The early 1740s found Robert Thomlinson anxiously staving off threats to this situation, occasioned first by an increase in dissenters in Swalwell and second by the early visits of John and Charles Wesley. In November 1740 he wrote to Mr Crowley's London agent seeking Crowley's support in quashing 'the Design of the Dessenters to set up a Conventicle in Swalwell' and erect a meeting house. One of the principal figures involved was Crowley's chief clerk at the Swalwell factory, and Thomlinson roundly denounced his plan 'to draw my People into the separation' and 'to set up a way of worship at Swalwell in opposition to that of his Masters'. Fearing that the dissenters would 'awe and influence', 'delude and entice', 'triumph and insult', and that 'a change in Religion may be introduced' among the Crowley workmen, he urged Crowley to intervene, 'for as his Agent depends upon his pleasure, so the fate of this scheme must depend upon his will'. And so it did, for on receipt

---

[226] Flinn, *Men of Iron*, 224; Hodgson, 'John Thomlinson', 134; Flinn, *Law Book*, 162 ff. Of 617 Winlaton families in 1788, only 56 were Church of Scotland, 3 Baptist, and 2 'Independent' in religion.
[227] DPD 'Bishop Chandler's Parochial Remarks on his Visitation'.

of a letter from his employer the chief clerk determined to withdraw his support for the plan and to 'go to Newcastle every Sunday, as he hath hitherto done'.[228]

Almost exactly two years later, Thomlinson was anxiously combating the influence of the Wesleys and 'one Williams', another Methodist preacher who had 'set my Parishioners a mading'. He had read John Wesley's sermons and journals and was full of contempt for 'these Enthusiasts'—'they all abound with crude incoherent stuff in their sermons and yet pretend to inspiration'. This time, however, he had no powerful ally on whom to call, though he was glad that Mr Bowes, who had gone to hear Charles Wesley out of curiosity, had found him 'a most nonsensical fellow'. He was equally happy to report to the Archdeacon of Northumberland that, 'by proper antidote against his poison', John Wesley's first visit to Whickham had 'done us little harm only carried of 3 or 4 of the meanest of our people', who had joined a Methodist society in Newcastle. Later visits appear to have increased Methodist strength, but by the end of December 1742 Thomlinson found that 'by the method that was taken their number is now dwindled to about 40—half of which are silly women and most of the rest mean ignorant men'.[229]

Thomlinson would perhaps have been cheered had he known that John Wesley had found his listeners in Whickham on his first visit 'exceeding quiet', self-satisfied, unmoved by his 'strong rough words', and kept awake only by the cold. He regarded them as 'dead, senseless, unaffected' even by the generous standards of nearby Tanfield, while at Swalwell he 'observed none that seemed to be much convinced: only stunned as if cut in the head'.[230]

A placid conformity seems indeed to have characterized much of the religious life of the parish. The wills of the parishioners continued to contain formal bequests of their souls well into the eighteenth century, but these rarely vibrate with individual conviction. The increasingly formulaic nature of such clauses is nicely indicated by the will of Edward Snowball, which commenced with the bequest of his soul 'into the hands of Almighty God hoping

[228] NRO ZAN M13/C7, 18 Nov. and 9 Dec. 1740.

[229] Ibid. 19 Oct., 6 Nov., and 23 Dec. 1742. The nature of 'the method that was taken' remains obscure.

[230] *The Journal of the Rev. John Wesley*, Everyman edn., 4 vols. (London, n.d.), i. 405 (26 Nov. and 28 Nov. 1742); 408 (28 Dec. 1742).

through the meritts, Death and passion of my Savior J C *etc*'.[231] By the 1720s, in fact, a substantial proportion of wills no longer contained a 'soul clause', and ten years later it was rare for them to do so. The last will and testament had become a secular affair. Dr Thomlinson, who was a keen supporter of the SPCK, was profoundly disappointed with the failure of his efforts 'to dispose and excite my parishioners to a liberal contribution', and found them unwilling to give much despite the reading out of letters of support from the King, the Archbishop of York, and the Bishop of Durham, two sermons on the subject of charity, and his own generous example.[232] The general tone of religious commitment in conformist Whickham may have been akin to that evidenced in old Sir James Clavering's complacent response to Ambrose Barnes when the latter spoke to him 'seriously and closely . . . concerning a life to come, and what a call old age is to prepare for it': '"Ay, cousin Barnes", sais Sir J., "you say true. I hope I shall be saved, for I never make visits on Sundayes, but keep within doors and read Dugdale's Baronage of England." '[233]

Enthusiasm seems to have been the prerogative of the dissenters, notably the Presbyterians of Swalwell, who eventually succeeded in their efforts to open a meeting-house in 1750 and thereafter extended support to John Wesley on his later visits to the area.[234] Even those few wills that display individual piety tend to come from this source. George Burrow, a smith, left money to a dissenting meeting in Newcastle. John Thompson, a Swalwell innkeeper, whose extraordinary will of 1744 consists of an impassioned twenty-one-line dedication of his soul followed by a four-line bequest of all his goods to his wife, was another man of deep religious conviction. Among his witnesses were Peter Armstrong, a former Crowley clerk, and John Hornsby, another Crowley clerk, who had endeavoured to sustain the plan for a meeting-house in Swalwell in 1740 despite his master's disapproval. Almost certainly, Thompson was a dissenter.[235]

---

[231] DPD Probate, Will of Edward Snowball (1736).

[232] NRO ZAN M13/C7, 29 June 1742.

[233] W. H. D. Longstaffe (ed.), *Memoirs of the Life of Mr Ambrose Barnes*, Surtees Soc. no. 50 (Durham, 1866), 52.

[234] Bourn, *Whickham*, 108. A minister was maintained from 1752. The old Presbyterian chapel could seat 300; *Wesley's Journal*, ii. 460–1.

[235] DPD Probate, Wills of George Burrow (1734), John Thompson (1744); NRO ZAN M13/C7, 9 Dec. 1740.

As for the broader industrial population of the parish, we do not know how assiduous they were in the performance of their religious duties beyond the baptisms of their children, their weddings, and the burial of their dead. Nor can we say how great a part religious values played in their lives. Edward Chicken took it for granted in *The Collier's Wedding* that pitmen 'came to church but very rare', and rested on the sabbath day 'from evry thing but drink and play'. He expected his readers to smile in recognition when he described colliers in church behaving 'as in a common hall', for 'some perhaps that were threescore / Was never twice in church before'.[236] Such was the public image of the miners, and perhaps the most significant thing about it was that at this point in the eighteenth century it was a matter for amusement rather than pious outrage. It was so even at the dinner table of Dr Thomlinson; when one of his guests observed in 1717 that in France Protestants could not be buried in consecrated ground 'but Moliere said nine foot deep was not Christian ground', a wag remarked, 'So, . . . colliers might sware etc., they were not on Christian ground.'[237]

Nevertheless, it would be unwise to underestimate either the cultural influence of the Church in the eighteenth-century coalfield or the role of the clergy in parish society. In time Wesley found hearers enough among the pitmen of Tyneside. They flocked to hear him on Gateshead Fell in April 1765 'from all parts . . . such a thirst have they after the good word'.[238] And among the labouring poor of Whickham there were those listed in 1764 who could be described as 'religious', like William Wigham and his wife, 'both old, very honest, industrious and religious, but very poor', while many more were at least 'sober, industrious'. Who, we might wonder, were the 'meanest of our people', 'silly women' and 'mean ignorant men' described by Dr Thomlinson as responsive to the Methodist incursion of 1742?[239]

Again, there was more to the influence of the church than formal attendance at services or overt piety. It could be felt also in the background assumptions of personal conduct and in tacit definitions of the world. Nor were the ministrations of the clergy

[236] Chicken, *Collier's Wedding*, 4, 18.
[237] Hodgson, 'John Thomlinson', 91.
[238] *Wesley's Journal*, iii. 211.
[239] DRO D/ST 336/7. In 1793 the Methodists and Dissenters of Whickham were again dismissively described as 'all of low Ranke': DPD DR XVII/1.

confined to the walls of the church. Some at least of the curates of Whickham were pastorally active among the work-people of the parish. Robert Thomlinson wrote of 'the greatness of the cure' and the need for a prospective curate to have 'a disposition to visit the sick which are commonly numerous'. He spoke warmly of Edmund Lodge, formerly chaplain to the Crowley works, who died of pneumonia exacerbated by preaching twice one Sunday at Whickham and Winlaton 'with a cold upon him'. John Bouche was said to lack a university degree, but to be an effective pastor, 'a mighty worthy sober and Good Man'.[240] The letters signed by curates of Whickham recommending deserving cases to the consideration or charity of the gentry also say much for the continuing role of these men, and of the church which they represented, in the lives of those placed in their care.[241]

Those who did come into direct contact with the church, especially the children, were left in no doubt as to the nature not only of their religious, but also of their social duties. Crowley's 'Laws' laid down that his workmen's children were to be taught the catechism of the Church of England and that their teacher was 'to take care to make his scholars show due respect to their superiors'. Scholars in the parochial free school were likewise to be instructed in the Bible, the Prayer Book, the catechism, and the *Whole Duty of Man*. Copies of the latter work, together with large numbers of other tracts lying 'undespos'd' in his study, were mentioned in Dr Thomlinson's draft will with the intention that they be distributed in the parish 'among the poorer Sort that can read', and a similar evangelical intention must have underlain the distribution twenty years later of Bishop Synge's *Essay Towards Making the Knowledge of Religion easy To the meanest Capacity*. It was printed in 'Large Letter *for the Curious, Aged and such as cannot use a smaller Print*'. Those who read it would have learned the basic tenets of the faith 'in very plain language and brought within the Compass of one Hour's reading' and their family duties. In addition, they were counselled 'to be patient and contented in all Estates and Conditions of Life', to submit to providence, and to 'behave themselves not

---

[240] NRO ZAN M13/C7, 18 Nov. 1740, 19 Oct. 1742; DPD DR ii 'Boxes of Visitation Papers (fragments) 1668–1770', Letter of William Williamson, rector, 26 Apr. 1762.

[241] e.g. DPD Probate, Letter with will of Adam Rochester (1686); DRO D/ST 323, 317.

only with Faithfulness and Diligence but also with Obedience and Respect' towards their masters and with 'Honour and Reverence ... Submission and Obedience' towards their rulers.[242] All this must be counted as part of the pervasive influence of an institution that retained centrality in the life of the parish. Colliers might come to church 'but very rare', but the local society in which they dwelt was far from being 'unchurched'.

6. DEPENDENCE AND INDEPENDENCE, RIOT AND NEGOTIATION

Clearly, industrial Whickham was not a society lacking in structure or cohesiveness, and the lives of its inhabitants can hardly be said to have lain outside the controlling influences of the gentry, the clergy, and the officers of the parish. If it can reasonably be described, by the later seventeenth century, as an industrial class society in its essential structures, it was none the less one in which social relations were very largely conducted in what might appear to be traditional forms. Whickham was firmly administered by a vestry of gentlemen and criss-crossed by vertically aligned ties of paternalism and deference. The economic relationship of capital and labour had not been stripped of personalized connections between employers and employees, and the force of such relationships was still underpinned by an ideology of subordination.

This was a context in which the old dialectic of deference could work well enough, synthesizing a simultaneous awareness of social differentiation from, and personal identification with, one's social superiors into an acceptance of subordination.[243] And so, no doubt, it did, often enough. Indeed, this might look like an essentially stable socioeconomic environment, successfully adapted to contain the conflicts of interest unleashed by economic and social change, a topography of social relations which might appear 'as imposing and established as the hills'.[244]

[242] Flinn, *Law Book*, 155; NRO ZAN M13/C7, Letter of 28 Apr. 1741, Will following letter of 7 Aug. 1738; Synge, *Essay*, v, 25, 26. See also n. 83 above.
[243] H. Newby, *The Deferential Worker* (London, 1977), ch. 8.
[244] Quoting R. Porter, *English Society in the Eighteenth Century* (London, 1982), 35.

But of course it was not; for there was another side to the story. Not all inhabitants of Whickham were equally involved, let alone enveloped, in the web of social and ideological bonds described above. Areas of independence existed within the social structure. The rector of Whickham might be able to scotch the initial attempt of the dissenters of Swalwell to build a meeting house; but he could not do so indefinitely. There were men prepared to push ahead. Nor could he prevent his own churchwarden (a partial conformist 'who never comes to the sacrament') from repeatedly entertaining the Wesleys on their visits to the area.[245] A tenant-farmer waggonman might be bound by his lease to lead his landlord's coal when the latter required it. Yet not all waggonmen were tenants, and not all tenants were equally subservient to their landlords' will. Some could lead when and for whom they chose, or would insist upon terms that satisfied their own interests—as did some of the Clavering waggonmen in 1710 and again in 1713, leaving their employers fuming at their ingratitude, 'impudence', 'baseness', and 'petty treason'.[246]

There were also alternative definitions of the social situation to those offered by the catechism, the *Whole Duty of Man*, or Bishop Synge. These were sometimes overtly political and ideological. Whickham lay close enough to Newcastle, a city in the vanguard of English urban development with a vigorous political life and an active local press in the early eighteenth century. It was certainly not insulated from the ideological currents of the day. James Clavering, an enthusiastic Whig, was a regular reader of the *Spectator*, the *Evening Post*, the *Postman*, and the *Flying Post*, as well as pamphlets received from his London agent. He was devoted to the maintenance of English 'religion, laws and liberty' and expressed 'an utter aversion to popery and arbitrary power'. A generation later Mr Arthur, first dissenting minister at Swalwell, was described as 'a real Friend and strenuous Asserter of the Cause of Liberty'. Such ideas were certainly current in the parish in the first half of the eighteenth century—Henry Liddell wrote approvingly that Whickham was 'much exalted above the rest of its

[245] NRO ZAN M13/C7, 23 Dec. 1742. In the later 1740s and afterwards John Wesley attracted large congregations on his visits (especially in Swalwell and Winlaton): *Wesley's Journal*, i. 546; ii. 13, 14, 227, 381, 460–1; iii. 61, 211.
[246] Dickinson, *Clavering Correspondence*, 102; Ncle. UL MISC MSS 10, 6 Feb. 1712/13.

neighbourhood' in the political enlightenment of its leading inhabitants, applauding the zeal of those 'true patriots' and 'publick spiritts'—and they continued to receive the endorsement of authority. By 1760 the landscape was dignified by George Bowes's column and his gilded statue of 'British Liberty'.[247]

Moreover, there was also in industrial Tyneside a vernacular tradition with which such elements of the libertarian ideology of the Augustan age could interact. The truculent independence and hostility to arbitrary dealings which had animated the copyholders of Whickham in the early seventeenth century reflected values that had lost none of their vitality despite changing circumstances. Thomas Bewick was brought up in the 1750s to respect 'bold, independent and honest men', and he found examples enough of the type among the cottagers and 'labouring men' of his neighbourhood, several of them pitmen. These people, he recalled, 'held the neighbouring gentry in the greatest estimation and respect', but they also preserved 'an honest and independent character', held views of their own, sought to avoid 'being ever numbered with the parish poor', and could exhibit in most singular fashion what Bewick regarded as 'the force of innate natural pride'.[248] Bewick's account of the temper of the labouring men of his boyhood might be dismissed as the nostalgic reminiscence of an aged radical. Yet he provided detailed individual examples to support his case, including some of the earliest pen-portraits of individual pitmen that survive to us; and the existence of the pride and independent spirit of which he wrote can be effectively documented in other ways.

There were alternative influences, therefore, upon the attitudes and demeanour of the people of industrial Tyneside in general, and of Whickham in particular, to paternalism, deference, an ideology of submissiveness propagated by the established church, and the carrots and sticks of the civil parish. The very existence of such alternative cultural resources could render the dialectic of deference vulnerable. The tranquillity of social relations, however, depended not simply on attitudes, but on *power*. Independence of spirit would avail little without a complementary capacity to dispute the terms of subordination.

This truism is amply demonstrated in the developing Poor Law

---

[247] Ibid. 12 Aug. 1712, 2 Sept. 1712, and *passim*; *Newcastle Courant*, 20 Sept. 1760; Ellis, *Letters of Henry Liddell*, 148–9, 170.

[248] Bewick, *Memoir*, 30, 31, 35.

policy of Whickham's 'Gentlemen of the Vestry' and the treatment eventually meted out to the least powerful group among the parishioners, the dependent poor. Continued industrial development and the growth of the wage-dependent sector of the population inevitably created in Whickham an increase in the amount of life-cycle-related poverty which caused labouring families to become 'chargeable to the parish', above all in widowhood and old age. In fact, between the later 1670s and the early 1740s, the numbers of poor in receipt of regular 'allowances' almost trebled and the costs to the parish rose proportionately.[249] To this extent, Whickham participated in a trend towards mounting Poor Law expenditure which has beeen documented elsewhere in England and has been termed the 'growth of social welfare'.[250]

In Whickham, however, this process might be better described as a growing crisis of dependency. For while the numbers of the poor and the costs of their relief escalated, in Whickham (unlike some other parishes) the concentration of property ownership was such that the population of ratepayers remained fairly stable. Nor was the increased rate burden that they bore significantly relieved by the charities of the parish, which tended to disburse their funds not upon the core of regular paupers but more broadly throughout the population of work-people. Most of the ratepayers were probably well able to afford the sums at which they were assessed, though they had never been well disposed towards the prospect of an enhanced charge. Their growing dissatisfaction was perhaps further influenced by the time and trouble involved in administering an expanding relief system. Whatever the case, in 1750 a reappraisal of parish relief led to a decision by the vestry to establish a workhouse in Swalwell. Within a year it had been built, the position of workhouse master had been advertised and filled, and the core of the indigent population had been 'removed' to it.[251]

---

[249] DRO EP/Wh 18, EP/Wh 22, *passim*.

[250] Wales, 'Poverty, Poor Relief and the Life-Cycle', 354 ff.; Newman Brown, 'Poor Relief and Family Situation', 409–11; Slack, *Poverty and Policy*, ch. 8, esp. 173–82.

[251] DRO EP/Wh 19, 20, 22, 38; D/ST 243 (letter of Nicholas Walton to John Leaton, 11 Feb. 1751, informing him of the decision 'to remove the Poor tomorrow morning'). For the development of workhouse schemes as a cheaper and more efficient means of poor relief, see Slack, *Poverty and Policy*, 193 ff. Knatchbull's Act of 1723 permitted the union of parishes for the purpose of establishing workhouses and the refusal of relief to those unwilling to enter them.

The initial management system of the workhouse is obscure, beyond the fact that locks were purchased 'for keeping the Men and Women in their Own appartments'. It is clear that not every pauper had been removed to Swalwell, for the overseers for each quarter still made payments to certain 'out poor'. These, however, were much reduced in number, and the obligations of the overseers were principally discharged by payments to the workhouse master.[252] In 1756, with the advent of a new master, the vestry determined to pay him a fixed weekly sum for the maintenance of each 'Poor Person' and also to defray the costs of funerals (the clothing of the dead being delivered to the master for re-use 'as new Objects shall come into the House and require the same'). He in return undertook 'the comfortable support of the Poor' and was allowed (in lieu of salary) the crop of the garden and all profits accruing from the labour of the inmates in the 'Manufactory'. Provision was also made for the discharge of such inmates as 'may become capable of otherwise earning their bread'.[253]

Five years later, however, the system was drastically revised and extended. In May 1761 it was agreed with two Whickham weavers, Peter and John Rippon, that they would not only maintain the poor in the workhouse with 'Meat, Drinke and all other Things necessary', but would also undertake 'from Time to Time [to] contract or agree with all or any of the Poor Persons who are chargeable or that hereafter may become chargeable to the said Parish for such Weekly or other allowance to the said Poor Persons as shall be agreed upon for their support', and to maintain all those 'Poor Persons commonly called Out Poor . . . who shall not be thought Proper objects of Charity fitt to be maintained in the said Workhouse'. In addition the Rippons were to pay for pauper funerals and to be responsible for all removals to and from the parish. In effect, the entire responsibility for poor relief in Whickham had been farmed out to the two men, 'It being the Intent and Meaning of this Agreement . . . that neither the Churchwardens and Overseers of the Poor nor their successors shall . . . be put to any Expense of Maintaining the Poor of the said Parish or any other expense relating thereto' except a fixed weekly payment and an end-of-year bonus to the Rippons if they performed their contract well.

[252] DRO EP/Wh 19, disbursements 1751–6, *passim*.
[253] Ibid. 118–20. It is clear that candidates for the master's place were required to put forward a 'proposal'. The vestry considered several.

Furthermore, the Rippons were to enjoy 'the advantage of the Work, Labour and Service of the said Poor Persons who now are or that may hereafter be in the said Workhouse or chargeable to the said Parish'.[254]

This agreement admirably expressed the intentions of the vestry, and they attempted thereafter to adhere to its basic principles as a means of pegging the costs of poor relief. Identical contracts were entered into with Thomas Dobson, a joiner, in 1762 and 1763, and the overseers' accounts for those years consist largely of payments to the workhouse master. The problem of the burden of the 'out poor', however, soon reasserted itself, for Dobson lost money, and in 1764 and 1765 new agreements with John Rippon confined his duties to running the workhouse, payments to the out poor or 'extra poor' reappearing in the annual overseers' accounts. By 1768 their needs were once more getting out of hand, and in that year the vestry adopted another tactic and ordered 'that no person should be relieved out of the Workhouse except such as shall be Sick or thought by the Vestry not proper to be sent to the said Workhouse'. Thereafter the overseers' accounts contain few regular pensioners, and those who received such payments were specifically identified as 'sick' or otherwise 'needfull'. The problem of reducing the burden of the out poor had been solved, and in 1774 it was possible to reintroduce the total delegation of poor relief to contractors on the model of 1761, a policy described in the vestry minute as an agreement 'to lett the Maintenance of the Poor'.[255]

All this, of course, was done in the interests of economy and efficient resource management in the face of a mounting problem of dependency. But it also represented at best an abdication of direct personal responsibility for the parish poor on the part of the

[254] DRO EP/Wh 19, 168–70.

[255] ibid. 182–4, 297 [then 2nd pagination] 206, 216, 252, 328, 330, and annual accounts *passim*. The subsequent overseers' accounts for 1787–1826 (EP/Wh 20) consist largely of payments to the workhouse master, who presumably maintained the inmates of the workhouse and dealt directly with the 'out poor'. The 'letting' of poor relief clearly continued. From the 1780s expenditure increased in money terms, but in 1803 the numbers maintained in the workhouse (20) and the adults maintained outside (118), more than half of whom were described as being aged over 60 or otherwise disabled by injury or infirmity, totalled little more than those who had been regularly relieved in 1743. (*Abstract of the Answers and Returns Made pursuant to an Act, passed in the 43rd Year of His Majesty King George III*, 137–8). From the perspective of the vestry, the whole experiment had proved a modest success in pegging levels of dependency on the parish.

officers, who confined themselves increasingly to the levying of the rate and the making of recommendations to the workhouse masters. At worst, it was a hard-faced determination to restrict narrowly the recognition of need. Given the existence of such institutionalized parsimony, it is scarcely to be wondered at that there were so many candidates for Mrs Bowes's charity. Nor is it surprising that the system of relief came to alienate some of the poor profoundly, for it had become a threat to what little independence they retained and to their closest personal ties.

That this is no supposition can be evidenced from the experience of four women who applied to the workhouse master for relief in 1775. Ann Pattison was simply removed to Tanfield, 'having no proper claim upon this parish'. The wife of John Grey was more fortunate; she was offered a choice between workhouse places for herself and her husband (which meant separation), or relief during her present illness but no further allowance thereafter. Her decision is not recorded. Ann Brown, a weaver's wife, 'refused to go into the said House, and chose to accept Six Pence per week instead thereof she having Two Children the one eight and the other Three years of Age'. Presumably she preferred to stay with her family and manage on this pittance (less than a day's wage for a labourer), for the prospect before her was similar to that of an unnamed 'poor woman at Ferryhill with several children'. The latter was offered no out-relief, but allegedly was told 'That she would be received into the Workhouse and taken care of and that her Children should be Bound out or put into reputable Families'. She replied, 'What, would you sell my Children?' Of course, she misunderstood the purpose intended. But then again, perhaps she understood the spirit of what was intended only too well.[256]

Whatever the effect of the revised system of poor relief on the attitudes of the poor and on their perceptions of their 'betters' among the parish officers, they were in no position to dispute the terms of their subordination. At best they could endeavour, like Thomas Bewick's cottagers, not to be numbered among the parish poor, or at least to stay out of the workhouse. For the adult male industrial workers of the parish, however, it was different. They possessed the capacity to make their presence felt in a manner that could influence the demeanour of their social superiors towards them. They possessed that capacity, however, in different degrees,

[256] DRO EP/Wh 19, 344.

and they demonstrated it in a variety of ways and with varying long-term success.

Of all Whickham's industrial workers, those most closely over-looked by their masters and most enveloped in the ties and obligations of paternalism were 'Crowley's crew'. The Crowley system had been developed for the dual purpose of rendering the factory work-force 'a happy and flourishing people amongst their neighbours' and to ensure that they answered 'the end of their being paid'. From the point of view of the factory managers, it appears to have succeeded in both ends tolerably well. We have only one stray reference to industrial unrest among the work-force—a complaint in 1700 from the Winlaton master hoemakers of 'their hammermen combining together not to work'. For the rest, trouble at the factories in the early eighteenth century was usually no more serious than the necessity of disciplining drunken or idle clerks or of prosecuting the perpetrators of occasional thefts from the counting house, the warehouse, or the workshops. At the very end of the eighteenth century, 'Crowley's crew' enjoyed a less tranquil reputa-tion, but even then their unruliness took the form of 'Church and King' rioting, including in 1793 the hanging of Tom Paine in effigy—a political alignment not uninfluenced by their dependence for work upon naval contracts.[257] Even 'Crowley's crew', however, were not invariably contained within the boundaries of deference and subordination, as is well illustrated by a neglected incident of 1740 which presents them in a different light.

For the labouring poor of Tyneside, and indeed much of England, 1740 was one of the worst years of the eighteenth century. The poor harvest of 1739—so bad in Whickham that Robert Thomlinson's tenants were unable to pay their rents and he feared that 'many of them will be Broak'—was followed by an exceptionally severe winter. Both the Thames and the Tyne long remained frozen and the coal trade was brought to a halt. Nor did the late thaw in the spring of 1740 bring effective relief, for both the coal and grain trades remained unsettled, interrupted by adverse winds and dislocated by privateering occasioned by England's recent involve-ment in war. In the first six months of 1740 the price of rye and oats

---

[257] Flinn, *Men of Iron*, 206, 247, 250; id., *Law Book*, 11–12, 60–1, 89; PRO DURH 17/3, 17/4, 17/7. After 1815 'Crowley's crew' gained a more radical reputation as supporters first of the Reform Bill and later of Chartism.

doubled in Newcastle, and the population of the area faced both the immediate reality of dearth and the likelihood that their suffering would be prolonged by a second bad harvest.[258]

These circumstances formed the background to the worst breakdown of civil order in Newcastle's history. Early on the morning of 19 June, a body of pitmen from Heaton colliery marched in order into central Newcastle to protest at the price of grain and at the fact that despite local shortages the export of grain from the area was still being permitted (a consequence of the fact that prices in Scotland and continental Europe were even higher than those in England). By mid-morning a crowd of perhaps four hundred people had assembled at the Sandhill, and grain was seized from inns, granaries, and carts, and stockpiled there under guard. Meanwhile, a deputation of the protesters was received by the city magistrates at the Guildhall and it was agreed that prices would be reduced at the next market. The demonstrators then deposited the confiscated stocks of grain at the public weighhouse and dispersed.[259]

Next morning the crowd reassembled and found that many of the shops and market stalls that they had intended to buy from were closed. A renewed assault on the granaries began in which women and children played a prominent role. Matters, however, were still not out of hand. Many of those besieging the granaries were persuaded to leave empty-handed. New negotiations took place with the magistrates, and reduced prices for grain, peas, oatmeal, cheese, and butter were determined. A paper was then subscribed by seven men (six of them illiterate), declaring that they, 'on the Behalf of ourselves and the Rest of the Pitmen Waggonmen etc. now complaining of the present high price of corn', agreed to the 'aforementioned Regulation' and undertook 'that all persons shall be contented therewith and immediately return to their respective Habitations and Employments'.[260]

This should have resolved matters, but the suspicious crowd apparently remained, and the magistrates took the precautions of calling up the town guard, requesting military aid, and asking local

---

[258] NRO ZAN M13/C7, 7 Nov. 1739; J. Ellis, 'Urban Conflict and Popular Violence: The Guildhall Riots of 1740 in Newcastle-upon-Tyne', *International Review of Social History*, 25 (1980), 333–8. For the conditions of 1739–41 more generally and their effect on levels of crime in the south, see J. M. Beattie, *Crime and the Courts in England, 1660–1800* (Oxford, 1986), 207 ff.

[259] Ellis, 'Urban Conflict and Popular Violence', 341.

[260] Ibid. 342; TWA Keelmen's Papers 394/10.

coal-owners to summon their pitmen to help restore order. The Grand Allies in fact declined to co-operate, but next day, 21 June, Alderman Mathew Ridley, a city magnate, appeared with a guard of 60 horse and 300 foot. The town gates were occupied, the riot act was read, and the crowds were partly dispersed. The administration of the sale of food at cheap rates, however, was rendered difficult by the failure of local farmers to attend the market and by the flocking into Newcastle of people from the surrounding villages, all of them anxious to buy. In consequence, the magistrates ordered that the sale of cheap corn should be restricted to regular customers of the market dealers and to such townspeople and pitmen who could produce certificates to that effect.[261]

Thus far the events at Newcastle had presented a serious and extremely well organized, but not untypical, example of popular protest in the face of scarcity and high prices, a form of 'petitioning in strength and in deed' that was for the most part orderly—if clearly threatening—and which successfully evoked an appropriate conciliatory response from the authorities.[262] Thereafter, however, they became exceptional, for the authorities' response proved inadequate. Grain shipments bound for the Tyne were diverted by local merchants anxious to avoid the losses that would ensue from being obliged to sell cheap. Only a single shipload of rye arrived at the Quayside and it remained there unsold. Next, political rivalries among the magistrates led to a refusal to renew the authorization of the town guard. On 26 June the keelmen seized the moment and stopped all shipping on the river, following which a large crowd once more assembled at the Sandhill, demanding the distribution and sale of the grain standing at the Quayside. The magistrates agreed, but when Mr Ridley and a score or so of armed freemen attempted to make a passage to the Quayside, these 'White Stocking Gentlemen' were jostled by the angry crowd. Some of them lost their nerve and fired on the crowd, killing one demonstrator and wounding several more.

Immediately, pandemonium broke loose. The freemen were

[261] Ellis, 'Urban Conflict and Popular Violence', 342–3.

[262] Quoting J. Walter and K. Wrightson, 'Dearth and the Social Order in Early Modern England', *Past and Present*, 71 (1976), 41. The literature on this issue is now extensive. For particularly important contributions, see E. P. Thompson, 'The Moral Economy of the English Crowd in the Eighteenth Century', *Past and Present*, 50 (1971), and J. Walter, 'Grain Riots and Popular Attitudes to the Law: Maldon and the Crisis of 1629', in Brewer and Styles, *An Ungovernable People.*

disarmed, their weapons were smashed and thrown into the Tyne, and they themselves were pursued to the Guildhall. The angry crowd showed remarkable restraint in making no attack on the persons of their governors (some of whom were escorted home in mock triumph); but they demonstrated their contempt for the city magistracy by thoroughly and ferociously sacking the building that symbolized civic authority. The city remained out of control until the evening, when three companies of troops arrived from Morpeth, forerunners of a whole regiment that subsequently marched in from Berwick. Then the arrests began.[263]

These events provide a signal example of the negotiative manner in which popular grievances were customarily presented and handled in this period. But they underscore even more firmly the fragility of the common people's respect for authority when the patience that they were constantly admonished to observe was abused. A deep well of resentment existed which could erupt into action if the magistracy failed to live up to their own paternalistic rhetoric. Of particular interest to this study is the relatively neglected role of 'Crowley's crew' in the cycle of protest and riot in June 1740. Their participation not only adds a further dimension to our understanding of the complex events of that month, but also casts a good deal of light on the attitudes and behaviour of a substantial sector of Whickham's work-force.

Like other groups among the labouring poor of Tyneside, 'Crowley's crew' had suffered badly during the disastrous winter and spring of 1739–40—not least because the interruption of shipping had dislocating effects on the factories, which depended to a considerable degree upon imported raw materials and in turn supplied their finished products to southern customers and ware-houses.[264] How far the factory welfare system attempted to cope with their needs we do not know, but the ironworkers were clearly feeling the pinch of deprivation. In addition, they also appear to have felt resentment at the decision of 21 June to restrict sales in Newcastle's markets to holders of certificates, for the first sign of unrest among them came some two nights later. This involved a visit to Winlaton by one John Fairburn and fourteen other Swalwell workmen, 'some of whom blew a horn' to attract attention and then urged the Winlaton people to join them in a march on Newcastle 'to

[263] Ellis, 'Urban Conflict and Popular Violence', 343–4, 345–6.
[264] Flinn, *Men of Iron*, chs. 6–8.

settle, as some of them alleged, the prices of corn'. The proposal was
favourably received, but nothing came of it, since the chief agent at
Swalwell, on hearing of the plan to assemble, sent to his Winlaton
counterpart, urging him 'to use his best endeavours to prevent the
said people from coming to Swalwell'. This he successfully did.[265]

Early on the morning of 26 June, however, representatives of the
keelmen, who had initiated their blockade of the river, landed at
Swalwell to persuade the Crowley men to join them in Newcastle.
The chief agent, Mr Walters, was again quickly informed and put up
a notice at the gate of the factory square 'that any person who dared
to blow a horn or Rise or leave their work without proper leave
should be forthwith discharged'. The keelmen, however, had
meanwhile passed on to Winlaton, where they spread the word
among the workmen 'that unless they joined to Assist in Takeing
what corn Remained in Newcastle it would be ship'd of in the
Night Time and they . . . would be starved for want of Bread as well
as the Keelmen'. In consequence, 'a great number' of Winlaton men,
some of whom later claimed to have been persuaded and others to
have been intimidated by their neighbours, descended upon
Swalwell. There they found the gate of the square locked and
bolted. They forced it off its hinges, entered, 'and compelled every
one they found therein to join them'. One of the most prominent of
those involved in this intimidation was John Gilles, a smith, who
strode around the square 'with a naked sword in his hand'. By noon
'several hundred' people were assembled and set off for Newcastle.[266]

At this point, the leadership that must have lain behind the
purposeful assembly of this crowd became apparent, for at the first
crossroads the marchers were halted and addressed by John Leaton,
clerk to the Winlaton Chapel, who was also by virtue of his office
the clerk of the poor and schoolmaster, and may have been a
kinsman of the Leatons who served as viewers at Gibside. The gist
of his speech was a demand for discipline, for he 'made a
proclamation to All the Assembled that they were going to
Newcastle to Settle the price of corn but that no person . . . should
dare to take any thing at his own hands or go into any publick house
to call for drink without paying for the same', adding 'that they

---

[265] TWA Keelmen's Papers, 394/51, examination of Robert Charlton, 394/52,
exam. of Joseph Miles.
[266] Ibid. 394/51, exams. of Robert Charlton, Thomas Haycock.

should make no Disturbance But send a Petition to the Mayor'. They then set off again, only to be overtaken at Derwenthaugh by John Laidler, a staitheman, who spoke to them from horseback and attempted to persuade them to disperse. On their refusal to do so, he suggested that 'if they would desist from going into . . . Newcastle he would go to Mathew Ridley Esq. and remonstrate to him the Grevances they then complained of and bring them his Answer'. This offer was accepted and Laidler rode off ahead, followed by the crowd, who intended to await his return on the Gateshead side of the Tyne bridge. At Gateshead, however, they met 'severall women crying and who told them severall men were killed and wounded in Newcastle' and begged them to cross over 'and prevent further damage'.[267]

The activities of the Crowley men after their entry to the city seem to have varied, to judge by their subsequent depositions. A substantial number appear to have maintained their discipline, among them Robert Charlton and Joseph Miles of Swalwell. They witnessed keelmen and others 'Very Riotous and Committing Great Outrages', but declined, and threatened to oppose, the keelmen's proposal that they should join forces to pull down both the house of the mayor and Mr Ridley's Heaton Hall. On Sandhill they found John Laidler, who had been captured by hostile keelmen on his way back from Mr Ridley's house; they rescued him, and heard Ridley's answer 'that he would to the uttermost of his Power Endeavour to Prevail with the Merchants to lett them have Corn at the Low Prices', and 'would Do Every other thing Just and Reasonable for their Satisfaction'. This satisfied 'Crowley's crew' 'Even to a Man', and John Leaton thereupon produced from his pocket a petition 'wherein the prices of Severall sorts of Corn was set forth at the lowest prices that they the said Crowleys crew Desired to pay for the same'. After an altercation with a keelman who suggested setting the prices at 12*d.* a bushel less, a small party of Crowley men then accompanied Leaton and Laidler to Elswick where the mayor was found. He listened while William Macclen, a Winlaton Mill tailor, read out the petition, told them 'that he was no Corn Merchant but that he would Do his utmost Endeavour to Ease the poor and their the said Crowleys crew's complaints', and gave them a guinea. And with that they set off home.

<hr/>

[267] Ibid. 394/51, exams. of Robert Charlton, Thomas Richardson.

Rather different was the experience of John Turner, who arrived late, went to the Guildhall, and met several Crowley men there who asked him 'to be Aiding and Assisting to them in destroying the windows . . . belonging to the Guildhall'. Anthony Hatherick, James Scott, and Thomas Greenfield looked around the town and then spent the night together in an alehouse. Thomas Richardson stayed with the main body until the deputation set off to find the mayor, watched the systematic destruction of the Guildhall for a quarter of an hour, and then ran into Joseph Graham, a waggonman of his acquaintance, and had three quarts of ale with him in various pubs—all of which, he insisted, he had paid for.[268]

Despite the best efforts of the Crowley system to mould a tractable and docile work-force, 'Crowley's crew' thus showed themselves fully conversant with the tradition of popular protest in conditions of scarcity and ready enough to participate in it, albeit some were clearly more forward than others if the stories of initial intimidation are to be credited. They were clearly willing to accept the leadership and counsels of restraint of intermediate figures in the hierarchy of authority such as John Leaton and John Laidler, and their dealings with such notables as Mathew Ridley and the mayor were respectful. Nevertheless, they defied the threats of their own managers in order to protest at all, they wrecked their factory gates, and they presented their grievances in a form that was more demanding than deferential. They had a sense of their legitimate rights in a time of crisis, and they were not slow to advance their claim to fair treatment through the forceful tradition of collective petitioning which was the only form of negotiation with authority open to most of the labouring people of their day. 'They claimed the right', in Robert Malcolmson's phrase, 'to twist gentlemen's arms'.[269]

Some of them paid for it, for in the aftermath of 26 June the chief agent at Swalwell was asked to provide the names of the participants, 'Distinguishing as much as may be those that were compell'd from those that came voluntarily and particularly mentioning the principal inciters or Ring leaders'. He did so willingly, sending in a list of twenty-three names on which 'bad

---

[268] TWA Keelman's Papers, 394/51, exams. of Robert Charlton, John Turner, Anthony Haderick, James Scott, Thomas Greenfield, Thomas Richardson, 394/52, exam. of Joseph Miles.

[269] Malcolmson, *Life and Labour*, 131.

ones' and 'notorious offenders' were specially marked.[270] Though only twelve Crowley workmen were subsequently indicted, it seems unlikely that the remainder kept their jobs at the factories. Nevertheless, they had won their point. In the months after the riots the authorities of Newcastle kept their promises to endeavour to redress the grievances presented to them by 'Crowley's crew'. They acted diligently to enforce an order in council, issued, ironically, on 26 June, to ban the export of grain for the duration of the crisis. More, they extended it, despite the protests of local grain merchants, to encompass coastwise shipments.

Nor did they pursue a vindictive policy in the punishment of the rioters. Despite extensive investigations, the compilation of lists of known rioters, and the drawing up of numerous indictments, relatively few men were actually tried at the assizes of 1740 and 1741. Only five—including one Crowley workman—were convicted for their part in the Guildhall riot of 26 June and sentenced to seven years' transportation each. Examples were made, therefore, but, given the gravity of the offence, the authorities' response was one of considerable restraint. This may have indicated a measure of genuine sympathy with the grievances of the rioters; equally, it may have represented a discreet extension of mercy in the face of their recently demonstrated power.[271]

While 'Crowley's crew' could defy their employers and confront their rulers to express their grievances as a body, the full possibilities for constructing an alternative conception of selfhood to that proffered them by their social superiors and religious mentors, and for expressing it in organized action, were to be realized by the pitmen. For of all the varied sectors of Whickham's industrial labour force, it was they who were least susceptible to the controlling influences of their masters.

Despite the introduction of the miners' bond, the pitmen remained a highly mobile group—a fact sufficiently attested by the impossibility of reconstituting satisfactorily the family histories of more than a handful of the scores of pitmen known to have worked in the collieries of Whickham. For this reason, the pitmen were only partially and temporarily integrated into parish life and the

---

[270] TWA Keelmen's Papers, 394/10, 394/12.
[271] Ellis, 'Urban Conflict and Popular Violence', 346–9. We are grateful to Dr Ellis for information on the fate of the Crowley workmen who were arrested.

constraints that it could impose. Though they too would be required to prove settlement at such time as they fell upon the parish, in sickness, disability, or old age, there was a very real sense in which for much of their lives their parish was the coalfield as a whole.

Again, although the pitmen can be characterized as a group of workers who were wholly proletarianized, they were also regarded, and regarded themselves, as 'a community of the skilled'.[272] Working a pit in an 'orderly' manner, hewing good 'round' saleable coal, and avoiding the numerous hazards of underground work that threatened life, limbs, and profits required experience, judgement, and skill. Employers valued those skills, paid well for them, and sought to retain them. Moreover, the manner in which they were exercised gave the pitmen a great deal of independence in the conduct of their work. Hewers worked singly and unsupervised, each man in his own 'bord'—four yards wide, according to the specifications of the Bucksnook viewer in 1726, and with four yards' 'piller' separating it from his next neighbour. Subject always to the quality of the workings, it was the speed and skill of the individual that determined both the level of his earnings and the hours that he worked. These were matters that had 'sociological import'.[273]

It was in such a context that the skills of the pitman were passed on—not by formal apprenticeship, but from father to son, brother to brother, trusted adult to frightened child, by candlelight or in darkness, sometimes in danger. Little wonder that the mythology grew that pitmen could only be 'bred', not made; that men adequate to the job could never be recruited from an adult population. Little wonder that the word 'pitman', which was in general use in the north-east by the early eighteenth century, came to mean more to those knowledgeable in the coal trade than 'workman' or 'collier'. It carried 'meanings of social bearing' and intimations of value.[274] All this contributed to the reputation of the pitmen as a proud, truculent, and singularly difficult group of employees; conscious

[272] Colls, *Pitmen*, 12.

[273] Flinn, *Coal Industry*, 329, 441; Buxton, *British Coal Industry*, 20; Welborne, *Miner's Unions*, 11, 14; NEIMME, T. E. Forster Collection, Shelf 49, Vol. 5 'View Book', 16. Cf. Shelf 18, 'Richard Peck's View Book, 1710–35', 22; Ashton and Sykes, *Coal Industry*, 32.

[274] Colls, *Pitmen*. 12. For the mythology of the 'bred pitmen' see ibid. 13–15 and Flinn, *Coal Industry*, 339 ff.

of their own skills and worth, sensitive about their wages and conditions, ready to seize on any advantage in their dealings with their masters, and liable to engage in small-scale stoppages whenever they had a grievance.

How long this had been so it is impossible to say. As early as 1633 the burgesses of Newcastle had expressed their apprehension at being surrounded by an industrial population 'apt to turn everye pretence and colour or grievance into uproare and seditious mutinye', and five years later it was feared that the distress occasioned by the stop of the coal trade would lead to rioting in the town.[275] These, however, were generalized allegations about the entire industrial work-force, including the mariners of the collier fleets and above all the keelmen of Newcastle's Sandgate.

The keelmen did indeed have a history of engagement in large-scale industrial conflict, traceable back to at least 1654, when they struck over their wages and were suppressed by troops.[276] Five years later they successfully blockaded the Tyne while they negotiated over a petition of grievances with the magistrates, before being once more suppressed. In 1677 they addressed the mayor and aldermen in peremptory terms over matters relating to wages, conditions, and market malpractices, introducing their 'petition' with the sentence, 'Wee presume to inform your worships what our Demands is which wee hope is Reasonable and Legall.'[277] Between 1701 and 1750, these 'Headstrong Folks', as George Bowes called them, struck successfully on at least six occasions, as well as precipitating the riot of 26 June 1740 and fighting a running battle with the Hostmen's Company over the mismanagement of the funds of the keelmen's charity founded in 1699.[278]

In contrast, only one act of collective resistance to their employers can be definitely attributed to the miners of Tyneside before 1700: a petition of 1662, described in the hostmen's records as having been drawn up 'in the name of at least 2000 workmen in the Cole pits' and originally 'intended to be presented to his

[275] Howell, *Newcastle-upon-Tyne*, 57; *CSPD, 1638–9*, 260.
[276] Howell, *Newcastle-upon-Tyne*, 292–3.
[277] TWA Keelmen's Papers, 394/1.
[278] DRO D/ST 356/23. The first clear case of industrial conflict between master and men in Whickham (if we exclude the activities of the copyholder wainmen) involved the riotous seizure of Charles Montague's staithe at Swalwell in July 1696 by 19 Newcastle labourers and 5 Whickham labourers. No further details are known, but it is very likely that the men involved were keelmen: DRO Q/S I/51.

Majesty'. This apparently complained 'of the wrong done unto them by the Cole Owners and their Overmen in not paying them their wages or forceing them to take corne or other Comodities at rates farr above the markett price to their great oppression', and the hostmen responded by ordering all coal-owners to pay their workmen any arrears due to them and to let them have their wages in future 'in ready money soe as there be noe just cause given them to complaine'.[279] For the rest, the records appear to be silent on the subject of industrial conflict, and in Whickham specifically the colliery workmen appear only incidentally, or as the auxiliaries of or witnesses for coal-owners engaged in disputes among themselves.

This contrast might be more apparent than real. Given the structure of employment in the seventeenth-century industry, such grievances as emerged would have tended to be between individual miners, or groups of men, and the subcontracting overmen who employed them. They would be less likely to leave records than disputes involving the keelmen, which directly affected the navigation of the Tyne. But the contrast may have lain also in the situations of the two groups. The miners were both fragmented into independent working units and geographically dispersed. They had less occasion to formulate a collective sense of grievance, or to express it in large-scale action, than the keelmen, who were employed by a limited number of Newcastle fitters, worked the river together, lived near one another for the most part, and very often shared a Scottish origin.

By the early eighteenth century, however, we can assert with more confidence that the pitmen belonged to the same antagonistic industrial culture as the keelmen. Indeed, they shared a significant ritual. 'These people have a particular manner of giving a pledge for their standing by one another on any occasion,' wrote Robert Harley of the keelmen in 1723, 'which is by spitting on a stone.'[280] 'The Ringleaders among them,' wrote an anonymous correspondent of the Durham pitmen in 1738, 'after exaggerating what they look upon as a Grievance, and proposing the Means of redressing it, spit upon a Stone, and all that are of their Sentiments do the same, which they esteem as binding as the most solemn Oath; and the Compact

---

[279] Dendy, *Hostmen*, 127. Fynes, *Miners*, 9–10, states wrongly that this petition concerned grievances over ventilation, an error in which he is followed by Webb, *Durham Miners*, 2, and Nef, ii. 172.

[280] Quoted in Fewster, 'Keelmen,', 25.

imply'd thereby is that none shall work, till their pretended Grievance is redress'd.'[281]

The pitmen, like the keelmen, found occasion enough to spit on stones. The author of the *Compleat Collier* warned his readers in 1708 that the hewers and barrowmen would 'confederate under Ground' to cheat their masters by sending up underfilled corves. The Tyneside coal-owners complained to Parliament in 1713 that with rising food prices the pitman 'accordingly sets a vallue upon his Laboure and all this goes out of the Coalowner's Pocket'.[282] Moreover, with the advent of the more centralized and vigilant management of the early eighteenth century, we find the independent evidence to support such allegations. At Tanfield colliery in May 1727 the men of several pits ceased work on a complaint regarding their payment by their overmen and refused to return to work for ten days, 'several of them threaten[ing] such others as are willing to Work'. When an attempt was made to arrest three ringleaders it was resisted, and the sheriff's officer, the owner's agent, and several overmen were pursued across Tanfield Moor to Burnopfield, close by Gibside, by a crowd led by three hewers 'who in their way raised severall shouts . . . to Get others to Join them'. The luckless officials were eventually besieged there by a crowd of two hundred, 'the Men Armed with Clubs and the Women with Stones who Gave them Great Abuse and threatened . . . that if they offered to take away any Men from thence they would knock them down'.[283]

Such drama was perhaps rare, but that constant minor friction was a perennial accompaniment to colliery life is evidenced by some of the unusually detailed 'daily presentments' that survive for the Gibside/Northbanks colliery itself in 1723–4. In the week ending 7 November 1723 the overmen reported that the men had refused to work at Dent's pit on Tuesday and Wednesday and at West pit on Friday and Saturday. In both cases they were said to be 'steaking for

[281] *Gloucester Journal*, 16 May 1738. We owed this reference to Dr R. W. Malcolmson. Cf. Brand, *Observations*, 101 n.: 'Boys have a custom (*inter se*) of *spitting* their *Faith*, or as they call it here, their *Saul* (*Soul*) when required to make Asservations in a Matter of Consequence.—In *combinations* of the Colliers etc. in the North, for the Purpose of raising their Wages, they are said to *spit on a Stone together*, by way of cementing their confederacy.—We have too a kind of popular Saying, when Persons are of the same Party, or agree in Sentiment, "they spit upon the same Stone"' (emphasis in original).

[282] *Compleat Collier*, 38; Hughes, *North Country Life*, 158.

[283] DRO D/ST 298, informations of Thomas Smith and others.

a barryman', i.e. demanding an extra man to sled their coal to the eye of the pit. Four months later, in March 1723, the week began well on the sixth with the men 'making ready for topp coal', but work was then interrupted 'by reason of raine' and by the tenth and eleventh the men were 'steaking for a penny a score', i.e. demanding a higher rate, presumably for difficult work on a new seam.[284] Without the chance survival of these fragmentary records, such incidents would be wholly concealed from us. They indicate well the kind of realities that could lead Ann Clavering to snort in exasperation, 'To be perfectly quiet I'm convinced is beyond the reach of a collier. The devill has possessed our men I believe.'[285]

It was perhaps partly in response to the 'unquiet' nature of day-to-day industrial relations that the pitman's bond gradually developed over the early eighteenth century into a far more complex document. The earliest bonds have been described as 'primitive and limited' in nature, concerned simply with binding men to work for a year in a given colliery and laying down the rates of wages to be paid.[286] The surviving bonds of the early eighteenth century, however, and the incidental references we have to the terms of bonds in use elsewhere, show a clear trend towards greater elaboration.

Coal-owners anxious to maximize production during periods of 'fighting trade', or equally anxious to maintain a steady and secure output in times of 'regulation' so as to achieve their quotas, inserted clauses aimed at imposing on their workers a greater degree of labour discipline. Bonds came to stipulate a minimum five-day week; to set penalties for absenteeism; to lay down precise rules for 'orderly' working; to insist that corves be properly filled and that only quality coal cut 'round' be sent to the surface; to require obedience to the directions of the overmen and viewers—all this on pain of fines for breach of regulations. At Northbanks in 1741, for

[284] DRO D/ST 246.
[285] Dickinson, *Clavering Correspondence*, 67–8. For an important discussion of the 'highly charged industrial relations atmosphere' in the collieries of early 18th-c. Scotland, 'in which strikes are never far from the surface and where other forms of collier non-co-operation were endemic', see C. Whatley, ' "The Fettering Bonds of Brotherhood": Combination and Labour Relations in the Scottish Coal-Mining Industry c.1690–1775', *Social History*, 12 (1987), 141–6. Whatley finds in this evidence 'deeply embedded traditions of collective activity which surfaced whenever opportunities for material advances were perceived, or when the need for mutual defence arose'.
[286] Flinn, *Coal Industry*, 352. Cf. Scott, 'Miner's Bond', 57, 60.

example, the men agreed to work 'Diligently and faithfully' for
George Bowes 'and no other person' from 23 December until 11
November next. The barrowmen or putters were to send up corves
'more than woodfull' and none that were improperly filled (fine 1*s*.)
and to include no 'unclean Cole' (fine 1*d*. per corf). Hewers were
required to obey all orders given them by the overman, and if
working in pits with horsedrivers to stay underground until only
'Ten sticks of each daies workings' remained to be drawn to the
bank.

There were no-strike clauses too. At West Hartford any man
refusing to work or 'in any way Instrumentall in hindering any
other workeman to worke in the said Colliery so that the said pitt or
pitts shall be laid in', was to pay 1*s*. a day for the first offence, 2*s*. a
day for the second offence, and so on for 'any greater number of days'.
At Northbanks the very first article of the bond empowered the
owner to deduct 1*s*. 'for Every day which they or any one of them
Disturbeth the said Work or procure or put on any other persons so
to do or Insist upon more wages than what are hereinafter agreed to
be paid whereby the working of any part of the said Colliery shall
be obstructed or hindered'.

Such clauses doubtless had some influence in reducing the level of
minor disputes. Yet the elaboration of the bond was very far from
being a completely one-sided development, for the greater complexity of the clauses inserted derived also from the inclusion of
items that were clearly in the men's interests and probably reflected
their initiative. Such clauses, for example, might lay down the size
of the corf to be filled—38 inches by 33 inches for the 'Topp Coal'
and slightly smaller for the 'French Coal' at Northbanks, where an
iron gauge was also to be provided for checking the corves. In
addition, the scale of payments agreed could be extremely elaborate,
including not only different rates for particular types of work, but
also different rates for specific seams; at Northbanks there were five
different rates for hewers working particular seams or pits. At West
Hartford in 1722 a clause was interlined after the initial drafting of
the bond (perhaps after negotiation?), laying down that, if a stated
target output was exceeded, new wage rates could be settled with
the viewer provided they were 'just and reasonable'.[287]

---

[287] Based upon details of bonds in Welbourne, *Miner's Unions*, 13; Scott, 'Miner's
Bond', 57 ff.; Colls, *Pitmen*, 45; Ashton and Sykes, *Coal Industry*, 88; DRO Q/S
OB 8, 488–9; DRO D/ST 72/15, 344/22.

The implication is that, while the coal-owners certainly endeavoured to use the disciplinary power of the bond to their own advantage, the relationship of the pitmen to their masters was in the final analysis a negotiated one—a reality stated clearly enough in the fact that the formal title of what was popularly known as the bond was 'Articles of Agreement'. Moreover, as the bonding system developed and spread across the coalfield, it came to have certain distinct advantages for the men. It offered temporary security of employment, for the owners were anxious to retain men even during trade stoppages; and if it promoted a degree of industrial paternalism, so much the better—the pitmen could appreciate a good employer. But its more fundamental significance lay in the fact that the binding days provided an occasion for collective bargaining on an annual basis which the men no less than the owners could turn to their benefit, especially under the leadership of the most experienced, shrewd, and articulate of the hewers.[288] The men did not subscribe until the articles of the bond were formally inscribed, and, given the competition for their labour, and the existence of alternatives within walking distance, they had no need to subscribe unless the articles suited them.

Even beyond this, however, the bond assisted in the creation of a larger, albeit temporary, identity for the men as a colliery workforce, as distinct from the crew of a particular overman's pit. It defined them as members of an industrial community involved in a common relationship to a particular owner and set of managers. It sharpened awareness of agreements and entitlements. Given the frequent mobility of at least a substantial part of the labour force, it could also enhance awareness of the pay and conditions to be found throughout the coalfield—matters of no small interest to men paid by the score of corves of coal cut. It provided a basis for the evaluation of particular managements and a moment at which to challenge them, and it contained the potential to create an enhanced sense of collective identity and shared interests at the level of the coalfield as a whole.

The bond, which had a role to play in creating the conditions for the development of industrial paternalism in a coalfield parish such as Whickham, clearly also had a marked contribution to make, in its

---

[288] This is recognized by Flinn, *Coal Industry*, 396, and by Colls, *Pitmen*, 68, 71, who argued that 'the Bond was, after all, a bargain of sorts', and the outcome of myriad 'local hagglings'.

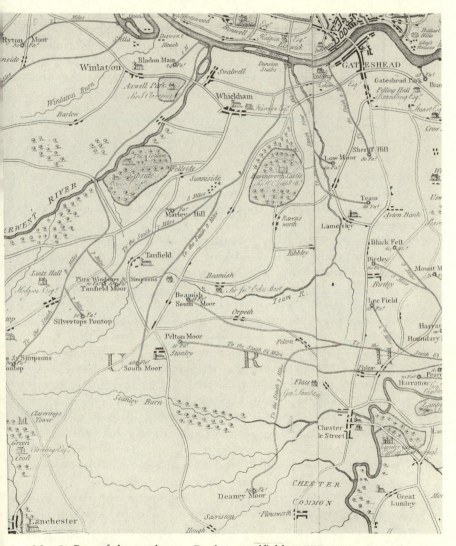

MAP 5. Part of the north-west Durham coalfield *c*.1787

Source: John Gibson, *Plan of the Collieries on the Rivers Tyne and Wear* (London, 1787)

developing form, to what can broadly be termed the political education of the pitmen. They were labouring men, subject ultimately to the insecurities and weaknesses of their market position. But they were also pitmen, members of a mobile regional community of skill. While their labour was in demand and they had health and strength, they had the independence individually to choose the relationships of subordination into which they entered and the power collectively to influence their terms. This was the essence of their distinctive position not only in Whickham but also in the society of the coalfield as a whole.

7. 'MUTINOUS PITMEN'

The social relations of Whickham were thus subject to sets of countervailing forces: paternalism and deference, independence and negotiation, co-operation and conflict, sympathy and resentment, resignation and resistance. They were moulded partly by the structures and institutions of parochial life, and partly by the broader realities of the developing industrial society of which Whickham was a part. Here was no single fixed pattern, but a situation of diversity and dynamism as the dialectics of social relations coloured the experience of individual lives in different combinations, and at various times, or particular stages of the life-cycle. For the most part these forces doubtless existed in a rough and ready equilibrium, now tipping one way, now another, or coexisted in a kind of cultural counterpoint, one theme now dominant, now subdued. Their relative strength and resonance would be tested only in moment of crisis, in those significant events that pulled people out of the comfortable inconsistencies of everyday life, forcing them to stand back, to reflect, to choose, to act, or to accept.

Such moments and events revealed both the possibilities and the limitations of the situation. For Whickham's 'objects of charity' the crucial event might be the necessity of applying to the parish. For 'Crowley's crew', as we have seen, the point of crisis came with the privations of the late spring of 1740. For the pitmen it was reached on those occasions when the interests of masters and men were thrown into stark conflict. This might occur at the level of the single pit or the individual colliery; but on rare and singularly instructive occasions it took place at the level of the coalfield as a whole. For, as we have repeatedly emphasized, the miners' community was less that of the parish than of the coalfield across which they moved in the course of their working lives. Their experience and attitudes were governed not only by the localized structures of parish life, or by the variable quality of relations with the owners and managers of particular collieries, but also by the fortunes of the coal trade as a whole, its entrepreneurial politics and the more general managerial strategies to which they gave rise. Given these realities, the developing identity of this central group among the inhabitants of Whickham cannot be fully appreciated without reference to the broader context within which they lived and worked. If we are to explore further the making of that peculiar identity, we must shift the focus of our attention from the single parish, which has provided our point of entry into coalfield society, to consider the implications of larger events that involved Whickham and its people, and had a considerable bearing upon their lives, but were of regional, even national, significance.

Our first example is provided by the somewhat obscure events of 1731. In the previous year, George Bowes of Gibside had chosen to defect from the Grand Allies, the cartel of leading coal-owners which since 1726 had sought to stabilize prices and profits by agreeing to an annual apportionment of the Tyneside vend. Bowes's defection, which involved unilateral price-cutting in order to secure a greater market share, provoked a new outbreak of the 'fighting trade' and, for those owners least equipped to compete, a sharp fall in both sales and profits.[289]

One result of this situation was reduced levels of working at many pits throughout the north-east. From Wearside it was reported in late January 1731 that some coal-owners had agreed to deliver no coal until 20 February in order to drive up prices. As a result, 'Great numbers of the Wives and Children of the Coal Pit Men are begging about here . . . by Reason their Husbands have not their usual Work, and are forc'd to draw Coals about for small Pay, to prevent starving, Work more proper for Horses.' On Tyneside as late as May, the collieries of the Grand Allies were working only three-quarter time. The pitmen, however, were not released from

---

[289] For the situation of the coal trade in 1730–1, see Hughes, *North Country Life*, 236–46, and Cromar, 'Coal Industry', 202–3.

their bonds, for it was in the interests of the owners to retain them lest their labour be needed. The Wearside men were said to be 'desperate' for 'No-body will trust them'—i.e. advance them credit—yet 'if any of them elope to other work [they] are imprisoned.' Meanwhile, the Grand Allies kept their underemployed pitmen 'upon a day or two notice', so that if the market improved 'the workings may be Encreas'd'.[290]

The pitmen appear to have borne with this situation, for they had no option, but by early February they were given a more direct source of grievance. Some of the owners, in the attempt to reduce production costs, had apparently adopted the device of unilaterally increasing the size of their corves. From Durham it was reported on 7 February that 'This Week a great many Pit-men came and made Complaint, that their Owners would not give them *Sufficient Subsistence* for working their Coals; adding to their Corss much more Weight, by making them hold a Peck more, and putting iron Bows, when before they were wood, without a Farthing allowance of the Price.' The men were to be seen 'walking about our Streets in Numbers, not knowing where or how to get their Grievances redress of'.[291] A month later news came from Newcastle that the corves were now '(by the Report of the Maker) five pecks more', and that they were 'hardly to be drawn by Horses', an innovation that had led the pitmen to meet 'in great bodies' and to resolve 'not to work a Coal till the Corfe or Basket is reduc'd to its primary Size'.[292]

The pitmen may have been spitting on stones, but it appears that on this occasion they did not act upon their resolution, for there is no evidence that strikes took place in the spring or summer. It was scarcely a propitious time for a withdrawal of labour. With the approach of the customary binding time in the late autumn, however, the men acted to put pressure on the owners at the moment when they were rendered most vulnerable.

The trouble began on the Wear on 25 October, when a crowd of more than a hundred pitmen forced an entry to the drainage engine house of the Earl of Scarborough's Newbottle colliery and 'broke several lead pipes by which the Engine was hindered from working'.

---

[290] *Ipswich Journal*, 6 Feb. 1731. Cf. *Gloucester Journal*, 9 Feb. 1731. We owe these and subsequent references to these newspapers to Dr R. W. Malcolmson. NRO Armstrong Papers, 725 F49.   [291] *Gloucester Journal*, 24 Feb. 1731.
[292] *Ipswich Journal*, 6 Mar. 1731. Cf. *Gloucester Journal*, 2 Mar. 1731.

They then held the engine house for a day and a night and 'gave Publick notice' to the engineer and viewer 'that if the Engine was repaired or set to work before they had brought their Masters to their Terms they wou'd pull it down to the Ground and murder [the engineer]'. Subsequent attempts to repair the engine were hindered by the pitmen, though they did not perform their murderous threat. After three weeks' interruption of drainage, the Earl's steward 'was obliged to submit to the unreasonable Demands of the said Pittmen, otherwise the Colliery would have inevitably been drowned and lost'. Meanwhile, similar attacks took place on the fire engines used to drain Murton and Bowes Biddick collieries on 2 November, and on these occasions the pitmen also carried away numbers of corves which they proceeded to 'burn and destroy'—a sufficient indication of the grievance at issue. Attacks also took place on the storehouses of staithemen, which were plundered of ale, wine, and victuals.[293]

News of these events spread rapidly. On 9 November John Yorke of Richmond wrote to his brother-in-law James Clavering, 'I perceive the colliers are become very uneasie and troublesome.' Four days later it was reported in London 'that the pitmen have rose against the Coal-Owners . . . and that the Damage they have done to the Gentlemen upon the River Weare was very considerable'. By then, however, a letter to Lord Scarborough had already been received in the capital and passed on to Whitehall. Troops were authorized to march on the coalfield and the local magistrates were ordered to enquire into the cause of the 'Tumult', to 'take all proper and legall methods for apprehending those . . . who are most mutinous and bringing them to justice', and to forward the resulting 'informations' to the government.[294]

It is from one of those informations, taken from Thomas Tinn, pitman, of Whickham Fellside, that we learn of events in the 'western collieries' following the rising of the Wearside men. According to Tinn, on Thursday 11 November he and other pitmen 'laid in the works' at two pits at Causey colliery and then made their way to Beckley 'in order to Force the Men to desist from Working'. No intimidation was necessary, however, for the pits there were

---

[293] PRO SP 36/25, fos. 81–6. We are grateful to Dr R. W. Malcolmson for first drawing our attention to this source. Cf. Colls, *Pitmen*, 204–5, who describes these events, though without discussing the broader industrial context.

[294] Dickinson, *Clavering Correspondence*, 171; *Gloucester Journal*, 16 Nov. 1731 (report from London, dated 13 Nov.); PRO SP 36/25, fo. 71.

already 'laid in', and the men moved on to Crook Field 'and stopp'd the Horses at one Pitt there, and obliged the Banksman to draw the men to Bank'. They then proceeded to Bucksnook 'and by Force Laid in a Pitt' there. On Friday 12 November, Tinn attended 'a meiting of Several Pittmen . . . belonging to most of the Collierys thereabouts' at Tinkler Row on Blackburn Fell, close to Marley Hill. There 'it was resolved that two Pittmen belonging to each Colliery should go in a Body to the Owners of the said Collierys to complain of certain Grievances which they thought they lay under'. Though no details of this meeting survive, the outcome was apparently that 'the Gentlemen desired that they would come down the next day to Ravensworth Castle', seat of the Liddells, 'where their Complaints shou'd be heard and remedied if Just'. The men, however, did not go to Ravensworth on either Saturday or Sunday, and matters stood still over the weekend. On Monday the fifteenth Tinn, together 'with several others to the Number of about Two Hundred came to Ravensworth Castle . . . in order to speak with the owners of the said Collierys'. They were greeted, however, with a reading of 'the Kings Proclamation against Rioters' and a declaration by the owners 'that if they would come in a peaceable manner they sho'd be heard'.

Clearly, matters were reaching an impasse. The men, for whatever reason, declined to present their grievances in what the owners regarded as an appropriate manner, and the owners were unwilling to negotiate until they did so. On Tuesday Tinn stayed at home in Fellside, but other local men 'to the Number of about Three Hundred' went down to Chester-le-Street on the Wear 'in order to Consult with the Pittmen there'. This consultation between the Tyne and Wear men was apparently at the invitation of five Wearside pitmen who had come over the day before, presumably after the Ravensworth Castle debacle, and told the men of the western collieries that 'they wondered to see their Ginns and Corves undestroyed, and that if they would go to Chester several Pittmen in that Neighbourhood would return with them and ffire the corves and break open Cellars for them'. Whatever the specific cause, men were gathering at Chester-le-Street on Tuesday 16 November, and early the next day Tinn himself went down 'and Joyned the Body at Chester which was composed of Tyne Water and Wear Water Men to the Number of Near one Thousand'. (Among them were also five Lumley pitmen, employed at three separate Wearside collieries, who said they had been roused that morning by a group of men who 'told them that they had been rid down by Several Ten tale Men belonging to the River of Tyne' and 'insisted that they shod goe along with them . . . and Swore that if they refused so to doe that they wou'd break their Windows and Household goods and wou'd then take them . . . away by force'.)

At about eleven o'clock on the morning of Wednesday 17 November the men moved off, 'with a design to throw down all Ginns and Corves wherever they found them standing and to resist in case of opposition'. This plan was attributed to 'the Wear Water Men, who said they would do the Work'. At Urpeth, however, they were met by what they regarded as a superior force raised by the magistrates. The pitmen, many of whom were perhaps half-hearted, dispersed, and some were subsequently taken prisoner and questioned.[295] Nothing more is known of these events, except that on Sunday 21 November eight companies of foot arrived at Newcastle from Berwick with instructions 'to quell our mutinous Pitmen'. As news of the troops' approach reached the area the men apparently 'began to disperse and file off by Degrees', and by 25 November it could be said that 'now we hear but little of them'. The troops were expected to winter in the area as a precautionary measure 'to observe the Motions of these People', but the pitmen's 'rising' seems to have faded away as quickly as it had begun.[296]

The actual events of 1731 remain in many ways frustratingly obscure. But for a handful of newspaper reports and Home Office papers, we would know almost nothing of them.[297] Even with these to hand, we do not know exactly how many collieries were involved in this first recorded mass strike of the pitmen of the northern

---

[295] PRO SP 36/25, fos. 79–84. The source of much of this information, Thomas Tinn, appears briefly in our family reconstitution study. Neither he nor his wife Martha was baptized in Whickham, and they did not marry there. They enter the record only with the baptism of their children in Dec. 1731 and Feb. 1734, and nothing more is known of them. At the time of the pitmen's action Martha Tinn was more than seven months pregnant, an indication of the kind of imperatives activating men whose subsistence was threatened.

[296] Northampton Mercury, 13 Dec. 1751 (report from Newcastle, dated 25 Nov.). We are grateful to Dr R. W. Malcolmson for this reference.

[297] There is no mention of the strike in the Newcastle Courant, or in the London Evening Post, the Gentleman's Magazine, or the Historical Register for 1731. The London Journal for 27 Nov. 1731 contains a single reference—a letter from Edinburgh, dated 18 Nov., reporting that eight companies of troops had marched from Berwick on the previous day 'to suppress some tumultuous People near Durham'.

coalfield. How many of Thomas Tinn's neighbours among the pitmen of Fellside participated in these dramatic events? What happened in the collieries where no 'outrages' took place to draw the attention of newspaper correspondents? We do not know. Yet the limited information that does survive as to the nature of the 1731 strike is very revealing.

In the first place, certain characteristic attitudes are revealed which have also been observed among other groups of eighteenth-century workmen engaged in industrial conflict, above all a powerful sense of certain basic entitlements: to a decent subsistence; to consideration of their interests and those of their families; to a degree of control over their pay and conditions of work and the right to protest against and if necessary resist arbitrary treatment by their employers.[298] Again, it reveals the capacity of the pitmen to organize themselves to present their grievances and further their cause almost a century before the emergence of the first formal trade unions in the coalfield. Clearly, they already possessed a strong sense of collective identity at the sub-regional level—as is indicated by their self-description as 'Tyne Water Men' and 'Wear Water Men'. And equally clearly, those two bodies of men were sufficiently aware of their broader common interest to co-operate in the furtherance of their cause. Their combination on this, as on other occasions, may have been 'informal and ephemeral', but none the less it showed that 'real flair for extemporary organization' which has been identified as equally characteristic of the pitmen's conduct in industrial disputes.[299] They began, it seems, with complaints of their grievances in a petitionary manner, a form of behaviour that has been described as 'deferential in the context of employee–employer relations, though entirely in keeping with the formal tradition of class relations in the eighteenth century'.[300] But there was little that was deferential about threats to strike as early as March 1731, about the activities on the Wear in late October and early November, or about the demeanour of the 'Tyne Water Men' before their employers at Ravensworth Castle. Clearly, they were willing to negotiate, but equally, they intended to negotiate while placing their employers under duress, both by a prior withdrawal of labour and by the forced shutdown of drainage machinery.

At the same time, the events of 1731 reveal the weaknesses of the

---

[298] Malcolmson, *Life and Labour*, 126.
[299] Flinn, *Coal Industry*, 396, 411.　　　[300] Ibid. 402.

pitmen's position. In the first place, their situation was crucially dependent on the state of the market for coal and for their labour. This was the fundamental cause of their sufferings and was quite beyond their control. Again, it governed their bargaining position with their masters. In the circumstances of the winter and spring of 1730–1 the coal-owners were able to manipulate the restraining power of the bond to their own advantage and to impose upon their bonded labour force an arbitrary change in their conditions of work which had immediate implications for their pay. The owners could ignore their initial protests and, even in the face of the strike in the autumn, clearly felt little compunction to negotiate with the angry pitmen unless the latter adopted a posture of greater deference than they were willing to assume. Faced with that resolution, the pitmen had little option but to submit to their masters' determination of whether or not their grievances were just, or to embark upon a peripatetic riot which was immediately met by the armed force of the state. At that point the pitmen clearly recognized the limits of their own capacity to resist. As they well knew, in the final resort 'almost any kind of demonstration or threatening activity by miners during strikes was sufficient to allow their arrest', and the coal-owners, despite (or perhaps because of) their paternalistic self-image, were only too willing to call in the troops against 'mutinous' subordinates.[301]

It is an awareness of these general realities that has led to an historiographical concentration on the violence and military intervention that so often accompanied industrial disputes on the Tyne and in the coalfield generally, both in 1731 and later. Early historians of the coalfield, albeit sympathetic to the plight of the pitmen, set the pattern. Fynes wrote of men 'goaded by a sense of wrong' who united to 'inflict grievous damage to life and property', 'committing extravagances', the desperate acts of an uneducated population, and yet finding themselves 'none the better for their resistance'. Webb found the pitmen brutalized, exploited yet 'powerless', and Turner wrote of a work-force whose 'rudimentary organization' was inadequate to ameliorate their condition, leaving them to seek redress only in 'violence and uprising'.[302]

---

[301] For the general weakness of the legal position of the miners in the period and the use of troops, see ibid. 408.

[302] Fynes, *Miners*, 9, 10, 12; Webb, *Durham Miners*, 21; Turner, 'English Coal Industry', 13.

This tradition of interpretation was consonant with the image of the pitmen as 'a race apart', and like that hostile stereotype it persists, albeit in more sophisticated form. M. W. Flinn, while recognizing that there was much bluster, melodramatic threat, and ritual in industrial relations, nevertheless concludes that, 'in the absence of formalized negotiations, labour relations were necessarily conducted against a background of near violence'. To Robert Colls, most recent historian of the northern pitmen, the sabotage and intimidation of 1731 appear 'characteristic of coalfield protest in the eighteenth and early nineteenth centuries', essentially at one with the individual acts of malicious damage to collieries by aggrieved pitmen which can be found in the records of the courts or newspaper reports.[303] More, he regards such activities not only as 'characteristic' of the pitmen but also as part of a broader tradition of riot, confrontation, and direct action that embraced also the keelmen's strikes, the Guildhall riot of 1740, and the militia riots of 1760. It was a tradition of brief, violent protest that drew the attention of complacent gentlemen to popular grievances, and it could work well enough in eliciting eventually a conciliatory response. But it was a world removed from the 'disciplined mass actions' that became more common in the period after 1790 as the reciprocity of traditional social and industrial relations crumbled and the pitmen haltingly stumbled along the path to organized trade unionism and political consciousness.[304]

Of course, there is much truth in the view that the actions of the pitmen, on this as on other occasions, drew upon and incorporated elements of a broader and older tradition of popular protest. It will already be apparent that the events of 1731 displayed distinct parallels with the riots of 1740, which, until the débâcle of 26 June, were in many ways highly traditional in form. Again, the pitmen certainly belonged to the same industrial culture as the keelmen, and indeed they may have learned something from them. Yet to lay too much stress upon these shared characteristics, and more generally to emphasize the violence of the pitmen's strike, is to risk missing the significance of those distinctive features of the pitmen's action which derived from the distinctiveness of their situation.

[303] Flinn, *Coal Industry*, 410; Colls, *Pitmen*, 206 ff. Cf. Turner's reference to 'numerous outrages' in 'English Coal Industry', 14. For instances of individual acts of sabotage, see *Newcastle Courant*, 6 Feb. 1762; *Newcastle Journal* 1, 8, 15, 22, and 29 Nov. 1740; PRO DURH 17/6; DRO Q/S OB 10, 113.
[304] Colls, *Collier's Rant*, 74; id., *Pitmen*, 209 ff. and 237.

In the first place, this *was*, as is apparent even in the inadequate documentation available, a well organized and disciplined mass action. The Tyne Water men chose delegates by colliery and approached the coal-owners as one interest group collectively entering into negotiations with another. The Wear Water men also must have been sufficiently well organized to plan the meeting at Chester-le-Street, and sufficiently conscious of the shared grievances of pitmen across the coalfield to invite the participation of their fellows to the north-west. The Chester-le-Street gathering itself and subsequent events have the air of a muster and a march, rather than of the inchoate outpouring of a rabble. All this surely reflected the structuring influence of the employment system under the miners' bond and the sense of common identity of a highly mobile work-force.

Secondly, the violence that was employed should be neither exaggerated nor misunderstood. Intimidation of fellow-workers, be it tacit or overt, is ugly, but it is as inseparable from the conduct of a large-scale strike as conscription is from the conduct of a major war; its presence in 1731 (or at Winlaton and Swalwell in 1740) is not a unique feature of eighteenth-century industrial relations. For the rest, the pitmen's violence was both limited and purposeful. There is no mention in the evidence of actual violence against any person. Indeed, the Tyne Water men appear to have been remarkably restrained even in venting their anger on the offending corves and the pithead gins, so much so as to invite the taunts of the emissaries from Wearside. As for the Wear men, their initial attacks on colliery machinery were explicitly intended to help force their masters to terms, and it is very much to the point that the Newbottle attack had succeeded in this objective by 14 November. The joint march from 'Chester' was clearly intended to accomplish the same purpose on a larger scale, while also providing the satisfaction of burning the corves, an action with both symbolic and practical significances.

A final notable characteristic of 1731 was that, to the best of our knowledge, action of this kind was exceptional. We would suggest that it was exceptional not because the pitmen still lacked the self-awareness or organizational capacity for large-scale industrial action, but precisely because they *did* possess a formalized arena for negotiation which usually rendered such actions unnecessary. It was at the annual binding season that their relationships to their employers were usually settled, in the rituals of blandishment and

coyness that preceded the subscribing of a colliery bond. It is surely
not without significance that the pitmen had every reason to believe
that they had made bad bargains the year before and that trouble
broke out during the actual binding season of 1731. That it came to
violence at the end may be attributable not only to the men's deep
resentments of what had been forced on them, but also to the fact
that they were in a bad bargaining position in the autumn of 1731,
facing intransigent masters who had to be given an offer that they
could not refuse.

Nor did the pitmen necessarily fail in that purpose. Although
they melted away before a force that they neither could nor
seemingly wished to oppose, they seem to have maintained some
form of solidarity. The magistrates' investigations produced very
few 'informations', and most of those came from victims of, rather
than participants in, the 'outrages'. The court records of the area
contain no evidence whatsoever that any pitman was prosecuted.[305]
Moreover, a subsequent reference to the year's troubles by one
informed party, James Clavering's brother-in-law, suggests some
sort of prolonged process of accommodation across the subsequent
binding season. 'I shall be glad to hear that peace is settled among
the colliers', he wrote as late as 7 December.[306] Perhaps the violence
was over, but the settlement was still in train; and it may be no
accident that the next pitmen's bond that survives, that of Northbanks in 1741, provided meticulously detailed specifications of the
size of corves to be used and states that an iron rule is to be available
for the measurement of the corf.[307]

Put into context, therefore, the outbreaks of violence that
accompanied the pitmen's 'mutiny' of 1731 take on a different
complexion. Indeed, we might go further and reverse the traditional
interpretation, based on such incidents treated in isolation, by
arguing that the remarkable thing about industrial relations in the
eighteenth-century coalfield was the general *lack* of violence. That
relative tranquillity may have been the outcome not of an essential
harmony of interests, nor of the deference elicited by paternalistically
inclined coal-owners, but of the fact that the labouring population
was sufficiently 'mature' and well organized to direct conflict into

---

[305] No evidence of prosecution survives among the Durham assize records for
1732 (PRO DURH 17/4), or in the quarter sessions order book for that year (DRO
Q/S OB 8). The actual sessions rolls for 1731–2 do not survive.
[306] Dickinson, *Clavering Correspondence*, 172.   [307] DRO D/ST 344/22.

forms of action that were characterized less by riot than by negotiation.[308]

Furthermore, experiences such as those of 1731 were doubtless highly educative for all concerned, and they could reverberate long after the settlement of the specific grievances at issue because they affected the consciousness of all those involved. Coal-owners faced with industrial sabotage, be it collective, purposeful, and tactical or merely individual and malicious, were not slow to secure a sheaf of statutes to protect their plant against aggrieved pitmen; equally, they shored up their legal position with regard to the punishment of breaches of labour contracts.[309] As for the pitmen, 1731 would have taught them (if they needed the lesson) both the limits of paternalism and the willingness of their employers to sacrifice their interests. In resisting their masters, they might also have learned the strengths and weaknesses of their own position. Their power to harass the coal-owners and to 'distress the trade' on a grand scale had certainly been demonstrated, as had the benefits of co-operation between collieries and between the two rivers. On the other hand, they had been reminded of the limits of their power to oppose men behind whom stood the apparatus of the state, of the need to avoid provoking military intervention, and of the dependence of their bargaining position upon the general condition of the coal trade. All this may have made them the more aware of the significance of the annual binding as an institutional means of mediating their relationship with their masters. That this was probably so is certainly most powerfully suggested by the next and greatest crisis of industrial relations in the eighteenth-century coalfield, the strike of 1765. The issue was the pitman's bond itself.

The great pitmen's 'Insurrection' or 'Stand' of 1765 was occasioned by a rumour or 'common fame', circulating in the coalfield in the earlier part of the year, that the coal-owners of the Tyne and Wear had agreed among themselves 'that no coal owner should hire another's man unless they produced a certificate of leave from their last master'.[310] This rumour was given plausibility by the fact that

---

[308] For a similar point, made in a different context, see Ellis, 'A Dynamic Society', 217.   [309] Boyd, Coal Pits and Pitmen, 14; Flinn, Coal Industry, 408.

[310] London Chronicle, 21–24 Sept. 1765 (letter from Sunderland, dated 19 Sept. and signed 'B'). Cf. Gentleman's Magazine, 35 (1765), 430. The Gentleman's Magazine's account of the strike was heavily dependent on B's letter, which was hostile to the pitmen.

since the mid-century the industry had experienced increasing competition for skilled labour. The reason for this was that the frontier of the coalfield was once more on the move. In the middle years of the century the spread of steam-powered drainage and haulage systems, and the development of new ventilation techniques, made it possible to exploit the rich, deep seams that lay in the eastern part of the coalfield—seams that had previously been inaccessible. By mid-century, rising demand from London encouraged the coal-owners to undertake the massive investment required in exploiting these seams, and a rash of new sinkings spread gradually in the area to the north and east of Newcastle and on the coastal plain of County Durham.[311]

To the pitmen, these new collieries, with their thick seams and state-of-the-art technology for drainage, haulage, and ventilation, offered a golden opportunity. In the older collieries, such as those of Whickham and the nearby Western collieries in which some of Whickham's pitmen worked, the earning capacity of the men was hampered by the increasing difficulties and irregularity of their work. As early as 1739, a colliery viewer commented of the western collieries in general that 'the ways are lengthened every year, but some Pits are going off'. This was certainly true at the Gibside–Northbanks–Marley Hill complex. In 1742 one of Mr Leaton's assistants had observed that it 'would not be amiss' to cut production at those pits producing low-quality pan coal, but he was anxious not to 'loose any of best men because I expect we may work some Maine Coale this summer'. As we have seen, fortnightly output was low by the best standards of the day at Gibside/ Northbanks in the 1720s and again in 1752. Well paid as they were by comparison with agricultural workers, the Northbanks pitmen were earning less than they could. Where work proved exceptionally difficult, or was rendered 'slack' by the quota system of the Grand Allies, a colliery could be in the situation, as one former pitman put it to George Bowes in 1759, of 'having too many hands more than could make Sufficient Bread for their families at that time'.[312]

[311] Flinn, *Coal Industry*, 22. For a more detailed account, see Cromar, 'Economic Power and Organization', 113 ff.

[312] NEIMME, Buddle Papers, Vol. 14, 365; DRO D/ST 235, 262. A batch of paybills survives for Northbanks pits in 1764 in D/ST 336. Unfortunately, these prove insufficiently full in their coverage of the working year to permit systematic comparison with the 1752 evidence analysed in ch. 3 above. The general impression, as might be expected, is of a declining level of activity at Northbanks–Marley Hill, even as compared with the less than optimum situation of 1752.

In contrast, the new collieries extended the prospect of higher, or at least more regular, earnings because the one part of the productive process that had *not* been transformed was coal-face work.[313] Moreover, the new collieries also provided the potential of an enhanced 'family wage', since they offered increased opportunities for the employment of young boys underground, in the operation of ventilation shutters, horse-leading, and the like.[314] To the owners of the longer-established collieries, however, these new developments presented not only opportunities but also serious threats. They were ready enough to invest in new sinkings, and some of them did so. But they also faced new and powerful competition, a gradual disintegration of the Grand Allies' stabilizing hegemony over production, and the necessity of struggling to protect their existing investment in collieries, waggonways, and dead rents.[315] It was a daunting prospect, and one rendered no more pleasing by the further need to compete for the skilled labour of pitmen who were once more in high demand.

Throughout the later 1750s and early 1760s, newspaper advertisements placed by colliery managers in the Newcastle papers tempted the pitmen with offers of immediate employment, 'good Encouragement', 'constant Employment', and 'Great Encouragement'.[316] Nor were they usually punctilious in specifying that they sought only unbound pitmen. These years also saw the placing of advertisements regarding pitmen who had 'eloped' or 'absented themselves', threatening legal penalties against any with the temerity to employ them.[317] Though the wage-rates paid to hewers

---

[313] Gabriel Jars reported that, at the new 600-foot-deep pit at Walker in 1765, the hewers, who were able to work standing upright, could cut as much as 30 corves of coal in a 6- or 7-hour day, the usual output being 20–5 corves per man: G. Jars, *Voyages metallurgiques ou recherches et observations sur les mines*, 3 vols. (Lyons, 1774–81), i. 192–3.

[314] Ashton and Sykes, *Coal Industry*, 173–4. Jars, *Voyages Metallurgiques*, i. 193, describes the many 'petits garcons' who worked 14-hour days with the horses at Walker.

[315] Cromar, 'Economic Power and Organization', 118, 122; Buxton, *British Coal Industry*, 37.

[316] *Newcastle Courant*, 4 June 1757, 25 Mar. 1758, 3 June 1758, 21 Jul. 1759, 15 Sept. 1759, 6 Oct. 1759, 25 Oct. 1760, 17 and 24 Nov. 1764; *Newcastle Journal*, 24 Dec. 1757; *Newcastle Chronicle*, 8 and 15 June 1765. NRO ZAN M13/D30, letter no. 46 (Jan. 1702), makes it clear that in contemporary usage 'encouragement' meant financial reward.

[317] e.g. *Newcastle Journal*, 27 Jan. 1749/50 and 28 Apr. 1750; *Newcastle Courant*, 6 Oct. and 1 Dec. 1764.

undoubtedly rose at older collieries such as Northbanks, the attractiveness of working conditions at the new pits proved decisive, and inevitably skilled labour drifted towards the eastern mines. In particular, competition at binding times intensified[318]—so much so that by the early 1760s matters were reaching a crisis point. In 1762 the Delavels of south Northumberland were paying men binding 'earnests', on subscription of the bond, of between one-and-a-half and two guineas, while in 1764 some Wearside gentlemen were reported to have paid earnests of two, three, and even four guineas, 'being in great want of pitmen'. Traditionally, the earnest had been merely a token sum to spend on drink—at Northbanks in 1741 it had been 6*d*.[319]

These were the circumstances that gave credence to the rumour that the owners had agreed among themselves to bind only such men as were released by a certificate from their former masters. This notion, according to one observer, spread 'like wildfire' across the coalfield: 'and as no coal owner that had his interest in view would grant such a certificate to a pitman as long as he had any occasion for his service, it was called a binding during the will of his master, consequently a species of slavery unknown in a free country'. Accordingly, 'on or about' 14 August 1765, the pitmen ceased work almost simultaneously at every colliery on the Tyne and Wear. Their choice of date was probably influenced by the fact that 13 August had been the binding day at the Grand Allies' collieries in the previous year. On 14 August, then, the men of the biggest coal-owning partnership on the Tyne were out of their bonds. The only exception to the general stoppage was apparently Hartley in south Northumberland, where the pitmen, 'having been treated with the greatest humanity and tenderness by Thomas Delavel Esq', elected to work on. For the rest, it was reported on 30 August that 'not one of the pitmen will work'.[320]

Meanwhile, the strike was consolidated by action to close the waggonways and prevent the transportation of coal stockpiled at

---

[318] The general tone is illustrated by some of the advertisements of binding days, which promised not only high earnings and prompt payment, but also improved working conditions: see e.g. *Newcastle Courant*, 25 Oct., 17 Nov., and 24 Nov. 1764.

[319] Colls, *Pitmen*, 49; *London Chronicle*, 21–4 Sept. 1765; DRO D/ST 344/22.

[320] *London Chronicle*, 10–12 and 21–4 Sept. 1765; Cromar, 'Economic Power and Organization', 122; *Lloyd's Evening Post*, 2–4 and 9–11 Sept. 1765. All future references to newspaper reports of the strike are to the editions of the stated dates of 1765, unless otherwise specified.

the pitheads to the riverside staithes. It was probably at about this time that the Fellside quarter of Whickham and the immediately adjacent stretches of the Tanfield Way witnessed the most dramatic local incidents of the strike. In at least three separate attacks in Whickham, Tanfield, and Lamesley, groups of men of up to thirty strong stopped, overturned, and broke up nineteen waggons belonging to Mrs Mary Bowes, Henry Liddell, Edward Simpson, and the Earl of Bute, scattering their contents and assaulting several of the drivers.

Of the fourteen participants in these events who were subsequently named in court proceedings, nine can be identified among the registration and employment records of Whickham in the preceding decade. One of the two ringleaders who were subsequently imprisoned, Joseph Blacklock the younger, who led the riots in Whickham and Lamesley, was said to be from Causey in 1766 when he was bound to be of good behaviour on his release from prison; but he had married in Whickham in 1758 and was the son and namesake of a Northbanks pitman of the preceding generation. The other, Aaron Wilson, was described as a pitman from Tanfield chapelry. He probably lived, like the sureties to his recognizance, in Burnopfield, close to Gibside Park—a supposition supported by the fact that when he was initially arrested he and his accomplice John Kirkley were rescued by a riotous assault upon the sheriff's officers in Whickham, instigated by their respective wives and Wilson's unmarried sister.[321]

These incidents enter the historical record only by virtue of the subsequent prosecutions, but much the same must have been happening all over the waggonway network of the region, for on 2 September it was reported from Newcastle that hundreds of ships lay idle in the northern ports, and that 'the keels are all laid by, the waggons are stopp'd, and the ways broke up and destroy'd'. In the capital, the price of coal soared.[322]

---

[321] DRO Q/S OB 13, pp. 40, 69, 84. The additional information on participants is derived from our name indexes and family reconstitution. The exact dates of the waggonway attacks in Whickham, Lamesley, and Tanfield were not stated in the quarter sessions order book.

[322] *London Evening Post*, 7–10 Sept. Cf. *Annual Register*, 8 (1765), 131. For coal prices, see *Lloyd's Evening Post*, 4–6 Sept. Following the arrival of a collier fleet on 9 Sept., very few colliers were reported reaching London until the second week of October—a sufficient testimony to the effectiveness of the strike: ibid. 26 Aug.–9 Oct., *passim*.

By this time the owners had grasped the full seriousness of the unprecedented situation, and on 31 August a printed handbill was put out 'By Order of the Gentlemen in the COAL TRADE on the Rivers TYNE and WEAR'. It earnestly recommended the pitmen 'to go immediately to their WORK as they are obliged by Law to do, till the Expiration of their present Bonds', and assured them 'that each Pitman shall receive a Discharge in Writing, if he shall require it, that he may be at Liberty to engage in the service of any other Master; and that no Agreement is entered into by the Gentlemen of the Coal Trade, to refuse any Pitman, on Account of his having served in any other Colliery the Year before'.[323]

This rapid climbdown should have resolved matters, had the dispute remained confined to the pitmen's initial grievance. But already events were taking a new turn. In late August and early September, a number of meetings apparently took place between the owners and the representatives of the men, leading to hopes that their differences 'were as good as compromised'. Such expectations, however, were swiftly disappointed when it became apparent that the men had 'taken it into their heads to stand out' and to press their advantage. At each meeting, it was reported, 'the pitmens demands rose', and by 2 September it was known in Newcastle that they were insisting on the 'grand article' that all existing bonds should be delivered up and that there should be a general rebinding. This, however, was a proposal that the coal-owners could not contemplate. As one of their sympathizers explained, 'were [the pitmen] all to be bound together', rather than sporadically over two or three months, 'at the expiration of their bonds, it would always be in their power to distress the trade, by refuseing to go to work till whatever they might please to desire was complied with'.[324]

The issue was now clear-cut. This was not a strike over wages, as was sometimes alleged but was repeatedly denied by informed parties:[325] it was a struggle over the balance of power between the concentrated forces of capital and labour across the entire northern

---

[323] PRO SP 37/4, no. 46.

[324] *Lloyd's Evening Post*, 6–9 and 9–11 Sept. Cf. *London Chronicle*, 10–12 Sept. For the new demands, see reports from Newcastle of 2 Sept. in ibid. 7–10 Sept. and *London Evening Post*, 7–10 Sept. A fuller account was given by 'B' in *London Chronicle*, 21–4 Sept.

[325] For the assumption that the strike was a straightforward wage dispute, see e.g. *London Chronicle*, 5–7 Sept.; *Lloyd's Evening Post*, 2–4 Sept. For statements to the contrary, see ibid. 20–3 Sept. and *Newcastle Journal*, 21 Sept., 28 Sept., 5 Oct.

coalfield. While the issue most certainly had implications for the earnings of the pitmen, and these can scarcely have been far from their thoughts, it was essentially a struggle over authority, and in particular over the proper relationship between masters and men. The pitmen, having successfully resisted what they believed to be an attempt to abrogate the bargaining power given them by the annual binding, had gone on the offensive to demand an enhanced bargaining power of a kind that the coal-owners had carefully avoided conceding in the past. It was a situation reminiscent, though in a transformed context, of the struggle between the copyholders of Whickham and the Grand Lessees almost a century and a half earlier. Indeed, one of the coal-owners chose to describe it to the Earl of Northumberland in terms remarkably similar to those used by his Jacobean predecessors. Having acquitted the coal-owners of 'any Imputation of Blame' in the matter, he declared that this was 'an affair of most serious Consequence to the Public', for 'the whole now turns upon this single point, whether the Pitmen are to be at Liberty to set the Die on the whole kingdom that has occasion to buy coals'.[326] That the coal-owners themselves had repeatedly proved only too willing to attempt just that in the past was beside the point; what he truly meant to express was his apprehension that the pitmen might succeed in 'setting the die' upon the kingdom, beginning with their masters.

Faced with this impasse, the response of the coal-owners was twofold. First, they placed an advertisement in the *Newcastle Journal* of 7 September, which was repeated in that paper and two other local papers on 14 and 21 September, declaring that 'most of the Bound Pitmen . . . have lately deserted their respective Employments, before the Expiration of their Bonds, and refuse to return or serve out their respective Times', and requesting all persons to refrain from employing them 'till they have performed their Bond Service to their present Masters, as they have not till then a Right to serve any other'.[327] Next they employed troops to police the coalfield. During the period of negotiation with the pitmen, soldiers had apparently been sent for as a precautionary measure, and three troops of dragoons had arrived in Newcastle from York on 2 September. There is no evidence of their use, however, until

[326] PRO SP 37/4, no. 48.
[327] *Newcastle Journal*, 7, 14, and 21 Sept.; *Newcastle Courant*, 14 and 21 Sept.; *Newcastle Chronicle*, 21 Sept.

12 September, when a correspondent from Newcastle wrote to a friend in York, 'I never thought much of the stop by the pitmen till this evening, when the drums beat to arms, and I find a strong party of soldiers is marched out of the town.'[328]

The deployment of these troops had probably been decided upon earlier that day at a meeting between the magistrates of the area and the gentlemen of the coal trade. Mr Blackett, the mayor, wrote afterwards to the Earl of Northumberland to inform him that the magistrates and gentlemen were unable to resolve the situation and to request the advice and assistance of government 'in a matter of so very great national consequence'. Next day, the coal-owner J. B. Ridley followed up this representation in a letter explaining to the Earl why the striking pitmen could not be proceeded against under the provisions of the Masters and Servants Act in 1747. The expedient of taking a servant before a justice for committal to the house of correction for not more than one month, he argued, was 'very well, where two or three or a dozen men desert their Service, and has been many times properly executed with good effect, but where there is a general combination of all the Pitmen to the Number of 4000, how can this measure take effect?' It would be impossible to seize all the guilty men and difficult enough to take a few, for they would make a 'formidable resistance'. Even if twenty or forty could be so punished, the prospect of a month in the house of correction would not 'carry with it the least Appearance of Terror so as to induce the remaining Part of so large a Number to Submit'. On the contrary, the men confined 'wou'd be treated as Martyrs for the good Cause and be supported and caressed and . . . brought home in Triumph'. Given the gravity of the situation, the impossibility of 'bringing the men to Reason by fair means and Persuasions', the threats reportedly made by 'the Wear Water Men as they are called' to destroy colliery machinery, and the breaking of a coal gin that very day at Sir Ralph Milbanke's colliery, Ridley urged that 'something more than the powers vested in the hands of the Magistracy of the three Counties appears most absolutely necessary for the sake of the whole Community'. He suggested that some 'extraordinary Exertion of Power be used'. This letter having been passed on to the Secretary of War, on 17 September three more troops of dragoons were ordered to proceed to Durham or to

---

[328] *Lloyd's Evening Post*, 9–11 Sept., 18–20 Sept.; *London Evening Post*, 7–10 Sept.; *London Chronicle*, 5–7 Sept.

quarters near Newcastle, in order to suppress or prevent 'outrages' by the pitmen.[329]

Before 13 September, in fact, there had been no 'outrages' beyond the cutting of the waggonways early in the strike. That situation, however, was shortly to change. For the response of the pitmen to the impasse was also twofold, and its first manifestation came in outbreaks of violence at a number of collieries. Since this violence was highlighted in the subsequent *Gentleman's Magazine* and *Annual Register* accounts of the strike, and has been much emphasized in most of the brief historical accounts of the events of 1765, it is as well to be precise about exactly what is known to have occurred. There are, in fact, only three documented incidents. On the morning of 13 September Sir Ralph Milbanke was able to get some of his pitmen to work. That afternoon a body of pitmen came to his colliery, cut the gin ropes, broke some machinery, and threw it down the pits, threatening also to return later and fire the colliery.[330] On the night of 17–18 September a pit at Pelton Common colliery belonging to Mr Jennison was 'wilfully and maliciously set on fire'.[331] On the same night, in the Auckland area of County Durham, others among the Wearside men 'burnt the utensils of many pits and set fire to the coals above and below ground, notwithstanding some parties of soldiers had been disposed in such a manner that it was expected they would have prevented them'. This was perhaps the most serious act of sabotage and the closest the pitmen came to putting into effect the resolution reported of a body of pitmen at Chester-le-Street on 13 September to destroy 'all the collieries they come at'.[332]

These incidents were serious enough, but they scarcely support the judgements of subsequent historians that in 1765 'riot and destruction swept along the whole Tyne valley', or that the strike, which began peaceably, 'did eventually open out into tumult and

---

[329] *Calendar of Home Office Papers, 1760–65*, 598, 600; PRO SP 37/4, no. 48.

[330] *London Chronicle*, 17–19 Sept. Cf. *Lloyd's Evening Post*, 16–18 Sept.

[331] *Newcastle Chronicle*, 21 Sept. Cf. *Lloyd's Evening Post*, 25–7 Sept.

[332] *London Chronicle*, 17–19 Sept., 28 Sept.–1 Oct. (report from Auckland, dated 24 Sept., referring to 'last' Tuesday, i.e. Tues. 17 Sept.). Cf. *Lloyd's Evening Post*, 27–30 Sept. It is striking that, as in 1731, the serious violence occurred on the Wear. Perhaps industrial relations were more bitter on Wearside. No other 'outrage' is recorded save the receipt of a threatening letter by Alderman Bell of Newcastle: *Newcastle Chronicle*, 28 Sept., 5 Oct.; *Newcastle Courant*, 28 Sept., 5 Oct. Cf. *London Evening Post*, 21–4 Sept.

violence'.[333] Contemporary local observers were of a quite different
opinion. A letter from Newcastle, condensed in *Lloyd's Evening
Post* on 16 September, reported that 'the pitmen still refuse to work;
they commit no disorders; some of them are gone into the country
to harvest-work, others lurk about the fields'.[334] An editorial in the
Newcastle Journal for 21 September, while deploring the intimidation of men willing to work by 'the Threatenings and lawless
Attacks of the more obstinate and violent' who had been 'guilty of
very rude and illegal Proceedings', insisted that 'in general, at other
Times' the pitmen had 'behaved themselves very peaceably and
quietly, so that no Body seems afraid of any mischief from the
Men'. On Wearside it was said that there was 'no act of violence
committed' until the firing of pits on 17 September, a month into
the strike.[335] It seems possible, in fact, that it was the deployment of
troops by the coal-owners that actually triggered the violence of
13–17 September by escalating the dispute. The Newcastle correspondent whose letter recorded the soldiers' march from the city on
12 September hinted as much. Prior to that event he had 'never
thought much of the stop', but seeing the troops march out made
him 'fear much mischief will be done soon'.[336] He was right. In the
main, however, the pitmen appear to have maintained the discipline
of the strike. Indeed, with regard to the one working colliery in the
coalfield, Thomas Delavel's Hartley, they were remarkably chival-
rous, allegedly informing that gentleman that they would not
molest his workings, 'being so satisfied with his behaviour to his
own people'.[337]

The response of their anonymous leaders to the coal-owners'
initiatives was of a quite different nature to the violence of a
minority in the coalfield: they appealed to public opinion and
engaged, both directly and through their sympathizers, in the

---

[333] Welbourne, *Miner's Unions*, 21; Colls, *Pitmen*, 237. These incidents have
figured prominently in the historiography because they were widely reported in
London and subsequently incorporated into two general accounts of the strike: that
of the *Gentleman's Magazine*, 35 (1765), 441, 448 (which greatly exaggerates the
report of pit burning from Auckland and misdates the incident to 24 Sept.), and that
of the *Annual Register*, 8 (1765), 131 (which generalizes the violence). These reports
have been drawn on frequently in the brief discussions previously accorded to the
events of 1765. In contrast, the Hammonds, who give a somewhat fuller account of
1765 in *The Skilled Labourer*, 12–17, were aware that the violence was limited.

[334] *Lloyd's Evening Post*, 16–18 Sept.
[335] *Newcastle Journal*, 21 Sept.; *London Chronicle*, 28 Sept.–1 Oct.
[336] *Lloyd's Evening Post*, 18–20 Sept.   [337] Ibid. 23–5 Sept.

'alternative politics' of the eighteenth century. On 14 and 21 September the coal-owners' newspaper advertisements were answered by the publication of a statement made by, or on behalf of, the pitmen themselves. This began with a denial of the 'scandalous and false reports' that they had broken their bonds, insisting that most of the men had been bound in late August 1764 and the remainder in early September; since their bonds were customarily for eleven months and fifteen days, they regarded themselves as free. In addition, the coal-owners were accused of attempting to prolong their bonds until 11 November 1765, and of placing their own advertisements in order to prevent the men from seeking alternative work so as 'to reduce the industrious Poor . . . to the greatest Misery; as all the Necessaries of Life are at such exorbitant Prices, that it is impossible for them to support their Families without using some other lawful Means, which they will and are determined to do'. The statement then repeated the allegation that the owners had secretly agreed 'not to employ any other Pitman that has served in any other Colliery the year before', which would oblige the men 'to serve in the same Colliery for Life; which they conjecture will take away the ancient Character of this Kingdom as being a free Nation'. This being the case, they were determined not to work for any of the coal-owners 'till they be fully satisfied that the said Article is dissolved, and new Bonds and Agreements made and entered into for the Year ensuing'.[338]

The general maintenance of discipline and the pitmen's public statement of their case were perhaps crucial to the eventual outcome of the strike. For, given the men's stubborn refusal to return to work and the general lack of occasion for coercion of the kind so much hoped for by the coal-owners, the focus of attention shifted to the battle for public opinion. On 14 and 17 September an open letter to the coal-owners, sent from Newcastle and signed 'A Collier', was published in both the *London Chronicle* and *London Evening Post*. Its author, who was almost certainly no collier, denounced the coal-owners' decision 'to summon the soldiery where no riotous proceedings have appeared' as 'indiscrete', 'guilty', and 'contemptibly fearful'. 'To brave the honest hearts of an industrious and distressed multitude by a superiority of force', he asserted, 'is enough to irritate them to deeds of desperation as

[338] *Newcastle Courant*, 14 and 21 Sept.; *Newcastle Journal*, 14 and 21 Sept.; *Newcastle Chronicle*, 21 Sept.

this army has all the appearance of a resolution to suppress their just and honest rage.' He asked how they, 'whom affluence and plenty have crowned with a profusion of blessings', could deny 'a trifling addition to their hire' to men who lived in 'poverty and want, danger and frequent death'. Finally, he asked how 'A lady so lately celebrated in our Papers for compassion to her tenants' could 'deny that lenient benevolence to her deplorable and starving Pitmen'.[339]

The letter from 'A Collier', with its themes of the misuse of military force, the hardships of the pitmen, and the callous indifference of the coal-owners, was to set the tone of a debate that raged for the next fortnight. Other letters from Newcastle abstracted in *Lloyd's Evening Post* informed the public that 'impartial people think the masters have brought this upon themselves, by endeavouring to break through an old custom'; that 'in a country which boasts its Liberty, it is an odd way of deciding differences between masters and servants by Dragoons'; that 'the sending a body of troops against [the pitmen] is a measure but little approved by the considerate part of the people'; and that it was considered 'an extraordinary circumstance to knock a set of poor men on the head because they will not quietly submit to be starved'. On the same theme, one 'Y.E.' wrote to the *London Chronicle* declaring his dismay at the use of the dragoons against 'the poor pitmen' and his vexation 'as an Englishman, as a man born in a free country, to see the fashion daily more and more prevailing of sending out a regular military force to oppose every commotion of the people'. Such tactics, he believed 'must end in a total subversion of our Freedom, or else be productive of some violent convulsion'.[340] Meanwhile, another letter to *Lloyd's* presented an extremely sympathetic version of the pitmen's case against the coal-owners, adding for good measure that even under the traditional bonding system the terms were 'very hard, when it is considered these eleven months are intended to deprive them of a settlement, to prevent their being troublesome to parishes, while the rich Coal-Owners are not, however, rich enough to provide for their own Poor, though, from the misfortunes which daily happen in the pits

[339] *London Chronicle*, 12–14 Sept. Cf. *London Evening Post*, 14–17 Sept. This was followed by the same author's 'A Second Letter to the Coalowners' in *London Evening Post*, 19–21 Sept., which was even more rhetorical and included a thinly veiled attack on the Earl of Bute.

[340] *Lloyd's Evening Post*, 16–18 Sept., 18–20 Sept.; *London Chronicle*, 28 Sept.–1 Oct.

to fathers of families etc. the real objects of charity, which this country swarms with, are very numerous'.[341]

It was in vain that one 'B' of Sunderland wrote to denounce the collier's letter, and to present what seems indeed to have been a fairly 'true and impartial account' of the strike from the coal-owners' perspective (though one that declined to comment on whether the owners truly had intended to bind at the will of the master).[342] Nor did it serve any purpose for another defender of the owners to point out (correctly) that the pitmen were among the best paid workmen in the country and that the owners supplied them with cheap corn in years of scarcity. The hunt was up for the coal-owners, and two London papers published in full a further denunciation of their character and an appeal for sympathy for their pitmen, penned by Richard Atkinson. In his view, the pitmen, far from being turbulent and idle, were 'infinitely more to be pitied than condemned'. 'Cut off from the light of heaven for sixteen or seventeen hours a day,' he argued, 'they are obliged to undergo a drudgery which the veriest slave in the plantations would think intolerable, for the mighty sum of fourteen pence; and in their old age are cast off to the inevitable wretchedness both of poverty and disease.' Yet the owners misrepresented these men as idle and extravagant, since, 'the more they are kept down, the more their Masters will be enabled to venture ten thousand guineas on a favourite horse, or the accidental turn of a Card'. The 'sensible part of the kingdom', he continued, would appreciate that 'a man who has but seven shillings a week to support himself, a wife and four or five children, can have no mighty matter to squander away extravantly at an alehouse or at any other place of recreation'.[343]

In the London press the owners undoubtedly lost the moral battle, and the London papers were also having great influence in the north, as is indicated by the decision of the editor of the *Newcastle Journal* to publish a conciliatory editorial on 21 September. This was occasioned by the 'declamatory Letters and Paragraphs' in the metropolitan press and his own receipt of several letters containing 'Matter more likely to inflame than reconcile the Parties at Variance'. His intention was clearly to cool the

---

[341] *Lloyd's Evening Post*, 20–3 Sept.
[342] *London Chronicle*, 21–4 Sept., and *London Evening Post*, 24–6 Sept.
[343] *Lloyd's Evening Post* 24–7 Sept., and *Public Ledger*, 26 Sept. Atkinson's letter was provoked by the second defence of the coal-owners alluded to above.

temperature of the debate. He deplored the extravagant behaviour of some of the pitmen, but praised the restraint of most. At the same time, he sought to correct the view 'that the *Stand* of the Pitmen is occasioned by their being beat down in their wages'. 'It is well known', he continued, 'that the Pitmen's wages are abundantly sufficient, and they themselves make not the least Complaint on that Account: But some other Terms and Conditions seem to be the Matter in Dispute; and whether there is any real Foundation For it, is best known to those Gentlemen who hire and employ them.' For his part, the editor was most concerned to lament the loss to rich and poor alike occasioned by the long continuance of the strike.[344]

The owners, in fact, had already taken the hint, influenced perhaps not only by their losses but also by the rumour that an enquiry might be instigated into the grievances of the pitmen which were now 'the general topic of conversation' in the capital.[345] On 21 September they published in the Newcastle papers a solemn declaration, 'in the most public Manner', that there neither was nor was ever intended to be any agreement among themselves to refuse to employ one another's pitmen, accompanied by the statement 'that they require no more from the Pitmen than that they shall perform the Conditions of there present Bonds'. This advertisement, which was reprinted a week later and published also in *Lloyd's Evening Post* (alongside an abstract of the pitmen's advertisement) for the information of the London public, was in effect a weary return to the position of 31 August.[346] It remained to be seen, however, whether the pitmen could be persuaded to accept the owners' word and to abandon their own more ambitious demands. Two more attempts to facilitate that process were to be published in the Newcastle press, and both in their different ways illustrate nicely the exasperation of men used to the exercise of authority in the face of obstinate insubordination.

The first was a hectoring rebuttal of the charges against the coal-owners laid by the letter from 'A Collier'. Its author, who was clearly engaged in the industry and possibly a viewer, traced the origins of the dispute to the 'extravagant' gratuities of recent years, and the pitmen's obstinacy to the fact that they had been 'spoiled

---

[344] *Newcastle Journal*, 21 Sept.
[345] *London Evening Post*, 21–4 Sept.; *Lloyd's Evening Post*, 25–7 Sept.
[346] *Newcastle Chronicle*, 21 and 28 Sept.; *Newcastle Journal*, 21 and 28 Sept.; *Newcastle Courant*, 21 Sept.; *Lloyd's Evening Post*, 25–7 Sept.

and debauched by People of inferior virtue'. He denied the
allegations made against the coal-owners 'which have catch'd the
Patriotic Zeal of the Public' and saw all of them as introduced only
to be 'made Use of as a Stalking Horse, in order to come at the Gold
in Hand at the next Binding; and that all might be free at one Time
of the Year, when the Works and Demand for Coals are at the
Height and consequently when the Pitmen could most injure the
Public by a Stop or lay their Employers under Contribution'. The
attempt to achieve this, supported by 'the Advice and Opinion of
nine-tenths of the Public', had reduced the pitmen 'from a State of
being able to procure all the decent Necessities of Life by an honest
Industry' into a lamentable condition. Yet their masters had behaved
with leniency towards them and had done 'every Thing . . . that
would satisfy any impartial By-stander'. The essential lesson to be
learned by those who supported the pitmen was 'that many People
must labour for the bare necessities of Life (as I have done) or no large
State or community can subsist', a message pushed home by a brief
excursion into Roman history to warn against the risks of declension
from 'Virtuous Industry' into luxury, corruption, and degeneracy.[347]

The second open letter, signed by 'A friend to Liberty and the
industrious Poor', adopted a paternalistic tone of sympathetic
condescension and was addressed directly to the pitmen. It was
prefaced with a quotation from Pope:

Order is heaven's first law, and that confess'd
Some must be nobler, wiser, greater, best,

and it began: 'My lads . . .' Its author assured the men that their
fears that they were to be made 'slaves for life' were an
'unaccountable infatuation'; 'For know, my lads, neither the coal-
owners, nor any other set of men in Great Britain, thank God, can,
nor dare attempt to deprive the lowest Englishman of his liberty.'
He urged them to accept their masters' 'most solemn, public, signed
declaration', for 'believe me you ought to be satisfied with that'. He
warned them that if they were not, and stood out, they would
forfeit sympathy, and pity, and lacking work might come to want
and crime and then 'the civil power will lay hold on you, and you all
then know the terrible consequences'. He instructed them that their
demand for a cancellation of all bonds was
a most unreasonable and unconscionable request; and if granted, I should
not be surprized at your *spitting on a stone*, and *smashing your souls*, once a

---

[347] *Newcastle Journal*, 28 Sept.

month at least, not to strike a stroke;—the country would then exactly resemble a family where the servants govern and bear rule; and I think every body knows where that is the case, what confusion and disorder prevail.

Finally, he too rounded off with 'a little piece of true history' from ancient Rome to illustrate the dire consequences of plebeian insubordination.[348]

How much ice either of these contributions to industrial relations would have cut with the pitmen is hard to say. Of considerably greater significance was the reopening of negotiations indicated by a letter of 27 September, which declared that the 'great misunderstanding that has so long subsisted between the Coal-owners and the Pitmen ... is this day in great forwardness towards being reconciled and it is thought it will be finally settled tomorrow'. The next day brought contradictory reports from Newcastle; one that the men were going back, another that 'the Pit-men still hold out'.[349] Perhaps both were true. By 4 October, however, it could be reported that 'all parties seem reconciled'. Half the men laid idle by the 'stick' of the pitmen had gone back to work over the previous three days and the remainder were due to start on Monday 7 November, 'as they have all entered into bonds for that purpose'. These bonds, however, entered into for the ensuing year, were 'to take date at the expiration of their present bonds'.[350]

The great 'stick', then, had ended in a stand-off. The owners had repudiated the intentions attributed to them of seeking to undermine the pitman's bond in its established form. The men, who were said to have 'stood it out as long as they well could', had accepted new bonds without insisting on a simultaneous binding. To the editor of the *Newcastle Courant* their differences were 'happily adjusted', and the *Journal* reported that the coal trade was 'going on with its former spirit'.[351]

---

[348] *Newcastle Chronicle*, 5 Oct. This letter was described by the editor as having been intended for insertion in the previous week's paper, but published belatedly 'as it may not be altogether too late for the service it was intended'. The author's 'piece of true history' included the fable of how the limbs mutinied against the belly and consequently pined and decayed until 'they found upon cool reflection that they not only were dependent on the belly for their welfare, but for their very existence' and so returned to their 'respective employs' and 'got into a thriving condition again'.

[349] *Lloyd's Evening Post*, 30 Sept.–2 Oct. Cf. *Newcastle Chronicle*, 28 Sept.

[350] *Lloyd's Evening Post*, 7–9 Oct.; *Newcastle Chronicle*, 5 Oct.

[351] *Lloyd's Evening Post*, 7–9 Oct.; *Newcastle Courant*, 5 Oct.; *Newcastle Journal*, 5 Oct.

As with the strike of 1731, there is much that remains obscure about the pitmen's 'stand' of 1765, above all the precise nature of the miners' organization and leadership. Yet mysterious as some aspects of these events inevitably remain, they too are instructive. They demonstrate once more the pitmen's powerful sense of their collective identity and interest; their capacity for organized, effective, and remarkably sustained action across the whole coalfield; their tactical skill; their restraint; their articulate leadership; their realistic sense of what they could and could not hope to achieve; their rejection of deferential submissiveness; their subscription to, and ability to manipulate to their advantage, the libertarian ideology of the age. They were not, as one letter to a London paper put it, 'a rabble of Coal-heavers'.[352] They were pitmen, and they also conceived themselves to be free-born Englishmen.

Few of those who lent their public support to the pitmen's cause in the newspaper letter war of September 1765 appear to have recognized these characteristics. They were more inclined to pity and excuse the miners than to admire their resolution; readier to dwell rhetorically on their sufferings and on the iniquities of their oppressive masters than to appreciate their initiative or recognize their power. It was the owners and their local sympathizers who understood best the causes of the strike, the reasons for its prolongation, the formidable nature of the power of an organized work-force at a time of labour shortage, and the high stakes that were being played for in 1765. That understanding underlay their rapid climbdown over the men's initial grievance, their resistance to the pitmen's subsequent attempt to press their advantage, and their eventual willingness to embrace a compromise settlement. It also explains the leniency shown to the handful of pitmen who were eventually tried and convicted for their part in the 'outrages' of the strike.[353]

---

[352] *Lloyd's Evening Post*, 27–30 Sept.

[353] There is no evidence of prosecutions at the assizes of 1766. In October 1765 Aaron Wilson and his sister Mary were convicted at Durham quarter sessions for their part in the riots in Tanfield and Whickham, being sentenced to 6 months' imprisonment. In July 1766, Durham magistrates likewise sentenced Joseph Blacklock and one Thomas Lowry to fines of 1s. 8d. and 3 months' imprisonment for other waggonway riots in Whickham and Lamesley. The leniency of these sentences is striking when we consider that the same justices sentenced several offenders to 7 years' transportation for petty theft, and shortly afterwards a woman was sentenced to be whipped around Durham market place for stealing 6d. worth of coal from Sir

But was it, after all, merely a 'great misunderstanding'? We think not. In the Watson Collection of the North of England Institute of Mining and Mechanical Engineers there survives the notebook of an unidentified colliery viewer, who took notes at a meeting at the Whitehart in Chester-le-Street on 5 December 1764 and two subsequent meetings in Newcastle on 24 December 1764 and 5 January 1765. On these occasions the coal-owners of the Wear and Tyne separately, and then jointly, 'absolutely promised and agreed that they will not employ any person or persons concerned in any colliery belonging to any of the said Coal Owners . . . without their consent in writing', undertook that none would offer a binding earnest of above 1*s*., and established a commission to settle any differences arising. One of the men who subscribed the Tyne agreement was Mr Leaton, the viewer of the Gibside colliery. Among the Gibside estate papers there also survives a rough draft of 'A Certificate for Pitmen', which reads 'This is to certifie whom it may concern that H M is discharged from the service of Mrs Bowes and is at liberty to hire himself to any other person.'[354]

The men were right. The owners did intend to establish a binding during the will of the master. The 'stand' of 1765 may not have achieved all that the pitmen's leaders hoped, but it certainly scotched that plan. By doing so, it preserved the by now customary system of hiring; it ensured the continuance of a fair labour market in which the suppliers of labour enjoyed some semblance of power; and it defended the bargaining position which enabled the pitmen to render themselves the élite corps of labour in an expanding mining industry.[355]

As for the owners, they solved their own problems most effectively six years later with the establishment of the Limitation of the Vend, an agreement on the regulation of prices and production

Thomas Clavering. (DRO Q/S OB 13, 40, 41, 69, 84, 92, 121). Local newspapers reported the case of the Wilsons and two further trials at Alnwick in Oct. 1765: that of 7 pitmen and 2 women 'for laying off Mr Haxley's coalpit at the Westgate' (1*s.* fines and 1 month gaol), and that of 2 pitmen for assaulting an overman at Longbenton (small fines and several weeks' gaol): *Newcastle Journal* 19 Oct.; *Newcastle Chronicle*, 12 Oct.

[354] NEIMME, Watson Coll., Shelf 8, no. 13, 'View Book, 1734–70', unfol.; DRO D/ST 341/22. In addition, D/ST 347/17K contains two printed warrants for the apprehension of absconding pitmen. These, however, may have been of a type in use before 1765. They have blank spaces for the entering of personal details, and one for the date '176_ '.

[355] Flinn, *Coal Industry*, 393–4; Colls, *Pitmen*, 49–51, 74 ff.

which rendered the 'fighting trade' a thing of the past.[356] That achieved, they could themselves 'set the Die on the whole Kingdom that has occasion to buy coals', in Mr Ridley's phrase. And with the profits gouged from the consumers of the south, they could well afford to bear with, and even to value and mythologize, their proud, demanding, and exceedingly well paid work-force of 'true bred pitmen'.

Together, the settlement established in the wake of the 'stand' of 1765 and the Limitation of the Vend laid the basis of a general peace in the coalfield for a generation. During that generation the collieries of Whickham itself faded into insignificance. But the characteristic patterns of social relations which we have seen in the making through our focus on Whickham and its environs, and the identities, attitudes, and expectations that informed them, were both consolidated and advanced. They were central aspects of the accumulated experience of industrial life which was both to animate and to contain the renewed struggles between capital and labour in the changing conditions of the nineteenth century.[357]

[356] Buxton, *British Coal Industry*, 38; Flinn, *Coal Industry*, 256, 260; Colls, *Pitmen*, 54; W. J. Hausman, 'Market Power in the London Coal Trade: The Limitation of the Vend, 1770–1845', *Explorations in Economic History*, 21 (1984).

[357] For developments after 1790, see Colls, *Pitmen*, 102–3 and *passim*. Since we have been critical of Colls's account of the earlier 18th-c. pitmen on a number of points, we should stress our admiration for his important book. Our point is simply that the developments that he traces take on a new resonance when placed in a fuller context of preceding realities. In the north-east it may well be the case, as Whately has written of Scotland, that developments in the pitmen's organization at the turn of the 19th c. 'may in reality not have been the beginning but rather the continuation of long-established traditions': Whately, 'Fettering Bonds', 141.

Conclusion

The struggle of man against power is the struggle of memory against forgetting.

Milan Kundera, *The Book of Laughter and Forgetting* (1980)

IN the preceding four chapters we have attempted to reconstruct some eight generations of life in Whickham from a variety of distinctive perspectives. Each of these directs attention to a particular dimension of the history of the parish. Each also endeavours to add a layer to our understanding of an unfolding process of economic and social change. We have examined the world the coal-owners created and the world the copyholders lost; the differentials of occupation, income, living standards, and life chances which characterized the industrial order that emerged in Whickham; the patterns of personal and social relations that gave it meaning and coherence. Throughout, we have tried to explain the course of Whickham's development, to convey something of the complexity and historical contingency of that process, and to capture something of its texture as human experience: its benefits and costs, the ways in which it impinged upon the lives of individuals and groups, the contributions that they made in turn to the restless dynamic of economic development and social structuring.

Our argument needs no laboured recapitulation. It is contained within our analytical narrative of Whickham's development. Some central themes, however, can be singled out for emphasis.

First, however extraordinary and exceptional its nature, however intimately localized in its specific details, Whickham's history was most emphatically part of a larger process of national significance. The growth of the northern coalfield was a direct consequence of the growth of London and of the tightening of the commercial bonds that linked the regional economies of England to the metropolis. By virtue of its geology, its geographical location, its previous involvement in coal production, and its availability (thanks to the Grand Lease) for exploitation, Whickham was firmly incorporated into a national market. This central fact was to govern not only its specific development, but also its relationship to the neighbouring parishes which shared, at least in part, its experience. Social change in Whickham marched to the drumbeat of the coal trade. And it marched in step with neighbouring settlements in an emerging industrial region in which parochial diversity was subordinate to a common experience which shaped the lives and identities of a substantial part of its inhabitants.

Social change in Whickham was in some respects swift and catastrophic—an aspect of its history vividly symbolized in the devastated fields and commons repeatedly described from the 1620s to the 1780s. In other respects, however, it was slow, uneven, piecemeal, incremental. It involved radical recastings of the economic and social structures of the parish, each in response to a fresh wave of industrial development. But the implications of these changes were apprehended only slowly and unevenly by Whickham's people. There was a disjuncture between the pace of economic development and its impact in the structuring of social relationships and identities. To sink a pit or build a waggonway took weeks or months. The reshaping of basic relationships and the recasting of fundamental attitudes took decades, even generations. The pace of change was set by the imperatives of profitability in capitalist enterprises of a singularly advanced nature, and its initiatives came time and again from men responsive to such pressures. The occupational and social structures called into being by the coal industry were those of an industrial class society. Yet to a very large extent, social relations were conducted in an older idiom, adapted only slowly and partially to the realities of new structural contexts. And even those novel institutions that did much both to institute social change and to routinize shifts in social relations—the Poor Laws, the laws of the Crowley firm, the managerial structure of the collieries, the pitman's bond—were unmistakably inflected with the accents of the past.

Whickham's history, taken as a whole, can be said to have reflected both a developing interaction and a perennial tension between the precocious 'modernity' of its economic and social structures and the enduring force of social traditions, attitudes, and expectations that its people shared with the 'pre-industrial' world.

The ultimately creative nature of this dynamic becomes clear in some of those significant events that allow us to break into the process of change, to obtain a firmer purchase on the structuring of social relations over time: the crushing of the copyholders' initiative of 1619–20, the riot of 1740, the dissenters' efforts to establish their meeting-house, the 'reform' of the poor relief system, the strikes of 1731 and 1765. More commonly, it was hidden in the quotidian messiness of life, part of the untidiness of history as it is lived from day to day, but a reality none the less, and one that gave a distinctive cast to the society of the coalfield, channelling the new, remoulding the familiar.

In Whickham, as elsewhere, historical time was 'a medium of continuity as well as of change'.[1] The interaction between the two was central to the making of the industrial society of Tyneside to which Whickham's history has provided a point of access. It informed the accumulating experience of industrial life which shaped the social identities not only of the parish but also of the region.

What impressed observers, however, was the new. Their attention was drawn to the coalfield by the significance of the coal trade in the metropolitan economy, and by a growing appreciation (born of periodic stoppages in that trade) of the peculiar and unquiet nature of the industrial society that had emerged to supply it. As outsiders they saw, or read about, the massive industrial undertakings, the scarred and harrowed landscape, the swarming 'sooty faces' speaking an unintelligible dialect, the settlements of unchurched 'Vulgar', the disturbing spectacle of an industrial workforce now sacking the Guildhall of Newcastle, now rising in desperate fury against the oppressions visited on them by callous plutocrats. It was a markedly partial, and in the main inaccurate, image of the coalfield and its people, but it was an undeniably powerful one.

By the mid-eighteenth century, the people of the northern coalfield (in common with those of less prominent mining regions) had acquired a peculiar symbolic significance among evangelicals and reformers. Some of them had caught the eye and the imagination of the public, evoking fear or pity, apprehension or indignation, according to taste. Already the process of broader public recognition was underway whereby 'the arduous and

[1] Abrams, *Historical Sociology*, 178.

dangerous business of getting coal' was to achieve 'a place in the national consciousness like that of no other industry'.[2]

And yet, with that very recognition, they were also deprived of their history. They were symbols not of a long, and in many ways successful, adaptation to the demands of new productive forms, but of disorder and anomic antagonisms, of oppression and ruthless exploitation. Nor was that perception essentially changed when the developments of the nineteenth century made the pitmen of the north into symbols of a different kind. By virtue of their early organization, their morally inspired leadership, and their disciplined and determined attempts to defend and advance their interests in an industry of vital significance, they were recognized as one of the 'charter groups' of organized labour.[3] Yet these characteristics also were perceived as novel consequences of a recent transformation, lacking any historical depth. Nor could such depth be provided by historians who relied for their account of preceding realities on the writings of the same observers who had initiated the denigration of the people of the coalfield as a 'race apart'.

The old stereotype of coalfield society makes for a nice, simple kind of history: a transition from isolation, dislocation, neglect, oppression, and incoherent rage to inspiration, organization, and purposeful resistance. But it does not give the people of the early coalfield their due. For of course, the coalfield settlements that were described in so pejorative and uncomprehending a manner by the moral entrepreneurs of the late eighteenth and early nineteenth centuries had a history. It was, as we have tried to show, a long and complex history, and one that deeply imprinted itself upon the attitudes, values, and social relationships of their inhabitants.

That history matters. It matters because neglect of the social history of the coalfield inevitably narrows our understanding of the processes of economic development which culminated in an industrial revolution. It matters because such neglect impoverishes our historical grasp of the complex dynamic that created the first industrial society. And it matters in itself; for only by recovering it can we rescue the working people of one of the most advanced

---

[2] B. F. Duckham, Introduction to Galloway, *Annals*, 6.
[3] For the concept of 'charter groups', see T. H. Breen, 'Creative Adaptations: Peoples and Cultures', in J. P. Greene and J. R. Pole (eds.), *Colonial British America: Essays in the New History of the Early Modern Era* (Baltimore, 1984), 205.

sectors of a nascent industrial order from 'the enormous condescension of posterity'.[4]

To be sure, they *were* something of a race apart, in the extraordinary environment they inhabited, the nature of their work, and the structure of their society. But they cannot be collectively characterized as ignorant, brutalized, feckless, or divorced from the values and conventional structures of the society of their day. That they were so depicted was partly in consequence of the ignorance and condescension of both their detractors and their sympathizers. But it was also because a proportion of them, the pitmen above all, had proved able to gain for themselves and their families, albeit for a brief period of the life-cycle, a degree of material indulgence denied to most of the labouring poor of their day. Moreover, they had also secured a degree of independent bargaining power which loosened their dependence on the good opinion of their 'betters'. These characteristics were not unique in the Georgian world, but they were not common. And they were certainly not given. They were the outcome of individual and collective action within an historically constructed set of power relationships. They were won.

Some of those who had won and defended these qualities were probably among the work-people observed by William Hutchinson on his ride through Whickham. Sooty faces indeed, but sooty faces who might cast their eyes over the treetops of Gibside's 'Elysian shades' and invest George Bowes's statue of British Liberty with their own significances, for their own reasons.

[4] E. P. Thompson, *The Making of the English Working Class* (London, 1963), 13.

BIBLIOGRAPHY

1. MANUSCRIPT SOURCES

British Library

Additional MSS, 40747–40748, Bowes Papers

Harleian MSS, 6850, no. 39, 'Coalmen of Newcastel answering the objections etc.'

Lansdowne MSS, 66, nos. 84, 86, 87, Papers concerning leases of mines in Whickham and Gateshead; 67, no. 22, 'Reasons against the Imposition uppon Newcastle Coales'; 156, no. 109, 'Touching Greenlaw Landes and colemines'

Durham Cathedral, Dean and Chapter Library

Hunter MSS, fo. 22/17, Ship Money assessment, 1636

Raine MSS, 81, Archdeacon of Durham's Visitation, 1697

Sharp Collection, 167, Bishop Cosin's Survey of the Bishopric of Durham, 1662

Durham County Record Office

D/CG, Whickham deeds

D/ST, Strathmore Papers

EP/Wh, Parochial records of Whickham

Quarter Sessions
  Q/R LV, Victuallers' recognizances
  Q/R/W, Wage rate assessments
  Q/S I, Indictments
  Q/S OB, Order Books
  Q/S OP, Process Books
  Q/S/P, Petitions

Durham University Department of Palaeography and Diplomatic (DPD)

Archdeacon of Durham
  DR VIII/1, Act Book 'Ex Officio', 1600–19
  'Archdeacon of Durham, Act Book 1572–76' (Prior's Kitchen)
  'Archdeacon of Durham, Act Book 1685–1705' (Prior's Kitchen)

Consistory Court
  DR ii, Visitation Books
  DR iii, Act Books
  DR iv, Act Books 'Ex Officio'
  DR v, Deposition Books
  DR xvii/1, 'Diocese Book, 1793'
  'Consistory Court Book of Acts Ex Officio, 1619–21' (Prior's Kitchen)
  'Consistory Court Book of Acts Ex Officio, 1662–72' (Prior's Kitchen)
  'Fragments of Durham Chancellor's Visitations, *c.*1634–7' (Prior's Kitchen)

Church Commission MSS
  Box 20, no. 189721, Whickham Rental *c.*1563–5
  Box 204, no. 244145, Parliamentary Survey of Brinkburne Colliery
  Box 205, nos. 244227–39, Copies of Durham Chancery Case papers, 1619–21; no. 244329, Memorandum on leases of Whickham coal mines
  Box 208, nos. 244891–4, Copies of Durham Chancery orders, 1634–5
  Box 209, nos. 245007–11, Copies of Exchequer Case papers

Halmote Court
  DDR HC iii F 18–23, Whickham Halmote Court Books
  Halmote Court Rentals, Box 11, Bundle 5, nos. 193323, 193324 (Whickham rentals, 1600 and *c.*1638)
  Halmote Court M6, Whickham enclosure awards

Probate records
  Original wills and inventories
  Registers of wills and inventories
  Probate bonds

Durham Chancery Records
  Chancery Decree Award no. 10
  'Bishop Chandler's Parochial Remarks on his Visitation' (photocopy of original in Newcastle-upon-Tyne Central Library)
  'Returns made by James Pilkington, bishop of Durham, to the Privy Council, . . . 1563' (photocopy of BL Harleian MSS 594, fos. 186–95)

Gateshead Public Library (GPL)

Cotesworth MSS
Ellison MSS

Lambeth Palace Library

Comm. XII a/4, Commonwealth Church Survey

North of England Institute of Mining and Mechanical Engineers (NEIMME), Newcastle-upon-Tyne

Bell Collection
Buddle Papers
T. E. Forster Collection
Johnson Collection
Watson Collection
Shelf 18, 'Richard Peck's View Book, 1710–35'
Tracts, vol. 29, 'Queries concerning the state of the Pitmen' (MS of *c*.1800 bound at end of volume)

Northumberland Record Office

Armstrong Papers
Cookson Papers
ZAN M13/C7, Letter Book and Accounts of Dr Robert Thomlinson of Whickham, 1720–48
ZAN M13/D30, Crowley MS Letter Book, 1700–03

Public Record Office

Clerks of Assize
    ASSI 44/3–8, North East Circuit Assize Indictments, 1649–60
    ASSI 45, North East Circuit Assize Depositions

Chancery
    C 2, 3, 6–10, Chancery Proceedings

Exchequer
    E 134, Exchequer Depositions
    E 179, Exchequer Lay Subsidies

Palatinate of Durham
    DURH 2, Durham Chancery, Bills and Answers
    DURH 4, Durham Chancery, Entry Books of Decrees and Orders
    DURH 5, Durham Chancery, Decrees, Orders, and Reports
    DURH 7, Durham Chancery, Depositions
    DURH 16, Clerk of the Crown, Crown Books (Assize orders)
    DURH 17, Clerk of the Crown, Indictments (Durham Assizes)
    DURH 19, Clerk of the Crown, Presentments, Jury Panels, and Proceedings at Assizes

Court of Requests
    REQ 2, Proceedings Eliz.–Jac. I

Court of Star Chamber
  STAC 8, Proceedings Jac. I

State Papers
  SP 36/25, Home Office Papers, 1731
  SP 37/4, Home Office Papers, 1765

Suffolk Record Office (Ipswich)

HAI/GD/4/13–15, 'Copy of the Inventory of the late Mr Alderman Crowley's Estate, 1728'

Tyne and Wear Archives

Keelmen's Papers, 394/1–53
Newcastle Common Council Books, 589/4–6

University of Newcastle-upon-Tyne Library

MISC MSS 10, Clavering Letter Book
MISC MSS 85, Montague Papers

2. CONTEMPORARY PRINTED BOOKS AND NEWSPAPERS

Abstract of the Answers and Returns Made pursuant to an Act, passed in the 43rd Year of His Majesty King George III, intitled 'An Act for procuring Returns relative to the Expence and Maintenance of the Poor in England (London, 1805).

BELL, J. (ed.), *Rhymes of the Northern Bards: Being a Curious Collection of old and new Songs and Poems Peculiar to the Counties of Newcastle-upon Tyne, Northumberland and Durham* (Newcastle, 1812).

BOURNE, H., *The History of Newcastle-upon-Tyne* (Newcastle, 1736).

BRAND, J., *Observations on Popular Antiquities: Including the whole of Mr Bourne's Antiquitates Vulgares* (Newcastle, 1777).

CHICKEN, E., *The Collier's Wedding*, 10th edn. (Liverpool, 1779).

ELLIS, W., *News from Newcastle* (London, 1651).

GIBSON, E., *Codex Juris Ecclesiastici Anglicani*, 2nd edn. (Oxford, 1761).

GIBSON, J., *Plan of the Collieries on the Rivers Tyne and Wear* (London, 1787).

GRAINGER, J., *General View of the Agriculture of the County of Durham* (London, 1794).

HUTCHINSON, W., *The History and Antiquities of the County Palatine of Durham*, 3 vols. (Newcastle, 1785–94).

JARS, G., *Voyages metallurgiques ou recherches et observations sur les mines*, 3 vols. (Lyons, 1774–81).

SWINBURNE, H., *A Treatise of Testaments and Last Wills* (London, 1635).

SYNGE, E., *An Essay Towards making the Knowledge of Religion easy to the meanest Capacity* (London, 1760).

YOUNG, A., *A Six Months Tour through the North of England*, 3 vols. (London, 1771).

Newspapers and periodicals

   The Annual Register
   The Gentleman's Magazine and Historical Chronicle
   The Historical Register
   Lloyd's Evening Post and British Chronicle
   The London Chronicle or Universal Evening Post
   The London Evening Post
   The London Journal
   The Newcastle Chronicle
   The Newcastle Courant
   The Newcastle Gazette
   The Newcastle Journal
   The Public Ledger

3. EDITIONS OF MANUSCRIPTS AND CONTEMPORARY PRINTED WORKS,
AND CALENDARS

Acts of the Privy Council of England, 1598–1631.

Anon., *The Compleat Collier* (London, 1708; 2nd edn. London, 1845).

BEWICK, T., *Memoir of Thomas Bewick Written By Himself 1822–1828* (London, 1961).

Calendar of Border Papers, 1595–1603.

Calendars of Home Office Papers, 1760–5, 1766–89.

Calendars of State Papers Domestic, Elizabeth I to William III.

DEFOE, D., *A Tour Through the Whole Island of Great Britain*, Everyman edn., 2 vols. (London, 1962).

DENDY, F. W. (ed.), *Extracts from the Records of the Merchant Adventurers of Newcastle-upon-Tyne*, ii, Surtees Soc., no. 101 (Durham 1899).

—— (ed.), *Extracts from the Records of the Company of Hostmen of Newcastle-upon-Tyne*, Surtees Soc., no. 105 (Newcastle, 1901).

DICKINSON, H. T. (ed.), *The Correspondence of Sir James Clavering*, Surtees Soc., no. 178 (Durham, 1967).

ELLIS, J. M. (ed.), *The Letters of Henry Liddell to William Cotesworth*, Surtees Soc., no. 197 (Durham, 1987).

FLINN, M. W. (ed.), *The Law Book of the Crowley Ironworks*, Surtees Soc., no. 167 (Durham, 1956).

FURNIVALL, F. J. (ed.), *Harrison's Description of England*, pt. I, New Shakspere Soc., 6th ser., 1 (London, 1877).

GRAY, W., *Chorographia: or, A Survey of Newcastle-upon-Tyne in 1649* (Antiquarian Society of Newcastle-upon-Tyne, Newcastle, 1813).

HAIR, P. E. H. (ed.), 'Coals and Rails: The Autobiography of Anthony Errington', unpublished typescript, n.d.

Historical Manuscripts Commission Reports (HMC), Salisbury.

HODGSON, J. C. (ed.), *Wills and Inventories from the Registry at Durham*, pt. III, Surtees Soc., no. 112 (Newcastle, 1906).

—— (ed.), 'The Diary of the Rev. John Thomlinson', in *Six North Country Diaries*, Surtees Soc., no. 118 (Durham, 1910).

—— (ed.), 'The Northern Journeys of Bishop Richard Pococke', in *North Country Diaries*, 2nd ser., Surtees Soc., no. 124 (Durham, 1915).

HUDDLESTON, C. R. (ed.), *Durham Recusants' Estates, 1717–1778*, Surtees Soc., no. 173 (Newcastle, 1962).

KIRBY, D. A. (ed.), *Parliamentary Surveys of the Bishopric of Durham*, ii, Surtees Soc., no. 185 (Gateshead, 1972).

LONGSTAFFE, W. H. (ed.), *Memoir of the Life of Mr Ambrose Barnes*, Surtees Soc., no. 50 (Durham, 1866).

MORRIS, C. (ed.), *The Illustrated Journeys of Celia Fiennes 1685–c.1712* (London and Exeter, 1982).

Parliamentary Papers, 1842.

RAINE, J. (ed.), *The Injunctions and other Ecclesiastical Proceedings of Richard Barnes, Bishop of Durham from 1575 to 1587*, Surtees Soc., no. 22 (Durham, 1850).

THIRSK, J. and COOPER, J. P. (eds.), *Seventeenth-Century Economic Documents* (Oxford, 1972).

WELFORD, R. (ed.), *Records of the Committees for Compounding, etc. with Delinquent Royalists . . . 1643–1660*, Surtees Soc., no. 111 (Newcastle, 1905).

WESLEY, J., *The Journal of the Rev. John Wesley*, Everyman edn., 4 vols. (London, n.d.).

WOOD, H. M. (ed.), *Durham Protestations*, Surtees Soc., no. 135 (Durham, 1922).

—— (ed.), *Wills and Inventories from the Registry at Durham*, pt. IV, Surtees Soc., no. 142 (Newcastle, 1929).

4. BOOKS AND ARTICLES

ABRAMS, P., *Historical Sociology* (Shepton Mallet, 1982).

APPLEBY, A. B., *Famine in Tudor and Stuart England* (Stanford and Liverpool, 1978).

ARKELL, T., 'Multiplying Factors for Estimating Population Totals from the Hearth Tax', *Local Population Studies*, 28 (1982).

—— 'A Student's Guide to the Hearth Tax: Some Truths, Half-Truths and Untruths', in N. Alldridge (ed.), *The Hearth Tax: Problems and Possibilities* (Humberside College of Higher Education, Hull, 1983).

—— 'The Incidence of Poverty in England in the Later Seventeenth Century', *Social History*, 12 (1987).

—— 'Some Regional Variations in the Household Structure of English Society in the Later Seventeenth Century', in R. M. Smith (ed.), *Regional and Spatial Demographic Patterns in the Past* (Oxford, 1990).

ASHTON, T. S. and SYKES, J., *The Coal Industry of the Eighteenth Century*, 2nd edn. (Manchester, 1964).

BARLEY, M. W., 'Rural Housing in England', in J. Thirsk (ed.), *The Agrarian History of England and Wales*, iv, *1500–1640* (Cambridge, 1967).

BEATTIE, J. M., *Crime and the Courts in England, 1660–1800* (Oxford, 1986).

BECKETT, J. V., *Coal and Tobacco: The Lowthers and the Economic Development of West Cumberland, 1660–1760* (Cambridge, 1981).

BENNETT, J. M., '"History that Stands Still": Women's Work in the European Past', *Feminist Studies*, 14 (1988).

BLAKE, J. B., 'The Medieval Coal Trade of North East England: Some Fourteenth-Century Evidence', *Northern History*, 2 (1967).

BLANCHARD, I. S. W., 'Commercial Crisis and Change: Trade and the Industrial Economy of the North-East, 1509–1532', *Northern History*, 8 (1973).

BOTHAM, F. W. and HUNT, E. H., 'Wages in Britain during the Industrial Revolution', *Economic History Review*, 2nd ser., 40 (1987).

BOULTON, J., *Neighbourhood and Society: A London Suburb in the Seventeenth Century* (Cambridge, 1987).

BOURN, W., *Whickham Parish: Its History, Antiquities, and Industry* (Carlisle, 1893).

BOWDEN, P., 'Agricultural Prices, Farm Profits, and Rents', in J. Thirsk (ed.), *The Agrarian History of England and Wales*, IV, *1500–1640* (Cambridge, 1967).

BOYD, R. N., *Coal Pits and Pitmen: A Short History of the Coal Trade and the Legislation Affecting It*, 2nd edn. (London, 1895).

BRASSLEY, P., 'Northumberland and Durham', in J. Thirsk (ed.), *The Agrarian History of England and Wales*, v, *1640–1750*, 2 pts. (Cambridge, 1985).

BREEN, T. H., 'Creative Adaptations: Peoples and Cultures', in J. P. Greene and J. R. Pole (eds.), *Colonial British America: Essays in the New History of the Early Modern Era* (Baltimore, 1984).

BULMER, M. I. A., 'Sociological Models of the Mining Community', *Sociological Review*, 23 (1975).

BUXTON, N. K., *The Economic Development of the British Coal Industry* (London, 1978).

CAMPBELL, M., *The English Yeoman under Elizabeth and the Early Stuarts* (New Haven, Conn., 1942).

CANNADINE, D., 'The Past and the Present in the English Industrial Revolution 1880–1980', *Past and Present*, 103 (1984).

CHARLES, L. and DUFFIN, L. (eds.), *Women and Work in Pre-Industrial England* (London, 1985).

CHAYTOR, M., 'Household and Kinship: Ryton in the Late 16th and Early 17th Centuries', *History Workshop Journal*, 10 (1980).

CHURCH, R., *et al.*, *The History of the British Coal Industry*, iii, *1830–1913: Victorian Pre-eminence* (Oxford, 1986).

CLARK, A., *The Working Life of Women in the Seventeenth Century* (London, 1919).

CLARK, P. and SLACK, P., *English Towns in Transition*, 1500–1700 (Oxford, 1976).

COLEMAN, D. C., *Industry in Tudor and Stuart England* (London, 1975).

COLLS, R., *The Collier's Rant: Song and Culture in the Industrial Village* (London, 1977).

—— *The Pitmen of the Northern Coalfield: Work, Culture, and Protest, 1790–1850* (Manchester, 1987).

CRESSY, D., 'Social Status and Literacy in North-East England, 1560–1630', *Local Population Studies*, 21 (1978).

—— 'Kinship and Kin Interaction in Early Modern England', *Past and Present*, 113 (1986).

CROMAR, P., 'The Coal Industry of Tyneside 1771–1800: Oligarchy and Spatial Change', *Economic Geography*, 53 (1977).

—— 'The Coal Industry on Tyneside, 1715–1750', *Northern History*, 14 (1978).

DIETZ, B., 'The North-East Coal Trade, 1550–1750: Measures, Markets, and the Metropolis', *Northern History*, 22 (1986).

ELLIOTT, N. R., 'A Geographical Analysis of the Tyne Coal Trade', *Tijdschrift voor Economische en Social Geografie*, 59 (1968).

ELLIS, J., 'The Poisoning of William Cotesworth, 1725', *History Today*, 28 (1978).

—— 'Urban Conflict and Popular Violence: The Guildhall Riots of 1740 in Newcastle-upon-Tyne', *International Review of Social History*, 25 (1980).

—— 'A Bold Adventurer, the Business Fortunes of William Cotesworth, c.1668–1726', *Northern History*, 17 (1981).

—— *A Study of the Business Fortunes of William Cotesworth, c.1668–1726* (New York, 1981).

—— 'A Dynamic Society: Social Relations in Newcastle-upon-Tyne 1660–1760', in P. Clark (ed.), *The Transformation of English Provincial Towns, 1600–1800* (London, 1984).

FEWSTER, J. M., 'The Keelmen of Tyneside in the Eighteenth Century, Part I', *Durham University Journal*, NS, 19 (1957).

FINLAY, R., *Population and Metropolis: The Demography of London 1580–1650* (Cambridge, 1981).

—— and SHEARER, B., 'Population Growth and Suburban Expansion', in A. L. Beier and R. Finlay (eds.), *London 1500–1700: The Making of the Metropolis* (London, 1986).

FLINN, M. W., *Men of Iron: The Crowleys in the Early Iron Industry* (Edinburgh, 1962).

—— , with the assistance of David Stoker, *The History of the British Coal Industry*, ii, *1700–1830: The Industrial Revolution* (Oxford, 1984).

FORDYCE, W., *The History and Antiquities of the County Palatine of Durham*, 2 vols. (Newcastle, 1857).

FYNES, R., *The Miners of Northumberland and Durham: A History of their Social and Political Progress* (Newcastle, 1873; reprinted Wakefield, 1971).

GALLOWAY, R., *Annals of Coal Mining and the Coal Trade* (London, 1899; reprinted Newton Abbot, 1971).

GIDDENS, A., *Central Problems in Social Theory: Action, Structure, and Contradiction in Social Analysis* (London, 1979).

GITTINGS, C., *Death, Burial, and the Individual in Early Modern England* (London, 1984).

HAMMOND, J. L., and HAMMOND, B., *The Skilled Labourer 1760–1832* (London, 1919).

HARRIS, F. R., *The Life of Edward Montagu, KG, First Earl of Sandwich (1625–1672)*, 2 vols. (London, 1912).

HARRISON, R., 'Introduction', in R. Harrison (ed.), *The Independent Collier: The Coal Miner as Archetypal Proletarian Reconsidered* (Hassocks, Sx, 1978).

HAUSMAN, W. J., 'Market Power in the London Coal Trade: The Limitation of the Vend, 1770–1845', *Explorations in Economic History*, 21 (1984).

HODGSON, R. I., 'Agricultural Improvement and Changing Regional Economies in the Eighteenth Century', in A. R. H. Baker and J. B. Harley (eds.), *Man Made The Land: Essays in English Historical Geography* (Newton Abbot, 1973).

—— 'The Progress of Enclosure in County Durham, 1550–1870', in H. S. A. Fox and R. A. Butlin (eds.), *Change in the Countryside* (London, 1978).

—— 'Demographic Trends in County Durham, 1560–1801: Data Sources and Preliminary Findings with Particular Reference to North Durham',

University of Manchester School of Geography, Research Papers, no. 5 (1978).

HOSKINS, W. G., *The Midland Peasant: The Economic and Social History of a Leicestershire Village* (London, 1957).

—— 'The Rebuilding of Rural England, 1570–1640', in *id.*, Provincial England (London, 1965).

HOUSTON, R. A., 'Illiteracy in the Diocese of Durham, 1663–89 and 1750–62: The Evidence of Marriage Bonds', *Northern History*, 18 (1982).

—— 'Coal, Class, and Culture: Labour Relations in a Scottish Mining Community 1650–1750', *Social History*, 8 (1983).

HOWELL, R., *Newcastle-upon-Tyne and the Puritan Revolution: A Study of the Civil War in Northern England* (Oxford, 1967).

HUGHES, E., 'The First Steam Engine in the Durham Coalfield', *Archaeologia Aeliana*, 27 (1949).

—— *North Country Life in the Eighteenth Century: The North-East, 1700–1750* (Oxford, 1952).

HUNT, C. J., *The Lead Miners of the Northern Pennines in the Eighteenth and Nineteenth Centuries* (Manchester, 1970).

INGRAM, M., *Church Courts, Sex, and Marriage in England, 1570–1640* (Cambridge, 1987).

JAMES, M., *Family, Lineage, and Civil Society: A Study of Society, Politics, and Mentality in the Durham Region 1500–1640* (Oxford, 1974).

KERRIDGE, E., *Agrarian Problems in the Sixteenth Century and After* (London, 1969).

—— 'The Coal Industry in Tudor and Stuart England: A Comment', *Economic History Review*, 2nd ser., 30 (1977).

KIRBY, D. A., 'Population Density and Land Values in County Durham during the Mid-Seventeenth Century', *Trans. Institute of British Geographers*, 57 (1972).

LANGTON, J., *Geographical Change and Industrial Revolution: Coal Mining in South West Lancashire, 1590–1799* (Cambridge, 1979).

LAQUEUR, T., 'Bodies, Death, and Pauper Funerals', *Representations*, 1 (1983).

LASKER, G. W. and ROBERTS, D. F., 'Secular Trends in Relationship as Estimated by Surnames: A Study of a Tyneside Parish', *Annals of Human Biology*, 9 (1982).

LASLETT, P., 'Mean Household Size in England since the Sixteenth Century', in P. Laslett and R. Wall (eds.), *Household and Family in Past Time* (Cambridge, 1972).

—— 'Introduction: Comparing Illegitimacy over Time and between Cultures', in P. Laslett, K. Oosterveen, and R. M. Smith (eds.), *Bastardy and its Comparative History* (London, 1980).

LEE, C. E., 'The World's Oldest Railway', *Trans. Newcomen Society*, 25 (1945–7).

LEVINE, D., *Family Formation in an Age of Nascent Capitalism* (London, New York, San Francisco, 1977).

—— and WRIGHTSON, K., 'The Social Context of Illegitimacy in Early Modern England', in P. Laslett, K. Oosterveen, and R. M. Smith (eds.), *Bastardy and its Comparative History* (London, 1980).

LEWIS, M. J. T., *Early Wooden Railways* (London, 1970).

MALCOLMSON, R. W., 'A Set of Ungovernable People', in J. Brewer and J. Styles (eds.), *An Ungovernable People: The English and their Law in the Seventeenth and Eighteenth Centuries* (London, 1980).

—— *Life and Labour in England 1700–1780* (London, 1981).

MCCORD, N., *North-East England: An Economic and Social History* (London, 1979).

NEF, J. U., *The Rise of the British Coal Industry*, 2 vols. (London, 1932).

NEWBY, H., *The Deferential Worker* (London, 1977).

NEWMAN BROWN, W., 'The Receipt of Poor Relief and Family Situation: Aldenham, Hertfordshire, 1630–90', in R. M. Smith (ed.), *Land, Kinship and Life-Cycle* (Cambridge, 1984).

PAGE, W. (ed.), *The Victoria County History of the County of Durham*, ii (London, 1907).

POLLARD, S., *The Genesis of Modern Management: A Study of the Industrial Revolution in Great Britain* (London, 1965).

POLLOCK, L., ' "Teach Her to Live under Obedience": The Making of Women in the Upper Ranks of Early Modern England', *Continuity and Change*, 4 (1989).

PORTER, R., *English Society in the Eighteenth Century*, (London, 1982).

PRIESTLEY, U. and CORFIELD, P., 'Rooms and Room Use in Norwich Housing, 1580–1730', *Post-Medieval Archaeology*, 16 (1982).

RICHARDSON, M. A., *The Local Historian's Table Book of Remarkable Occurrences*, 2 vols. (Newcastle, 1841).

RULE, J., *The Experience of Labour in Eighteenth Century Industry* (London, 1981).

RUSHTON, P., 'Women, Witchcraft, and Slander in Early Modern England: Cases from the Church Courts at Durham, 1560–1675', *Northern History*, 18 (1982).

—— 'Property, Power and Family Networks: The Problem of Disputed Marriage in Early Modern England', *Journal of Family History*, 11 (1986).

SCHOFIELD, R. S., 'The Measurement of Literacy in Pre-Industrial England', in J. Goody (ed.), *Literacy in Traditional Societies* (Cambridge, 1968).

—— 'An Anatomy of an Epidemic: Colyton, November 1645 to November

1646', in L. Bradley (ed.), *The Plague Reconsidered*, supplement to *Local Population Studies* (1977).

SCOTT, H., 'The Miner's Bond in Northumberland and Durham', *Proceedings of the Society of Antiquaries of Newcastle-upon-Tyne*, 4th ser., 11 (1947).

SEDGWICK, R. (ed.), *The History of Parliament: The House of Commons 1715–1754*, 2 vols. (London, 1970).

SHARPE, J. A., *Crime in Early Modern England, 1500–1750* (London, 1984).

SLACK, P., 'Mortality Crises and Epidemic Disease in England, 1485–1610', in C. Webster (ed.), *Health, Medicine and Mortality in the Sixteenth Century* (Cambridge, 1979).

—— *The Impact of Plague in Tudor and Stuart England* (London, 1985).

—— *Poverty and Policy in Tudor and Stuart England* (London, 1988).

SMAILES, A. E., *North England* (London and Edinburgh, 1960).

SMOUT, T. C., *A History of the Scottish People, 1560–1830* (Glasgow, 1969).

SPUFFORD, M., 'First Steps in Literacy: The Reading and Writing Experience of the Humblest Seventeenth-Century Spiritual Autobiographers', *Social History*, 4 (1979).

SURTEES, R., *The History and Antiquities of the County Palatine of Durham*, 4 vols. (London, 1816–40).

SWEEZY, P., *Monopoly and Competition in the English Coal Trade, 1550–1850* (Cambridge, Mass., 1938).

TAWNEY, R. H., *The Agrarian Problem in the Sixteenth Century* (London, 1912).

THIRSK, J., *Economic Policy and Projects: The Development of a Consumer Society in Early Modern England* (Oxford, 1978).

THOMAS, B., 'Was There an Energy Crisis in Great Britain in the 17th Century?' *Explorations in Economic History*, 23 (1986).

THOMAS, K., *Religion and the Decline of Magic: Studies in Popular Beliefs in Sixteenth and Seventeenth Century England* (London, 1971).

—— *Man and the Natural World: Changing Attitudes in England, 1500–1800* (London, 1983).

THOMPSON, E. P., *The Making of the English Working Class* (London, 1963).

—— 'Time, Work-Discipline and Industrial Capitalism', *Past and Present*, 38 (1967).

—— 'The Moral Economy of the English Crowd in the Eighteenth Century', *Past and Present*, 50 (1971).

—— 'Patrician Society Plebeian Culture', *Journal of Social History*, 7 (1974).

—— 'Folklore, Anthropology, and Social History', *Indian Historical Review*, 3 (1978).

TREVOR-ROPER, H. R., 'The Bishopric of Durham and the Capitalist Reformation', *Durham University Journal*, 38, NS, 8 (1945–6).

TUCK, R., 'Civil Conflict in School and Town, 1500–1700', in B. Mains and A. Tuck (eds.), *Royal Grammar School, Newcastle-upon-Tyne: A History of the School in its Community* (Stocksfield, 1986).

TURNER, R., 'The English Coal Industry in the Seventeenth and Eighteenth Centuries', *American Historical Review*, 28 (1921).

WALES, T., 'Poverty, Poor Relief and the Life-Cycle: Some Evidence from Seventeenth-Century Norfolk', in R. M. Smith (ed.), *Land, Kinship, and Life-Cycle* (Cambridge, 1984).

WALTER, J., 'Grain Riots and Popular Attitudes to the Law: Maldon and the Crisis of 1629', in J. Brewer and J. Styles (eds.), *An Ungovernable People* (London, 1980).

—— and WRIGHTSON, K., 'Dearth and the Social Order in Early Modern England', *Past and Present*, 71 (1976).

WATTS, S. J. and WATTS, S. J., *From Border to Middle Shire: Northumberland, 1586–1625* (Leicester, 1975).

WEATHERILL, L., *Consumer Behaviour and Material Culture in Britain, 1660–1760* (London and New York, 1988).

WEBB, S., *The Story of the Durham Miners* (London, 1921).

—— and WEBB, B., *English Local Government from the Revolution to the Municipal Corporations Act*, i, *The Parish and the County* (London, 1906).

WELBOURNE, E., *The Miners' Unions of Northumberland and Durham* (Cambridge, 1923).

WHATLEY, C., ' "The Fettering Bonds of Brotherhood": Combination and Labour Relations in the Scottish Coal-Mining Industry c.1690–1775', *Social History*, 12 (1987).

WILLIAMSON, B., *Class, Culture, and Community: A Biographical Study of Social Change in Mining* (London, 1982).

WRIGHTSON, K., 'The Nadir of English Illegitimacy in the Seventeenth Century', in P. Laslett, K. Oosterveen, and R. M. Smith (eds.), *Bastardy and its Comparative History* (London, 1980).

—— *English Society 1580–1680* (London, 1982).

—— 'Kinship in an English Village: Terling, Essex 1550–1700', in R. M. Smith (ed.), *Land, Kinship and Life-Cycle* (Cambridge, 1984).

WRIGHTSON, K., and LEVINE, D., *Poverty and Piety in an English Village: Terling, 1525–1700* (New York, San Francisco, London, 1979).

—— 'Death in Whickham', in J. Walker and R. Schofield (eds.), *Famine, Disease, and the Social Order in Early Modern Society* (Cambridge, 1989).

WRIGLEY, E. A., 'A Simple Model of London's Importance in Changing English Society and Economy, 1650–1750', *Past and Present*, 37 (1967).

—— 'Marriage, Fertility, and Population Growth in Eighteenth-Century England', in R. B. Outhwaite (ed.), *Marriage and Society: Studies in the Social History of Marriage* (London, 1981).

—— 'Urban Growth and Agricultural Change: England and the Continent in the Early Modern Period', *Journal of Interdisciplinary History*, 15 (1985).

—— *Continuity, Chance, and Change: The Character of the Industrial Revolution in England* (Cambridge, 1988).

—— and SCHOFIELD, R. S., *The Population History of England, 1541–1871: A Reconstruction* (London, 1981).

5. UNPUBLISHED DISSERTATIONS AND PAPERS

BRASSLEY, P. W., 'The Agricultural Economy of Northumberland and Durham in the Period 1640–1750', B.Litt. thesis (Oxford, 1974).

CROMAR, P., 'Economic Power and Organization: The Development of the Coal Industry on Tyneside 1700–1828', Ph.D. thesis (Cambridge, 1975).

ELLIS, J., 'Combinations in the Newcastle Coal Trade in the Early Eighteenth Century', unpublished paper, n.d.

HORTON, P. H., 'The Administrative, Social and Economic Structure of the Durham Bishopric Estates, 1500–1640', M.Litt. thesis (Durham, 1975).

ISSA, C., 'Obligation and Choice: Aspects of Family and Kinship in Seventeenth-Century County Durham', Ph.D. thesis (St Andrews, 1987).

GLOSSARY

Adit
A drainage channel driven through to a hillside at a level lower than the mine, permitting free drainage by gravity.

Banksman
An official responsible for surface operations at the pithead.

Bord and pillar
The customary method of working a coal seam in the north-east. 'Bords' were the 'work-rooms' driven through the seams by hewers (q.v.). Large 'pillars' of unwrought coal were left to support the roof. The result was a chequerboard pattern of workings.

Chaldron
A customary measurement of coal. The size of the chaldron varied between collieries and over time, a source of much confusion. See ch. 1 n. 94.

Coal wain
A cart used for the transportation of coal from the pithead to the riverside staithes (q.v.), usually drawn by two oxen and two horses.

Copyholder
A customary tenant of manorial land who held land by 'copy of court roll' and 'according to the custom of the manor'.

Corf
A basket of willow rods used to transport coal underground and to the surface.

Corver
A maker of corves.

Earnest
A sum of money paid to pitmen on their subscription of the miners' bond of a colliery.

Fitter
A shipping agent who arranged the sale of coal to shipmasters on behalf of coal-owners. Fitters owned keels and employed keelmen (q.v.).

Fother
A customary measurment of coal, varying in size. See ch. 2, n. 39.

Gin
A wooden horse-drawn engine, erected at the pithead for drawing coal or for drainage purposes.

Grieve
The principal officer of the manor, equivalent to a bailiff, elected annually by the tenants from among their own number.

Hewer
A miner who cut coal at the face.

Hostman
A member of Newcastle-upon-Tyne's company

	of Merchant Venturers, or from 1600 of the Hostmen's Company. Hostmen enjoyed the exclusive right to trade in coal from the Tyne.
Keelman	Men and boys employed transporting coal in keel boats from the riverside staithes (q.v.) to collier fleets moored at the mouth of the Tyne.
Level	Tunnel giving access from the pit shaft to the coalface.
Overman	A miner with responsibility for the working of an individual pit. Initially overmen were semi-independent subcontractors. Later they became salaried middle-management employees of the coal-owners, reporting to the colliery viewer (q.v.).
Pan coal	Small coal considered of insufficient quality for 'sea sale', commonly sold to fuel the salt-pans at Shields.
Putter	A miner employed dragging corves of coal cut by hewers (q.v.) from the coal-face to the pit shaft. Sleds were used for this purpose.
Sea coal	Coal sent to market by sea transport.
Sinker	A miner employed in the sinking of pit shafts.
Staithe	A riverside wharf at which coal was transferred from wains or waggons to keel boats.
Staitheman	An official in charge of the operation of a staithe.
Stithe	Foul air in coal-workings.
Sworn men	Officers of the manor, elected annually by the tenants to assist the grieve (q.v.) in his duties.
Ten	A measurement of coal, comprising ten Newcastle chaldrons (q.v.).
Vend	The coal marketed either by an individual colliery or by all sea-sale collieries on the Tyne.
Viewer	An expert mining engineer, employed by coal-owners as a colliery manager and/or consultant engineer.
Waggonman	A term used to describe either a contractor supplying horses and drivers for the waggonways or simply a driver.
Waggonway	A wooden railway linking collieries to the staithes (q.v.). Coal was transported down the waggonway in horse-drawn waggons.
Waggonwright	A craftsman employed in the construction and maintenance of waggonways.

Wailing (or wealing)	The sorting and screening of coal at the pithead or staithe (q.v.), a task usually performed by women.
Wainman	The driver of a coal wain.
Wayleave	The right to cross land when transporting coal to the staithes (q.v.) by coal wain (q.v.) or waggonway (q.v.).

INDEX